THE UNIVERSITY OF CHICAGO
ORIENTAL INSTITUTE PUBLICATIONS
VOLUME 124

Series Editors
Thomas A. Holland
and
Thomas G. Urban

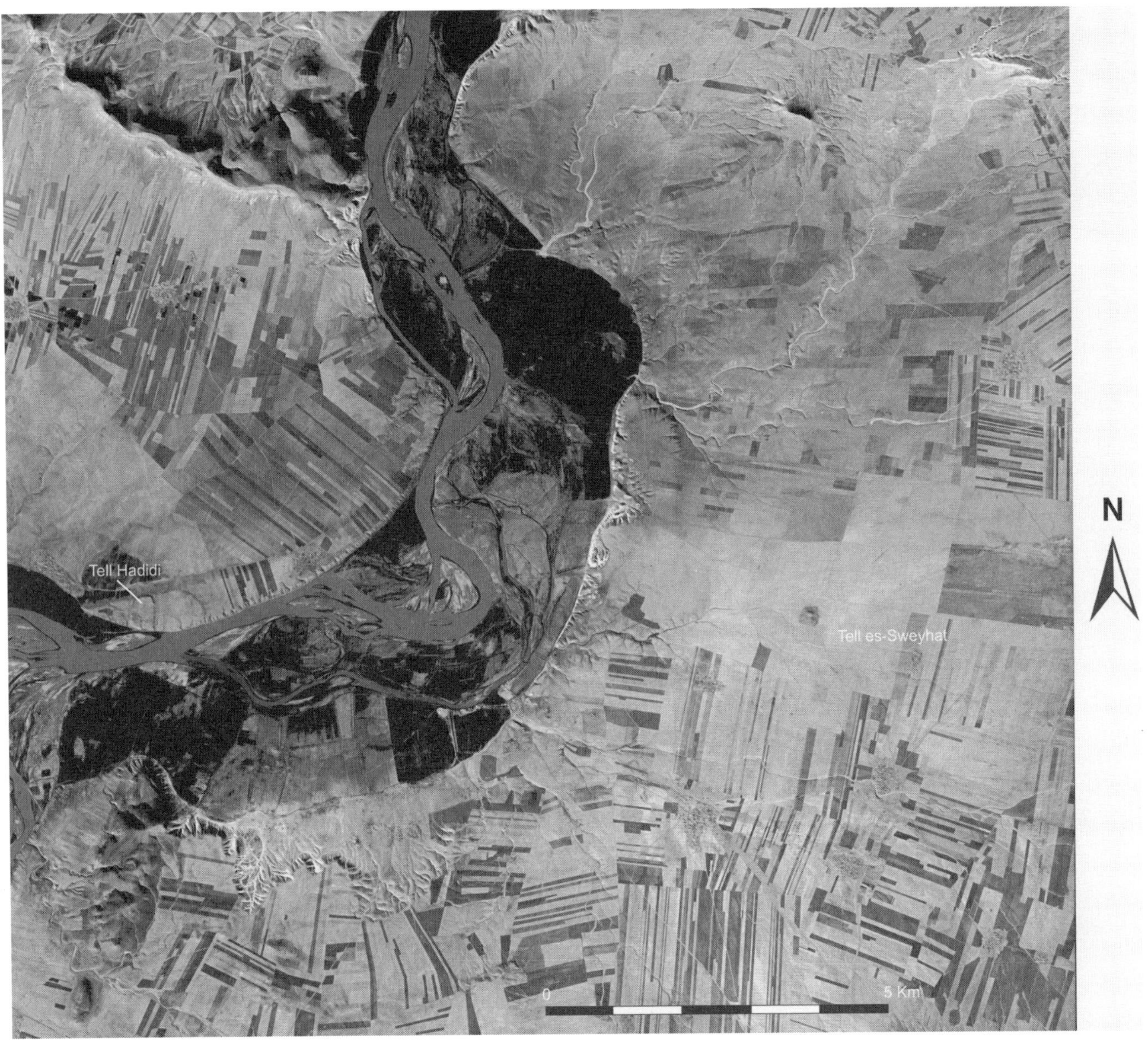

The Immediate Area of Tell es-Sweyhat Showing the Main Terrace of the Euphrates River around Tell es-Sweyhat and the Heavily Re-worked Alluvial Plain of the Euphrates (River Flow from North to Southwest). Produced by Jason Ur, Oriental Institute CAMEL Laboratory; Courtesy of U.S. Geological Survey

**EXCAVATIONS AT TELL ES-SWEYHAT, SYRIA
VOLUME 1**

ON THE MARGIN OF THE EUPHRATES

SETTLEMENT AND LAND USE AT TELL ES-SWEYHAT AND IN THE UPPER LAKE ASSAD AREA, SYRIA

by

TONY J. WILKINSON

with contributions by

NAOMI F. MILLER, CLEMENS D. REICHEL, *and* DONALD WHITCOMB

ORIENTAL INSTITUTE PUBLICATIONS • VOLUME 124
THE ORIENTAL INSTITUTE OF THE UNIVERSITY OF CHICAGO
CHICAGO • ILLINOIS

Library of Congress Control Number: 2004104597
ISBN: 1-885923-29-5
ISSN: 0069-3367

The Oriental Institute, Chicago

.

Series Editors' Acknowledgments

The assistance of Lindsay DeCarlo, Katie L. Johnson, Leslie Schramer, and Alexandra Witsell is acknowledged in the production of this volume.

Printed by Edwards Brothers, Ann Arbor, Michigan

TABLE OF CONTENTS

LIST OF ABBREVIATIONS

Bibliographical Abbreviations

CAD	*The Assyrian Dictionary of the Oriental Institute of the University of Chicago.* A. Leo Oppenheim et al., editors. Chicago: The Oriental Institute, 1956–
DOG	Deutsche Orient-Gesellschaft
Deir ez-Zur	*Symposium International: Histoire de Deir ez-Zur et ses Antiquités.* Deir ez-Zur, 2–6 October 1983. République Arabe Syrienne, Ministère de la Culture, Direction Générale des Antiquités et des Musées
FAO	Food and Agriculture Administration of the United Nations
1974	*FAO-UNESCO Soil Map of the World* 1: *Legend.* Paris: United Nations Educational, Scientific and Cultural Organization
1977	*FAO-UNESCO Soil Map of the World* 7: *South Asia.* Paris: United Nations Educational, Scientific and Cultural Organization
Holland, *Sweyhat* 2	*Excavations at Tell es-Sweyhat* 2: *Archaeology of the Bronze Age, Hellenistic, and Roman Remains from an Ancient Town on the Euphrates River.* Thomas A. Holland. Oriental Institute Publications 125. Chicago: The Oriental Institute, in press.
TAVO	Tübinger Atlas des Vorderen Orients
UNEP	United Nations Environment Programme

General Abbreviations

app.	appendix
a.s.l.	above sea level
A.D.	*anno Domini*
B.C.	before Christ
B.P.	before the present
ca.	*circa*, about, approximately
CAMEL	Center for the Archaeology of the Middle Eastern Landscape, The Oriental Institute of the University of Chicago
cc.	cubic centimeter(s)
cf.	*confer,* compare
cm	centimeter(s)
COHMAP	Cooperative Holocene Mapping Project
cont.	continued
ED	Early Dynastic
ed.	editor, edition, edited by
e.g.	*exempli gratia*, for example
EBA	Early Bronze Age
et al.	*et alii*, and others
etc.	*et cetera*, and so forth
f(f).	and following
FAO	Food and Agriculture Organization of the United Nations

fig(s).	figure(s)
fn.	footnote
g	gram(s)
ha	hectare(s)
H/W	Holland/Whitcomb 1972 survey (site number)
ICARDA	International Center for Agricultural Research in the Dry Areas
i.e.	*id est*, that is
ibid.	*ibidem*, in the same place
indet.	indeterminate
kg	kilogram(s)
km	kilometer(s)
LBA	Late Bronze Age
LC	Late Chalcolithic
m	meter(s)
MASCA	Museum Applied Science Center for Archaeology, University of Pennsylvania
MBA	Middle Bronze Age
mm	millimeter(s)
n(n).	note(s)
n/a	not applicable
n.a.	not available
no(s).	number(s)
p(p).	page(s)
pers. comm.	personal communication
pl(s).	plate(s)
PPNA	Pre-pottery Neolithic A
PPNB	Pre-pottery Neolithic B
sp.	species
SPOT	Système pour l'Observation de la Terre
sq(s).	square(s)
SS	prefix for Sweyhat Survey number
str.	stratum
T	prefix for Van Loon Tabqa Survey number (up to 554); Wilkinson Tabqa Survey number (above 554)
UNESCO	United Nations Educational, Scientific, and Cultural Organization
var.	variety

LIST OF PLATES

Frontispiece: The Immediate Area of Tell es-Sweyhat Showing the Main Terrace of the Euphrates River around Tell es-Sweyhat and the Heavily Re-worked Alluvial Plain of the Euphrates (River Flow from North to Southwest). Produced by Jason Ur, Oriental Institute CAMEL Laboratory; Courtesy of U.S. Geological Survey

1. Upper Lake Assad from Tell Jouweif (SS 8), ca. 1991

2. Upper Lake Assad, Looking toward Jebel Aruda (T 527) from Tell Sheikh Hassan (T 523), ca. 1991

3. View West from Shams ed-Din toward the Main Terrace of the Euphrates on the West Bank, Autumn 1992

4. Euphrates Valley South of Tell es-Sweyhat (SS 1), View Looking North Across Relict Early Floodplain with Tell Jouweif (SS 8) to Left of Center

5. View across the Southeastern Portion of the Lower Town of Tell es-Sweyhat (SS 1) and Cultivated Steppe beyond, toward Limestone Escarpment to East, Autumn 1974

6. Valley Fill of Northern Wadi Showing Upper Loam Overlying Gravel Fill

7. Spout and Collecting Basin of Wine Press p 101b near SS 26

8. Treading Floor and Collecting Basin of Wine Press 22 p 103, Cut in Limestone along Floor of Euphrates Bluffs

9. Limestone Quarries along Limestone Bluffs of Euphrates Valley to North of SS 28

10. Pock-marked Area of Plundered Early Bronze Age Tombs to East of Shams ed-Din Southern Site and Cemeteries (SS 22)

11. Vaulted Tomb Cut in Limestone of Euphrates Bluffs near SS 27

12. Vaulted Tomb Cut in Limestone of Euphrates Bluffs near SS 27

13. Early Bronze Age Southern Site and Cemeteries at Shams ed-Din (SS 22) Visible as Low Gray Rise

14. Roman Site of SS 29 on West Bank of Euphrates River with Modern Tombs and Rows of Weathered Stones of Building Walls

15. Middle Bronze Age Floors and Associated Walls Exposed by Erosion at Tell Jouweif (SS 8)

16. Satellite Photograph of Tell es-Sweyhat (SS 1) Showing the Faint Trace of the Outer Enclosure Wall around the Central Tell

LIST OF TABLES

ACKNOWLEDGMENTS

The results described in this report have been distilled from some thirty years of research, and necessarily the list of acknowledgments must be long. First I must thank Dr. Thomas Holland for inviting me to participate in the initial phase of the Tell es-Sweyhat project in the early 1970s and supporting what at that time seemed a rather eccentric exercise of off-site archaeology. Special thanks must also go to Dr. Afif Bahnassi, Director General of Antiquities and Museums of the Syrian Arab Republic, and to Dr. Adnan Bounni, Director of Excavations, Department of Antiquities and Museums, Damascus. Dr. Bounni is to be thanked for granting permission for the surveys and providing prompt permission for the salvage operation at Tell Jouweif.

I am also grateful to Donald Whitcomb for supplying me with documentation of his early reconnaissance surveys around Tell es-Sweyhat as well as kindly contributing the pottery reports included herein. At all times both Tom Holland and Donald Whitcomb have freely provided data and advice, and their encouragement and support have contributed immeasurably to the present volume. In the field I also benefited from the advice and help of the late Leon Marfoe (to whom this volume is dedicated), as well as from the presence of Richard Zettler (University of Pennsylvania Museum) and Michael Danti. Michael's dissertation considerably extends the scope of the original Sweyhat model to allow for the pastoral economy. Thanks also go to Naomi F. Miller (MASCA, University of Pennsylvania Museum), who provided prompt analysis of the carbonized plant remains from Tell Jouweif, the results of which are described in *Chapter 8*, and which should be read in conjunction with her work on the remains from Tell es-Sweyhat as well as other sites in the region.

Fieldwork was initially funded by the Tell es-Sweyhat Project which itself was sponsored by the Ashmolean Museum, Oxford, with additional support from the Birmingham City Museums and Art Gallery, The British Museum, the C. H. W. John's Fund, The Fitzwilliam Museum, The Manchester Museum, The Merseyside County Museums, The Museum and Art Gallery Service of the Bolton Arts Department, the Royal Ontario Museum, The British Academy, and The Cambridge University Museum of Archaeology and Ethnology. Funding for the later phases of fieldwork during 1991 and 1992 was provided by the National Geographic Society (Grant 4900-92) as well as by the Oriental Institute, Chicago. I am most grateful to the Oriental Institute and its recent directors — William Sumner, Gene Gragg, and Gil Stein — for their considerable encouragement and support during the compilation and production of this report.

Clemens Reichel contributed the impressively detailed gazetteer (*Appendix B*), which enabled the analysis provided in *Chapter 9* to be more comprehensive than otherwise would have been the case. Tom Holland and Tom Urban are to be thanked for help and assistance during the editorial process. I owe Tom Urban a great debt of gratitude for guiding the report through the final stages of production and his assistants: Leslie Schramer, Alexandra Witsell, and Katie Johnson are to be congratulated for their patience in dealing with a heavy and often unruly manuscript. Thanks also go to Carrie Hritz and Colleen Coyle for the considerable amount of time they invested on some of the key figures in the text, and to Jason Ur for processing the satellite images. Additional figures were drafted by my wife Eleanor Barbanes, to whom I am immensely grateful for providing help, advice, and inspiration during the production of this report. An earlier version of this report benefited from valuable commentary by Glenn Schwartz, and I also wish to thank John Larson, archivist at the Oriental Institute for speedily and efficiently making available key maps and photographs of the area in question.

Tony J. Wilkinson
Edinburgh, October 2003

BIBLIOGRAPHY

Adams, Robert McC.
1978   "Strategies of Maximization, Stability and Resilience in Mesopotamian Society, Settlement and Agriculture." *Proceedings of the American Philosophical Society* 122: 329–35.

Adamthwaite, Murray R.
2001   *Late Hittite Emar: The Chronology, Synchronisms, and Socio-Political Aspects of a Late Bronze Age Fortress Town.* Leuven: Peeters Press.

Admiralty War Staff Intelligence Division
1917   *Handbook of Mesopotamia* 4: *Northern Mesopotamia and Central Kurdistan.* Oxford: Naval Intelligence Division.

Ainsworth, William Francis
1888   *A Personal Narrative of the Euphrates Expedition: Conducted in 1835,* Volumes 1 and 2. London: Kegan Paul, Trench and Co.

Akahane, Sadayuki
1998   "Environmental and Archaeological Setting of the Middle Khabur Region." In *Excavations at Tell Umm Qseir in the Middle Khabur Valley, North Syria,* edited by Akira Tsuneki and Yutaka Miyake, pp. 4–13. Tsukuba: Department of Archaeology, University of Tsukuba.

Akkermans, Peter M. M. G.
1984   "Archäologische Geländebegehung im Baliḫ-Tal." *Archiv für Orientforschung* 31: 188–90.

1988a   "The Period V Pottery." In *Hammam et-Turkman* 1: *Report on the University of Amsterdam's 1981–84 Excavations in Syria,* Volume 1, edited by Maurits N. van Loon, pp. 287–349. Publications de l'Institut historique-archéologique néerlandais de Stamboul 63. Istanbul: Netherlands Historical and Archaeological Institute.

1988b   "An Updated Chronology for the Northern Ubaid and Late Chalcolithic Periods in Syria: New Evidence from Tell Hammam et-Turkman." *Iraq* 50: 109–45.

1989a   "Halaf Mortuary Practices: A Survey." In *To the Euphrates and Beyond: Archaeological Studies in Honour of Maurits N. van Loon,* edited by Odette M. C. Haex, Hans H. Curvers, and Peter M. M. G. Akkermans, pp. 75–88. Rotterdam: A. A. Balkema.

1989b   "The Neolithic of the Balikh Valley, Northern Syria: A First Assessment." *Paléorient* 15: 122–34.

1989c   "Tradition and Social Change in Northern Mesopotamia during the Later Fifth and Fourth Millennium B.C." In *Upon This Foundation: The 'Ubaid Reconsidered,* edited by Elizabeth F. Henrickson and Ingolf Thuesen, pp. 339–67. Copenhagen: Museum Tusculanum Press.

1993   *Villages in the Steppe: Later Neolithic Settlement and Subsistence in the Balikh Valley, Northern Syria.* International Monographs in Prehistory Archaeological Series 5. Ann Arbor: International Monographs in Prehistory.

1999   "Pre-Pottery Neolithic B Settlement Patterns along the Balikh and Euphrates, Fact or Fiction?" In *Archaeology of the Upper Syrian Euphrates: The Tishrin Dam Area,* edited by Gregorio del Olmo Lete and Juan-Luis Montero Fenollós, pp. 523–33. Proceedings of the International Symposium in Barcelona, 28–30 January 1998. Aula Orientalis, Supplementa 15. Barcelona: Editorial Ausa.

Akkermans, Peter M. M. G.; José Limpens; and Richard H. Spoor
1993   "On the Frontier of Assyria: Excavations at Tell Sabi Abyad, 1991." *Akkadica* 84–85: 1–52.

Akkermans, Peter M. M. G., and Marie le Mière
1992   "The 1988 Excavations at Tell Sabi Abyad, a Later Neolithic Village in Northern Syria." *American Journal of Archaeology* 96: 1–22.

Akkermans, Peter M. M. G., and Marc Verhoeven
1995   "An Image of Complexity: The Burnt Village at Late Neolithic Sabi Abyad, Syria." *American Journal of Archaeology* 99: 5–32.

Akkermans, Peter M. M. G., and F. A. M. Wiggermans
1995   "The Middle Assyrian Texts from Tell Sabi Abyad, Syria." Paper presented at the Rencontre Assyriologique Internationale, 1995, in Leuven, Belgium.

Akkermans, Peter M. M. G., and Beatrice Wittman
1993   "Khirbet esh-Shenef 1991: Eine späthalafzeitliche Siedlung im Balikhtal, Nordsyrien." *Mitteilungen der Deutschen Orient-Gesellschaft zu Berlin* 125: 143–66.

Alcock, Susan E.
1993   *Grecia Capta: The Landscapes of Roman Greece.* Cambridge: Cambridge University Press.

1994   "Breaking up the Hellenistic World: Survey and Society." In *Classical Greece: Ancient Histories and Modern Archaeologies,* edited by Ian Morris, pp. 171–90. Cambridge: Cambridge University Press.

Alcock, Susan E.; John F. Cherry; and Jack L. Davis
1994   "Intensive Survey, Agricultural Practice and the Classical Landscape of Greece." In *Classical Greece: Ancient Histories and Modern Archaeologies,* edited by Ian Morris, pp. 137–70. Cambridge: Cambridge University Press.

Algaze, Guillermo
1990   *Town and Country in Southeastern Anatolia,* Volume 2: *The Stratigraphic Sequence at Kurban Höyük.* Edited by Guillermo Algaze. Oriental Institute Publications 110. Chicago: The Oriental Institute.

1993   *The Uruk World System: The Dynamics of Expansion of Early Mesopotamian Civilization.* Chicago: University of Chicago Press.

1999   "Trends in the Archaeological Development of the Upper Euphrates Basin of Southeastern Anatolia During the Late Chalcolithic and Early Bronze Ages." In *Archaeology of the Upper Syrian Euphrates: The Tishrin Dam Area,* edited by Gregorio del Olmo Lete and Juan-Luis Montero Fenollós, pp. 535–72. Proceedings of the International Symposium in Barcelona, 28–30 January 1998. Aula Orientalis, Supplementa 15. Barcelona: Editorial Ausa.

Algaze, Guillermo; Ray Breuninger; and James Knutstad
1994   "The Tigris-Euphrates Archaeological Reconnaissance Project: Final Report of the Birecik and Carchemish Dam Survey Areas." *Anatolica* 20: 1–96.

Algaze, Guillermo; Adnan Mısır; and Tony J. Wilkinson
1992   "Şanlıurfa Museum/University of California Excavations and Surveys at Titriş Höyük, 1991: A Preliminary Report." *Anatolica* 18: 33–60.

Ali, Hassan Mohammed
1955   *Land Reclamation and Settlement in Iraq.* Baghdad, Republic of Iraq: Baghdad Printing Press.

Alley, R. B.; P. A. Mayewski; T. Sowers; M. Stuiver; K. C. Taylor; and P. U. Clark
1997   "Holocene Climatic Instability: A Prominent, Widespread Event 8200 yr Ago." *Geology* 25: 483–86.

Altaweel, Mark
2003   "The Roads of Ashur and Nineveh." *Akkadica* 124: 221–29.

Amiet, Pierre
1976   *L'art d'Agadé au Musée du Louvre.* Paris: Éditions des Musées nationaux.

Andreae, Bernd
1957   *Farming, Development and Space: A World Agricultural Geography.* Berlin and New York: de Gruyter.

Anonymous
1978/79a "Ǧabal Arūda." *Archiv für Orientforschung* 26: 177.

1978/79b "Tall al-ʿAbd." *Archiv für Orientforschung* 26: 177.

1978/79c "Tall Mumbaqat." *Archiv für Orientforschung* 24: 168–71.

Armstrong, James A., and Richard L. Zettler
1997   "Excavations on the High Mound (Inner Town)." In *Subsistence and Settlement in a Marginal Environment: Tell es-Sweyhat, 1989–1995 Preliminary Report,* edited by Richard L. Zettler, pp. 11–33. Museum Applied Science Center for Archaeology Research Papers in Science and Archaeology 14. Philadelphia: University of Pennsylvania Museum of Archaeology and Anthropology.

Arnaud, Daniel
1986   *Emar 6: Recherches au pays d'Aštata: Textes sumériens et accadiens,* Tome 3: *Texte.* Éditions Recherche sur les Civilisations; Synthèse 18. Paris: Éditions Recherche sur les Civilisations.

1991   *Textes Syriens de l'Âge du Bronze Récent.* Barcelona: Editorial Ausa.

Ashtor, Eliyahu
1976   *A Social and Economic History of the Near East in the Middle Ages.* London: Collins.

Astour, Michael C.
1988   "The Geographical and Political Structure of the Ebla Empire." In *Wirtschaft und Gesellschaft von Ebla,* edited by Harmut Waetzoldt and Harald Hauptmann, pp. 139–58. Heidelberger Studien zum Alten Orient 2. Heidelberg: Heidelberger Orientverlag.

1992   "An Outline of the History of Ebla (Part 1)." In *Eblaitica: Essays on the Ebla Archives and Eblaite Language,* Volume 3, edited by Cyrus H. Gordon, pp. 3–82. Winona Lake: Eisenbrauns.

Ault, Bradley A.
1999   "*Koprones* and Oil Presses at Halieis: Interactions of Town and Country and the Integration of Domestic and Regional Economies." *Hesperia* 68: 549–73.

Avissar, Miriam
1996   "The Medieval Pottery." In *Yoqneʿam 1: The Late Periods,* edited by A. Ben-Tor, Miriam Avissar, and Y. Portugali, pp. 75–172. Qedem Reports 3. Jerusalem: Institute of Archaeology, Hebrew University of Jerusalem.

Azouri, Ingrid, and Christopher Bergman
1980   "The Halafian Lithic Assemblage of Shams ed-Din Tannira." *Berytus* 28: 127–43.

Bachelot, L.
1999   "Les données archéologique de l'Âge du Bronze Récent dans la vallée du Haut Euphrate." In *Archaeology of the Upper Syrian Euphrates: The Tishrin Dam Area,* edited by Gregorio del Olmo Lete and Juan-Luis Montero Fenollós, pp. 333–61. Proceedings of the International Symposium in Barcelona, 28–30 January 1998. Aula Orientalis, Supplementa 15. Barcelona: Editorial Ausa.

Ball, Warwick
2000   *Rome in the East: The Transformation of an Empire.* London: Routledge.

Bar-Matthews, Mira; Avner Ayalon; and Aharon Kaufman
1998   "Middle to Late Holocene (6,500 Yr. Period) Paleoclimate in the Eastern Mediterranean Region from Stable Isotopic Composition of Speleothems from Soreq Cave, Israel." In *Water, Environment and Society in Times of Climatic Change,* edited by Arie S. Issar and Neville Brown, pp. 203–14. Water Science and Technology Library 31. Dordrecht, Netherlands: Kluwer Academic Publishers.

Bartl, Karin
1994   *Frühislamische Besiedlung im Balīḫ-Tal/Nordsyrien.* Berliner Beiträge zum Vorderen Orient 15. Berlin: Dietrich Reimer Verlag.

1996   "Balīḫ Valley Survey: Settlements of the Late Roman/ Early Byzantine and Islamic Period." In *Continuity and Change in Northern Mesopotamia from the Helle-*

nistic to the Early Islamic Period, edited by Karin Bartl and Stefan R. Hauser, pp. 333–48. Proceedings of a colloquium held at the Seminar für Vorderasiatische Altertumskunde at the Freie Universität Berlin, 6–9 April 1994. Berliner Beiträge zum Vorderen Orient 17. Berlin: Dietrich Reimer Verlag.

Bartl, Karin, and Stefan R. Hauser, editors
1996   *Continuity and Change in Northern Mesopotamia from the Hellenistic to the Early Islamic Period*. Proceedings of a colloquium held at the Seminar für Vorderasiatische Altertumskunde at the Freie Universität Berlin, 6–9 April 1994. Berliner Beiträge zum Vorderen Orient 17. Berlin: Dietrich Reimer Verlag.

Beaumont, Peter
1996   "Agricultural and Environmental Changes in the Upper Euphrates Catchment of Turkey and Syria and Their Political and Economic Implications." *Applied Geography* 16: 137–57.

Becker, Helmut; Jörg Fassbinder; and Faris Chouker
1994   "Magnetische und elektrische Prospektion in Munbāqa/Ekalte 1993." *Mitteilungen der Deutschen Orient-Gesellschaft zu Berlin* 126: 65–80.

Bell, Gertrude Lowthian
1911   *Amurath to Amurath*. New York: E. P. Dutton.

Bell, Gertrude Lowthian, and Sir William Mitchell Ramsay
1909   *The Thousand and One Churches*. London: Hodder and Stoughton.

Ben Mechlia, N.
1993   "Variations in the Crop Area and Yield of Barley in Relation to Rainfall under a Mediterranean Climate." In *The Agrometeorology of Rain-fed Barley-based Farming Systems*, edited by M. Jones, G. Mathys, and D. Rijks, pp. 121–26. Aleppo: International Center for Agricultural Research in the Dry Areas Publications.

Bernbeck, Reinhard
1993   *Steppe als Kulturlandschaft: Das 'Aǧīǧ-Gebiet Ostsyriens vom Neolithikum bis zur islamischen Zeit*. Berliner Beiträge zum Vorderen Orient Ausgrabungen 1. Berlin: Dietrich Reimer Verlag.

Besançon, Jacques; André Delgiovine; Michel Fontugne; Claude Lalou; Paul Sanlaville; and Jean Vaudour
1997   "Mise en évidence et datation de phases humides du Pléistocène Supérieur dans la région de Palmyre (Syrie)." *Paléorient* 23: 5–23.

Besançon, Jacques, and Paul Sanlaville
1981   "Aperçu géomorphologique sur la vallée de l'Euphrate Syrien." *Paléorient* 7: 5–18.

Bintliff, John L., and Anthony M. Snodgrass
1988   "Off-site Pottery Distributions: A Regional and Interregional Perspective." *Current Anthropology* 29: 506–13.

Birkeland, Peter W.
1974   *Pedology, Weathering and Geomorphological Research*. London: Oxford University Press.

Blaikie, Piers M., and Harold Brookfield
1987   *Land Degradation and Society*. London: Methuen.

Blumler, M. A.
1996   "Ecology, Evolutionary Theory and Agricultural Origins." In *The Origins and Spread of Agriculture and Pastoralism in Eurasia*, edited by David R. Harris, pp. 25–50. London: University College London Press.

Boerma, Jan A. K.
1988   "Soils and Environment of Tell Hammam et-Turkman." In *Hammam et-Turkman* 1: *Report on the University of Amsterdam's 1981–84 Excavations in Syria*, Volume 1, edited by Maurits N. van Loon, pp. 1–11. Publications de l'Institut historique-archéologique néerlandais de Stamboul 63. Istanbul: Netherlands Historical and Archaeological Institute.

2001   "Environmental Conditions." In *Selenkahiye: Final Report on the University of Chicago and University of Amsterdam Excavations in the Tabqa Reservoir, Northern Syria, 1967–1975*, edited by Maurits N. van Loon, pp. 2.5–2.23. Publications de l'Institut historique-archéologique néerlandais de Stamboul 91. Istanbul: Netherlands Historical and Archaeological Institute.

Boese, Johannes
1986/87 "Excavations at Tell Sheikh Hassan: Preliminary Report on the 1987 Campaign in the Euphrates Valley." *Les Annales Archéologiques Arabes Syriennes* 36/37: 67–101.

1987/88 "Excavations at Tell Sheikh Hassan: Preliminary Report on the 1988 Campaign in the Euphrates Valley." *Les Annales Archéologiques Arabes Syriennes* 37/38: 158–87.

1995   *Ausgrabungen in Tell Sheikh Hassan* 1: *Vorläufiger Berichte über die Grabungskampagnen 1984–1990 und 1992–1994*. Schriften zur Vorderasiatischen Archäologie 5. Saarbrücken: Saarbrücker Druckerei und Verlag.

Boessneck, Joachim, and Joris Peters
1988   "Tierknochen- und Molluskenfunde aus dem Grabungsbereich 'Kuppe' in Tall Munbāqa." *Mitteilungen der Deutschen Orient-Gesellschaft zu Berlin* 120: 51–58.

Boessneck, Joachim, and Angela von den Driesch
1986   "Tierknochen- und Molluskenfunde aus Mumbāqa." *Mitteilungen der Deutschen Orient-Gesellschaft zu Berlin* 118: 147–60.

Bolton, F. E.
1991   "Tillage and Stubble Management." In *Soils and Crop Management for Improved Water Use Efficiency in Rain-fed Areas*, edited by H. C. Harris, P. J. M. Cooper, and M. Pala, pp. 39–47. Proceedings of an international workshop in Ankara, Turkey, 15–19 May 1989. International Center for Agricultural Research in the Dry Areas Publications 247. Aleppo: International Center for Agricultural Research in the Dry Areas Publications.

Bottema, Sytze
1984   "The Composition of Modern Charred Seed Assemblages." In *Plants and Ancient Man: Studies in*

Palaeoethnobotany, edited by Willem van Zeist and W. A. Casparie, pp. 207–12. Proceedings of the Sixth Symposium of the International Work Group for Palaeoethnobotany in Groningen, 30 May–3 June 1983. Rotterdam: A. A. Balkema.

1989   "Notes on the Prehistoric Environment of the Syrian Djezireh." In *To the Euphrates and Beyond: Archaeological Studies in Honour of Maurits N. van Loon*, edited by Odette M. C. Haex, Hans H. Curvers, and Peter M. M. G. Akkermans, pp. 1–16. Rotterdam: A. A. Balkema.

1995   "Holocene Vegetation of the Van Area: Palynological and Chronological Evidence from Söğütlülü, Turkey." *Vegetation History and Archaeobotany* 4: 187–93.

Bottema, Styze, and Willem van Zeist
1981   "Palynological Evidence for the Climatic History of the Near East, 50,000–6,000 B.P." In *Préhistoire du Levant: Chronologie et organisation de l'espace depuis les origines jusqu'au VIe millénaire*, edited by Jacques Cauvin and Paul Sanlaville, pp. 111–32. Actes du Colloque International Centre National de la Recherche Scientifique 598. Paris: Centre National de la Recherche Scientifique.

Bottema, Sytze, and Henk Woldring
1990   "Anthropogenic Indicators in the Pollen Record of the Eastern Mediterranean." In *Man's Role in the Shaping of the Eastern Mediterranean Landscape*, edited by Sytze Bottema, G. Entjes-Nieborg, and Willem van Zeist, pp. 231–64. Rotterdam: A. A. Balkema.

Bounni, Adnan
1973   *Sauvegarde des Antiquités du Lac du Barrage de l'Euphrate*. Damascus: Direction Générale des Antiquités et des Musées.

1974a   "'Anab as-Safinah." In *Antiquités de l'Euphrate: Exposition des découvertes de la campagne internationale de sauvegarde des antiquités de l'Euphrate*, edited by Adnan Bounni, pp. 29–32. Damascus: Direction Générale des Antiquités et des Musées.

1974b   *Antiquités de l'Euphrate: Exposition des découvertes de la campagne internationale de sauvegarde des antiquités de l'Euphrate*. Damascus: Direction Générale des Antiquités et des Musées.

1974c   "Travaux des fouilles: Tell al-'Abd." In *Antiquités de l'Euphrate: Exposition des découvertes de la campagne internationale de sauvegarde des antiquités de l'Euphrate*, edited by Adnan Bounni, pp. 25–28. Damascus: Direction Générale des Antiquités et des Musées.

1979a   "Campaign and Exhibition from the Euphrates in Syria." In *Archaeological Reports from the Tabqa Dam Project, Euphrates Valley, Syria*, edited by David Noel Freedman, pp. 1–7. Annual of the American Schools of Oriental Research 44. Cambridge: American Schools of Oriental Research.

1979b   "Preliminary Report on the Archeological Excavations at Tell al-'Abd and 'Anab al-Safinah (Euphrates), 1971–1972." In *Archaeological Reports from the Tabqa Dam Project, Euphrates Valley, Syria*, edited by David Noel Freedman, pp. 49–61. Annual of the American Schools of Oriental Research 44. Cambridge: American Schools of Oriental Research.

Bowden, M. J.; R. W. Kates; P. A. Kay; W. E. Riebsame; R. A. Warrick; D. L. Johnson; H. A. Gould; and D. Weiner
1981   "The Effect of Climate Fluctuations on Human Populations: Two Hypotheses." In *Climate and History: Studies in Past Climate and Their Impact on Man*, edited by T. M. L. Wigley, M. J. Ingram, and G. Farmer, pp. 479–513. Cambridge: Cambridge University Press.

Braidwood, Robert J.
1937   *Mounds in the Plain of Antioch: An Archaeological Survey*. Oriental Institute Publications 48. Chicago: University of Chicago Press.

Braidwood, Robert J., and Linda S. Braidwood
1960   *Excavations in the Plain of Antioch 1: The Earlier Assemblages, Phases A–J*. Oriental Institute Publications 61. Chicago: University of Chicago Press.

Brengle, K. G.
1982   *Principles and Practices of Dryland Farming*. Colorado: Associated Universities Press.

Bridel, Philippe; Clemens Krause; Hanspeter Spycher; Rolf A. Stucky; Peter Suter; and Suzanne Zellweger
1974   *Tell el Hajj in Syrien: Zweiter vorläufiger Bericht, Grabungskampagne 1972*. Bern: Hans Jucker.

Bridel, Philippe, and Rolf A. Stucky
1980   "Tell el Hajj, place forte du limes de l'Euphrate." In *Le Moyen Euphrate: Zone de contacts et d'échanges*, edited by Jean Claude Margueron, pp. 349–53. Actes du colloque de Strasbourg, 10–12 mars 1977. Travaux du Centre de Recherche sur le Proche-Orient et la Grèce Antiques 5. Leiden: E. J. Brill.

Brown, A. G.
1997   *Alluvial Geoarchaeology: Floodplain Archaeology and Environmental Change*. Cambridge: Cambridge University Press.

Bryson, R. A., and D. A. Baerris
1967   "Possibilities of Major Climatic Modification and Their Implications: North-west India, a Case Study." *Bulletin of the American Meteorological Society* 48: 136–42.

Buccellati, Giorgio
1990a   "From Khana to Laqê: The End of Syro-Mesopotamia." In *De la Babylonie à la Syrie, en passant par Mari: Mélanges offerts à Monsier J.-R. Kupper à l'occasion de son 70e anniversaire*, edited by Ö. Tunca, pp. 228–53. Liege: University of Liege.

1990b   "'River Bank,' 'High Country,' and 'Pasture Land': The Growth of Nomadism on the Middle Euphrates and the Khabur." In *Tall al-Ḥamīdīya 2*, edited by Seyyare Eichler, Markus Wäfler, and David Warburton, pp. 87–117. Symposium on Recent Excavations in the Upper Khabur Region in Berne, 9–11 December 1986. Orbis Biblicus et Orientalis, Series

Archaeologica 6. Freiburg: Universitätsverlag; Göttingen: Vandenhoeck & Ruprecht.

1997 "Amorites." In *The Oxford Encyclopedia of Archaeology in the Near East*, Volume 1, edited by Eric M. Meyers, pp. 107–11. Oxford: Oxford University Press.

Buitenhuis, Hijlke

1983 "The Animal Remains of Tell Sweyhat, Syria." *Palaeohistoria* 25: 131–44.

1988 *Archeozoölogisch Onderzoek Langs de Midden-Eufraat: Onderzoek van het faunamateriaal uit zes nederzettingen in Zuidoost-Turkije en Noord-Syrië daterend van ca. 10.000 BP tot 1400 AD.* Amsterdam: Rijksuniversiteit Groningen.

Bull, Ian D.; Richard P. Evershed; and Phillip P. Betancourt

2001 "An Organic Geochemical Investigation of the Practice of Manuring at a Minoan Site on Pseira Island, Crete." *Geoarchaeology* 16: 223–42.

Bull, I. D.; I. A. Simpson; P. F. van Bergen; and R. P. Evershed

1999 "Muck '-n' Molecules: Organic Geochemical Methods for Detecting Ancient Manuring." *Antiquity* 73: 86–96.

Burckhardt, John Lewis

1822 *Travels in Syria and the Holy Land.* Reprint 1992. London: Darf.

Burdon, David J., and Chafic Safadi

1963 "Ras-al-Ain: The Great Karst Spring of Mesopotamia: An Hydrogeological Study." *Journal of Hydrology* 1: 58–95.

Burghardt, Andrew F.

1959 "The Location of River Towns in the Central Lowland of the United States." *Annals of the Association of American Geographers* 49: 305–23.

1971 "A Hypothesis about Gateway Cities." *Annals of the Association of American Geographers* 61: 269–85.

Buringh, Peter

1960 *Soils and Soil Conditions in Iraq.* Baghdad, Republic of Iraq: Ministry of Agriculture.

1979 *Introduction to the Study of Soils in Tropical and Subtropical Regions.* Wageningen, Netherlands: Center for Agricultural Publication and Documentation.

Butzer, Karl W.

1995 "Environmental Change in the Near East and Human Impact on the Land." In *Civilizations of the Ancient Near East*, Volume 1, edited by Jack M. Sasson, pp. 123–51. New York: Simon & Schuster Macmillan.

1997 "Sociopolitical Discontinuity in the Near East c. 2200 B.C.E: Scenarios from Palestine and Egypt." In *Third Millennium B.C. Climate Change and Old World Collapse,* edited by Hasan Nüzhet Dalfes, George Kukla, and Harvey Weiss, pp. 245–96. Proceedings of the North Atlantic Treaty Organization Advanced Research Workshop on Third Millennium B.C. Abrupt Climate Change and Old World Social Collapse in Kemer, Turkey, 19–24 September 1994. North Atlantic Treaty Organization Advanced Science Institutes Series 1; Global Environmental Change 49. Berlin: Springer.

Calvet, Yves, and Bernard Geyer

1992 *Barrages antiques de Syrie.* Collection de la Maison de l'Orient Méditerranéen 21; Série Archéologique 12. Lyon: Maison de l'Orient Méditerranéen.

Cameron, Averil

1993 *The Mediterranean World in Late Antiquity, AD 395–600.* London: Routledge.

Campbell, Stuart

2000 "Questions of Definition in the Early Bronze Age of the Tishrin Dam." In *From the Euphrates to the Caucasus: Chronologies for the 4th–3rd Millennium B.C,* edited by Catherine Marro and Harald Hauptmann, pp. 53–63. Actes du colloque d'Istanbul, 16–19 décembre 1998. Varia Anatolica 11. Paris: Institut français d'études anatoliennes d'Istanbul de Boccard.

Carter, Elizabeth, and Andrea Parker

1995 "Pots, People and the Archaeology of Death in Northern Syria and Southern Anatolia in the Latter Half of the Third Millennium B.C." In *The Archaeology of Death in the Ancient Near East*, edited by Stuart Campbell and Anthony Green, pp. 96–116. Oxbow Monograph 51. Oxford: Oxbow Books.

Carter, Stephen, and Richard Tipping

1997 "Geoarchaeological Studies." In "Jerablus-Tahtani, Syria, 1996: Preliminary Report," by Edgar Peltenburg, Stuart Campbell, Stephen Carter, Fiona M. K. Stephen, and Richard Tipping, pp. 15–16. *Levant* 29: 1–18.

Casana, Jesse

2003 "The Archaeological Landscape of Late Roman Antioch." In *Culture and Society in Later Roman Antioch* (Papers from a Colloquium, London, 15 December 2001), edited by Janet A. R. Huskinson and Isabella Sandwell, pp. 102–25. Oxford: Oxbow Books.

Cauvin, Jacques

1978 *Les premiers villages de Syrie–Palestine du IXème au VIIème millénaire avant J.C.* Collection de la Maison de l'Orient Méditerranéen Ancien 4; Série Archéologique 3. Lyon: Maison de l'Orient; Paris: Diffusion de Boccard.

1978/79 "Tall Murēbiṭ und Tall Šēḫ Hassan." *Archiv für Orientforschung* 26: 159–60.

1979 "Les fouilles de Mureybet (1971–1974) et leur signification pour les origines de la sedentarisation au Proche-Orient." In *Archaeological Reports from the Tabqa Dam Project, Euphrates Valley, Syria,* edited by David Noel Freedman, pp. 19–48. Annual of the American Schools of Oriental Research 44. Cambridge: American Schools of Oriental Research.

1980 "Le Moyen-Euphrate au VIIIe millénaire d'après Mureybet et Cheikh Hassan." In *Le Moyen Euphrate: Zone de contacts et d'échanges,* edited by Jean Claude Margueron, pp. 21–34. Actes du colloque de Strasbourg, 10–12 mars 1977. Travaux du Centre de Recherche sur le Proche-Orient et la Grèce Antiques 5. Leiden: E. J. Brill.

Charles, Henri

1939   *Tribus moutonnières du Moyen-Euphrate.* Documents d'Études Orientales 8. Beirut: Institut Français de Damas.

1942   *La sédentarisation entre Euphrate et Balikh.* Beirut: Les Éditions des Lettres Orientales.

Chisholm, Michael

1979   *Rural Settlement and Land Use: An Essay in Location.* London: Hutchinson.

Civil, Miguel

1994   *The Farmer's Instructions: A Sumerian Agricultural Manual.* Barcelona: Editorial Ausa.

Clarke, Graeme W.

1984/85   "Syriac Inscriptions from the Middle Euphrates." *Abr-Nahrain* 23: 73–82.

1994   "Jebel Khalid on the Euphrates: The Acropolis Building." *Mediterranean Archaeology* 7: 69–75.

1999a   "Tell Jebel Khalid." In *Archaeology of the Upper Syrian Euphrates: The Tishrin Dam Area,* edited by Gregorio del Olmo Lete and Juan-Luis Montero Fenollós, pp. 227–36. Proceedings of the International Symposium in Barcelona, 28–30 January 1998. Aula Orientalis, Supplementa 15. Barcelona: Editorial Ausa.

1999b   "The Upper Euphrates Valley during the Hellenistic-Roman Period." In *Archaeology of the Upper Syrian Euphrates: The Tishrin Dam Area,* edited by Gregorio del Olmo Lete and Juan-Luis Montero Fenollós, pp. 637–42. Proceedings of the International Symposium in Barcelona, 28–30 January 1998. Aula Orientalis, Supplementa 15. Barcelona: Editorial Ausa.

Clarke, Graeme W., and Peter Connor

1995   "Jebel Khalid on the Euphrates: 1993 Season." *Mediterranean Archaeology* 8: 119–24.

Clarke, A. L., and J. S. Russell

1977   "Crop Sequential Practices." In *Soil Factors in Crop Production in a Semi-arid Environment,* edited by John Samuel Russell and Emmet Lewis Greacen, pp. 279–300. St. Lucia: University of Queensland Press and The Australian Society of Soil Science.

Clawson, Marion H.; Hans H. Landberg; and Lyle T. Alexander, editors

1971   *The Agricultural Potential of the Middle East.* New York: Elsevier.

Clère, Jacques; Patrice Adeleine; and Denise Ferembach

1985   "Étude anthropologique des mandibules de Cheikh Hassan." *Cahiers de l'Euphrate* 4: 265–73.

Cocks, P. S.; E. F. Thompson; K. Somel; and A. Abd el-Moneim

1988   *Degradation and Rehabilitation of Agricultural Land in North Syria.* Aleppo: International Center for Agricultural Research in the Dry Areas Publications.

Cooke, Ronald U., and Richard W. Reeves

1976   *Arroyos and Environmental Change in the American South-west.* Oxford: Clarendon Press.

Cooper, Elisabeth N.

1998   "The EB–MB Transitional Period at Tell Kabir, Syria." In "Natural Space, Inhabited Space in Northern Syria (10th–2nd Millennium B.C.)," edited by Michel Fortin and Olivier Aurenche. Actes du colloque tenu à l'Université Laval in Québec, 5–7 mai 1997. Travaux de la Maison de l'Orient 28. *Bulletin of the Canadian Society for Mesopotamian Studies* 33: 271–80.

2001   "Archaeological Perspectives on the Political History of the Euphrates Valley during the Early Second Millennium B.C." In *Canadian Research on Ancient Syria,* edited by Michel Fortin, pp. 79–86. Canadian Society for Mesopotamian Studies 36. Toronto: Canadian Society for Mesopotamian Studies.

Cooper, P. J. M.

1991   "Fertilizer Use, Crop Growth, Water Use and Water Use Efficiency in Mediterranean Rain-fed Farming Systems." In *Soils and Crop Management for Improved Water Use Efficiency in Rain-fed Areas,* edited by H. C. Harris, P. J. M. Cooper, and M. Pala, pp. 135–52. Proceedings of an international workshop in Ankara, Turkey, 15–19 May 1989. International Center for Agricultural Research in the Dry Areas Publications 247. Aleppo: International Center for Agricultural Research in the Dry Areas Publications.

Cooper, P. J. M., and E. Bailey

1990   "Livestock in Mediterranean Farming Systems, a Traditional Buffer Against Uncertainty: Now a Threat to the Agricultural Resource Base." Paper presented at the World Bank Symposium, Risk in Agriculture, 9–10 January, 1990, in Washington, D.C.

Córdoba, J. M.

1988   "Prospección en el valle de río Baliḫ (Siria): Informe provisional." *Aula Orientalis* 6: 149–88.

Costa, Paolo M., and Tony J. Wilkinson

1987   "The Hinterland of Sohar: Archaeological Surveys and Excavations within the Region of an Omani Seafaring City." *Journal of Oman Studies* 9: 1–238.

Courty, Marie-Agnès

1994   "Le cadre paléogéographique des occupations humaines dans le bassin du Haut-Khabur (Syrie du nord-est): Premiers résultats." *Paléorient* 20: 21–59.

1998   "The Soil Record of an Exceptional Event at 4000 B.P. in the Middle East." In *Natural Catastrophes during Bronze Age Civilisations: Archaeological, Geological, Astronomical, and Cultural Perspectives,* edited by Benny J. Peiser, Trevor Palmer, and Mark E. Bailey, pp. 93–108. British Archaeological Reports, International Series 728. Oxford: Archaeopress.

Cribb, Roger

1991   *Nomads in Archaeology.* Cambridge: Cambridge University Press.

Crowfoot, Grace M.

1957   "Late Roman A, B, and C Wares." In *The Objects from Samaria,* edited by John Winter Crowfoot, Grace M. Crowfoot, and Kathleen M. Kenyon, pp. 357–64. Samaria-Sebaste 3. London: Palestine Exploration Fund.

Crowfoot, John Winter; Grace M. Crowfoot; and Kathleen M. Kenyon
1957 *The Objects from Samaria.* Samaria-Sebaste 3. London: Palestine Exploration Fund.

Cruells, W.
1998 "The Halaf Levels of Tell Amarna (Syria): First Preliminary Report." *Akkadica* 106: 1–21.

Culican, William, and Thomas L. McClellan
1983/84 "El-Qitar: First Season of Excavations, 1982–83." *Abr-Nahrain* 22: 29–63.

Curtin, Philip D.
1984 *Cross-Cultural Trade in World History.* Cambridge: Cambridge University Press.

Curtis, John
1989 *Excavations at Qasrij Cliff and Khirbet Qasrij.* Saddam Dam Report 10; British Museum Western Asiatic Excavations 1. London: British Museum Press.

Curtis, John, and Anthony Green
1997 *Excavations at Khirbet Khatuniyeh.* Saddam Dam Report 11. London: British Museum Press.

Curvers, Hans H.
1988 "The Period VII Pottery." In *Hammam et-Turkman* 1: *Report on the University of Amsterdam's 1981–84 Excavations in Syria,* Volume 2, edited by Maurits N. van Loon, pp. 397–455. Publications de l'Institut historique-archéologique néerlandais de Stamboul 63. Istanbul: Netherlands Historical and Archaeological Institute.

1989 "The Beginning of the Third Millennium in Syria." In *To the Euphrates and Beyond: Archaeological Studies in Honour of Maurits N. van Loon,* edited by Odette M. C. Haex, Hans H. Curvers, and Peter M. M. G. Akkermans, pp. 173–93. Rotterdam: A. A. Balkema.

1991 The Balikh Drainage in the Bronze Age. Ph.D. dissertation, University of Amsterdam.

Curvers, Hans H., and Glenn M. Schwartz
1997 "Umm el-Marra, a Bronze Age Urban Center in the Jabbul Plain, Western Syria." *American Journal of Archaeology* 101: 201–39.

Czichon, Rainer M., and Peter Werner
1998 *Tall Munbāqa-Ekalte* 1: *Die Bronzezeitlichen Kleinfunde.* Wissenschaftliche Veröffentlichung der Deutschen Orient-Gesellschaft 97; Ausgrabungen in Tall Munbāqa-Ekalte 1. Saarbrücken: Saarbrücker Druckerei und Verlag.

Dalley, Stephanie
1993 "Nineveh after 612 B.C." *Altorientalische Forschungen* 20: 134–47.

Danti, Michael D.
1997 "Regional Surveys and Excavations." In *Subsistence and Settlement in a Marginal Environment: Tell es-Sweyhat, 1989–1995 Preliminary Report,* edited by Richard L. Zettler, pp. 85–94. Museum Applied Science Center for Archaeology Research Papers in Science and Archaeology 14. Philadelphia: University of Pennsylvania Museum of Archaeology and Anthropology.

2000 Early Bronze Age Settlement and Land Use in the Tell es-Sweyhat Region, Syria. Ph.D. Dissertation, University of Pennsylvania.

Danti, Michael D., and Richard L. Zettler
1998 "The Evolution of the Tell es-Sweyhat (Syria) Settlement System in the 3rd Millennium B.C." In "Natural Space, Inhabited Space in Northern Syria (10th–2nd Millennium B.C.)," edited by Michel Fortin and Olivier Aurenche. Actes du colloque tenu à l'Université Laval in Québec, 5–7 mai 1997. Travaux de la Maison de l'Orient 28. *Bulletin of the Canadian Society for Mesopotamian Studies* 33: 209–28.

Dar, Shimon
1986 *Landscape and Pattern: An Archaeological Survey of Samaria 800 B.C.E.–636 C.E,* Volumes 1 and 2. British Archaeological Reports, International Series 308. Oxford: British Archaeological Reports.

Davis, P. H., editor
1967 *Flora of Turkey,* Volume 2. Edinburgh: Edinburgh University Press.

Dixon, John C.
1994 "Duricrusts." In *Geomorphology of Desert Environments,* edited by Athol D. Abrahams and Anthony J. Parsons, pp. 82–105. London: Chapman and Hall.

Dornemann, Rudolph H.
1978 "Tell Hadidi: A Bronze Age City on the Euphrates." *Archaeology* 31: 20–26.

1979 "Tell Hadidi: A Millennium of Bronze Age City Occupation." In *Archaeological Reports from the Tabqa Dam Project, Euphrates Valley, Syria,* edited by David Noel Freedman, pp. 113–51. Annual of the American Schools of Oriental Research 44. Cambridge: American Schools of Oriental Research.

1980 "Tell Hadidi: An Important Center of the Mitannian Period and Earlier." In *Le Moyen Euphrate: Zone de contacts et d'échanges,* edited by Jean Claude Margueron, pp. 217–34. Actes du colloque de Strasbourg, 10–12 mars 1977. Travaux du Centre de Recherche sur le Proche-Orient et la Grèce Antiques 5. Leiden: E. J. Brill.

1981 "The Late Bronze Age Pottery Tradition at Tell Hadidi, Syria." *Bulletin of the American Schools of Oriental Research* 241: 29–47.

1981/82 "Tell Hadidi." *Archiv für Orientforschung* 28: 218–23.

1983 "The Syrian Euphrates Valley as a Bronze Age Cultural Unit, Seen from the Point of View of Mari and Tell Hadidi." *Deir ez-Zur* 63–73.

1985 "Salvage Excavations at Tell Hadidi in the Euphrates River Valley." *Biblical Archaeologist* 48: 49–59.

1988 "Tell Hadidi: One Bronze Age Site among Many in the Tabqa Dam Salvage Area." *Bulletin of the American Schools of Oriental Research* 270: 13–42.

1989 "Comments on Small Finds and Items of Artistic Significance from Tell Hadidi and Nearby Sites in the Euphrates Valley, Syria." In *Essays in Ancient Civilization Presented to Helene J. Kantor,* edited by Albert

Leonard, Jr., and Bruce Beyer Williams, pp. 59–75. Studies in Ancient Oriental Civilization 47. Chicago: The Oriental Institute.

1990   "The Beginning of the Bronze Age in Syria in Light of Recent Excavations." In *Resurrecting the Past: A Joint Tribute to Adnan Bounni,* edited by Paolo Matthiae, Maurits N. van Loon, and Harvey Weiss, pp. 85–100. Publications de l'Institut historique-archéologique néerlandais de Stamboul 67. Istanbul: Netherlands Historical and Archaeological Institute.

1992   "Early Second Millennium Ceramic Parallels between Tell Hadidi-Azu and Mari." In *Mari in Retrospect: Fifty Years of Mari and Mari Studies*, edited by Gordon D. Young, pp. 77–112. Winona Lake: Eisenbrauns.

1993   "Tell Hadidi." In *L'Eufrate e il tempo: Le civiltà del medio Eufrate e della Gezira siriana,* edited by Olivier Rouault and Maria Grazia Masetti-Rouault, pp. 183–84. Milano: Electa.

1997   "Hadidi, Tell." In *The Oxford Encyclopedia of Archaeology in the Near East*, Volume 2, edited by Eric M. Meyers, pp. 453–54. Oxford: Oxford University Press.

Dossin, Georges
1974   "Le site de Tuttul-sur-Balîḫ." *Revue d'Assyriologie et d'Archéologie Orientale* 68: 25–34.

Drews, Robert
1993   *The End of the Bronze Age: Changes in Warfare and the Catastrophe ca. 1200 B.C.* Princeton: Princeton University Press.

Ducos, Pierre
1968   "The Animal Remains from Selenkaḥiye." *Les Annales Archéologiques Arabes Syriennes* 18: 33–34.

1973   "La faune de Tell Selenkahiye: Note préliminaire sur les ossements de la campagne de 1972." *Les Annales Archéologiques Arabes Syriennes* 23: 160.

Duff, B.; P. E. Rasmussen; and R. W. Smiley
1995   "Wheat/Fallow Systems in Semi-arid Regions of the Pacific NW America." In *Agricultural Sustainability: Economic, Environmental and Statistical Considerations,* edited by Vic Barnett, Roger Payne, and Roy Steiner, pp. 85–109. New York: John Wiley.

Egami, Namio; Sei-ichi Masuda; and Tayuka Iwasaki
1979   *Rumeilah and Mishrifat: Excavations of Hellenistic Sites in the Euphrates Basin 1974–1978.* Preliminary Report of Archaeological Researches in Syria 1. Tokyo: Ancient Orient Museum.

Eichler, Seyarre; Dieter Robert Frank; Dittmar Machule; Gerlinde Mozer; and Wilfried Pape
1984   "Ausgrabungen in Tall Munbāqa 1983." *Mitteilungen der Deutschen Orient-Gesellschaft zu Berlin* 116: 65–93.

Eidem, Jesper, and Rahel Ackermann
1999   "The Iron Age Ceramics from Tell Jurn Kabir." In *Iron Age Pottery in Northern Mesopotamia, Northern Syria and South-Eastern Anatolia*, edited by Arnulf Hausleiter and Andrzej Reiche, pp. 309–24. Papers presented at the meetings of the international "table ronde" at Heidelberg, 1995, and Nieborów, 1997, and other contributions. Altertumskunde des Vorderen Orients 10. Münster: Ugarit-Verlag.

Eidem, Jesper, and Karin Pütt
1994   "An Iron Age Site on the Euphrates: The First Season of Excavations at Tell Jurn Kabir (Syria)." *Orient Express* 1994: 8–9.

Eidem, Jesper, and David Warburton
1996   "In the Land of Nagar: A Survey around Tell Brak." *Iraq* 58: 51–64.

Einwag, Berthold
1993   "Vorbericht über die archäologische Geländebegehung in der Westğazira." *Damaszener Mitteilungen* 7: 23–43.

Einwag, Berthold; Kay Kohlmeyer; and Adelheid Otto
1995   "Tell Bazi: Vorberichte über die Untersuchungen 1993." *Damaszener Mitteilungen* 8: 95–124.

Einwag, Berthold, and Adelheid Otto
1999   "Tall Bazi." In *Archaeology of the Upper Syrian Euphrates: The Tishrin Dam Area,* edited by Gregorio del Olmo Lete and Juan-Luis Montero Fenollós, pp. 179–91. Proceedings of the International Symposium in Barcelona, 28–30 January 1998. Aula Orientalis, Supplementa 15. Barcelona: Editorial Ausa.

Ergenzinger, Peter J.; W. Frey; H. Kühne; and H. Kurschner
1988   "The Reconstruction of Environment, Irrigation and Development of Settlement on the Habur in North-east Syria." In *Conceptual Issues in Environmental Archaeology,* edited by J. Bintliff, D. A. Davidson, and E. G. Grant, pp. 108–28. Edinburgh: Edinburgh University Press.

Ergenzinger, Peter J., and Hartmut Kühne
1991   "Eine regionales Bewässerungssystem am Ḫābūr." In *Die Rezente Umwelt von Tall Šēḫ Ḥamad und Daten zur Umweltrekonstruktion der assyrischen Stadt Dūr-Katlimmu,* edited by Hartmut Kühne, pp. 163–90. Berichte der Ausgrabung Tall Šēḫ Ḥamad/Dūr-Katlimmu 1. Berlin: Dietrich Reimer Verlag.

Evershed, R. P.; P. H. Bethell; P. J. Reynolds; and N. J. Walsh
1997   "5ß-Stigmastanol and Related 5ß-Stanols as Biomarkers of Manuring: Analysis of Modern Experimental Material and Assessment of the Archaeological Potential." *Journal of Archaeological Science* 24: 485–95.

Fales, Frederick Mario
1990   "The Rural Landscape of the Neo-Assyrian Empire: A Survey." *State Archives of Assyria Bulletin* 4: 81–142.

Fedele, Francesco G.
1990   "Man, Land and Climate: Emerging Interactions from the Holocene of the Yemen Highlands." In *Man's Role in the Shaping of the Eastern Mediterranean Landscape,* edited by Sytze Bottema, G. Entjes-Nieborg, and W. van Zeist, pp. 31–42. Rotterdam: A. A. Balkema.

de Feyter, T.
1989   "The *Aussenstadt* Settlement of Munbaqa, Syria." In *To the Euphrates and Beyond: Archaeological Studies*

in Honour of Maurits N. van Loon, edited by Odette M. C. Haex, Hans H. Curvers, and Peter M. M. G. Akkermans, pp. 237–56. Rotterdam: A. A. Balkema.

Finet, André

1972   "Aperçu sur les fouilles Belges du Tell Kannâs." *Les Annales Archéologiques Arabes Syriennes* 22: 63–74.

1973   "Les fouilles du secteur Ouest au Tell Kannâs." *Archiv für Orientforshung* 24: 171–75.

1974   "Tell Qannas." In *Antiquités de l'Euphrate: Exposition des découvertes de la campagne internationale de sauvegarde des antiquités de l'Euphrate*, edited by Adnan Bounni, pp. 71–75. Damascus: Direction Générale des Antiquités et des Musées.

1975   "Les temples sumériens du Tell Kannâs." *Syria* 52: 157–74.

1977   "Les briques marquées du Tell Kannâs." *Annuaire de l'Institut de Philologie et d'Histoire Orientales et Slaves* 21: 37–52.

1979   "Bilan provisoire des fouilles belges du Tell Kannâs." In *Archaeological Reports from the Tabqa Dam Project, Euphrates Valley, Syria*, edited by David Noel Freedman, pp. 79–95. Annual of the American Schools of Oriental Research 44. Cambridge: American Schools of Oriental Research.

1980   "L'apport du Tell Kannas à l'histoire Proche-Orientale, de la fin du 4e millénaire à la moitié du 2e." In *Le Moyen Euphrate: Zone de contacts et d'échanges,* edited by Jean Claude Margueron, pp. 107–15. Actes du colloque de Strasbourg, 10–12 mars 1977. Travaux du Centre de Recherche sur le Proche-Orient et la Grèce Antiques 5. Leiden: E. J. Brill.

1993   "Gli scavi belgi di Tell Kannas." In *L'Eufrate e il tempo: Le civiltà del medio Eufrate e della Gezira siriana,* edited by Olivier Rouault and Maria Grazia Masetti-Rouault, pp. 143–44. Milan: Electa.

Finkbeiner, Uwe

1994   "Abd." In "Archaeology in Syria," edited by Harvey Weiss, pp. 101–58. *American Journal of Archaeology* 98: 116–17.

1995   "Tell el-ʿAbd: Vorläufiger Bericht über die Ausgrabungen 1992–1993." *Damaszener Mitteilungen* 8: 51–83.

1997   "ʿAbd." In "Archaeology in Syria," edited by Harvey Weiss, pp. 97–148. *American Journal of Archaeology* 101: 97–100.

Finkelstein, Israel

1988   *The Archaeology of the Israelite Settlement*. Jerusalem: Israel Exploration Society.

1995a   "The Great Transformation: The 'Conquest' of the Highlands Frontiers and the Rise of the Territorial States." In *The Archaeology of Society in the Holy Land,* edited by Thomas E. Levy, pp. 349–65. London: Leicester University Press.

1995b   *Living on the Fringe: The Archaeology and History of the Negev, Sinai, and Neighbouring Regions in the*

Bronze and Iron Ages. Monographs in Mediterranean Archaeology 6. Sheffield: Sheffield Academic Press.

Fleming, Daniel E.

1993   "A Limited Kingship: Late Bronze Emar in Ancient Syria." *Ugarit-Forshungen* 24: 59–71.

Florea, N., and Kh. al-Joumaa

1998   "Genesis and Classification of Gypsiferous Soils of the Middle Euphrates Floodplain, Syria." *Geoderma* 87: 67–85.

Food and Agriculture Organization of the United Nations

1974   *FAO-UNESCO Soil Map of the World* 1: *Legend*. Paris: United Nations Educational, Scientific and Cultural Organization.

1977   *FAO-UNESCO Soil Map of the World* 7: *South Asia*. Paris: United Nations Educational, Scientific and Cultural Organization.

Frangipane, Marcella, and Alba Palmieri

1989   "Aspects of Centralization in the Late Uruk Period in the Mesopotamian Periphery." *Origini* 14: 539–60.

Frank, Dieter Robert

1975   "Versuch zur Rekonstruktion von Bauregeln und Maßordnung einer nordsyrischen Stadt des vierten Jahrtausends: Untersucht anhand von Grabungsergebnissen der Deutschen Orient-Gesellschaft in Ḥabūba Kabīra: Ernst Heinrich zum 75. Geburtstag." *Mitteilungen der Deutschen Orient-Gesellschaft zu Berlin* 107: 7–16.

Frank, Dieter Robert; Dittmar Machule; Ursula Wittwer; and Markus Wäfler

1982   "Tall Munbāqa 1979." *Mitteilungen der Deutschen Orient-Gesellschaft zu Berlin* 114: 7–70.

Frankel, Rafael

1999   *Wine and Oil Production in Antiquity in Israel and Other Mediterranean Countries*. Journal for the Study of the Old Testament/American Schools of Oriental Research, Monographs 10. Sheffield: Sheffield Academic Press.

Franken, H. J.

1978   "Pottery from a Middle Bronze Age Tomb near Tell Hadidi on the Euphrates." In *Archaeology in the Levant: Essays for Kathleen Kenyon*, edited by Peter Roger Stuart Moorey and Peter Parr, pp. 67–75. Warminster: Aris and Phillips.

1983   "Four Large Projects of the Institute." *Newsletter University of Leiden, Department of Pottery Technology* 1: 4–5.

Freedman, David Noel, editor

1979   *Archaeological Reports from the Tabqa Dam Project, Euphrates Valley, Syria*. Annual of the American Schools of Oriental Research 44. Cambridge: American Schools of Oriental Research.

Frumkin, Amos; Israel Carmi; Israel Zak; and Mordeckai Magaritz

1994   "Middle Holocene Environmental Change determined from the Salt Caves of Mount Sedom, Israel." In *Late Quaternary Chronology and Paleoclimates of the Eastern Mediterranean*, edited by Ofar Bar-Yosef and

Renee S. Kra, pp. 315–32. Tucson: Radiocarbon, University of Arizona Press; Cambridge: American School of Prehistoric Research.

Gaffney, Vince, and Martin Tingle

1985 "The Maddle Farm (Berks.) Project and Micro-Regional Analysis." In *Archaeological Field Survey in Britain and Abroad*, edited by Sarah Macready and F. H. Thompson, pp. 67–73. Occasional Paper 6. London: Society of Antiquaries.

Gallant, Thomas W.

1986 "'Background Noise' and Site Definition: A Contribution to Survey Methodology." *Journal of Field Archaeology* 13: 403–18.

1991 *Risk and Survival in Ancient Greece: Reconstructing the Rural Domestic Economy.* Stanford: Stanford University Press.

Gerber, Christoph

1996 "Die Umgebung des Lidar Höyük von hellenistischer bis frühislamischer Zeit: Interpretation der Ergebnisse einer Geländebegehung." In *Continuity and Change in Northern Mesopotamia from the Hellenistic to the Early Islamic Period*, edited by Karin Bartl and Stefan R. Hauser, pp. 303–32. Proceedings of a colloquium held at the Seminar für Vorderasiatische Altertumskunde at Freie Universität Berlin, 6–9 April 1994. Berliner Beiträge zum Vorderen Orient 17. Berlin: Dietrich Reimer Verlag.

Gerritsen, Fokke A.

1996 "Hellenistic and Roman-Parthian Pottery from the Balikh Valley, Northern Syria." *Oudheidkundige Mededelingen uit het Rijksmuseum van Oudheden te Leiden* 76: 93–108.

Gerritsen, Fokke A.; Jennifer A. MacCormack; Glenn M. Schwartz

2000 "Survey in the Jabbul Plain." In "Excavation and Survey in the Jabbul Plain, Western Syria: The Umm el-Marra Project 1996–1997," by Glenn M. Schwartz, Hans H. Curvers, Fokke A. Gerritsen, Jennifer A. MacCormack, Naomi F. Miller, and Jill A. Weber, pp. 447–55. *American Journal of Archaeology* 104: 419–62.

Geyer, Bernard

1985 "Geomorphologie et occupation du sol de la Moyenne Vallée de l'Euphrate dans la region de Mari." *Mari Annales de Recherches Interdisciplinaires* 4: 27–39.

Geyer, Bernard, and J. Besançon

1996 "Environnement et occupation du sol dans la vallée de l'Euphrate syrien durant le Néolithique et le Chalcolithique." *Paléorient* 22: 5–15.

Geyer, Bernard, and Yves Calvet

2001 "Les steppes arides de la Syrie du Nord au Bronze ancien ou 'la première conquête de l'est.'" In *Conquête de la steppe et appropriation des terres sur les marges arides du croissant fertile*, edited by Bernard Geyer, pp. 55–67. Travaux de la Maison de l'Orient Méditerranéen 36. Lyon: Maison de l'Orient Méditerranéen — Jean Pouilloux.

Geyer, Bernard, and Jean-Yves Monchambert

1987 "Prospection de la Moyenne vallée de l'Euphrate: Rapport préliminaire: 1982–1985." *Mari Annales de Recherches Interdisciplinaires* 5: 293–344.

Geyer, Bernard, and Marie-Odik Rousset

2001 "Les steppes arides de la Syrie du Nord à l'époque byzantine ou 'la ruée vers l'est.'" In *Conquête de la steppe et appropriation des terres sur les marges arides du Croissant Fertile*, edited by Bernard Geyer, pp. 111–21. Travaux de la Maison de l'Orient Méditerranéen 36. Lyon: Maison de l'Orient Méditerranéen — Jean Pouilloux.

Gibson, McGuire, and Tony J. Wilkinson

1995 "The Dhamār Plain, Yemen: A Preliminary Study of the Archaeological Landscape." Papers from the twenty-eighth meeting of the Seminar for Arabian Studies at Oxford, 21–23 July 1994. *Proceedings of the Seminar for Arabian Studies* 25: 159–83.

Göyünç, Nejat, and Wolf-Dieter Hütteroth

1997 *Land an der Grenze: Osmanische Verwaltung im heutigen türkisch-syrisch-irakischen Grenzgebiet im 16. Jahrhundert.* Istanbul: Eren Yayıncılık.

Golvin, L.

1980 "À la recherche de la cité médiévale de Bālis (Moyen-Euphrate)." In *Le Moyen Euphrate: Zone de contacts et d'échanges*, edited by Jean Claude Margueron, pp. 389–96. Actes du colloque de Strasbourg, 10–12 mars 1977. Travaux du Centre de Recherche sur le Proche-Orient et la Grèce Antiques 5. Leiden: E. J. Brill.

Gommes, R.

1993 "Current Climate and Population Constraints on World Agriculture." In *Agricultural Dimensions of Global Climate Change,* edited by Harry M. Kaiser and Thomas E. Drennen, pp. 67–86. Delray Beach, Florida: St. Lucie Press.

Goodfriend, Glenn A.

1990 "Rainfall in the Negev Desert during the Middle Holocene, Based on ^{13}C of Organic Matter in Land Snail Shells." *Quaternary Research* 34: 186–97.

1991 "Holocene Trends in ^{18}O in Land Snail Shells from the Negev Desert and Their Implications for Changes in Rainfall Source Areas." *Quaternary Research* 35: 417–26.

Gorny, Ronald L.

1995 "Viticulture and Ancient Anatolia." In *The Origins and Ancient History of Wine,* edited by Patrick E. McGovern, Stuart J. Fleming, and Solomon H. Katz, pp. 133–74. Food and Nutrition in History and Anthropology 11. Amsterdam: Gordon and Breach.

Goudie, Andrew

1986 *The Human Impact on the Natural Environment.* Cambridge: Massachusetts Institute of Technology Press.

Grainger, John D.

1990 *The Cities of Seleukid Syria.* Oxford: Clarendon Press.

Greene, Kevin

1986 *The Archaeology of the Roman Economy.* Berkeley: University of California Press.

Gregory, P. J.
1991   "Concepts of Water Use Efficiency." In *Soils and Crop Management for Improved Water Use Efficiency in Rain-fed Areas*, edited by H. C. Harris, P. J. M. Cooper, and M. Pala, pp. 9–20. Proceedings of an international workshop in Ankara, Turkey, 15–19 May 1989. International Center for Agricultural Research in the Dry Areas Publications 247. Aleppo: International Center for Agricultural Research in the Dry Areas Publications.

Gremmen, W. H. E., and Sytze Bottema
1991   "Palynological Investigations in the Syrian Ǧazīra." In *Die rezente Umwelt von Tall Šēḫ Ḥamad und Daten zur Umweltrekonstruktion der assyrischen Stadt Dūr-Katlimmu,* edited by Hartmut Kühne, pp. 105–16. Berichte der Ausgrabung Tall Šēḫ Ḥamad/Dūr-Katlimmu 1. Berlin: Dietrich Reimer Verlag.

Grossman, David
1971   "Do We Have a Theory for Settlement Geography? The Case for Ibo Land." *The Professional Geographer* 23: 197–203.

Guest, Evan, editor
1966   *Flora of Iraq: Introduction.* Flora of Iraq 1. Baghdad, Republic of Iraq: Ministry of Agriculture.

Guérin, Alexandrine
1996   "L'occupation abbaside de Nasibin, typologie et chronologie préliminaires de la céramique prospectée en surface." In *Continuity and Change in Northern Mesopotamia from the Hellenistic to the Early Islamic Period*, edited by Karin Bartl and Stefan R. Hauser, pp. 377–400. Proceedings of a colloquium held at the Seminar für Vorderasiatische Altertumskunde at Freie Universität Berlin, 6–9 April 1994. Berliner Beiträge zum Vorderen Orient 17. Berlin: Dietrich Reimer Verlag.

Guler, M., and M. Karaca
1988   "Agroclimatological Criteria for Determining the Boundaries of Fallow Practice." In *Winter Cereals and Food Legumes in Mountainous Areas,* edited by J. P. Srivastava, S. Varma, and M. Tahir. Proceedings of an international symposium on Problems and Prospects of Winter Cereals and Legumes Production in the High-Elevation Areas of West Asia, Southeast Asia, and North Africa in Ankara, Turkey, 6–10 July 1987. Aleppo: International Center for Agricultural Research in the Dry Areas Publications.

Gustavson-Gaube, Carrie
1981   "Shams ed-Din Tannira: The Halafian Pottery of Area A." *Berytus* 29: 9–182.

Haex, Odette M. C.; Hans H. Curvers; and Peter M. M. G. Akkermans, editors
1989   *To the Euphrates and Beyond: Archaeological Studies in Honour of Maurits N. van Loon.* Rotterdam: A. A. Balkema.

Halstead, Paul
1989   "The Economy Has a Normal Surplus: Economic Stability and Social Change among Early Farming Communities of Thessaly, Greece." In *Bad Year Economics: Cultural Responses to Risk and Uncertainty,* edited by Paul Halstead and John O'Shea, pp. 68–80. Cambridge: Cambridge University Press.

Hammade, Hamido, and Yayoi Koike
1992   "Syrian Archaeological Expedition in the Tishreen Dam Basin: Excavations at Tell al-ʿAbr 1990 and 1991." *Damaszener Mitteilungen* 6: 109–75.

Hanbury-Tenison, Jack
1983   "The 1982 Flaked Stone Assemblage at Jebel Aruda, Syria." *Akkadica* 33: 27–33.

Hannestad, Lise
1983a   *Ikaros: The Hellenistic Settlements* 2: *The Hellenistic Pottery Catalogue and Plates*, Volume 2. Jutland Archaeological Society Publications 16. Aarhus: Jysk Arkaeologisk Selskab.

1983b   *Ikaros: The Hellenistic Settlements* 2: *The Hellenistic Pottery from Failaka*, Volume 1. Jutland Archaeological Society Publications 16. Aarhus: Jysk Arkaeologisk Selskab.

Harlan, Jack R.
1995   *The Living Fields: Our Agricultural Heritage.* Cambridge: Cambridge University Press.

Harper, Richard P.
1975   "Excavations at Dibsi Faraj, Northern Syria, 1972–1974: A Preliminary Note on the Site and Its Monuments." *Dumbarton Oaks Papers* 29: 319–38.

1980   "Athis-Neocaesareia-Qasrin-Dibsi Faraj." In *Le Moyen Euphrate: Zone de contacts et d'échanges*, edited by Jean Claude Margueron, pp. 327–48. Actes du colloque de Strasbourg, 10–12 mars 1977. Travaux du Centre de Recherche sur le Proche-Orient et la Grèce Antiques 5. Leiden: E. J. Brill.

Harris, H. C.
1991   "Implications of Climatic Variability." In *Soils and Crop Management for Improved Water Use Efficiency in Rain-fed Areas*, edited by H. C. Harris, P. J. M. Cooper, and M. Pala, pp. 21–34. Proceedings of an international workshop in Ankara, Turkey, 15–19 May 1989. International Center for Agricultural Research in the Dry Areas Publications 247. Aleppo: International Center for Agricultural Research in the Dry Areas Publications.

Harris, H. C.; A. E. Osman; P. J. M. Cooper; and M. J. Jones
1991   "The Management of Crop Rotations for Greater Water Use Efficiency." In *Soils and Crop Management for Improved Water Use Efficiency in Rain-fed Areas,* edited by H. C. Harris, P. J. M. Cooper, and M. Pala, pp. 237–50. Proceedings of an international workshop in Ankara, Turkey, 15–19 May 1989. International Center for Agricultural Research in the Dry Areas Publications 247. Aleppo: International Center for Agricultural Research in the Dry Areas Publications.

Harrison, Sandy P., and Gunnar Digerfeldt
1993   "European Lakes as Palaeohydrological and Palaeoclimatic Indicators." *Quaternary Science Reviews* 12: 233–48.

Hausleiter, Arnulf, and Andrzej Reiche, editors
1999   *Iron Age Pottery in Northern Mesopotamia, Northern Syria and South-Eastern Anatolia.* Papers presented at the meetings of the international "table ronde" at Heidelberg, 1995, and Nieborów, 1997, and other contributions. Altertumskunde des Vorderen Orients 10. Münster: Ugarit-Verlag.

Hawkins, J. David
1995   "The Political Geography of North Syria and South-East Anatolia in the Neo-Assyrian Period." In *Neo-Assyrian Geography*, edited by Mario Liverani, pp. 87–101. Quaderni di Geografia Storica 5. Rome: Università di Roma.

Heinrich, Ernst
1970a   "Bericht über die von der Deutschen Orient-Gesellschaft mit Mitteln der Stiftung Volkswagenwerk in Habuba Kabira und in Mumbaqat unternommenen archäologischen Untersuchungen." *Les Annales Archéologiques Arabes Syriennes* 20: 25–44.

1970b   "Mumbaqat." In "Bericht über die von der Deutschen Orient-Gesellschaft mit Mitteln der Stiftung Volkswagenwerk in Habuba Kabira und in Mumbaqat unternommenen archäologischen Untersuchungen," edited by Ernst Heinrich, pp. 25–44. *Les Annales Archéologiques Arabes Syriennes* 20: 37–39.

1970c   "Mumbaqat." In "Zweiter vorläufiger Bericht über die von der Deutschen Orient-Gesellschaft mit Mitteln der Stiftung Volkswagenwerk in Ḥabuba Kabira und in Mumbaqat unternommenen archäologischen Untersuchungen (Herbstkampagne 1969), erstattet von Mitgliedern der Mission," by Ernst Heinrich, Wido Ludwig, Eva Strommenger, Ruth Opificius, and Dietrich Sürenhagen, pp. 27–85. *Mitteilungen der Deutschen Orient-Gesellschaft zu Berlin* 102: 72–78.

Heinrich, Ernst; Wido Ludwig; Eva Strommenger; Ruth Opificius; and Dietrich Sürenhagen
1970   "Zweiter vorläufiger Bericht über die von der Deutschen Orient-Gesellschaft mit Mitteln der Stiftung Volkswagenwerk in Ḥabuba Kabira und in Mumbaqat unternommenen archäologischen Untersuchungen (Herbstkampagne 1969), erstattet von Mitgliedern der Mission." *Mitteilungen der Deutschen Orient-Gesellschaft zu Berlin* 102: 27–85.

Heinrich, Ernst; Hansjörg Schmid; Hans-Christian Kara; Eva Strommenger; Dietrich Sürenhagen; Giesela Hecker; Ursula Seidl; Dittmar Machule; and Dieter Rentschler
1971   "Dritter vorläufiger Bericht über die von der Deutschen Orient-Gesellschaft mit Mitteln der Stiftung Volkswagenwerk in Ḥabūba Kabira und Mumbaqat unternommenen archäologischen Untersuchungen (Herbstkampagne 1970), erstattet von Mitgliedern der Mission." *Mitteilungen der Deutschen Orient-Gesellschaft zu Berlin* 103: 5–58.

Heinrich, Ernst; Eva Strommenger; Dieter Robert Frank; Wido Ludwig; Dietrich Sürenhagen; Eva Töpperwein; Hansjörg Schmid; Jan-Christoph Heusch; Kay Kohlmeyer; Dittmar Machule; Markus Wäfler; and Thomas Rhode

1973   "Vierter vorläufiger Bericht über die von der Deutschen Orient-Gesellschaft mit Mitteln der Stiftung Volkswagenwerk in Ḥabuba Kabira (Ḥububa Kabira, Herbstkampagnen 1971 und 1972 sowie Testgrabung Frühjahr 1973) und in Mumbaqat (Tall Munbaqa, Herbstkampagne 1971) unternommenen archäologischen Untersuchungen, erstattet von Mitgliedern der Mission." *Mitteilungen der Deutschen Orient-Gesellschaft zu Berlin* 105: 5–68.

1974   "Vierter vorläufiger Bericht über die von der Deutschen Orient-Gesellschaft mit Mitteln der Stiftung Volkswagenwerk in Ḥabuba Kabira (Ḥububa Kabira, Herbstkampagnen 1971 und 1972 sowie Testgrabung Frühjahr 1973) und in Mumbaqat (Tall Munbaqa, Herbstkampagne 1971) unternommenen archäologischen Untersuchungen, erstattet von Mitgliedern der Mission (Fortsetzung)." *Mitteilungen der Deutschen Orient-Gesellschaft zu Berlin* 106: 5–97.

Heinrich, Ernst; Einar von Schuler; Hansjörg Schmid; Wido Ludwig; Eva Strommenger; and Ursula Seidl
1969   "Bericht über die von der Deutschen Orient-Gesellschaft mit Mitteln der Stiftung Volkswagenwerk im Euphrattal bei Aleppo begonnenen archäologischen Untersuchungen, erstattet von Mitgliedern der Expedition." *Mitteilungen der Deutschen Orient-Gesellschaft zu Berlin* 101: 27–67.

Heinzelin, J. de
1967   "Supplement A: Investigations on the Terraces of the Middle Euphrates." In *The Tabqa Reservoir Survey 1964*, by Maurits N. van Loon, pp. 22–26. Damascus: Direction Générale des Antiquités et des Musées.

Heusch, Jan-Christoph
1980   "Tall Habuba Kabira im 3. und 2. Jahrtausend: Die Entwicklung der Baustruktur." In *Le Moyen Euphrate: Zone de contacts et d'échanges*, edited by Jean Claude Margueron, pp. 159–78. Actes du colloque de Strasbourg, 10–12 mars 1977. Travaux du Centre de Recherche sur le Proche-Orient et la Grèce Antiques 5. Leiden: E. J. Brill.

Hide, Christine M.
1990   "Archaeobotanical Remains from Tell es-Sweyhat, Northwest Syria." Museum Applied Science Center for Archaeology Ethnobotanical Laboratory Report 7. Philadelphia: University of Pennsylvania Museum of Archaeology and Anthropology.

Hillman, Gordon C.
1973a   "Agricultural Productivity and Past Population Potential at Aşvan." *Anatolian Studies* 23: 225–40.

1973b   "Agricultural Resources and Settlement in the Aşvan Region." *Anatolian Studies* 23: 217–24.

1981   "Reconstructing Crop Husbandry Practices from Charred Remains of Crops." In *Farming Practice in British Prehistory*, edited by Roger J. Mercer, pp. 123–62. Edinburgh: University of Edinburgh Press.

1984   "Interpretation of Archaeological Plant Remains: The Application of Ethnographic Models from Turkey." In *Plants and Ancient Man: Studies in Palaeoethno-*

botany, edited by Willem van Zeist and W. A. Casparie, pp. 1–42. Proceedings of the Sixth Symposium of the International Work Group for Palaeoethnobotany in Groningen, 30 May–3 June 1983. Rotterdam: A. A. Balkema.

1996   "Late Pleistocene Changes in Wild Plant-Foods Available to Hunter-Gatherers of the Northern Fertile Crescent: Possible Preludes to Cereal Cultivation." In *The Origins and Spread of Agriculture and Pastoralism in Eurasia*, edited by David R. Harris, pp. 159–203. Washington, D.C.: Smithsonian Institution Press.

2000   "Overview: The Plant-Based Components of Subsistence in Abu Hureyra 1 and 2." In *Village on the Euphrates: From Foraging to Farming at Abu Hureyra*, edited by Andrew M. T. Moore, G. C. Hillman, and A. J. Legge, pp. 416–22. Oxford: Oxford University Press.

Hillman, Gordon C.; Susan M. Colledge; and David R. Harris
1989   "Plant-Food Economy during the Epipaleolithic Period at Tell Abu Hureyra, Syria: Dietary Diversity, Seasonality, and Modes of Exploitation." In *Foraging and Farming: The Evolution of Plant Exploitation*, edited by David R. Harris and Gordon C. Hillman, pp. 240–68. One World Archaeology 13. London: Unwin Hyman.

Hole, Frank
1991   "Middle Khabur Settlement and Agriculture in the Ninevite 5 Period." *Canadian Society for Mesopotamian Studies Bulletin* 21: 17–30.

1994   "Environmental Instabilities and Urban Origins." In *Chiefdoms and Early States in the Near East: The Organizational Dynamics of Complexity*, edited by Gil J. Stein and Mitchell S. Rothman, pp. 121–51. Monographs in World Archaeology 18. Madison: Prehistory Press.

1997   "Evidence for mid-Holocene Environmental Change in the Western Khabur Drainage, Northeastern Syria." In *Third Millennium B.C. Climate Change and Old World Collapse*, edited by Hasan Nüzhet Dalfes, George Kukla, and Harvey Weiss, pp. 39–66. Proceedings of the North Atlantic Treaty Organization Advanced Research Workshop on Third Millennium B.C. Abrupt Climate Change and Old World Social Collapse in Kemer, Turkey, 19–24 September 1994. North Atlantic Treaty Organization Advanced Science Institutes Series 1; Global Environmental Change 49. Berlin: Springer.

in press   "Preliminary Report on the Joint American-Danish Archaeobiological Sampling of Sites in the Khabur Basin (1990)." *Les Annales Archéologiques Arabes Syriennes*.

Holland, Thomas A.
1976   "Preliminary Report on Excavations at Tell es-Sweyhat, Syria, 1973–74." *Levant* 8: 36–70.

1977   "Preliminary Report on Excavations at Tell es-Sweyhat, Syria, 1975." *Levant* 9: 36–65.

1980   "Incised Pottery from Tell Sweyhat, Syria and Its Foreign Connections." In *Le Moyen Euphrate: Zone de contacts et d'échanges*, edited by Jean Claude Margueron, pp. 127–57. Actes du colloque de Strasbourg, 10–12 mars 1977. Travaux du Centre de Recherche sur le Proche-Orient et la Grèce Antiques 5. Leiden: E. J. Brill.

in press   *Excavations at Tell es-Sweyhat 2: Archaeology of the Bronze Age, Hellenistic, and Roman Remains from an Ancient Town on the Euphrates River*. Oriental Institute Publications 125. Chicago: The Oriental Institute.

Holland, Thomas A., and Richard L. Zettler
1991   "Sweyhat." In "Archaeology in Syria," edited by Harvey Weiss, pp. 683–740. *American Journal of Archaeology* 95: 717–19.

Holling, C. S.
1986   "The Resilience of Terrestrial Ecosystems: Local Surprise and Global Change." In *Sustainable Development of the Biosphere*, edited by William C. Clark and R. E. Munn, pp. 292–320. Cambridge: Cambridge University Press.

Holod, Renata
1978   "Ceramics." In *City in the Desert: Qasr al-Hayr East*, by Oleg Grabar, Renata Holod, James Knustad, and William Trousdale, pp. 110–37. Harvard Middle Eastern Monographs 23/24. Cambridge: Harvard University Press.

d'Hont, Olivier
1994   *Vie quotidienne des 'Agedat*. Damascus: Institut Français d'Études Arabes de Damas.

Hütteroth, Wolf-Dieter
1990   "Villages and Tribes of the Ğezīra under Early Ottoman Administration (16th Century): A Preliminary Report." *Berytus* 38: 179–84.

Ibach, Robert D., Jr.
1987   *Archaeological Survey of the Hesban Region*. Hesban 5. Berrien Springs: Andrews University Press.

Ionides, Michael George
1937   *The Régime of the Rivers Euphrates and Tigris: A General Hydraulic Survey of Their Basins*. London: E. and F. N. Spon.

Issawi, Charles
1988   *The Fertile Crescent 1800–1914: A Documentary Economic History*. Oxford: Oxford University Press.

Jabbour, E., and M. Naji
1991   "Soil and Crop Management for Improved Water Use Efficiency in Rain-fed Areas of Syria." In *Soils and Crop Management for Improved Water Use Efficiency in Rainfed Areas*, edited by H. C. Harris, P. J. M. Cooper, and M. Pala, pp. 159–67. Proceedings of an international workshop in Ankara, Turkey, 15–19 May 1989. International Center for Agricultural Research in the Dry Areas Publications 247. Aleppo: International Center for Agricultural Research in the Dry Areas Publications.

Jamieson, Andrew Stewart

1993   "The Euphrates Valley and Early Bronze Age Ceramic Traditions." *Abr-Nahrain* 31: 36–92.

1999   "Neo-Assyrian Pottery from Tell Ahmar." In *Iron Age Pottery in Northern Mesopotamia, Northern Syria and South-Eastern Anatolia*, edited by Arnulf Hausleiter and Andrzej Reiche, pp. 287–308. Papers presented at the meetings of the international "table ronde" at Heidelberg, 1995, and Nieborów, 1997, and other contributions. Altertumskunde des Vorderen Orients 10. Münster: Ugarit-Verlag.

Jammous, B., and D. Stordeur

1996   "Jerf al-Ahmar." In *Syrian-European Archaeology Exhibition: Working Together*, edited by Sultan Muhesen, Najah Attar, and Alan Waddams, pp. 27–30. Damascus National Museum, 30 May–11 July 1996. Damascus: Éditions de l'Institut Français d'Études Arabes de Damas.

Janssen, B. H.

1970   *Soil Fertility in the Great Konya Basin, Turkey.* Wageningen, Netherlands: Center for Agricultural Publication and Documentation.

Jas, Remko M., editor

2000   *Rainfall and Agriculture in Northern Mesopotamia.* Proceedings from the third MOS Symposium in Leiden, 21–22 May 1999. MOS Studies 3; Publications de l'Institut historique-archéologique néerlandais de Stamboul 88. Istanbul: Netherlands Historical and Archaeological Institute.

Jean, Charles-F.

1948   "Lettres de Mari IV Transcrites et traduites." *Revue d'Assyriologie et d'Archéologie Orientale* 42: 53–78.

Johns, C. H. W.

1901   *An Assyrian Doomsday Book, or, Liber Censualis of the District Round Harran in the Seventh Century B.C.* Assyriologische Bibliothek 17. Leipzig: J. C. Hinrichs.

Johnson, Gregory A.

1981   "Monitoring Complex System Integration and Boundary Phenomena with Settlement Size Data." In *Archaeological Approaches to the Study of Complexity*, edited by Sander Ernst van der Leeuw, pp. 143–88. Amsterdam: University of Amsterdam.

Jones, M. J.

1993   "Barley-based Farming Systems of the Mediterranean." In *The Agrometeorology of Rain-fed Barley-based Farming Systems*, edited by M. J. Jones, pp. 129–44. Aleppo: International Center for Agricultural Research in the Dry Areas Publications.

Kaegi, Walter E.

1992   *Byzantium and the Early Islamic Conquests.* Cambridge: Cambridge University Press.

Kalsbeek, J.

1980   "La céramique de série du Djebel ʿAruda (à l'époque d'Uruk)." *Akkadica* 20: 1–11.

Kampschulte, Ingrid, and Winfried Orthmann

1984   *Gräber des 3. Jahrtausends v. Chr. im syrischen Euphrattal 1: Ausgrabungen bei Tawi 1975 und 1978.* Saarbrücker Beiträge zur Altertumskunde 38. Bonn: Dr. Rudolf Habelt.

Karstens, Karsten

1990   "Ein Rollsiegel aus Tall Munbāqa." *Mitteilungen der Deutschen Orient-Gesellschaft zu Berlin* 122: 43–44.

1992   "Rollsiegel aus Tall Munbāqa/Ekalte 1990." *Mitteilungen der Deutschen Orient-Gesellschaft zu Berlin* 124: 41–43.

Kaul, R. N., and D. C. P. Thalen

1979   "South-west Asia." In *Arid-Land Ecosystems: Structure, Functioning and Management,* Volume 1, edited by D. W. Goodall and R. A. Perry, pp. 213–71. International Biological Programme 16. Cambridge: Cambridge University Press.

Kennedy, David, editor

1998   *The Twin Towns of Zeugma on the Euphrates: Rescue Work and Historical Studies.* Journal of Roman Archaeology Supplementary 27. Portsmouth: Journal of Roman Archaeology.

Kennedy, David, and Derrick Riley

1990   *Rome's Desert Frontier from the Air.* London: B. T. Batsford.

Kennedy, Hugh

1992   "The Impact of Muslim Rule on the Pattern of Rural Settlement in Syria." In *La Syrie de Byzance à l'Islam: VIIᵉ–VIIIᵉ siècles*, edited by Pierre Canivet and Jean-Paul Rey-Coquais, pp. 291–98. Actes du colloque d'international Lyon, Maison de l'Orient Méditerranéen et Institut du Monde Arabe à Paris, 11–15 septembre 1990. Damascus: Institut Français de Damas.

Kerbe, Jehad

1987   *Climat, Hydrologie et Aménagements Hydro-agricoles de Syrie*, Volumes 1 and 2. Talence: Diffusion Presses Universitaires de Bordeaux.

Klengel, Horst

1992   *Syria 3000 to 300 B.C.: A Handbook of Political History.* Berlin: Akademie-Verlag.

Koelling, Sabine, and Joachim Kunze

1986   "Analyse von Metallproben aus Tall Munbāqa." *Mitteilungen der Deutschen Orient-Gesellschaft zu Berlin* 118: 161–63.

Kolars, John F., and William A. Mitchell

1991   *The Euphrates River and Southeast Anatolia Development Project.* Carbondale: Southern Illinois University Press.

Kouchoukos, Nicholas Thomas

1998   Landscape and Social Change in Late Prehistoric Mesopotamia. Ph.D. dissertation, Yale University.

Krause, Clemens; Kurt Schuler; and Rolf A. Stucky

1972   *Tell el Hajj in Syrien: Erster vorläufiger Bericht: Grabungskampagne 1971.* Basel: Hans Jucker.

1973 "Erster vorläufiger Bericht über die auf Tell el Hajj durchgeführten schweizerischen archäologischen Ausgrabungen: Erstattet von Mitgliedern der Mission." *Les Annales Archéologiques Arabes Syriennes* 23: 161–200.

Kühne, Hartmut
1980 "Das Nordost-Tor von Tell Mumbāqat." In *Le Moyen Euphrate: Zone de contacts et d'échanges*, edited by Jean Claude Margueron, pp. 203–15. Actes du colloque de Strasbourg, 10–12 mars 1977. Travaux du Centre de Recherche sur le Proche-Orient et la Grèce Antiques 5. Leiden: E. J. Brill.

1995 "The Assyrians on the Middle Euphrates and the Ḫābūr." In *Neo-Assyrian Geography*, edited by Mario Liverani, pp. 69–85. Quaderni di Geografia Storica 5. Rome: Università di Roma.

Küster, Hansjörg
1989 "Bronzezeitliche Pflanzenreste aus Tall Munbāqa." *Mitteilungen der Deutschen Orient-Gesellschaft zu Berlin* 121: 85–91.

Kuhrt, Amélie
1995 "The Assyrian Heartland in the Achaemenid Period." In *Dans les Pas des Dix-Mille: Peuples et pays du Proche-Orient vus par un Grec*, edited by Pierre Briant, pp. 239–54. Actes de la Table Ronde Internationale à Toulouse, 3–4 février 1995. Pallas 43. Toulouse: Presses Universitaires du Mirail.

Kutzbach, John E.; G. Bonan; J. A. Foley; and S. P. Harrison
1996 "Vegetation and Soil Feedbacks on the Response of the African Monsoon to Orbital Forcing in the Early to Middle Holocene." *Nature* 384: 623–26.

Landmann, Günter; Andreas Reimer; Gerry Lemcke; and Stephan Kempe
1996 "Dating Late Glacial abrupt Climate Changes in the 14,750 yr long Continuous Varve Record of Lake Van, Turkey." *Palaeogeography, Palaeoclimatology, Palaeoecology* 122: 107–18.

Lázaro, Ana I.
1988 "The Period X Pottery." *Hammam et-Turkman* 1: *Report on the University of Amsterdam's 1981–84 Excavations in Syria*, Volume 2, edited by Maurits N. van Loon, pp. 499–559. Publications de l'Institut historique-archéologique néerlandais de Stamboul 63. Istanbul: Netherlands Historical and Archaeological Institute.

Lebeau, Marc
1983 *La céramique de l'âge du fer II–III à Tell Abou Danné et ses rapports avec la céramique contemporaine en Syrie*. Centre de recherche d'archéologie orientale Université de Paris 2; Éditions Recherche sur les Civilisations 12. Paris: Éditions Recherche sur les Civilisations.

2000 "Stratified Archaeological Evidence and Compared Periodizations in the Syrian Jezirah during the Third Millennium B.C." In *From the Euphrates to the Caucasus: Chronologies for the 4th–3rd Millennium B.C.*, edited by Catherine Marro and Harald Hauptmann, pp. 167–92. Actes du colloque d'Istanbul, 16–19 décembre 1998. Varia Anatolica 11. Paris: Institut Français d'Études Anatoliennes d'Istanbul de Boccard.

Lehmann, Gunnar
1996 *Untersuchungen zur späten Eisenzeit in Syrien und Libanon: Stratigraphie und Keramikformen zwischen ca. 720 bis 300 v. Chr.* Altertumskunde des Vorderen Orients 5. Münster: Ugarit-Verlag.

1998 "Trends in the Local Pottery Development of the Late Iron Age and Persian Period in Syria and Lebanon, ca. 700 to 300 B.C." *Bulletin of the American Schools of Oriental Research* 311: 7–37.

Leisten, Thomas
1999/2000 "Balis: Preliminary Report on the Campaigns 1996 and 1998." *Berytus* 44: 35–55.

Lemcke, Gerry, and Michael Sturm
1997 "Trace Element Measurements as Proxy for the Reconstruction of Climate Changes at Lake Van (Turkey): Preliminary Results." In *Third Millennium B.C. Climate Change and Old World Collapse*, edited by Hasan Nüzhet Dalfes, George Kukla, and Harvey Weiss, pp. 653–78. Proceedings of the North Atlantic Treaty Organization Advanced Research Workshop on Third Millennium B.C. Abrupt Climate Change and Old World Social Collapse in Kemer, Turkey, 19–24 September 1994. North Atlantic Treaty Organization Advanced Science Institutes Series 1; Global Environmental Change 49. Berlin: Springer.

Lewis, Norman N.
1987 *Nomads and Settlers in Syria and Jordan 1800–1980*. Cambridge: Cambridge University Press.

1988 "The Balikh Valley and Its People." In *Hammam et-Turkman* 1: *Report on the University of Amsterdam's 1981–84 Excavations in Syria*, Volume 2, edited by Maurits N. van Loon, pp. 683–95. Publications de l'Institut historique-archéologique néerlandais de Stamboul 63. Istanbul: Netherlands Historical and Archaeological Institute.

Liverani, Mario
1992 *Studies on the Annals of Ashurnasirpal* 2: *Topographical Analysis*, Volume 2. Quaderni di Geografia Storica 4. Rome: Università di Roma.

1995 *Neo-Assyrian Geography*. Quaderni di Geografia Storica 5. Rome: Università di Roma.

1996 "Reconstructing the Rural Landscape of the Ancient Near East." *Journal of the Economic and Social History of the Orient* 39: 1–41.

Lloyd, Seton
1938 "Some Ancient Sites in the Sinjar District." *Iraq* 5: 123–42.

Lloyd, Seton, and William Brice
1951 "Harran." *Anatolian Studies* 1: 77–111.

Lloyd, Seton, and Nuri Gokçe
1953 "Sultantepe." *Anatolian Studies* 3: 27–51.

Logar, Nuša
1996   "Die Keramik und andere Kleinfunde." In *Resafa* 4: *Die Große Moschee von Resafa-Ruṣāfat Hišām*, edited by Dorothée Sack, pp. 77–110. Mainz am Rhein: Philipp von Zabern.

Loizides, P.
1980   "Crop Rotations under Rain-fed Conditions in a Mediterranean Climate in Relation to Soil Moisture and Fertilizer Requirements." In *Rain-fed Agriculture in the Near East and North Africa*, edited by the Food and Agriculture Organization of the United Nations, pp. 23–38. Proceedings of the Food and Agriculture Organization Regional Seminar in Amman, 5–10 May 1979. Rome: Food and Agriculture Organization of the United Nations.

Loomis, R. S.
1983   "Crop Manipulations for Efficient Use of Water: An Overview." In *Limitations to Efficient Water Use in Crop Production*, edited by Howard M. Taylor, Wayne R. Jordan, and Thomas R. Sinclair, pp. 345–74. Madison: American Society of Agronomy.

Ludwig, Wido
1980   "Mass, Sitte und Technik des Bauens in Habuba Kabira-Süd." In *Le Moyen Euphrate: Zone de contacts et d'échanges,* edited by Jean Claude Margueron, pp. 65–74. Actes du colloque de Strasbourg, 10–12 mars 1977. Travaux du Centre de Recherche sur le Proche-Orient et la Grèce Antiques 5. Leiden: E. J. Brill.

Ludwig, Wido, and Eva Strommenger
1970   "Ausgrabungen in Ḥabuba Kabira und Mumbaqat." *Archiv für Orientforschung* 23: 131–34.

Lupton, Alan
1996   *Stability and Change: Socio-political Development in North Mesopotamia and South-east Anatolia 4000–2700 B.C.* British Archaeological Reports, International Series 627. Oxford: Tempus Repartum.

Lüth, Friedrich
1989   "Ein neuer Typus halbmondförmiger Axtklingen aus Nordsyrien." In *To the Euphrates and Beyond: Archaeological Studies in Honour of Maurits N. van Loon,* edited by Odette M. C. Haex, Hans H. Curvers, and Peter M. M. G. Akkermans, pp. 167–72. Rotterdam: A. A. Balkema.

Lyon, Jerry D.
2000   "Middle Assyrian Expansion and Settlement Development in the Syrian Jazira: The View from the Balikh Valley." In *Rainfall and Agriculture in Northern Mesopotamia*, edited by Remko M. Jas, pp. 89–126. Proceedings from the third MOS Symposium in Leiden, 1999. MOS Studies 3, Publications de l'Institut historique-archéologique néerlandais de Stamboul 88. Istanbul: Netherlands Historical and Archaeological Institute.

Lyonnet, Bertille
1996   "La prospection archéologique de la partie occidentale du Haut-Khabur (Syrie du Nord-est): Méthodes, résultats et questions autour de l'occupation aux IIIe et IIe millénaires av. N.È." In *Mari, Ébla et les hourrites dix ans de travaux,* edited by Jean-Marie Durand, pp. 363–76. Actes du colloque international à Paris, mai 1993. Amurru 1. Paris: Éditions Recherche sur les Civilisations.

Machule, Dittmar
1984   "Tall Munbaqa 1983." *Archiv für Orientforschung* 31: 160–62.

1993/94   "Tall Munbāqa 1988–1993." *Archiv für Orientforschung* 40/41: 241–43.

1994   "Tall Munbāqa/Ekalte 1993." *Mitteilungen der Deutschen Orient-Gesellschaft zu Berlin* 126: 63–64.

Machule, Dittmar; Mathias Benter; Joachim Boessneck; Angela von den Driesch; Teunis Cornelis de Feyter; Karsten Karstens; Heinz-Helmut Klapproth; Sabine Koelling; Joachim Kunze; Ömer Tezeren; and Peter Werner
1987   "Ausgrabungen in Tall Munbāqa 1985." *Mitteilungen der Deutschen Orient-Gesellschaft zu Berlin* 119: 73–134.

Machule, Dittmar; Mathias Benter; Rainer M. Czichon; Iris Gerlach; Azad Hamoto; Heinz Klapproth; Wilfried Pape; and Peter Werner
1991   "Ausgrabungen in Tall Munbāqa/Ekalte 1989." *Mitteilungen der Deutschen Orient-Gesellschaft zu Berlin* 123: 71–93.

Machule, Dittmar; Mathias Benter; Rainer M. Czichon; Iris Gerlach; and Peter Werner
1992   "Ausgrabungen in Tall Munbāqa/Ekalte 1990." *Mitteilungen der Deutschen Orient-Gesellschaft zu Berlin* 124: 11–40.

Machule, Dittmar; Mathias Benter; Rainer M. Czichon; Karsten Karstens; Heinz Klapproth; Walter Mayer; Wilfried Pape; and Peter Werner
1988   "Ausgrabungen in Tall Munbāqa 1986." *Mitteilungen der Deutschen Orient-Gesellschaft zu Berlin* 120: 11–50.

Machule, Dittmar; Mathias Benter; Rainer M. Czichon; Marta Luciani; Mohammad Miftah; Wilfried Pape; and Peter Werner
1993   "Ausgrabungen in Tall Munbāqa/Ekalte 1991." *Mitteilungen der Deutschen Orient-Gesellschaft zu Berlin* 125: 69–101.

Machule, Dittmar; Mathias Benter; Rainer M. Czichon; Winfried Pape; and Peter Werner
1990   "Ausgrabungen in Tall Munbāqa 1988." *Mitteilungen der Deutschen Orient-Gesellschaft zu Berlin* 122: 9–42.

Machule, Dittmar; Mathias Benter; Rainer M. Czichon; and Peter Werner
1996   "Tall Munbāqa/Ekalte 1994." *Mitteilungen der Deutschen Orient-Gesellschaft zu Berlin* 128: 11–32.

Machule, Dittmar; Rainer M. Czichon; and Peter Werner
1989   "Ausgrabungen in Tall Munbāqa 1987." *Mitteilungen der Deutschen Orient-Gesellschaft zu Berlin* 121: 65–77.

1994   "Tall Munbāqa/Ekalte 1992." *Mitteilungen der Deutschen Orient-Gesellschaft zu Berlin* 126: 51–62.

Machule, Dittmar; Karsten Karstens; Heinz-Helmut Klapproth; Gerlinde Mozer; Wilfried Pape; Peter Werner; Walter Mayer; Ruth Mayer-Opificius; and Michael Mackensen
1986   "Ausgrabungen in Tall Munbāqa 1984." *Mitteilungen der Deutschen Orient-Gesellschaft zu Berlin* 118: 67–145.

Machule, Dittmar, and Dieter Rentschler
1971   "Arbeiten in Mumbaqat und Beobachtungen in der Umgebung." In "Dritter vorläufiger Bericht über die von der Deutschen Orient-Gesellschaft mit Mitteln der Stiftung Volkswagenwerk in Ḥabūba Kabira und Mumbaqat unternommenen archäologischen Untersuchungen (Herbstkampagne 1970), erstattet von Mitgliedern der Mission," by Ernst Heinrich, Hansjörg Schmid, Hans-Christian Kara, Eva Strommenger, Dietrich Sürenhagen, Giesela Hecker, Ursula Seidl, Dittmar Machule, and Dieter Rentschler, pp. 5–58. *Mitteilungen der Deutschen Orient-Gesellschaft zu Berlin* 103: 48–58.

Machule, Dittmar, and Markus Wäfler
1978   "Tall Munbāqa 1978." *Mitteilungen der Deutschen Orient-Gesellschaft zu Berlin* 110: 73–76.

1983   "Tall Munbaqa 1968–1979." *Les Annales Archéologiques Arabes Syriennes* 33: 123–29.

Machule, Dittmar; Markus Wäfler; and Thomas Rhode
1974   "Mumbaqat (Tall Munbaqa) Herbstkampagne 1971." In "Vierter vorläufiger Bericht über die von der Deutschen Orient-Gesellschaft mit Mitteln der Stiftung Volkswagenwerk in Ḥabuba Kabira (Ḥububa Kabira, Herbstkampagnen 1971 und 1972 sowie Testgrabung Frühjahr 1973) und in Mumbaqat (Tall Munbaqa, Herbstkampagne 1971) unternommenen archäologischen Untersuchungen, erstattet von Mitgliedern der Mission (Fortsetzung)," by Ernst Heinrich, Eva Strommenger, Dieter Robert Frank, Wido Ludwig, Dietrich Sürenhagen, Eva Töpperwein, Hansjörg Schmid, Jan-Christoph Heusch, Kay Kohlmeyer, Dittmar Machule, Markus Wäfler, and Thomas Rhode, pp. 5–97. *Mitteilungen der Deutschen Orient-Gesellschaft zu Berlin* 106: 6–52.

Mainguet, Monique
1991   *Desertification: Natural Background and Human Mismanagement.* Springer Series in Physical Environment 9. Berlin: Springer.

Mairs, L. D.
1995   "Jebel Khalid: Preliminary Archaeozoology Report." *Mediterranean Archaeology* 8: 124–27.

Mallowan, Max E. L.
1946   "Excavations in the Baliḫ Valley, 1938." *Iraq* 8: 111–59.

Marfoe, Leon
1990   "An Overview of Horizontal Exposures." In *Town and Country in Southeastern Anatolia* 2: *The Stratigraphic Sequence at Kurban Höyük,* edited by Guillermo Algaze, pp. 185–209. Oriental Institute Publications 110. Chicago: The Oriental Institute.

Margueron, Jean Claude
1980   *Le Moyen Euphrate: Zone de contacts et d'échanges.* Actes du colloque de Strasbourg, 10–12 mars 1977. Travaux du Centre de Recherche sur le Proche-Orient et la Grèce Antiques 5. Leiden: E. J. Brill.

1982   "Aux marches de l'empire hittite: Une campagne de fouille à Tell Faq'ous (Syrie), citadelle du pays d'Ashtata." In *La Syrie au Bronze Récent,* pp. 47–66. Extraits de la 27 Rencontre Assyriologique Internationale de Paris, juillet 1980. Paris: Éditions Recherche sur les Civilizations.

1988   "Espace agricòle et aménagement régional à Mari au début du IIIᵉ millénaire." Irrigation and Cultivation in Mesopotamia 1. *Bulletin on Sumerian Agriculture* 4: 49–60.

1989   "Emar et Faq'ous." In *Contributions français à l'archéologie syriennes 1969–1989.* Damascus: Institut Français d'Archéologie du Proche-Orient.

1995   "Emar, Capital of Aštata in the Fourteenth Century B.C.E." *Biblical Archaeologist* 58: 126–38.

Margueron, Jean-Claude, and M. Sigrist
1997   "Emar." In *The Oxford Encyclopedia of Archaeology in the Near East,* Volume 2, edited by Eric M. Meyers, pp. 236–39. Oxford: Oxford University Press.

Marro, Catherine, and Harald Hauptmann, editors
2000   *From the Euphrates to the Caucasus: Chronologies for the 4th–3rd Millennium B.C.* Actes du colloque d'Istanbul, 16–19 décembre 1998. Varia Anatolica 11. Paris: Institut Français d'Études Anatoliennes d'Istanbul de Boccard.

Masuda, Sei-ichi
1983   "Terracota House-Models Found at Rumeilah." *Les Annales Archéologiques Arabes Syriennes* 33: 153–60.

Matthers, John, editor
1981   *The River Qoueiq, Northern Syria and Its Catchment: Studies Arising from the Tell Rifa'at Survey 1977–79.* British Archaeological Reports, International Series 98. Oxford: British Archaeological Reports.

Matthews, Victor Harold
1978   *Pastoral Nomadism in the Mari Kingdom (ca. 1830–1760 B.C.).* American Schools of Oriental Research, Dissertation Series 3. Cambridge: American Schools of Oriental Research.

Matthiae, Paolo
1980   *Ebla: An Empire Rediscovered.* Translated by Christopher Holme. London: Hodder and Stoughton.

Maxwell Hyslop, R.; J. du Plat Taylor; M. V. Seton Williams; and J. d'A. Waechter
1942   "An Archaeological Survey of the Plain of Jabbul, 1939." *Palestine Exploration Quarterly* 74: 8–40.

Mayer, Walter
1990   "Der antike Name von Tall Munbāqa, die Schreiber und die chronologische Einordnung der Tafelfunde: Die Tontafelfunde von Tall Munbāqa 1988." *Mitteilungen der Deutschen Orient-Gesellschaft zu Berlin* 122: 45–66.

1993   "Die Tontafelfunde von Tall Munbāqa/Ekalte: 1989 und 1990." *Mitteilungen der Deutschen Orient-Gesellschaft zu Berlin* 125: 103–06.

Mayer-Opificius, Ruth
1989   "Eine Siegelabrollung aus mittelsyrischer Zeit auf Tontafeln aus Tall Munbāqa." *Mitteilungen der Deutschen Orient-Gesellschaft zu Berlin* 121: 79–84.

Mazzoni, Stefania
1995   "Settlement Pattern and New Urbanization in Syria at the Time of the Assyrian Conquest." In *Neo-Assyrian Geography*, edited by Mario Liverani, pp. 181–91. Quaderni di Geografia Storica 5. Rome: Università di Roma.

McClellan, Thomas L.
1984/85 "El-Qitar: Second Season of Excavations, 1983–84." *Abr-Nahrain* 23: 39–72.

1986   "El-Qitar: Third Season of Excavation, 1984–85." *Abr-Nahrain* 24: 83–106.

1992   "12th Century B.C. Syria: Comments on H. Sader's Paper." In *The Crisis Years: The 12th Century B.C. from Beyond the Danube to the Tigris*, edited by William A. Ward and Martha Sharp Joukowsky, pp. 164–73. Dubuque: Kendall/Hunt.

1997   "Qitar, el-." In *The Oxford Encyclopedia of Archaeology in the Near East*, Volume 4, edited by Eric M. Meyers, pp. 389. Oxford: Oxford University Press.

1998   "Tell Banat North: The White Monument." In *About Subartu: Studies Devoted to Upper Mesopotamia*, edited by Marc Lebeau, pp. 243–69. Subartu 4. Turnhout, Belgium: Brepols.

McClellan, Thomas L., and Anne Porter
in press "Archaeological Surveys of the Tishreen Dam Flood Zone." *Les Annales Archéologiques Arabes Syriennes.*

McCorriston, Joy
1992   "The Halaf Environment and Human Activities in the Khabur Drainage, Syria." *Journal of Field Archaeology* 19: 315–33.

1995   "Preliminary Archaeobotanical Analysis in the Middle Habur Valley, Syria and Studies of Socioeconomic Change in the Early Third Millennium B.C." *Canadian Society for Mesopotamian Studies Bulletin* 29: 33–46.

McNicoll, Anthony W.; Phillip C. Edwards; Jack Hanbury-Tenison; J. B. Hennessy; Timothy F. Potts; Robert H. Smith; Alan G. Walmsley; and Pamela Watson
1992   *Pella in Jordan 2: The Second Interim Report of the Joint University of Sydney and College of Wooster Excavations at Pella 1982–1985*. Mediterranean Archaeology, Supplement 2. Sydney: Meditarch.

McQuigg, J. D.
1981   "Climate Variability and Crop Yield in High and Low Temperate Regions." In *Food-Climate Interactions*, edited by Wilfrid Bach, Jürgen Pankrath, and Stephen Henry Schneider, pp. 121–37. Proceedings of an International Workshop held in Berlin (West), 9–12 December 1980. Dordrecht, Netherlands: D. Reidel.

Meijer, Diederik J. W.
1986   *A Survey in Northeastern Syria.* Publications de l'Institut historique-archéologique néerlandais de Stamboul 58. Istanbul: Netherlands Historical and Archaeological Institute.

Métral, Françoise
2000   "Managing Risk: Sheep-Rearing and Agriculture in the Syrian Steppe." In *The Transformation of Nomadic Society in the Arab East,* edited by Martha Mundy and Basim Musallam, pp. 123–44. University of Cambridge Oriental Publications 58. Cambridge: Cambridge University Press.

Meyer, Jan-Waalke
1982   "Zusammenfassende Ergebnisse der Ausgrabungen in Halawa/Syrien 1979–1980." *Archiv für Orientforschung Beiheft* 19: 237–43.

1987/88 "Halawa 1986–1987: Les fouilles sur le tell Halawa A." *Les Annales Archéologiques Arabes Syriennes* 37/38: 242–50.

1991   *Gräber des 3. Jahrtausends v. Chr. in syrischen Euphrattal 3: Ausgrabungen in Šamseddin und Djerniye.* Schriften zur Vonderasiatischen Archäologie 3. Saarbrücken: Saarbrücker Druckerei und Verlag.

1996   "Offene und geschloßene Siedlungen: Ein Beitrag zur Siedlungsgeschichte und historischen Topographie in Nordsyrien während des 3. und 2. Jts. v. Chr." *Altorientalische Forschungen* 23: 132–70.

Meyer, Jan-Waalke, and Winfried Orthmann
1983   "Halawa 1980–1982." *Les Annales Archéologiques Arabes Syriennes* 33: 93–110.

Meyer, Jan-Waalke, and Alexander Pruß
1994   *Ausgrabungen in Halawa 2: Die Kleinfunde von Tell Halawa A.* Schriften zur Vorderasiatischen Archäologie 6. Saarbrücken: Saarbrücker Druckerei und Verlag.

Middleton, Nick, and David Thomas
1992   *World Atlas of Desertification.* United Nations Environment Programme. London: Edward Arnold.

Millar, Fergus
1993   *The Roman Near East 31 B.C.–A.D. 337.* Cambridge: Harvard University Press.

Miller, Naomi F.
1983   Economy and Environment of Malyan, a Third Millennium B.C. Urban Center in Southern Iran. Ph.D. dissertation, University of Michigan.

1984   "The Use of Dung as Fuel: An Ethnographic Example and an Archaeological Application." *Paléorient* 10, no. 2: 71–79.

1986   "Vegetation and Land Use." In "The Chicago Euphrates Archaeological Project 1980–1984: An Interim Report," by Guillermo Algaze, K. Ataman, M. Ingraham, Leon Marfoe, M. McDonald, Naomi F. Miller, C. Snow, Gil J. Stein, Bruce Verharen, Patricia Wattenmaker, Tony J. Wilkinson, and K. Aslıhan Yener, pp. 37–148. *Anatolica* 13: 85–89, 119–20.

1990a   "Archaeobotanical Perspectives on the Rural-Urban Connection." In *Economy and Settlement in the Near East: Analyses of Ancient Sites and Materials*, edited by Naomi F. Miller, pp. 79–83. Museum Applied Science Center of Archaeology Research Papers in Science and Archaeology, Supplement to Volume 7. Philadelphia: University of Pennsylvania Museum of Archaeology and Anthropology.

1990b   "Clearing Land for Farmland and Fuel: Archaeobotanical Studies of the Ancient Near East." In *Economy and Settlement in the Near East: Analyses of Ancient Sites and Materials*, edited by Naomi F. Miller, pp. 71–78. Museum Applied Science Center for Archaeology Research Papers in Science and Archaeology, Supplement to Volume 7. Philadelphia: University of Pennsylvania Museum of Archaeology and Anthropology.

1991   "The Near East." In *Progress in Old World Palaeoethnobotany: A Retrospective View on the Occasion of 20 Years of the International Work Group for Palaeoethnobotany*, edited by Willem van Zeist, Krystyna Wasylikowa, and Karl-Ernst Behre, pp. 133–60. Rotterdam: A. A. Balkema.

1993   "Tell Jouweif: Flotation Samples from the 1992 Excavation." Museum Applied Science Center for Archaeology Ethnobotanical Laboratory Report 12. Philadelphia: University of Pennsylvania Museum of Archaeology and Anthropology.

1996   "Plant Remains from Umm al-Marra, Syria, 1994 and 1995." Museum Applied Science Center for Archaeology Ethnobotanical Laboratory Report 19. Philadelphia: University of Pennsylvania Museum of Archaeology and Anthropology.

1997a   "Farming and Herding along the Euphrates: Environmental Constraint and Cultural Choice (Fourth to Second Millennia B.C.)." In *Subsistence and Settlement in a Marginal Environment: Tell es-Sweyhat, 1989–1995 Preliminary Report*, edited by Richard L. Zettler, pp. 123–32. Museum Applied Science Center for Archaeology Research Papers in Science and Archaeology 14. Philadelphia: University of Pennsylvania Museum of Archaeology and Anthropology.

1997b   "Sweyhat and Hajji Ibrahim: Some Archaeobotanical Samples from the 1991 and 1993 Seasons." In *Subsistence and Settlement in a Marginal Environment: Tell es-Sweyhat, 1989–1995 Preliminary Report*, edited by Richard L. Zettler, pp. 95–122. Museum Applied Science Center for Archaeology Research Papers in Science and Archaeology 14. Philadelphia: University of Pennsylvania Museum of Archaeology and Anthropology.

2002   "Tracing the Development of the Agropastoral Economy in Southeastern Anatolia and Northern Syria." In *The Dawn of Farming in the Near East*, edited by Rene T. J. Cappers and Sytze Bottema, pp. 85–94. Studies in Early Near Eastern Production, Subsistence, and Environment 6. Berlin: Ex Oriente.

Miller, Naomi F., and Tristine Lee Smart
1984   "Intentional Burning of Dung as Fuel: A Mechanism for the Incorporation of Charred Seeds into the Archeological Record." *Journal of Ethnobiology* 4: 15–28.

Minnis, Paul E.
1985   *Social Adaptation to Food Stress: A Prehistoric Southwestern Example*. Chicago: University of Chicago Press.

Molina, Manuel
1999   "Goods Distribution in the Upper Euphrates from the Perspective of the Tell Qara Quzaq Excavations." In *Archaeology of the Upper Syrian Euphrates: The Tishrin Dam Area*, edited by Gregorio del Olmo Lete and Juan-Luis Montero Fenollós, pp. 471–78. Proceedings of the International Symposium in Barcelona, 28–30 January 1998. Aula Orientalis, Supplementa 15. Barcelona: Editorial Ausa.

Molist Montaña, Miquel
1994   "Halula." In "Archaeology in Syria," edited by Harvey Weiss, pp. 101–58. *American Journal of Archaeology* 98: 105–06.

1996   *Tell Halula (Siria) un Yacimiento Neolítico del Valle Medio del Éufrates Campañas de 1991 y 1992*. Informes Arqueológicos 4. Barcelona: Ministerio de Educacion y Cultura Instituto del Patrimonio Histórico Español.

Moore, Andrew M. T.
1975   "The Excavation of Tell Abu Hureyra in Syria: A Preliminary Report." *Proceedings of the Prehistoric Society* 41: 50–77.

1989   "The Transition from Foraging to Farming in Southwest Asia: Present Problems and Future Directions." In *Foraging and Farming: The Evolution of Plant Exploitation*, edited by David R. Harris and Gordon C. Hillman, pp. 620–31. One World Archaeology 13. London: Unwin Hyman.

1992   "The Impact of Accelerator Dating at the Early Village of Abu Hureyra on the Euphrates." *Radiocarbon* 34: 850–58.

Moore, Andrew M. T., and G. C. Hillman
1992   "The Pleistocene to Holocene Transition and Human Economy in SW Asia: The Impact of the Younger Dryas." *American Antiquity* 57: 482–94.

Moore, Andrew M. T.; G. C. Hillman; and A. J. Legge
2000   *Village on the Euphrates: From Foraging to Farming at Abu Hureyra*. Oxford: Oxford University Press.

Moorey, Peter Roger Stuart
1980   *Cemeteries of the First Millennium B.C. at Deve Höyük, near Carchemish, Salvaged by T. E. Lawrence and C. L. Woolley in 1913*. British Archaeological Reports, International Series 87. Oxford: British Archaeological Reports.

Moortgat-Correns, Ursula
1972   *Die Bildwerke vom Djebelet el Beda in ihrer räumlichen und zeitlichen Umwelt*. Berlin: Walter de Gruyter.

Morandi Bonacossi, Daniele

2000a   "Marina ša Šadê, Marinâ, Burmarina: The Many Names of an Assyrian Town on the Euphrates." In *Patavina Orientalia Selecta*, edited by Elena Rova, pp. 221–30. History of the Ancient Near East/Monographs 4. Padova: Sargon Srl.

2000b   "The Syrian Jezireh in the Late Assyrian Period: A View from the Countryside." In *Essays on Syria in the Iron Age*, edited by Guy Bunnens, pp. 349–96. Ancient Near Eastern Studies, Supplement 7. Leuven: Peeters Press.

Mortimore, Michael

1989   *Adapting to Drought: Farmers, Famines and Desertification in West Africa*. Cambridge: Cambridge University Press.

1998   *Roots in the African Dust: Sustaining the Sub-Saharan Drylands*. Cambridge: Cambridge University Press.

Mulders, M. A.

1969   *The Arid Soils of the Balikh Basin (Syria)*. Rotterdam: Drukkerij.

Muraoka, Takamitsu

1984/85   "Two Syriac Inscriptions from the Middle Euphrates." *Abr-Nahrain* 23: 83–89.

Musil, Alois

1927   *The Middle Euphrates: A Topographical Itinerary*. American Geographical Society Oriental Explorations and Studies 3. New York: American Geographical Society.

1928   *Palmyrena: A Topographical Itinerary*. American Geographical Society Oriental Explorations and Studies 4. New York: American Geographical Society.

Netser, Michael

1998   "Population Growth and Decline in the Northern Part of Eretz-Israel during the Historical Period as Related to Climatic Changes." In *Water, Environment and Society in Times of Climatic Change*, edited by Arie S. Issar and Neville Brown, pp. 129–45. Water Science and Technology Library 31. Dordrecht, Netherlands: Kluwer Academic Publishers.

Neumann, J., and S. Parpola

1987   "Climatic Change and the Eleventh–Tenth-Century Eclipse of Assyria and Babylonia." *Journal of Near Eastern Studies* 46: 161–82.

Nicholson, Sharon E.

1995   "Variability of African Rainfall on Interannual and Decadal Timescales." In *Natural Climate Variability on Decade-to-Century Time Scales*, edited by Climate Research Committee, Board on Atmospheric Sciences and Climate, Commission on Geosciences, Environment, and Resources, pp. 32–43. Papers presented at a Workshop, 21–25 September 1992. Washington, D.C.: National Academy Press.

Nierlé, M.-C.

1982   "Mureybet et Cheikh Hassan (Syrie): Outillage de mouture et de broyage (9ème et 8ème millénaires)." *Cahiers de l'Euphrate* 3: 177–215.

Nieuwenhuyse, Olivier

2000   "Halaf Settlement in the Khabur Headwaters." In *Prospection Archéologique du Haut-Khabur Occidental (Syrie du N.È.)*, edited by Bertille Lyonnet, pp. 151–260. Bibliothèque archéologique et historique de l'Institut français d'archéologie de Beyrouth 155. Beirut: Institut Français d'Archéologie du Proche-Orient.

Nordblom, Thomas L.

1983   *Livestock-Crop Interactions: The Decision to Harvest or to Graze Mature Grain Crops*. Discussion Paper 10, Farming Systems Program. Aleppo: International Center for Agricultural Research in the Dry Areas Publications.

Northedge, Alastair

1981   "Selected Late Roman and Islamic Coarse Wares." In *The River Qoueiq, Northern Syria, and Its Catchment: Studies Arising from the Tell Rifa'at Survey 1977–79*, Volume 2, edited by John Matthers, pp. 459–71. British Archaeological Reports, International Series 98. Oxford: British Archaeological Reports.

Oates, David; Joan Oates; and Helen McDonald

1997   *Excavations at Tell Brak 1: The Mitanni and Old Babylonian Periods*. London: British School of Archaeology in Iraq; Cambridge: McDonald Institute Monographs.

Oates, Joan

1959   "Late Assyrian Pottery from Fort Shalmaneser." *Iraq* 21: 130–46.

1982   "Archaeological Evidence for Settlement Patterns in Mesopotamia and Eastern Arabia in Relation to Possible Environmental Conditions." In *Palaeoclimates, Palaeoenvironments, and Human Communities in the Eastern Mediterranean Region in Later Prehistory*, Volume 2, edited by John L. Bintliff and Willem van Zeist, pp. 359–93. British Archaeological Reports, International Series 133. Oxford: British Archaeological Reports.

Oded, Bustenay

1979   *Mass Deportations and Deportees in the Neo-Assyrian Empire*. Wiesbaden: Ludwig Reichert Verlag.

L'Office Arabe, editor

1969   Étude documentaire sur l'agriculture syrienne. Damascus, Syria: L'Office Arabe.

Oguchi, T., and C. T. Oguchi

1998   "Mid-Holocene Floods of the Syrian Euphrates inferred from 'Tell' Sediments." In *Palaeohydrology and Environmental Change*, edited by Gerardo Benito, Victor R. Baker, and Kenneth John Gregory, pp. 307–16. Chichester: Wiley.

del Olmo Lete, Gregorio, and Juan-Luis Montero Fenollós

1999   *Archaeology of the Upper Syrian Euphrates: The Tishrin Dam Area*. Proceedings of the International Symposium in Barcelona, 28–30 January 1998. Aula Orientalis, Supplementa 15. Barcelona: Editorial Ausa.

Oram, Peter A., and Cornelis de Haan
  1995   *Technologies for Rain-fed Agriculture in Mediterranean Climates: A Review of World Bank Experiences.* World Bank Technical Paper 300. Washington, D.C.: The World Bank.

Orssaud, Dominique
  1980   "Céramique." In "Déhès (Syrie du Nord) Campagnes I–III (1976–1978)," by Jean-Pierre Sodini, Georges Tate, Bernard Bavant, Swantje Bavant, Jean-Luc Biscop, and Dominique Orssaud, pp. 1–305. *Syria* 57: 234–66.

Orthmann, Winfried
  1974   "Moumbaqat." In *Antiquités de l'Euphrate: Exposition des découvertes de la campagne internationale de sauvegarde des antiquités de l'Euphrate*, edited by Adnan Bounni, pp. 62–65. Damascus: Direction Générale des Antiquités et des Musées.

  1975   "Bericht über die dritte Grabungskampagne 1973 in Mumbaqat." *Les Annales Archéologiques Arabes Syriennes* 25: 129–53.

  1976   "Mumbaqat 1974: Vorläufiger Bericht über die von der Deutschen Orient-Gesellschaft mit Mitteln der Stiftung Volkswagenwerk unternommenen Ausgrabungen." *Mitteilungen der Deutschen Orient-Gesellschaft zu Berlin* 108: 25–44.

  1978/79   "Tall Ḥalāwa." *Archiv für Orientforschung* 26: 157–59.

  1981   *Halawa 1977 bis 1979: Vorläufiger Bericht über die 1. bis 3. Grabungskampagne.* Saarbrücker Beiträge zur Altertumskunde 31. Bonn: Rudolf Habelt Verlag.

  1981/82   "Tall Ḥalāwa." *Archiv für Orientforschung* 28: 223–26.

  1982   "Ausgrabungen in Halawa 1978." *Les Annales Archéologiques Arabes Syriennes* 32: 143–76.

  1984   "Tall Halawa 1982." *Archiv für Orientforschung* 31: 142–46.

  1985   "Art of the Akkade Period in Northern Syria and Mari." *Mari Annales de Recherches Interdisciplinaires* 4: 469–74.

  1989   *Halawa 1980 bis 1986: Vorläufiger Bericht über die 4.–9. Grabungskampagne.* Saarbrücker Beiträge zur Altertumskunde 52. Bonn: Rudolf Habelt Verlag.

Orthmann, Winfried, and Hartmut Kühne
  1974   "Mumbaqat 1973: Vorläufiger Bericht über die von der Deutschen Orient-Gesellschaft mit Mitteln der Stiftung Volkswagenwerk unternommenen Ausgrabungen." *Mitteilungen der Deutschen Orient-Gesellschaft zu Berlin* 106: 53–97.

Orthmann, Winfried, and Elena Rova
  1991   *Gräber des 3. Jahrtausends v. Chr. im syrischen Euphrattal 2: Ausgrabungen in Wreide.* Schriften zur Vorderasiatischen Archäologie 2. Saarbrücken: Saarbrücker Druckerei und Verlag.

Pabot, H.
  1956   Rapport au Gouvernement de Syria sur l'écologie et ses applications. Rome: Food and Agriculture Organization of the United Nations.

Pala, M.; A. Matar; A. Mazid; and K. el-Hajj
  1992   "Wheat Response to Nitrogen and Phosphorous Fertilization under Various Environmental Conditions of Northern Syria." In *Fertilizer Use Efficiency under Rain-fed Agriculture in West Asia and North Africa*, edited by John Ryan and Abdallah Matar, pp. 92–105. Proceedings of the Fourth Regional Workshop in Agadir, Morocco, 5–10 May 1991. Aleppo: International Center for Agricultural Research in the Dry Areas Publications.

Palmer, Carol
  1998   "'Following the Plough': The Agricultural Environment of Northern Jordan." *Levant* 30: 129–65.

Parry, M. L.
  1986   "Some Implications of Climatic Change for Human Development." In *Sustainable Development of the Biosphere*, edited by William C. Clark and R. E. Munn, pp. 378–409. Cambridge: Cambridge University Press.

Parry, M. L., and T. R. Carter
  1988   "The Assessment of the Effects of Climatic Variations on Agriculture: Aims, Methods and Summary of Results." In *The Impact of Climatic Variations on Agriculture: Assessments in Semi-Arid Regions,* Volume 2, edited by M. L. Parry, T. R. Carter, and N. T. Konijin, pp. 11–96. Dordrecht, Netherlands: Kluwer Academic Publications.

Peltenburg, Edgar; Diane Bolger; Stuart Campbell; Mary Anne Murray; and Richard Tipping
  1996   "Jerablus-Tahtani, Syria, 1995: Preliminary Report." *Levant* 28: 1–25.

Peltenburg, Edgar; Stuart Campbell; Stephen Carter; Fiona M. K. Stephen; and Richard Tipping
  1997   "Jerablus-Tahtani, Syria, 1996: Preliminary Report." *Levant* 29: 1–18.

Peregrine, Peter N.; Andrew Bell; Matthew Braithwaite, and Michael D. Danti
  1997   "Geomagnetic Mapping of the Outer Town." In *Subsistence and Settlement in a Marginal Environment: Tell es-Sweyhat, 1989–1995 Preliminary Report*, edited by Richard L. Zettler, pp. 73–84. Museum Applied Science Center for Archaeology Research Papers in Science and Archaeology 14. Philadelphia: University of Pennsylvania Museum of Archaeology and Anthropology.

Perrin de Brichambaut, G., and C. C. Wallén
  1963   *A Study of Agroclimatology in the Near East.* World Meteorological Organization Technical Note 56. Geneva: World Meteorological Organization.

Poidebard, Antoine
  1934   *La trace de Rome dans le désert de Syrie: Le limes de Trajan á la conquête arabe: recherches aériennes (1925–1932)*, Volumes 1 and 2. Paris: P. Geuthner.

Pollock, Susan, and Cheryl Coursey
1995   "Ceramics from Hacinebi Tepe: Chronology and Connections." *Anatolica* 21: 101–41.

Porter, Anne
1995   "The Third Millennium Settlement Complex at Tell Banat: Tell Kabir." *Damaszener Mitteilungen* 8: 125–63.

1999   Mortality, Monuments and Mobility: Ancestor Traditions and the Transcendence of Space. Ph.D. dissertation, University of Chicago.

Porter, Anne, and Thomas L. McClellan
1998   "The Third Millennium Settlement Complex at Tell Banat: Results of the 1994 Excavations." *Damaszener Mitteilungen* 10: 11–63.

Postgate, J. Nicholas
1985   Review of *Die Orts- und Gewässernamen der mittelbabylonischen und mittelassyrischen Zeit*, by Khaled Nashef. *Archiv für Orientforschung* 32: 95–101.

1995   "Assyria: The Home Provinces." In *Neo-Assyrian Geography*, edited by Mario Liverani, pp. 1–17. Quaderni di Geografia Storica 5. Rome: Università di Roma.

Poyck, A. P. G.
1962   *Farm Studies in Iraq: An Agro-Economic Study of the Agriculture in the Hilla-Diwaniya Area in Iraq.* Mededelingen van de Landbouwhogeschool te Wageningen 62. Wageningen, Netherlands: H. Veenman & Zonen.

Rabo, Annika
1986   *Change on the Euphrates: Villagers, Townsmen and Employees in Northeast Syria.* Stockholm Studies in Social Anthropology 15. Stockholm: University of Stockholm.

al-Radi, Selma, and Helga Seeden
1974   "Shams ed-Din Tannira." In *Antiquités de l'Euphrate: Exposition des découvertes de la campagne internationale de sauvegarde des antiquités de l'Euphrate*, edited by Adnan Bounni, pp. 59–61. Damascus: Direction Générale des Antiquités et des Musées.

1980   "The AUB Rescue Excavations at Shams ed-Din Tannira." *Berytus* 28: 88–126.

Randsborg, Klavs
1991   *The First Millennium A.D. in Europe and the Mediterranean: An Archaeological Essay.* Cambridge: Cambridge University Press.

Rapp, A.
1987   "Reflections on Desertification 1977–1987: Problems and Prospects." *Desertification Control Bulletin* 15: 27–33.

Rasmussen, P. E., and H. P. Collins
1991   "Long-term Impacts of Tillage, Fertilizer, and Crop Residue on Soil Organic Matter in Temperate Semiarid Regions." *Advances in Agronomy* 45: 93–134.

Raymond, André, and Jean-Louis Paillet
1995   *Bālis 2: Histoire de Bālis et fouilles des îlots 1 et 2.* Damascus: Institut Français de Damas.

Reade, Julian E.
1968   "Tell Taya 1967: Summary Report." *Iraq* 30: 234–64.

1973   "Tell Taya 1972–73: Summary Report." *Iraq* 35: 155–87.

Renfrew, Jane M.
1973   *Palaeoethnobotany: The Prehistoric Food Plants of the Near East and Europe.* New York: Columbia University Press.

Retallack, Greg John
1990   *Soils of the Past: An Introduction to Paleopedology.* Boston: Unwin Hyman.

Ribot, Jesse C.
1996   "Climatic Variability, Climatic Change and Vulnerability: Moving Forward by Looking Back." In *Climate Variability, Climate Change, and Social Vulnerability in the Semi-arid Tropics*, edited by Jesse C. Ribot, Antonio Rocha Magalhās, and Stahis S. Panagides, pp. 1–10. Cambridge: Cambridge University Press.

Richards, Keith
1982   *Rivers: Form and Process in Alluvial Channels.* London: Methuen.

Riederer, Josef
1976   "Kupfergeräte aus Ḥabūba Kabīra und Mumbaqat Untersuchungsbericht." *Mitteilungen der Deutschen Orient-Gesellschaft zu Berlin* 108: 23–24.

Rifai, Mahmoud Faisal
1990   "Water Lifting Practices in Aleppo District before Motorisation." In *Techniques et pratiques hydro-agricoles traditionelles en domaine irrigué: Approche pluridisciplinaire des modes de culture avant le motorisation en Syrie,* Volume 2, edited by Bernard Geyer, pp. 313–20. Actes du colloque de Damas, 27 juin–1 juillet 1987. Bibliothèque archéologique et historique de l'Institut français d'archéologie de Beyrouth 136. Paris: Librairie Orientaliste Paul Geuthner.

Rihaoui, Abdul Kader
1965   "Étude préliminaire sur la sauvegarde des monuments dans la région du barrage de l'Euphrate." *Les Annales Archéologiques de Syrie* 15: 99–111.

Roaf, Michael, and Robert Killick
1987   "A Mysterious Affair of Styles: The Ninevite 5 Pottery of Northern Mesopotamia." *Iraq* 49: 199–230.

Roberts, Neil
1982   "Lake Levels as an Indicator of Near Eastern Palaeoclimates: A Preliminary Appraisal." In *Palaeoclimates, Palaeoenvironments, and Human Communities in the Eastern Mediterranean Region in Later Prehistory,* Volume 1, edited by John L. Bintliff and Willem van Zeist, pp. 235–67. British Archaeological Reports, International Series 133. Oxford: British Archaeological Reports.

Roberts, Neil, and H. E. Wright, Jr.
1993   "Vegetational, Lake-level, and Climatic History of the Near East and South-west Asia." In *Global Climates*

since the Last Glacial Maximum, edited by H. E. Wright, Jr., J. E. Kutzbach, T. Webb III, W. F. Ruddiman, F. A. Street-Perrott, and P. J. Bartlein, pp. 194–220. Minneapolis: University of Minnesota Press.

Rösner, U., and F. Schäbitz

1991   "Palynological and Sedimentological Evidence for the Historic Environment of Khatouniye, Eastern Syrian Djezire." *Paléorient* 17, no. 1: 77–87.

Roodenberg, J. J.; Tony J. Wilkinson; and S. Bayrı-Baykan

1984   "Surveys and Soundings at Kumartepe: An Interim Report." *Anatolica* 11: 1–16.

Rosen, Arlene Miller

1997   "The Geoarchaeology of Holocene Environments and Land Use at Kazane Höyük, S.E. Turkey." *Geoarchaeology* 12: 395–416.

Rosen, Arlene Miller, and Paul Goldberg

1995   "Paleoenvironmental Investigations." In "Titris Höyük, a Small EBA Urban Center in SE Anatolia: The 1994 Season," by Guillermo Algaze, Paul Goldberg, Diedre Honça, Timothy Matney, Adnan Mısır, Arlene Miller Rosen, Duncan Schlee, and Lewis Somers, pp. 13–64. *Anatolica* 21: 32–37.

Rossmeisl, Inge

1989   "Late Bronze Age Pottery of Tell Sabi Abyad." In *Excavations at Tell Sabi Abyad: Prehistoric Investigations in the Balikh Valley, Northern Syria,* edited by Peter M. M. G. Akkermans, pp. 337–56. Balikh Valley Archaeological Project Monograph 1; British Archaeological Reports, International Series 468. Oxford: British Archaeological Reports.

Rothman, Mitchell S.

2001a   "The Local and the Regional: An Introduction." In *Uruk Mesopotamia and Its Neighbors: Cross-cultural Interactions in the Era of State Formation*, edited by Mitchell S. Rothman, pp. 3–26. Santa Fe: School of American Research Press.

2001b   *Uruk Mesopotamia and Its Neighbors: Cross-cultural Interactions in the Era of State Formation*. Santa Fe: School of American Research Press.

Rouault, Olivier, and Maria Grazia Masetti-Rouault

1993   *L'Eufrate e il tempo: Le civiltà del medio Eufrate e della Gezira siriana*. Milano: Electa.

Rowton, Michael B.

1973   "Urban Autonomy in a Nomadic Environment." *Journal of Near Eastern Studies* 32: 201–15.

1974   "Enclosed Nomadism." *Journal of Economic and Social History of the Orient* 17: 1–30.

Russell, Edward W.

1961   *Soil Conditions and Plant Growth*. Ninth edition. London: Longman.

Sader, Hélène

1992   "The 12th Century B.C. in Syria: The Problem of the Rise of the Aramaeans." In *The Crisis Years: The 12th Century B.C. from Beyond the Danube to the Tigris*, edited by William A. Ward and Martha Sharp Joukowsky, pp. 157–63. Dubuque: Kendall/Hunt.

Sanlaville, Paul

1985   *Holocene Settlement in North Syria: Résultats de deux prospections archéologiques effectuées dans la région du nahr Sajour et sur la haut Euphrate syrien*. Edited by Paul Sanlaville. Maison de l'Orient Méditerranéen Centre National de la Recherche Scientifique-Université Lyon 2; Archaeological Series 1; British Archaeological Reports, International Series 238. Oxford: British Archaeological Reports.

1992   "Changements climatiques dans la péninsule arabique durant le Pléistocène supérieur et l'Holocène." *Paléorient* 18, no. 1: 5–26.

Schloen, J. David

1995   The Patrimonial Household in the Kingdom of Ugarit: A Weberian Analysis of Ancient Near Eastern Society. Ph.D. dissertation, Harvard University.

Schneider, Ellen

1999   "Die eisenzeitliche Keramik von Tell Sheikh Hassan (Syrien)." In *Iron Age Pottery in Northern Mesopotamia, Northern Syria and South-Eastern Anatolia*, edited by Arnulf Hausleiter and Andrzej Reiche, pp. 325–46. Papers presented at the meetings of the international "table ronde" at Heidelberg, 1995, and Nieborów, 1997, and other contributions. Altertumskunde des Vorderen Orients 10. Münster: Ugarit-Verlag.

Schneider, Gerwulf

1989   "A Technological Study of North-Mesopotamian Stone Ware." *World Archaeology* 21: 30–50.

Schumm, Stanley Alfred

1963   "Sinuosity of Alluvial Channels on the Great Plains." *Bulletin of the Geological Society of America* 74: 1089–1100.

1977   *The Fluvial System*. New York: Wiley-Interscience.

Schwartz, Glenn M.

1994   "Before Ebla: Models of Pre-State Political Organization in Syria and Northern Mesopotamia." In *Chiefdoms and Early States in the Near East: The Organizational Dynamics of Complexity*, edited by Gil J. Stein and Mitchell S. Rothman, pp. 153–74. Monographs in World Archaeology 18. Madison: Prehistory Press.

2001a   "The Pottery from Selenkahiye 1972, 1974, and 1975." In *Selenkahiye: Final Report on the University of Chicago and University of Amsterdam Excavations in the Tabqa Reservoir, Northern Syria, 1967–1975*, edited by Maurits N. van Loon, pp. 223–325. Publications de l'Institut historique-archéologique néerlandais de Stamboul 91. Istanbul: Netherlands Historical and Archaeological Institute.

2001b   "Syria and the Uruk Expansion." In *Uruk Mesopotamia and Its Neighbors: Cross-cultural Interactions in the Era of State Formation*, edited by Mitchell S. Rothman, pp. 233–64. Santa Fe: School of American Research Press.

Schwartz, Glenn M., and Hans H. Curvers
1992   "Tell al-Raqā'i 1989 and 1990: Further Investigations at a Small Rural Site of Early Urban Northern Mesopotamia." *American Journal of Archaeology* 96: 397–419.

Schwartz, Glenn M.; Hans H. Curvers; Fokke A. Gerritsen; Jennifer A. MacCormack; Naomi F. Miller; and Jill A. Weber
2000   "Excavation and Survey in the Jabbul Plain, Western Syria: The Umm el-Marra Project 1996–1997." *American Journal of Archaeology* 104: 419–62.

Schwartz, Glenn M., and Harvey Weiss
1992   "Syria, ca. 10,000–2000 B.C." In *Chronologies in Old World Archaeology,* Volume 1, edited by Robert W. Ehrich, pp. 221–43. Third edition. Chicago: University of Chicago Press.

Seeden, Helga
1978/79 "Šams ad-Dīn Tannira." *Archiv für Orientforshung* 26: 165–66.

1982   "Ethnoarchaeological Reconstruction of Halafian Occupational Units at Shams ed-Din Tannira." *Berytus* 30: 55–95.

Seidl, Ursula
1969   "Mumbaqat." In "Bericht über die von der Deutschen Orient-Gesellschaft mit Mitteln der Stiftung Volkswagenwerk im Euphrattal bei Aleppo begonnenen archäologischen Untersuchungen, erstattet von Mitgliedern der Expedition," by Ernst Heinrich, Einar von Schuler, Hansjörg Schmid, Wido Ludwig, Eva Strommenger, and Ursula Seidl, pp. 27–67. *Mitteilungen der Deutschen Orient-Gesellschaft zu Berlin* 101: 65–67.

1971   "Kleinfunde." In "Dritter vorläufiger Bericht über die von der Deutschen Orient-Gesellschaft mit Mitteln der Stiftung Volkswagenwerk in Ḥabūba Kabira und Mumbaqat unternommenen archäologischen Untersuchungen (Herbstkampagne 1970), erstattet von Mitgliedern der Mission," by Ernst Heinrich, Hansjörg Schmid, Hans-Christian Kara, Eva Strommenger, Dietrich Sürenhagen, Giesela Hecker, Ursula Seidl, Dittmar Machule, and Dieter Rentschler, pp. 5–58. *Mitteilungen der Deutschen Orient-Gesellschaft zu Berlin* 103: 43–48.

Sheets, Payson, and Thomas L. Sever
1991   "Prehistoric Footpaths in Costa Rica: Transportation and Communication in a Tropical Rainforest." In *Ancient Road Networks and Settlement Hierarchies in the New World*, edited by Charles D. Trombold, pp. 53–65. Cambridge: Cambridge University Press.

Shukla, Jagadish
1995   "On the Initiation and Persistence of the Sahel Drought." In *Natural Climate Variability on Decade-to-Century Time Scales*, edited by Climate Research Committee, Board on Atmospheric Sciences and Climate, Commission on Geosciences, Environment, and Resources, pp. 44–47. Papers presented at a Workshop, 21–25 September 1992. Washington, D.C.: National Academy Press.

Snell, Daniel C.
1983/84 "The Cuneiform Tablet from el-Qiṭār." *Abr-Nahrain* 22: 159–70.

Sodini, Jean-Pierre; Georges Tate; Bernard Bavant; Swantje Bavant; Jean-Luc Biscop; and Dominique Orssaud
1980   "Déhès (Syrie du Nord) Campagnes I–III (1976–1978)." *Syria* 57: 1–304.

Stein, Gil J.
1987   "Regional Economic Integration in Early State Societies: Third Millennium B.C. Pastoral Production at Gritille, Southeast Turkey." *Paléorient* 13, no. 2: 101–11.

1999   "Material Culture and Social Identity: The Evidence for a 4th Millennium B.C. Mesopotamian Uruk Colony at Hacınebi, Turkey." *Paléorient* 25, no. 1: 11–22.

Stewart, B. A.; O. R. Jones; and P. W. Unger
1993   "Moisture Management in Semiarid Temperate Regions." In *Agriculture and Environmental Challenges: Proceedings of the Thirteenth Agricultural Sector Symposium,* edited by Jitendra P. Srivastava and Harold Alderman, pp. 67–80. Washington, D.C.: The World Bank.

Stockton, C. W., and D. M. Meko
1990   "Some Aspects of the Hydroclimatology of Arid and Semiarid Lands." In *Human Intervention in the Climatology of Arid Lands*, edited by Donald R. Haragan, pp. 1–26. Contribution of the Committee on Desert and Arid Zones Research 25. Albuquerque: University of New Mexico Press.

Stordeur, D.
1996   "Jerf al-Ahmar and the PPNA Horizon in the Middle Euphrates." Paper presented at the International Colloquium on the Syrian Djezireh. *Deir ez-Zor* 22–25.

Strommenger, Eva
1969   "Die Funde." In "Bericht über die von der Deutschen Orient-Gesellschaft mit Mitteln der Stiftung Volkswagenwerk im Euphrattal bei Aleppo begonnenen archäologischen Untersuchungen, erstattet von Mitgliedern der Expedition," by Ernst Heinrich, Einar von Schuler, Hansjörg Schmid, Wido Ludwig, Eva Strommenger, and Ursula Seidl, pp. 27–67. *Mitteilungen der Deutschen Orient-Gesellschaft zu Berlin* 101: 54–64.

1970   "Kleinfunde." In "Zweiter vorläufiger Bericht über die von der Deutschen Orient-Gesellschaft mit Mitteln der Stiftung Volkswagenwerk in Ḥabuba Kabira und in Mumbaqat unternommenen archäologischen Untersuchungen (Herbstkampagne 1969), erstattet von Mitgliedern der Mission," by Ernst Heinrich, Wido Ludwig, Eva Strommenger, Ruth Opificius, and Dietrich Sürenhagen, pp. 27–85. *Mitteilungen der Deutschen Orient-Gesellschaft zu Berlin* 102: 61–71.

1971   "'Keramik' and 'Terrakottaplastik.'" In "Dritter vorläufiger Bericht über die von der Deutschen Orient-Gesellschaft mit Mitteln der Stiftung Volkswagenwerk in Ḥabūba Kabira und Mumbaqat unternommenen archäologischen Untersuchungen (Herbstkampagne

1970), erstattet von Mitgliedern der Mission," by Ernst Heinrich, Hansjörg Schmid, Hans-Christian Kara, Eva Strommenger, Dietrich Sürenhagen, Giesela Hecker, Ursula Seidl, Dittmar Machule, and Dieter Rentschler, pp. 5–58. *Mitteilungen der Deutschen Orient-Gesellschaft zu Berlin* 103: 21–34.

1973 "Ausgrabungen in Ḥabuba Kabira und Mumbaqat." *Archiv für Orientforschung* 24: 168–71.

1974 "Habouba Kabira." In *Antiquités de l'Euphrate: Exposition des découvertes de la campagne internationale de sauvegarde des antiquités de l'Euphrate*, edited by Adnan Bounni, pp. 55–58. Damascus: Direction Générale des Antiquités et des Musées.

1974/77 "Ḥabuba Kabira 1973 bis 1975." *Archiv für Orientforschung* 25: 256–58.

1975 "Habuba Kabira-Sud 1974." *Les Annales Archéologiques Arabes Syriennes* 25: 155–64.

1976 "Fünfter vorläufiger Bericht über die von der Deutschen Orient-Gesellschaft mit Mitteln der Stiftung Volkswagenwerk in Ḥabūba Kabīra unternommenen archäologischen Untersuchungen (Kampagnen 1973, 1974, 1975)." *Mitteilungen der Deutschen Orient-Gesellschaft zu Berlin* 108: 5–22.

1979 "Ḥabuba Kabira-Tall," pp. 72–77. In "Ausgrabungen der Deutschen Orient-Gesellschaft in Ḥabuba Kabira," by Eva Strommenger. In *Archaeological Reports from the Tabqa Dam Project, Euphrates Valley, Syria*, edited by David Noel Freedman, pp. 63–78. Annual of the American Schools of Oriental Research 44. Cambridge: American Schools of Oriental Research.

1980 *Habuba Kabira: Eine Stadt vor 5000 Jahren: Ausgrabungen der Deutschen Orient-Gesellschaft am Euphrat in Habuba Kabira, Syrien.* Sendschrift der Deutschen Orient-Gesellschaft 12. Mainz am Rhein: Philipp von Zabern.

Strommenger, Eva, and Max Hirmer

1962 *Fünf Jahrtausende Mesopotamien: Die Kunst von den Anfängen um 5000 v. Chr. bis zu Alexander dem Grossen.* Munich: Hirmer.

Strommenger, Eva, and Dietrich Sürenhagen

1970 "Die Grabung in Ḥabuba Kabira-Süd." In "Zweiter vorläufiger Bericht über die von der Deutschen Orient-Gesellschaft mit Mitteln der Stiftung Volkswagenwerk in Ḥabuba Kabira und in Mumbaqat unternommenen archäologischen Untersuchungen (Herbstkampagne 1969), erstattet von Mitgliedern der Mission," by Ernst Heinrich, Wido Ludwig, Eva Strommenger, Ruth Opificius, and Dietrich Sürenhagen, pp. 27–85. *Mitteilungen der Deutschen Orient-Gesellschaft zu Berlin* 102: 59–61.

Stucky, Rolf A.

1972 "Tell el-Hajj." *Archiv für Orientforschung* 23: 175.

1974 "Tell el-Hajj." In *Antiquités de l'Euphrate: Exposition des découvertes de la campagne internationale de sauvegarde des antiquités de l'Euphrate*, edited by Adnan Bounni, pp. 94–98. Damascus: Direction Générale des Antiquités et des Musées.

1975 "Tell el-Hajj 1972." *Les Annales Archéologiques Arabes Syriennes* 25: 165–81.

Sürenhagen, Dietrich

1973 "Friedhöfe in Ḥabuba Kabīra-Süd." In "Vierter vorläufiger Bericht über die von der Deutschen Orient-Gesellschaft mit Mitteln der Stiftung Volkswagenwerk in Ḥabuba Kabira (Ḥububa Kabira, Herbstkampagnen 1971 und 1972 sowie Testgrabung Frühjahr 1973) und in Mumbaqat (Tall Munbaqa, Herbstkampagne 1971) unternommenen archäologischen Untersuchungen, erstattet von Mitgliedern der Mission," by Ernst Heinrich, Eva Strommenger, Dieter Robert Frank, Wido Ludwig, Dietrich Sürenhagen, Eva Töpperwein, Hansjörg Schmid, Jan-Christoph Heusch, Kay Kohlmeyer, Dittmar Machule, Markus Wäfler, and Thomas Rhode, pp. 5–68. *Mitteilungen der Deutschen Orient-Gesellschaft zu Berlin* 105: 33–38.

1975 "Die Euphrat-Expedition der D. O. G." In *Le temple et le culte,* edited by E. van Donzel, P. H. E. Donceel-Voute, A. A. Kampman, and M. J. Mellink, pp. 5–9. Compte rendu de la vingtième Rencontre Assyriologique Internationale à Leiden, 3–7 juillet 1972. Publications de l'Institut historique-archéologique néederlandais de Stamboul 37. Istanbul: Netherlands Historical and Archaeological Institute.

1978 *Keramikproduktion in Ḥabūba Kabira-Süd.* Berlin: Verlag Bruno Hessling.

1986 "The Dry Farming Belt: The Uruk Period and Subsequent Developments." In *The Origins of Cities in Dry-Farming Syria and Mesopotamia in the Third Millennium B.C.,* edited by Harvey Weiss, pp. 7–43. Guilford, Connecticut: Four Quarters Publishing.

Sweet, Louise E.

1974 *Tell Ṭoqaan: A Syrian Village.* Anthropological Papers, Museum of Anthropology, University of Michigan 14. Ann Arbor: University of Michigan.

Tate, Georges

1992 *Les campagnes de la Syrie du nord du IIe au VIIe siècle: Un exemple d'espansion démographique et économique à la fin de l'antiquité,* Volume 1. Bibliothèque archéologique et historique de l'Institut français d'archéologie de Beyrouth 133. Paris: Librairie Orientaliste Paul Geuthner.

1997 "The Syrian Countryside during the Roman Era." In *The Early Roman Empire in the East*, edited by Susan E. Alcock, pp. 55–71. Oxbow Monograph 95. Oxford: Oxbow Books.

Thalen, D. C. P.

1979 *Ecology and Utilization of Desert Shrub Rangelands in Iraq.* The Hague, Netherlands: W. Junk.

Thissen, Laurens C.

1985 "The Late Chalcolithic and Early Bronze Age Pottery from Hayaz Höyük." *Anatolica* 12: 75–130.

Tomita, Toru

1998 "Late Chalcolithic Chronology in Syria and Northern Mesopotamia." In *Excavations at Tell Umm Qseir in the Middle Khabur Valley, North Syria: Report of the*

1996 Season, edited by Akira Tsuneki and Yutaka Miyake, pp. 197–201. Al-Shark 1. Tsukaba, Japan: Department of Archaeology, Institute of History and Anthropology, University of Tsukaba.

Tonghini, Cristina
1996   "Recent Excavation at Qal'at Ja'bar: New Data for Classifying Syrian Fritware." In *Continuity and Change in Northern Mesopotamia from the Hellenistic to the Early Islamic Period,* edited by Karin Bartl and Stefan R. Hauser, pp. 287–300. Proceedings of a colloquium held at the Seminar für Vorderasiatische Altertumskunde at Freie Universität Berlin, 6–9 April 1994. Berliner Beiträge zum Vorderen Orient 17. Berlin: Dietrich Reimer Verlag.

Townsend, C. C., and Evan Guest, editors
1966   *Flora of Iraq,* Volume 2. Baghdad, Republic of Iraq: Ministry of Agriculture.

Trokay, Madeleine
1981   "Les cônes d'argile du Tell Kannâs." *Syria* 58: 149–71.

Tsoar, H., and Y. Yekutieli
1993   "Geomorphological Identification of Ancient Roads and Paths on the Loess of the Northern Negev." *Israel Journal of Earth Sciences* 41: 209–16.

Tübinger Atlas des Vorderen Orients
1985   Land Utilization Maps A X no. 4 and B I 16 and 17. Wiesbaden: Ludwig Reichert Verlag.

Uerpmann, Hans-Peter
1982   "Faunal Remains from Shams ed-Din Tannira, a Halafian Site in Northern Syria." *Berytus* 30: 3–52.

Ur, Jason A.
2002   "Settlement and Landscape in Northern Mesopotamia: The Tell Hamoukar Survey 2000–2001." *Akkadica* 123: 57–88.

2003   "CORONA Satellite Photography and Ancient Road Networks: A Northern Mesopotamian Case Study." *Antiquity* 77: 102–15.

van der Kooij, Gerrit
1982   "Some Ethnographical Observations of Archaeological Impact at the Village Hadidi in Syria." *Lettres d'Information Archéologie Orientale* 5: 80–84.

van der Leeuw, Sander Ernst
1974   "Sondages à Ta'as, Hadidi et Jebel 'Aruda." In *Antiquités de l'Euphrate: Exposition des découvertes de la campagne internationale de sauvegarde des antiquités de l'Euphrate,* edited by Adnan Bounni, pp. 76–82. Damascus: Direction Générale des Antiquités et des Musées.

1976   *Studies in the Technology of Ancient Pottery.* Two volumes. Amsterdam: University of Amsterdam.

van Driel, Govert
1977   "De Uruk-Nederzetting op de Jebel Aruda: Een voorlopig Bericht (stand eind 1976)." *Phoenix* 23: 42–64.

1980   "The Uruk Settlement on Jebel Aruda: A Preliminary Report." In *Le Moyen Euphrate: Zone de contacts et d'échanges,* edited by Jean Claude Margueron, pp. 75–93. Actes du colloque de Strasbourg, 10–12 mars 1977. Travaux du Centre de Recherche sur le Proche-Orient et la Grèce Antiques 5. Leiden: E. J. Brill.

1981/82   "Ǧabal 'Arūda." *Archiv für Orientforschung* 28: 245–46.

1982   "Tablets from Jebel Aruda." In *Zikir Šumim: Assyriological Studies Presented to F. R. Kraus on the Occasion of his Seventieth Birthday,* edited by G. van Driel, Th. J. H. Krispijn, M. Stol, and K. R. Veenhof, pp. 12–25. Leiden: E. J. Brill.

1983   "Seals and Sealings from Jebel Aruda 1974–1978." *Akkadica* 33: 34–62.

1984   "Ǧabal 'Arūda 1982." *Archiv für Orientforschung* 31: 134–37.

1993   "Gebel Aruda." In *L'Eufrate e il tempo: Le civiltà del medio Eufrate e della Gezira siriana,* edited by Olivier Rouault and Maria Grazia Masetti-Rouault, pp. 139–42. Milano: Electa.

van Driel, Govert, and Carol van Driel-Murray
1979   "Jebel Aruda 1977–1978." *Akkadica* 12: 2–28.

1983   "Jebel Aruda: The 1982 Season of Excavation, Interim Report." *Akkadica* 33: 1–26.

van Lerberghe, Karel
1996   "The Beydar Tablets and the History of the Northern Jazirah." In *Administrative Documents from Tell Beydar (Seasons 1993–1995),* edited by Farouk Ismail, Walther Sallaberger, Philippe Talon, and Karel van Lerberghe, pp. 119–26. Subartu 2. Turnhout, Belgium: Brepols.

van Liere, W. J.
1960/61   "Observations on the Quaternary of Syria." Berichten van de Rijksdienst voor het Oudheidkundig bodemonderzoek Jrg.: 10–11.

1963   "Capitals and Citadels of Bronze–Iron Age Syria in Their Relationship to Land and Water." *Les Annales Archéologiques de Syrie* 13: 109–22.

van Liere, W. J., and J. Lauffray
1954/55   "Nouvelle prospection archéologique dans la Haute Jezireh Syrienne." *Les Annales Archéologiques de Syrie* 4/5: 129–48.

van Loon, Maurits N.
1967   *The Tabqa Reservoir Survey 1964.* Damascus: Direction Générale des Antiquités et des Musées.

1968a   "First Results of the 1967 Excavations at Selenkahiye." *Les Annales Archéologiques Arabes Syriennes* 18: 21–32.

1968b   "The Oriental Institute Excavations at Mureybiṭ, Syria: Preliminary Report on the 1965 Campaign, Part 1: Architecture and General Finds." *Journal of Near Eastern Studies* 27: 265–82.

1969a   "New Evidence from Inland Syria for the Chronology of the Middle Bronze Age." *American Journal of Archaeology* 73: 276–77.

1969b "New Sites in the Euphrates Valley." *Archaeology* 22: 65–68.

1973 "First Results of the 1972 Excavations at Tell Selenkahiye." *Les Annales Archéologiques Arabes Syriennes* 23: 145–58.

1977/78 "First Results of the 1974 and 1975 Excavations at Selenkahiye near Meskene, Syria." *Les Annales Archéologiques Arabes Syriennes* 27/28: 165–85.

1978/79 "Tall Salankaḥīya." *Archiv für Orientforschung* 26: 169–70.

1979 "1974 and 1975 Preliminary Results of the Excavations at Selenkahiye near Meskene, Syria." In *Archaeological Reports from the Tabqa Dam Project, Euphrates Valley, Syria,* edited by David Noel Freedman, pp. 97–112. Annual of the American Schools of Oriental Research 44. Cambridge: American Schools of Oriental Research.

2001 *Selenkahiye: Final Report on the University of Chicago and University of Amsterdam Excavations in the Tabqa Reservoir, Northern Syria, 1967–1975.* Edited by Maurits N. van Loon. Publications de l'Institut historique-archéologique néerlandais de Stamboul 91. Istanbul: Netherlands Historical and Archaeological Institute.

van Loon, Maurits N., and Diederik J. W. Meijer

1988 "Forward." In *Hammam et-Turkman* 1: *Report on the University of Amsterdam's 1981–84 Excavations in Syria,* Volume 1, edited by Maurits N. van Loon, pp. xxv–xxix. Publications de l'Institut historique-archéologique néerlandais de Stamboul 63. Istanbul: Netherlands Historical and Archaeological Institute.

van Oosterom, E. J.; S. Ceccarelli; and J. M. Peacock

1993 "Yield Response of Barley to Rainfall and Temperature in Mediterranean Environments." *Journal of Agricultural Science* 121: 307–13.

van Zeist, Willem

1968 "A First Impression of the Plant Remains from Selenkahiye." *Les Annales Archéologiques Arabes Syriennes* 18: 35–36.

1973 "Preliminary Botanical Results of the 1972 Season at Selenkahiye." *Les Annales Archéologiques Arabes Syriennes* 23: 159.

1994 "Some Notes on Second Millennium B.C. Plant Cultivation in the Syrian Jazira." In *Cinquante-deux réflexions sur le Proche-Orient ancien: Offertes en hommage à Léon de Meyer,* edited by H. Gasche, M. Tankret, C. Janssen, and A. Degraeve, pp. 541–49. Mesopotamian History and Environment, Occasional Publications 2. Leuven: Peeters Press.

van Zeist, Willem, and J. A. H. Bakker-Heeres

1982 "Archaeobotanical Studies in the Levant 1: Neolithic Sites in the Damascus Basin: Aswad, Ghoraifé, Ramad." *Palaeohistoria* 24: 165–256.

1984 "Archaeobotanical Studies in the Levant 3: Late-Palaeolithic Mureybit." *Palaeohistoria* 26: 171–99.

1985 "Archaeobotanical Studies in the Levant 4: Bronze Age Sites on the North Syrian Euphrates." *Palaeohistoria* 27: 247–316.

van Zeist, Willem, and Willemina Waterbolk-van Rooijen

1989 "Plant Remains from Tell Sabi Abyad." In *Excavations at Tell Sabi Abyad: Prehistoric Investigations in the Balikh Valley, Northern Syria,* edited by Peter M. M. G. Akkermans, pp. 325–35. Balikh Valley Archaeological Project Monograph 1; British Archaeological Reports, International Series 468. Oxford: British Archaeological Reports.

1996 "The Cultivated and Wild Plants." In *Tell Sabi Abyad: The Late Neolithic Settlement: Report on the Excavations of the University of Amsterdam (1988) and the National Museum of Antiquities Leiden (1991–1993) in Syria,* Volume 2, edited by Peter M. M. G. Akkermans, pp. 521–50. Publications de l'Institut historique-archéologique néerlandais de Stamboul 76. Istanbul: Netherlands Historical and Archaeological Institute.

van Zeist, Willem; Willemina Waterbolk-van Rooijen; and S. Bottema

1988 "Appendix 2: Some Notes on the Plant Husbandry of Tell Hammam et-Turkman." In *Hammam et-Turkman* 1: *Report on the University of Amsterdam's 1981–84 Excavations in Syria,* Volume 2, edited by Maurits N. van Loon, pp. 705–15. Publications de l'Institut historique-archéologique néerlandais de Stamboul 63. Istanbul: Netherlands Historical and Archaeological Institute.

van Zeist, Willem, and H. Woldring

1978 "A Postglacial Pollen Diagram from Lake Van in East Anatolia." *Review of Palaeobotany and Palynology* 26: 249–76.

de Vaux, R., and A.-M. Steve

1950 *Fouilles à Qaryet el-'Enab, Abū Gôsh, Palestine.* Paris: Librairie Victor Lecoffre.

Venturi, F.

1998 "The Late Bronze Age II and Early Iron Age Levels." In *Tell Afis (Syria): The 1988–1992 Excavations on the Acropolis,* edited by S. M. Cecchini and Stefania Mazzoni, pp. 123–62. Recherche di Archeologia del Vicino Oriente 1. Pisa: Edizioni ETS.

Vesilind, R. J.

1993 "The Middle East's Water: Critical Resource." *National Geographic* 183: 38–70.

Vidal, F. S.

1978 "Utilization of Surface Water by Northern Arabian Bedouins." In *Social and Technological Management in Dry Lands: Past and Present, Indigenous and Imposed,* edited by Nancie L. Solien González, pp. 111–26. American Association for the Advancement of Science Selected Symposium 10. Boulder: Westview Press.

Villard, Pierre

1987 "Un conflit d'autorités à propos des eaux du Balîh." *Mari Annales de Recherches Interdisciplinaires* 5: 591–96.

Vita-Finzi, Claudio, and Eric S. Higgs
1970   "Prehistoric Economy in the Mount Carmel Area of Palestine: Site Catchment Analysis." *Proceedings of the Prehistoric Society* 36: 1–37.

von Schuler, Einar; Hansjörg Schmid; Wido Ludwig; and Eva Strommenger
1969   "Die Frühjahrskampagne 1969 in Ḥabuba Kabira." In "Bericht über die von der Deutschen Orient-Gesellschaft mit Mitteln der Stiftung Volkswagenwerk im Euphrattal bei Aleppo begonnenen archäologischen Untersuchungen, erstattet von Mitgliedern der Expedition," by Ernst Heinrich, Einar von Schuler, Hansjörg Schmid, Wido Ludwig, Eva Strommenger, and Ursula Seidl, pp. 27–67. *Mitteilungen der Deutschen Orient-Gesellschaft zu Berlin* 101: 37–64.

von Soden, Wolfram
1982   "Eine altbabylonische Urkunde (79 MBQ 15) aus Tall Munbāqa." *Mitteilungen der Deutschen Orient-Gesellschaft zu Berlin* 114: 71–77.

von Thünen, Johann Heinrich
1966   *The Isolated State.* Translated by Carla M. Wartenberg. London: Pergamon.

Wachholtz, Rolf
1996   *Socio-Economics of Bedouin Farming Systems in Dry Areas of Northern Syria.* Farming Systems and Resource Economics in the Tropics 24. Kiel: Wissenschaftsverlag Vauk.

Wachholtz, Rolf; T. L. Nordblom; and G. Arab
1992   "Characterization of Year-round Sheep Feeding and Grazing Calenders of Bedouin Flocks in the NW Syrian Steppe." In *International Center for Agricultural Research in the Dry Areas Annual Report for 1992: Pasture, Forage and Livestock Program,* pp. 215–29. Aleppo: International Center for Agricultural Research in the Dry Areas Publications.

Wäfler, Markus
1974   "Keramik," and "Ausgewählte Kleinfunde." In "Vierter vorläufiger Bericht über die von der Deutschen Orient-Gesellschaft mit Mitteln der Stiftung Volkswagenwerk in Ḥabuba Kabira (Ḥububa Kabira, Herbstkampagnen 1971 und 1972 sowie Testgrabung Frühjahr 1973) und in Mumbaqat (Tall Munbaqa, Herbstkampagne 1971) unternommenen archäologischen Untersuchungen, erstattet von Mitgliedern der Mission (Fortsetzung)," by Ernst Heinrich, Eva Strommenger, Dieter Robert Frank, Wido Ludwig, Dietrich Sürenhagen, Eva Töpperwein, Hansjörg Schmid, Jan-Christoph Heusch, Kay Kohlmeyer, Dittmar Machule, Markus Wäfler, and Thomas Rhode, pp. 5–97. *Mitteilungen der Deutschen Orient-Gesellschaft zu Berlin* 106: 30–45.

1980   "Der Becher MBQ 26/35–62 (= 71 MBQ 59)." *Mitteilungen der Deutschen Orient-Gesellschaft zu Berlin* 112: 9–11.

1982   "Zu den Siegelabrollungen auf Tontafelurkunde 79 MBQ 15 aus Tall Munbaqa." *Mitteilungen der Deutschen Orient-Gesellschaft zu Berlin* 114: 78.

Waelkens, Marc; Norman Herz; and Luc Moens
1992   *Ancient Stones: Quarrying, Trade and Provenance: Interdisciplinary Studies on Stones and Stone Technology in Europe and Near East from the Prehistoric to the Early Christian Period.* Acta Archaeologica Lovaniensia Monographiae 4. Leuven: Leuven University Press.

Walker, D., and G. Singh
1993   "Earliest Palynological Records of Human Impact on the World's Vegetation." In *Climate Change and Human Impact on the Landscape: Studies in Palaeoecology and Environmental Archaeology,* edited by F. M. Chambers, pp. 101–08. London: Chapman and Hall.

Wallén, C. C.
1967   "Aridity Definitions and Their Applicability." *Geografiska Annaler* 49: 367–84.

Watson, Oliver
1999   "Report on the Glazed Ceramics." In *Ar-Raqqa* 1: *Die frühislamische Keramik von Tall Aswad,* edited by Peter A. Miglus, pp. 81–87. Mainz am Rhein: Philipp von Zabern.

Wattenmaker, Patricia
1987   "Town and Village Economies in an Early State Society." *Paléorient* 13, no. 2: 113–22.

Weber, Jill A.
1997   "Faunal Remains from Tell el-Sweyhat and Hajji Ibrahim." In *Subsistence and Settlement in a Marginal Environment: Tell es-Sweyhat, 1989–1995 Preliminary Report,* edited by Richard L. Zettler, pp. 133–67. Museum Applied Science Center for Archaeology Research Papers in Science and Archaeology 14. Philadelphia: University of Pennsylvania Museum of Archaeology and Anthropology.

Weiss, Harvey; M.-A. Courty; W. Wetterstrom; F. Guichard; L. Senior; R. Meadow; and A. Curnow
1993   "The Genesis and Collapse of Third Millennium North Mesopotamian Civilization." *Science* 261: 995–1004.

Whitcomb, Donald
1990/91   "Glazed Ceramics of the Abbasid Period from the Aqaba Excavations." *Transactions of the Oriental Ceramic Society* 55: 43–65.

White, K. D.
1970   "Fallowing, Crop Rotation and Crop Yields in Roman Times." *Agricultural History* 44: 281–90.

White, P. F.; T. T. Treacher; and A. Termanini
1997   "Nitrogen Cycling in Semi-arid Mediterranean Zones: Removal and Return of Nitrogen to Pastures by Grazing Sheep." *Australian Journal of Agricultural Research* 48: 317–22.

Whiting, Robert
1979   "Brief Discussion of Tablets from Area H," pp. 145–46; and "Catalogue of Tablets Excavated at Tell Hadidi," pp. 146–49. In "Tell Hadidi: A Millennium of Bronze Age City Occupation," by Rudolph H Dornemann. In *Archaeological Reports from the*

Tabqa Dam Project, Euphrates Valley, Syria, edited by David Noel Freedman, pp. 113–51. Annual of the American Schools of Oriental Research 44. Cambridge: American Schools of Oriental Research.

Wilkinson, Tony J.

1975   "The Physical Environment of Dibsi Faraj: A Preliminary Study." In "Appendix A: Excavations at Dibsi Faraj, Northern Syria, 1972–1974: A Preliminary Note on the Site and Its Monuments," edited by Richard P. Harper, pp. 334–38. *Dumbarton Oaks Papers* 29: 319–38.

1978   "Erosion and Sedimentation along the Euphrates Valley in Northern Syria." In *The Environmental History of the Near and Middle East since the Last Ice Age*, edited by William Charles Brice, pp. 215–26. London: Academic Press.

1982   "The Definition of Ancient Manured Zones by Means of Extensive Sherd-Sampling Techniques." *Journal of Field Archaeology* 9: 323–33.

1989   "Extensive Sherd Scatters and Land-Use Intensity: Some Recent Results." *Journal of Field Archaeology* 16: 31–46.

1990   *Town and Country in Southeastern Anatolia 1: Settlement and Land Use at Kurban Höyük and Other Sites in the Lower Karababa Basin*. Oriental Institute Publications 109. Chicago: The Oriental Institute.

1993   "Linear Hollows in the Jazira, Upper Mesopotamia." *Antiquity* 67: 548–62.

1994   "The Structure and Dynamics of Dry-Farming States in Upper Mesopotamia." *Current Anthropology* 35: 483–520.

1995   "Late-Assyrian Settlement Geography in Upper Mesopotamia." In *Neo-Assyrian Geography*, edited by Mario Liverani, pp. 139–59. Quaderni di Geografia Storica 5. Rome: Università di Roma.

1996   "Sabi Abyad: The Geoarchaeology of a Complex Landscape." In *Tell Sabi Abyad: The Late Neolithic Settlement: Report on the Excavations of the University of Amsterdam (1988) and the National Museum of Antiquities Leiden (1991–1993) in Syria*, Volume 1, edited by Peter M. M. G. Akkermans, pp. 1–24. Publications de l'Institut historique-archéologique néerlandais de Stamboul 76. Istanbul: Netherlands Historical and Archaeological Institute.

1997   "Environmental Fluctuations, Agricultural Production and Collapse: A View from Bronze Age Upper Mesopotamia." In *Third Millennium B.C. Climate Change and Old World Collapse*, edited by Hasan Nüzhet Dalfes, George Kukla, and Harvey Weiss, pp. 67–106. Proceedings of the North Atlantic Treaty Organization Advanced Research Workshop on Third Millennium B.C. Abrupt Climate Change and Old World Social Collapse in Kemer, Turkey, 19–24 September 1994. North Atlantic Treaty Organization, Advanced Science Institute Series 1; Global Environmental Change 49. Berlin: Springer.

1998   "Water and Human Settlement in the Balikh Valley, Syria: Investigations from 1992–1995." *Journal of Field Archaeology* 25: 63–87.

1999   "Holocene Valley Fills of Southern Turkey and Northwestern Syria: Recent Geoarchaeological Contributions." *Quaternary Science Reviews* 18: 555–71.

2000a   "Archaeological Survey of the Tell Beydar Region, Syria, 1997: A Preliminary Report." In *Tell Beydar: Environmental and Technical Studies*, edited by Karel van Lerberghe and Gabriella Voet, pp. 1–37. Subartu 6. Turnhout, Belgium: Brepols.

2000b   "Regional Approaches to Mesopotamian Archaeology: The Contribution of Archaeological Surveys." *Journal of Archaeological Research* 8: 219–67.

Wilkinson, Tony J., and Eleanor Barbanes

2000   "Settlement Patterns in the Syrian Jazira during the Iron Age." In *Essays on Syria in the Iron Age*, edited by Guy Bunnens, pp. 397–422. Ancient Near Eastern Studies, Supplement 7. Leuven: Peeters Press.

Wilkinson, Tony J., and Thomas A. Holland

1992   *Syrian Jazira Landscape Studies at Tells Sweyhat and Sabi Abyad*. Report to the National Geographic Society, Grant 4900-92.

Wilkinson, Tony J.; B. Monahan; and D. J. Tucker

1996   "Khanijdal East: A Small Ubaid Site in Northern Iraq." *Iraq* 58: 17–50.

Wilkinson, Tony J., and D. J. Tucker

1995   *Settlement Development in the North Jazira, Iraq: A Study of the Archaeological Landscape*. Iraq Archaeological Reports 3. Warminster: Aris and Phillips.

Willcox, George

1996   "Evidence for Plant Exploitation and Vegetation History from Three Early Neolithic Pre-pottery Sites on the Euphrates (Syria)." *Vegetation History and Archaeobotany* 5: 143–52.

Williams, Martin A. J., and Robert C. Balling, Jr.

1996   *Interactions of Desertification and Climate*. London: E. Arnold.

Williamson, T. M.

1984   "The Roman Countryside: Settlement and Agriculture in N.W. Essex." *Britannia* 15: 225–30.

Wirth, Eugen

1971   *Syrien: Eine geographische Landeskunde*. Wissenschaftliche Länderkunden 4/5. Darmstadt: Wissenschaftliche Buchgesellschaft.

Wolman, M. G., and L. B. Leopold

1957   "River Floodplains, Some Observations on Their Formation." *United States Geological Survey, Professional Paper* 282C: 87–107.

Woolley, C. Leonard

1953   *A Forgotten Kingdom: A Record of the Results Obtained from the Recent Important Excavation of Two Mounds, Atchana and al Mina, in the Turkish Hatay*. Baltimore: Penguin Books.

Yakir, Dan; Arie Issar; Joel Gat; Eilon Adar; Peter Trimborn; and Joseph Lipp

1994   "^{13}C and ^{18}O of Wood from the Roman Siege Rampart in Masada, Israel (AD 70–73): Evidence for a Less Arid Climate for the Region." *Geochimica et Cosmochimica Acta* 58: 3535–39.

Yener, K. Aslıhan; Christopher Edens; Timothy P. Harrison; J. Verstraete; and Tony J. Wilkinson

2000   "The Amuq Valley Regional Project 1995–1998." *American Journal of Archaeology* 104: 163–220.

Yener, K. Aslıhan; Tony J. Wilkinson; Scott Branting; E. S. Friedman; J. D. Lyon; and Clemens D. Reichel

1996   "The Oriental Institute Amuq Regional Projects, 1995." *Anatolica* 22: 49–84.

Young, Gordon D., Jr., editor

1992   *Mari in Retrospect: Fifty Years of Mari and Mari Studies.* Winona Lake: Eisenbrauns.

Zaccagnini, C.

1975   "The Yield of the Fields at Nuzi." *Oriens Antiquus* 14: 181–225.

Zeder, Melinda A.

1995   "The Archaeobiology of the Khabur Basin." *Bulletin of the Canadian Society for Mesopotamian Studies* 29: 21–32.

1998   "Environment, Economy and Subsistence on the Threshold of Urban Emergence in Northern Mesopotamia." In "Natural Space, Inhabited Space in Northern Syria (10th–2nd Millennium B.C.)," edited by Michel Fortin and Olivier Aurenche. Actes du colloque tenu à l'Université Laval in Québec, 5–7 mai 1997. Travaux de la Maison de l'Orient 28. *Bulletin of the Canadian Society for Mesopotamian Studies*: 55–67.

1999   "The Role of Pastoralism in the Development of Specialized Urban Economies in the Ancient Near East." Paper presented at the Annual Meetings of the Society for American Archaeology, March 1999, in Chicago.

Zettler, Richard L.

1997   "Introduction," pp. 1–10; "Surface Collections and Excavations in the Lower Town and Lower Town South," pp. 35–72; and "Conclusions," pp. 169–71. In *Subsistence and Settlement in a Marginal Environment: Tell es-Sweyhat, 1989–1995 Preliminary Report*, edited by Richard L. Zettler. Museum Applied Science Center for Archaeology Research Papers in Science and Archaeology 14. Philadelphia: University of Pennsylvania Museum of Archaeology and Anthropology.

Zettler, Richard L., and Naomi F. Miller

1995   "Searching for Wine in the Archaeological Record of Ancient Mesopotamia of the Third and Second Millennia B.C." In *The Origins and Ancient History of Wine*, edited by Patrick E. McGovern, Stuart J. Fleming, and Solomon H. Katz, pp. 123–31. Food and Nutrition in History and Anthropology 11. Amsterdam: Gordon and Breach.

Zohary, Michael

1966   *Flora Palaestina* 1: *Text: Equisetaceae to Moringaceae.* Jerusalem: Israel Academy of Sciences and Humanities.

1. INTRODUCTION

1.A. INTRODUCTION TO THE SURVEY

The present study forms part of my long-term research strategy that is aimed at examining the growth of towns, rural settlements, and the rural landscape over much of the last ten thousand years. Emphasis is upon the retrieval of information from surface surveys, and at the same time, the integration of cultural change within both the local environmental context and long-term environmental change. It must be emphasized that the surveys under discussion, collectively called the Sweyhat Survey, were small and rather detailed studies of some 60 sq. km of land around Tell es-Sweyhat and the thirty sites therein on the east bank of the Euphrates River; the surveys were conducted in 1974, 1991, and 1992. Sweyhat Survey site numbers are designated with the prefix SS (= Sweyhat Survey; see *Appendix A: Sweyhat Survey Site Catalog*). The survey area is nested within a broader "area of interest," which comprises the area of the upper Lake Assad (formerly Lake Tabqa) salvage project. I have not surveyed the broader area, which covers some 350 sq. km downstream of the Tishrin Dam (fig. 1.1A), but I have visited many of the sites. Thus the survey area constitutes some 15–19% of the area surrounding Lake Assad. Although an area that covers only some 60 sq. km can hardly be considered to be representative of the entire region, the above sample fraction is sufficient to place some confidence in its representativeness. More importantly, the detailed surveys have provided crucial information on some

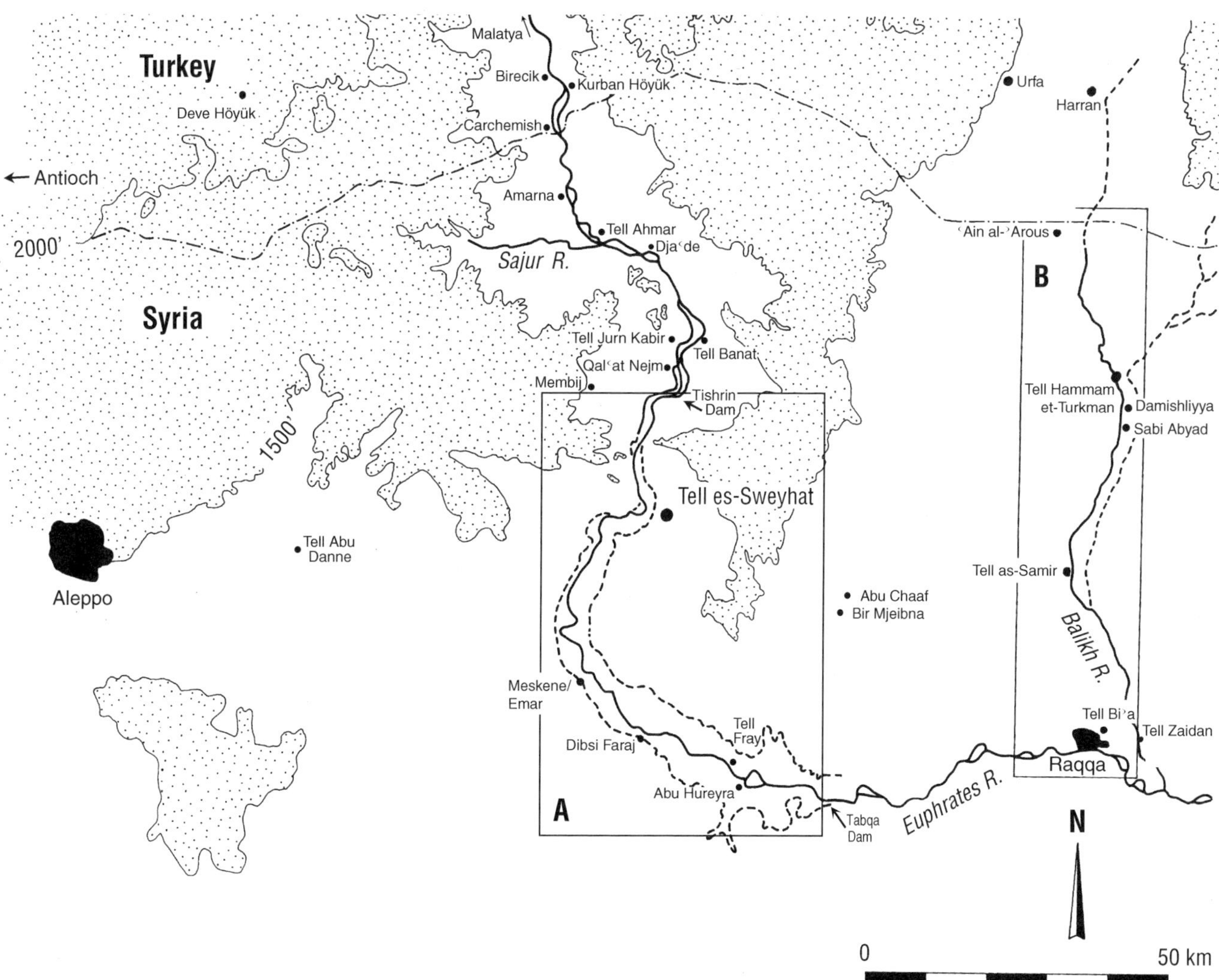

Figure 1.1. Map of North Central Syria Showing Location of (*A*) the Lake Tabqa (renamed Lake Assad) Salvage Area and (*B*) the Valley of the Balikh River

hitherto little-documented periods in the area and have also provided much-needed control for the archaeology of the greater reservoir area. In addition, the surveys have supplied a wealth of data on off-site archaeology and landscape features in general. Because these surveys and their publication span virtually my entire career in archaeology, they encompass a significant shift in both field techniques and my theoretical approach to the subject. I hope this variation is not too evident in the text that follows.

Tell es-Sweyhat was first recorded as a significant site in 1972 as a result of a brief reconnaissance of the east bank of the Lake Assad rescue area by Thomas A. Holland and Donald Whitcomb (Holland 1976). Three excavation campaigns followed, sponsored by the Ashmolean Museum, Oxford, and various British museums and universities in 1973, 1974, and 1975, of which the writer was a participant in 1974 (Holland 1976, 1977). A gap of fourteen years followed until 1989, when excavations resumed as a joint project directed for the Universities of Chicago and Pennsylvania by Holland and Richard L. Zettler, respectively (Zettler 1997: 1–10). The results of the excavations conducted by the Oriental Institute team, as well as earlier campaigns directed by Holland, appear in the companion report to this volume (Holland, *Sweyhat* 2).

In order to set the Bronze Age site, Tell es-Sweyhat, within a broader regional context, the upper Lake Assad reservoir area is also described, at a rather summary level, and the basic trends in settlement are sketched. Unfortunately, however, owing to the loss of an unknown but probably considerable part of the archaeological record, initially as a result of the erosion by the Euphrates River, and more recently submerged beneath the rising waters of the lake, the archaeological record is incomplete. This makes the admittedly slender record of the Sweyhat Plain much more valuable. To strengthen the picture derived from archaeological survey, the site is placed within its geomorphological and landscape context by reference to several surveys conducted across the plain from the early 1900s to the early 1990s. By examining the region at a range of scales, from the individual trench, through the site territory, and ultimately to the region of Lake Assad, and by supplementing the discussions with relevant data gathered from surveys, excavations, and studies of other Near Eastern sites and regions, I hope to achieve a more well-rounded picture of an Early Bronze Age community than would be achieved by excavation alone. To help the reader cope with the sometimes wide-ranging discussions, as many sites as possible have been added to the various maps herein. Because no one map can effectively display all the sites, the site names have been indexed by both page number and the figure in which they are located (see *Index of Geographical Names*).

1.B. THE RECORD OF EARLIER SURVEYS

The history of archaeological survey in Syria extends back to the earliest systematic survey in the region, that of Robert J. Braidwood in the Amuq Plain (then located in Syria, but now part of the Turkish province of Hatay). The Braidwood survey, more than most early surveys, paid considerable attention to the recovery and recording of sites of all sizes (Braidwood 1937). Since then many surveys have been more haphazard and appear to have been aimed at finding sites to dig rather than to obtain a systematic record of long-term settlement history. It is not necessary to list here all surveys conducted in western Syria (for a summary, see Matthers 1981: 1–6), but it is worth noting that already by 1939, the Jabbul Plain, between the Euphrates River and Aleppo, had been surveyed (Maxwell Hyslop et al. 1942).

After a long period, a fundamental development in the archaeological investigation of the middle Euphrates Valley was the launch by the Directorate General of Antiquities, Damascus, in 1963 of the rescue project behind the proposed Tabqa Dam. Located near Medinat al-Thawra, the dam was anticipated to result in a lake some 80 km long with a maximum width of 8 km. An archaeological survey, directed by Abd el-Kader Rihaoui (1965) in 1963 for the Directorate General of Antiquities, proceeded ahead of dam construction and was followed in the summer of 1964 by the survey of Maurits van Loon (1967). Van Loon's survey was considerably aided by the availability of aerial photographs and 1:25,000 maps that enabled an extensive, but not necessarily complete, inventory to be made of all significant sites that were to be lost within the area of the projected Lake Assad (see *Appendix B: Site Gazetteer*).

Surveys in the region since van Loon's survey include: the Qoueiq survey, north of Aleppo, in 1977–1979 (Matthers 1981); the survey of the upper Euphrates and Sajur Valleys in Syria in 1977 and 1979 (Sanlaville 1985: 41–98); the survey of the Balikh Valley in 1983 (Akkermans 1993; Curvers 1991; Akkermans 1984, fig. 1.1); the survey of the lower Euphrates Valley north of Jerablus in Turkey in 1989 (Algaze, Breuninger, and Knutstad 1994); and the survey of the Tishrin Dam area immediately upstream of the upper Lake Assad survey area conducted during the late 1980s (McClellan and Porter, in press). Most recently, the survey of the Jabbul Plain provides valuable comparative data for a climatically marginal area away from the main river valley (Gerritsen, MacCormack, and Schwartz 2000: 447–55). More sporadic results come from surveys of the Balikh Valley (Córdoba 1988) and of the western Jazirah between the Balikh and the Euphrates Rivers (Einwag 1993). In terms of geomorphology, a considerable amount of the Euphrates Valley has been mapped (Geyer and Monchambert 1987; Geyer 1985; Besançon and Sanlaville 1981), although the upper Lake Assad area still lacks a comprehensive and detailed geomorphological study.[1]

With the construction of a second major dam within the Tishrin Gorge (between Jebel Khalad [T 552] and al-Qitar in fig. 9.1) upstream of the Tabqa Dam, an additional 60 km length of the Euphrates Valley was flooded by another reservoir. Details of many of the sites inundated during the late 1990s are provided in the major report by del Olmo Lete and Montero Fenollós (1999).

Initially, excavations in the Lake Assad area were confined to a small number of sites; for example, early campaigns were sponsored by the Oriental Institute at Tell Mureybit (T 504) in 1965 (van Loon 1968b) and Selenkahiye (T 507) in 1967 (also in 1974 and 1975 by the University of Amsterdam; van Loon 1979); by a Belgian team directed by André Finet at Tell Kannas (T 508) in 1967 (Finet 1979, 1975, 1973), and a project directed initially by Ernst Heinrich for the Deutsche Orient-Gesellschaft at Tell Habuba Kabira (T 509), and then continued by Eva Strommenger in 1973 (Strommenger 1979; Heinrich et al. 1973; Strommenger 1971; Heinrich 1970c). The rescue project became even larger and more international when it fell under the patronage of UNESCO in 1971. As a result the pace of excavation quickened considerably and numerous new excavations were started for virtually all archaeological periods (for summaries, see Margueron 1980; Freedman 1979).[2]

The Tell es-Sweyhat survey was initiated in autumn 1974 (see Holland 1976: 68–70), and following a gap of some eighteen years, was continued during two brief supplementary seasons in 1991 and 1992. Initial surveys were aimed more towards geomorphological mapping, but because numerous unexpected archaeological features were frequently observed, the survey did not proceed along predictable lines. Building upon an earlier study of the site territory by Whitcomb and the site survey of Holland and Whitcomb (Holland, *Sweyhat* 2), the 1974 survey demonstrated that archaeological features were extremely common in the territory of Tell es-Sweyhat, with the result that the study rapidly evolved into an on-site and off-site survey, of which geomorphology was but a component. Because of the inadequacy of the survey site records of the 1974 season, the 1991 and 1992 seasons were aimed at providing a more systematic collection and recording of sites and checking some of the initial field results. Of particular interest was the reappraisal of extensive sherd scatters that were sampled and mapped in greater detail than during the original field season (summarized in Wilkinson 1982). The overall research objective of the 1991 and 1992 surveys was to examine interrelationships between changes in settlement and land use through time. Building upon the work of Michael Chisholm (1979), an attempt was made to map site territories empirically as an alternative to the inferential methods of traditional site catchment analysis as exemplified by Claudio Vita-Finzi and Eric Higgs (1970). Moreover, it was considered that the location of a major site in such a climatically marginal area would provide a valuable indicator of fluxes of settlement that in turn could potentially be related to long-term historical trends in ancient upper Mesopotamia. In fact, despite its small size, the survey area makes a rewarding case study of the colonization of climatically marginal land. At present, there is continuing debate regarding the relationship between fluctuations in settlement and climate during the later part of the third millennium B.C. (e.g., Weiss et al. 1993). Consequently the presence, and apparent growth, of a major center in such a vulnerable area during an apparent desiccation phase is of considerable interest. It suggests that just as in many semi-arid areas today, there is no simple relationship between the survival of settlement during phases of inclement climate. Instead there is now a substantial school of thought which argues that populations in such areas buffer their economies against climatic catastrophes. In other words, social and economic conditions can either contribute to the preconditions for collapse or settlement decline (Ribot 1996) or conversely can allow climatic fluctuations to be overridden by human action. Clearly, with its marginal location and clear evidence for episodes of advance and retreat of settlement, the area around Tell es-Sweyhat makes an ideal case study for the examination of such opposing schools of thought.

---

1. *Section 2: The Physical Environment* herein, while providing a basic geomorphological framework, does not claim to be exhaustive. Rather geomorphology has been employed to illustrate key processes that have operated along the Euphrates Valley which are relevant to an understanding of the archaeological record.

2. Two site numbering systems are employed herein: first, the numbering system of van Loon's survey which assigns T 501–T 556 to sites to be affected by the building of the Tabqa Dam, which I have continued up to T 591 (i.e., T 557–T 591; see table B.2), and second, that of the Sweyhat Survey which are referred to as SS 1 to SS 30 (*Appendix A: Sweyhat Survey Site Catalog*).

My survey objectives during 1991 and 1992 were primarily to check and record sites of all sizes within the immediate area of Tell es-Sweyhat and to analyze the landscape archaeology with particular reference to changing route systems, land use patterns, and Holocene geomorphology. It was also decided to place the site within the context of the upper Lake Assad area by the compilation of a gazetteer of all known sites north of the bend in the Euphrates River (located near Selenkahiye [T 507]), and by placing them within a broader environmental context. These data, compiled primarily by Clemens Reichel as a site gazetteer (*Appendix B: Site Gazetteer*), are also discussed in *Section 9: Tell es-Sweyhat in Its Regional Context.*

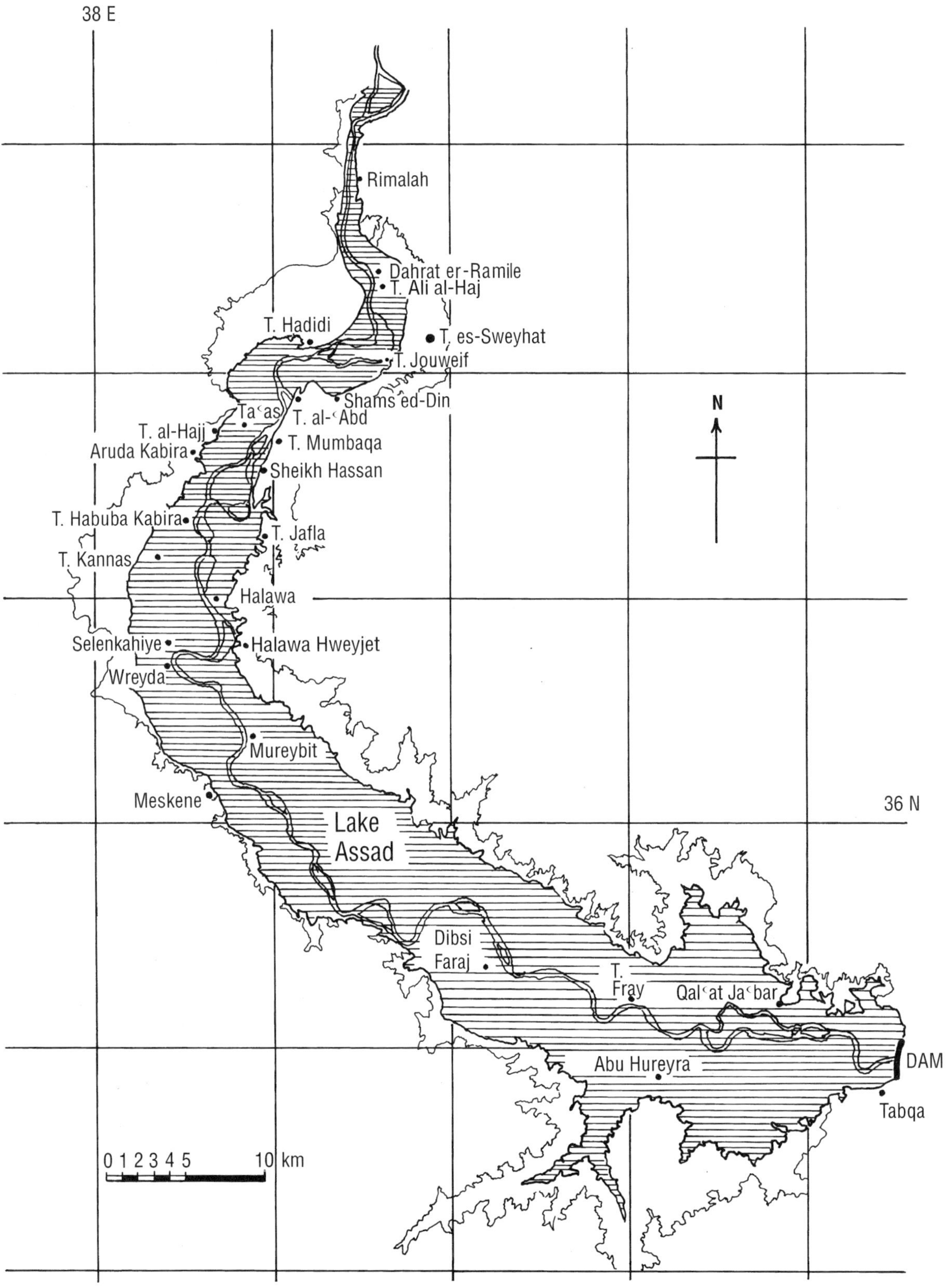

Figure 1.2. Main Sites within the Upper Lake Assad Area

Survey was mainly restricted to the river terrace around Tell es-Sweyhat, the adjacent floodplain (to the west), and the steppic escarpment immediately to the east. In addition, in 1991 and 1992 short visits were made to the opposite (Shamiyah or west) bank of the Euphrates River north of Tell Hadidi (T 548, now submerged) to record plundered Roman tombs and sites along that bank of the river. Details of these and other sites recorded during the intensive survey are supplied in *Section 5: The Archaeological Landscape II* and *Appendix A: Sweyhat Survey Site Catalog*. More recently, further surveys together with excavations of selected sites within the territory of Tell es-Sweyhat have been conducted by Michael Danti (Danti 2000: 266–79; 1997). Danti's surveys, conducted in 1996 and 1997, included the area of steppe on the escarpment, as well as part of the upland steppe and tributary wadis of the Wadi al-Fayyed that extend between the Euphrates Valley and the Balikh Valley to the east. The survey area was subdivided into 5 km quadrants and a total of twenty-eight archaeological sites between the early third millennium B.C. and nineteenth century A.D. were recorded. The survey, although restricted to only part of this large area of steppe, has provided valuable information on possible agro-pastoral communities, especially those which date to the Early Bronze Age.

1.C. THE LAKE ASSAD AREA IN THE RECENT PAST

The Syrian Euphrates Valley was visited by numerous European travelers during the nineteenth and early twentieth centuries, but few ventured past Tell es-Sweyhat. Of those that did, Gertrude Bell provides a reasonable description of the area. Otherwise, most visitors tended to travel past Balis (modern Meskene) on their way from Aleppo to Deir az-Zor and Baghdad. These travelers do, however, give some valuable insights into the traditional economy, which in turn provides a guide to aspects of the ancient economy. Here I treat the visits in chronological order and supplement them with observations on historical geography made by Wolf-Dieter Hütteroth (1990), Nejat Göyünç and Wolf-Dieter Hütteroth (1997), and Norman Lewis (1987) (for site locations, see fig. 9.1).

J. L. Burckhardt (1822: 48), during his original journey down the Euphrates River, describes the area between Meskene and Raqqa as having extensive bedouin flocks grazing its fine pasture, but with no permanent villages. To this may be added William Ainsworth's observations on the verdant natural history, which in addition to a rich bird life included animals such as wild boar, jackals, and foxes. Riparian vegetation of aspen/poplar-type trees as well as mulberry and a dense tamarix undergrowth were noted farther downstream towards Raqqa, but again there is no mention of permanent cultivation or villages (Ainsworth 1888).

In February/March 1909, Gertrude Bell, following a circuitous route from Aleppo to Konya via Baghdad, made observations on the archaeology and landmarks of the east bank of the Euphrates River (Bell 1911). During her short visit she took the opportunity to record a number of sites and make some valuable observations on the area. Her brief but acute observations indicate a wild and desolate terrain, the only evidence of farming being in the area of ʿAnab and Tell Jifneh where "occasionally a small bit of ground had been scratched with the plough and sown with corn" (Bell 1911: 47). According to her informants and also inferable from her general silence on the matter, sedentary settlement was minimal along the east bank of the Euphrates River. Rather, the area was the domain of various nomadic groups such as the Beni Saʿid (a subdivision of the Beni Fahl) and the "Weldeh" (Walda), supplemented later in the season by the arrival of large numbers of ʿAnayzah after their water supplies had been used up. In general, the area was so bereft of firewood that charcoal had to be carried for fuel, and it was not until within about one hour of Raqqa that sufficient tamarisk bushes were available to provide fuel. Of the sites and places mentioned in the area were "Rumeilah" (T 554, Rimalah), close to the site of the projected Tishrin Dam, and a "Shems ed Dîn," near where she spent a night (location uncertain, but it could have been, or near to, Tell Jouweif [SS 8]). At "Shems ed Dîn," which she described as being a grassy area of higher ground with the foundations of stonebuilt houses, she noted a heap of cut stones of an entablature carved with dentils and palmettes, perhaps the foundations of a Roman tower tomb. Also mentioned as she continued downstream were "Tell ez Zaher" (T 536, Shams ed-Din Central Tell), now mostly submerged by the lake; the hill of "Sheikh Sîn"; the area of "Jernîyeh," now the site of a village and a thriving Suq al-Ahad (Sunday market). She climbed "Tell Gaʾrah" where she noted the foundations of a fort, and she recorded the important Bronze Age site of "Tell Munbayah" (T 534, Tell Mumbaqa), the ramparts of which she sketched. She observed, but did not visit, "Sheikh ʾArûd" (T 527, Jebel Aruda) on the west side of the river but did visit "Tell Sheikh Hassan" (T 523, Sheikh Hassan), "ʿAnab," and "Tell Jifneh." Curiously she observed that several tombs between "Tell Munbayah" and "Tell Murraibet" (T 504, Tell Mureybit) incorporated basalt "mills," that is, stones for milling corn (Bell 1911: 63). The local bedouin claimed not to know what they were, which implies that they were rotary rather than saddle querns, implying that perhaps a canal with water mills was once active along this east bank of the river.

Writing only three and six years later, on two separate trips, Alois Musil described significantly more cultivated terrain in the area of Meskene and Abu Hureyra (T 545; fig. 1.2). Numerous cultivated fields were noted, some of which were irrigated by water obtained either by diesel pump (Musil 1927: 193) or by animal-powered hoists that operated over three seven-hour shifts per day (Musil 1928: 179). These bucket and pulley type systems were characteristically used along the Euphrates River until the 1930s; they were powered by oxen, horse, or camel and were usually employed for summer crops, of which a single system could irrigate about 1 ha (Rifai 1990: 314). Such simple systems may have been in use because the ever-shifting channel did not make investment in waterwheels worthwhile. By contrast, along more stable and less erosive rivers, such as the Balikh, Khabur, and Sajur, water-powered waterwheels were in use (Rifai 1990: 314). As Musil traveled from Meskene towards the northwest, the amount of cultivation in evidence was significant, and traveling over a rolling stony plain towards Habuba Kabira (T 509/513) and Khafje Saghire (T 515) he notes that much of the plain was under cultivation (Musil 1928: 191). It is not entirely clear whether the contrast between the east and west banks of the river was quite as marked as given by Bell and Musil, but from other records it appears that sedentary settlement was increasing rapidly, both from the direction of Aleppo and Raqqa, thereby leaving the east bank as more of a backwater.

There has been a tendency for the Jazirah (i.e., the area between the Euphrates and Tigris Rivers) to be described as virtually unoccupied since around the time of the Mongol invasions, but detailed analysis of Ottoman *defterler* (fiscal conscriptions of the Ottoman administration) indicates that during the sixteenth century, the upper Khabur Valley, for example, was rather well populated with sedentary occupation, villages, and cultivation extending to only a little short of the present limit of cultivation.[3] To the south of this sedentary zone, cultivated land often devoted to the growing of millet extended as linear ribbons along the permanent rivers (Hütteroth 1990: 180). Cultivation was often by semi-nomadic tribes, presumably living by means of a dual economy described by Michael Rowton (1974, 1973) as "dimorphic." Fiscal units in this southern zone were recorded as *nahr*, literally "river," but reasonably interpreted in this context as canals. According to Ottoman records, Deir az-Zor and two smaller places were occupied, but little else. By analogy, it seems reasonable to expect that much of the area around the great bend of the Euphrates River was also occupied, although perhaps sparsely, hence the occasional ruined village noted by various travelers may simply be the remains of early Ottoman settlements. In the view of both Hütteroth 1990 and Lewis 1988, such settlement tended to occur under periods of relative security and prosperity; therefore, in the seventeenth, eighteenth, and nineteenth centuries, when administrative control faltered, the area reverted largely to pastoral nomadism until the early twentieth century when settlement revived as the Jazirah again fell under increased administrative control.

In the intervening seventeenth and eighteenth centuries, the boundary of sedentary occupation appears to have retreated to the north and west (the Shamiyah) of Tell es-Sweyhat, while the pastoral zone was in the Jazirah and the desert to the south (the Badiyah). The Jazirah and Badiyah, being the bedouin territory, were occupied seasonally. Most pastoralists were found to the south in the desert area during the winter and in the summer were within the Euphrates Valley, or on the fringes of the settled zone where farming and grazing communities mingled (Lewis 1987: 1). During the nineteenth century, when political control appears to have been weak, the boundary between sedentary occupation and the tribal nomadic areas was between Aleppo and Meskene extending northeast towards Membij, thereafter extending to a little south of Tell Ahmar (Lewis 1987: 16). In general the Dhahab River, some 40 km east of Aleppo, was regarded as the long-term limit of rain-fed cultivation, but the potential quality of farmland well to the east was occasionally noted by travelers. By the late nineteenth century a large tract of land on the west bank of the Euphrates River opposite Tell es-Sweyhat was occupied by the estates of Sultan Hamid, with the result that this area became the de facto limit of rain-fed cultivation. However, the east bank in the region of Tell es-Sweyhat certainly remained unoccupied into the early twentieth century (as noted by Bell 1911: 38) and apparently continued to be semi-nomadic or nomadic until after 1940, when the law of the tribes defined the Euphrates Valley opposite Tell es-Sweyhat as the limit of cultivation. Farther north the boundary then crossed the Euphrates Valley to the Jazirah in the vicinity of Qalʿat Nejm so as to include the dry steppe behind Tell Ahmar within the settled zone (Lewis 1987, map 2).

In the late nineteenth century when security was weak, it was necessary for farmers near the margins of the sedentary zone to make payments (*khuwah*) to tribes in addition to any government taxes (Lewis 1987: 37). Economies in this zone were not only weakened by such dual payments, but also by their distance from suitable markets. In fact the cost of transport was so great that, except in dry years when cereals were in short supply, it was uneconomic to sell grain to the main areas of food consumption in western Syria. Thus millet, which fetched some 12 *piastres* a *shunbul*

---

3. Hütteroth 1990: 179; Göyünç and Hütteroth 1997. For a more detailed analysis of the limit of rain-fed cultivation in the Jazirah, see *Section 2.A: Introduction to the Regional Environment.*

(ca. 6–8 liters) in Aleppo in 1888, cost 10 *piastres* a *shunbul* to transport it the three days journey from even the closest part of the Euphrates Valley. Clearly then, even without the problems of hostilities with the bedouin, the area suffered from a negative feedback process whereby without large urban markets it was uneconomic to produce surplus grain for sale, but under prevailing circumstances there was no chance of urban centers growing up. However, after the 1940s, when the area was under stable administrative control, the population of the Jazirah increased rapidly and at present has numerous towns. Raqqa, for example, went from a police post, established in the 1880s, to a town of some 5,000 in 1930, to a population of 80,000 in 1980 (Rabo 1986: 15). As a result of this massive growth of settlement, the area is now densely populated with villages of all sizes, and rain-fed cultivation extends across much of the Jaziran steppe even to areas south of the river where rain-fed cultivation has been at times illegal and certainly is extremely marginal. Nevertheless, recent studies of satellite imagery show that the present-day limit of rain-fed cultivation still conforms fairly closely to the theoretical line established by climatologists (Perrin de Brichambaut and Wallén 1963), and only to the west of Raqqa does dry-farming extend beyond that limit (Beaumont 1996: 149).

Despite the massive increase in sedentary settlement and the integration of the region into the modern commercial economy (often heavily reliant upon cash-cropping of irrigated cotton), the area still supports some pastoral elements. For example, in the late 1970s, Rabo observed near Raqqa that in the early spring families with sufficient sheep or goats headed out to the steppe to join their flocks. In this case, however, the transhumant cycle was rather small, camps usually being located within 5–15 km from the village.[4] Such a flexible life-style has a long precedent in this marginal area and Lewis (1988) has recorded for the Balikh Valley a classic dimorphic society with pastoralists heading out to the steppe in the winter/spring and returning to their fields (both irrigated and dry farmed) for sowing and harvesting. Herein lies the flexibility of such life-styles because by relying on both cultivation and pasture, dimorphic communities can turn failed crops over to sheep for grazing in a bad year but can provide for both cereal requirements and animal products in normal years. Such flexibility is crucial to an understanding of the ebb and flow of settlement in this region (Rowton 1974, 1973).

1.D. THE AREA TODAY

During the 1970s, the area of Tell es-Sweyhat appeared bleak, arid, and uninviting for settlement. Nevertheless, partly owing to local population growth, but fueled considerably by the in-migration of people displaced by the growing lake, and others from farther afield, the population grew substantially so that by the 1990s the plain was dotted by villages large and small. The landscape is dominated by the cultivation of wheat and barley, which must depend upon the capricious annual rainfall. By the 1980s the river terrace surrounding Tell es-Sweyhat was covered by a patchwork of long strip fields arranged within roughly rectilinear blocks. Increasingly common are small vegetable gardens and orchards that receive their water either from groundwater pumped from the local aquifer or from nearby Lake Assad. Surrounding the main area of villages and their fields on the north, east, and southeast was an undulating area of steppic plateau, primarily devoted to pasture, but also to occasional low yield cereal cultivation.

The Tell es-Sweyhat excavation team lived in the village of Nafileh, a modest sprawling village located ca. 2 km southeast of the tell. Villages on the floodplain, on the other hand, were constructed on a more circular plan with houses rather more densely packed than those of the gravel terraces, perhaps to conserve fertile agricultural soil (van der Kooij 1982: 83). At Nafileh, the extensive courtyard houses were initially all of mudbrick, built with foundations of local limestone. The inhabitants owned flocks of sheep and also worked in the fields, but because some land was owned by landowners from neighboring villages, it was not always obvious who owned the land. During the campaigns of the 1970s, the economy was more traditional with fewer pumps than in the 1990s; as a result irrigated vegetable gardens were virtually absent. The original village water supply was from a village well, from which water was hauled, usually by horse. By 1989, pumping had taken over with the result that the water table was lowered and water salinity had risen to the point that it was only suitable for irrigation and the more sturdy (or less discerning) goats (see also *Section 2.D: Water Resources*).

---

4. Similar movements were observed by the writer in 1995, at which time shepherds with their flocks left the middle Euphrates Valley east of Raqqa to pasture their flocks on fields in the central Balikh Valley.

Villages in the area of Lake Assad were all of fairly recent occupation. On the west bank of the river the village of Hadidi appears to have been occupied for about 100–150 years and could trace its ancestry back to the Walda bedouin that had displaced the Beni Saʿid and become peasant farmers (van der Kooij 1982). Nafileh, on the other hand, was of much more recent origin and local inhabitants point to its establishment during the twentieth century.

1.E. ARCHAEOLOGICAL AND HISTORICAL CONTEXT

The archaeological record for the upper Lake Assad area is not as continuous as might be expected, partly because an unknown number of sites located upon the floodplain have been eroded away, are buried beneath floodplain deposits or sediments washed from side wadis, or lie buried beneath overlying cultural occupations (see *Section 2: The Physical Environment*). The area therefore resembles the lower Euphrates Valley area near Deir az-Zor, with its perforated and for some periods at least, rather sparse archaeological record (Geyer and Monchambert 1987). Further details of the cultural record from sites within the Lake Assad area are supplied in *Section 9: Tell es-Sweyhat in Its Regional Context* as well as in *Appendices A* and *B*. Here only noteworthy features of the occupation phases and political history are summarized in order to highlight certain significant processes that influenced settlement trends.

With the exception of several lacunae, the archaeological record extends back to the Upper Paleolithic (10000–8300 B.C.). This is indicated by remains equivalent to the Natufian at Abu Hureyra (T 545, within the eastern part of the flooded zone; Moore, Hillman, and Legge 2000; Moore 1975). Early and late Pre-pottery Neolithic A (PPNA) levels (ca. 8300–8000 and 8000–7600 B.C.) occur across the river at Mureybit (T 502–504) and Tell Sheikh Hassan (T 523) (*Appendix B: Site Gazetteer*), as well as a small area of early and rather more extensive later Pre-pottery Neolithic B (PPNB) remains at Abu Hureyra (Moore, Hillman, and Legge 2000). To this must be added the important Pre-pottery Neolithic A site of Jerf al-Ahmar (T 559), located immediately upstream of the site of the Tishrin Dam.[5] Early ceramic Neolithic remains were also found at Abu Hureyra in the form of Amuq A related pottery, but interestingly, early ceramic sites (ca. 6000–5500 B.C.) are not as common as in the Balikh Valley where Akkermans noted at least six significant occupations (1993, fig. 5.11). Whether this is because riverine erosion has removed prehistoric sites from the Euphrates floodplain or because conditions for settlement were more favorable in the Balikh Valley is not clear, but the former explanation seems more likely (see *Section 2.B: The Euphrates Terraces*; Akkermans 1999). Although one Halafian site (Shams ed-Din Tannira [T 562]; Seeden 1982; al-Radi and Seeden 1980) was excavated, the record is sparse and is only slightly more obvious than in the middle Euphrates Valley downstream where Halafian sites were found to be entirely absent (Geyer and Monchambert 1987: 318). The situation is somewhat improved for the Ubaid period, with excavated buildings from Tell Sheikh Hassan, occupation at Mureybit, ʿAnab as-Safinah (T 557), and sherds from Tell al-Hajj (T 517, *Appendix B: Site Gazetteer*), supplemented by two small Chalcolithic sites, both virtually flat, recorded on the west bank of the Euphrates River. Both sites, SS 25 and 30 (*Appendix A: Sweyhat Survey Site Catalog*), were found during the surveys in the 1990s and provide a useful record of local Ubaid and early Late Chalcolithic (i.e., pre-Uruk contact phase) ceramics. A remarkable increase in settlement occurred during the Middle and Late Uruk periods, when major occupations appear at Tell Sheikh Hassan, Habuba Kabira (T 509/513), Tell Kannas (T 508), and Jebel Aruda (T 527), plus a number of other sites (see *Appendix B: Site Gazetteer*). The contrast with the sparse record of previous phases reinforces the impression that settlement was of adventitious groups that somehow imposed themselves upon the area, a topic that is returned to in *Section 9.B: Long-term Trends in Settlement*.

Some measure of settlement continuity at the regional level can be discerned in the early third millennium B.C., when Tell Hadidi (T 548), first, and then the Sweyhat Plain were occupied. This period was the forerunner of a substantial increase in settlement that continued through the third millennium within the upper Lake Assad area. There is little reason here to elaborate on the details of occupations, but Tells Hadidi, Sweyhat, al-ʿAbd, Mumbaqa (T 534), Habuba Kabira (T 509), Halawa A and B (T 519A and B), Shams ed-Din Southern Site and Cemeteries (SS 22), Selenkahiye (T 507), as well as the cemeteries at Tawi (T 522) and Shams ed-Din are just some of the Early Bronze Age sites of significance. However, although the upswing in archaeological excavations has resulted in a significant

---

5. Originally discovered in 1989 by Thomas McClellan, this site was more recently excavated by a Franco-Syrian team (Jammous and Stordeur 1996).

increase in our knowledge of the third millennium material cultures, the chronology is far from settled (Schwartz and Weiss 1992). For this volume a chronology is summarized in *Section 6: The Ceramic Sequence from Surveyed Sites.*

As we enter the period of textual records, the area of Lake Assad can be viewed within a wider historical context. Tell es-Sweyhat was apparently within the orbit of Ebla (modern Tell Mardikh) (Astour 1988: 154), but unlike Tell Hadidi (T 548), there has been no textual evidence to suggest a name for the site. Excavations at Tell Hadidi yielded more than a dozen Late Bronze Age tablets, two of which refer to the city of Azu (Dornemann 1979: 146). Astour (1988: 148) suggests that for the period of the Ebla archives Azu was a royal city under the administration of Ebla.[6] If this was the case, then Tell es-Sweyhat, which was only slightly smaller than Tell Hadidi, might also have been a royal city. Although one of the Tell Hadidi letters does mention "villages of the city of Azu," Tell es-Sweyhat cannot have numbered among them because it was not occupied during the Mitannian period. Consequently the closest one can come to a name for Tell es-Sweyhat is the client kingdom of Burman, which based on Early Bronze Age texts from Ebla has been conjectured to have been situated on the east bank of the Euphrates River to the east-northeast of Azu (Tell Hadidi; Meyer 1996: 169; Astour 1992: 27, 34–35).

The excavated evidence that places a major growth phase of Tell es-Sweyhat in the final quarter of the third millennium enables the site to be seen within the context of both the demise of Tell Leilan in the Khabur Valley, and probably the later phases of urbanization within the Karababa area farther upstream alongside the Euphrates River in Turkey. A significant part of Tell es-Sweyhat's occupation appears to postdate the destruction of Palace G at Ebla (modern Tell Mardikh) and must therefore be contemporaneous with Mardikh period IIB2 or even IIIA. The significance of this and the decline of Ebla after Palace G is elaborated in later sections. In the Early Bronze Age a considerable growth in settlement appears to have occurred in the Lake Assad area, but whether this was fueled by trade, the existence of suitable political circumstances, or other factors is unclear.

The location of Tell es-Sweyhat in such a marginal position appears to have been unsustainable in the long term, with the result that the site as well as several other Early Bronze Age centers went into a major decline during the first half of the second millennium B.C. From both the archaeology and the albeit meager yield of texts from sites in the region, it is clear that the area of Lake Assad remained of significance through most of the second millennium. With the decline of the kingdom of Ebla in the second millennium, administration must have been split between Ebla, Yamhad (modern Aleppo), Carchemish, as well as Mari to the southeast (E. N. Cooper 2001; Astour 1988: 147). Despite such political partitioning, both textual and archaeological data attest to the continuation of trade throughout the region during the early second millennium B.C. (E. N. Cooper 2001: 83).

In addition to the large number of thirteenth century tablets from Emar (modern Meskene), Tell Hadidi (T 548), Mumbaqa (T 534, probably ancient Ekalte; Klengel 1992: 84, n. 2), and Tell Fray (T 532) have also yielded cuneiform texts. On the west bank, Tell al-Hajj (T 517) has been equated with Arazik = Aeaziqu, a place referred to in the Alalakh texts, on the basis of its equation with Roman Eragiza. In terms of the political geography, by the Late Bronze Age Emar fell within the orbit of the Hittite administration at Carchemish. Ashtata, the region controlled by Emar, extended along the west bank of the Euphrates River, whereas on the east bank the area surrounding Tell es-Sweyhat fell within the former Mitannian state. At this time although the administrative tentacles of the Middle Assyrian state may have reached as far west as the Euphrates Valley within the Tishrin Dam area, the realistic western limit seems to have been closer to the Balikh River. Thus the presence of Middle Assyrian ceramics at Sandaliye Maqbara on the west bank of the Euphrates River opposite Tell Banat (Eidem and Ackermann 1999: 315; Einwag, Kohlmeyer, and Otto 1995: 105) suggests that some influence may have extended this far west. That the Emar region had administrative links with the north is reinforced by the presence of Qal'at Ferq'ous, a hilltop fortification between Dibsi Faraj (T 541) and Emar (modern Meskene).[7] This has been proposed as a hilltop fortification established by Murshili II and equipped with a Hittite garrison (Klengel 1992: 116; Margueron 1982). Tablets from Tell Fray (ancient Jaharišša, Yakharisha, or Iaharisa) located in the floodplain southeast of Meskene (and now flooded beneath the waters of the lake), suggest that this site was a stronghold of Ashtata and was therefore administratively under Carchemish. It therefore seems reasonable to suggest that the Sweyhat area fell under Hittite control during the period when the Assyrian

----

6. According to a re-reading of text TM. 75.G.2367, originally published by Pettinato in Astour 1992, n. 160, which relates to a military campaign between Mari and Ebla (ibid., pp. 26ff.).

7. I originally noted Qal'at Ferq'ous in 1973 during fieldwork at Dibsi Faraj (T 541). This site was then reported to the director of excavations at that site, Richard Harper, who communicated its presence to the French mission then working at Meskene. Brief excavations were subsequently conducted at Qal'at Ferq'ous by the French mission (see Margueron 1982).

Empire was extending westward in the thirteenth century.[8] Then at a slightly later date Tell es-Sweyhat may have been located towards or a little beyond the western boundary of the Middle Assyrian Empire, a point that is consistent with results from recent excavations at Sabi Abyad in the Balikh Valley. Such major changes in the political geography between the Early Bronze Age, when the Sweyhat area fell within the kingdom of Ebla, the Middle Bronze Age, when it occupied a boundary zone between Yamhad (modern Aleppo) and Mari, the earlier part of the Late Bronze Age, when it must have been under Carchemish, and the later Late Bronze Age, when it may have intermittently been administered from Assur, must have had a significant influence on the pattern of settlement in the area (see *Section 9.B: Long-term Trends in Settlement*).

Although the excavations at Tell es-Sweyhat do not provide evidence on the question of the decline in settlement in western Syria during the late second millennium, archaeological surveys at least enable us to examine critically current notions on this question as well as on the thorny problem of Aramaean origins (McClellan 1992; Sader 1992).

In the mid-ninth century B.C., Shalmaneser III annexed Bit Adini into the growing empire and presumably along with it the Jaziran east bank of the Euphrates River. Liverani (1992) notes that Bit Adini was probably administered by a local king of an Aramaic dynasty, and that at this time it probably sent tribute to the Assyrian capital (Liverani 1992). In the reigns of both Shalmaneser III (858–824 B.C.) and Tiglath-Pileser III (744–727 B.C.) the area seems to have been close to the frontier of the empire, which could explain the dearth of archaeological remains of the Iron Age (see *Section 7.F: The Iron Age*).

Little can be said about the area during the approximately 200 years of Achaemenid rule. This may simply be because both the Achaemenid administration and the material culture changed little from their Neo-Assyrian predecessors (Curtis 1989: 52; Moorey 1980: 128). It is therefore difficult to assess whether there was an Achaemenid presence at all. Grainger, employing very sketchy archaeological evidence, argues for a retreat of the limit of settlement during this period (1990: 18–20), and certainly a number of sites such as Umm al-Marra and Abu Danne, to the east of Aleppo, were deserted at this time. On the other hand, using a range of textual and archaeological evidence, others (e.g., Kuhrt 1995; Dalley 1993) have argued for northern Iraq, that there was continuity of occupation and administration, at least on certain key sites. This point is echoed by Moorey who points out that Achaemenid administrative centers were often on strong points characterized by long periods of occupation and may not therefore be particularly conspicuous (1980: 128–29). Therefore, for the upper Lake Assad area, we expect (and indeed find) that the remains of the period between the Iron Age/Neo-Assyrian occupations and the Seleucids are elusive. This pattern changes abruptly with the arrival of the Seleucids (333–364 B.C.), who as a result of their conspicuous material assemblage are readily recognizable during both survey and excavation. Although the location of the major crossing point of the Euphrates River, Thapsacus, is still a matter of debate, other Seleucid sites, unfortunately not known by their original names, have been recorded. These include a number of smaller sites within the survey area as well as the major Greek site of Jebel Khaled (T 552), currently being excavated by an Australian team (Clarke and Connor 1995). This apparently purely Greek site, which may in fact be a Macedonian colony laid out on a Hippodamian grid, occupies a well-defended hilltop overlooking the Euphrates River near the Tishrin Dam site (Clarke 1994; *Appendix B: Site Gazetteer*). It eloquently demonstrates that with the arrival of the Greeks, the area, although presumably retaining a significant Aramaean presence, must have received a significant Hellenistic cultural influence and was probably under Seleucid administration.

Following the period of the Seleucid Empire during the third and second centuries B.C., the spread of a Roman administrative presence was gradual. For the region of Lake Assad, Roman occupation did not necessarily mean total Roman control, therefore, during the late republic and early empire (i.e., late first century B.C. and early first century A.D.) when the Roman provinces were primarily located in the area of the northern Levantine coast, areas inland simply consisted of a patchwork of local states ruled variously by kings, tetrarchs, or ethnarchs, who although in treaty relationships with Rome, administered their own territories (Kennedy and Riley 1990: 29). At other times the Euphrates River north of the great bend must have formed the boundary between Rome and Parthia, which places the sites described in the survey in a key area of political flux. More concrete evidence of Roman control can be recognized at Tell al-Hajj (T 517: Eragiza) which was a small Roman fort downstream of which extended, at intervals, a number of watchstations. This continued to the fort of Dibsi Faraj (T 541) and beyond (Clarke 1999b: 640). The Sweyhat area seems to have been ignored or passed over by historical sources, perhaps because of its location within a backwater

---

8. As indicated in Kühne 1995, fig. 2; see also Postgate 1985: 97 for alternative reconstruction that relates to the eleventh century B.C. but also predates the discovery of the Middle Assyrian material from Sabi Abyad (Akkermans, Limpens, and Spoor 1993; Postgate 1995, fig. 2).

away from key routes. For example, even when the area was securely within the empire, during the period of existence of the Roman province of Osrhoene, travelers would cross the Euphrates River at Zeugma (to the north near modern Birecik in Turkey), continue to the headwaters of the Balikh River, then proceed to join the Euphrates River at Nicephorium/Calinicum located by modern Raqqa (Millar 1993: 440). From at least the third century A.D., nomadic elements then appear to have become increasingly important, especially as the administrative grip on the region weakened (Kennedy and Riley 1990: 37). This theme of alternations between increased and lessened nomadic influence must have remained an important factor in the development of settlement throughout the first millennium A.D., although as is evident in the discussions below, the Sweyhat Plain remained moderately densely settled for much of this time, only going into terminal decline around A.D. 1000 or shortly thereafter.

In general it appears that the area of land occupied by sedentary peoples increased considerably between the first century B.C. and the end of the third century A.D. (Tate 1997: 55), so that by the fifth and sixth centuries A.D. many parts of the Levant and western Syria had attained a very high population density (Netser 1998; Cameron 1993: 177; Randsborg 1991: 47–49). As a result, many parts of the Near East had attained unprecedented levels of settlement, population, productivity, and wealth by or just after the fourth century A.D. (Ball 2000: 243). Nevertheless, one of the key features to have become evident from archaeological surveys in recent years is that in addition to the landscape being rather crowded, there was a high degree of variation in the rural settlement density. This increase is exemplified for the area around Urfa (southern Turkey), which seems to have gained population rapidly in the Late Roman/Early Byzantine period and then declined shortly thereafter (Wilkinson 1990: 143), whereas other areas to the south, for example, in the Balikh Valley, grew rapidly in population during the Early Islamic period (Bartl 1996, 1994). Such rapid fluctuations are not surprising within a zone that formed the frontier (*thughūr*) between the Byzantine Empire and the expanding Early Islamic realm, and it is reasonable to expect that the Sweyhat area also may have been subjected to acute social and political stresses during the Late Antique and Early Islamic periods.

With the Islamic conquests, the Euphrates River appears to have formed the boundary between the Byzantine Empire and the expanding Islamic state. Significantly, in A.D. 637 John Kateas, the Byzantine governor of Osrhoene, within which Tell es-Sweyhat was situated during the Late Roman/Early Byzantine period, made a pact with the Muslim general 'Iyad bin Ghanm that committed the Byzantines to a payment of 100,000 gold nomismata[9] annually to the Muslims. This was on the condition that they would not cross the Euphrates River, which formed the border between the two polities. However, when Heraclius heard of this arrangement Kateas was replaced by Ptolemaios, 'Iyad crossed the Euphrates River, and the province of Mesopotamia fell to the Muslims (Kaegi 1992: 159–60).

It is interesting that despite the rapid fluctuations of political conditions which prevailed, from the survey evidence as described in *Section 9.B: Long-term Trends in Settlement*, the Sweyhat area shows a broad ebb and flow of settlement that does not reflect the apparent shifts in the political framework. This stability is, however, inherent in the nature of the survey record, which is frequently insensitive to short-term fluctuations in social and political conditions.

The onset of Islamic rule during the seventh century witnessed considerable fluctuations in population, although unfortunately this is difficult to discern for the Sweyhat area because the written sources tend to concentrate mainly upon population centers such as Balis (modern Meskene), located on the west bank of the Euphrates River just around the big bend, and slightly outside the area treated here. At the time of the Muslim conquests we hear of the migration of population from Balis (Ashtor 1976: 13), but by the Umayyad period significant investments were being made so that Prince Maslama (709/710–718/719), son of Abdal Malik, dug a canal from the Euphrates River near Balis (Harper 1975: 324) and established at least one new village between Aleppo and Balis (Ashtor 1976: 62). In addition, a second canal was dug on the east bank as well (H. Kennedy 1992). Because of its position on the west bank of the Euphrates River, Balis was within Syria, but the area of Sweyhat, being on the east bank, would have lain within the Jazirah. During the tenth century Balis was a river port that lay at the intersection of major land routes, and the Muslim geographers tell us something of conditions in the Early Islamic period. Thus Ibn Hawkal writing in the tenth century A.D. describes the town as having gardens between the town and the river, and that the chief crops of its lands were wheat and barley. Ibn Hawkal's report and the presence of the Nahr al-Maslama canal emphasize that at this time the floodplain of the Euphrates River was cultivated (and presumably settled), a point that is relevant to an understanding of the economy of the region for other periods as well. Overall, it is possible to make a case that under the Umayyads there was an expansion of settlement, which in some areas even extended farther than it did during the height of Roman prosperity (H. Kennedy 1992: 297).

---

9. 1 nomismata equal to approximately 1 gold solidus (i.e., the main gold unit of the Late Roman Empire).

With the Mongol invasions of the early thirteenth century we can assume that the area may have suffered considerably. Thus Ibn Ash-Shihna relates that Balis (modern Meskene) lost most or all of its inhabitants at this time (Ashtor 1976: 288). After the conquest of the Mongols the area west of the Euphrates River came under the administration of the Mamluks (mid-thirteenth century to 1517), whereas large areas of eastern Syria presumably became primarily the domain of pastoral nomads. At this time the most powerful tribe was the Yeminite al-Fadl, and other tribes included the Bani Kilab and Bani Khalid (Ashtor 1976: 280, 285). The Mamluk period continued to be one characterized by considerable flux of population, and emigration continued from Balis to the more prosperous centers in western Syria and Egypt (Ashtor 1976: 289).

It would be wrong, however, to caricature the Jazirah after the Mongol invasion as being a barren wasteland dominated exclusively by nomadic tribes. Rather, by the sensitive use of early Ottoman *defterler*, Wolf Hütteroth and colleagues have been able to show that during the first century of Ottoman administration (e.g., in the sixteenth century A.D.) much of the Jazirah must have been an area of relative security and prosperity (Göyünç and Hütteroth 1997; Hütteroth 1990), and it seems reasonable to expect that such conditions prevailed in at least parts of the upper Lake Assad area as well. Nevertheless, as shown below, within the intensive survey area of the Sweyhat Plain, the area does appear to have gone into a terminal decline a short time after the Early Islamic period.

2. THE PHYSICAL ENVIRONMENT

2.A. INTRODUCTION TO THE REGIONAL ENVIRONMENT

The Jazirah forms an arc of dry steppe extending from the Euphrates River in the west through to the Tigris River in the east (fig. 2.1). Currently most of this region falls within Syria, the remainder being within modern Turkey and Iraq. It forms an undulating plateau between 350 and 500 m above sea level developed upon Tertiary sedimentary rocks punctuated by rare outcrops of volcanic hills. Soils of the northern dry-farming zone are mainly calcic xerosols[10] characterized by a horizon of calcium carbonate accumulation at depths of >30 cm below the soil surface (FAO 1974). To the south these grade into xerosols with gypsic subsurface B horizons and ultimately into the gypsic yermosols of the true desert. In the northernmost areas where rainfall is >500 mm, calcic xerosols are replaced by chromic luvisols in which the calcium carbonate B horizon is less well developed. In general these soils are fertile, and given sufficient rainfall, they only require applications of nitrogen and phosphorous to give sustained high crop yields (FAO 1977: 68).

The original vegetation of the region is difficult to reconstruct owing to the heavily degraded state of the present landscape, but it probably would have fallen into the following zones: lands away from the river were probably mainly comprised of grassy steppe with scattered trees of pistachio (*Pistachia*), hawthorn (*Crataegus*), and almond (*Amygdalus*), or shrubs such as *Artemisia*, *Tamarix*, or various types of Chenopodiaceae (see *Section 8: The Ancient Agricultural Economy*; Hide 1990; also Kaul and Thalen 1979: 245; Guest 1966; Pabot 1956). Valley floors may have exhibited a similar vegetation, grading into a riverine woodland dominated by willow or poplar (*Salix/Populus*). Overgrazing, mainly from sheep and cattle, as well as fuel cutting and dry farming, have significantly reduced the number of good species, so that less palatable species such as *Anabasis syriaca*, *Astragalus spinosa*, and *Cornulaca* sp. have become dominant (Middleton and Thomas 1992: 42). Such degradation has a long history extending back to at least 5000 B.C. (McCorriston 1992; Miller 1990a–b). More detail now comes from a recent reconstruction of the regional vegetation by Gordan Hillman (Moore, Hillman, and Legge 2000, fig. 3.7). This reconstruction places Tell es-Sweyhat within Hillman's zone 4, namely the terebinth-almond woodland steppe zone. This area receives too little rainfall for oak woodland but nevertheless would have supported a scatter of drought tolerant trees such as pistachio (terebinth), almonds, and hawthorn. On the floodplain where more water was available a riverine forest would have been present.

The Jaziran climate is a semi-arid variant of the Mediterranean climate. It features hot, dry summers and cool, or cold, wet winters in which a snow cover can sometimes occur. Rainfall varies from 500 to 700 mm in the north to 150 mm or less within the desert, the limit of viable dry farming being in the region of 200–300 mm rainfall per annum depending on hydrology and other local conditions (fig. 2.1). Inter-annual fluctuations of rainfall are considerable, varying from >60% in the desert to 20–30% in the moister areas of western Syria (Perrin de Brichambaut and Wallén 1963; Kerbe 1987, map 1). Because most precipitation comes from cool season (October–April) westerly depressions, a moderately high region wide correlation of rainfall occurs such that, for example, when Aleppo receives a high rainfall, distant places such as Kamishli also register high falls, and vice versa (see *Section 3.D: Climate and Rain-fed Agriculture*). Under current conditions of general circulation a drought in one area will probably, but not necessarily, be matched by drought over most of upper Mesopotamia. As a result during serious famines in antiquity, if inhabitants took to the road to move to lands of plenty, they would probably have had to flee a long way to find food (see, e.g., Jean 1948: 70, for an example from cuneiform texts).

Although no long-term climatic records are currently available for the immediate vicinity of Tell es-Sweyhat, by relating rainfalls for specific years from stations at Membij, Abu Hureyra (T 545), Raqqa, Meskene, and Jarniyah to a twenty-nine year record from Aleppo and Kamishli, it is possible to estimate the local mean annual rainfall as approximately 250 mm. This amount of rainfall places the site very close to the limit of viable dry farming, which according to Perrin de Brichambaut and Wallén (1963) is very close to Tell es-Sweyhat.

---

10. Using the terminology of the FAO soil classification system (FAO 1974); according to more traditional systems approximate equivalents are as follows: calcic xerosols = brown calcimorphic soils; yermosols = gray desert soils; chromic luvisols = terra rossa (Buringh 1979).

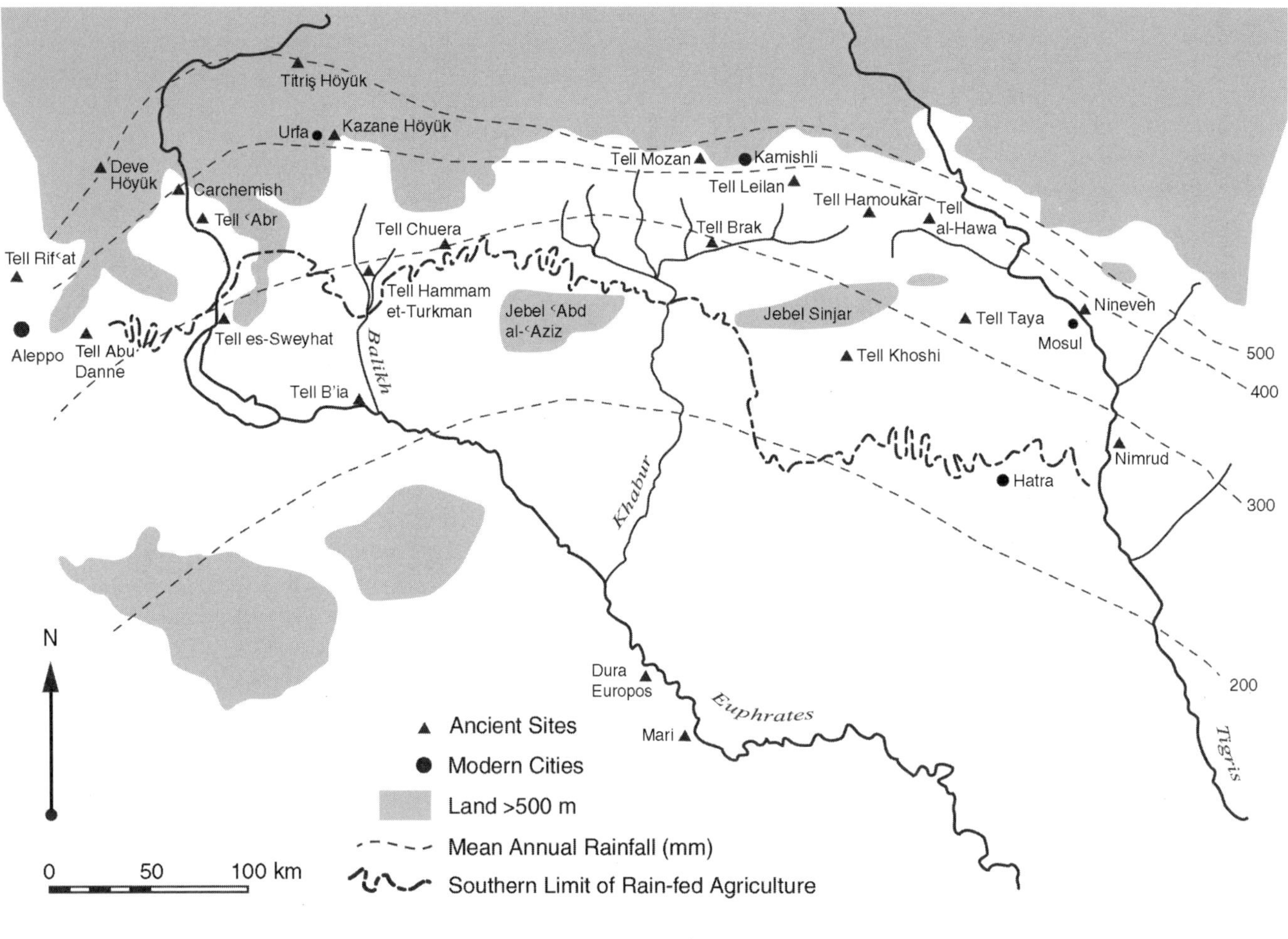

Figure 2.1. Jazirah of Syria Showing Approximate Rainfall Isohyets (in mm per Annum) and Tell es-Sweyhat in Relation to the Limit of Rain-fed Cultivation. From TAVO Map A X 4

2.A.1. CLIMATE AND CLIMATIC CHANGE

A considerable amount has been written concerning climatic fluctuations in the Near East over the past 10,000–12,000 years (i.e., during the Holocene; Butzer 1995; Courty 1994; Hole 1994; Roberts and Wright 1993; Sanlaville 1992; Bottema 1989), and little point is gained in repeating these statements. However, because the data are of critical importance to the sustenance of a site like Tell es-Sweyhat in such a marginal environment, it is necessary to at least review the debate and to draw from it some key conclusions.

The semi-arid Jazirah has a subtle and ambiguous record of environmental change, in part because of the lack of large sediment-bearing lakes, good pollen sequences, or well-preserved biotic material. Most records come from alluvial sequences, local slope deposits, from interstratified soils, or from soils buried beneath occupation strata. Although recent developments in soil analysis, particularly soil micro-morphology, are providing valuable new insights into possible environmental or climatic fluctuations (Courty 1998, 1994) the records from different data sources are still contradictory.

At present two extreme schools of thought regarding climate and climate change exist, with a number of intermediate views. On the one hand, a number of paleobotanists, particularly Sytze Bottema and co-workers, consider that in the Jaziran region, the modern climate was established some 6,000 years ago (i.e., during the Late Chalcolithic/Uruk period), and since that time no significant climatic changes have taken place (Gremmen and Bottema 1991: 111–12). On the other hand, an increasing body of data is beginning to challenge this suggestion, particularly the most recent results from Lake Van in the Euphrates headwaters (see below) and from northern Syria. In the latter area, soil micro-morphological analysis of alluvial sediments and soils suggests that a number of significant climatic fluctuations occurred through the last 10,000 years (Courty 1994). One such phase includes an abrupt climate change posited to have occurred around 2200 B.C.[11] which is suggested to have precipitated large-scale societal collapse immediately after the Akkadian period (Weiss et al. 1993; Courty 1994). Overall, the climate fluctuations of Marie-Agnès Courty comprise an Early Holocene (i.e., before 8,000 B.P.) moist and warm phase; a marked arid phase between ca. 8,000 and 7,000 B.P.; increased moisture again between 7,000 and 5,000 B.P. (i.e., during the Ubaid and Uruk periods); a gradual deterioration with increased aridity during 5,000–3,800 B.P. (i.e., during the later Uruk and early to middle third millennium B.C.), followed by a dramatic drying episode at ca. 3,800 B.P. or slightly earlier (i.e., ca. 2200–2350 B.C.). According to Courty, Weiss, and colleagues (Weiss et al. 1993), this period of extreme aridity continued for 200 to 300 years. It was then followed by more stable conditions similar to those of the present day which continued from the Middle Bronze Age time to the present day. Clearly such a scenario is relevant to the establishment and continuation of Tell es-Sweyhat, and the significance of this is examined in more detail in *Section 9.G: Long-term Settlement and Environmental Change.*

A more nuanced view comes from Butzer who suggests that despite a number of climatic anomalies (including the late third millennium event noted by Courty), no clearly defined climatic trend has occurred during the past 5,000 years (Butzer 1997; Butzer 1995: 138). A complicating factor is that not only are many of the climatic indicators used in the region rather insensitive to climatic fluctuations, but also climatic trends may be in opposite directions in different areas. This is further complicated by the fact that in the Euphrates Valley of Syria, communities experience both the local climate, in the form of the regional weather, together with the effects of a water supply that reflects climatic fluctuations of the Anatolian Plateau much farther to the north. Members of the COHMAP[12] team have expressed this view most clearly with data suggesting that between 9,000 and 6,000 B.P., the well-substantiated moist sub-pluvial conditions of southern Arabia were contemporaneous with somewhat drier conditions in much of Anatolia. The area between (namely northern Syria/Iraq and the Jazirah) must have then experienced indeterminate climatic conditions (Roberts and Wright 1993). On the other hand, the record of Dead Sea water levels and the nearby salt caves indicate wetter intervals before 7,000 B.P. and between ca. 5,000 and 4,000 B.P., with drier episodes after around 4,150 B.P. (Frumkin et al. 1994). An even clearer record is now available for Soreq Cave near Jerusalem that again shows a drying phase after ca. 4,150 B.P. (Bar-Matthews, Ayalon, and Kaufman 1998: 211). The latter arid phase approximately coincides with the drying recorded for the Van cores, which suggests that this trend extended over a large area of the Near East.

Relevant to an assessment of past climate change is what constitutes the "normal" climate, and how does one recognize a significant climatic deviation from this. Climate can exhibit regular periodic or quasi-periodic variations, in which there is no long-term change, but variability on the scale of a few years, a decade, or perhaps centuries. Similarly, for example, mean rainfall can remain constant, but variability can increase with higher peak precipitation and lower lows. Finally, measurable climatic change can occur in the form of an abrupt discontinuity or a more gradual change in climatic parameters. Apart from the well-attested Late Glacial changes between 14,000 and 8,000 B.P., episodes dubbed the little ice age, the Medieval warm episode, and the Middle Holocene wet period of Arabia, northwest India, and northeast Africa are now fairly well attested, at least on a regional scale.

Of relevance to the environment of the Sweyhat area is the record from sediments within Lake Van, which being located near the source of the Euphrates River in eastern Turkey has been a key contributing area to the flow of that river. The re-coring of Lake Van in 1990 has produced a revised sedimentary record that indicates an annual accumulation of lake sediments (varves) that not only supply an apparently accurate chronology in terms of calender years, but also provide a record of varying sediment supply into the lake (Landmann et al. 1996). This work is supplemented by the geochemical studies of varved sediments by Lemcke and Sturm (1997). The new chronological framework provides a control for the important Lake Van pollen sequence originally published by van Zeist and Woldring (1978) as well as the related sequence from the neighboring marsh of Söğütlü (Bottema 1995). The recalibration of this formerly insecurely-dated vegetation sequence results in a much more coherent record as follows.

Following a slightly warm but semi-arid late glacial interstadial between 14,000 and 12,000 B.P.[13] (van Zeist and Woldring's 1978, zone 1) conditions became cooler and drier between ca. 12,000 and 9,000 B.P., with minimal tree coverage (zones 2 and 3). This phase includes the cold and dry Younger Dryas interval. Between 9,000 and 8,000 B.P. (zone 4) tree cover expanded at the expense of shrubs and herbs, a progression that continued until ca. 6,700 B.P. (ca. 4800 B.C.), when woodland and forest reached its maximum extent. This growth of woodland, caused by increased at-

---

11. Or some 150 years earlier according to Courty (1998: 98).

12. COHMAP refers to the Cooperative Holocene Mapping Project, dedicated to mapping the earth's climate at different times during the Holocene period.

13. This is equivalent to the Bolling and Allerod phases of European chronologies.

mospheric moisture and a longer, warmer growing season, resulted in a well-vegetated environment that persisted in a relatively stable state from ca. 6,700 to 3,400 B.P. (i.e., 4800 to 1450 B.C., or during Ubaid, Uruk, and the Early and Middle Bronze Ages). A progressive but fluctuating decline in tree cover that is clearly evident after 3,400 B.P. (1450 B.C.), could be the result of either increased aridity or human activities. Significantly, the rise of the Urartian state, with its increased demands on land and fuel, probably accounts for this decline in tree cover during the final two zones (7 and 8) of the pollen diagram. The geochemical record of Lemcke and Sturm (1997) that has been used to provide a record of inferred atmospheric humidity provides a slightly different picture of climatic conditions on the plateau. This record indicates a distinct Younger Dryas cold and dry period between 10,000 and 11,000 B.P., a more humid Chalcolithic period which continued into the first part of the third millennium B.C., followed by a progressively drier late third and second millennium B.C. (see *Section 9.G: Long-term Settlement and Environmental Change* for further details). For the moment the Lake Van record and that from Soreq Cave in Israel (Bar-Matthews, Ayalon, and Kaufman 1998) appear to be the most temporally and climatically reliable; therefore, these are used as a base line climatic record against which the archaeological record is compared. It must be emphasized that the Lake Van record relates to an area some 470 km to the northeast of Tell es-Sweyhat on the Anatolian Plateau, and the climatic record of Lemcke and Sturm does make a number of assumptions concerning the carbonate and isotope geochemistry that may be subject to revision. Nevertheless, the carbon and oxygen isotope record from Soreq Cave, some 600 km to the south of Tell es-Sweyhat, does provide a similar record, with a moist (but variable) Chalcolithic period up until ca. 4,150 B.P. followed by a somewhat drier climate after that (Bar-Matthews, Ayalon, and Kaufman 1998).

The new varve sequence from Lake Van has provided a well-dated geochemical signal of past humidity for some 14,000 years (now subject to some revisions for the period 14,000–9,000 B.P.). This indicates that following a Middle Holocene phase of slightly moister conditions, atmospheric humidity decreased gradually during the final third of the third millennium B.C. (Lemcke and Sturm 1997, fig. 5). Such a Middle Holocene moist interval, followed by Late Holocene drying is also supported by lake levels in Europe and the eastern Mediterranean (Harrison and Digerfeldt 1993) as well as the above-mentioned record from Soreq Cave. In terms of the sedimentary signal from Lake Van, a significant increase in both sedimentation rates and preservation of opaline silica in the sediments occurred around 5,100 B.P. and between 6,200 and 4,000 B.P. (Landmann et al. 1996: 116). This increase, according to the analysts, would conform to the period of maximum atmospheric warmth and humidity during the Middle Holocene, a phase well represented in southern Arabia and also suggested by Courty (1994) for the Syrian Jazirah and adjacent regions. In addition, the signatures of calcium carbonate, organic carbon, biogenic opal (SiO_2), and "lithogenics" (other mineral inclusions) become more variable from around 6,700 B.P. (ca. 4750 B.C.), or more clearly from 5,400 B.P. (3450 B.C.), that is, during the Ubaid and Uruk periods. Although the pollen record suggests fairly stable vegetation conditions at this time, sedimentary inputs into the lake become more variable. Although possibly caused by variations in climate, this sedimentary fluctuation could equally stem from changing runoff and sedimentation within the catchment of Lake Van as a result of increased human activities during these periods. If this sedimentary variation is evidence of a more fluctuating environment, this fluctuation could have had a considerable impact on human communities that would have had to contend with perhaps drier years, increased flood peaks, more winter snow, or summer heat. Because settlements in marginal environments such as that at Tell es-Sweyhat are very vulnerable to fluctuations in climate, anything that would increase their amplitude further is of significance (for a related discussion, see Hole 1994).

Unfortunately, compared with the array of information from Lake Van, data sources from within the Jazirah are slender. Several sources suggest increased moisture during the Middle Holocene. These include increased stream flow for the areas of Titriş Höyük (Rosen and Goldberg 1995) and Kazane Höyük (Rosen 1997), and in the area of Jebel ʿAbd al-ʿAziz, Syria (Hole 1997). In addition, raised water tables occurred in the fourth millennium B.C. at Kurban Höyük in Turkey (Wilkinson 1990), and for the fourth, fifth, and sixth millennia in northern Iraq (Wilkinson and Tucker 1995). In the Euphrates Valley to the north of Tell es-Sweyhat, evidence for substantially increased floods comes from later fourth and third millennium B.C. levels at Jerablus Tahtani (Peltenburg et al. 1997; Peltenburg et al. 1996) and Ubaid levels at Tells ʿAbr and Kosak (Oguchi and Oguchi 1998). Farther east the lower Khabur Valley provides evidence for a major geomorphological change from an unstable sand bed braided channel to a meandering channel within a predominantly silt floodplain. This change, which took place around 6,000 B.P., that is, before the Uruk period (Ergenzinger and Kühne 1991), may have been caused by increased erosion of topsoil within the Khabur Valley. This erosion resulted in a floodplain rich in silt and clay, which in turn caused the river to meander more[14]

---

14. In general, when river floodplains are dominated by sand and gravel, the river has a braided multi-thread channel pattern, which can shift to a sinuous single-thread channel if the floodplain materials then become dominated by silt and clay (Schumm 1963).

(Schumm 1963). To the east of the lower Khabur Valley the pollen sequence at Buara, near the Syria/Iraq border, although yielding no significant changes in vegetation, did exhibit a peat deposit radiocarbon-dated to 5,730 ± 120 B.P.; although not associated with a noticeably aquatic flora, the presence of this and localized organic material for a depth of some 50 cm below suggests increased waterlogging prior to this date. Within the Wadi Radd in the eastern Khabur Basin a pollen core suggests a brief period of increased moisture contemporary with the Roman occupation of the area (Rösner and Schäbitz 1991).

On face value, the above data provide supporting evidence for increased moisture during the fifth and fourth millennia B.C. (i.e., in the Late Chalcolithic; Courty 1994, phase 3), in the form of raised water tables, increased stream discharge (either as perennial flow or higher flood peaks), or increased soil waterlogging (table 2.1 at end of section). However, the evidence may be blurred by increased human impact on the landscape, with decreasing vegetation causing higher runoff and peak floods in river channels, localized erosion of soils, as well as a decline in water tables and spring flow[15] (Butzer 1995). In the Jazirah of southern Turkey and northern Syria, this Chalcolithic phase of stable, more verdant landscapes, and reliable stream flow appears to have been replaced in the later part of the third millennium B.C. by valley environments characterized by more erratic flow regimes, occasional evidence for accelerated erosion and deposition (as at Kurban Höyük; Wilkinson 1990), and increased incision of valley floors (Wilkinson 1999; Rosen 1997; Rosen and Goldberg 1995).

As population in the Jazirah increased and became more nucleated into settlements of up to 100 ha area (Wilkinson 1994, table 2), human impact on the landscape appears to have increased. Consequently, smaller rivers, such as the Khabur, Balikh, and Sajur, could have suffered increased abstraction of water for irrigation and therefore artificially-depressed flow regimes. Palynology in the Near East indicates that significant impacts on the vegetation cover may not have occurred until around the second millennium B.C. (Bottema and Woldring 1990). Given that initial human impacts on vegetation in other parts of the Old World fall within the range sixth–seventh millennium B.P. in Indonesia, southeast Asia, and perhaps ninth millennium B.P. for India (Walker and Singh 1993, fig. 9.1), these impacts in the Near East seem remarkably late in date. It seems more likely that, as in the eastern Mediterranean, some influence on soil erosion and runoff was experienced perhaps as early as 5000 B.C. (Butzer 1995: 144), but that our data sources are not yet good enough to show this clearly.[16] By way of illustration, paleobotanical data suggest significant environmental degradation by the Halafian period (McCorriston 1992) in the Khabur Valley or certainly by the Early Bronze Age in the Turkish Euphrates Valley (Miller 1990a). It is likely that at least during the later part of the Holocene, the climate signal had become increasingly blurred by human impacts on the landscape. This issue is addressed again in *Section 9.G: Long-term Settlement and Environmental Change*.

Even though sedimentary and soil records are hard pressed to differentiate between climate change and human impacts, cuneiform texts provide glimpses of episodes of climatic uncertainty, if not significant climatic change. Such texts provide a gloomy record of, for example, the Middle to Late Assyrian transition, during which drier conditions with droughts and famines occurred at roughly ten year intervals in the eleventh and tenth centuries B.C. These drier phases were then followed by a moister spell during the early first millennium B.C. (Neumann and Parpola 1987). In comparison, a 1,000 year tree ring record from an area of comparable climate in Morocco shows that clusters of dry years signifying major droughts (defined as at least six years of drought) occurred usually once or twice in six of the last ten centuries (Stockton and Meko 1990, fig. 1.15). If conditions comparable to those of the last millennium in Morocco prevailed in upper Mesopotamia, it is likely that between five and ten droughts of this order would have occurred during the millennium-long Early Bronze Age. Such episodes would only be compounded by outbreaks of infectious disease or plague that could episodically result in significant population decline (Issawi 1988: 96–97). Whether global patterns of climate change, random fluctuations, or local human influence were pervasive, it is clear that the food production system of a site such as Tell es-Sweyhat should be assessed within a context of a dynamic environment. Furthermore, the ability of the system to withstand shocks in terms of extreme and unpredictable events, or to override them, becomes crucial to the survival of the community.

---

15. The Kurban Höyük evidence of a declining water table was originally (and could still be) attributed to this process (Wilkinson 1990: 26–32).

16. Perhaps because in the Jazirah environmental degradation started so early in the Holocene there is no good "pristine" environment to act as a convincing yardstick.

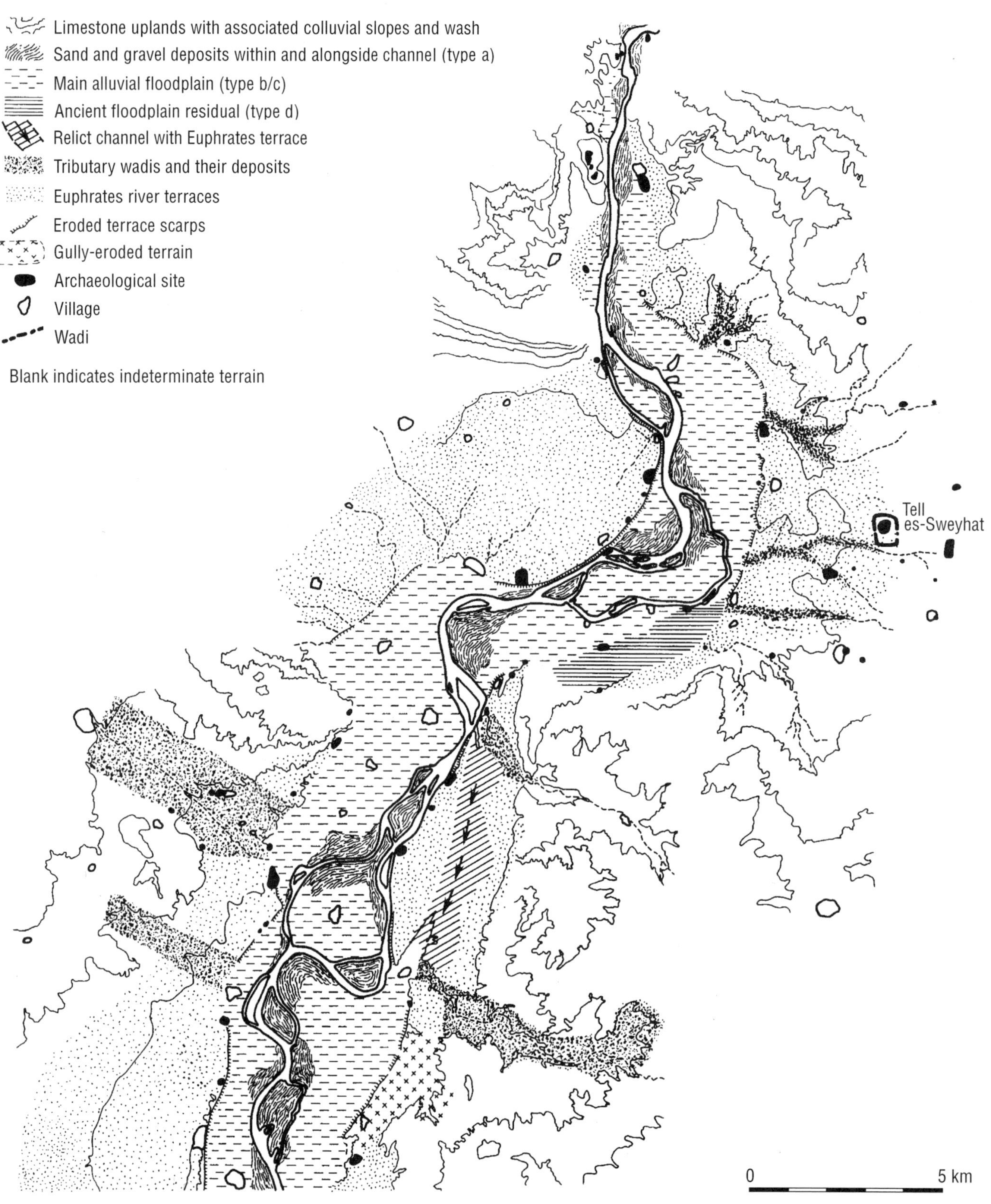

Figure 2.2. Sketch Map of the Geomorphology of the Upper Lake Assad Area

2.A.2. THE GEOMORPHOLOGY OF THE UPPER LAKE ASSAD AREA

The location of Tell es-Sweyhat on a dry river terrace some 3 km away from the Euphrates floodplain provided a large area of potential cultivation or grazing but offered few other obvious incentives for settlement. However, by indicating which part of the settlement record might be missing as a result of erosion or sedimentation, the geomorphological record makes it possible to estimate where gaps may be in the original settlement pattern, placing other site locations in a more realistic context. Because natural and human processes are often interdependent, emphasis here is upon interactions between humans and natural agencies. Such interactions are particularly crucial to our understanding of hollow ways (see *Section 5.D: Linear Hollows*) as well as to the off-site "field scatters" described in *Section 4.D: Off-site Sherd Distribution.*

Tell es-Sweyhat is situated roughly in the center of a broad crescentic embayment on the east bank of the Syrian Euphrates River (fig. 2.2). The plain, which measures roughly 10 km north–south and 7 km east–west, is surrounded to the north, east, and south by the Jaziran Plateau and on the west by the Euphrates River. The local bedrock is a soft, white chalk-like Tertiary limestone capped by a light brown, sandy, thin-bedded limestone that forms the capping over the plateau surface at roughly 500 m above mean sea level. The limit of the plain is effectively formed by the steep slopes of the plateau, which are cut into the chalk and grade progressively into gentle rock-cut slopes and ultimately into the general level of the Sweyhat Plain (fig. 2.3). These rock-cut slopes either have a cover of thin soils overlain by a broken crust of secondary calcium carbonate or fine and coarse deposits washed from the adjacent hills. In turn, the slopes are cut by occasional wadis incised to a depth of 1–4 m and which then flow across the terrace area to the west to join the Euphrates River. The Sweyhat Plain forms one of a suite of Pleistocene terraces indicated in figure 2.2. In the area of Tell es-Sweyhat, the geomorphology can be classified into the following subdivisions.

2.B. THE EUPHRATES TERRACES

2.B.1. THE MAIN TERRACE

The broad expanse of plain that surrounds Tell es-Sweyhat and which merges with the lower rock-cut slopes forms part of the main terrace complex of the Euphrates Valley. This broad, very gently sloping bench results from the erosion of the underlying limestone by an arm of the Euphrates River. The bench is covered by up to 7.0 m of dark gray, black, green, and blue gravels[17] of Anatolian provenance that are now cemented to form a conglomerate. In turn, on top of these channel gravels are deposits of Euphrates sand and silt finally overlain by locally-derived soil wash and wadi gravel from the adjacent terrace and hills. A conspicuous feature of the terrace between SS 25 and Shajara Saghira (SS 29) (on the west bank; see fig. 7.1 for site locations) and around Mishrifat (SS 16A), Ramalah (SS 16B),

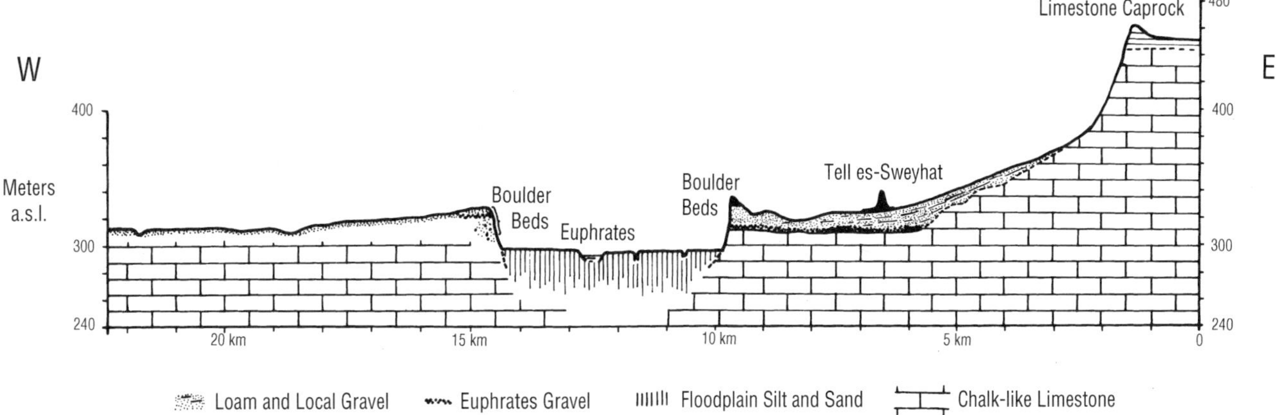

Figure 2.3. Geological Cross Section through the Floodplain, Plateau, and River Terraces of the Euphrates River

17. These Euphrates gravels derive from a wide range of rock types that include basic and acidic igneous rocks, metamorphics, lavas, and a wide range of sedimentary rocks. Gravels are well rounded and from their color and rounding are readily distinguished from the more angular and dominantly sedimentary sediments of the local accumulations.

and SS 16C (on the east bank) are deposits of massive limestone boulders. Individual boulders range in size from 0.8 to 2.0 m long axis, with occasional examples attaining 5.0 m. Most are of the brownish limestone that caps the plateau, but occasional white limestone boulders are also represented. The boulders are not confined to a single bed but on the west bank appear to comprise an aggrading sequence of Euphrates deposits that form the main west terrace (fig. 2.3). Such massive boulders suggest the occurrence of a Pleistocene flood event of extreme power, but because the boulders are locally derived and no long-distance transport of rocks is evident, the event may not have been a single flood operating within the entire Euphrates basin. Rather they may relate to erosion and perhaps the cutting of the Tishrin Gorge located some 10 km upstream (at present day Jerf al-Ahmar [T 559]). These beds are archaeologically significant because the resultant litter of large stones in places mimics the pattern of stones that occur on archaeological sites, thus providing occasional false sites. Elsewhere, where the boulders have been gathered up in antiquity for building purposes, they do form real walls within genuine archaeological sites, for example, at Hellenistic and Roman Mishrifat, Ramalah, SS 16C, and Shajara Saghira.

The surface of the plain at ca. 325 m above sea level is slightly above a former bed level of the Euphrates River, which at ca. 320 m is itself some 30 m above the present channel level. This terrace forms part of a persistent feature in the region described as the main terrace, or the Shajara Formation, and is dated to the mid-late Pleistocene.[18] In reality, this terrace can be subdivided into a number of different morphological features as follows: to the west of the river at 314–318 m and 320–328 m and to the east of the river at 320–330 m (in the north), 320–325 m (in the vicinity of Tell es-Sweyhat), and 330–332 m along the bluffs, a topographic unit that attains a local maximum elevation of 350 m near the village of Mishrifah Saghir. The lower extension of the terrace is sometimes referred to as the Mureybit Formation.

If one accepts that the lowest surface (that to the west of the river) is the youngest, it follows that the general trend of Pleistocene channel movement has been from east to west, with the present channel occupying a course slightly to the west of center. The modern channel is now constrained within a narrow gorge upstream near Jerf al-Ahmar (T 559) and Ramalah (SS 16B), located some 7–8 km to the northwest of Tell es-Sweyhat. A second gorge, slightly less narrow, occurs downstream near Shams ed-Din (Sites SS 22, T 536, and T 562). Such constraints, both upstream and downstream, effectively limit the amount of lateral movement that can occur, and today the channel is contained within a trough some 3 km wide and 20–50 m deep.

2.B.2. THE ALLUVIAL PLAIN

The Euphrates floodplain is a dynamic feature comprising a 200 m wide channel and associated sub-channels of a braided but locally meandering channel system. These channels migrate back and forth across the alluvial plain, re-working earlier deposits as well as trimming valley-side bluffs, archaeological sites, occasional quarries, tombs, and rock-cut wine presses (see *Section 5: The Archaeological Landscape II*). The 32 km length of the valley from Halawa Hweyjet (T 511B) to Jerf al-Ahmar (T 559) (fig. 9.1) contains a sometimes multiple channel with a relatively low sinuosity (mean sinuosity = 1.28, maximum = 1.60) and a gravel bed.[19] Minor channels or anabranches leave and re-join the channel periodically over lengths of between 3 and 6 km. Near Dibsi Faraj (T 541) sinuosities greater than 1.5 can be observed for relict meanders in the fine floodplain sediments of the southern edge of the valley (fig. 2.4, see n. 7). Near the Roman/Byzantine/Early Islamic citadel of Dibsi Faraj (figs. 1.2 and 2.4), a sinuous medieval or post-medieval channel (now relict) erased the Early Islamic canal, the Nahr al-Maslama, and reworked the floodplain. This relict channel meandered more than the present one, which in the recent past developed the less sinuous braided planform. Similar relict meanders are evident in the alluvial plain near Raqqa (Besançon and Sanlaville 1981, map 1). The presence of both sinuous and non-sinuous channel reaches today (fig. 2.2) suggests that both types of channel may coexist. However, because non-sinuous channels seem much more pervasive today, it is likely that sinuous channels are characteristic of the pre-modern floodplain. Because less sinuous braided channels are associated with coarse floodplain sediments and a predominance of coarse sediment transport along the stream bed (Schumm 1977), it is possible

---

18. See Besançon and Sanlaville 1981; de Heinzelin 1967; van Liere 1960/61. This terrace is also referred to as terrace Q3 of Upper Pleistocene date according to the geological map of Syria (Boerma 2001, fig. 2.1), and also terrace Q_{II} (Geyer and Besançon 1997).

19. Sinuosity is defined as the ratio of channel length to valley length, i.e., Lc/Lv where Lc = the length along the main channel and Lv = the overall length along the main valley. Very mean-

dering channels have a high sinuosity in the region of 2–3, whereas rivers with braided channels have sinuosities between 1.5 and 1 (a straight channel being that with a sinuosity of 1) (Schumm 1977). Note that downstream near Dibsi Faraj (T 541), channel sinuosity in 1960 was approximately 1.4, whereas partial traces of relict meanders shown in figure 2.4 yielded sinuosities of 1.32, 1.5, and 2.3.

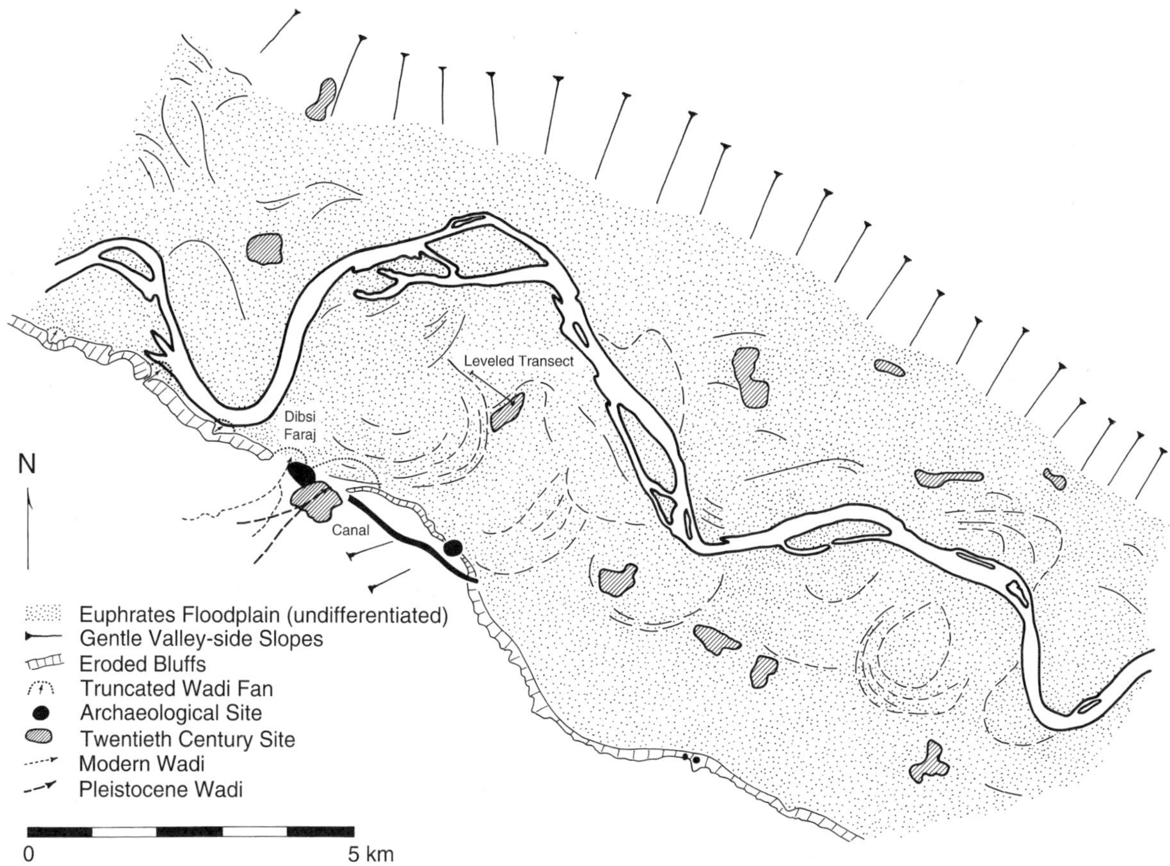

Figure 2.4. Relict Meanders of the Euphrates River in the Area of Dibsi Faraj (T 541). For Location, See Figure 1.2

that the change in river regime may result from increased flood peaks and transport of coarse sediment in recent times.[20] Such a pattern could be accounted for by more extreme climatic conditions of recent years but equally could result from increased flood peaks precipitated by increased settlement and de-vegetation in the upper Euphrates Valley over the last 200 or so years. On the other hand, re-mobilization of sediment stored in the riverine plain upstream may have increased the sediment load and initiated a new phase of braided channel development.

Crucial to human settlement in this zone is the height of the floodplain surface above flood level. In most years the level of the Euphrates River fluctuates from low water in August, September, and October to as much as 6 m above this minimum in April or May after the Anatolian spring snowmelt (Kolars and Mitchell 1991: 90–91). Instrumental leveling at Dibsi Faraj (T 541) some 40 km downstream of Tell es-Sweyhat showed that permanent settlement was not lower than 5.4 m above the minimum water level but more frequently was more than 6 m above minimum level (fig. 2.5). In the area of Tell es-Sweyhat the numerous villages that existed on the floodplain prior to the development of Lake Assad (fig. 2.2), other things being equal, must also have been at an equivalent elevation above flood level. Furthermore, the presence of Tell Jouweif (SS 8) and Shams ed-Din Central Tell (T 536) on a single enclave of relict floodplain suggests that the enclave predates the occupation of the sites and when occupied was also above the level of flooding. Both Tell Jouweif and Shams ed-Din Central Tell appear to date from at least the early third millennium B.C. (*Sections 6* and *8*) whereas Qubab (T 501) on an enclave of relict floodplain to the south was Byzantine in date according to van Loon (1967). Using the evidence of floodplain sediments and morphology in tandem with the presence

---

20. Braided channels occur in "high-energy fluvial environments with steep valley gradients, large and variable discharges [...], dominant bed-load transport, and non-cohesive banks lacking stabilization by vegetation" (Richards 1982: 211). In addition they are associated with increased width-depth ratios. If valley slope is assumed to have remained constant, a change from a meandering to a braided channel implies an increase in the dis- charge of bed material, and perhaps an increase in water discharge as well, or both in combination (Richards 1982: 255). In the Euphrates Valley near Tell es-Sweyhat the braided system varied from islands that were relatively stable and which must have persisted for many decades or centuries, to unstable shoals and sandy islands.

of human settlements, both ancient and modern, four types of morphological units can be recognized within the pre-Lake Assad floodplain (from lowest/youngest to highest/oldest [Types *b* and *c* are undifferentiated in fig. 2.2]):

Type *a*   Near channel level, sandy riverine deposits; flooded in most years.

Type *b*   Undifferentiated floodplain with modern fields; flooded in occasional years.

Type *c*   Higher floodplain with modern fields and villages; only flooded in exceptional years; equivalent to the "terrasse historique" (Qoo) of Geyer and Besançon 1997.

Type *d*   Ancient floodplains, such as that behind Tell Jouweif (SS 8); rarely flooded and encroached along eastern edge by aggrading wadi fans; equivalent to terraces Qoa and Qob of Geyer and Besançon 1997, namely the Early Holocene and Bronze Age terraces respectively.

Sections through the Type *c* floodplain near Dibsi Faraj (T 541) revealed that floodplain levels had risen by both deposition within the river channel (*Appendix C: Selected Soil and Sediment Descriptions: Section 1* [2.5–5.2 m]) and as vertical accretions of silt outside its banks (0–2.5 m) as a result of overbank floods, in this case interfingering with deposits washed from the nearby limestone bluffs (cf. Wolman and Leopold 1957). Field data suggest that rather than being evidence of riverine incision, the floodplain terraces, Types *c* and *d*, are products of gradual accretion associated with an essentially stable channel level.[21] In general the silt, sand, and loam deposits of the alluvial plain showed very little evidence of soil formation (soil structure, secondary accumulations of minerals, development of soil horizons), or surface scatters of potsherds (see *Section 4.B: Off-site Sherd Scatters*). The alluvial plain seems to have been deposited relatively recently, probably within the last 1,000 or 2,000 years. During the Early to Middle Holocene, the alluvial plains may have been covered by a riverine forest of poplar, ash, and occasional elms probably with intervening backswamps of abandoned channels filled with various types of reeds and rushes (Moore, Hillman, and Legge 2000: 70–71).

In most areas, lateral erosion by the river has kept the adjacent bluffs trimmed and vertical, but in the vicinity of Tell Jouweif (SS 8) and Shams ed-Din Central Tell (T 536) gentle degraded slopes merge with the old floodplain (Type *d*). Wadis grade down to this level and their sediment load has accumulated upon it as broad spreads of off-white silts, sand, and gravel. Just visible within the southeastern part of this floodplain residual is a line of low relict bluffs of Euphrates conglomerate and gravel that were eroded presumably when the river last passed through this area. This enclave of ancient floodplain terrace was bounded on the riverward side by low bluffs within the floodplain. The Type *d* floodplain is the only area of demonstrably ancient floodplain that exists in the area; elsewhere continuous channel shifts have scoured away the floodplain and trimmed the bluffs, as well as presumably any sites that were originally present. Of the two sites recorded on this enclave (Tell Jouweif and Shams ed-Din Central Tell; fig. 2.6), the

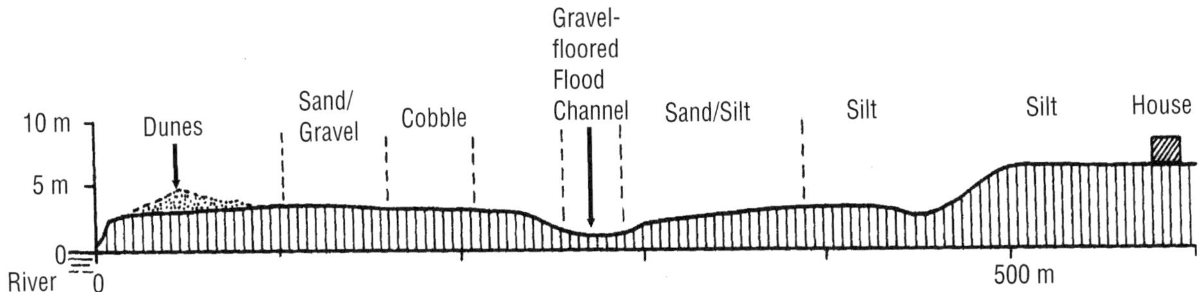

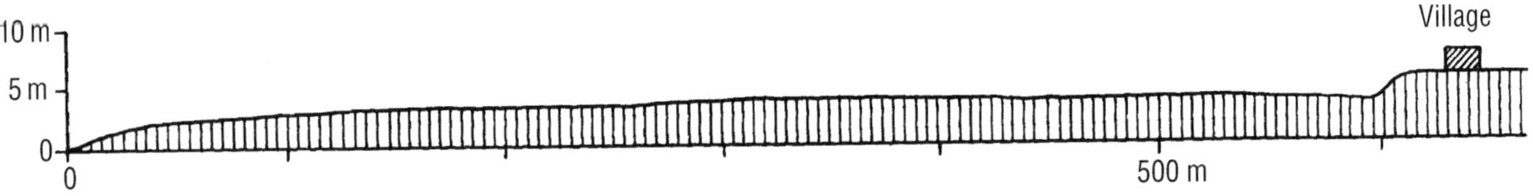

Figure 2.5. Leveled Profile of the Euphrates Alluvial Plain near Dibsi Faraj (T 541)

---

21. This inference is supported by a more detailed study of flood-plain aggradation, published by Richard Tipping for the site of Jerablus Tahtani (Peltenburg et al. 1997).

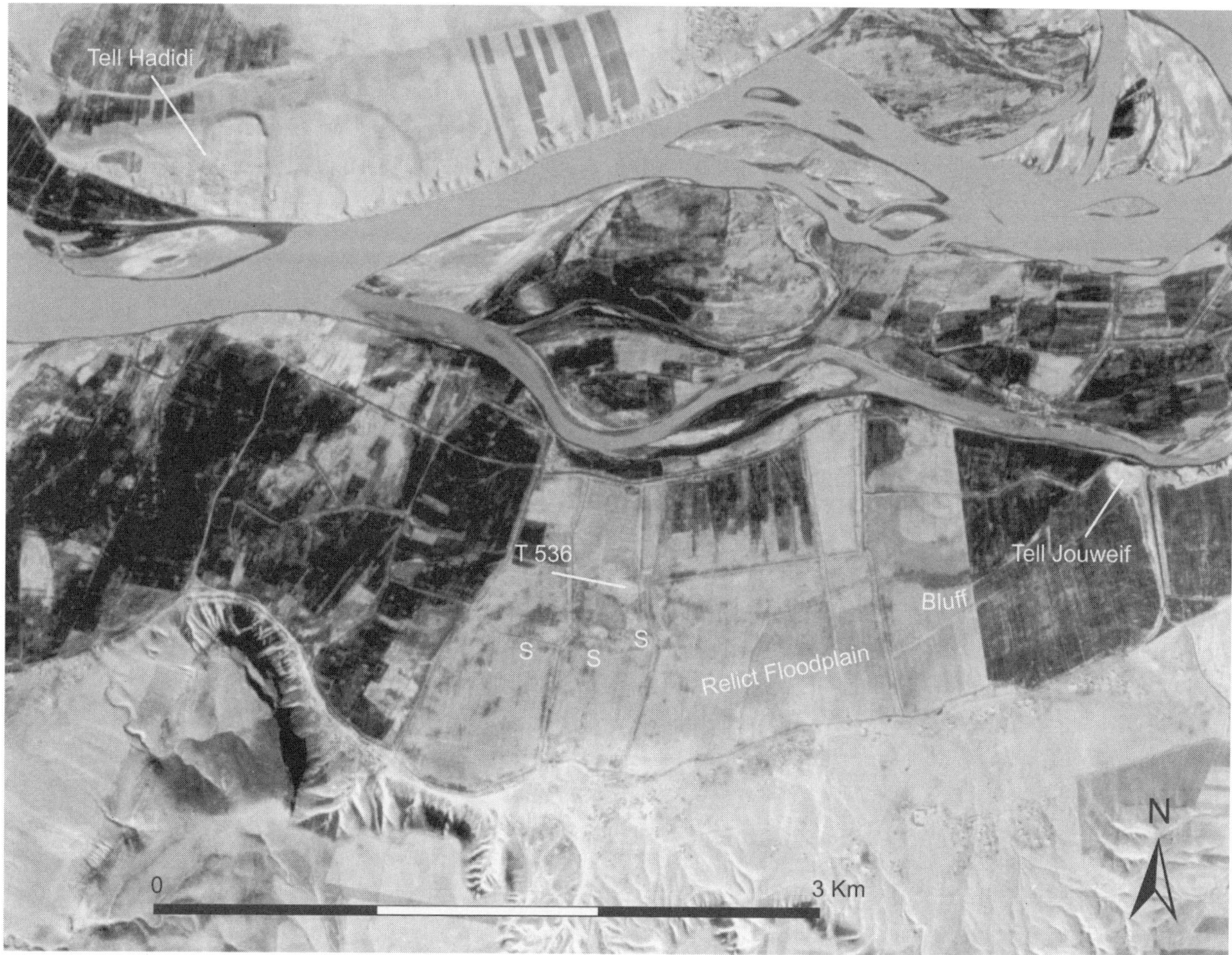

Figure 2.6. CORONA Satellite Image of the Area around Tell Jouweif (SS 8) and Shams ed-Din Central Tell (T 536) Showing Additional Small Sites (Light-colored Patches: S) on the Relict Euphrates Floodplain. Note the Very Low Bounding Riverine Bluff to the Southwest of Tell Jouweif. Produced by Jason Ur, Oriental Institute CAMEL Laboratory; Courtesy of U.S. Geological Survey

latter has not been dated. The earlier levels at Tell Jouweif, which must lie on the floodplain silts, can be dated to approximately the early third millennium B.C., thereby suggesting that this floodplain predates about 3000 B.C. Long-term erosion by the Euphrates River can therefore easily explain the paucity of prehistoric sites within the area of Lake Assad.[22] This impression is reinforced by CORONA satellite images that show the pale-colored patches of several possible sites in the same floodplain enclave around Tell Jouweif and Shams ed-Din Central Tell (fig. 2.6).

There are few deep sections through the valley floor to provide information on sedimentary conditions through the Holocene. However, upstream of Tell es-Sweyhat near the Turkish border, fluviatile gravels of the Euphrates Valley at ca. 5 m above present floodplain level are associated with the site of Jerablus Tahtani. Similar high-energy sediments occur in Ubaid levels at Tells ʿAbr and Kosak a little downstream from Jerablus Tahtani (Oguchi and Oguchi 1998) and in post-Chalcolithic levels in the Khabur Valley (Akahane 1998). These elevated and high-energy sediments all attest to major increases in flood magnitude during the Middle Holocene through to the later third millennium B.C. These events, the latter of which appear roughly contemporaneous with other later third millennium B.C. sedimentary transitions within the Euphrates catchment at Kurban Höyük, Titriş Höyük, and the upper Balikh Valley, again appear to be a manifestation of increased amplitude of flow. The sedimentary transitions at the Turkish sites may reflect the impact of changing atmospheric humidity[23] intensified by environmental stress resulting from increased population

---

22. See Brown (1997: 280–81) for general discussion of preservation potential on floodplains.

23. In this case the floods could reflect increased rainfall, decreasing rainfall (associated with increased inter-annual variability), or simply increased incidence of storms. In the case of a decrease in rainfall, vegetation would potentially be decreased and the in-

ter-annual variability of the rainfall would increase, both of which may have exacerbated flood levels. Alternatively, increased annual rainfall may have resulted in an increase in protective vegetation. Therefore, of these options, the third seems most likely. This increased incidence of storms may or may not have been associated with changes in the mean annual rainfall.

and/or urbanization. Consequently, increased runoff, decreased rainfall interception via vegetation, lowered groundwater levels, and channeled flow along tracks, ditches, and canals may all have produced conditions that amplified flow fluctuations and created conditions that favored localized incision. A similar amplification of a long return interval flood by changes in land use may also have contributed to the elevated flood peaks recorded at Jerablus Tahtani, Tell ʿAbr, and Tell Kosak (for further discussion of third millennium environmental change, see *Section 9.G: Long-term Settlement and Environmental Change*).

2.B.3. TRIBUTARY WADIS AND VALLEY FILLS

The river terrace around Tell es-Sweyhat is crossed by three wadi systems that follow roughly parallel courses from the plateau to the Euphrates River (figs. 2.7–2.8). Although these wadis show some resemblance to canals and were originally mapped as such, there was no evidence that these were dug features. Thus the wadis lacked upcast mounds alongside them, there was no evidence for them ever having flowed year round, and they do not flow from the area of springs or relict springs.[24] The two wadi systems to the north and center, although forming continuous valleys, lack active channel beds along their entire length. The third, Wadi Nafileh to the south, has a continuous gravel bed with cobbles as large as 15 cm across, a size which suggests that peak flows can be powerful in some years. The northern and southern wadis have asymmetric valley cross profiles 3–5 m in depth (fig. 2.8), whereas the central system exhibits much lower relief so that only along its south bank is there any discernible terrace. None of these wadis show evidence of deliberately excavated channels, nor are banks of upcast present as might be expected along canals. The central wadi has, however, been modified considerably as a result of the growth of Tell es-Sweyhat and associated wall construction. The wadis become better defined and incised towards the Euphrates as a result of the migration of "knick points" or points of incision away from the main river (see below).

2.B.3.1. THE NORTHERN WADI

The northern wadi flows past Khirbet Aboud al-Hazu (SS 6) and Khirbet Aboud al-Hazu 2 (SS 19) and has the following sequence of deposits exposed at the headcut immediately downstream of Khirbet Aboud al-Hazu (from bottom to top, fig. 2.9a):

Deposit *a*   Strongly cemented chalk breccia on eroded limestone wadi bed.

Deposit *b*   90–120 cm thick. Lenses and strings of poorly sorted fluvial gravel within a matrix of silty and sandy loam. These are of local provenance and form a discontinuous deposit across the about 50 m width of the valley.

Deposit *c*   Upper fill of about 60 cm of brown silt loam with rare stones. Two wheel-thrown potsherds, but undiagnostic, were at 40 and 60 cm depth. Calcium carbonate concretions were evident near the interface with Deposit *b* along the southern valley edge.

Deposit *a*, from its stratigraphic position and strong cementation, probably results from wadi flow during the Late Pleistocene or Early Holocene. Deposit *b* indicates down valley episodic flow of moderate energy. Similar beds downslope included cobbles of 20–25 cm within a brown silt matrix, reddened at depth. The presence of a rim of a chaff-tempered vessel, apparently prehistoric, at 115 cm within the cobbles, suggests that these are of prehistoric date or later. The absence within Deposits *b* and *c* of mottles resulting from oxidation or reduction, as well as shells of freshwater molluscs, also supports that flow was intermittent, presumably taking place after winter rains. Deposit *c* represents a phase when down valley flow was overtaken by lateral movement of soil from the adjacent slopes into the valley bottom. The presence of wheel-thrown potsherds indicates a Bronze Age or post-Bronze Age date. Such local soil wash, which was probably initiated by increased plowing within the wadi catchment during the third millennium B.C., probably continued episodically through the following 4,000 years whenever soil disturbance increased available sediment for erosion.

2.B.3.2. THE CENTRAL WADI

Excavation of Trench S3 (= sounding T.1) in a very shallow break in the eastern enclosure wall of Tell es-Sweyhat (fig. 2.10) revealed that the original wadi had been 2.2 m deeper during the Early Bronze Age. The sequence was as follows (fig. 2.10, from top to bottom; see also Holland, *Sweyhat* 2, for ceramics from this sequence):

---

24. I am grateful to Donald Whitcomb for supplying me with his original aerial photograph map that identified, in addition to the wadi systems, a large number of sites and off-site features as well as the southern extension of Tell es-Sweyhat.

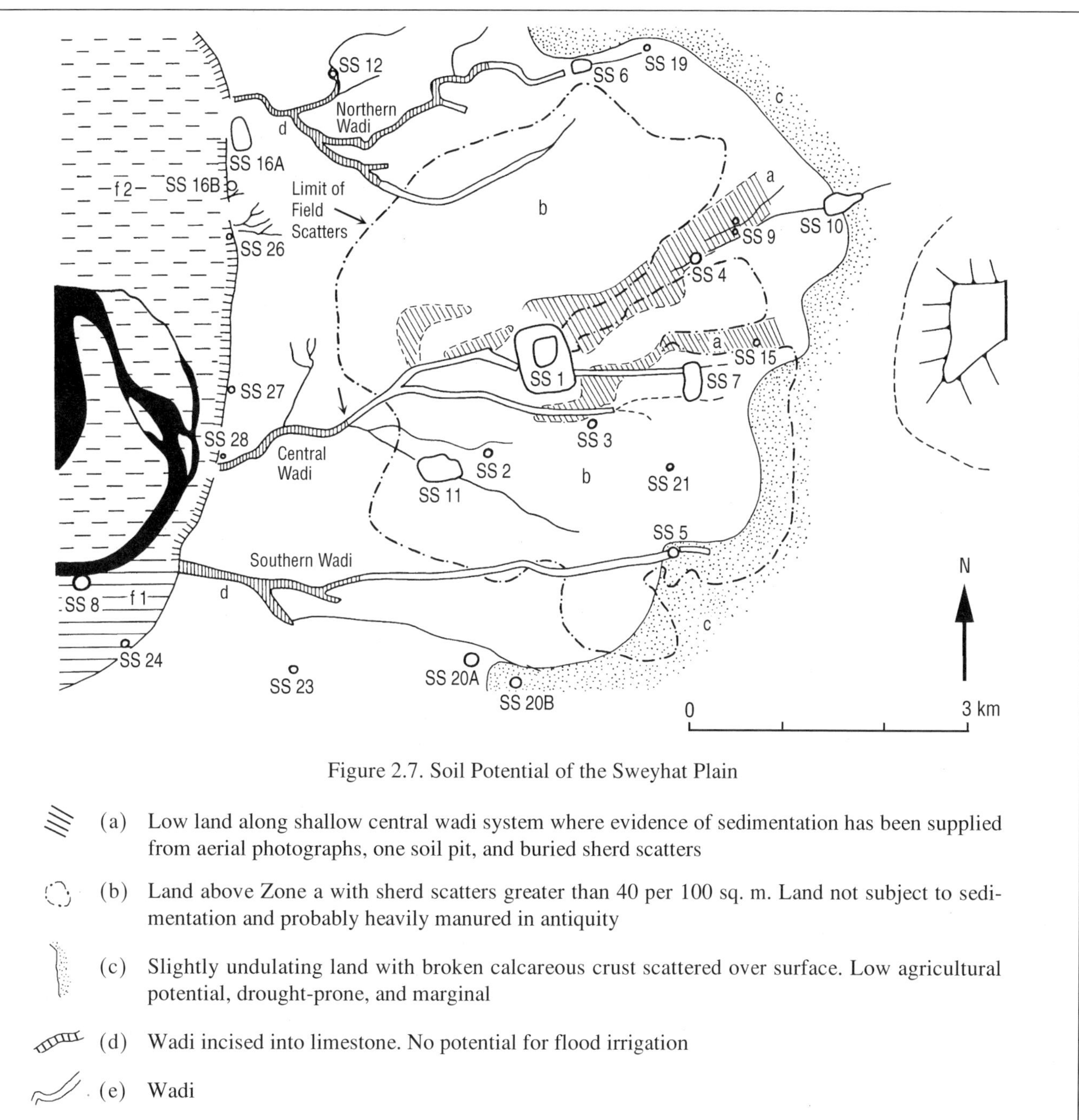

Figure 2.7. Soil Potential of the Sweyhat Plain

(a) Low land along shallow central wadi system where evidence of sedimentation has been supplied from aerial photographs, one soil pit, and buried sherd scatters

(b) Land above Zone a with sherd scatters greater than 40 per 100 sq. m. Land not subject to sedimentation and probably heavily manured in antiquity

(c) Slightly undulating land with broken calcareous crust scattered over surface. Low agricultural potential, drought-prone, and marginal

(d) Wadi incised into limestone. No potential for flood irrigation

(e) Wadi

(f1) Ancient Euphrates floodplain

(f2) Recent floodplain

0–60 cm	Strong brown sandy loam with weak subangular structure and occasional soft calcium carbonate concretions. Ash at ca. 40 cm
60–100/120 cm	Very pale brown sandy loam with occasional pieces of disintegrated mudbrick and occasional charcoal flecks below. Thin mud floor, locally plastered at 80 cm
100/120–220 cm	Stones of limestone, 10–30 cm long axis, with abundant potsherds in interstices. Probably a collapsed wall or a wall foundation
160–210 cm (to east)	Mudbrick with strong brown and pale olive mottles
210–230 cm	Strong brown sandy loam; two small lenses of fine gravel, maximum size 1 cm, mainly of local limestone

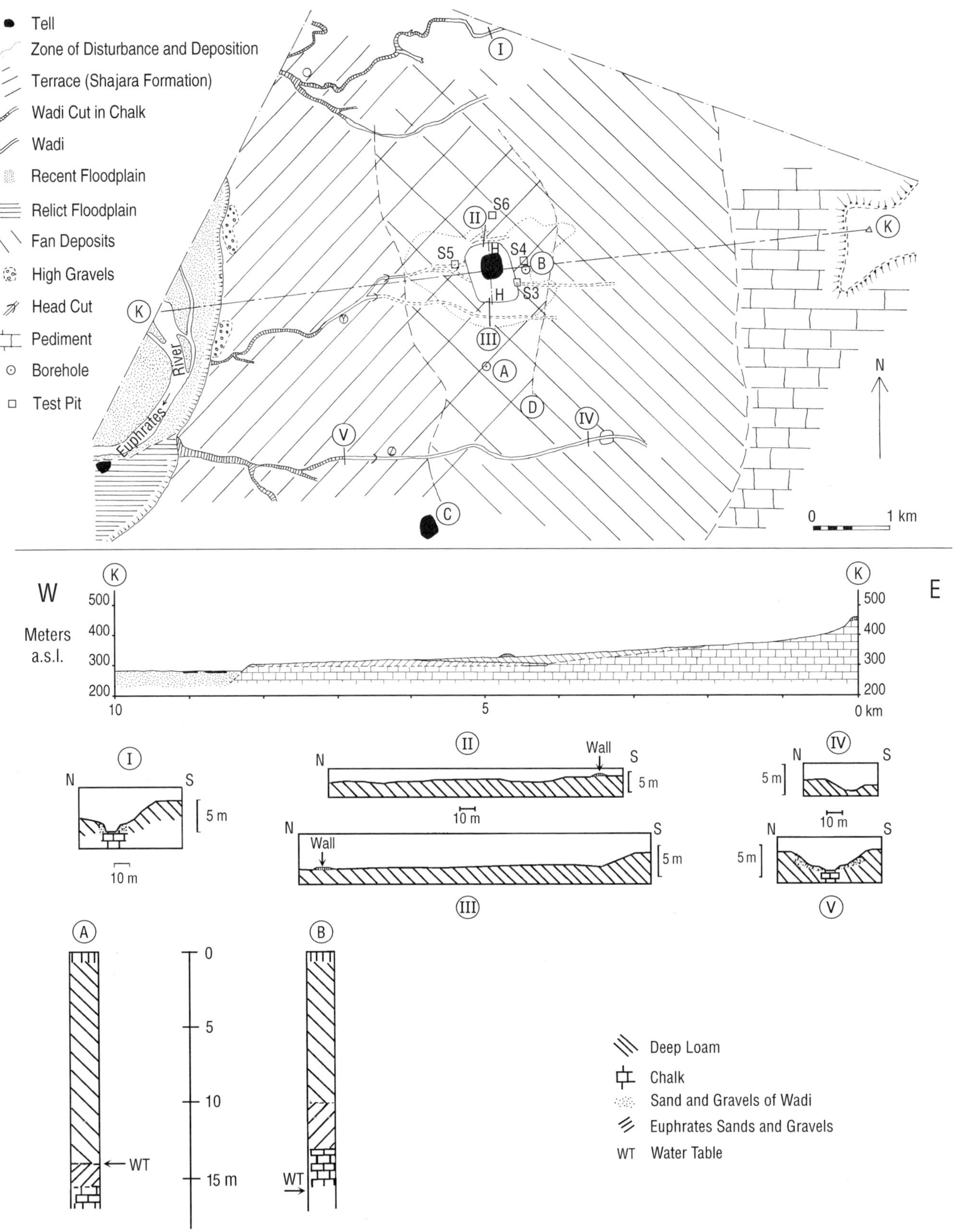

Figure 2.8. Top: Location of (*A–B*) Boreholes, (*I–V, K*) Sections, and (*S3–S6*) Trenches in the Area of Tell es-Sweyhat; (*C*) Represents the Western Limit of the Fan Deposits upon which Tell es-Sweyhat was Built; (*D*) Represents the Eastern Limit of the Buried Terrace Gravels Deposited by the Euphrates River (the Shajara Formation). Below: (*I–V, K*) Various Cross Sections and (*A–B*) Boreholes through the Plain. Vertical Scale Exaggerated in Sections I–V

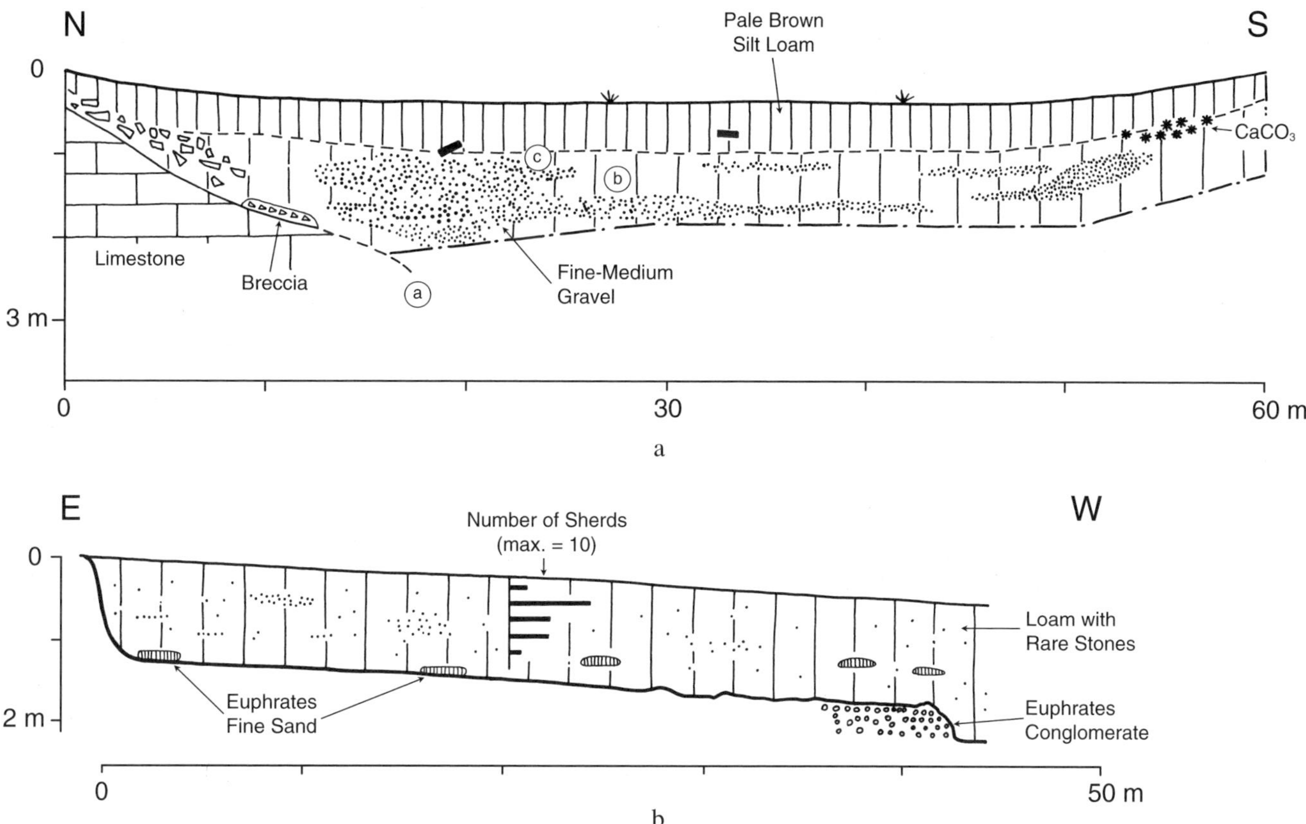

Figure 2.9. (*a*) Cross Section across Northern Wadi (*b*) Long Profile of Central Wadi Showing Valley Fills

The basal fine gravel was deposited by episodic low-moderate energy flow along the wadi's axis. Olive and red-dish yellow mottles between 160 and 200 cm suggest localized waterlogging (probably in the presence of organic mat-ter), which may have occurred even after the wadi ceased to flow. Thus the wadi may have been a conduit for subsur-face seepage. The abundant late Early Bronze Age occupation deposits between 100 and 210 cm demonstrate the pres-ence of occupation and/or associated dumping in the immediate vicinity. After occupation ceased, that is, at depths of less than 100 cm, the wadi bed gradually aggraded with loam fill interrupted by periodic occupation, probably of post-Bronze Age date. This upper fill indicates a final phase of sustained low energy sedimentation, which infilled the pre-vious wadi void with fine sediments.

Downstream, below the headcut position (indicated by arrow in fig. 2.7), the fill of the central wadi comprised a sandy loam and loam with occasional stones or gravel "strings" (fig. 2.9b). The stones and gravel were of Euphrates type and comprised igneous and metamorphic rocks of Anatolian provenance.

This deposit indicates occasional low to moderate energy flows along the wadi, with a significant proportion of fine sediment being washed from the adjacent terrain. Stones of local provenance were not transported along the chan-nel, which implies that the main source of bedload was from the vicinity of the headcut as a result of the progressive migration eastwards of the headcut (see below). Potsherds, moderately abraded but not water rolled were from wheel-thrown vessels of post-3000 B.C. date. They were distributed throughout the top 80 cm of alluvial fill with a peak at 20–40 cm depth (fig. 2.9b). The abundance of such sherds on the surrounding fields (see *Section 4.D: Off-site Sherd Distribution*) suggests that they could have been washed from the surrounding terrain rather than from Tell es-Sweyhat ca. 2 km to the east. The sherds, being of undiagnostic plain simple wares, only allow the fill to be described as post-Early Bronze Age in date.

Aerial photographs indicate spreads of pale sedimentation, apparently calcareous silts, to the east, north, and west of Tell es-Sweyhat. Where these spreads are found, field inspection indicated that the wadi channels are sufficiently unbounded to allow water to spread over the land surface, a significant factor in bringing moisture to the land. The soil mark to the east conforms to a broad area of silt aggradation that occurred upstream of Tell es-Sweyhat, as confirmed by soil pits and surface sherd sampling (*Section 4.C: Off-site Sampling Technique*). This accumulation to the east of the lower town enclosure wall appears to have partly obscured it so that now this is the least visible part of the Bronze Age fortification.

2.B.3.3. THE SOUTHERN WADI: WADI NAFILEH

This is probably the most active wadi on the Sweyhat terrace today. The fill, which includes a partly consolidated basal cobble horizon approximately 1 km downstream of Nafileh, suggests that in the past, as is the case today, this was an active wadi of moderately high energy flow. An overlying sandy loam horizon containing three potsherds, unlike those in the northern and central wadis, did not spread across the entire wadi as in the northern and central wadis. Thus, down valley flow was probably always greater than lateral wash from the adjacent land surface.

2.B.4. INTERACTION OF EUPHRATES FLOW AND WADI EROSION

The frequent lateral movements of the Euphrates River, which have kept most bluffs trimmed and vertical, have also eroded the wadi fans that debouch on the floodplain. As a result, when the river is at a distance from the wadi mouth, fans build up on the floodplain and aggradation can occur within the wadi bed. When the Euphrates River swings through and erodes the wadi fan, the wadi bed can be lowered by as much as 6 m so that wadi slope and power are increased, the wadi is rejuvenated, and an incision works its way rapidly away from the Euphrates River. Such rejuvenations, which expose the full geological sequence of the wadi deposits, can occur every few decades or centuries and account for the deeply eroded lower courses of some wadis. Where the floodplain is an ancient and stable feature, such as behind Tell Jouweif (SS 8), wadis attain a state of long-term stability and incision is less pronounced. Because of such local effects it is unwise to interpret wadi incisions simply in the light of climatic change; instead, the very dynamic local circumstances of wadi and main channel erosion may drive the process of incision. Such processes may also enhance certain human-induced features such as the hollow ways indicated in figure 5.1.

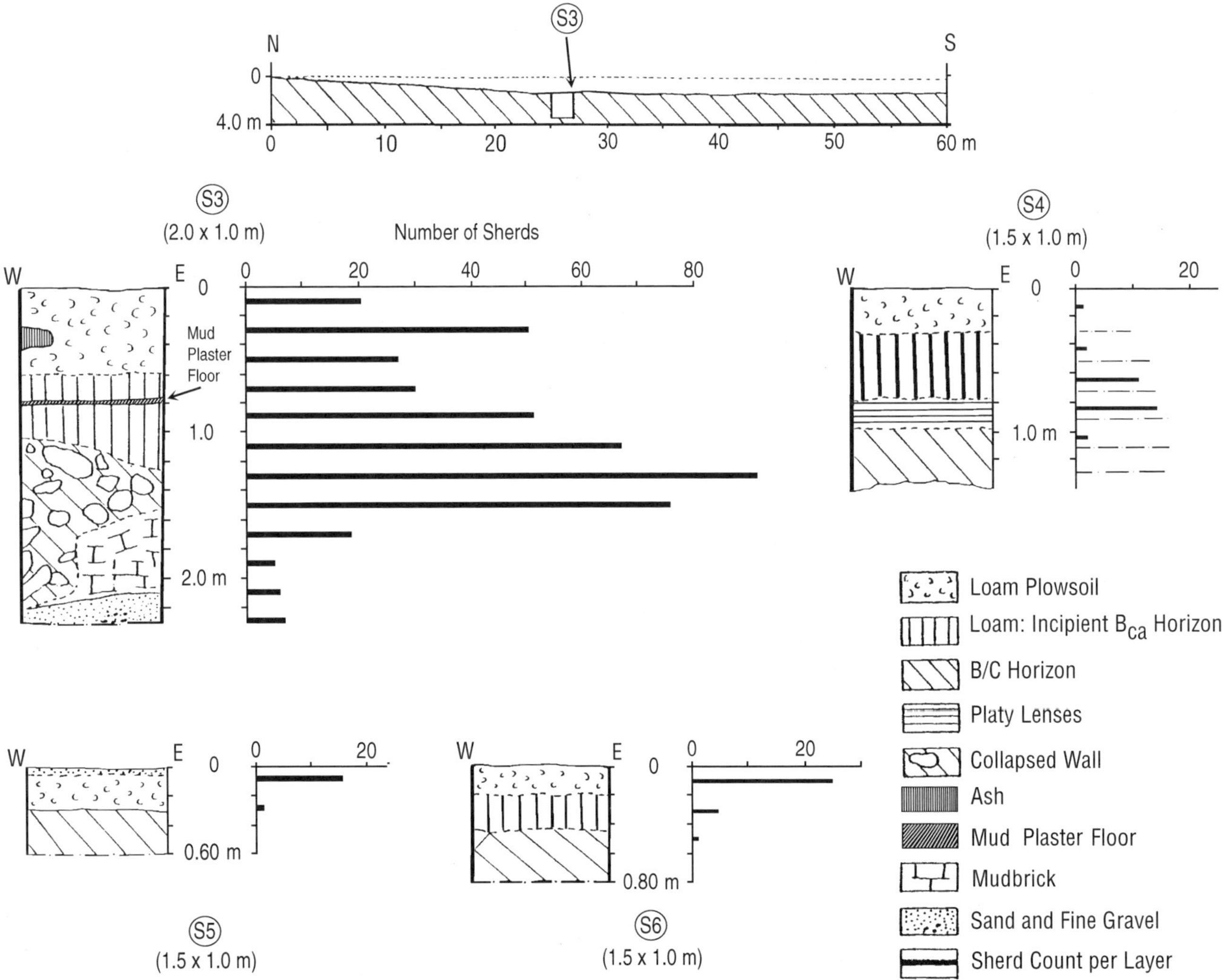

Figure 2.10. Sections Recorded in Trenches S3 to S6 in the Vicinity of Tell es-Sweyhat

2.C. THE SOILS

The soils over most of the Sweyhat Plain are developed on a deep sequence of reddish yellow loams primarily washed from the hills to the east. In the vicinity of Tell es-Sweyhat these local deposits attain a depth of some 10–13 m and overlie sands and gravels of the Euphrates terrace. These fluvial sands and gravels fade out rapidly to the east and south and do not extend beyond Nafileh (where they occur at ca. 20 m) or to the southeast of Tell Othman (SS 20A, fig. 2.7).

The upper part of this local sedimentary cover has developed a soil profile as a result of several thousands of years of weathering. This *calcic xerosol* [25] consists of a horizon enriched with soft white calcium carbonate concretions, which is weakly developed at depths below 20 cm, and in places, a second horizon of gypsum that occurs at depths below 40 cm. The presence of soft calcium carbonate concretions within post-Bronze Age sediments such as the second horizon of soil test Trench S4 (40–80 cm, figs. 2.8, 2.10) demonstrates that such horizons have been actively developing during the past 5,000 years. Within the time scale under consideration, landscape forming processes are therefore not static. A representative profile from Nafileh indicating salient features of the local soils is described in *Appendix C: Selected Soil and Sediment Descriptions: Section 3*; descriptions of profiles of Trenches S5 and S6 (fig. 2.10) are provided in *Appendix C: Selected Soil and Sediment Descriptions: Sections 5–6*.

The angular calcareous stones that litter the eastern part of the plain and form an impediment to plowing (*c* in fig. 2.7) may be part of a relict calcrete (calcareous crust). However, the only in situ calcrete horizon distinguished was a small exposure alongside the Wadi Nafileh that was visible in 1974.

Evidence for sedimentary and soil conditions that existed prior to the growth of the tell came from Trench IC excavated on the main tell in 1974 (fig. 2.11 and *Appendix C: Selected Soil and Sediment Descriptions: Section 2*). Below the lowest cultural deposits of the tell were 60 cm of loam and sand with occasional charcoal flecks and one ash layer, overlying a buried soil A (topsoil) horizon (14 in fig. 2.11). This horizon belonged to a buried soil profile, the subsoil of which included secondary gypsum. The sediments between the base of the tell and the buried soil (i.e., 2–13 in fig. 2.11) accumulated as a result of episodic low energy fluvial flow alternating with the accumulation of loams, the latter being deposited in the vicinity of some human activity. Sand layers 4, 7, and 8 may have been deposited by a combination of low energy wadi flow and wind action. The elevation of the base of Trench IC suggests that such flow deposits accumulated within a gentle depression, the surface of which was 1 to 2 m below the general level of the plain. The presence of a subsoil horizon enriched in gypsum crystals (*Appendix C: Selected Soil and Sediment Descriptions: Section 2*, layer 15) suggests that the soil environment prior to occupation (i.e., fourth millennium B.C. and earlier) was semi-arid like that of the present day. The localized low energy wadi flow and perhaps aeolian activity would also suggest that the environment was similar to that of today. Unlike semi-arid areas of southern Arabia where a pre-third millennium moist interval is well attested by a dark gray humic palaeosol, the soil below Tell es-Sweyhat lacks such evidence (contrast with the Thayyilah soils of Yemen [Fedele 1990]). For a similar soil profile exposed beneath the eastern lower town, see *Appendix C: Selected Soil and Sediment Descriptions: Section 4*.

In contrast to the stone-littered slopes of the eastern plain, the area surrounding Tell es-Sweyhat has deep soils of high potential fertility. These soils are equivalent to the medium to deep phases of the reddish brown soils of the upper Jazirah in Iraq (Buringh 1960), which have limiting factors for agricultural production as follows.

Factor *1*   Low, unreliable rainfall.

Factor *2*   Undulating land sheds water more rapidly, therefore producing lower yields than more gently sloping terrain. This gently-sloping land is therefore characterized by higher moisture infiltration, which results in higher yields.

Factor *3*   The shallow depth of many soils.

Factor *4*   The presence of soil crusts.

Factor *1* is uniform over the plain. East and southeast of a line linking sites Khirbet Aboud al-Hazu (SS 6), SS 4, Khirbet al-Hamrah (SS 7), Nafileh Village (SS 5), Tell Othman (SS 20A), and SS 20B, the undulating terrain has

---

25. According to the FAO soil classification (FAO 1977, 1974). These soils are the calciorthids of Boerma 2001, which are named according to the United States scheme of soil classification.

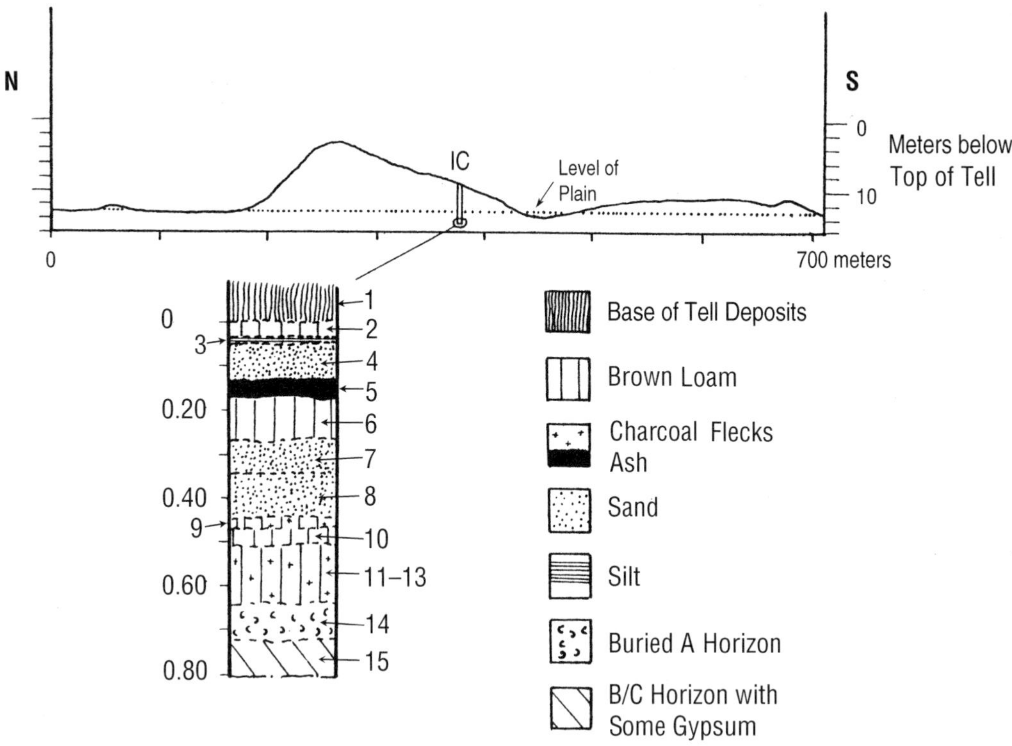

Figure 2.11. Section in Trench IC through Base of Tell

thinner soils with a relict and broken crust (*c* in fig. 2.7). Here soils have a lower moisture-holding capacity and in general are more susceptible to drought.

On the alluvial fans and outwash deposits that form along the boundary between the steppe and the Euphrates floodplain soils are rich in gypsum ($CaSO_4$), which can comprise 38–78% of the subsoil gypsic horizon (Florea and al-Joumaa 1998). Although such soils are usually under pasture today, in the past they may have been irrigated, but this would have been most effective if local groundwater was applied. On the other hand, if non-local waters (such as Euphrates river water) had been used, this would have resulted in excessive loss of gypsum, with possibly harmful effects (ibid., p. 82).

On the floodplain itself soil horizon development is often limited as a result of the relatively recent age of the soils. However, in lower parts of the plain, as well as those areas with poor drainage, soils can be moderately saline.

2.C.1. TOPOGRAPHY, MOISTURE SHEDDING, AND MOISTURE CONSERVATION

The above assessment of soil limitations by Buringh can however operate to the advantage of local farmers by enhancing soil moisture in those areas that receive runoff from nearby slopes. Soil texture and infiltration capacity being equal, on undulating land where heavy rainfall can runoff and be lost to the soil, soil moisture and crop yields are lower. On flatter terrain where less rainfall is lost to runoff (and indeed some may be gained from upslope) soil moisture is higher and crop yields commensurably greater. For example, studies in northern Iraq show that undulating land can have significantly lower crop yields than flatter terrain (Ali 1955: 147). Applying these results to the Sweyhat area it is possible to posit a three-tiered system of land productivity (fig. 2.7).

Type *a* Lowest lands in the vicinity of Tell es-Sweyhat would probably gain moisture as a result of overbank flow from wadis. As a result, such areas of enhanced moisture concentration may have produced higher crop yields and would be less likely to suffer crop failure.

Type *b* Flatter areas around Tell es-Sweyhat but more than 2 m above adjacent wadi bottoms would lose less water to runoff than Type *a* terrain, and yields could be expected to be higher. On the other hand, some runoff might be lost to the lowest Type *a* land.

Type *c* Undulating land around the fringes of the plain would have higher loss from runoff and crops would receive less moisture with the result that yields would be lower.

From the above summary of what is undoubtedly a very complex situation, it can be seen that rainfall fluctuations, land use practice, and topography can have a considerable influence on soil moisture and crop yields. As a result, the actual production of crops in this marginal zone varies. Some fields are truly marginal and only yield worthwhile crops in good years, whereas others are much more productive. During periods of maximum production, however, when cereal cultivation might spread to the most marginal soils and when there would be a temptation to dispense with the fallow year, there would be more likelihood of crop failure than when the most reliable soils were cropped under a resilient fallowing regime (see *Section 3.E: Land Use and Risk Management*). In reality one might expect that any one Bronze Age household would have had land holdings in a range of different terrain types in order to spread the risk of crop failure.

2.D. WATER RESOURCES

Five main types of water resources are available to be tapped within 5 km of Tell es-Sweyhat: direct rainfall, flood runoff, the Euphrates River, natural seepages, and wells. In earlier times the relative importance of these sources may have been different from today owing to environmental change, the overutilization of water using modern technology, and different factors of social organization. Of the above, direct rainfall cannot be effectively used for domestic purposes unless concentrated by runoff.

2.D.1. FLOOD RUNOFF

Apart from the presence, in 1974, of one or two small vegetable plots in wadi floors, there is little evidence today for the use of wadi runoff. However, low ground fringing the main wadi systems probably received occasional inundations of floodwater and the presence of a possible water-collection basin at Early Islamic Khirbet al-Hamrah (SS 7) suggests that episodic wadi flow may have been collected in the past. The 25 m diameter basin-like feature, although probably designed to collect flow from the adjacent wadi, was ambiguous in its form and may have simply been the hollow remaining from an infilled well.[26] A more elongated feature along the northern wadi through the same site had adjacent upcast mounds that included limestone fragments. This feature may have been either a cistern or a well dug down to the underlying limestone. Although the large Early Islamic site of Khirbet Dhiman[27] (SS 11) lacked basins, the location of this site on a shallow wadi suggests that runoff either could have supplied some domestic water or could have been used for limited runoff agriculture adjacent to the wadi. The resemblance between these wadi basins and so-called *muhāfirs* of the north Arabian desert may be significant (Vidal 1978) and suggests that these sites may have developed alongside artificially constructed water holes. *Muhāfirs*, which are constructed along wadis often in locations where wadi flow is slowed by a widening of the bed or the junction of a secondary wadi, consist of shallow depressions surrounded by a low crescentic or circular mound of upcast. By acting as water holes for flocks, camels, and humans they provide logical foci for habitation, so the growth of Khirbet al-Hamrah adjacent to such a feature seems reasonable. Furthermore, the presence of potential watering areas for flocks hints that a significant pastoral component may have existed at such sites. Although earlier sites may also have developed alongside similar features, it is likely that older basins would have become infilled by flood sediments deposited from the wadi. On the other hand, given the ease of well construction in the area, it is unlikely that either Khirbet al-Hamrah or Khirbet Dhiman would have drawn all of their domestic water from runoff, and it is probable that both runoff and wells contributed to their sustenance.

The evidence for Bronze Age floodwater utilization is even more problematic. The potential area for floodwater runoff farming around Tell es-Sweyhat is indicated in figure 2.7 (category *a* land). To the northeast, near SS 9 Mound A, a 10 m long wall of limestone boulders located adjacent to the wadi floor may have been used to channel wadi runoff. Although this wall of boulders was evidently ancient, it was undated, therefore it can only be used to demonstrate that runoff agriculture probably existed, but at an unknown date. Consequently neither the potential area of soil moisture enhancement nor the wall at SS 9 Mound A can be used as evidence for runoff agriculture during the Bronze Age. Nevertheless, allowances should be made for such practices in the ancient economy.

---

26. Alternatively, such hollows may have been originally dug to supply mudbrick for house construction at the site (Wilkinson and Tucker 1995: 27–35).

27. Khirbet Dhiman (SS 11) for consistency is spelled here as it was originally published. Later information suggests that some local people refer to the site as Khirbet Dhima, which can therefore be regarded as an alternative spelling.

None of the above systems can have extended over a very large area and they can best be viewed as localized techniques employed to supplement the major cultivation activity of dry farming.

2.D.2. THE EUPHRATES RIVER

At Birecik, some 85 km upstream within Turkey, the flow of the Euphrates River varies from a minimum in August or September of around 150–300 cubic meters per second and high flows in March or April of up to 3,400–4,400 cubic meters per second. This results in mean annual flows of between 484 and 1,356 cubic meters per second, with a longer term mean flow of about 856 cubic meters per second (Kolars and Mitchell 1991, tables 5.2 and 6.5, based on Clawson, Landberg, and Alexander 1971).

Being located more than 3 km from the site, it is unlikely that the Euphrates River would have been used for supplying domestic water to the inhabitants of Tell es-Sweyhat. Although the floodplain could have been irrigated, the vertical rise through which it was necessary to raise irrigation water was such that canals would have been required to be sufficiently long to allow the canal to "rise" relative to the river up to the higher floodplain levels. Calculations made for such an Islamic canal at Dibsi Faraj (T 541) near Meskene suggest that in order to rise the 3–5 m vertical distance that was necessary, a canal would have been required to be 8.5 to 20.0 km in length. The irrigation of lower floodplain levels by shorter canals would have resulted in considerable crop losses due to annual flooding that would have inundated the lower levels of the floodplain where the crops were growing. Although not excluding opportunistic or short canal irrigation, this factor would have confined its application either to restricted areas of winter/spring crops or for a limited range of summer crops. Such land could have been farmed by the inhabitants of Tell es-Sweyhat, but their exploitation would have been much more efficient from sites like Tell Jouweif (SS 8) or SS 27 on or adjacent to the floodplain. Further information on irrigation potential within the upper Lake Assad area is supplied in *Section 3.C: Irrigation Agriculture*.

2.D.3. SEEPAGES

Within a zone immediately adjacent to the Euphrates bluffs and extending up to 2 km to the east, seepages of water were evident along the lower wadi courses where incision had exposed the underlying limestone. The seepage water is today too brackish for domestic use and is now restricted to the watering of flocks of sheep and goats.

2.D.4. WELLS

Boreholes and modern wells indicate that the water table falls steadily relative to ground level away from the Euphrates bluffs, reaching some 48 m 7 km to the east (fig. 2.12). Qualitative tests as well as conversations with the local inhabitants in 1974 indicate that water quality improves inland. The water was slightly brackish, but drinkable, within the Euphrates gravel at Tell Othman (SS 20A) and in boreholes near Tell es-Sweyhat, but farther to the east, where the water table was partly in limestone, it was more drinkable.[28] In the vicinity of the modern village of Nafileh where the depth to water table was 20–25 m, the work entailed to lift the water would have made it feasible to irrigate only small areas of land.

According to conversations with the borehole engineers and judging by the limited catchment area of the plain, water table recharge was probably quite low. Nevertheless, it would have been sufficient for traditional techniques of agriculture, and it is only today, with the use of diesel pumps, that water tables as well as water quality are declining.

The only evidence for wells from the Tell es-Sweyhat excavations came from Operation 9 within the lower town. There a stone-lined water conduit and a plastered basin may have been part of a water distribution system. These were in the vicinity of a patch of cobbles of Euphrates provenance (Zettler 1997: 45). Normally present in the Sweyhat area at depths of 10–12 m below ground level, such gravels are likely to be upcast from the excavation of wells down to the water-bearing gravel layers. To judge by the presence of wells at comparable sites within the Jazirah, at Kurban Höyük (Algaze 1990: 48, fig. 43), and Tell al-Hawa (Wilkinson and Tucker 1995, chapter 4), the prime source of domestic water at Tell es-Sweyhat would also have been wells or water holes. Although pebbles from the underlying Euphrates gravel were occasionally scattered over the surface away from the site, no mounds of sediment upcast by well con-

---

28. Since 1974, however, there has been a marked decline in water
    quality as a result of overpumping. This has caused the water
    table to fall and water to become more saline.

struction were evident, and if they ever did exist they must have subsequently been plowed into oblivion. Analogy with the hinterland of Early Islamic Sohar in Oman suggests that wells for irrigation can reach depths of at least 14 m, and that such wells could sustain gardens of 1–2 ha (Costa and Wilkinson 1987: 45). Because Tell es-Sweyhat falls within the range of depth where well irrigation is feasible, this technique remains a possibility. However, in view of the lack of evidence for well upcast, the use of this technique cannot be confirmed.

2.E. CONCLUSION

Evidence for Holocene environmental change in the upper Lake Assad area is equivocal, but this may partly be a result of either the lack of suitable sections, or that diagnostic deposits were not visible within the available sections. The wadi bed breccia (indicated at *a* in figure 2.9a) suggests that conditions may have been moister in the Late Pleistocene or Early Holocene, but the lack of datable evidence for this horizon weakens its value. Gypsic horizons, within both the buried soil at the site (i.e., Area IC, 15 in fig. 2.11; see above and *Appendix C: Selected Soil and Sediment Descriptions: Section 2*) and in modern soils, suggest that in the fourth millennium B.C., the area had a marginal semi-arid climate little different from today. Although there is evidence for waterlogging in Trench S3 (fig. 2.10), this does not necessarily relate to higher water tables and instead may simply result from ponding of floodwater behind the outer enclosure wall. This does not mean that there has been no environmental change, just that the fairly insensitive indicators employed do not indicate it.

On the other hand, the northern and central wadis show good evidence of a post-Bronze Age phase of valley aggradation in their middle and upper reaches. This may be ascribed to plowing in antiquity, which encouraged the accumulation of copious plow wash in valley floors. For such accumulations to take place down valley, sediment delivery from the fields and surrounding slopes must have exceeded the capacity of fluvial flow to transport it, with the result that aggradation occurred and no significant channel was eroded. In contrast, the southern (Nafileh) wadi lacks evidence for a change of regime except for a colluvial fill that has developed across part of the valley.

The location of Tell es-Sweyhat on the central wadi system appears to be significant because that wadi, although the least powerful of the three throughout the Holocene, was the most likely to overflow and flood the surrounding terrain. Such floods from the least powerful wadi would have been controllable and would have enhanced soil moisture over a fairly broad area. Therefore although there is no evidence that irrigation ever took place, crop yields could have

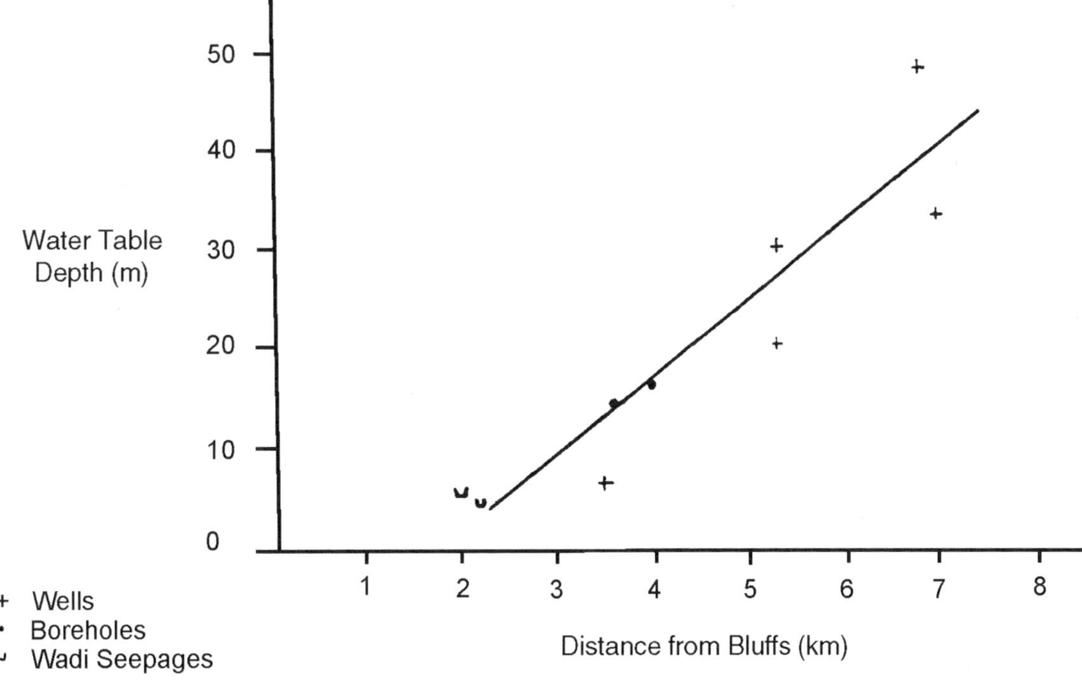

Figure 2.12. Groundwater and Ground Level along an East–West Transect through the Plain. Distance Measured in Kilometers Eastward from the Euphrates Bluffs

been significantly improved and crop failures minimized along a restricted zone of the central wadi (fig. 2.7). Further-more, such occasionally flooded terrain would have been ideal for the grazing of flocks of sheep and goats. As is evident from soil profiles, the more elevated areas away from wadis would be above the level of flooding and would represent agriculturally marginal areas of greater risk for cultivation.

The above sketch suggests that a zone along the central wadi would have provided a logical focus for grazing, crop production, and settlement during the earlier (and perhaps final) phase of settlement but would have been insufficient to provision a town like Tell es-Sweyhat during its maximum size. This point is elaborated below in *Sections 3 and 4*.

Although opportunities for irrigation along the Euphrates River would have been limited, canal irrigation may well have taken place in suitable areas during various periods (see *Section 3.C: Irrigation Agriculture*). On the terrace, dry farming must have formed the mainstay of the local farming economy, but soil moisture enhancement by means of runoff could have taken place along the main wadis. Well irrigation, if employed, would only have been capable of irrigating limited areas.

Finally, and crucial to an understanding of the settlement of the region, is the question of the completeness of the settlement record on the floodplain, and when was it first occupied by sedentary settlement. In his publication on the environmental conditions of the Selenkahiye (T 507) area, J. A. K. Boerma (2001: 2.19), asserts that because no pre-Roman settlement occurred on the floodplain, we can assume that valley floor occupation was not possible before Roman times because the valley floor was too wet. He continues by suggesting that the supposition that older occupation may have been present, but that the remains have been eroded away is mere speculation. Consequently, he continues, "we may safely assume that the valley floor had the character of a floodplain at the time Selenkahiye came into existence, and that it was not permanently inhabitable." This argument for non-settlement before the Roman period can be countered by the following lines of evidence.

- Pre-Roman settlement does, in fact, occur on the earlier levels of the floodplain as at Tell Jouweif (SS 8: *Sections 6.A: Pottery of the Chalcolithic to Late Roman Periods* and *8: The Ancient Agricultural Economy: Biological Remains*), as well as upstream within the Tishrin Dam area at the sites of Tell Kabir (Porter 1999) and Jerablus Tahtani (Peltenburg et al. 1997; Peltenburg et al. 1996). Moreover, although Geyer and Besançon (1996) suggest that the actual floodplain of the Euphrates River downstream of its junction with the Khabur River may have been somewhat hostile for settlement, they demonstrate that sites of PPNB, Halaf, Ubaid, and Uruk date do occur on the remains of the ancient Holocene terrace (Qoa). Overall, pre-Roman settlements can be found along the Syrian Euphrates River but only on low residuals of the Early to Middle Holocene (i.e., 11000–2000 B.C.) floodplain that have survived erosion by this very mobile river.

- Geoarchaeological surveys by the author during the early 1970s in the area of Dibsi Faraj (T 541) demonstrated that the Euphrates River had been actively eroding laterally, especially to the south, and had sliced through a number of archaeological sites leaving upstanding sections or exposing cultural debris below fan gravels issuing from side wadis. Moreover, Akkermans (1999) observes that a number of prehistoric sites do lie buried beneath alluvium or colluvial material washed from slopes and side wadis at various points along the Syrian Euphrates River,[29] thereby again indicating that settlement did in fact occur at the level of the floodplain.

- Finally, lengths of Islamic and Roman period canals around and upstream of Dibsi Faraj (T 541) have been removed by fluvial erosion, along with their associated floodplain. This again suggests that there has been considerable re-working of the floodplain. In the lower Lake Assad area lateral erosion by the Euphrates River appears to have been mainly toward the southern edge of the valley leaving the northern edges more liable to slow but steady aggradation (Wilkinson 1978).

To conclude, it seems evident that there are far fewer prehistoric settlements along the Euphrates Valley in the upper Lake Assad area than within the less geomorphologically dynamic tributary of the Balikh Valley (Akkermans 1999). This point and the evidence summarized above indicate that at least the slightly higher and older parts of the floodplain were occupied to some degree from the prehistoric period onwards, and that the absence of settlement is not because conditions made it impossible for people to live in these locations, but simply because erosion has erased many sites and sedimentation has obscured others. Of course, it is impossible to estimate how many sites may have been present, either on the floodplain or along its fringes, but this potential loss is crucial for an understanding of the overall demographic trends discussed in *Section 9: Tell es-Sweyhat in Its Regional Context*.

---

29.   For example, Halaf levels near Tell Amarna (Tishrin Dam area) are close to the level of the floodplain and appear to have been buried by sediments brought in from side wadis. This burying has resulted in the pre-Halaf virgin soil being some 3.30 m below modern field level (Cruells 1998).

Table 2.1 Valley Fill Sequences for Part of Northwest Syria and South Turkey Showing a Possible Middle Holocene Phase of Moister Valley Environments and Later Holocene Drying or Increased Human Impacts (from Wilkinson 1999)

B.C.	6000	5000	4000	3000	2000	1000	0 A.D.	1000	2000
	I	I	I	I	I	I	I	I	I
Amuq (Turkey)	Instability		????	I‹Dry lake ›I		???	I‹ Amuq Lake		
Orontes (Atchana)		I‹ Stable aggrading———— ›I clay floodplain			? ?		Moderate-energy floodplain		
Euphrates and Khabur (Syria)	Braided channel				Meandering channel			Braided and meandering	
Tell es-Sweyhat (Syria)				I‹—Plow wash————————					
Lower Balikh (Syria)		Moderate perennial flow		I‹—Local canals water conflict	I‹—Regional canals				
Kazane Höyük (Turkey)		Moderate, stable perennial flow		Declining, more erratic flow					
Titriş Höyük (Turkey)				Stable flow	Declining, more erratic flow	Plow wash			
Kurban Höyük (Turkey)				Higher water table	Wells I‹Accelerated aggradation				
	I	I	I	I	I	I	I	I	I
	8,000	7,000	6,000	5,000	4,000	3,000	2,000	1,000	0 B.P.

3. LAND USE AND THE AGRICULTURAL ECONOMY

3.A. INTRODUCTION

This section places traditional agricultural practice within an environmental framework for the area of Lake Assad. From its location some 3 km away from the Euphrates floodplain, Tell es-Sweyhat appears to have relied primarily upon rain-fed cultivation, but the irrigable Euphrates alluvial plain as well as zones of soil moisture enhancement along wadi floors, as described in *Section 2.B: The Euphrates Terraces,* would have provided additional areas of potential agricultural production. Here, following a brief description of the regional environment, some aspects of irrigation practice along the Euphrates River are considered. A more detailed treatment of rain-fed agriculture is provided by reference to relationships between crop yield, strategies of crop management, and climatic fluctuations. A key factor to be examined is the tendency for societies in this agriculturally marginal environment to fluctuate between a fairly resilient[30] state when population is low and a highly productive state but with unstable economies that exhibit a greater propensity to suffer crop failure– when population densities increase.

3.B. THE TRADITIONAL ECONOMY

Villages in the area of Tell es-Sweyhat gain their support from a combination of rain-fed cultivation of cereals, pasturing of flocks of sheep and goats, and cash income earned from migrant labor. More details on the cultivation economy are provided below (see climate and rain-fed agriculture), but in terms of pastoral economy, at both Nafileh (the village near Tell es-Sweyhat) and Tell Hadidi (T 548) on the west bank of the Euphrates River, the domestic fauna was dominated by sheep and goats, with the inevitable sprinkling of dogs nominally acting as guardians to the household flocks. Van der Kooij notes for the village of Hadidi that fat-tailed sheep were herded near the village in wintertime, but during summer were taken several kilometers away from the village. While in the village milking took place twice a day near the home, in the summer it was once a day in the fields (van der Kooij 1982: 83). In April the flocks were sometimes allowed to graze the half-grown grain (presumably to thin out the grains), and following the harvest they were allowed to graze the stubble. The limit of the present-day exploitation territory at Hadidi was estimated to be approximately 1.5 km from the village. Within this area were situated all basic resources, namely drinking water, irrigation canals, dry-farming fields, main grazing areas, and the graveyard. In addition to most of the villagers who lived within the village from May onwards a few families lived outside the village within black bedouin tents. The reasons given for this shift of residence were that living in tents away from the village made one closer to the rain-fed cereal fields for harvesting, as well as to the summer grazing on fields, the latter making milking as well as the processing of milk products that much easier (ibid., p. 84).

Further insights into the traditional economy can be gleaned from Sweet's (1974) study of Tell Toqaan near Aleppo where two different animal groups were observed. First was a "peasant group" which comprised working animals used for power, that is for plowing, operating irrigation wheels, threshing, and carrying grain to market. Such animals were cattle and oxen, the non-descript village horse, donkeys, mules, horses, and occasionally camels. In addition, village animals included dogs and cats, small household flocks of sheep/goats (ibid., pp. 89–90), together with, in pre-Islamic times, presumably pigs. Second, visiting pastoral nomads would appear in the village after the harvest with their larger flocks, consisting primarily of sheep, with a few goats and occasional camels for transport. It might therefore be expected that in areas such as Lake Assad with a long-term dimorphic economy, settlement faunal collections might also break down into similar assemblages. However, preliminary analysis suggests that instead the breakdown is according to environment, with the more mixed economies occurring farther to the north along the Euphrates River in

---

30. Resilience, being the ability of a biological system to maintain its structure and pattern of behavior in the face of disturbance, contrasts with stability, being a state of equilibrium towards which a system constantly returns. Thus resilience emphasizes a concern for long-term survival even at the expense of numerical strength (for discussion, see Holling 1986: 296–97; Adams 1978).

Turkey, and a sheep/goat dominated economy (with some wild species) occurring in drier areas farther to the south (Weber 1997, appendix 8.7). This appearance of a strong component of sheep/goat husbandry in the upper Lake Assad area occurs in parallel with the emergence of a more specialized pastoral economy in the third millennium B.C. farther to the east in the Khabur Valley (Zeder 1998).

With the completion of the Tabqa Dam in 1974, the valley floor immediately to the west of Tell es-Sweyhat was flooded by the rising waters of Lake Assad. The flooding resulted in the displacement of the inhabitants of floodplain villages as well as the loss of a large area of fertile, cultivable fields, which had been mainly devoted to cash cropping of cotton. Interestingly, in 1992, following the decline of the Euphrates flow from Turkey, the lake level dropped and the former floodplain (the *zor*) was exposed, revealing new deposits of silt and clay and some riparian vegetation that developed during other brief low water phases. This area, specifically known to the inhabitants of Nafileh as Hawijah, was then devoted to the cultivation of a summer/autumn crop of beans (*lubija*). No irrigation was practiced because the former lake shore or lake bed deposits were sufficiently moist to sustain a single crop. The process of planting appears to have been identical to that noted by van der Kooij at Hadidi in 1974, where a woman and her daughter made random holes into the un-tilled alluvial soil, dropped a bean seed into each, and scraped the earth back over to cover the hole (van der Kooij 1982: 82). Cropping in the Sweyhat *zor* was quite labor-intensive with the result that the inhabitants of Nafileh and other villages (particularly women and children) moved temporarily to the *zor* to tend the fields and pick the crop. Most lived in small, temporary structures of branches and reeds, returning only to the village on occasional days off.

The now diminished lake, which formed little more than a slightly extended Euphrates channel, continued to furnish the new growth industry of the lake, namely, net fishing for the apparently significantly enlarged fish population. This rapid adjustment to valley floor bean cultivation, as well as the acquisition of the otherwise novel craft of net fishing from boats, underscores the ability of these traditional and supposedly conservative communities to adapt to changing circumstances. Therefore, when assessing the archaeological record for past societies in the area, one should adopt a flexible perspective and be prepared to see considerable changes in the land use record. No single settlement-land use model should be expected to operate through the extended time periods under consideration.

3.C. IRRIGATION AGRICULTURE

Because Tell es-Sweyhat is situated close to the limit of rain-fed cultivation one might assume that the Euphrates River would have been harnessed as a key source of irrigation water. However, van Liere (1963: 115) disputes this point of view by noting that many major tells were preferentially located near the junction of tributary valleys (e.g., the Balikh and Khabur) with the main Euphrates Valley. Such a situation, van Liere suggests, was able to benefit from the potential supply of more manageable irrigation waters from the tributary valley, rather than the Euphrates River which exhibits high, poorly timed floods and was difficult to control. Evidence from cuneiform texts supports this argument to some extent, at least for ancient Tutul (Tell Bi'a) which clearly did receive its waters from the Balikh River (Dossin 1974; Villard 1987). It does not necessarily follow, however, that all Euphrates Valley tells beyond the limit of rain-fed cultivation received irrigation water in that manner.

Within the rescue area of Lake Assad there are remains of large Early Islamic irrigation canals between Abu Hureyra (T 545) and Dibsi Faraj (T 541; Wilkinson 1975). Others near Habuba Kabira (T 509/513) and at Tell Fray (T 532) (figs. 1.2, 3.1; Bounni 1979a) may be earlier, with the latter being perhaps as early as Late Bronze Age. In addition, the presence of wine presses (see *Section 5.A: Wine Presses*) on the floodplain near Tell es-Sweyhat, as well as the mention of vineyards at Late Bronze Age Emar (Fleming 1993: 64, 66) in an area that cannot support vineyards using rainfall alone, suggests that there was some reliance on irrigation on the valley floor. Most convincing, however, are textual records of fields by the river as well as of irrigated land. Thus the Emar texts occasionally refer to fields with their edge against the Euphrates River (Arnaud 1986, text no. 3), or even in the course of the river, presumably on land on the lower parts of the floodplain that was liable to annual flooding (Arnaud 1991: 99, text no. 55). Moreover, Liverani (1996: 32) infers that the elongate fields at Emar were oriented with their long axes at right angles to the river, and also that they were not irrigated directly from it. This orientation implies that canals were probably employed to direct water to such fields on the floodplain in the vicinity of Emar, and the absence of the remains of relict canals today implies that riverine sedimentation or erosion has either obscured or erased them. Overall, a compelling case can be made that the floodplain back to at least the Late Bronze Age was a center of agricultural activity with long

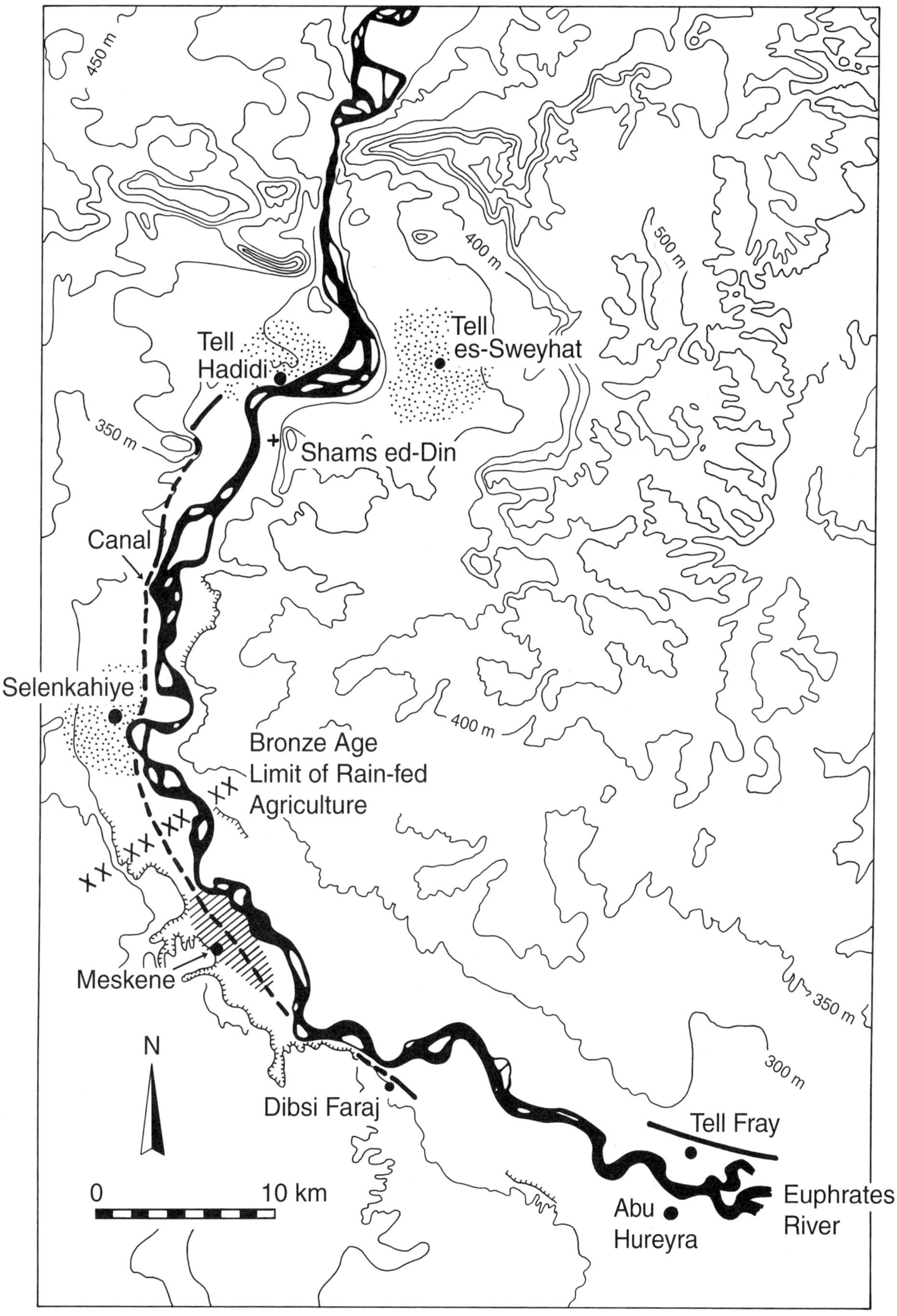

Figure 3.1. Bronze Age Tells Associated with Areas of Rain-fed Cultivation (Stipple) in the Upper Lake Assad Area in Relation to Probable Irrigated Land on the Euphrates Floodplain around Emar (Hatched). The Approximate Limit of Rain-fed Agriculture Is Inferred to Lie between these Two Land Use Types. Solid and Broken Lines Indicate Ancient Canals Dated to the Late Bronze Age (to the North of the Euphrates River) and Roman/Islamic Periods (to the South of the River)

strip fields, at least some irrigated lands, as well as perhaps vineyards and canals. Nevertheless, it is also apparent that the agricultural system was vulnerable to lack of water (either from drought, conflict, or because the irrigation systems failed) because there are ample references to "years of distress" (Adamthwaite 2002: 133–75).

For Emar, the presence of irrigated agriculture on the floodplain is supported by the catchment of the ancient site itself, which falls mainly within the floodplain (hatched area in fig. 3.1), the only nearby dry-farming land being thin and poor soils on the high rolling steppe to the south. Emar's location is in marked contrast to most Bronze Age settlements farther to the north that are located amid cultivable rain-fed lands of the main Euphrates terrace. Certainly van Liere's (1963) doubts regarding the ancient irrigation economy have some justification, namely that the river was too big to be controlled by Bronze Age techniques, the groundwater was too saline, and the spring floods came too late for winter crops and too early for summer crops. Nevertheless, texts from Tell Fray (T 532) suggest that its canal (which was visible in the floodplain until inundated by the rising lake) was in use during the later second millennium B.C. (Bounni 1979a: 7). Canal irrigation systems therefore appear to have been in use from the Bronze Age to the period of use of the Dibsi canal in the Early Islamic period (see *Section 2.D.2: The Euphrates River*), and that canals were sufficiently long to "raise" the water to a sufficient elevation above the river for long-term irrigation, but without excess damage being incurred. It can therefore be argued that irrigated cultivation must at least be allowed for in the floodplain zone, and that it might have proved crucial to many local economies, especially during the Late Bronze Age, Roman, and Islamic periods. In *Section 2.B.2: The Alluvial Plain* it is suggested that the mobile erosive Euphrates River has probably removed much of the floodplain, so the absence of settlement sites, agricultural lands, and canals in this zone is hardly surprising.

If irrigation did occur on the floodplain, the obvious point of reference is the lower Euphrates Valley at Terqa and Mari where a floodplain irrigation economy must have existed during the third and second millennia B.C., if not earlier (Margueron 1988; Geyer and Monchambert 1987). In his analysis of the Terqa landscape, Buccellati (1990a) defines three zones of water access in the valley floor (the *zor* in local Arabic usage).

- The zone with greatest access to river water is a zone (Akkadian *ušallum*) that is also subject to flooding.

- Beyond a bounding levee and parallel to the river was a generally flat area that could receive irrigation water via canals that took their water from the river upstream (*ugārum*).

- Finally, at still higher levels would be an area too high for riverine irrigation (*nābalum*), but which would receive water by other means, perhaps wells or runoff from the local wadi flow.

Such a system could have equally applied to the upper Lake Assad area because each zone corresponds to a particular geomorphological sub-unit recognizable within the suite of floodplain sediments.

- The first zone would form what I have termed the near channel level (Zone *a*, *Section 2.B.2: The Alluvial Plain*) which comprises sandy riverine deposits and is flooded in most years.

- The second zone (*ugārum*) would form Zones *b* and *c*, namely the undifferentiated floodplain with modern fields, and the higher floodplain with fields and villages, which only receive Euphrates floodwater in occasional or exceptional years.

- Finally the third zone would be the higher older floodplain terraces with aggrading alluvial fans (Zone *d*, *Section 2.B.2: The Alluvial Plain*).

The foregoing suggests that irrigation could have occurred within the floodplain but the evidence for it would have been removed by erosion, along with many archaeological sites that were dependent upon it. Such an economy would, however, only directly benefit sites on or alongside the floodplain, and sites like Tell es-Sweyhat, being situated away from the floodplain zone, would have had to derive the bulk of their sustenance from a combination of rain-fed cultivation and pasture. The remainder of this section examines the practices and problems of rain-fed cultivation and pasture use in this marginal environment.

3.D. CLIMATE AND RAIN-FED AGRICULTURE

When examining the agricultural regime of a marginal region such as that prevailing around Tell es-Sweyhat, it is essential to consider what effects "normal" climatic fluctuations have on agriculture, especially over extended periods of time. Particularly relevant is the positive effect of appropriate soil management on the conservation of moisture and plant nutrients, as well as the deleterious effect of sustained cultivation and cropping on soil quality. In the long term, the latter factors can result in soil degradation and ultimately crop failure. The themes of sustainability of production versus soil degradation are constantly reiterated in the literature on desertification, and although it would be unwise to view human influences as the sole cause behind desertification, the interaction between land use and climate is a crucial factor in the assessment of settlement in areas of marginal rain-fed cultivation. For example, although the Sahelian drought of 1968–1984 could have been precipitated by a climatic drought, many consider it to have been a crisis that was pre-conditioned by economic and political factors over the previous decade and was then triggered by a run of exceptionally dry years (Mainguet 1991: 6–16; Rapp 1987; Goudie 1986: 46). In such cases, the increased vulnerability of land use systems was arguably a necessary pre-condition for the Sahelian famines but was not a sufficient condition. Without the prolonged drought the disaster would not have occurred, but if the economic system had been less stressed it would have been more resilient and the effects of the drought might have been lessened (Parry 1986: 382).

Similarly, it is feasible that in the rain-fed farming zone of the Near East, as urban centers grew in the third millennium B.C., changes in agricultural production might have increased the fragility of land use systems that would have increased the likelihood of crop failure and the propensity to population collapse. Such a concept is clearly relevant to the region under investigation. By determining the potential likelihood of such intrinsic reasons for collapse it should then be possible to assess the magnitude of external events that might be necessary to precipitate collapses of still higher magnitude.

Mean annual rainfall, on its own, is not a totally reliable guide to potential crop growth, so it is necessary to examine climatic fluctuation in conjunction with the interaction between landforms, soils and land use, and annual rainfall. Both mean annual rainfall and its year-to-year variability are important to crop growth in a rain-fed farming regime. Where rainfall is more regular and reliable, it is possible to grow cereal crops with annual rainfall as low as 180 mm, whereas where it is less regular and reliable, rainfall in any one year may need to be as high as 230 mm (Wallén 1967). Using the statistic of rainfall interannual variability combined with mean annual rainfall, Perrin de Brichambaut and Wallén (1963) and Wallén (1967) have defined a limit to dry farming in the Middle East. Tell es-Sweyhat lies on, or very close to this boundary, but today it is clear that cereal farming can spread beyond this limit, almost as far as Raqqa with an annual rainfall of around 183 mm (ten year record). This extension is partly due to socioeconomic factors that enable large landowners to absorb some of the risk of crop failure in order to recoup a profit during wet years. This risk is unacceptable to subsistence farmers in a traditional economy who must minimize risk by guaranteeing a certain minimal yield each year. According to the TAVO survey,[31] the present limit of rain-fed cultivation can be subdivided into an inner (i.e., northern) zone of wheat, barley, and legume cultivation within the moist steppe (dominant, partial, or sporadic cultivation), and an outer (i.e., southern) zone of wheat and barley cultivation characterized by high yield uncertainty (again divided into three subunits). Tell es-Sweyhat falls within this outer zone of partial cultivation and is fringed to the east by steppe pasture (some of which is now under cultivation) and to the west again by the wheat and barley areas of the outer zone. Within a short distance, on the west bank of the Euphrates River, the inner zone of wheat, barley, and legumes is evident, and it is within this zone that sustained rain-fed agriculture associated with more certain yields prevails. On the other hand, the high risk outer zone extends more than 50 km to the southeast, and it is within this zone that risk of crop failure is at its highest (table 3.1).

Archaeological data can be marshaled to estimate the limit of long-term settlement, although because the data rarely indicate the nature of the land use system, this evidence must be employed with caution. During the late glacial period (9500–9000 B.C.), carbonized plant remains from Upper Paleolithic and Neolithic Abu Hureyra (T 545) on the Euphrates River suggest that a forest-steppe boundary existed a little to the west, probably just to the west of the bend in the river (Moore and Hillman 1992; Moore 1989). For a short period before 6000 B.C., in the eastern Jazirah of Iraq, a number of settlements extended well to the south of the present limit of rain-fed cultivation into the area around Hatra (Oates 1982). In contrast, within the Balikh Valley, a short distance east of Tell es-Sweyhat, a marked bunching of sites occurs in the northern part of the valley within what is today the zone of rain-fed cultivation. The presence of this concentration of sites during the ceramic Neolithic and Halaf periods (i.e., until ca. 4500 B.C.) suggests that a southern limit of rain-fed prehistoric settlement existed in the region of Tell Hammam et-Turkman (Wilkinson 1998: 71–72). More southerly Halaf sites within the rain-fed zone exhibited a larger percentage of wild animals within their faunal sample (33% at Khirbet esh-Shenef in the Balikh Valley and 55% at Shams ed-Din Tannira on the Euphrates floodplain southwest of Tell es-Sweyhat [fig. 3.1; Uerpmann 1982]). This higher percentage suggests that these communities were probably not entirely dependent upon cultivation but must have relied partly on wild game procured from the dry steppe. Such sites may be regarded as having been near the margin of rain-fed cultivation. Beyond this

---

31. TAVO 1985, map A X 4, 1:2,000,000.

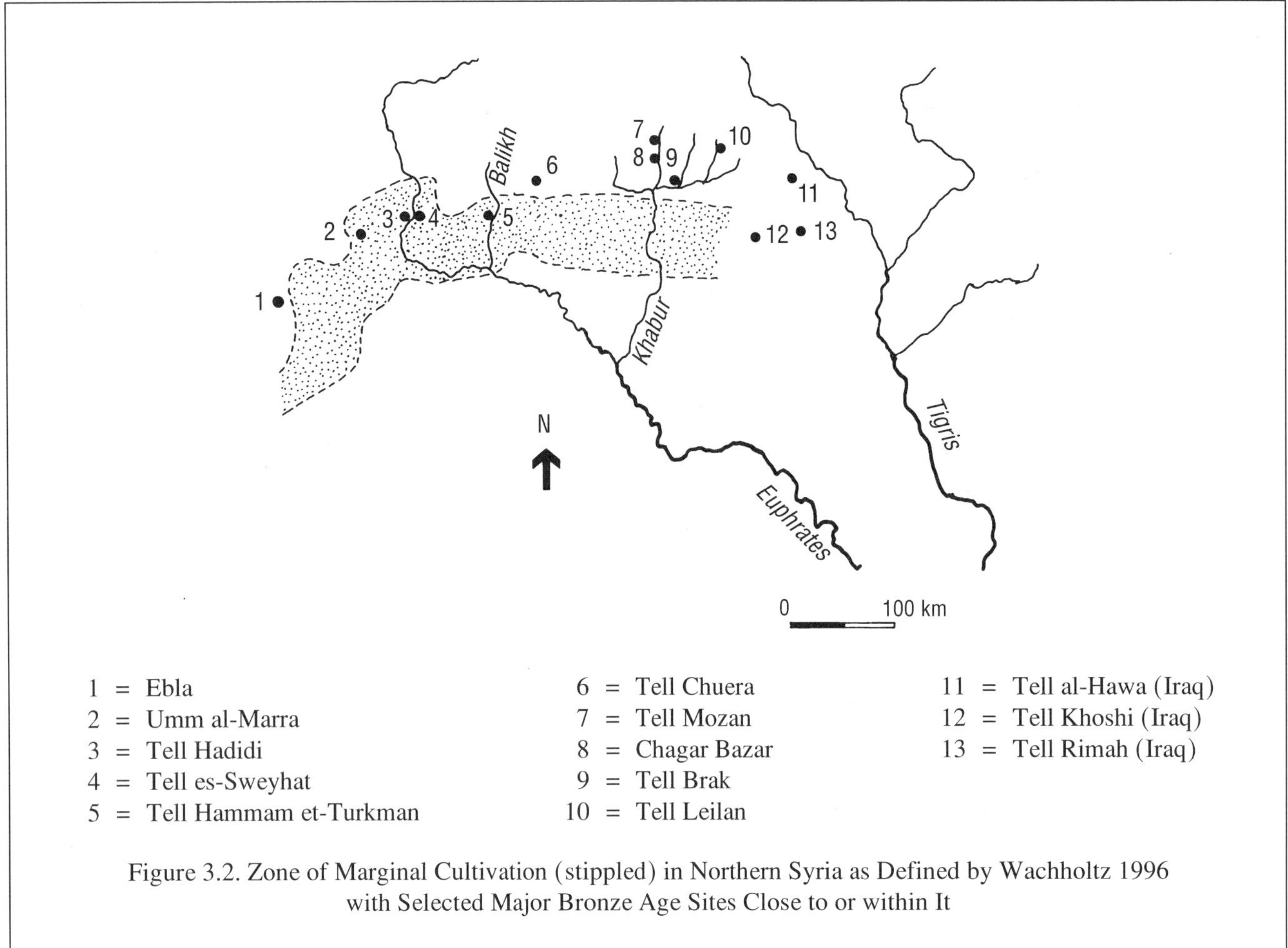

Figure 3.2. Zone of Marginal Cultivation (stippled) in Northern Syria as Defined by Wachholtz 1996 with Selected Major Bronze Age Sites Close to or within It

limit occasional small sites as well as major settlements such as Mounbateh/Tell Sawwan in the Balikh Valley were perhaps sustained, in part, by irrigation. Similar bunching of settlements can be observed in the upper Balikh Valley within Syria during the Early Bronze Age, and in general the distribution of archaeological sites suggests a long-term limit for presumably rain-fed settlement that is not much different from that of today. This limit is illustrated most clearly by the distribution of earlier Chalcolithic, Late Chalcolithic, Uruk, and Early Dynastic sites in upper Mesopotamia.[32] These sites, although occupied during a relatively moist period,[33] fall either close to the present limit of rain-fed cultivation or a short distance to the north of it. In summary, the present limit of rain-fed cultivation, although apparently occurring during a slightly more arid climate than that of the Chalcolithic, lies some distance to the south of the limit of settlement that occurred during moister times. This difference must reflect the modern commercialized economy that allows farmers to take greater risks than in ancient times when it was a priority to obtain basic subsistence needs first and to minimize risk of crop failure. Such complications in the relationship between ancient settlement and climate are echoed in the southern Levant, where Finkelstein notes similar contradictions between the limit of settlement and the prevailing environment (1995a: 31–35). In general, a broad zone of marginal cultivation and steppe rangeland can be defined as indicated in figure 3.2 (based on Wachholtz 1996, fig. 2.1). This area, which contains within it the limit of rain-fed cultivation, includes not only Umm al-Marra, but also Tell Hadidi (T 548), Tell es-Sweyhat, and Tell Hammam et-Turkman.

In terms of the ecology of the agricultural economy, northern Syria can be subdivided into five zones as follows (Cocks et al. 1988; Pabot 1956; see also fig. 3.3 based on Jones 1993, fig. 3). These zones are associated with crop yield (in this case cereals) that declines significantly from north to south (table 3.1). Tell es-Sweyhat appears to lie close to the border between Zones *3* and *4*.[34]

---

32. That is representing a range from Halaf until about 2600 B.C.; data from TAVO 1985, map B I 16 and 17.

33. Courty's (1994) phase 3, namely, Halaf, Ubaid, and Uruk, falling roughly between 5000 and 3000 B.C. This also conforms to other indicators of increased moisture as noted above.

34. See also Wachholtz 1996 for a discussion of the marginal zone to the southeast of Aleppo.

Zone *1a*   With rainfall greater than 600 mm, this area exhibits a wide range of crops. In Turkey, Zone *1a* is characterized predominantly by wheat, barley, and lentils grown in alternating years, with vineyards occupying marginal soils (Wilkinson 1990).

Zone *1b*   Rainfall between 350 and 600 mm and not less than 300 mm in two of every three years. Main crops comprise wheat, chick-peas, lentils, fruit, vegetables, and non-irrigated summer crops.

Zone *2*   Mean rainfall of 250–300 mm, and above 250 mm in two of every three years. Crops comprise barley, wheat, some food legumes, and summer crops; livestock herding, mainly sheep and goats, is of increasing importance.

Zone *3*   Mean annual rainfall greater than 250 mm and not less than 250 mm in one year out of two. Barley and livestock (mainly sheep and goats) are the main products; wheat is also grown but food legumes are of little importance.

Zone *4*   With average rainfall between 200 and 250 mm, and not less than 200 mm during half the years, barley and sheep or goats remain the primary products, barley being mainly grown to feed flocks.

Zone *5*   Even less rainfall than Zone *4* and extending into true desert, this area is not used for cultivation but is used for grazing, primarily by nomadic or semi-nomadic pastoralists.

Where mean annual rainfall exceeds about 325 mm wheat is the main cereal, although barley may be important on poorer soils (Jones 1993: 131). Farther south barley predominates until the pastoral Zone *5* takes over. The present-day limit of dry farming is very ragged and depends on a range of cultural and economic factors as well as on local soil and hydrological conditions (fig. 2.1). For example, soils along wadis may remain moist for greater parts of the year with the result that lobes of rain-fed farming (albeit benefiting from enhanced soil moisture levels) extend southward into the true desert. In drier areas most land is under barley, usually with an alternating year of fallow, but increasingly being grown as an annual crop. Significantly, the increased proportion of barley that appears in records of carbonized plant remains from Tell Hammam et-Turkman and neighboring sites after the third millennium B.C. can be interpreted as being the result of the extension of cereal cultivation out of the floodplain and on to the drier soils on the higher terraces beyond.

Because crop production is not viable every year, grazing of animals increases towards the southern limit of Zone *4*, and in some years barley is not even harvested but is directly grazed by the sheep and goats. This underscores the elasticity of such economies, in which the production of plant foods for human consumption is not necessarily the pri-

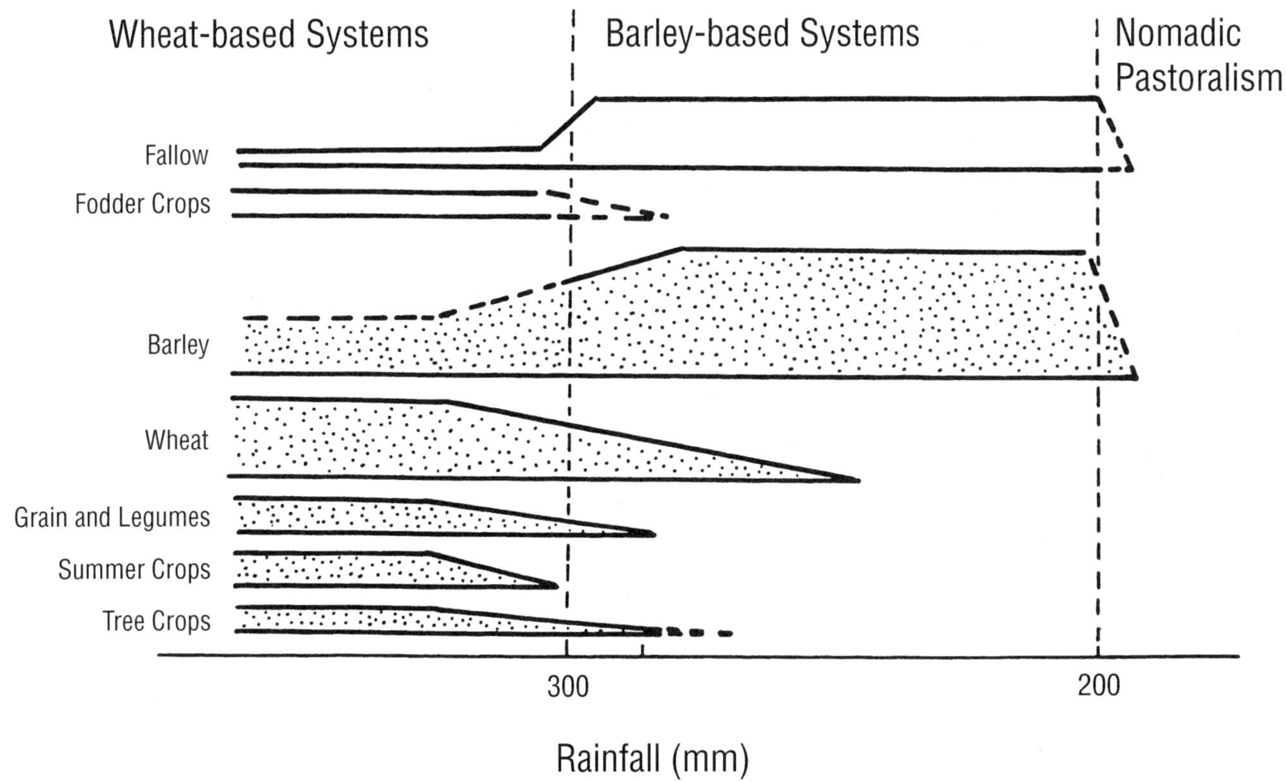

Figure 3.3. Agro-ecological Zones in Northern Syria (re-drawn after Jones 1993: 130)

mary goal of the inhabitants. Rather, there is a flexible policy towards food crops such that standing barley is often regarded as an enhanced animal feed rather than a failed food crop (Nordblom 1983; Wachholtz 1996). If necessary, and depending upon grain availability, animals can then be exchanged for grain produced in more productive areas. Thus today at least, we see a range of agricultural practices within upper Mesopotamia and a necessary degree of interdependence between adjacent zones. As a result of this flexible strategy of grazing standing barley in dry years, it should be appreciated that the perception of crop failure is much more blurred than it would be for a true commercial economy. Such factors of resilience and related feedback mechanisms are elaborated below.

Table 3.1. Mean Barley Yields for Agricultural Zones *1–5*, 1979–89
(based on Cooper and Bailey 1990; Oram and de Haan 1995, table 3.1)

Agricultural Zone	*1*	*2*	*3*	*4*	*5*
Mean annual rainfall (mm)	>350	250–350	>250	200–250	<200
Mean barley yield (kg/ha)	1,367	885	576	480	359
Co-efficient of variation (%)	37	51	81	103	114
% of years with no harvest	0	1	36	46	64
Barley area (ha within Syria)	43,000	646,000	580,000	867,000	400,000
Mean share of barley production 1979–89 (%)	16	42	17	8	6

As noted above, Tell es-Sweyhat lies very close to the limit of economic dry farming. Although we have no knowledge of what the Bronze Age rainfall was, it is possible as a first approximation, to examine how the twentieth-century rainfall record may affect crop yields.

Extended time periods of climatic statistics are not available for upper Mesopotamia, but a forty-five year record from Mosul in combination with thirty year runs for Kamishli and Aleppo, and an even shorter run for Hasseke, provide a general picture of rainfall conditions over a broad area for much of this century. Thus Mosul, with mean annual rainfall of 384 mm and a wide inter-annual fluctuation, rarely experienced rainfall less than 250 mm in any wet season (Wilkinson and Tucker 1995, fig. 4).[35] Five-year running means suggest two broad medium range variations (i.e., greater than ten years duration), an earlier one between 1927 and 1937 of rather lower rainfall, followed by a moister (albeit wildly fluctuating) episode between the late 1930s and the early 1950s. Unfortunately, disruptions in rainfall records around 1960 make interpretations beyond this point difficult. Whether such dry and moist periods represent significant climatic trends or not is debatable and rather may simply be an example of "persistence" in which runs of dry or wet years can appear grouped together over relatively short time periods (Gommes 1993: 72).

When the climatic statistics from stations to the west, northeast, and east of Tell es-Sweyhat are compared, a general pattern with rises and falls of rainfall is similar at all three stations (fig. 3.4).[36] This broad correlation of rainfall across north Syria, northern Iraq, and southern Turkey is supported by scatter diagrams which demonstrate that, in general, a high rainfall year in one area is matched by a high rainfall year elsewhere, and vice versa (fig. 3.5). This pattern implies that if any given community experienced a severe drought and famine, there is little chance that the deficit could be met by importing grain from other parts of the region (Wilkinson 1997: 70–71). However, the correlation is not particularly strong, and the deviations from this trend are instructive. As indicated in figure 3.4 in occasional years rainfall (and presumably crop yield) in Aleppo was significantly higher than in Kamishli. In such cases, bearing in mind the problems of the high cost of overland transport of bulk products, and the possibility of ambush from other hungry communities, it is possible that a desperate community in the Khabur Valley could import food from west of the Euphrates River. In other words, occasional disparities in rainfall, in turn, could lead to disparities in the food supply that potentially could encourage the flow of bulk foodstuffs.[37] Such years are illustrated in figure 3.5d, which

---

35. Rainfall is calculated in terms of hydrological years so that all rainfall that falls within any given wet season is calculated together.

36. Aleppo and Kamishli have mean annual rainfall of 334 and 444 mm respectively.

37. Although the above analysis suggests the potential for movement of food, owing to the high cost of overland transport of bulk foods in early economies, it remains debatable whether such transfers were a commonplace feature of the economy.

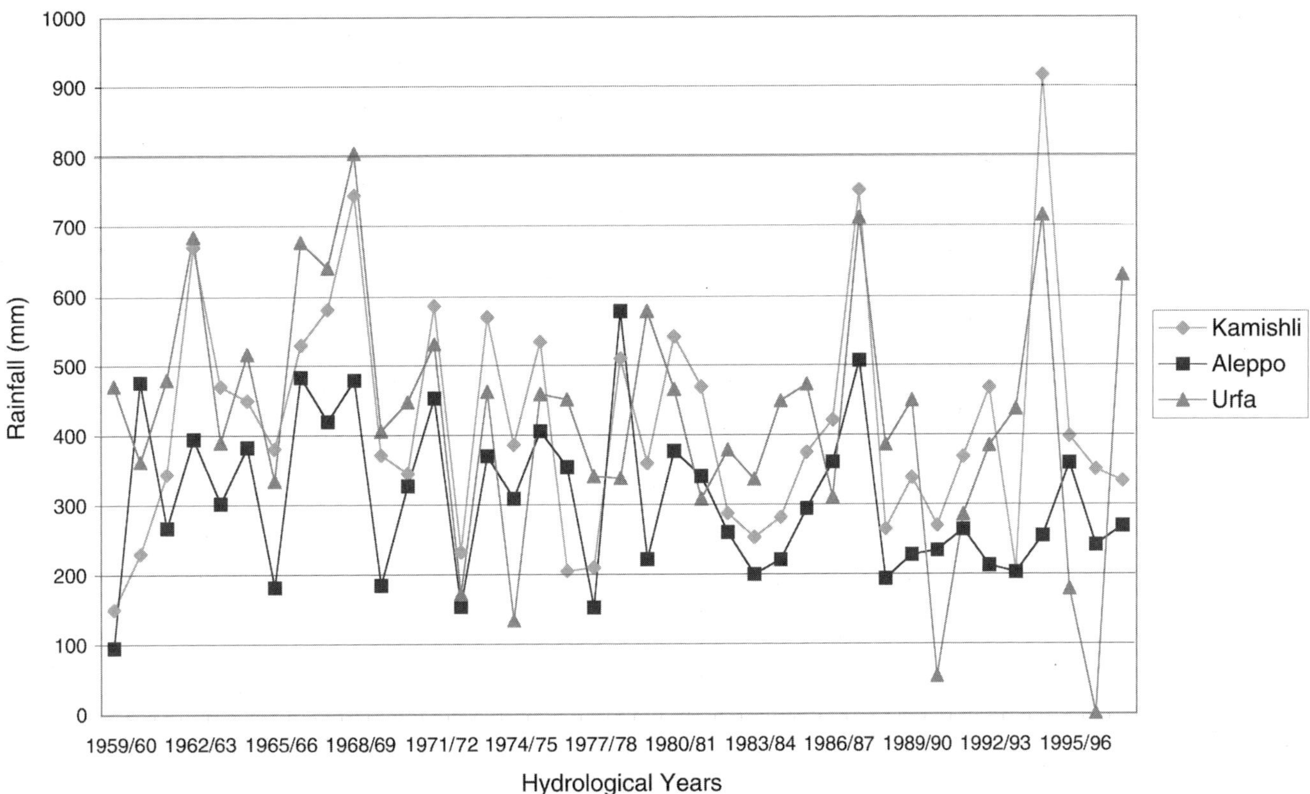

Figure 3.4. Annual Rainfall for Kamishli (Northeastern Syria), Aleppo (Northwestern Syria),
and Urfa (Turkey) from 1959 to 1998

shows for Aleppo and Urfa (between which Tell es-Sweyhat is situated) those years in which Aleppo received significantly more rainfall than Urfa and vice versa.

The foregoing statistics demonstrate that both Aleppo and Mosul are in marginal locations, but in neither case do the climatic records show runs of critically dry years. Nevertheless, Tell es-Sweyhat, with rainfall of around 250 mm, would experience more years with significantly lower rainfall as well as occasional "back-to-back" pairs of dry years either of which could have produced major crop deficits.[38]

In the context of human perceptions and land use, Parry (1986) suggests three scales of climatic fluctuation:

1. Climatic variability, that is the year-to-year differences in climatic variables to which economic and social systems generally adjust

2. Medium-term climatic changes (of duration 10–200 years) to which society probably needs to adapt in order to avoid undesirable impact

3. Long-term climatic changes which occur on scales too large to be considered significant for the planning horizons of most societies (Parry 1986: 380)

In addition, of course, extreme events, either short-term or of longer duration, can have a major impact on crop production systems.

Most case studies comparing crop yield and climate show a marked positive relationship with rainfall (Parry and Carter 1988: 29) so that crop yield increases when rainfall is high and decreases in drier years. However, such a straightforward correlation between climate and land use should not be assumed. Rather, for cereal crops, two main components influence yield variability, namely, technological change and climatic variability (see below), to which must be added an often significant amount of random "noise" (McQuigg 1981:122). In the case of the traditional economy, technology could be represented by the introduction of irrigation (if that is possible), by enhanced fertilizer

---

38. Pairs of dry years occurred at Mosul in 1927/28–1928/29 and
    1923/24–24/25.

utilization, terrace construction, or other innovations. Although without detailed off-site or soil surveys it may be difficult to assess the contribution of technological innovations, they cannot be ignored. Therefore, during times of food
stress, the introduction of key innovations to either raise crop yields or maintain sustainability sufficiently to override
minor climate fluctuations may have been crucial to community survival.

Technological factors can complicate the relationship between climate and crop production, and recent data from
Syria indicate that it is possible to account for between 50% and 70% of the variability in wheat and barley yields by
various estimates of seasonal rainfall (van Oosterom, Ceccarelli, and Peacock 1993; Harris 1991: 24). Using computer
simulation, Harris has shown that simulated grain yield correlates well with rainfall, but rather less with length of
growing season. Hence at Muslimiyah, a test station of ICARDA,[39] rainfall accounted for 85% of variations in simulated crop yield (Harris 1991: 31). Other climate factors that can significantly influence crop yields are seasonal distribution of rainfall, length of growing season, and temperature. For example, frost can damage crops when they are actively growing, and extreme high temperatures in spring, especially when associated with high winds, can be equally
damaging.

Similar correlations between grain yield and climate were obtained in Tunisia, where in the arid zone (<350 mm
per annum) there was a strong linear correlation of barley yield with rainfall from September to May (Ben Mechlia
1993: 122). However, in slightly wetter areas (rainfall >450 mm per annum), the scatter of points is greater and there
is a plateau at 15 quintals/ha (i.e., 1,500 kg/ha), which Ben Mechlia regards as the probable maximum barley yield in
Tunisia under present growing conditions. Farther south where rainfall is <250 mm, the use of runoff collection and
other methods of soil moisture enhancement result in a lower correlation between winter rainfall and barley yield. Applying such principles to northern Syria, it is feasible that there might be less correlation between rainfall and crop
yield in the moist steppe areas of Zone *1*, as well as in the drier areas (Zones *4–5*), while the intermediate Zones *2–3*
would be expected to register the strongest correlations. This is relevant to Tell es-Sweyhat because the presence of
zones of soil moisture enhancement along wadis, as in Tunisia, would provide relatively high yields in drier years.

A pragmatic way of comparing the relationship between land use and climate is to examine the twentieth-century
extension of settlement and cultivation that occurred throughout the Jazirah with the modern rainfall data. For example, various historical sources for part of northern Iraq indicate that in 1938 the limit of cultivation in northwest Iraq
extended only a short distance south of the Jebel Sinjar. During the following forty years a massive southward colonization occurred until by the 1970s settlement reached some 50–75 km south of its former limit. This colonization is ascribed to the sedentarization of Shammar bedouin (Wilkinson and Tucker 1995; Thalen 1979: 297), although it was almost certainly encouraged as well by the run of moist years that occurred in the 1940s and 1950s. The unsustainability
of such land use practices is emphasized by attempts by various governments to restrain cultivation to within the
moister northern areas of the steppe so that today a line established by the government of Iraq has managed to restrict
cultivation within the northern band. In the Balikh Valley north of Raqqa, satellite images and topographic maps indicate a similar southward shift in cultivation, in this case between 1945 and 1980 (Lewis 1988). This area, forming part
of Rowton's (1973) zone of dimorphic chiefdoms, originally consisted of steppe grazing away from the valley and
cultivated and often irrigated enclaves along the river. Thus pastoralism co-existed with cultivation, each of which required different climatic conditions. The resilience of such communities is emphasized by the severe winter of 1911,
during which, although some 80% of the sheep in the vilayet of Aleppo died from cold or hunger, human survival was
possible because harvests were moderately good (Lewis 1988: 689). Gradually, however, this dual economy was replaced by sedentarization of nomadic groups and the movement of people out from the valleys, resulting in the massive extension of cropland of the 1930s, 1940s, and 1950s (Lewis 1988: 692). Although this extension of settlement is
ascribed to conditions when a central government ensured secure, peaceful, and economic conditions, again the preva-
lence of moister winters at this time must have allowed settlement to take place. Thus an extension of settlement into
more marginal lands has seen the replacement of a resilient traditional dual economy by cereal monoculture, cash
crops along the river, and a considerable reliance on migratory labor. The southward colonization took place under
both favorable political and economic conditions and improved rainfall. By replacing the resilient traditional system by
a fragile rainfall dependent monoculture, the system has become more vulnerable to crop failure. This in turn has been
made yet more likely because of soil degradation that decreases potential crop yields by removing soil and lessening its
soil moisture-holding capacity. Finally, the unrealistic extension of cultivation into more marginal lands again makes
such systems extremely vulnerable to collapse.

---

39. International Center for Agricultural Research in the Dry Areas
     (Aleppo). I am especially grateful to the staff of ICARDA, par-
ticularly Tom Nordblom and Scott Christiansen, for providing
valuable reference material on dry-farming systems.

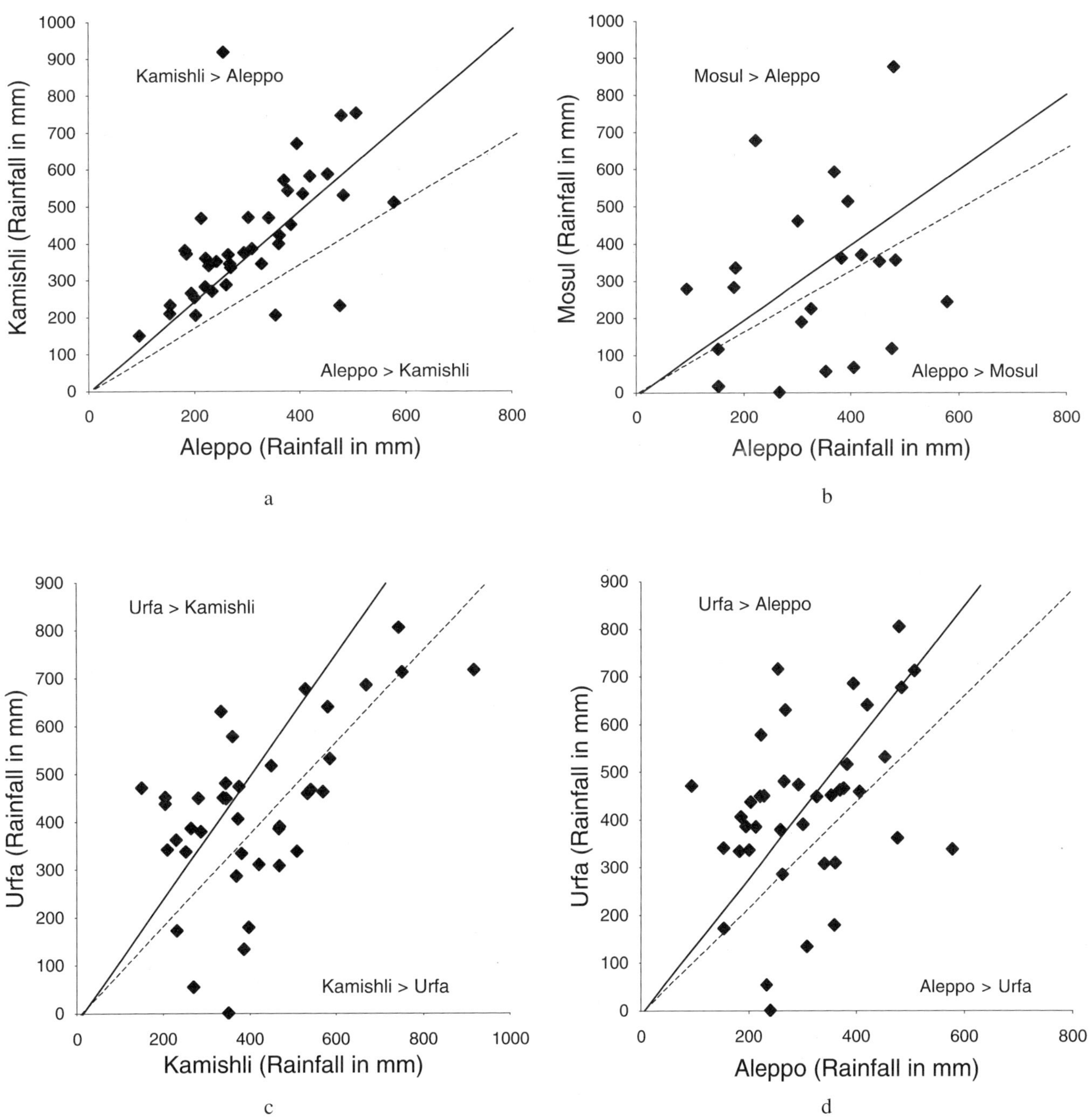

Figure 3.5. Scatter Diagrams Showing Annual Rainfall (*a*) at Kamishli and Aleppo from 1959 to 1998, (*b*) at Mosul and Aleppo from 1959 to 1980, (*c*) at Kamishli and Urfa from 1959 to 1998, and (*d*) at Urfa and Aleppo from 1959 to 1998

3.E. LAND USE AND RISK MANAGEMENT

In addition to climate, soil conditions and crop management practices can significantly influence yields and therefore human carrying capacity. Deep soils provide significant reservoirs of soil moisture, and if root systems are long enough to penetrate to below 100 cm these lower horizons can supply crucial water at times of soil moisture deficit. For example, crop yield data from northern Iraq indicate that on dry-farmed lands near Tell ʿAfar, thinner soils on the rolling steppe provided significantly lower cereal yields than the deeper soils of the plain (Ali 1955: 147).

A more widespread but controversial method of increasing crop production is the practice of fallowing, which entails leaving some land uncultivated in alternate cropping years (in Syria 14–16 months). As a result, the portion of rain that falls on the uncropped land, rather than being consumed by crop growth, is held over for the next cropping year. The resultant bonus (normally in the range 10–25% of annual rainfall) can be crucial by supplying supplementary soil moisture especially in dry years. However, because both nutrients and moisture can be limiting factors on crop growth it is not always clear which factor provides the bonus in crop growth (Loomis 1983: 359). Nevertheless, on the American Great Plains, fallow can strongly reduce the risk of crop failure as well as the relative variability over years and in one area, failed crops (defined in this case as <400 kg/ha) were obtained in ten years out of twenty-seven of continuous wheat, but never after fallow (Loomis 1983: 360).

In Syria fallowing is a long-continued tradition in areas receiving <300 mm annual rainfall (Harris et al. 1991: 238), and in the Mediterranean region the practice certainly goes back to the Roman period (White 1970). In upper Mesopotamia fallowing was practiced in the Neo-Assyrian period (early first millennium B.C.; Fales 1990: 119). It is also considered to have been a normal cropping practice as far back as the fifteenth century B.C. and probably earlier at Nuzi in northeast Iraq (Zaccagnini 1975: 219–20). An explicit reference in a Neo-Assyrian cuneiform text declares:

> "… he shall have the use of the field for six years, three under cultivation and three in fallow" (*CAD karapḫu*; see also Johns 1901)

Although the efficacy of fallowing has been disputed by some authorities including Loizides (1980) who concluded that fallow in Mediterranean climates does not result in any significant increases in the amount of water available for the next crop, more detailed studies at ICARDA demonstrated that storage of rainwater does take place in fallow land during rainy years (Jabbour and Naji 1991: 163). In certain cases the moisture carry-over may seem meager, with perhaps as little as 8% of the previous winter season's rain being stored after a dry year, or as much as 31% being available after a wet year (Oram and de Haan 1995: 17). Therefore, if a dry year follows a wet year the moisture surplus from the wet year provides a safety net for the dry year. This, although crucial for traditional or subsistence economies, is less important for modern day farmers integrated into the national economy. On the other hand, if there are two years of drought, moisture carry-over is negligible and the drought effect can be severe. The difference between crop yields of biennially fallowed land and monoculture (fertilized or unfertilized) is indicated in figure 3.6 (from Cocks et al. 1988, table 4, with additional rainfall data from Aleppo). Not only does continuous cropping of cereals result in lower yields, when grown without fertilizers, the practice usually results in declining yields after a few years, a result that argues in favor of fallowing (Oram and de Haan 1995: 17). Deeper soils (i.e., those >90 cm) are more effective for fallowing than shallow soils owing to the reservoir effective of soil moisture stored at depths greater than 1 m (Harris et al. 1991: 239; based on Guler and Karaca 1988).

The use of the fallow year in farming practice can be demonstrated for a reconstructed rainfall pattern sequence at Tell es-Sweyhat as follows. The annual rainfall data from 1959/60 until 1997/98 for Kamishli (northeastern Syria), Urfa (southern Turkey), and Aleppo (to the west of the Euphrates River), are shown in figure 3.4. The data are plotted according to hydrological years, that is, from September to August, so that a full winter season's rainfall is included in each data point rather than being split by two calendar years. Both Kamishli and Aleppo are significantly wetter than Tell es-Sweyhat, but Sweyhat is closer to the latter station. On the basis of the correlation between the two curves (fig. 3.5a), a rainfall curve can be simulated for Tell es-Sweyhat based upon an estimated mean annual rainfall of 250 mm per annum; this would have run approximately parallel to the curve of the nearer station, Aleppo. Thus the simulated rainfall data, based upon the mean rainfall at Aleppo are:

> Tell es-Sweyhat annual rainfall = Aleppo annual rainfall × 250/334 = 0.75
>
> 0.75 being the ratio of the two mean annual rainfalls

It is immediately apparent from the simulated curve (fig. 3.7), that if 200 mm is accepted as the minimum annual rainfall for an acceptable crop,[40] crop failures would have occurred in 1965/66, 1969/70, 1972/73, 1978/79, 1983/84, 1988/89, and 1989/90. Such a series of crop failures, which are unlikely to be sustainable over a long period of time, underscore the marginal location of Tell es-Sweyhat.

If, however, 20% of the fallow year moisture is carried over, the mean annual rainfall rises to 301 mm (effective equivalent) and the amplitude of the curve is reduced so that virtually no crop failures occur (fig. 3.7). This smoothing is partly because of the nature of the climatic fluctuations themselves, namely, that any given dry year (e.g., 1969/70 or 1973/73) is usually preceded by a significantly wetter year such that the carry-over figure is fairly substantial.

---

40. An oversimplification, but sufficient for the present heuristic example.

Although only a simulation, the above example emphasizes the importance of the fallow year. If it were dispensed with, crop failures would be much more likely compared with the less productive but more sustainable and resilient fallowing system.

For fallowing to operate effectively, weeding or plowing is necessary to keep the fallow clean of weeds that can otherwise deplete soil moisture reserves. Because fallowed soils subjected to wetting and drying cycles can result in rapid nitrification (Russell 1961: 304), the practice can result in soil deterioration, which in the long term can counteract the advantages of soil moisture conservation and nutrient accumulation. Alternatively, fallowing can reduce the incidence of soil-borne diseases, so that in Syria, where continuous cereal growing is practiced, increases in infestation of crops can occur (Harris et al. 1991: 241).

If fallow was operating successfully to conserve soil moisture, a drought such as that of 1969/70 would have been less serious than the one in 1983/84 because of the preceding wet year in 1968/69 (fig. 3.7). On the other hand, at Hasseke, which is one of the drier stations of the Jazirah, a dry period from 1958/59 to 1960/61 would be potentially serious not because of its extremity but because moisture carry-over during the fallow year would be from dry year to dry year, with the result that the percentage carry-over would probably be insufficient to save crop failure. Fallowing can therefore be seen to be less effective in drier parts of the Jazirah where extreme dry years may be preceded by moderately dry years.

As a complement to fallowing, the application of fertilizer or manure can significantly enhance crop growth. Both phosphorus and nitrogen provide substantial increases in dry matter and grain yield, and by increasing the growth of the plant canopy, shading can result and water use efficiency is increased (P. J. M. Cooper 1991: 139; Gregory 1991: 13). By increasing root development, fertilizer applications may increase the ability of the plant to extract water from the soil in the spring and early summer growth periods (P. J. M. Cooper 1991: 139), or from soil moisture reserves at depth. On the other hand, by encouraging early growth, which can outstrip the available soil moisture, manure applica-

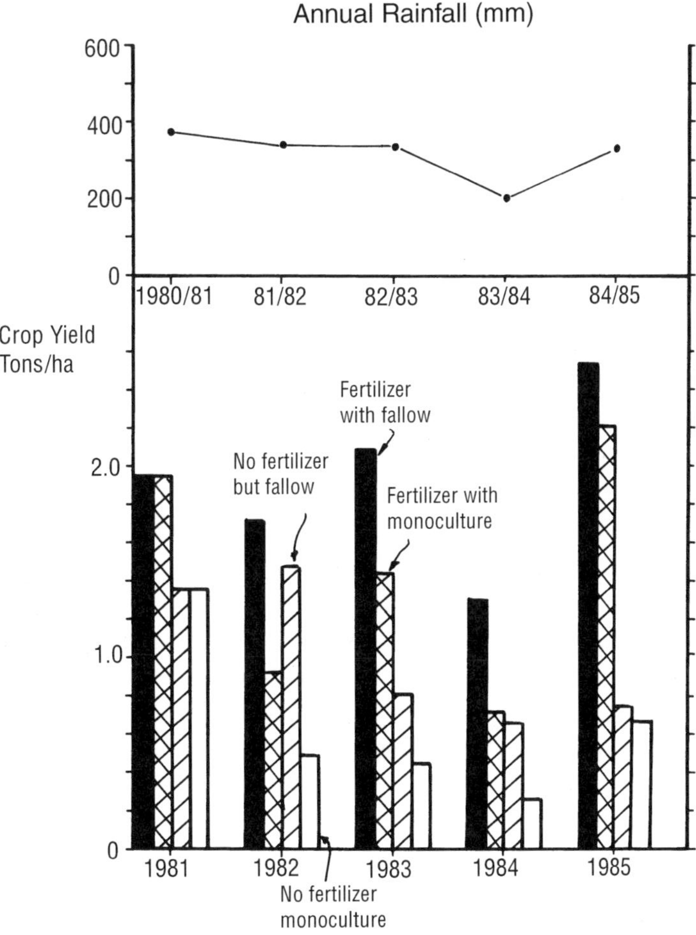

Figure 3.6. Barley Yield (tons/ha) under Different Crop Management Systems in Part of Northern Syria Compared with Rainfall for the Same Years at Aleppo (top). Based on Data in Cocks et al. 1988 with Additional Climatic Data

tions can result in soil drought and the death of the crop (Halstead *apud* Palmer 1998: 150). Cropping trials in Syria indicate that positive responses to phosphate applications can occur in all parts of the dry-farming zone, even in dry areas (Oram and de Haan 1995; P. J. M. Cooper 1991, figs. 5–6), although where there is a previous history of extensive use of fertilizers, response to renewed phosphate applications may be negligible (Pala et al. 1992: 98). Nitrogen, on the other hand, appears to be more effective in moister areas or in wetter years, as is the response to fertilizer applications in general (Pala et al. 1992: 97). Because of the absence of chemical fertilizers in antiquity, nitrogen and phosphate enhancement would have to come either from manure or from compost, ashes, and other nutrients applied as a soil dressing or by the grazing of animals. The last named practice, attested in the irrigated lands of southern Mesopotamia from Sumerian times (Civil 1994), may not, however, have been sufficient to replace lost nutrients in rain-fed farming lands that did not benefit from rejuvenating accumulations of silt. Although in the past the effectiveness of manure applications to arid soils has been questioned owing to the dryness of the soil (Buringh 1960: 252–53), when applied as compost to moist soils such additions would have been effective. Traditionally, farmers usually become aware of the deleterious effect of manuring under dry conditions that can "heat" the soil causing die off of young plants. Therefore, during years of extreme drought, such as those that recently occurred in West Africa, farmers sell their manure rather than applying it to the fields (Mortimore 1989: 64–66, 100). On the one hand, application of manure during dry conditions could form a negative feedback effect by encouraging crop growth, which in turn would withdraw water thereby depressing yields, whereas, by not applying badly needed humic matter to the soil, the soil would become degraded and less likely to sustain high yields in the long term. In general, by adding badly needed humic material to the soil, manure or compost applications would also offset the loss of organic matter mineralized during fallowing and in turn would increase the structural stability and moisture-holding capacity of the soil, thus further enhancing crop growth.

An alternative way of raising production is by extending the area sown. This is possible because in many rain-fed farming areas farmers are able to judge from the amount of autumn rain (i.e., October to December) the degree of risk entailed in planting. If the autumn is wet the following crop may be expected to be good, and if labor is available, larger areas can be sown. In northern Iraq autumn rainfall provides a rough indicator of expected annual rainfall. Rainfall in September to December is approximately correlated with the rainfall in that hydrological year. As autumn rains usually provide between 20% and 40% of total yearly rainfall, this is not sufficient to guarantee fully a successful crop or to act as a predictor of crop failure, but by judging the situation in late February (by which time some 65% of annual rainfall has been received; Thalen 1979: 53), the likelihood of crop failure can be roughly gauged. As a result farmers can choose, if failure seems certain, either not to sow at all or to sow and then to turn the crop over to grazing. Later in the season farmers can then recoup part of their loss by selling off spare animals and purchasing grain on the market.

In addition to the above, crop management techniques that can mitigate the effect of dry years include the variation of:

1. Total cropped area and distribution of crops
2. Amount of intercropping
3. Plant density
4. Substitution of crops with low moisture demands
5. Date of planting, as well as use of mulches to preserve soil moisture

However, in such a marginal, semi-arid environment the degree of flexibility in crop management practices is rather limited.

Of the above techniques, fallow and fertilization can mitigate some of the worst effects of drought and here I suggest an ordering of traditional cropping practices from those that are most liable to crop failure (Practice *A*) to those that favor soil moisture conservation, nutrient recycling, water use efficiency, and sustainable yields (Practice *D*).

Practice *A*   Cereals planted annually. In this practice soil nutrient reserves are not replenished and there is no capability of carrying over soil moisture from one season to the next. This system, *sometimes* provides more cereal production simply because the land is cropped every year. It is especially vulnerable following dry years, however, when there is no soil moisture to act as a reserve.

Practice *B*   Cereals planted with an intervening fallow year. As a result of the carrying over of soil moisture, this ancient system can mitigate some effects of drought, but by encouraging the mineralization of soil organic matter, it can also result in long-term deterioration of the soil.

Practice *C*   Annual cropping in conjunction with the application of manure. Although this may improve water use efficiency, as well as soil structure and moisture retention properties, by dispensing with the fallow year, soil moisture reserves are depleted thus increasing the likelihood of crop failure in dry years.

Practice *D*   Planting with an alternating fallow year in combination with the application of manure and/or composts. Manure and composts, in addition to their other virtues, should replace or improve organic matter lost as a result of mineralization during the fallow year.

Of the above, Practice *D* may well have been the most sustainable in antiquity.

3.F. LAND USE AND SOIL DEGRADATION

Of the land use practices described above, fallowing, although beneficial in the short term, by encouraging depletion of organic matter and the associated mineralization of nitrogen, leads to situations that are unstable in the long term (Harris et al. 1991: 241; Clarke and Russell 1977: 287; Stewart, Jones, and Unger 1993: 71). Not only are nutrients lost, but soil structure also deteriorates and soils become more vulnerable to deflation. In turn, by removing the lighter soil fractions (silt/clay aggregates and organic matter) further deterioration of the soil can result. The existence of extensive areas of unvegetated (fallowed) land, either plowed to discourage weeds, or unplowed and crusted, can then encourage either wind or water erosion (Blaikie and Brookfield 1987: 131). Similarly, rapid declines in organic nitrogen and carbon can result if crop residues are not returned to the soil, a situation which is exacerbated by the increased soil erosion that can take place on clean fallow (Bolton 1991). In antiquity, if more crop residues or stubble were removed by grazing animals for stall feeding of animals, or as temper for mudbrick, fuel, and so forth, fertility would decline and erosion hazard would increase. This is a further negative feedback process that might result during Bronze Age urbanization and which would need to be addressed in order to avoid long-term declines in crop productivity.

The problematic role of fallowing in the context of long-term soil degradation is summed up by the following statement concerning sustainable agriculture in a semi-arid area of the northwest United States (my italics):

> As highlighted by the analysis of the long-term trials, a major limitation of the wheat/fallow system is the accelerated loss in soil organic matter which accompanies the non-productive part of this rotational pattern. The high oxidation soil rate is not balanced by an equivalent return of organic residues during the cropping portion of the rotation. In cases where residues are removed or burned, the decline in soil organic matter is accelerated. And while use of both organic and inorganic soil amendments in conjunction with improved cultivars enhances the biological sustainability of the system, increasing input costs combined with static wheat prices makes the system *economically* unsustainable (Duff, Rasmussen, and Smiley 1995: 108).

Today the northern dry-farmed steppe within Syria is subject to moderate soil erosion from water, whereas areas farther to the south are more prone to eolian degradation (Middleton and Thomas 1992: 42–45). As a result of long-

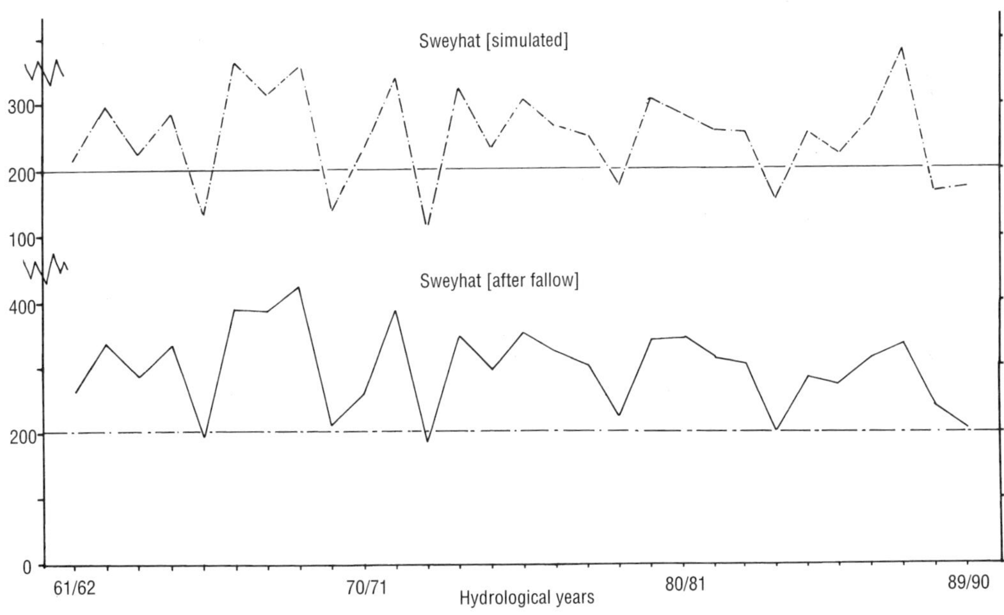

Figure 3.7. Influence of Fallowing on Effective Rainfall for Tell es-Sweyhat: Top, without Fallow (i.e., when Land is Cultivated Every Year); Below, Taking into Account a Fallow Year that Carries over Some Soil Moisture

term, often human-induced degradation, organic matter decreases gradually in topsoils so that marginal soils under native pasture exhibit most organic matter, more severely eroded marginal lands less, improved cultivation with farmyard manure less, and cultivated land (un-manured) least (Cocks et al. 1988, table 5). Organic matter is important for crop growth because it:

1. Is a major source of inorganic nutrients and microbial energy
2. Serves as an ion exchange medium and can hold water and nutrients in an available form
3. Promotes soil aggregation and root development
4. Improves water infiltration and water use efficiency (Rasmussen and Collins 1991: 94)

In semi-arid environments soil organic matter is particularly important because of its high impact on water conservation, nutrient availability, and stabilization of yields (Rasmussen and Collins 1991: 97). Thus, any farming system in the rain-fed farming zone that results in long-term loss of soil organic matter also results in a gradual decline and increased fluctuation in crop yields.

Such is the pressure on land today that dust storms are frequent and the recent expansion of cultivation has resulted in eolian deposits forming over former grazing lands, as well as, for example, covering railway tracks in the Khabur Valley (Middleton and Thomas 1992: 44–45). Today periodic dust storms testify to the massive mobilization of topsoil that can occur from extensive areas of plowed steppe.

The increase in population that occurred through the Late Holocene in the marginal dry-farming zone of upper Mesopotamia, by requiring the expansion of cultivated land, must have encouraged soil degradation. This increase, together with the large-scale removal of vegetation both by grazing animals and for fuel, must have contributed to the present-day heavily degraded landscape. Such processes of vegetation removal, by influencing surface albedo (reflectivity), can also result in complex feedback mechanisms that in turn can influence microclimate. For example, when shade-giving plants and trees are removed, the terrain can reflect more solar radiation, which ultimately under certain circumstances decreases surface temperature and in turn reduces a stable microclimate with a decreased tendency to generate clouds and convective rainfall (Williams and Balling 1996: 63). This "Charney hypothesis," although controversial, suggests that desert conditions can be reinforced as a result of vegetation removal (Kaul and Thalen 1979: 258; Kutzbach et al. 1996). Conversely, increased surface reflectivity can induce a complex range of responses that can include increased surface warming which in turn may either encourage the development of localized convectional rain or further drying (Williams and Balling 1996: 69). Whether such conditions were initiated under ancient conditions is of course debatable, but it is possible that increased intensity of cultivation during the third millennium B.C. may have encouraged the development of periodic dust storms. By increasing atmospheric dust, these may also have encouraged a number of feedback mechanisms that, in turn, may have influenced local climate (Bryson and Baerris 1967: 141; Nicholson 1995; Shukla 1995). Unfortunately, because of uncertainties regarding the direction and significance of such mechanisms it is as yet difficult to determine whether they would have reinforced already dry conditions or would have ameliorated them.

3.G. THE ROLE OF PASTORALISM

Because earlier regional studies by the author in the area of Tell es-Sweyhat concentrated on the physical remains of settlement and land use, the pastoral component, which leaves a more ephemeral trace in the landscape, was not dealt with effectively. On the other hand, the study of excavated fauna, and more recently carbonized plant remains, have contributed important new data towards an understanding of the pastoral nomadism (*Section 8: The Ancient Agricultural Economy;* Zeder 1998; Miller 1997a, 1997b). Thus Zeder (1999: 4) points out that the development of highly specialized pastoral nomadism, dependent upon settled populations for their essential supplies, is specifically related to the growth of urban centers in the third millennium B.C. As more land was devoted to cultivation, sheep and goats could be moved farther away to outlying pastures, which would place them, and more importantly their owners, more removed from regulation by central authorities. Therefore, despite the problems of recognition of nomadic sites, it is evident that pastoralism must have made an important contribution to the economy of the region since at least the period of the Mari records and probably earlier. This is especially the case because of the precarious climatic circumstances for crop production (Danti and Zettler 1998: 210).

For the Balikh Valley in the nineteenth century, Lewis (1987) describes how at the end of winter or in the early spring people who normally resided in tent camps along the river moved with their sheep away from the valley on to steppe grazing beyond. Although some moved to the steppe desert to the south of the Euphrates Valley, most moved to the steppe pastures to the east or west of the Balikh Valley where the animals could graze on the newly grown vegetation. Similar patterns have been observed around Raqqa and Deir az-Zor farther down the Euphrates Valley. In the former area during the 1970s, families with more than fifteen sheep moved away from the Euphrates Valley in the early spring and pitched camp at a distance between 5 and 15 km from the village (Rabo 1986: 62). Similarly, the traditional pattern of transhumance southeast of Deir az-Zor was for the ʿAgedat tribe to remain in the river valley floodplain area in summer and autumn, and then to move out and utilize the grazing lands of the steppe to the north and south of the river some 20–50 km away in the winter and spring, extending farther away in dry years (d'Hont 1994: 209–17). Such patterns of movement may well have been practiced in antiquity in the Tell es-Sweyhat area, especially during periods of minimal sedentary settlement along the river.

Even the nomadic pastoralists depended to some degree on cropped land for part of the year, and recent studies show that today sheep belonging to bedouin groups consume a significant amount of cereal crop residues. For example, between Aleppo and the Euphrates Valley at the present time, the inhabitants operate strategies that range from virtually fully sedentary villagers on the edge of the steppe to nomadic (bedouin) pastoralists beyond the cultivated zone where rainfall is less than 200 mm per annum (Wachholtz, Nordblom, and Arab 1992: 217). Sheep belonging to each group rely on a combination of feeds that range from hand-fed grains and bran, through harvested and unharvested crops, to open steppe grazing. For the fairly dry year of 1990/91 (rainfall ca. 199 mm at Aleppo), grazing on native pastures on open steppe or common grazing was concentrated in March, April, and May, but this formed only a minor part of the flock's total food requirement for the year (ibid., p. 227). In the more sedentary parts of the agro-pastoral zone, unharvested (i.e., "failed") crops were grazed in April and May. This was not the case in the driest part of the area where the nomadic groups that occupied that region presumably did not have fields (ibid., fig. 3.10, p. 226). These groups continued to rely on grazing of pastures. Otherwise, for most of the summer from June through September, most communities relied on grazing of cereal straw on fields around villages. Nevertheless, in the moister village areas unharvested cereals continued to be grazed, a point that underscores their potential importance to the local village economy (ibid., fig. 3.10). In October/November grazing on cotton residues and maize (corn) stubble was important, whereas for December through March great reliance was placed upon feed of wheat and barley straw. Discounting the modern introduction of maize and cotton grazing in the autumn, it can be seen that for these communities there was a considerable reliance upon crops as feed. This was either in the form of stubble grazing (summer), hand-fed cereal straw (winter), or in the dire circumstances of a drier year (ca. 200 mm in this case) from unharvested crops.

Although such a high reliance on crops is unlikely to have been practiced in the Bronze Age, some reliance is to be expected. Thus texts in a dialect of Old Akkadian from Tell Beydar in the Khabur Valley mention the use of barley for hand-feeding oxen, donkeys, and sheep during the winter months (van Lerberghe 1996: 120–21). Even during the third millennium B.C. there must have been a significant amount of interdependence between the agricultural and pastoral sectors in most years. The high reliance on cereal stubble and straw for summer and winter feed, respectively, highlights the fact that any expansion of sheep and goat flocks must have increased the demand for feed crops around sedentary settlements (Danti 2000). Such activity would also have led to excessive grazing and potential degradation of pastures around the margins of the cultivated areas. Degradation does not simply result from plant removal by the ever-hungry animals and the erosive action of animal hooves, but also by the export of nutrients within the animals themselves, through their feces and urine. This is especially the case with nitrogen (White, Treacher, and Termanini 1997). Such exports depend on the movements and residence patterns of the flocks, so that where these are grazing on stubble and then bedded down elsewhere, there is a net export of nutrients to the latter area, but depending upon the residence time in each area. Such activities, although difficult to factor into land use models, suggest that increases in the number of sheep and goats may well lead to increases in degradation of the land unless careful attention is paid to the recycling of dung for fertilizer and for fuel, the latter leading to further recycling in the form of ash for fertilizer.

3.H. CONCLUSION

In the Tell es-Sweyhat area the ancient communities had a range of habitats that they could exploit. These included an area of potential irrigation along the Euphrates River for which we have precious little evidence, rain-fed cultivation on the fringing steppe that probably provided the bulk of plant foods, and pasture lands within the riverine zone, the cultivable steppe, and the upland beyond. The cultivable steppe, although productive in the short term, exhibits a susceptibility to degradation and declining yields in the long term. When cultivation spread on to more undulating lands characterized by lower soil moisture, violation of fallow would have had more severe repercussions than in the potentially moist soils of low lying areas. This illustrates that local knowledge gained probably over many generations was essential for the optimum production of rain-fed crops. Both systems must have directly influenced the pattern of long-term sedentary settlement, and indirectly the nomadic-pastoral economy. Only by understanding interactions between the sedentary and mobile communities can we hope to understand the pattern of archaeological settlement.

4. THE ARCHAEOLOGICAL LANDSCAPE I

4.A. SITE DEFINITION

The presence of Tell es-Sweyhat, a 30–40 hectare site set within a marginal environment some distance away from the Euphrates River, requires some explanation, both in terms of the physical environment (see *Section 2: The Physical Environment*) and the settlement geography of the region. A specific objective of the Sweyhat Survey was to establish how the site related to settlement patterns that preceded and followed it, to determine the size of contemporaneous settlements in order to place Tell es-Sweyhat within a coherent settlement hierarchy, and to compare the site and its subsistence base with that of other sites on the plain.

The surveyed area comprised the surrounding terrace plain, up to and including the Euphrates bluffs to the west and the fringing plateau scarp to the east (fig. 3.1). Before describing off-site features, it is necessary to outline the problem of site definition and to describe how occupation sites were recognized in the field. This was not simply a pedant's pilgrimage, but a necessary exercise because the closer one looked, the more archaeology became evident. Nevertheless, although there were some "gray" areas, it was eventually possible to distinguish what must have been sedentary occupation sites from non-habitation features related to other activities. The following is a summary of the main criteria for site definition and off-site sherd scatter; off-site features are described in *Section 5: The Archaeological Landscape II* in the order: wine presses, quarries, tombs, and linear hollows.

In terms of site morphology, the following classes of sites could be recognized (detailed descriptions of the Sweyhat Survey sites are provided in *Appendix A: Sweyhat Survey Site Catalog*). It should be emphasized that this rather arbitrary classification attempts to subdivide what is essentially a continuum of site forms:[41]

Tells

> The tells are the typical prominent mounds recorded by every Middle Eastern archaeological survey. With the exception of Tell es-Sweyhat, which is surrounded by a lower town, all are rather small (ca. 1 ha) and high, usually from 5 to 10 m in height. Their steep sides probably result from their being surrounded by enclosure walls. The tells in the area of Tell es-Sweyhat exhibit multi-period occupations with a significant Early Bronze Age component. Tells so classified are Tell es-Sweyhat, Tell Jouweif (SS 8), Tell Ali al-Haj (SS 17), and Tell Othman (SS 20A).

Low Tells

> In the Sweyhat area the low tells were about 1 ha in area and quite prominent, usually being from 2 to 3 m in height. All were Early Bronze Age (mainly early Early Bronze Age). Low tells include SS 2, Tell Hajji Ibrahim (SS 3), and SS 9.

Other Low Mounds

> Other low mounds were usually small mounds (<2 ha) with a low, rounded profile, of various dates: Early Bronze Age, Iron Age, and Hellenistic. Exceptionally Khirbet Aboud al-Hazu (SS 6) showed evidence of architecture in the form of an enclosure wall. Other low mounds include Nafileh Village (SS 5), Khirbet Aboud al-Hazu, Khirbet al-Hamrah 2 (SS 15), SS 20B, SS 21, Shams ed-Din Southern Site and Cemeteries (SS 22), and SS 26.

Low Late Sites with Traces of Walls and Buildings

> These comprise multiple low mounds with walls evident as lines of stones or linear mounds and courtyards within intervening depressions. Every site of this class was occupied during the past 2,000 years, and most were confined to a single period. Sites so classified include SS 4, Khirbet al-Hamrah (SS 7), Khirbet Haj Hassan (SS 10), Khirbet Dhiman (SS 11), SS 12, and Shajara Saghira (SS 29).

---

41. Numbers for sites of the Sweyhat Survey are designated SS 1 and so on, to distinguish them from the Tabqa survey sites of van Loon (up to T 556) and Wilkinson (T 557 and above); see also footnote 2.

Flat Sites

Flat sites have no discernible relief, but have sufficient occupation debris to warrant their being classified as habitation sites (in contrast to the ambiguous "other sites"). These sites include Ramalah (SS 16B), SS 23, SS 24, SS 25, SS 28, and SS 30.

Hilltop or Blufftop Sites

Located on eroded bluffs or hilltops, these sites are usually defined on two or three sides by deeply dissected wadis and are to be distinguished from sites such as Ramalah (SS 16B) that simply occupied the edge of plateaus or high terraces. These sites include SS 14, Mishrifat (SS 16A), and SS 27.

Other Habitation Sites

These miscellaneous sites are poorly defined on the ground and small; they include SS 13, Dahrat er-Ramile (SS 18), and Khirbet Aboud al-Hazu 2 (SS 19).

Field Scatters

Scatters of sherds dispersed over large areas of terrain, but without any traces of former sedentary occupation, are referred to as field scatters.

In addition to surface mounding, archaeological sites could be distinguished by their surface scatter of large limestone fragments, which by reference to the excavations at Tell es-Sweyhat appeared to be mainly derived from wall foundations. Such scatters were restricted in area and were predominantly confined to areas of archaeological mounding. In common with many areas of the Middle East, occupation sites were also distinguishable by their slightly grayer color, in contrast to the redder hue of the natural soils. Artifact scatters when devoid of other indicators of sedentary occupation (foundation stones, door sockets, and so on) presented a considerable dilemma by forming a virtually continuous spread across the entire plain. Initially during the first field season in 1974, such scatters were mistaken for true sedentary habitation sites, but later in the season as they proved to be more and more extensive, they became less plausible as "sites" per se, and steps were taken to describe and interpret them. Here, field scatters are considered before other off-site features, settlement distribution being treated in *Section 6.A: Pottery of the Chalcolithic to Late Roman Periods.*

Taken together the sites and off-site features provide a much more complete view of the ancient landscape than sites alone. Unfortunately, because off-site landscape features are difficult to date, it is not possible to break the landscape down into straightforward archaeological phases. In terms of function, however, the archaeological record can be subdivided as follows:

Sedentary Habitation

Mainly sedentary, represented by all thirty Sweyhat Survey sites (SS 1–30; Chalcolithic and later)

Transitory Habitation

Traces of possible nomadic encampments such as at SS 14. More sites of this type on the high steppe east of Sweyhat have been investigated by Michael Danti (1997)

Transport

As indicated by the described linear hollows (probably Early Bronze Age and later)

Land Use and Economy

As inferred from wine presses (Hellenistic, Roman, and Byzantine) and by off-site sherd scatters (Bronze Age, Hellenistic, Roman, Byzantine, and Early Islamic; see *Section 5: The Archaeological Landscape II*)

Economy and Building Materials

As inferred from the presence of quarries (mainly Hellenistic, Roman, and Byzantine)

Cemeteries

These are common and complement the record from the archaeological sites themselves (Early Bronze Age and later)

4.B. OFF-SITE SHERD SCATTERS

During preliminary fieldwork in 1974 it quickly became evident that the plain between archaeological sites was strewn with a low density, but ever-present scatter of sherds, and less commonly figurine fragments, flints, and small fragments of basalt querns. Although superficially resembling a low density artifact scatter of conventional archaeological sites, when traced in the field, rather than having a definable limit, the scatters simply appeared to spread virtually *ad infinitum*. Such "field scatters" are by no means unusual and since the original fieldwork was published (Holland 1976, appendix) they have shown up in Greece, Iran, Iraq, Oman, Turkey, and Britain.[42] In order to describe and interpret these scatters and to determine if they included any in situ habitation sites, a sample program was devised as follows.

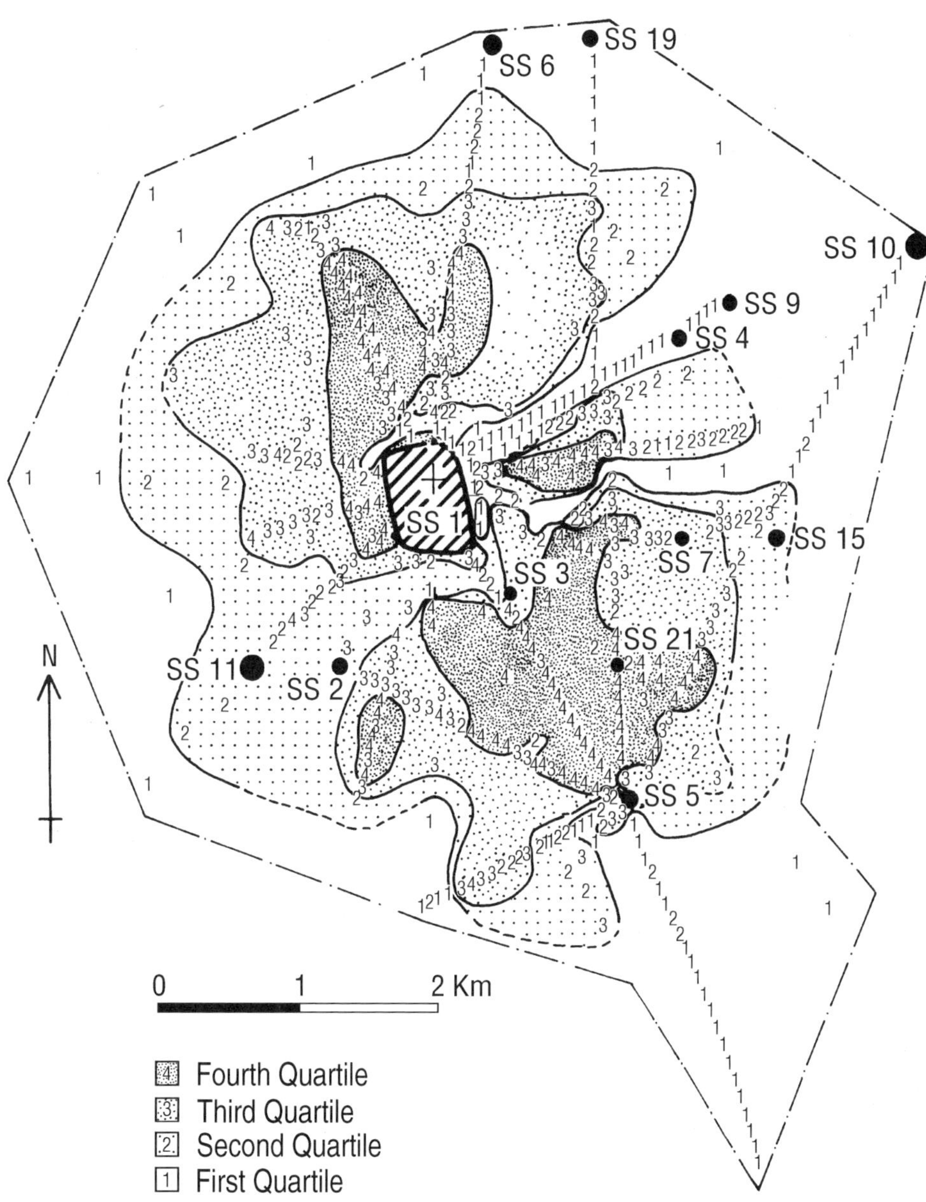

Figure 4.1. Distribution of Sherds on the Surface of Fields around Tell es-Sweyhat.
Data Derived from Off-site Sample Squares and Tally Counts

42. Wilkinson 1989; Bintliff and Snodgrass 1988; Gallant 1986;
Wilkinson 1982. For extended discussion, see Alcock, Cherry,
and Davis 1994; Wilkinson 1994, with commentaries.

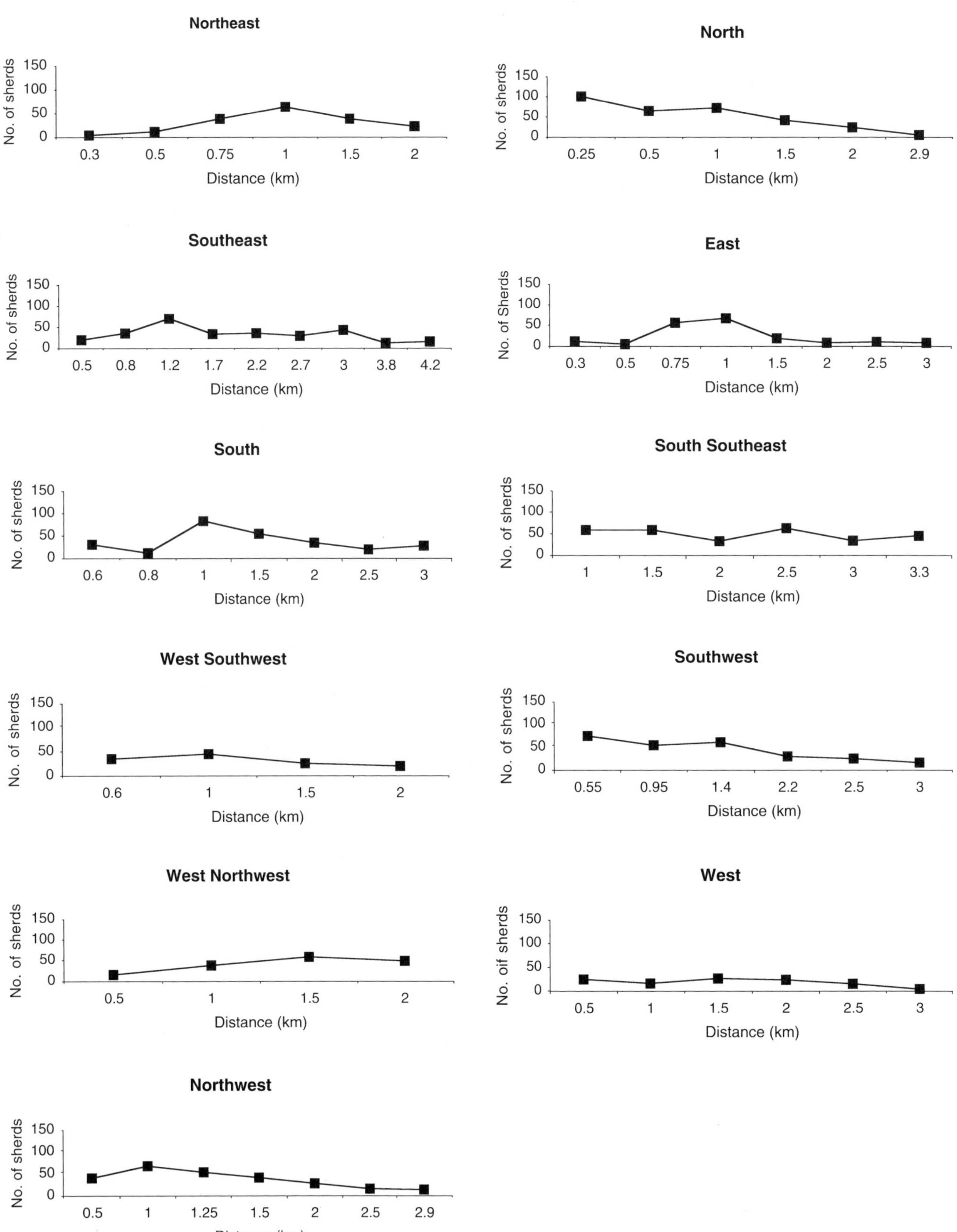

Figure 4.2. Sherd Density Graphs (in Terms of Number of Sherds per 100 sq. m) for Radial Transects around Tell es-Sweyhat Sampled during the 1974 Field Season. Note Horizontal Scale Varies

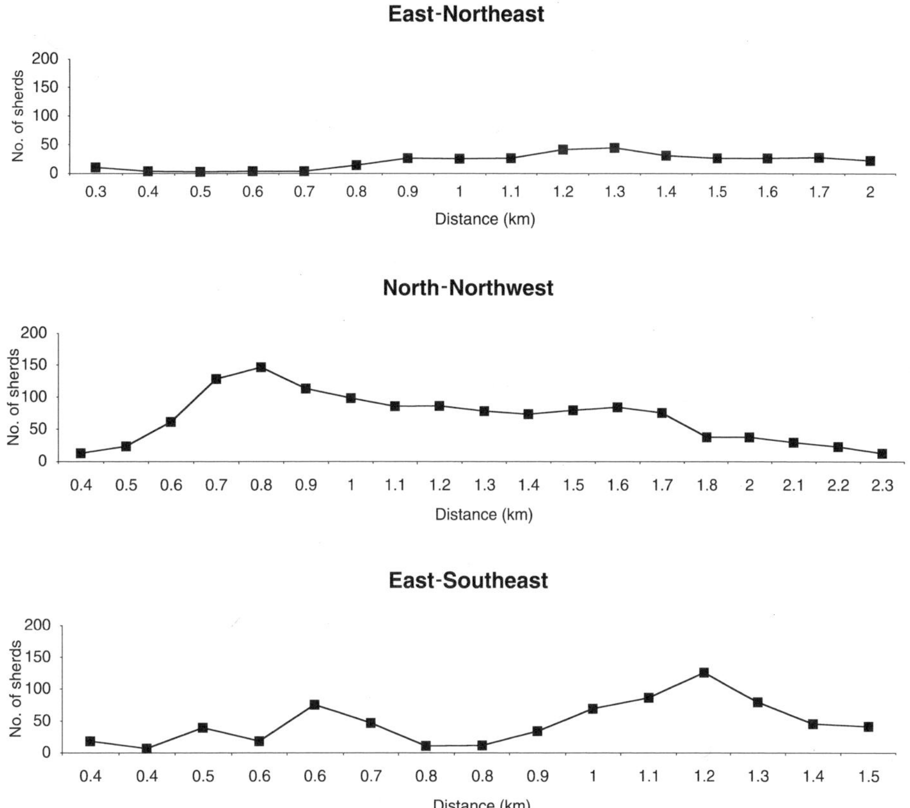

Figure 4.2. Sherd Density Graphs (in Terms of Number of Sherds per 100 sq. m) for Radial Transects around Tell es-Sweyhat Sampled during the 1974 Field Season. For *East-Southeast,* the Distances 0.4, 0.6, and 0.8 Occur Twice, Once for a Collection by Tony J. Wilkinson and the Second for a Collection by Leon Marfoe. Note Horizontal Scale Varies (*cont.*)

4.C. OFF-SITE SAMPLING TECHNIQUES

In 1974, surface collection of artifacts entailed laying out 10×10 m sample squares across the modern fields at intervals of initially 500 m, then later along selected alignments at 100 m intervals (figs. 4.1–2). Sample squares were positioned by pacing either from the main tell at Sweyhat or from its outer wall, along transects laid out radially by means of a prismatic (i.e., surveying) compass. The continuity of scatters between sample squares was noted, but no attempt was made at this time to record the sherd counts quantitatively between squares. Sampling appeared to be sufficiently accurate to describe the basic distribution of scatters. Within sample squares all sherds and other artifacts were collected, and after counting, body sherds were discarded at the point of collection, rims, bases, decorated sherds, handles, and other diagnostic features being taken back to the dig house for washing, marking, and later identification (see below). In 1991 a similar procedure was adopted for a smaller number of sample squares, primarily in order to check the 1974 results, but also to determine how ground conditions (plowing, fallowing, and other land use factors) affected sherd counts. Ideally we would have both weighed and counted all sherds in the field, but because there is a high correlation between the number of sherds and the overall weight (fig. 4.3), it was considered more practical in the field to use counts only.

Because surface collection was time consuming (about fifteen minutes per square) a more streamlined technique was introduced during the 1991 season. A tally counter was employed to click the number of observed sherds along a given alignment. At the same time, the number of paces walked were counted and the tally of sherds noted every 100 m. The technique (originally suggested by Warwick Ball for the Jazirah in Iraq), although less accurate than the sample square method and lacking the capability of providing diagnostic sherds, had the virtue of enabling large areas to be assessed in a short time as well as providing a more fine-grained pattern of sherd density.

Altogether, off-site recording techniques sampled 125 squares in 1974 and 33 in 1991. Furthermore, 392 tally count estimates were made in 1991 and 23 in 1992.

In order to determine the effect of land use on sherd counts, in 1991 paired sample squares were placed on contiguous parcels of plowed and unplowed as well as unplowed and fallowed land with the following results (table 4.1, fig. 4.4):

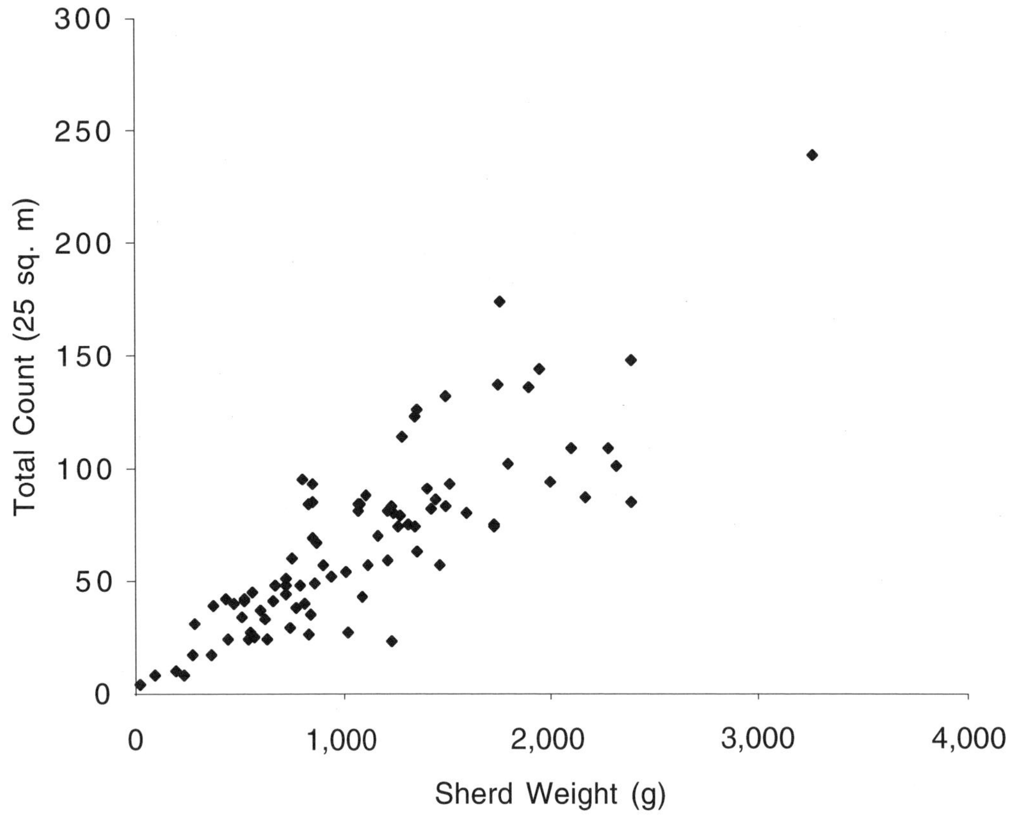

Figure 4.3. Scatter Diagram Showing Correlation between Total Sherd Count and Sherd Weight for
Tell es-Sweyhat Lower Town Survey. Data Collected by Lee Horne

Table 4.1. Sherd Densities from Fallow Land in 1991, Land Harvested in 1991, and Land Recently Plowed in 1991

Location (Square No.)	*Collection Condition*	*Number of Sherds*	*Mean*
Square 15. Near SS 21	Fallow 1991	100	
Square 17. Near SS 21	Fallow 1991	71	86
Square 16. Near SS 21	Harvested 1991*	68	
Square 18. Near SS 21	Harvested 1991*	78	73
Square 28. 400 m from Tell es-Sweyhat**	Harvested 1991	36	
Square 30. 600 m from Tell es-Sweyhat**	Harvested 1991	52	
Square 32. 800 m from Tell es-Sweyhat**	Harvested 1991	49	46
Square 29. 400 m from Tell es-Sweyhat**	Recently plowed 1991	29	
Square 31. 600 m from Tell es-Sweyhat**	Recently plowed 1991	43	
Square 33. 800 m from Tell es-Sweyhat**	Recently plowed 1991	28	33

*Plowed in 1990 and harvested in June/July 1991

**North of the northern outer wall of the Tell es-Sweyhat lower town

Although qualitative observations suggest that fallowed land (i.e., land that had lain unplowed for about one year) produced higher sherd counts than land cropped and harvested during the same year, when sherd counts were taken from the two land use types the difference was not significant (table 4.1, fig. 4.4; although obviously more samples are required). Samples collected from recently plowed land, however, showed consistently lower sherd counts than adjacent harvested squares because after plowing, loose soil partly obscures sherds, which then become progressively exposed by the blowing away of dry soil and by washing action of rain. With time and further weathering, sherds, rather than being contained within the soil, emerge to eventually become pedestaled on the exposed ground surface. As a result of this weathering effect, sherd counts tended to be higher on unplowed land (and perhaps higher still on fallow) than on plowed land. In addition, surface straw or weeds can obscure sherds and therefore depress sherd counts. Consequently, areas that were heavily obscured were avoided for sampling. In order to determine whether differences in sherd densities were real or merely reflected land use at the time of sampling, notes on the most recent cultivation regime were taken. By laying out sample squares on unplowed or fallowed land, some level of consistency was achieved. Nevertheless, occasional negative anomalies apparent on the scatter map (fig. 4.1) may result from sample squares being set out on plowed fields.

Tally counts, being made while walking, are susceptible to the surveyor's perception of the ground surface. Where stones were abundant on the surface there was simply too much information for the brain (mine at least) to absorb while walking, and sherd counts were apparently underrepresented. Being recorded constantly, however, tally counts indicated more detailed fluctuations in sherd density, so that, for example, wadi areas susceptible to overbank sedimentation sometimes exhibited significant lows on the tally count transects (marked W in fig. 4.5; see also fig. 4.6).

The transects showed that surface sherd density in between demonstrable archaeological sites was remarkably continuous and significantly lower than scatter densities recorded within the walls of Tell es-Sweyhat. There, surface collection in 1989 by Lee Horne employed 25 sq. m circular areas to give a roughly 1% sample coverage of the lower town. The ninety sample areas gave a mean count per area of 67 sherds, equivalent to 268 sherds per 100 sq. m; that is

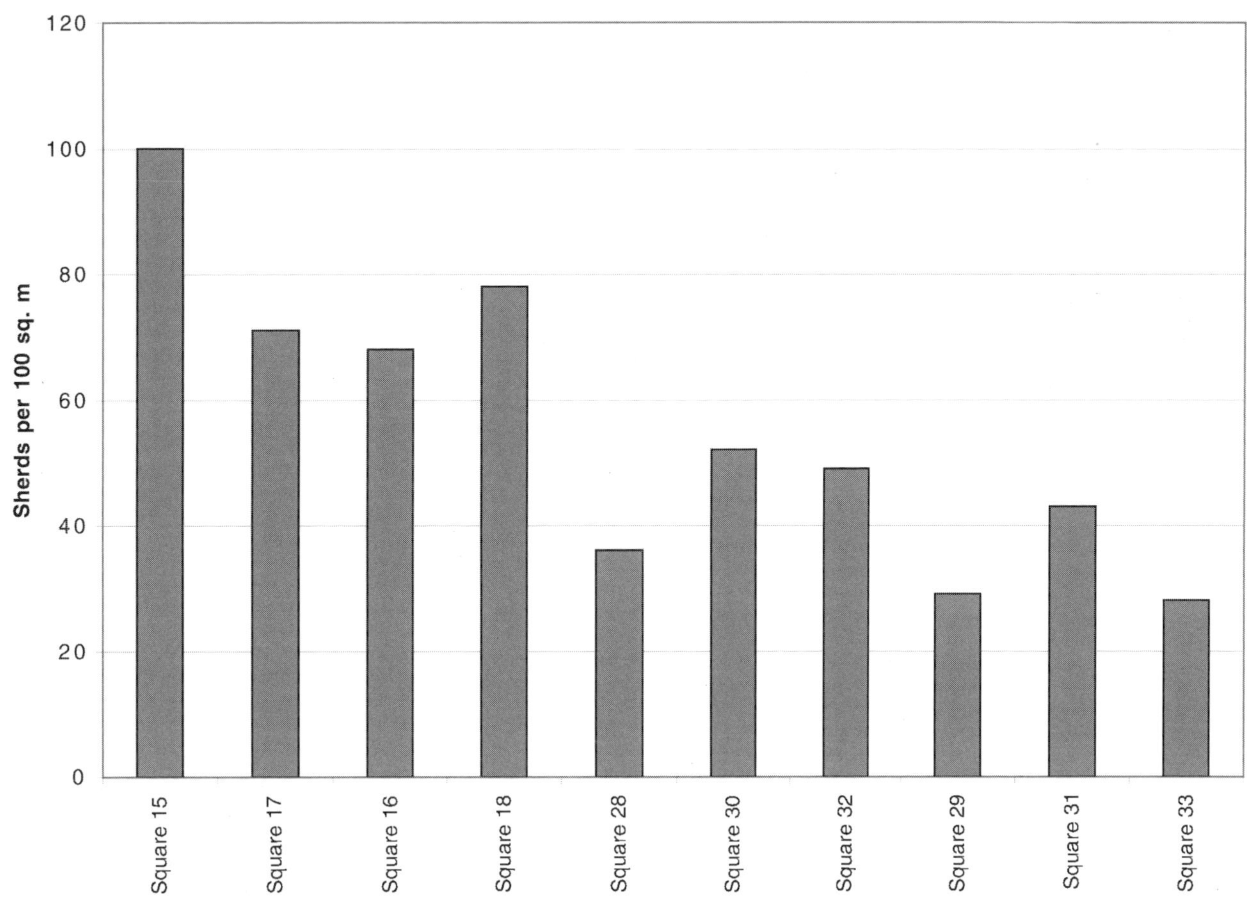

Figure 4.4. Sherd Densities on Different Types of Land Use — Fallow (Squares 15 and 17), Harvested (Squares 16*, 18*, 28, 30, and 32), and Recently Plowed (Squares 29, 31, and 33) — as Recorded in 1991. See Table 4.1 for Details

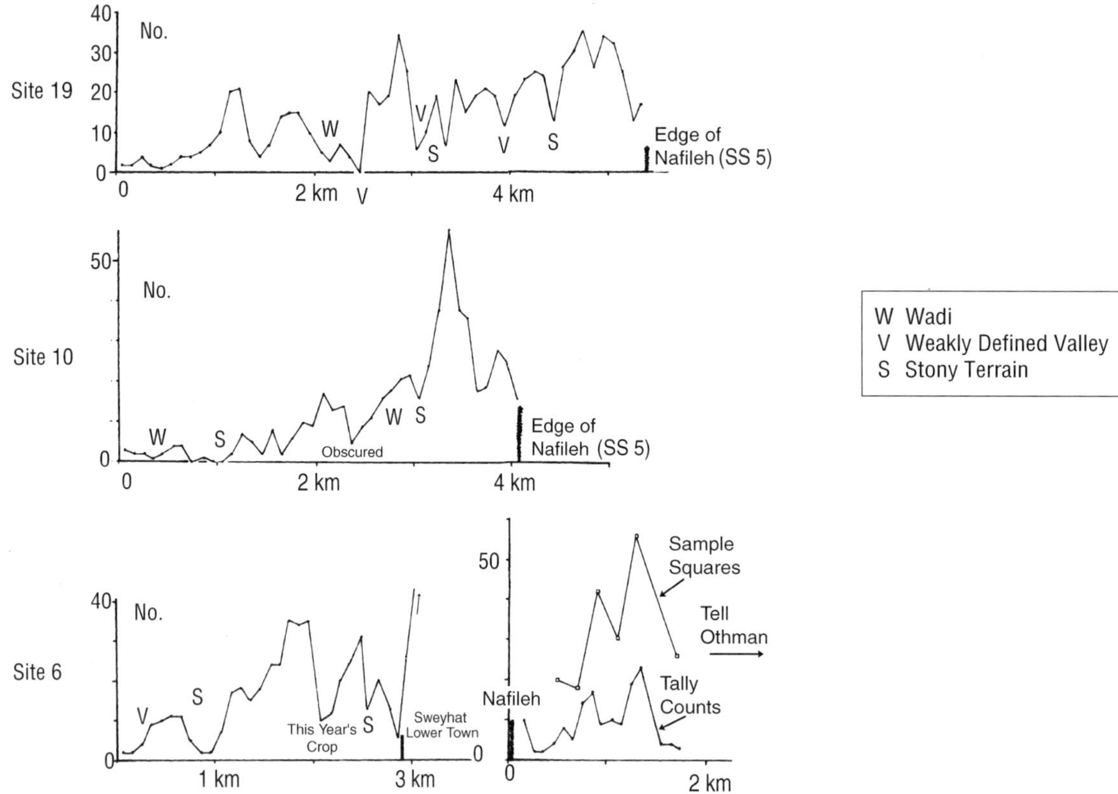

Figure 4.5. Tally Count Transects in Vicinity of Tell es-Sweyhat, 1991. Top: Khirbet Aboud al-Hazu 2 (SS 19) to Nafileh Village (SS 5); Center: Khirbet Haj Hassan (SS 10) to Nafileh (SS 5); Bottom Left: Khirbet Aboud al-Hazu (SS 6) to Tell es-Sweyhat Lower Town; Bottom Right: Tell Othman (SS 20A) to Nafileh Village (SS 5). For Transect Locations, See Figure 4.1

roughly seven times the mean density of field scatters (table 4.2).[43] Although minor sites, when walked over with a tally counter, registered higher sherd densities than field scatters, these densities were not nearly as high as those recorded at Tell es-Sweyhat. The distinctions between lower town sherd densities, off-site densities, and those from tally counts (both on- and off-site) are indicated in figure 4.7.

Table 4.2. Basic Statistics for On-site and Off-site Sherd Scatters

Type of Scatter	Number of Samples	Mean*	Standard Deviation	Minimum	Maximum
Sweyhat On-site Scatter [44]	90	268.0	162.0	16	956
Lower Town South [45]	42	134.0	—	4	324
Off-site Field Scatter	159	39.3	27.6	0	146

*Expressed in terms of sherds per 100 sq. m

Off-site scatters were consistent in entirely lacking any of the characteristics of archaeological sites: traces of mounding, plowed-out foundation stones, or grayish-hued soils were absent. Neither were marked concentrations of

43. I am grateful to Richard Zettler for providing this information; see also Zettler 1997: 35–37. An additional forty-two circles were placed in the lower town south, that is, in the area immediately south of the south enclosure wall, which showed that arti-

fact scatters in the area were much less than on the remainder of the lower town within the wall.

44. Zettler 1997: 35–37.

45. Zettler 1997: 35–37.

artifacts visible as might be expected from transient nomadic occupation (Cribb 1991: 176–80). Furthermore, excavation of Trenches S6 and S5 (figs. 2.8, 5.1; north and west of the outer town, respectively; see *Appendix C: Selected Soil and Sediment Descriptions: Sections 5* and *6*) demonstrated that sherds were distributed throughout the plow soil and that the soil was devoid of any evidence of in situ occupation. Upon excavation, sherd densities proved much higher than appeared from surface scatters because pottery was distributed throughout the plow soil (fig. 2.10, table 4.3).

Table 4.3. Excavated Sherd Counts from Two Trenches (S6 and S5; each 1.5 × 1.0 m; see *Appendix C: Selected Soil and Sediment Descriptions* for descriptions), Tabulated According to Sherds per sq. m and per 10 × 10 m Square Equivalent, Compared with Collected Surface Values from Adjacent 10 × 10 m Sample Squares

Trench Number	Surface Density per 100 sq. m	Sherd Density per 1 sq. m of soil	Equivalent per 100 sq. m	Difference between Surface and Subsurface Density
S6	72	20.66	2,066	×28
S5	46	11.33	1,133	×24

Because insufficient sample squares were collected in 1974 to provide a reliable sherd distribution map, it was necessary to combine both sample square and tally count data to create a composite sherd density map. This appeared feasible because of the good correlation (correlation coefficient of +0.75) between counts from sample squares and tally counts made across the same terrain (fig. 4.8). More subjectively, this correlation was supported by sherd density plots,

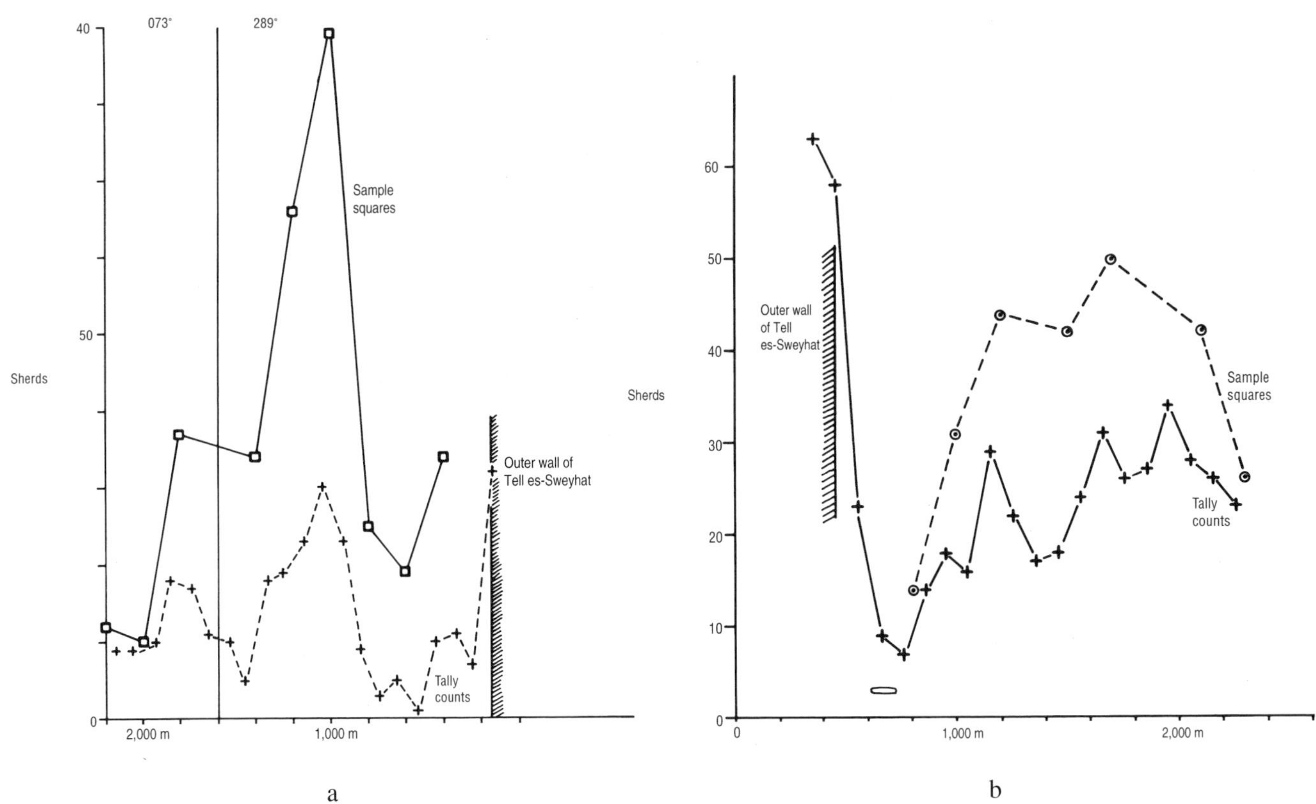

Figure 4.6. (*a–b*) Transects Made in 1991 and 1992 Showing Tally Counts and Sherd Scatter Densities along Transects away from Tell es-Sweyhat

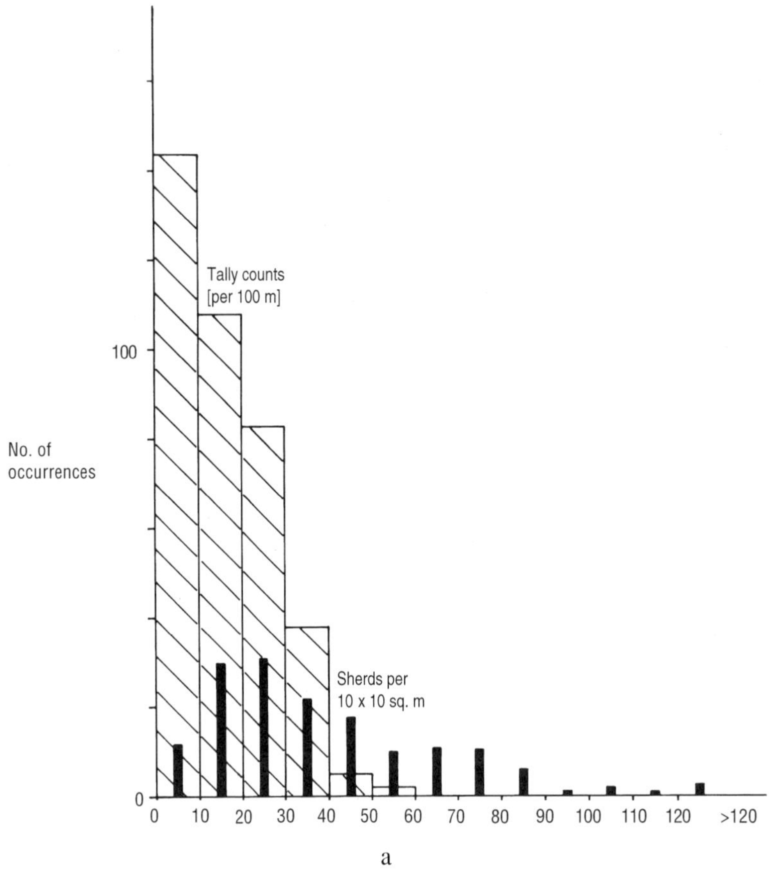

Tell es-Sweyhat

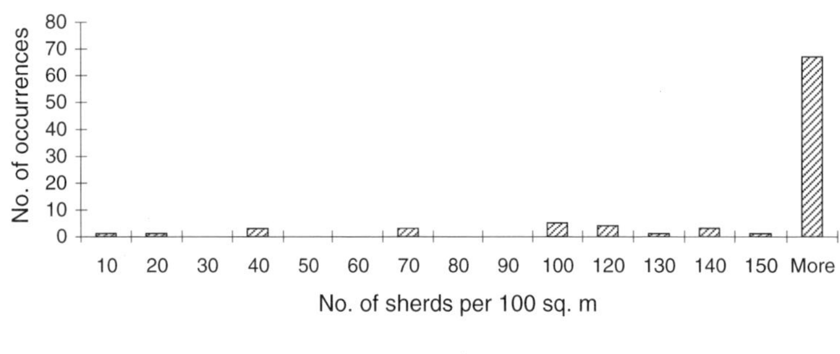

Tell es-Sweyhat

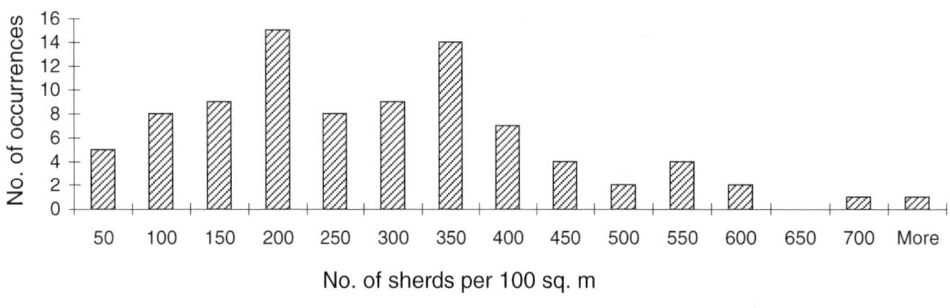

Figure 4.7. (*a*) Sherd Counts from Off-site 10×10 m Sample Squares (solid columns), from Tally-count Transects (open columns); (*b*–*c*) Sherd Counts from the Lower Town Survey of Lee Horne. Note that (*b*) and (*c*) Represent the Same Data Set but Are Plotted at Different Scales to Facilitate Comparison with (*a*)

which indicate a reasonable consistency between the two data sets (figs. 4.5–6). In order to "merge" the data from sample squares and tally counts, each data set was statistically ordered into their respective quartile ranges as follows:

Sample Squares (median = 33)	*Tally Counts (median = 14)*
Fourth quartile: 56–146	Fourth quartile: 24–58
Third quartile: 34–55	Third quartile: 15–23
Second quartile: 20–33	Second quartile: 7–14
First quartile: 0–19	First quartile: 0–6

The resultant map indicates sherd densities according to their first, second, third, and fourth quartile ranges, from which quartile contours have been interpolated as indicated in figure 4.1. This map provided a dense distribution of data points in which high sample square sherd densities corresponded to high tally counts and vice versa. This provides a more reliable distribution than that originally produced (Holland 1976, appendix; Wilkinson 1982, fig. 6), and one that differs from the original in a number of ways as follows.

4.D. OFF-SITE SHERD DISTRIBUTION

When sample squares are placed along radial transects they become more widely spaced with distance, so that this configuration is not ideal for providing a regular sample framework (e.g., interpolating contours). Nevertheless, the mapped distribution does allow the following general statements to be made about the distribution. Beyond a zone of low or uneven scatters adjacent to the outer walls, sherd scatter densities increase to a maximum between 1 and 2 km

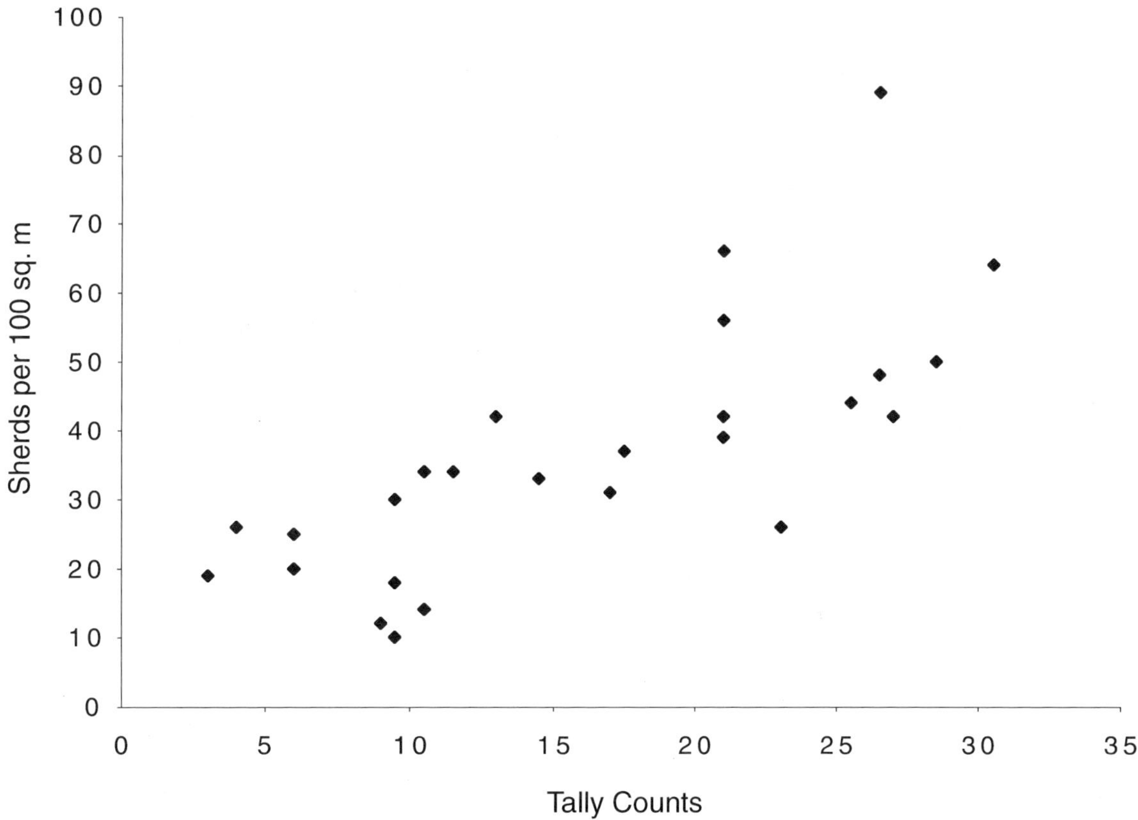

Figure 4.8. Scatter Diagram Showing Correlation between Field Scatter Sample Squares (Vertical Axis) and Tally Counts (Horizontal Axis) at Tell es-Sweyhat

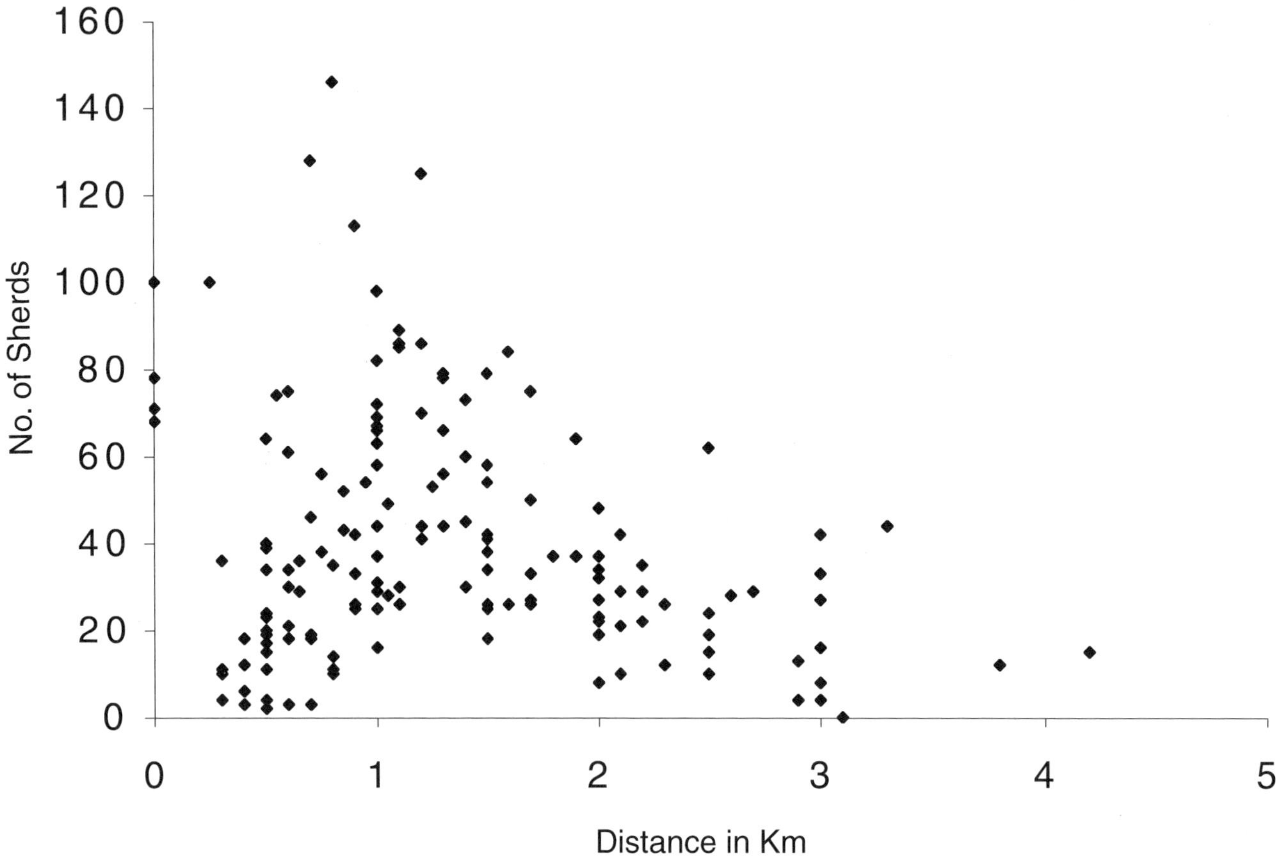

Figure 4.9. Scatter Plot Showing All Sherd Scatter Densities from Sample Squares around Tell es-Sweyhat. Vertical Axis,
Sherd Density per 100 sq. m; Horizontal Axis, Distance in Kilometers from Tell es-Sweyhat

from the main tell. Beyond 2.5 km, sherd density drops significantly, and beyond 3 km, although sherds are still
present they fall within the lowest quartile range (0–19 sherds per 100 sq. m). This pattern is evident both on the scatter map (fig. 4.1) and the scatter plot (fig. 4.9).

Maximum sherd densities (56–146 sherds per 100 sq. m) occupy a north-northwest–south-southeast axis, which is
partly accentuated by the presence of the late Early Bronze Age settlement of Nafileh Village (SS 5) and areas of low
sherd density to the west and southeast of Tell es-Sweyhat.

Areas of low sherd density fall into two classes: (1) Those that occur beyond 2.5 km from the tell, and which appear to represent a general decline in the overall density of surface sherds with distance from the site; and (2) those
near the outer walls of Tell es-Sweyhat or which occur along linear bands. The second class appears to correspond to
patterns of sedimentation along wadis and is best exemplified by the linear negative anomaly that extends between Tell
es-Sweyhat (SS 1) and SS 4 and 9 to the northeast. This feature was already recognized in 1974 when a Trench (S4)
was excavated some 150 m to the east of the eastern wall of Tell es-Sweyhat. The soil profile was as follows (fig.
2.10):

1.   0–30 cm: Light yellowish brown loam with weak subangular blocky structure, breaking to single grains. Plow soil

2.   30–72 cm: Brownish yellow loam with moderate subangular blocky structure. Occasional weak calcium carbonate soft
     concretions. Rare small stones; occasional biopores. Boundary at ca. 72 cm clear during excavation. Soil B horizon

3.   72–95 cm: Lenses of reddish yellow loam and white chalky silt with well-developed platy structure. Episode of low
     energy sedimentation

4.   95–135 cm: Reddish yellow sandy loam with fine subangular blocky structure and common gravel-size calcium car-
     bonate concretions varying from soft to hard. Occasional gravel. Buried soil B horizon

The pottery, which was collected in 20 cm spits, was virtually absent in the surface layers, but increased progressively through eleven sherds (50–70 cm; lower layer 2) to a maximum of fourteen sherds between 70 and 90 cm (layer
3, fig. 2.10). Sherds started to accumulate within the upper part of horizon 4 and increased progressively within the
silt-loam sedimentation that overlay it. Layer 3 is a moderately low energy water-lain deposit, perhaps resulting from

overbank flow from a wadi. The overlying deposit (2), which also contained sherds, was deposited in a tranquil environment that resulted in progressive aggradation during which soil forming processes were dominant and pre-existing sedimentary structures (if they had existed) were destroyed. This episode probably relates to the period when the outer wall of Tell es-Sweyhat was constructed and partly blocked and diverted the wadi flow. In such a case, the sherd scatter started to accumulate approximately when the wall was built (i.e., allowing for the time of the sedimentation event to spread as far east as this soil pit) and continued for a short while after its construction. Although it is not entirely clear whether horizons 3 or 4 were associated with ancient cultivation, Trench S4 does clearly demonstrate that low energy sedimentation has covered the sherd scatter. That this sherd horizon accumulated in the distant past can be inferred from the contained calcium carbonate accumulations in horizon 2. Although these carbonates have not been independently dated, even weak accumulations require at least 1,000 to 2,600 years to form (Birkeland 1974: 169, 271), therefore the underlying layers 3 and 4 are probably more than 1,000 to 2,600 years old.[46]

Other negative anomalies, less well defined, can be seen to the north of Khirbet al-Hamrah (SS 7), and to the north, east, and south of the town walls of Tell es-Sweyhat as follows:

1. Excavation of Trench S3 demonstrated that the increase in cultural material with depth could be related to occupation along the town wall (see *Section 2.B.3.2: The Central Wadi*), which was then covered by sedimentation that accumulated behind the wall and formed a spread upstream

2. The sparse scatters in the southwestern sector similarly may be related to aggradation along wadis (e.g., to the east of the central wadi; see *Section 2.B.3.2: The Central Wadi*)

3. An abrupt drop-off 1.2 km to the west of the lower town may have been caused by an accumulation of fine sediment that appears on aerial photographs as a pale amorphous image

Abrupt positive anomalies, attributable to human occupation, are less apparent and are limited to a peak recorded by tally counts in an area to the northwest of Tell es-Sweyhat. This area represents a probable site (SS 13), which included other distinguishing features such as large limestone fragments perhaps derived from wall foundations and a deeply hollowed limestone mortar or door socket.

A second anomaly lay immediately outside the southern wall of the lower town in an area originally recognized by Donald Whitcomb as a possible enclosure. This area, which was systematically surveyed by Michael Danti in 1991, exhibited sherd scatter densities intermediate between those of the surrounding field scatters and the lower town (table 4.2). Apart from a weak crop mark evident on the aerial photographs and a cluster of large limestone rocks within the sampled area, evidence for habitation was ambiguous. Nevertheless, excavation by Michael Danti in Operation 19B revealed the fragmentary footings of a 1.5 m wide stone wall, thereby potentially extending the area of the site to the south of the southern enclosure wall up to a maximum size of perhaps 40 ha (Zettler 1997: 51).

The decline in sherd scatter density with distance from Tell es-Sweyhat, although subject to wide fluctuations, registered a negative correlation of -0.237 with distance. The correlation is weak owing to the numerous low readings near the tell, but when readings that appear to result from sedimentation along wadis were removed, the correlation became significant at -0.68 (linear) and -0.72 (log-normal). However, because of the questionable practice of selectively removing low readings, no attempt has been made at additional regression analysis.

4.E. THE DATES OF THE OFF-SITE SHERD SCATTERS

Typological dating of the contained diagnostic sherds requires the assumption that the scatters accumulated shortly after the original pots were in use. If, however, the sherds had arrived on the fields at a considerably later date as a result of, for example, the fields being fertilized with nutrient-rich soils dug from the mound, the typological date would be too early. This problem is considered below.

The battered condition of the sherds, which implied a considerable residence time within the soil, also served as an impediment to dating. Of the 272 diagnostics collected in 1974, only 155 could be identified with any confidence. Where the sherds can be dated typologically, most appeared to be of Early Bronze Age date. Examination by Holland in 1975 and drawings of the 1992 collection (figs. 4.10–11) indicate that 84% of the datable sherds were Early Bronze Age in date. (Note that additional rim sherds from the 1974 season were drawn but these were mainly too small and

---

46. No Hellenistic or later sherds were recorded from these buried
    layers.

battered to be published.) These diagnostic sherds predominantly belonged to the later part of the period, which was contemporaneous with the Area IV buildings and the maximum extent of the lower town. In contrast, only 15% of the datable sherds were Hellenistic, Roman, or Early Islamic. These were usually more recognizable than the battered Early Bronze Age plain simple wares and included strap handles, glazed sherds, as well as one sherd of brittle ware.

According to figure 4.12, Early Bronze Age sherds tend to cluster around Tell es-Sweyhat, being especially common within the dense scatter to the north and northwest, but somewhat sparser to the south and east. Later sherds, on the other hand, are more common to the southwest and southeast, particularly within 1 km of the major Early Islamic sites of Khirbet Dhiman (SS 11) and al-Hamrah (SS 7) (fig. 4.13; table 4.4).

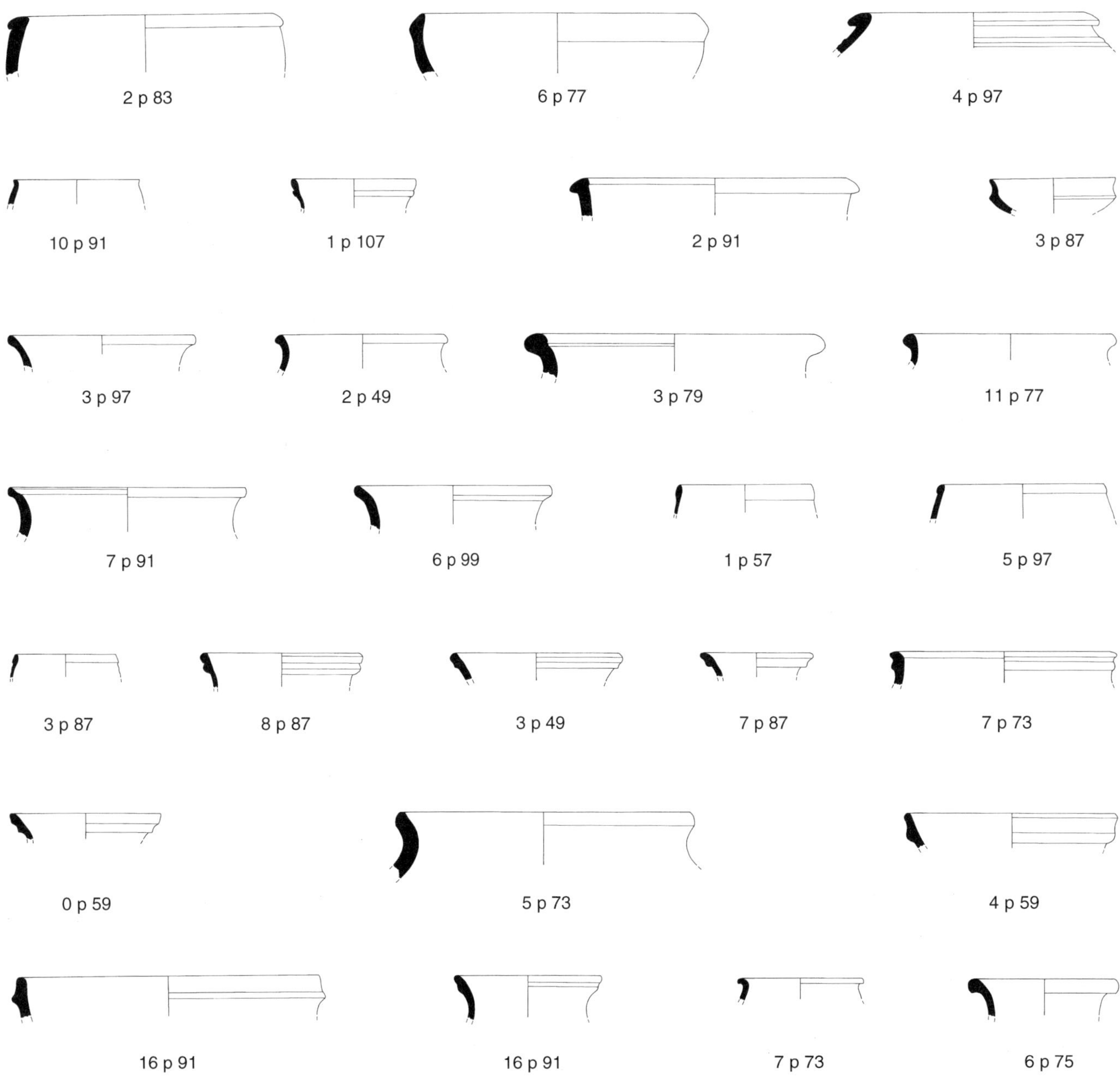

Figure 4.10. Some Diagnostic Sherds from the 1974 Field Scatter Collections by Thomas Holland around Tell es-Sweyhat. Scale 1:10

Table 4.4. Counts of Early Bronze Age and Post-Hellenistic Diagnostics from Field Scatters

Date	Total Diagnostics	Percentage within Islamic Circle*	Percentage within EBA Circle	Percentage of Total Diagnostics
Early Bronze Age	141	19%	35%	87%
Hellenistic to Early Islamic**	21	57%	10%	13%

*That is, from within 1 km radius of Khirbet Dhiman (SS 11) or Khirbet al-Hamrah (SS 7)

**Mainly Hellenistic to Early Islamic handles and glazed wares

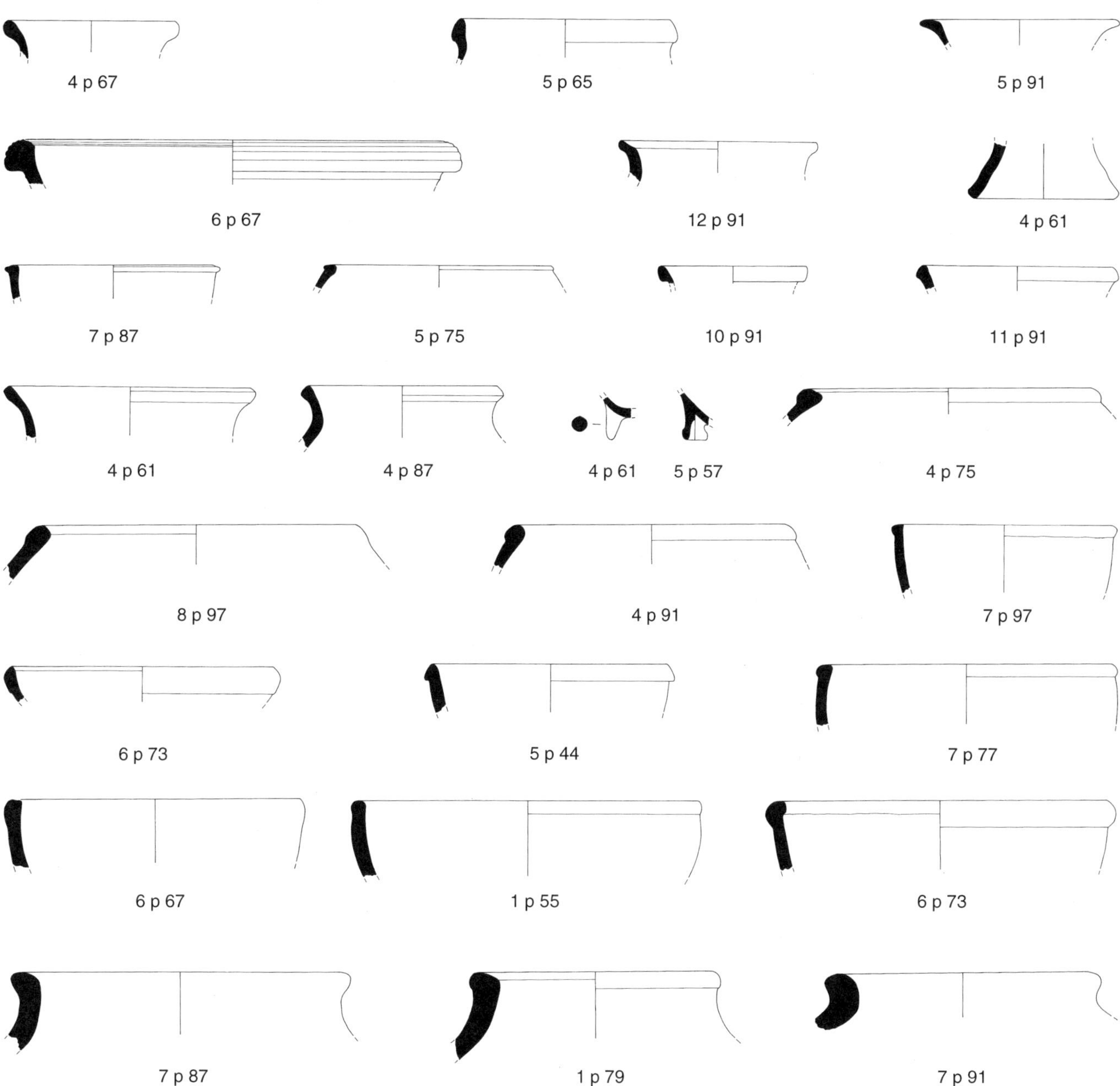

Figure 4.11. Some Diagnostic Sherds from the 1974 Field Scatter Collections by Thomas Holland around Tell es-Sweyhat (*cont.*). Scale 1:10

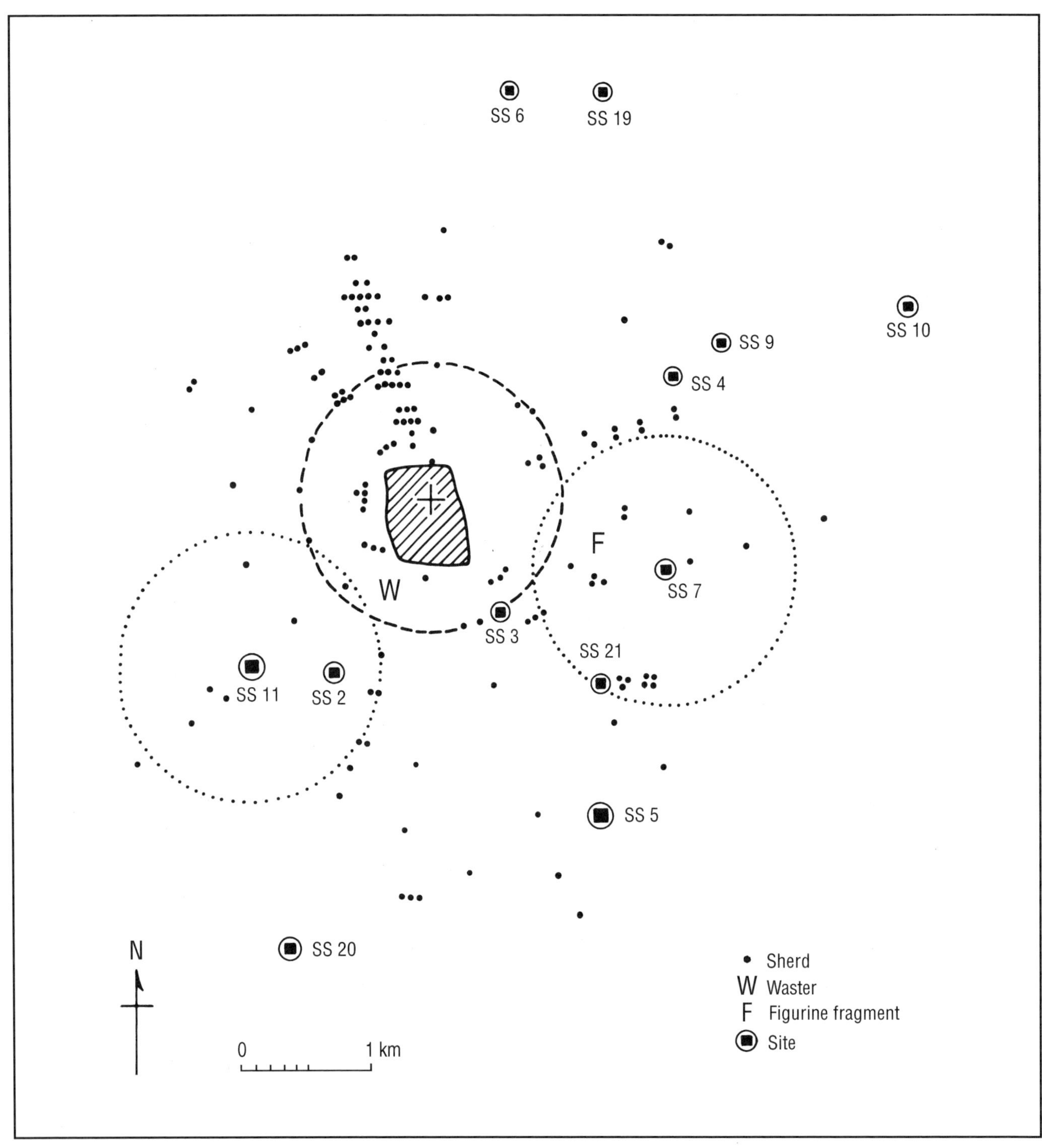

Figure 4.12. Distribution of Probable Early Bronze Age Diagnostic Sherds around Tell es-Sweyhat

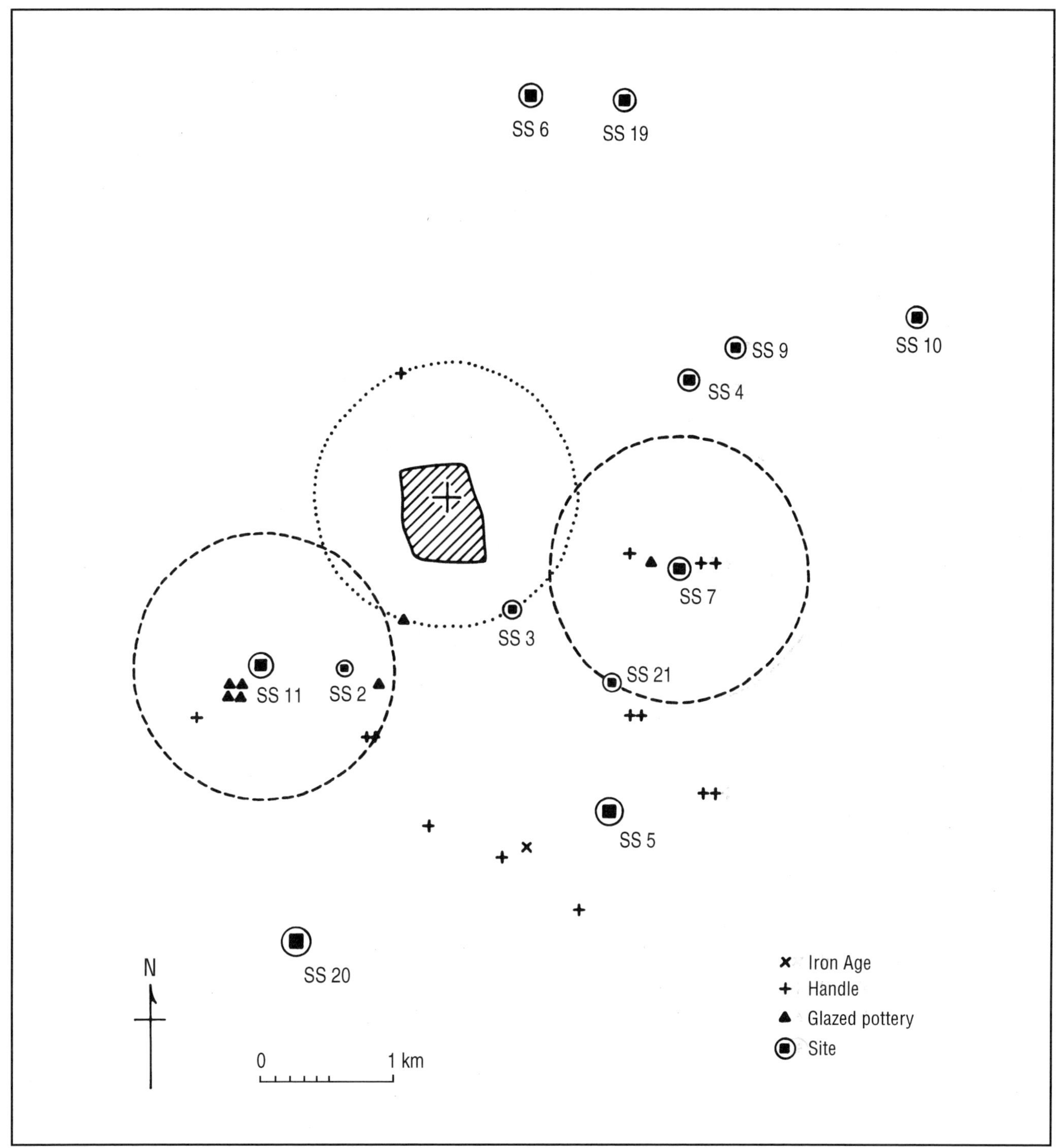

Figure 4.13. Distribution of Probable Hellenistic, Roman, Byzantine, and Early Islamic Diagnostic Sherds around Tell es-Sweyhat

4.F. DISCUSSION AND CONCLUSION

The off-site sampling program demonstrated that sherd scatters, although covering most of the plain, decrease significantly in density beyond 2.5 km from Tell es-Sweyhat. In places, the scatter has been buried by localized sedimentation, either adjacent to wadis or behind certain major obstructions such as the outer wall of the lower town at Tell es-Sweyhat. The sherds have probably remained in the plow soil for many thousands of years, with most arriving during the Early Bronze Age, and a minority belonging to the Hellenistic to Early Islamic periods. Sherd scatters occur over the deeper, calcareous, and cultivable stone-free loams that surround Tell es-Sweyhat and are much less common on the undulating stony and more marginal soils to the north (i.e., beyond Khirbet Aboud al-Hazu [SS 6]), east (beyond SS 7 and 9), and southeast (beyond Nafileh Village [SS 5]). Although a sample program was not conducted around Tell Othman (SS 20A) owing to disturbance resulting from a new road, qualitative observation also confirmed the presence of field scatters around this site. Short tally count transects conducted approximately 1 km to the west and south of Tell Othman showed that scatter densities fell within the lower two quartiles of the density range and thereafter declined to negligible amounts on the surrounding rolling upland.

The field scatters are both sparser and more evenly distributed than those associated with occupation sites and therefore cannot satisfactorily be explained in terms of sedentary occupation. Also, soil sections indicate that the sherds occupy the agriculturally mixed parts of natural calcareous xerosol soil profiles and do not appear to have been associated with evidence of sedentary occupation. The scatters are therefore interpreted as resulting from fertilization practices in antiquity which resulted in organic refuse being collected from adjacent settlements and spread on fields to enhance yields. Sherds, occasional fragments of basalt, some flints, and even rare figurine fragments that were contained in the rubbish then remain in the soil as the undecayed component. Similar scatters of various dates have been recorded in many parts of the Middle East, on both former irrigated and dry-farmed lands in Iran, Oman, Iraq, elsewhere in Syria (Ur 2002), and Turkey (Wilkinson 1989, 1982), as well as in Greece (Bintliff and Snodgrass 1988) and Britain (Gaffney and Tingle 1985; Williamson 1984). The Sweyhat area scatters appear, at face value, to be predominantly of Early Bronze Age date, that is, similar to those around Tell al-Hawa in northern Iraq (Wilkinson and Tucker 1995) as well as around Hamoukar in northeast Syria (Ur 2002). In other areas, field scatters are of different dates. Around Titriş Höyük and Kurban Höyük in southern Turkey, although scatters include Bronze Age sherds, most sherds are of Late Roman/Early Byzantine date (Algaze, Misir, and Wilkinson 1992; Wilkinson 1990). Around the Amuq Plain (Turkey) and along the Balikh Valley (Syria), scatters are almost exclusively late in date, being Hellenistic/Parthian through to Early Islamic (Wilkinson 1998; Yener et al. 1996: 66). Although late sherds do occur in the Sweyhat scatters, they are in a minority and occur in a restricted area.

Off-site artifact scatters can also result from the recent spreading of soil dug from occupation sites for use as fertilizer; therefore, patterns such as those around Tell es-Sweyhat should be viewed critically. In addition, low-density sherd scatters are produced by the presence of lower or outer town areas, cemeteries, random pot drops, specialist types of sites, and pastoral encampments;[47] therefore, it is necessary to establish by soil pits whether subsoil structures exist or may have existed, and whether scatters are continuous and extensive. Lower towns, plowed-out sites, and cemeteries usually produce scatters rich in large, unabraded sherds, whereas around Tell es-Sweyhat small highly abraded sherds dominate. Both soil test pits and continuity sampling were undertaken around Tell es-Sweyhat, and although the presence of smaller sites between transects cannot be discounted, it is quite clear that a significant amount of or most of the artifact scatters on the Sweyhat Plain are likely to have been produced as a result of the process of fertilization.

Since the 1970s, off-site sherd scatters have been demonstrated to be present in many parts the Old World. In addition, cesspits or manure pits have been recorded in excavated town areas in the East Mediterranean region (Ault 1999; Schloen 1995), and these can plausibly be interpreted as the repositories of manure prior to its being spread on the fields. In recent years a new technique that measures certain chemicals[48] as biomarkers has been used to detect faecal deposition and manuring around archaeological sites. Enrichment of these biomarkers is increased significantly over background levels as a result of manuring, and in modern trials they can be enhanced compared with, for example, total phosphate concentrations (Bull et al. 1999; Evershed et al. 1997: 493). Not only do different animals result in the accumulation of different faecal biomarkers (Bull et al. 1999: 87), but an increased signal of 5β stanols can still be detectable some 120 years after the application of farmyard manure ceased. Furthermore, raised concentrations of

---

47. For critical review of the interpretation of off-site sherd scatters, see Alcock, Cherry, and Davis 1994.

48. Lipids such as 5β stanols.

biomarkers are evident in 4,000 year old soils of agricultural terraces of early to middle Minoan date on Crete (Bull, Evershed, and Betancourt 2001; Bull et al. 1999: 92–93).

If manuring is accepted for the interpretation of the field scatters around Tell es-Sweyhat, it follows that, other things being equal, the density of sherds should be proportional to the quantity of settlement-derived waste applied to the fields. The observed decrease in sherd density beyond 2.5 km may therefore reflect a decline in manure application with distance that would accord with principles of conservation of effort. Many studies have shown how inputs (including manure applications) to intensively cultivated land drop off rapidly with increasing distance from the settlement (reviewed in Chisholm 1979). For example, as the amount of time expended in traveling increases, the amount of time remaining for labor decreases, and this decrease can affect both the type of crop grown and the output of produce. The significance of town-derived manure to the pre-industrial agricultural economy is emphasized by Heinrich von Thünen who points out that buying town manure is most economical for those areas immediately adjacent to the town; and with increasing distance from it the advantage of buying and applying such waste declines until at a certain distance it ceases to be used (von Thünen 1966). Even where manure does not need to be purchased, similar factors operate and numerous examples can be quoted of rings of intensively cultivated and manured lands surrounding settlements in traditional communities.[49]

In addition to conservation of effort, distribution of manure is also influenced by increased fallowing intervals with distance from the settlement (Hillman 1973b: 220). Hence, by decreasing the number of years that a given field is under crop (and also manured), the number of potsherds would be less, thereby resulting in a decline in pottery density away from the settlement.

To summarize, the following points favor the hypothesis that most of the off-site sherds scattered around Tell es-Sweyhat result from manuring in antiquity rather than from in situ occupation:

a.　The sherds do not form scatters like those on conventional sites

b.　Sherds are highly abraded unlike the large more intact fragments characteristic of true habitation sites

c.　Remains of foundation stones, door sockets, and large quern stones characteristic of occupation sites are absent. In exceptional cases small sites (such as SS 13) were evident, but these were recognizable by virtue of specific features such as the aforementioned stones

In addition, two points suggest that the sherd scatters are not of recent date:

d.　The pottery is of considerable antiquity, with most contained sherds being Early Bronze Age and a minority being of the Hellenistic–Early Islamic periods

e.　In one extensive area to the east of the lower town the sherd scatter is buried beneath sediments of demonstrable antiquity (Trench S4)

Those lands that appear to have received the greatest quantity of settlement-derived manure in the Early Bronze Age were the deeper low gradient and less stony soils within 2.5 km of Tell es-Sweyhat. The zones of potential flooding along wadis, although probably also heavily manured, did not register high surface sherd densities because an overlying deposit resulting from overbank sedimentation had probably obscured the sherds. However, the common occurrence of sherds throughout the valley fills (see *Section 2.B.3: Tributary Wadis and Valley Fills*) implies that sherds have been common on the surface over most of the surrounding plains. The least intensively manured lands were the stony, slightly undulating soils 3 km beyond Tell es-Sweyhat to the southeast, east, and north. The dearth of sherd scatters on these soils does not, of course, mean that such soils were uncultivated, but rather that settlement-derived manure was not applied in significant quantities. Between the Middle Bronze Age and Hellenistic period, which corresponded to a time of sparse sedentary settlement on the Sweyhat Plain, evidence for settlement-derived manuring was sparse. Evidence for a moderate level of renewed activity during the Early Islamic period or slightly earlier occurs, however, in the southwestern sector, that is, around Khirbet Dhiman (SS 11), and to the southeast near Khirbet al-Hamrah (SS 7). Again, intensive cultivation appears to have been restricted to the deeper, less stony soils. The implications of the sherd scatters to the overall understanding of settlement land use systems is discussed in *Section 9: Tell es-Sweyhat in Its Regional Context*.

49.　Wilkinson (1989, 1982); see, for example, Mortimore 1998, fig.
　　3.1.

5. THE ARCHAEOLOGICAL LANDSCAPE II:
WINE PRESSES, QUARRIES, TOMBS, AND LINEAR HOLLOWS

Compared with highland areas of, for example, Palestine (Dar 1986) or Yemen (Gibson and Wilkinson 1995), where off-site features occur in abundance, in the area of Tell es-Sweyhat off-site features occur sporadically within the landscape. Consequently they only provide a hint of the range of activities that took place in antiquity. However, if interpreted with caution they can contribute significantly to our knowledge of both the ancient society and the economy, by providing evidence on, for example, grape processing (now entirely absent), organized quarrying (now *ad hoc* or dependent upon imports), changing burial practice, and transport systems. Furthermore, because the more recent landscape features are most likely to survive, they should be seen as usually biasing our understanding towards the more recent social and economic activities.

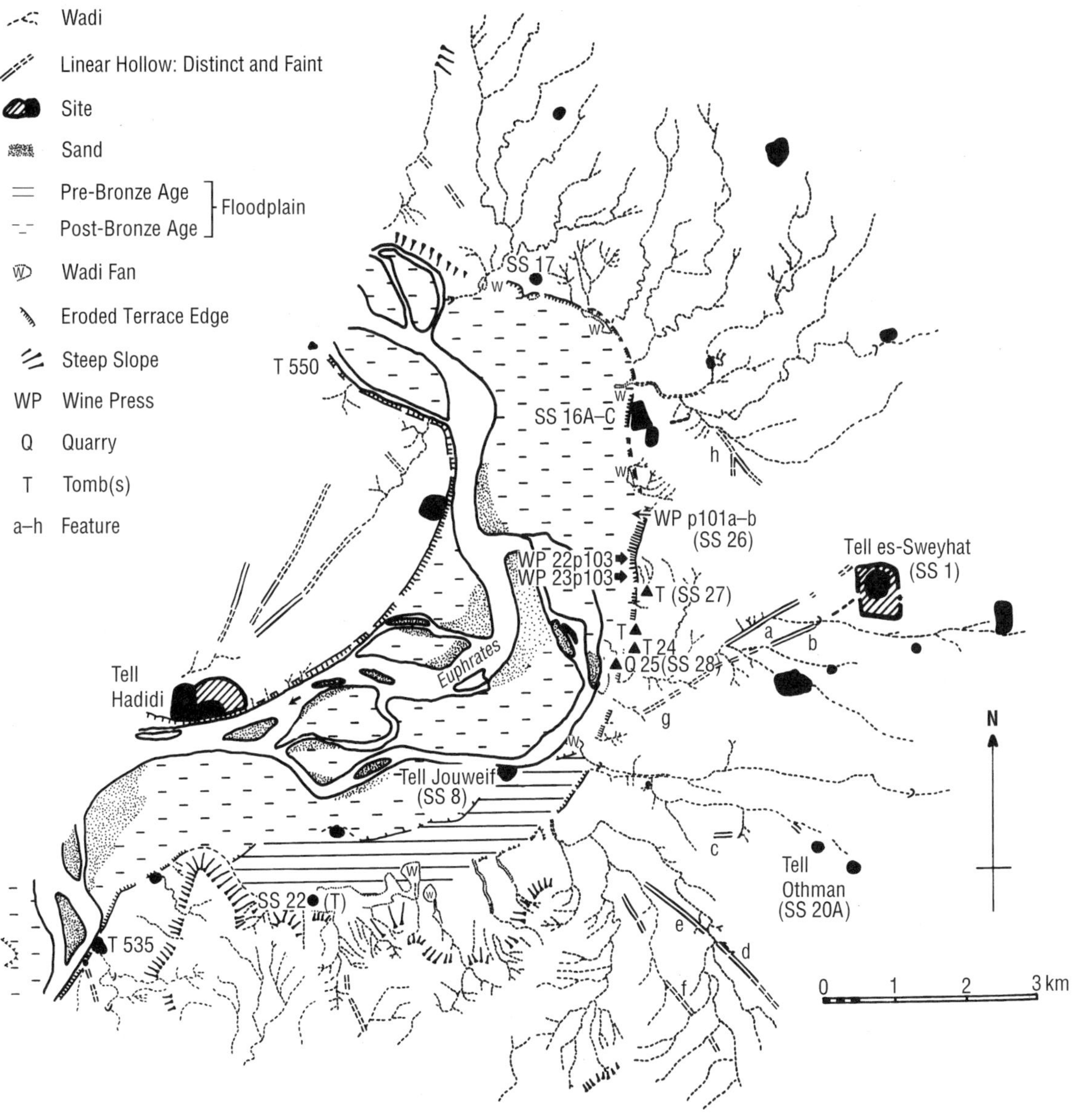

Figure 5.1. Landscape Map of Tell es-Sweyhat Area

75

5.A. WINE PRESSES

The occurrence of wine presses beyond the present limits of grape production raises interesting implications regarding the past environment in the region, but it is not clear whether their presence indicates environmental change or simply a shift from a grape producing to a non-grape producing culture.

The wine presses were all recorded in autumn 1992; all four were cut in white chalky limestone at the foot of eroded limestone bluffs along the east bank of the Euphrates River (fig. 5.1: WP 101a–b, 22, 23).

5.A.1. THE FEATURES

Of the four features, two were sufficiently complete to be described and reconstructed (fig. 5.2; pls. 7–8). The first (field reference p 101b) was located within SS 26, the small Late Iron Age and Late Roman/Byzantine site situated on the edge of the floodplain below eroded limestone bluffs. The second (22 p 103) was away from any visible site (although such a site may have been removed by riverine erosion) at an elevation of 1.5–2.0 m above the floodplain. Relevant dimensions of the wine presses are given in table 5.1.

Table 5.1. Dimensions of the Wine Presses

Field Reference	*Treading Floor Length**	*Treading Floor Width*	*Basin Length*	*Basin Width*	*Depth*
p 101a (SS 26)	1.5 m	0.6 m	—	—	—
p 101b (SS 26)	1.8 m	1.5 m	0.9 m	0.9 m	0.5 m
22 p 103	3.0 m	2.4 m	1.3 m	1.2 m	0.25 m
23 p 103	8.0 m	>5.0 m	—	—	—

*Length is taken parallel to the line of bluffs (i.e., roughly north–south), width is perpendicular.

Both comprised a pressing chamber or treading floor upslope, a small receiving tank downslope, and a linking channel (fig. 5.2). In p 101b this linking channel was an enclosed rock-cut pipe of dimensions 6 × 13 cm that led to a raised carved spout situated within the receiving basin (fig. 5.2a). In 22 p 103 the 10 cm wide channel was open and conducted the grape juice over a rock-cut bench into the receiving basin (fig. 5.2b). Unfortunately, the rock-cut chambers were partly filled with sediment so that the depths could not be determined without excavation. Approximate reconstructions were possible, however, using the level of the linking channel as a guide. Although different in detail, both must have functioned in a similar manner: grapes were pressed or trodden in the upper chamber and the juice flowed down the channel to be collected within the collection basin.

Two additional features, p 101a at SS 26 and 23 p 103 some distance away from any known site, appear to belong to treading floors; unfortunately, the receiving basins have either been eroded away or are obscured by sediment. The former (p 101a), which featured three subsidiary tanks to upslope, each with a linking channel to what appeared to be a treading area, is enigmatic, but it could conceivably be an example of what Frankel (1999, chapter 9) terms an improved winery.

5.A.2. INTERPRETATION AND SIGNIFICANCE OF THE WINE PRESSES

In Israel and Palestine the characteristic grape-pressing structure is the simple treading installation comprising an upper treading surface for the processing of the fruit, and a lower collecting vat that received the liquid via a channel or bore (Frankel 1999: 51). The structures are normally cut in bedrock. Mean areas for wine presses in Israel are 3.10 sq. m for the treading floor and 1.24 sq. m for the vat (ibid., p. 52). The treading floors of p 101a, p 101b, and 22 p 103 fall within the general range of examples cited by Frankel (ibid., chart 3). This is also the case for the extant vats, and p 101a falls within the commonest size class of Frankel's study, and 22 p 103 is not an uncommon size (ibid., chart 3). Similar tanks at Khirbet Buraq in Palestine (Dar 1986, pl. 24) have been interpreted as tanks for measuring the quantity of grapes prior to pressing. These and other examples from the West Bank of Palestine have been placed within a

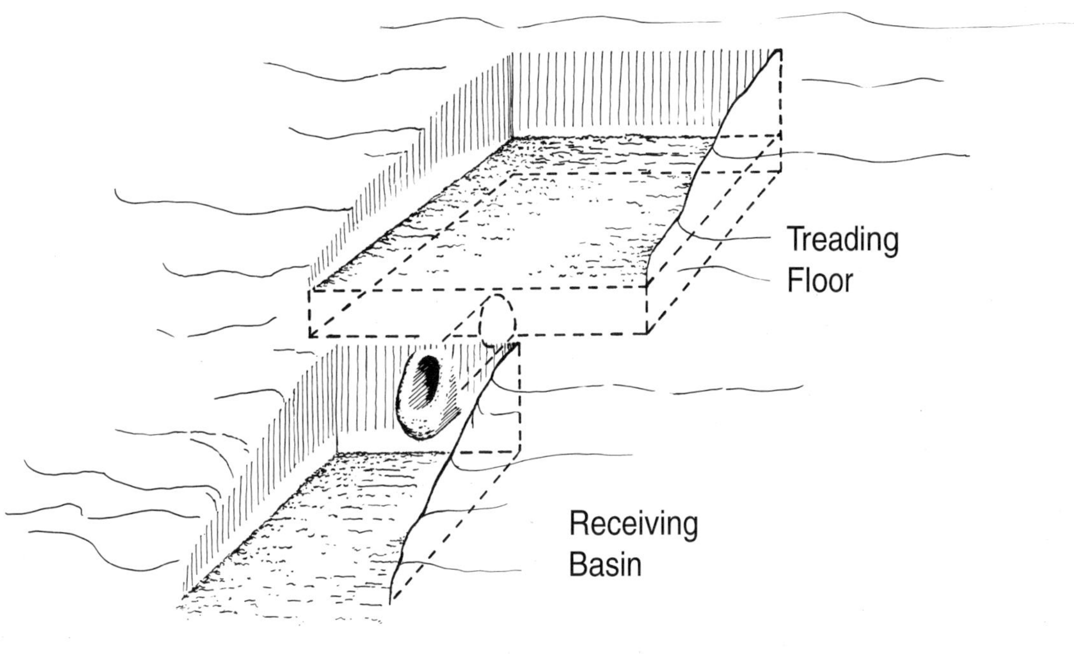

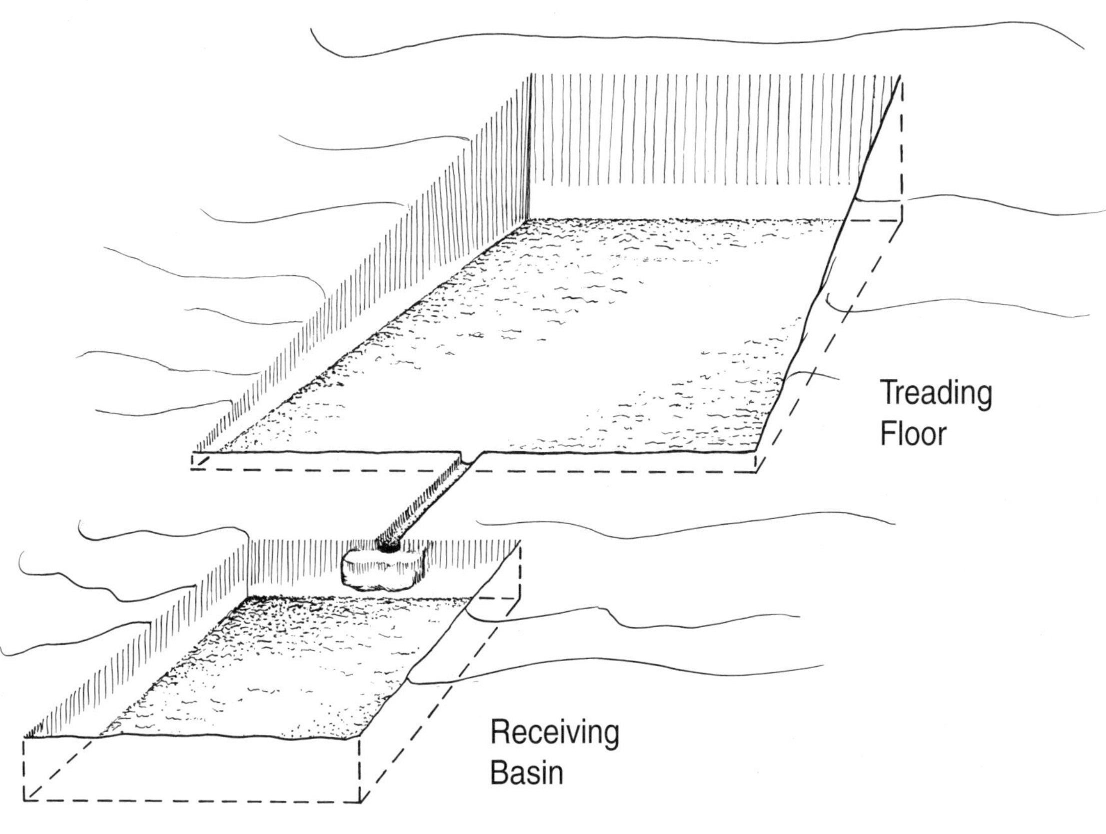

Figure 5.2. Three-dimensional Drawings of Wine Presses along the Euphrates Bluffs. (*a*) From SS 26 (p 101b): Upper Treading Floor 1.8 × 1.5 m, Lower Collecting Basin 0.9 × 0.9 × 0.5 m Deep; (*b*) Located approximately 700 m South of SS 26 (22 p 103): Upper Treading Floor 3.0 × 2.4 m, Lower Collecting Basin 1.20 × 1.30 × 0.25 m. Drawing by Eleanor Barbanes

context of settlements, roads, fields, and other agricultural installations (Dar 1986: 147–53). The West Bank examples are associated with settlement remains from Iron Age to Byzantine date and Dar has inferred that the smaller installations (which resemble those near Tell es-Sweyhat) belonged to small farmers and were associated with plots of land, perhaps 40–80 dunams in area (i.e., 4–8 ha; Dar 1986: 152). The largest example recorded from the Sweyhat area, with an upper chamber measuring at least 8 × 5 m, if it belonged to a wine press, would have been for producing much larger volumes of wine. Such a press might have belonged to an estate or a larger community (ibid., 152). Given the Late Iron Age to Byzantine date of SS 26, it seems probable that the two installations from that site fall within this range, but there is no direct evidence for dating, and it should be remembered that wine presses with rectangular treading floors can date from as early as the Early Bronze Age (Frankel 1999: 51).

Today the landscape of the Sweyhat area is a bare, heavily degraded steppe. Neither grapes nor olives are grown today, but this does not mean that they are incapable of growth because recent attempts have been made to reestablish olives in the area. The absence of grapes, lentils, and olives may simply be explained by the low rainfall. For example, modern agricultural statistics for the moist steppe region of southeastern Turkey show that both lentils and grapes progressively decline in importance towards the Syrian frontier, their place being taken by wheat and barley (Wilkinson 1990, fig. 2.4). At present in northern Syria, grape production (relying on rainfall alone) is confined to moister areas to the west of the Euphrates Valley, that is, within the long-term settled zone, but the presence of carbonized grape seeds at Abu Hureyra (T 545, Neolithic), Tell Hadidi (T 548, Late Bronze Age), Selenkahiye (T 507, Early Bronze Age), and Tell es-Sweyhat (Zettler and Miller 1995: 125) suggests the possibility of vines being grown in the area. Alternatively, it is possible that the grapes which supplied these wine presses on the floodplain were irrigated,[50] either from a canal that has now been eroded away by the Euphrates River or by wells tapping a shallow water table within the floodplain. In addition to the above palaeobotanical evidence for grapes in the region, Late Bronze Age real estate texts from Emar mention the presence of vineyards, including one that abutted the city (Fleming 1993, n. 47).

Tell es-Sweyhat falls within a region that was at least partly deserted during the medieval period or slightly later and remained largely under pastoral nomadism until it was recolonized in the twentieth century (Lewis 1988: 691). Because this recolonization was partly effected as a result of increased security in the region, which allowed investment in agriculture as well as mechanization to take place, changes in grape production should be seen within a sociopolitical context. Because of the operation of these political and social factors, it can be argued that during the Hellenistic to Byzantine period the area may have been within a cultural sphere in which grape production was part of everyday life and that since then a change in the social and political conditions has occurred so that in the recent past grapes have contributed little to the diet or social behavior.

With the available data, it is impossible to say when the abandonment of grape cultivation took place. However, a decline in grape production may have been coincident with decreasing demand for wine during the Islamic period. By the twelfth/thirteenth century, when the local population had declined considerably, grape production was probably significantly less or absent. Whatever the reasons behind the decline in grape production, the former presence of vineyards along the floodplain edge, perhaps even on the limestone bluffs that fringe the floodplain, suggests that the environment of the late first millennium B.C. and early mid-first millennium B.C. must have been significantly more verdant in appearance than that of today, even if the climate itself was not actually wetter.

In addition to the four wine presses, numerous rock-cut tombs (now sadly plundered), two stone quarries, and Tell Jouweif (SS 8) all exhibited riverward faces heavily eroded by the Euphrates River. This erosion provides further supporting evidence for the observation made in *Section 2.B.2: The Alluvial Plain* that much of the Euphrates floodplain has been reworked by the migrating meanders and channels of the river. The truncation of various features of Hellenistic to Byzantine date suggests that much of this erosion has taken place over the last 1,500 to 2,000 years.

5.B. QUARRIES

Two stone quarries were located at the foot of the limestone bluffs, 200–300 m to the north of SS 28 (fig. 5.1: Q 25). Each quarry comprised a broad rock-cut platform located 3–4 m above the present floodplain level. Evidence of block removal could be seen in the form of rectangular areas of roughly pecked limestone which apparently conformed

---

50.   For ancient Anatolia, Gorny (1995: 146) notes that while vineyards are occasionally associated with irrigation, "a regular and widespread practice of irrigating vineyards can not be substantiated from the (Hittite) texts."

to the likely size and shape of the removed block. Ghosts of individual blocks, which were evident as slightly different levels of pecked surface (pl. 9), enabled block dimensions to be estimated as 100–150 × 50–100 cm. The northern quarry, with dimensions of 30 × 15 m, was the most complete. Both quarries were obliquely cut by the eroded limestone slopes, the exposure of which was probably one of the original reasons for locating the quarries at this point. However, given the considerable mobility of the river channel, it is also possible that the quarries were located at a former riverside location so that it would be convenient to transport stone blocks to locations upstream and downstream. Although the blocks might have been used for building construction, the abundance of tombs, some of masonry construction, along the bluffs suggests that these quarries may also have supplied materials for tomb construction.

The quarries resemble other examples from the Near East in which ancient quarrymen have left distinctive patterns of rectilinear channels on selected rock outcrops, and Algaze, Breuninger, and Knutstad (1994) report similar examples from the area of Birecik on the Turkish Euphrates River. Such traces of shallow channels, by allowing the stone blocks to be undercut and ultimately severed, and by providing access points for the insertion of crowbars and other quarrying tools, enabled the blocks to be systematically removed. Elsewhere in the eastern Mediterranean, the use of such quarrying methods extends back to the third millennium B.C. (Waelkens, Herz, and Moens 1992). Although less well attested for the Near East at this time (ibid., p. 11), the presence of well-dressed ashlar masonry in Early Bronze Age tombs at Tell Banat (Porter 1999) and probable Early Bronze Age quarries near Titriş Höyük (Algaze, Misir, and Wilkinson 1992: 45) demonstrate that in the middle Euphrates Valley to the north of Lake Assad elaborate or large-scale quarrying techniques must extend back to at least the mid-third millennium B.C.

5.C. TOMBS

Rock-cut or masonry tombs are a common feature along the Euphrates bluffs where they have been exposed by long-continued erosion and more recently by plundering (fig. 5.1: T; pl. 10). As a result they are often conspicuous and a number of both on- and off-site tombs have been excavated and studied. Porter (1999: 363–420), for example, discusses significant mortuary groups along the Syrian Euphrates River at Jerablus Tahtani, Shioukh Tahtani, Rumeilah (near SS 17), Tell es-Sweyhat (SS 1), Tell Hadidi (T 548), Shams ed-Din Southern Site and Cemeteries (SS 22), Tawi (T 522), Halawa Tells A and B (T 519A and B), Wreyda (between T 506 and T 512), and Selenkahiye (T 507), as well as at Tell Banat itself. Porter's classification recognizes primary and secondary inhumations, stone cist graves, pit graves, shaft and chamber tombs, dolmens, as well as the massive built conical structures such as Tell Banat's White Monument. In the Early Bronze Age a wide variety of mortuary practices were used along the Euphrates River, and Carter and Parker (1995) identify pit burials, ossuaries, cists, burials in ceramic containers, gallery graves and dolmens, nodal shaft graves, and shaft tombs. Different styles of burial may be related to social practice and the way of life of the interred. This includes the rights of the inhabitants to the land and whether they were sedentary or mobile pastoralists (Porter 1999), the latter being regarded by Porter as an important practice in the Tell Banat/Tell es-Sweyhat area.

In general, although extensive tomb complexes have been exposed by plundering over the past fifty years, their date and relationship to the sites in the area often remains difficult to determine. This is especially the case for tombs that lack grave goods, which therefore remain undated. Alternatively, grave typology can be employed to date the tombs (e.g., Carter and Parker 1995, table 14.1; Porter 1999, table 2). Although many of the graves examined fell into the typological groups defined by Carter and Parker (1995, table 14.3), because such types appear to have been constructed during other periods as well, it does not necessarily follow that they are of Early Bronze Age date. The discovery of graves at Tell es-Sweyhat in 1993 has increased our knowledge considerably (Zettler 1997: 51–72).[51]

The following representative tomb types, of various dates, have been noted within the area of the Sweyhat survey. Representative examples are indicated on plates 11 and 12; locations of main tomb groups in the Sweyhat survey are indicated in figure 5.1.

---

51. The evidence for high status graves at Tell es-Sweyhat has been extended for the Tishrin Dam area by studies at Tell Banat by Thomas McClellan and Anne Porter.

Type *a*   Simple rectangular graves, ca. 200 × 50 cm in horizontal dimension; in the Sweyhat area usually cut into the limestone bedrock of eroded hillslopes. Erosion of the overlying soils and rock mean that no realistic depths can be given.

Type *b*   Shaft tombs (Carter and Parker 1995, type 7) consist of a square or rectangular shaft cut through the Euphrates terrace conglomerate into the underlying limestone. In the single recorded example, the upper shaft was lined with dressed limestone blocks that either were derived from the excavation of the underlying shaft and chamber (i.e., which presumably were cut in bedrock) or were brought from neighboring quarries. The shaft probably led down into tomb chambers of Type *c*.

Type *c*   Rock-cut vaulted chambers formed the most common and conspicuous tomb types along the bluffs, particularly in the area of SS 27 to the west of Tell es-Sweyhat. A well-constructed shaft tomb with rock-cut vaulted chambers was recorded below SS 27. From its position adjacent to this Early Bronze Age site (see *Section 7.D: The Mid-/Late and Late Early Bronze Age*), it can be suggested to be of similar date. The recorded example comprised a 3 × 3 m central rock-cut chamber, flanked by rock-cut arched vaults on each of three sides opposite what was probably an entrance. Each vaulted burial chamber measuring 200 × 50 cm was presumably intended for one inhumation (pl. 12). These chambers belong to Carter and Parker 1995, type 7b.

Type *d*   Simple rock-cut chambers (Carter and Parker 1995, type 2 "ossuaries"). One below the Early Bronze Age site of Nafileh Village (SS 5) is possibly of this date also.

A good example of a Roman/Byzantine rock-cut tomb was briefly recorded by myself and John Ellsworth in October 1991. The site was rather inaccessibly located some 50–70 m up steep limestone bluffs on the west bank of the river at Shash Hamdan (T 550). Sadly, by the time it was reported by the local inhabitants, it had been robbed not only of grave goods but even of the (presumably) better quality statues that formed a high relief element of the surrounding decorative frieze. The removal of these statues was brutally executed by cutting through the rock behind to leave a broad scalloped gouge in its place. The stolen reliefs were clearly destined for the antiquities market. Although the tomb was partly infilled by debris eroded from the adjacent slopes, a single rock-cut burial chamber could be recognized in the southwestern wall of the chamber.

Unfortunately, the absence of clearly related grave goods hinders the dating of most tombs. The vaulted chamber tombs (Type *c*) are similar to Early Bronze Age chamber burials with entrance shafts from Shams ed-Din South.[52] However, these also find close parallels in the Roman/Byzantine Grave E no. 2 near Rumeilah, which is situated between Tell Ali al-Haj (SS 17) and Ramalah (SS 16B). This tomb featured three funerary niches, each hollowed out around a central chamber (Egami, Masuda, and Iwasaki 1979: 9, pl. 19). Similarly, the Type *a* rectangular rock-cut slots might be equivalent to Meyer's cist graves, without the stone surround, or perhaps later features from Rumeilah (near SS 17). The latter, which were exposed from beneath overlying stone circles, were again shown to be Hellenistic or Roman.

During the earlier seasons of excavation at Tell es-Sweyhat, evidence for Bronze Age burials was limited to a single infant (or fetus) buried in a cooking pot in Area III (T. A. Holland, pers. comm.). Given the extensive scale of the Early Bronze Age cemeteries adjacent to Shams ed-Din Southern Site and Cemeteries (SS 22; Meyer 1991, fig. 3), similar occurrences could also have been anticipated around Tell es-Sweyhat. Such a discovery happened in 1993 as a result of the collapse of the ground in association with irrigation. This collapse exposed several tombs (Tombs 1–5) of which Tomb 1 was sealed by the outer fortification wall and therefore clearly pre-dated it (Zettler 1997: 56). The tombs consisted of chambers cut into the hard loam soil that underlay the Sweyhat Plain and they contained a rich assemblage of weapons (bronze daggers, ax blades, javelin point), jewelry, and clothing ornaments, as well as abundant ceramics among the remaining burials and food offerings. These Sweyhat tombs lacked the architectural sophistication of the tombs from Tell Banat and are probably contemporaneous with the later phases of Banat tomb 7 and later in date than the White Monument, Tell Banat's monumental conical structure (Porter 1999: 398; McClellan 1998). In terms of chronology Porter places the Sweyhat tombs in her phase 4 (ca. 2450–2300 B.C.; Porter 1999, table 1), while from the physical position of Tomb 1 and the grave goods, Zettler (1997: 56) sees them as being roughly equivalent to Amuq I–J or Kurban Höyük period IV, that is, falling in the third quarter of the third millennium B.C.

In addition to these plundered tombs, possible cemeteries can also be recognized in one or two locations on aerial photographs as groups of small, faint, subrounded features of apparently low relief. These may form the remains of ex-

---

52. Meyer 1991, figs. 10, 27; for summary, see *Appendix B: Site Gazetteer*; see also Shams ed-Din Southern Site and Cemeteries (SS 22); Carter and Parker 1995, type 7b.

tensive areas of cemeteries, but they have not been verified as cemeteries by excavation, nor have they been plundered by grave robbers.[53]

5.D. LINEAR HOLLOWS

Forming an anomalous element within the landscape are straight hollows or valleys. The lack of both a sinuous plan form and a dendritic pattern distinguishes these features from true wadis, but they do in part at least form part of the drainage net. Some linear hollows, such as Feature *h* to the northwest of Tell es-Sweyhat and Feature *a* to the southwest (fig. 5.1), form prominent topographic valleys, whereas others are nothing more than extremely shallow hollows with virtually no surface expression and are only recognizable from aerial photographs.

For example, Feature *e/d* (fig. 5.1) is remarkably subtle, being in places eroded along a slightly sinuous gully that then continues to the southeast as a straight albeit faint feature. Elsewhere, the feature appears as a very shallow topographic hollow or simply as an increase in the density of the cereal crop. Owing to the general absence of crops during the autumn survey season, vegetation marks were rarely evident to us, but during crop growth or ripening such features might be much more conspicuous. Feature *f* is even more subtle than Feature *e/d*, being only locally visible as a very shallow hollow. By initially recognizing linear hollows on aerial photographs, it was possible to locate them in the field, but it is unlikely that such features would have been recognized on the basis of their field characteristics alone.

Most hollows either radiate out from or lie between tells, the major features being: from Tell Hadidi (T 548), three radial hollows; from Tell es-Sweyhat, two or three hollows; from Tell Othman (SS 20A), one or two hollows; from Tell Jouweif (SS 8), three or four hollows. In addition a number of other features exist, all of which are oriented upon sites as can be seen in figure 5.1. Features *a* and *b/g* (fig. 5.1) between Tell es-Sweyhat and Tell Jouweif are particularly striking examples of their association with sites.

When hollows form part of the drainage net they can occur on trunk wadis or minor tributaries. Although on aerial photographs they mainly appear as broad shallow features, hollows can also act as a focus for gully erosion that results in localized narrow incisions. Their hollow form and relationship to the drainage net suggests that they conduct some runoff, but their often discordant relation to the drainage system and their tendency to cross from drainage basin to drainage basin (e.g., from Feature *g* to Feature *b*; fig. 5.1) suggest that other factors have also influenced their alignment.

There are two obvious explanations for such features: they are canals or they represent early roads or tracks that have been hollowed away by the passage of people and animals, reinforced by localized runoff and erosion.

If the linear hollows were canals, being excavated features, these should have shown evidence of banks of upcast alongside, especially where undulating terrain was traversed and deeper cuts would have been necessary to maintain an even grade. If the hollows had once conveyed water from a perennial source there should be evidence for such a source as well as perhaps scatters of shells of freshwater mollusks that inhabited such flows. In the case of the Sweyhat Plain there is no evidence of a water source at their upslope ends, and indeed the groundwater table slopes down relative to the general ground level (see below and fig. 2.12). Neither were freshwater mollusks found along linear hollows or wadis. If the hollows had been designed to conduct flood runoff, their gradient indicates that they would have taken it from the high and dry terrace towards the well-watered Euphrates floodplain. Finally, in places such as at Features *c*, *e*, and *f* (fig. 5.1), hollow ways can be seen to cross minor watersheds where it would have been necessary to construct deep cuttings or tunnels to maintain grade. No evidence of such installations could be seen either on the ground or in aerial photographs.

Alternatively, if the hollow ways were roads or tracks, they would be expected to radiate out from or run between sites. It is also well established that as a result of the passage of traffic, road surfaces become compacted, thus generating greater runoff and the concentration of overland flow along selected paths (Tsoar and Yekutieli 1993; Wilkinson 1993; Sheets and Sever 1991: 58–62). In addition, churning by the feet of humans and animals, as well as by occasional wheels of carts, disturbs the soil considerably and results in increased sediment yield from such areas. Flow concentration of normally dispersed overland flow has also been suggested as a likely course for valley trenching episodes

---

53. Similar features can also be recognized along the Balikh Valley,
    where they often occur on the low uncultivated terraces adjacent
    to the cultivated floodplain.

in the American Southwest, in which case a number of flow concentration features have been blamed, such as wagon roads, cattle trails, railroad embankments, canals, and other embankments (Cooke and Reeves 1976: 94–98).

To conclude, hollow ways or tracks seem the most likely explanation for the features around Tell es-Sweyhat. As a result of such flow concentrations, parts of the old track systems, particularly those on steeper terrain where runoff power was increased (Sheets and Sever 1991: 60), or those where soils were more readily compacted or disturbed, became a discordant element in the drainage net. Erosion resulting from flow concentration would be further increased by the rejuvenating effects of the migrating Euphrates River as discussed above. Similar features recorded elsewhere in the Jazirah have been interpreted as ancient routes (Ur 2002, 2003; Wilkinson 1993; Buringh 1960; van Liere and Lauffray 1954/55), and indeed they share many attributes with the hollow ways and sunken lanes of western Europe.

If the hollow ways represent roads, they indicate a significant amount of movement along selected paths, with the main routes being as follows:

1. Local routes around Tell Hadidi (T 548); the hollow way to the north is on the same line as a wadi. At least one of these may have been taking traffic to the north via the Euphrates Valley.

2. From Tell es-Sweyhat leading to the northwest (Feature *h*), continuing after a gap to the northwest of Tell Ali al-Haj (SS 17).

3. Two hollow ways trending to the southwest of Tell es-Sweyhat towards Tell Jouweif (SS 8) (Features *a*, *b*/*g*). The feature that skirts the northwestern corner of Tell es-Sweyhat (Feature *a*) can be suggested as part of a track running from at least Tell Jouweif, which perhaps continued to the northeast of Sweyhat to traverse the hills beyond via a low gap. One feature near Tell es-Sweyhat (Feature *b*) appears both in the field and in aerial photographs to lead towards the center of the western enclosure wall where presumably there was a gate.

4. A possible route leading west from Tell Othman (SS 20A) toward the bluffs north of Tell al-ʿAbd (T 535) (Feature *c*).

5. Two converging features heading towards Tell Jouweif (SS 8) from the southeast (Features *e*/*d*, *f*).

All sites associated with the above routes have significant Early/Middle Bronze Age occupation, which implies that the routes functioned at these times, but perhaps during other periods as well.

6. THE CERAMIC SEQUENCE FROM SURVEYED SITES

Tony J. Wilkinson and *Donald Whitcomb*

As noted in *Section 1.E: Archaeological and Historical Context*, despite the large number of excavations conducted over the last thirty years, the ceramic chronology for northern Syria remains incomplete. For example, the third millennium of the Euphrates Valley, although known in broad outline, has until recently lacked chronological definition.[54] In addition, ceramics of the late second millennium and early first millennium remain poorly understood, as does much of the first millennium up until the introduction of the distinctive Hellenistic wares. Considerable progress was made with the publication of the Tell Abu Danne sequence (Lebeau 1983), but this period still requires subdivision[55] and consequently it is difficult to recognize, from surface pottery alone, the development of Assyrian control in the region.

Here, where possible, ceramics are anchored with respect to the excavated sequence from Tell es-Sweyhat, amended where appropriate by other local sequences, for example, those from Tell Hadidi (T 548), Selenkahiye (T 507), Tell Banat, and Qara Qusak. More long-distance parallels have also been sought from Tell Mardikh (Ebla), as well as Kurban Höyük, Titriş Höyük, and the Amuq Plain. The broad chronological sequence referred to is given in table 6.1.

Surface pottery came primarily from haphazard sampling. Sites were walked and sherds were collected along parallel paths a few meters apart to ensure an even coverage and a maximum recovery of diagnostic sherds. Where topographic subdivisions were apparent, sites were subdivided into smaller collection units (e.g., A, B, C). During the sampling, attempts were made to make collection units less than 1 ha in area to ensure that if aggregate site areas were made for rough population estimates, the smallest unit area would not exceed 1 ha.

With the exception of a few multi-period mounds, most sites treated in this section provide single period or short-range occupations. Consequently, publication of pottery assemblages according to site seemed appropriate. This does not of course mean that each site is solely restricted to a single period, but in general the internal consistency of the types suggests that most sites illustrated here were occupied over a relatively brief span of time (perhaps a few generations or centuries) and that each was endowed with its own distinctive pottery assemblage. The most obvious exception to this is Tell Ali al-Haj (SS 17), which is included because it was one of the few sites to encompass much or all of the second millennium B.C. Tell Jouweif (SS 8) and Tell Othman (SS 20A) are also tell sites characterized by long occupational ranges, but the former site is dominated by early Middle Bronze Age forms from the upper occupation levels, whereas the latter has only a small collection of pottery. Table 6.1 summarizes the main sequences discussed here, as well as the main occupied phases of individual sites. Where more than one phase is represented on a site that assemblage is marked with two asterisks (**) in table 6.1; such assemblages obviously cannot be used to date other assemblages. In addition, table 6.2 provides tabulated data and cross references on the periodization adopted for the Early and Middle Bronze Ages.

The following discussion of the pottery sequence is according to occupation phase; where an equivalent occupation phase is present at Tell es-Sweyhat, appropriate cross reference is made according to the sequence at that site: Periods A to K (see *Section 1: Introduction to the Survey*, table 6.1, and Holland, *Sweyhat* 2). The earlier periods (Chalcolithic to Roman) are treated by me and the latest (Islamic) by Donald Whitcomb. The pottery illustrations (figs. 6:1–31), again arranged by site (see table 6.1), are accompanied by descriptive catalogs.

---

54. For a general four-stage chronology, see Jamieson 1993, and recent assessments by Porter 1999, Lebeau 2000, and other authors in Marro and Hauptmann 2000.

55. The publication of detailed comparanda by Lehmann (1998, 1996) as well as Hausleiter and Reiche (1999) have clarified the record for the Iron Age of Syria, but this period is still in need of further unambiguous subdivision.

Table 6.1. Pottery from Key Sites Illustrating the Main Periods of Occupation in the Sweyhat Survey Area

Sites (SS)	Sweyhat Period*	Survey Survey Period	Range of Occupation by Period	Figure Number
SS 30	—	II	Earlier Ubaid	6.1
SS 25	—	III	Late Chalcolithic	6.2
SS 2, 3**, 9, 21	J, K	V	Early Early Bronze Age	6.3–6
SS 5	G, F, E	VI–VII	Middle–Late Early Bronze Age	6.7
SS 24, 27	E, D	VII–VIII	Late Early Bronze Age/Middle Bronze Age	6.8–9
SS 8**	J–D	V–VIII	Early Bronze Age and Middle Bronze Age	6.10–12
SS 17**	D	VIII–X	Middle Bronze Age, Late Bronze Age, Iron Age	6.13–15
SS 15, 20B	—	X	Iron Age	6.16–17
SS 26**	B, A	X–XIII	Iron Age and Late Roman/Early Byzantine	6.18–19
SS 6	C, B	X–XI	Iron Age, Hellenistic, and Roman	6.20
SS 16B	C	X–XI	Iron Age–Hellenistic	6.20
SS 10	B	XII/XIII	Late Roman–Early Byzantine	6.21
SS 4	A	XIII–XIV	Early Byzantine/Early Islamic	6.22
SS 7, 11, 12	A	XIV	Early Islamic	6.23–30
SS 28	A	XV	Middle Islamic	6.31

*From Holland, *Sweyhat* 2

**Represents sites with clearly multi-period occupations

Sweyhat Survey Period	Corresponding Cultural Period	Sweyhat Period	Date[1]
I	Halaf	—	5600–5000 B.C.
II	Ubaid	—	5000–4200 B.C.
III	Late Chalcolithic	—	4200–3400 B.C.
IV	Uruk	K	3400–3000 B.C.
V	Early Early Bronze Age (= EB I–II[2])	G, H, J	3000–2600 B.C.
VI	Mid-Early Bronze Age (= EB III)	F, G	2600–2300 B.C.
VII	Late Early Bronze Age (= EB IV[3])	E, D–E	2300–2000 B.C.
VIII	Middle Bronze Age	D	2000–1600 B.C.
IX	Late Bronze Age	—	1600–1200 B.C.
X	Iron Age	—	1200–330 B.C.
XI	Hellenistic	C	330–50 B.C.
XII	Roman	B	50 B.C.–A.D. 350
XIII	Early Byzantine	—	A.D. 350–650
XIV	Early Islamic	A	A.D. 650–1000
XV	Middle Islamic	—	A.D. 1000–1300
XVI	Late Islamic	—	After A.D. 1300

[1]Note that chronological periods, in calender years, are approximate and generalized from various sources, including Schwartz and Weiss 1992 for the earlier periods and Millar 1993 for the Roman presence.

[2]According to Palestinian chronology.

[3]Late Early Bronze Age (Sweyhat Survey Period VII) includes the "Early Bronze Age–Middle Bronze Age" transition.

6.A. POTTERY OF THE CHALCOLITHIC TO LATE ROMAN PERIODS

Tony J. Wilkinson

6.A.1. UBAID AND LATE CHALCOLITHIC

No Halaf period sites were discovered within the survey area, and the nearest site of this period was just outside it at Shams ed-Din Tannira (T 562). Within the upper Lake Assad area the only site producing Ubaid pottery was ʿAnab as-Safinah (T 557; not collected, but see Bounni 1979b: 55), which yielded common western-related Ubaid sherds. In addition, the area of SS 30, located on the west bank of the Euphrates River, yielded a small assemblage of Ubaid-related wares as well as a number of painted Chalcolithic sherds of less clear attribution. This assemblage overlaps chronologically with that from the adjacent SS 25, and because both sites were exposed by recent disturbance and were spatially indeterminate, it remains possible that they simply form two components of the same extensive site. Because of this possible overlap, although the two assemblages are treated separately, they are discussed sequentially.

SS 30 (Sweyhat Survey Period II)

The ceramic assemblage from SS 30 consists of a range of straight-sided and flared-rim bowls with geometric designs executed in mat black, grayish brown, reddish brown, and red paint (fig. 6.1). Body sherds with curvilinear painted bands in brown or black mat paint (fig. 6.1:10–13) are of typically Ubaid type and the more complete painted profiles resemble vessels from Hammam et-Turkman period IV in the Balikh Valley. Specific parallels for the painted patterns are: figure 6.1:1 (Hammam et-Turkman period IV phase A: Akkermans 1988b, fig. 3:23) and figure 6.1:3 (Hammam et-Turkman period IV phase A: ibid., fig. 3:2, 14). The hatched or crosshatched diamonds occur in Amuq E contexts (Braidwood and Braidwood 1960, figs. 147, 149–50), which form part of an assemblage of "Ubaid-like monochrome painted ware" (ibid., fig. 181). Closer to Tell es-Sweyhat, hatched diamonds occur in level 7 at Tell ʿAbr (Hammade and Koike 1992, figs. 13–16). Although typical Ubaid pottery is often regarded as predominantly greenish gray mat-painted ware, a wide range of paint hues can occur; at Tell Hammam et-Turkman colors range from black to red, brown being the most common (Akkermans 1988b: 112–28). This situation is matched at SS 30, where of the recorded sherds more than 50% had red, brown, or orange mat paint. Although it is feasible that some of the reddish painted vessels with hatched diamonds may be related to local Halaf types (cf. Gustavson-Gaube 1981: 64, 110–11), the absence of distinctively Halaf forms, fabrics, and motifs supports an Ubaid date for the illustrated assemblage.

Fabrics are predominantly sand tempered, but some fine voids appear to be impressions of fine chaff. Vitrified bodies, a characteristic feature of southern Mesopotamian Ubaid pottery (Braidwood and Braidwood 1960: 181), also occur, and in both cases (fig. 6.1:1, 11) the surface decoration is of more typical Ubaid-like grayish brown mat paint. The one or two Late Chalcolithic forms that are evident (fig. 6.1:15–16) may be part of an outlying scatter from neighboring SS 25.

The collection from SS 30, small though it is, can best be paralleled in Hammam et-Turkman period IV phase A (Akkermans 1988b: 131), which is equivalent to phase E of the Amuq Plain and is datable roughly to the period 5000 to 4700/4600 calibrated B.C.

SS 25 (Sweyhat Survey Period III)

Unlike pottery from SS 30, that of SS 25 was predominantly undecorated, exceptions being the sparsely painted vessels figure 6.2:16 and 19. The general impression is that vessels were coarse and less well made than the earlier Ubaid wares of SS 30, but as Akkermans (1988b) notes, the lower firing of the Late Chalcolithic wares may simply have been a measure to conserve fuel by cutting down on the length of firing.

The commonest vessel form collected was the hemispherical bowl, which usually exhibited a scraped lower body. Often termed Coba bowls, after Coba Höyük in southern Anatolia, these have been recorded over a wide area of southern Turkey and northern Syria (Akkermans 1988a: 312). Related forms from SS 30 are figure 6.1:3–4, 6–7, 9, and 11, all of which have a scraped lower body. However, the more closed or incurving profiles of the SS 30 examples are more common in Late Ubaid levels (Hammam et-Turkman period IV phases C and D). Flint-scraped bowls with an open form are also evident from Late Chalcolithic Hayaz Höyük in the Karababa area of southeast Turkey (Thissen 1985, fig. 1),[56] and a range of similar bowls and jars from a buried alluvial context in the Atchana drain, Amuq Plain,

---

56. Dated to 3600 B.C. uncalibrated, this would also fall within the range 4400–3800 B.C. expected for ceramic of this phase.

has been radiocarbon dated to 4510–3980 calibrated B.C. (Yener et al. 2000, figs. 7–8). Furthermore, specific attributes such as the grooved rim of figure 6.2:2 (cf. Akkermans 1988b, fig. 7:108) and the tapering form of figure 6.2:8 (ibid., fig 7:106, 109) are diagnostic of Hammam et-Turkman period IV types of the Ubaid period.

Jars also show parallels with both Hammam et-Turkman period IV (cf. fig. 6.2:14 with Akkermans 1988a, pl. 94:284–85; pl. 95:290) and Hammam et-Turkman period V (fig. 6.2:13, 21–22; ibid., pls. 102–03). More distinctively Late Chalcolithic is what appears to be part of a carinated casserole of Amuq F type (fig. 6.2:30), the impact of which is lessened by the absence of the carination.

Pottery fabrics exhibit a greater degree of chaff temper than any other period recorded during the survey and most sherds showed at least some evidence of vegetable inclusions or their voids (see fig. 6.2 pottery descriptions for details). Again this feature is characteristic of Tell Hammam et-Turkman where chaff temper increases (as painting decreases) through the Ubaid to attain a preponderance in the Late Chalcolithic when 97% of the pottery was chaff tempered (Akkermans 1988b: 128).

In conclusion, the range of forms described for SS 25 clearly falls within the latest Ubaid and particularly the Late Chalcolithic periods of northern Syria as exemplified by the Tell Hammam et-Turkman sequence. The small percentage of painted pottery suggests a date contemporary with the later phases of period IV or period V at Tell Hammam et-Turkman, where painted pottery decreased throughout the Ubaid to attain a low percentage in Hammam et-Turkman period V (i.e., Late Chalcolithic). The appearance of significant chaff temper (albeit not in overwhelming quantities) also excludes a Hammam et-Turkman period IV phases A and B date (earlier Ubaid). However, the generally enclosed forms suggest a date before that of the more open Coba bowls of the Late Chalcolithic of Hayaz Höyük and Hammam et-Turkman period V. Also, the assemblage lacks the now well-attested chaff-tempered hammerhead bowls, casseroles, and jars of the full Late Chalcolithic (cf. Pollock and Coursey 1995) and Late Chalcolithic 2–3 forms of the Khabur Valley (Tomita 1998, fig. 84). Given the small sample size it is best to attribute the occupation to Hammam et-Turkman period IV phases C and D and period V. This corresponds to the Late Ubaid and the earlier stages of the Late Chalcolithic, that is to Late Chalcolithic 1 and 2 of the recent Santa Fe chronology (Rothman 2001a: 7; Schwartz 2001b: 236–37). Chronologically this period falls in the range ca. 4600 to 3800 calibrated B.C. In other words, SS 25 ceased to be occupied probably only one or two hundred years before the rise of the major Late Uruk settlement complex around Tell Sheikh Hassan (T 523) and Habuba Kabira South (T 513) around 3600 B.C. The significance of this absence of occupation is discussed in *Section 9: Tell es-Sweyhat in Its Regional Context*.

Table 6.2. Summary of Main Ceramic Periodization Used for the Bronze Age Sites of the Sweyhat Survey
(Note: Dates B.C. Are Approximate)

Date B.C.	Sweyhat Survey	Tell es-Sweyhat (Holland, Sweyhat 2)	Tell es-Sweyhat (Armstrong and Zettler 1997)	Hadidi * (Dornemann 1988, 1990)	Selenkahiye (Schwartz 2001a)	Euphrates (Jamieson 1993)	Tell Banat (Porter 1999)
	Period	Period	Phase			Horizon	Phase
3300–3100	V	J		Stratum 1–1		1A	1
3100–2900	V	H	1				2
2900–2700	V	H		Stratum 2–1		1B	2
2700–2600	V	G					2
2600–2500	VI	G	2	Stratum 2–2A			3
2500–2400	VI	G				2A	3
2400–2300	VI	F	3	Stratum 2–2B	Early		4
2300–2200	VII	E			Selenkahiye		5
2200–2100	VII	E	4	Area M	Late	2B	5
2100–2000	VII	D–E	4		Selenkahiye		6
2000–1900	VIII	D	5				
1900–1800	VIII	D	6	Area B			

*Dornemann chronology: Sweyhat Survey Periods and Corresponding Diagnostic Pottery Types (see table 6.3):

Sweyhat Survey Period V: Diagnostic Pottery Types A, B, C, E, F
Sweyhat Survey Period VI: Diagnostic Pottery Types D, G, H
Sweyhat Survey Period VII: Diagnostic Pottery Types I, J, K (continuing into Sweyhat Survey Period VIII)
Sweyhat Survey Period VIII: Diagnostic Pottery Types L, M, N, O

6.A.2. THE EARLY BRONZE AGE

Despite the large number of excavations conducted in the upper Lake Assad area over the last two decades, there is still no fully accepted ceramic sequence for the Late Chalcolithic and Early Bronze Age. Here reference is made to ceramic sequences derived from within the upper Lake Assad area, from Kurban Höyük in the Turkish Euphrates Valley, the Amuq Plain to the northwest, and the Balikh Valley to the east. The distinctive Ninevite V assemblage characteristic of northern Iraq and northeast Syria does not normally extend this far west and therefore cannot be used for dating. Most local parallels are drawn from Tell es-Sweyhat and Tell Hadidi (T 548), of which the latter, although probably the most complete sequence, is made less useful because it derives from a number of separate excavations rather than a superimposed stratigraphic sequence. Furthermore, some of the Hadidi assemblages derive from tombs, and these are not necessarily similar in form or ware to contemporaneous assemblages from domestic sites (Porter 1999: 290). Overall, because Bronze Age ceramic types of the Euphrates region frequently vary according to their context, the use of form alone may not be sufficient to pin down the ceramics to a specific period of time (Campbell 2000: 54–55). In the text that follows most ceramics appear to be defined from domestic and storage contexts and the distinctive range of high quality funerary wares seems to be underrepresented.

Table 6.2 summarizes the Early and Middle Bronze Age ceramic periods used in the upper Lake Assad area and in northern Syria in general. A major difference in chronological terminology between northwestern Syria on the one hand and northern Iraq on the other hinders the ceramic analysis, and the Levantine chronological subdivisions EB I through EB IVB do not relate comfortably to the upper Lake Assad area assemblages (see Schwartz and Weiss 1992: 236). Consequently they are included here only when they have been used in another sequence that is cited here. Because of this lack of a local sequence Jamieson (1993) attempts to reconcile these differences by describing four general third millennium B.C. ceramic horizons for the Euphrates region as follows:

Horizon 1A   Post-Uruk date, equivalent to Amuq phase G, represents the early phase of the Early Bronze Age

Horizon 1B   Part of the early Early Bronze Age, equivalent to Amuq phase H and later parts of the Ninevite V farther to the east

Horizon 2A   Represents development of new wares of increased technical sophistication and standardization that fall chronologically within the mid-third millennium B.C. and are equivalent to Amuq phase I

Horizon 2B   Represents continuation of Horizon 2A tradition, including the main phase of expansion at Tell es-Sweyhat, probably of Akkadian and post-Akkadian (Ur III) date. This horizon, according to Jamieson (1993), is equivalent to Amuq phase J and Tell Mardikh phases IIB1 and IIB2

Table 6.2. Summary of Main Ceramic Periodization Used for the Bronze Age Sites of the Sweyhat Survey (Note: Dates B.C. Are Approximate) (*cont.*)

Date B.C.	Sweyhat Survey	Kurban Höyük (Algaze 1990)	Amuq (Braidwood and Braidwood 1960)	Jazirah (Lebeau 2000)	Levant	SS Sites Occupied	Tell Hajji Ibrahim (Danti 2000)	Tell Mardikh (Matthiae 1980)
	Period	Phase	Phase	Early Jezirah			Phase	Phase
3300–3100	V		G	0	EB I	SS 2, SS 3,	A	
3100–2900	V			I	EB II	SS 9, SS 13,	B	
2900–2700	V	Vb				SS 19, and SS 21		
2700–2600	V		H	II		= 6		
2600–2500	VI			IIIa	EB III		C	
2500–2400	VI	IV				SS 5		
2400–2300	VI		I	IIIb		= 1	D	
2300–2200	VII			IV	EB IVA			
2200–2100	VII	III	J		EB IVA	SS 5, SS 24, and SS 27		IIB1–IIB2
2100–2000	VII			V	EB–MB	= 3		
2000–1900	VIII				MB I	SS 24, SS 27, SS 8,		
1900–1800	VIII		K		MB II	and SS 17 = 4		

Matthiae (1980: 95–111), working with materials from Ebla, places Mardikh phases IIB1 and IIB2 within EB IVA and B, which would therefore make horizon 2B of the Euphrates region also equivalent to EB IV. Jamieson (1993), however, anticipated that his sequence would eventually become subdivided. Such a subdivision has been attempted by Porter (1999), who divides the third millennium into six phases based on materials from Tell Banat.

Further terminological confusion arises from the imposition of the Palestinian Early Bronze Age terminology on ceramic assemblages from the Euphrates Valley. For example, what would be regarded by many Mesopotamian archaeologists as "Uruk" assemblages at Tell Hadidi (T 548) are classified as Early Bronze I by the excavator (Schwartz and Weiss 1992; Dornemann 1990). On the other hand, in southeast Turkey and northern Iraq respectively, *cyma recta* and Ninevite V-related assemblages have generally been placed within the early Early Bronze Age (Algaze 1990; Roaf and Killick 1987). This terminological confusion underscores the value of a local sequence and reference is therefore primarily made to those of Tell es-Sweyhat, Tell Hadidi, and Tell Banat, with additional reference being made to Schwartz and Weiss (1992). Here a general terminology is employed as follows:

Early Early Bronze Age:	Sweyhat Survey Period V; Sweyhat Periods G, H, and J
Mid-/Late Early Bronze Age:	Sweyhat Survey Period VI; Sweyhat Periods G and F
Late Early Bronze Age:	Sweyhat Survey Period VII; Sweyhat Periods E and D–E

However, because of the inevitable presence at some sites of pottery of more than one phase of occupation, to facilitate future re-analysis, I have chosen to illustrate as much of each assemblage as possible.

Although a key local reference sequence for the third millennium B.C. comes from the original soundings at Tell es-Sweyhat (Areas I and IIA), the lack of radiometric dates for this has made it necessary to seek additional parallels from Tell Hadidi (T 548) and other excavated sequences in the region. Because of its proximity and relative completeness, I have chosen the Tell Hadidi sequence as a reference as follows ([*(period)*] refers to Dornemann's [1988, 1990] periodization):

SWEYHAT SURVEY PERIOD IV

Hadidi Stratum 1 — Common beveled-rim bowls. Equivalent to Late Amuq F and part of Amuq G. Kurban Höyük period VI, defined as Late Chalcolithic at that site. [*EB I*]. The later parts of this (Hadidi stratum 1, level 4), includes part of Jamieson's (1993) horizon 1A and Porter's (1999) phase 1. No Uruk horizons with beveled-rim bowls were recognized on any of the surveyed sites, but this period is possibly present at Tell Hajji Ibrahim (SS 3), where Danti (2000, 1997) has exposed cultural levels dated to this phase. Beveled-rim bowls have also been recovered at Shams ed-Din Tannira (*Appendix B: Site Gazetteer*, T 562).

SWEYHAT SURVEY PERIOD V

Hadidi Stratum 2, Level 1 — Presence of *cyma recta* cups. Equivalent to Sweyhat Periods J, H, and part of G, Amuq G and H, and Kurban Höyük period V, that is, early Early Bronze Age. [*EB II*]. Jamieson (1993) horizon 1A and 1B and Porter (1999) phases 1 and 2.

SWEYHAT SURVEY PERIOD VI

Hadidi Stratum 2, Level 2 — From excavated levels. In addition a large group of vessels classified as Early Bronze Age III/IV by the excavator came from tombs; these include a strong presence of metallic wares; equivalent to Sweyhat Periods F and G and Kurban Höyük period IV, that is, mid-/late Early Bronze Age. [*EB III and IV*]. Jamieson (1993) horizon 2A; Porter (1999) phases 3 and 4.

SWEYHAT SURVEY PERIOD VII

Hadidi Stratum 4 — Corresponds to the later phases of the Tell es-Sweyhat Area IV building (i.e., Sweyhat Periods D and D–E), and also Kurban Höyük period III (i.e., late EBA and perhaps EB/MB). Jamieson (1993) horizon 2B and Porter (1999) phases 5 and 6. [*EB IV and EB–MB or MB I*].

THE EARLY EARLY BRONZE AGE (SWEYHAT SURVEY PERIOD V)

Given the paucity of unequivocal external parallels and the ambiguity of many of the forms, no spurious precision is attempted here; therefore, the following assemblages may be regarded as belonging to the first half of the third millennium B.C.[57] Since my completion of the Sweyhat Survey, Tell Hajji Ibrahim (SS 3) has been excavated to reveal three main occupation levels during the Early Bronze Age (Danti 2000, 1997). Phases A, B, and C belong to the Late Uruk and early Early Bronze Age phases, but in addition there is a later phase (D) that includes metallic wares,[58] only a few scraps of which were found on the surface during the initial survey. These demonstrate that occupation continued into the third quarter of the third millennium B.C.

Pottery from those sites considered to have been occupied during the early Early Bronze Age are illustrated in figures 6.3–6. Drawn sherds have been classified into a simple typology as tabulated (table 6.3). The small size of the collections limits the statistical validity of the counts and although the table probably includes some chronological variations, no attempt is made at this stage to provide subdivisions. Some idea of the chronological range becomes evident from the cited parallels.

Table 6.3. Key Early and Middle Bronze Age Diagnostic Sherds according to the Sweyhat Survey Sites

	Type A	Type B	Type C	Type D	Type E	Type F	Type G	Type H	Type I	Type J	Type K	Type L	Type M	Type N	Type O
SS 2	2	3	1	—	—	—	—	—	—	—	—	—	—	—	—
SS 3	—	1	—	—	—	—	—	—	—	—	—	—	—	—	—
SS 9	8	1	2	1	—	1	—	—	—	—	—	—	—	—	—
SS 13	—	—	3	—	—	—	—	—	—	—	—	—	—	—	—
SS 19	2	1	5	—	—	—	—	—	—	—	—	—	—	—	—
SS 21	—	1	3	1	4	4	—	—	—	—	—	—	—	—	—
SS 5	—	—	1	—	—	—	5	—	3	1	1	—	—	—	—
SS 8	1	1	3	—	—	—	—	2	—	6	2	6	3	1	2

Most sherds from SS 2, Tell Hajji Ibrahim (SS 3), SS 9, SS 13, Khirbet Aboud al-Hazu 2 (SS 19), and SS 21 were either wheel thrown or technologically indeterminate, but a minority were handmade (see figs. 6.3–6 pottery descriptions for details; pottery from SS 13 and Khirbet Aboud al-Hazu 2 not illustrated). Fabrics are predominantly "plain simple ware" or variants thereof, sherds being mainly pale brown, reddish brown, or greenish, usually with fine/medium sand temper. The sand was frequently, but not exclusively, of Euphrates provenance. Chaff temper was rare.

The distinctive beaded-rim jar (Type A, table 6.3; e.g., fig. 6.3:8–12) occurred at four sites. Its presence in levels corresponding to Sweyhat Periods G to J in Area IIA at Tell es-Sweyhat suggests an earlier Early Bronze Age date as does its common presence in phases B and C at Tell Hajji Ibrahim (SS 3) (Danti 2000, figs. 5.37–38). External parallels include examples from strata 1 and 2/1 at Tell Hadidi (T 548) (Dornemann 1988, fig. 5:18, 20, 21; fig. 6:10, 15), Halawa Tell B (T 519B; Orthmann 1981, pl. 57:1), Mumbaqa H6/H7 (Orthmann and Kühne 1974, fig. 5:4, 5), and

---

57. These types can now potentially be extended back to the late fourth millennium B.C. as a result of a program of radiocarbon dating of the excavated levels at Tell Hajji Ibrahim (SS 3). At that site similar ceramics to those of Survey Period V here (but with two beveled-rim bowls and occasional chaff-tempered wares) can be dated as follows (from earliest to latest): Phase A1 3358–3036 calibrated B.C.; Phase A2 3080–3015 calibrated B.C.; and Phase B 3031–2890 calibrated B.C. (Danti 2000, table 5.1). Thus the early Early Bronze Age occupations of sites on the Sweyhat Plain would appear to overlap chronologically with those of the southern Uruk colonization at Habuba Kabira South (T 513) (i.e., Survey Period IV). Approximate equivalences be-

tween Sweyhat Survey periods and those of Tell Hajji Ibrahim are given in table 6.2.

58. Here metallic ware is used in the same way as Algaze 1990: 326–27 and Zettler 1997: 59–72. That is, it is a highly fired ware with a fine, hard fabric and dense paste, usually gray, reddish, or orange in color. It has a metallic clinky ring, hence its name, but it is not necessarily fired to a sub-stoneware fabric as is the case for the stonewares farther to the northeast in the Jazirah (G. Schneider 1989). Schwartz (pers. comm., March 2000) prefers to refer to this ware as a gray spiral burnish ware.

Hammam et-Turkman period V phase A (Akkermans 1988a, pl. 103:65–66). Similar forms have also recently been published from Sweyhat Phase 1 levels in Operation 1 (Armstrong and Zettler 1997: 12–13 and 33, form i). All the above suggest a date range mainly falling within the first half of the third millennium B.C.

Among the large number of jar forms are some with distinctive interior hollows (Type B; e.g., fig. 6.3:1, 3–7). These occurred at six of the eight sites (table 6.3) and were found in similar contexts as Type A at Tell es-Sweyhat[59] (Areas 1 and IIA) and Halawa Tell A (T 519A). Again these are characteristic of Hajji Ibrahim phases B and C (Danti 2000, figs. 5.61–62). At Tell Hadidi (T 548) they occur in both strata 1 and 2/1 (Dornemann 1988, fig. 6:10, 15; fig. 7:17–18, 20), but the presence of similar vessels in stratum 2/2 (EB III) suggests that this is a long-lived form, a point confirmed by their common presence in period IV levels in area D at Tell Banat (Porter and McClellan 1998, fig. 11).

Simple open bowls (Type C) are common at the seven survey sites in question (e.g., fig. 6.5:19–20). Although numerically the most common type, the lack of a distinctive profile weakens them as a type fossil. Nevertheless, their frequency in the lower levels of Areas I and IIA at Tell es-Sweyhat (Sweyhat Periods H and J, and operation 1; Armstrong and Zettler 1997: 33, forms a and b) indicates that they predate the main later third millennium B.C. occupation of Tell es-Sweyhat (Sweyhat Periods E and F). Similar forms occur at Tell Hadidi (T 548) in strata 1, 2/1, and 2/2.

Less common but more distinctive are small bowls with neat externally beaded rims (Type D). In the Sweyhat sequence they appear to be slightly later in date than Types A, B, and C, being found in the middle parts of the Area I sequence. At Kurban Höyük they occur in early Early Bronze Age or mid-/late Early Bronze Age contexts (Algaze 1990, Kurban Höyük period V, pl. 44:Q–T, bowl 6b). Although at Tell Hadidi (T 548) the first occurrence of these bowls is in stratum 2/1 (Dornemann 1988, fig. 6:38), they increase in frequency in stratum 2/2 (ibid., fig. 7:24; fig. 8:2, 29, 39). Also suggestive of a slightly later date of occupation at some of the Sweyhat Survey Period V sites is the presence in phase C at Tell Hajji Ibrahim (SS 3) of bowls that resemble Type G (table 6.3; see also Danti 2000, fig. 5.42:I–J; fig. 5.52:J).

The other two types are less common, Type E occurring only at SS 21 (fig. 6.6:19–20) and Type F at SS 9 and 21 (fig. 6.6:13, 22). The distinctive Type E, which bears a slight resemblance to forms from Tell Hammam et-Turkman VI East (Curvers 1991, fig. 1:2, 4), can be tentatively dated to the early mid-third millennium B.C., a point that is confirmed by its presence at Hajji Ibrahim phases B and C (Danti 2000, fig. 5.20:D; fig. 5.60:B–C). The jar with a hollowed top (Type F) appears to be part of a suite of forms, some of which can be paralleled at fourth millennium contexts elsewhere, although a mid-third millennium date seems more likely (Algaze, pers. comm., 1997).

Individual sherds providing convincing external parallels include figure 6.3:20 from SS 2, a distinctive form found in early Early Bronze Age levels at Kurban Höyük (i.e., Kurban Höyük period V; Algaze 1990, pl. 20:H–J, bowl 9c), stratum 1 at Tell Hadidi (T 548) (Dornemann 1988, fig. 4:35), and Uruk levels at Habuba Kabira (T 509/513) (Sürenhagen 1978, table 20:28–34). Also, a sherd (fig. 6.3:2) from SS 2 appears in Kurban Höyük period VI levels (Algaze 1990, pls. 24:G, 39:C) and stratum 2/2 at Tell Hadidi. Although again this indicates an extended time range, it predates the main Period E occupation at Tell es-Sweyhat.

Least specific in form, but comprising a noteworthy group, are jars with simple rims. Again these would not be out of place in the lower levels of Tell es-Sweyhat Areas I and IIA, Hadidi strata 1, 2/1, and 2/2, nor Halawa Tell B (T 519B).

Notwithstanding the terminological confusion, the pottery from SS 2, Tell Hajji Ibrahim (SS 3), SS 9, SS 13, and Khirbet Aboud al-Hazu 2 (SS 19) can be seen to fall within strata 1 and 2/1 at Tell Hadidi (T 548) and Sweyhat Periods J, H, and early G, with some signs of a slightly later date for SS 21. In terms of the Kurban Höyük sequence these sites can be regarded as probably equivalent in date to Kurban Höyük period V (early EBA), although because of the parochial nature of pottery production and distribution at this time there is a limited number of parallels with the Kurban Höyük sequence. Types A and B may also occur in the equivalent of the local Late Chalcolithic/Uruk assemblage. Although the absence of Amuq F chaff-tempered wares, beveled-rim bowls, and southern Uruk indicators argue against a pre-third millennium B.C. date for the sites in question, the late fourth millennium B.C. dates from Tell Hajji Ibrahim argue for some overlap with the later phases of the Late Chalcolithic. Unfortunately, the slightly later diagnostic *cyma recta* cup, so familiar in the Kurban Höyük sequence, is scarce to the south of Carchemish (Algaze, pers. comm.) and is very rare at Tell Hadidi (T 548) (Dornemann 1988, fig. 6:36). Although a proto-*cyma recta* form can be distinguished at both Tell Hadidi (Dornemann 1988, fig. 6:33–34) and in the lower levels at Tell es-Sweyhat, none were found during the survey. SS 21 appears, on the basis of very tenuous parallels, to be slightly later than the above

---

59. See also Armstrong and Zettler 1997: 33, form h.

sites, with Types A and B being rare and E and F appearing more frequently. At present, the assemblage from this site appears to be positioned between that of SS 2, Tell Hajji Ibrahim, SS 9, SS 13, and Khirbet Aboud al-Hazu 2 on the one hand, and Nafileh Village (SS 5) on the other, that is, in the later part of the early third millennium B.C.

In general, the ceramics from this group of sites fall within the early third millennium B.C., namely in Porter's (1999) phases 1 and 2, but the presence of hollowed-rim jars (Type B) and the externally beaded small jar (Type D) may extend the group into Porter's phase 3 (Tell Banat period IV), that is, toward the middle of the third millennium B.C.

MID-/LATE EARLY BRONZE AGE (SWEYHAT SURVEY PERIOD VI)

Sweyhat Survey Period VI, which falls within the third quarter of the third millennium B.C., is roughly equivalent to the Akkadian period in Mesopotamia. Ceramically it is represented by a range of plain simple wares and metallic wares that were particularly common at Tell Hadidi (T 548), especially in tombs. At Tell es-Sweyhat this period appears to be represented by Sweyhat Periods F and G, at which time the site may have covered some 10–15 ha and also included a rich tomb (Tomb 5), also of this period (Zettler 1997: 51–72). Another site occupied during Sweyhat Survey Period VI, Tell Hajji Ibrahim (SS 3), yielded body sherds of a hard thin ware akin to Amuq H brittle orange ware (not illustrated). This phase has since been confirmed by excavation, which produced numerous metallic wares also of the mid-third millennium B.C. (Danti 2000, phase D; 1997: 91–92). Apart from these two occurrences, both evident primarily from excavations, little evidence for occupation of sites is known at this time, perhaps because the bulk of the population was housed within the growing settlements of Tell Hadidi and Tell es-Sweyhat. However, Nafileh Village (SS 5) provides a group of pottery that represents both this phase of the third quarter of the third millennium as well as the final quarter. Nafileh Village may therefore have been occupied at the time when Tell es-Sweyhat achieved its maximum size.

Nafileh Village (SS 5): Pottery from the Mid-/Late Third Millennium B.C. (Sweyhat Survey Periods VI–VII)

Nafileh Village (SS 5) provided a small collection of sherds that, according to external parallels, clearly postdates ceramics from SS 2, Tell Hajji Ibrahim (SS 3), SS 9, and SS 21. These sherds apparently do not fully belong to the Tell Hadidi "EB III" tradition, and metallic wares are absent. However, metallic wares, being frequently associated with funerary contexts, may be absent simply because there were no funerary contexts within the areas collected. Pottery is uniformly wheel-made with pale brown, greenish, or reddish sand-tempered fabrics and again can be described as plain simple ware. Counts of common forms are given in table 6.3. Nafileh Village was probably only briefly occupied, but owing to the presence of modern village houses and courtyards over part of the site, it was only possible to make a partial collection of pottery from the surface.

A common and distinctive form is the Type G bowl, which is a variant of the out-rolled rim bowl (Type D), already mentioned from the earlier Early Bronze Age sites (fig. 6.7:6–9). Although quite common in the Area IC sequence at Tell es-Sweyhat, this form is virtually absent from excavated levels in IIA. External parallels are common: At Tell Hadidi (T 548) the form begins in stratum 2/1 but increases in stratum 2/2. These bowls also occur in tombs E1 and L1 (EB III/IV) in association with metallic ware as well as in Early Bronze IV levels in area M. At Kurban Höyük, Type G bowls are again common (as bowl 9b) in both Kurban Höyük periods IV and III, where they are dated to the mid-/late Early Bronze Age and Early Bronze/Middle Bronze Ages, respectively (Algaze 1990, pls. 56:L–N, 100:D–M). At Tell Banat, variants of this form occur in both Banat periods III and IV but are more rounded and common in Banat III, which puts them in the range 2450–2300 B.C. as well as slightly later (Porter and McClellan 1998: 30).

The jar forms, on the other hand, provide parallels with Tell es-Sweyhat Area IV levels (Periods F to D–E): Type I = Holland 1976, fig. 9:21–22, 24; Type J = Holland 1977, fig. 7:1; Type K = ibid., fig. 7:5. Additional parallels can be cited from Kurban Höyük period III (i.e., EB/MB; cf. Algaze 1990, pls. 113, 114, jar 14), Early Bronze III/IV tomb L1 at Tell Hadidi (T 548) (Dornemann 1988, figs. 16:23, 26; 18:7–8), and Early Bronze IV levels at the same site (Jar I: Dornemann 1979, area M). At Ebla, Types I, J, and K are all common in Mardikh IIIA, dated by the excavator to the early second millennium (i.e., Middle Bronze I; Matthiae 1980, figs. 33, 35). The distinctive rilled jars (Type I, e.g., fig. 6.7:11–13) are common at Tell Kabir, which continued the Tell Banat sequence, where they represent occupation through Early Bronze IV into the Early Bronze/Middle Bronze transition phase (E. N. Cooper 1998, fig. 1:a–d), that is, during Porter (1999) phases 5 and 6 (ca. 2300–2000 B.C.).

The limited occurrence of Type G bowls within the Area IV (Periods F to D–E) levels at Tell es-Sweyhat, dated to the final quarter of the third millennium, suggests that the occupation at Nafileh Village (SS 5) predates this phase and may therefore be contemporary with Period F or late G at Tell es-Sweyhat. However, the jar forms, with their common parallels within Area IV, suggest that occupation at Nafileh Village also continued to at least partially overlap with that period when Tell es-Sweyhat attained its maximum size. The various simple jar forms, all in plain simple ware, can only be described as Early or Middle Bronze Age in date. Although jar forms I, J, and K can occur in both late Early Bronze Age and early Middle Bronze Age contexts, the closest parallels at Kurban Höyük for the assemblage lie in Kurban Höyük period III, but the absence of barrel jars from Nafileh Village (cf. SS 24 and Tell Jouweif [SS 8], below) precludes a Middle Bronze Age date. This would again support a later third millennium B.C. date for the Nafileh Village occupation.

Late Early Bronze Age and Early Middle Bronze Age Ceramics from SS 27 and SS 24 (Sweyhat Survey Periods VII–VIII)

Pottery assemblages from SS 24 and SS 27 appear to represent late third and early second millennium occupation. This sequence is then extended into the Middle Bronze Age by a succession of ceramics collected from the eroded face of Tell Jouweif (SS 8), which is described below. An important reference horizon for distinguishing late Early Bronze Age occupation is the large assemblage from Tell es-Sweyhat Area IV (Periods F, E, and D–E; Holland, *Sweyhat* 2), the pottery of which also appears characteristic of the main occupation of the lower town.[60] Although parallels with Kurban Höyük period III are evident, it is clear that a key Middle Bronze Age form, the barrel jar, is missing from the excavations at Tell es-Sweyhat, and therefore the presence or absence of this form is taken as an indicator of early Middle Bronze Age or later Early Bronze Age occupations, respectively, as long as this is not contradicted by other elements within the assemblage.

The small assemblage from SS 24 includes similar elements to that of SS 27. This assemblage demonstrates overlap with Period E occupation in Tell es-Sweyhat Area IV, as well as continuation into Period D (MBA). Representative of Periods E or D–E at Tell es-Sweyhat are the Type I jars (fig. 6.8:6, 13–14), which also show parallels at Kurban Höyük period III and Early Bronze /Middle Bronze Age transition levels at Tell Kabir (E. N. Cooper 1998, fig. 2:a–b). In addition, Middle Bronze Age occupation is represented by the Type L barrel jars, (fig. 6.8:1–3) as well as by the later phases of use of the Type I jar.

The larger assemblage from SS 27 includes Type G bowls (fig. 6.9:7, 21–22) and various other bowls (fig. 6.8:22, 24) also found in Period F and G assemblages at Tell es-Sweyhat. The same and related bowls (fig. 6.8:22–25) are paralleled in EB IV levels at Tell Hadidi (T 548), Area M (Dornemann 1979, fig. 15:28), but are more typical of post-Early Bronze Age horizons. Thus similar bowls occur in Middle Bronze Age levels at Umm al-Marra (Curvers and Schwartz 1997, fig. 24:3, 13–14). Distinctively Early Bronze Age is the small jar or bowl (fig. 6.9:5), which occurs in period III at Kurban Höyük (Algaze 1990, pl. 105:J–P, jar 5b), EB IV levels at Tell Hadidi (Dornemann 1979, area M), Late Selenkahiye (T 507; Schwartz 2001a, pls. 5A.9–10, type D9), and in Hammam et-Turkman period VI levels (Curvers 1988, fig. 18:46–47). This places it towards the end of the third millennium B.C., or more specifically within Porter's (1999) phase 5 (ca. 2300–2150 B.C.). Various Type I and J jar rims (fig. 6.9:9, 17–20) are also Kurban Höyük period III forms (cf. Algaze 1990, pl. 114, jar 17), which in the upper Lake Assad area can fall within the Early Bronze III/IV and Early Bronze/Middle Bronze Age transition (E. N. Cooper 1998, figs. 1:a–d, 2:a–b). The presence of a small number of barrel jars (fig. 6.9:16, 37–38; Type L and variants) suggests at least a minor component of Middle Bronze Age occupation. More specifically, this form, elsewhere described as neckless jars or kraters, first makes its appearance in the Early Bronze/Middle Bronze Age transition levels at Tell Kabir and increases thereafter to become very common in the Middle Bronze IIA (E. N. Cooper 1998: 276). The presence of a Middle Bronze Age component is also supported by the large potstand (fig. 6.9:8) with parallels in Kurban Höyük period III (Algaze 1990, pl. 129) and Hammam et-Turkman period VII (Curvers 1988, pl. 142:211).

Taken together, both SS 27 and SS 24 seem to be contemporaneous with Periods D–E and E at Tell es-Sweyhat and with the maximum extent of the lower town. However, the presence of barrel jars and other Middle Bronze Age forms at both sites suggests that occupation continued into the Middle Bronze Age (i.e., into Sweyhat Survey Period VIII or Sweyhat Period D). Further continuation of occupation into the second millennium B.C. is then represented by the longer Early Bronze Age and Middle Bronze Age sequence at nearby Tell Jouweif (SS 8).

---

60. But see Holland (*Sweyhat* 2) for a revised chronological subdivision of the Area IV building.

6.A.3. MIDDLE BRONZE AGE AND LATER ASSEMBLAGES

EARLY AND MIDDLE BRONZE AGE OCCUPATION AT TELL JOUWEIF (SS 8) (SWEYHAT SURVEY PERIODS V–VIII)

Occupation at Tell Jouweif (SS 8) continued the sequence of Nafileh Village (SS 5), SS 24, and SS 27 into approximately the middle of the second millennium B.C. Particularly evident is the use of comb-incised decoration on pottery, a feature particularly characteristic of northern Syria and Mesopotamia during the last quarter of the third millennium (Holland 1980: 142), and which continued on Middle Bronze II pottery from Tell Hadidi (T 548) (Dornemann 1979, fig. 22), al-Qitar (Culican and McClellan 1983/84), and other sites in the region.

The most common form recorded is the Type J jar (e.g., fig. 6.12:19–23, 28) with parallels ranging from Kurban Höyük period III (Algaze 1990, pl. 114:H–J, jar 17) to Middle Bronze II levels at Tell Hadidi (T 548) (Dornemann 1979, fig. 23:39–40). Another characteristic type is the Type L barrel jar (e.g., fig. 6.11:14) or variants with complexly formed rims (Types M, N, and O; table 6.3). Type L barrel jars were very common in Kurban Höyük period III levels (e.g., Algaze 1990, pls. 119–21, barrel 1b) but continue into Middle Bronze II at Tell Hadidi (Dornemann 1979, fig. 23:20) as well as at al-Qitar (McClellan 1986, fig. 9). Barrel jar variants (Types M, N, O) appear to continue as late as Middle Bronze II/Late Bronze at Mumbaqa (T 534) (e.g., fig. 6.12:17; cf. de Feyter 1989, fig. 5:1, 7). The distinctive grooved top form also has late analogs, being found in Tell Hadidi Middle Bronze II levels (fig. 6.10:12; cf. Dornemann 1979, fig. 22:18, 22). Unequivocal evidence of Early Bronze Age occupation appears in the form of the heavy Type H grooved rim storage jars (fig. 6.11:1–2). The two examples collected have clear parallels in Kurban Höyük period IV levels (Algaze 1990, pls. 69–70, jar 18) and rather less with the Kurban Höyük period III types. At Tell Hadidi (T 548) the form is dated to EB IV (cf. Dornemann 1979, fig. 16:3, 29; fig. 18:2). Figure 6.12:2 is an example of a type C.1.e bowl from late Selenkahiye (T 507), dated to the final quarter of the third millennium B.C. (Schwartz 2001a, pl. 5A.2).

Section recording conducted in conjunction with sampling of soils for carbonized plant remains demonstrated the existence of an upper stratum of mudbrick rooms (*Section 8.A: Introduction* and fig. 8.1), out of which had been thrown, as a result of modern plundering, large fragments of barrel and other storage jars. In addition to the standard Type L barrel jar (fig. 6.10:2, 8), several (e.g., fig. 6.11:10–11) comprised an evolved rim form described at al-Qitar as a "featured rim" (sometimes highly exaggerated; Culican and McClellan 1983/84: 51). At al-Qitar, these are probably dated to around the mid-second millennium B.C. Forms related to many of the evolved barrel jars illustrated in figures 6.10 and 6.11 come from the latest levels at Tell Habuba Kabira (T 509) (Strommenger 1971) and from Mumbaqa H4/H5 and H5/H6 (Wäfler 1974). This suggests that occupation at Tell Jouweif (SS 8) was contemporary with occupations at a number of fortified sites along the edge of, or overlooking, the Euphrates floodplain. However, the presence of the Middle Bronze Age building level at Tell Jouweif near the top of the tell and the absence of post-Middle Bronze Age pottery suggest that the site was not occupied much later than the middle of the second millennium.

Because Tell Jouweif (SS 8) was occupied over several periods, it is difficult to compare its surface collection with assemblages from small, apparently short-range sites. From the presence of a single Type A jar (fig. 6.12:18 from Site 8C) and some Type C open bowls, an early Early Bronze Age occupation is likely.[61] Mid-/late Early Bronze Age occupation is also attested from the presence of the Type H jars as well as a lugged cooking pot showing parallels with vessels from Kurban Höyük period IV levels (fig. 6.12:24; cf. Algaze 1990, pl. 93, jar 34). However, no examples of metallic ware were found. Occupation probably reached its peak during the late Early Bronze Age and Middle Bronze Age (i.e., up to MB II), and the common parallels with both Area IV ceramics at Tell es-Sweyhat and Early Bronze IV–Middle Bronze II levels at Tell Hadidi (T 548) indicate that the occupation at Tell Jouweif coincided with occupation at both sites. However, the virtual absence of barrel jars from Tell es-Sweyhat levels, together with the presence of many of these as well as other Middle Bronze II types at Tell Jouweif, demonstrates that occupation persisted at this riverside settlement longer than at Tell es-Sweyhat and well into the second millennium B.C.

---

61. This is confirmed by the original 1972 collections of Holland
    and Whitcomb which produced forms dating to Sweyhat Periods
    J through G (Holland, *Sweyhat* 2, fig. 6:14–18).

TELL ALI AL-HAJ (SS 17) (SWEYHAT SURVEY PERIODS VIII–X)

The deep deposits of this tell, combined with the fact that the site has been excavated, will eventually provide a long ceramic sequence. Excavations by a Japanese team exposed eight building levels of which the sixth and eighth revealed almost complete models of terra-cotta houses (Egami, Masuda, and Iwasaki 1979: 4); unfortunately, further details are lacking. In view of this lack of information, the following notes, combined with the illustrated pottery types collected from the mound and adjacent occupation areas (figs. 6.13–15), should provide a general impression of the overall sequence on the site and enable it to be related to other occupations in the area. However, because sampling relied on out-of-context collections, partly eroded from excavated or dumped areas, it is not clear whether the ceramics described above are representative of the entire sequence.

Although a number of probable Early and Middle Bronze Age forms were present, including the chronologically extended range Type I, J, K jars (fig. 6.13:7–9, 11–14), no substantial Early Bronze Age assemblage was noted. Of the forms illustrated, Type L barrel jars (fig. 6.13:3–4, 15–16) are probably of later Middle Bronze Age date or perhaps slightly later. In addition, the distinctive evolved barrel jars, called "featured rims" by McClellan (1984/85, see Tell Jouweif [SS 8]), exhibit parallels with the latest levels at Tell Habuba Kabira (T 509) as well as Middle Bronze Age levels at Mumbaqa (T 534); for example, see figure 6.13:18–19 (cf. Mumbaqa: Wäfler 1974 in H4/H5), figure 6.13:4 (cf. no. 21 in Mumbaqa H5/H6), and figure 6.13:4, 20–21 (in later levels at Tell Habuba Kabira: Strommenger 1969). This places them roughly within the middle of the second millennium, probably contemporary with the later levels at Tell Jouweif.

Significantly, there is a suggestion of occupation into the Late Bronze Age, although continuity of occupation throughout the second millennium cannot be demonstrated. Possible Late Bronze Age forms include a heavy squared storage jar rim of general Middle Assyrian type (fig. 6.15:3) and approximately paralleled at Sabi Abyad (Rossmeisl 1989, fig. XII.6:74), and jar rims with cordoned necks (fig. 6.15:6; cf. Rossmeisl 1989, fig. XII.3:34). Less specific is a plate (fig. 6.14:5) that is either Late Bronze Age or Iron Age in date (forms CP 1–3 from Tell Abu Danne; Lebeau 1983; see also Bachelot 1999, pls. 1–2 for related LBA forms) and bowl number 3 in figure 6.14 (ibid., pl. 2:4, also LBA).

Iron Age occupation is well documented with a hole-mouth jar (fig. 6.14:13) resembling MM 3, 4, and 5 from Tell Abu Danne, a large pithos rim (fig. 6.14:22; cf. examples common at Khirbet al-Hamrah 2 [SS 15] and SS 20B, described below), as well as a range of bowls (fig. 6.14:1–3; cf. Tell Abu Danne, BL 8 dated from 950 to 700 B.C.). A pair of carinated jars of Late Bronze Age, Iron Age, or even Achaemenid date are similar, but less pronounced in form to the carinated bowls of SS 26 described below. These vessels (fig. 6.14:10 and perhaps 11) resemble those from Jurn Kabir groups A and B (ca. eleventh–mid-ninth century B.C., according to Eidem and Ackermann 1999, fig. 4:2, also fig. 6:3), but also later according to the Tell Ahmar sequence (Jamieson 1999), where they are estimated to fall in the range 650–600 B.C. Also a platter (fig. 6.14:5) is paralleled in Jurn Kabir group B (Eidem and Ackermann 1999, fig. 6:6–7) as well as those from Iron Age levels at Tell Sheikh Hassan (T 523; Schneider 1999, fig. 4.1). Finally, a few Hellenistic types were also noted.

From the collected pottery it appears that there was substantial occupation in the Middle Bronze Age which apparently continued through the Late Bronze Age into the Iron Age. This makes the site one of the few in the area to show evidence of occupation through the later second millennium into the early first millennium B.C.

IRON AGE POTTERY FROM KHIRBET AL-HAMRAH 2 (SS 15) AND 20B (SWEYHAT SURVEY PERIOD X)

With the exception of Tell Ali al-Haj (SS 17), no sites within the intensive survey area produced Late Bronze Age pottery, and it seems likely that the Sweyhat Plain was abandoned during most of the Middle and Late Bronze Age. Nevertheless, occupation continued or recommenced along the river during the Late Bronze Age at Mumbaqa (T 534), Tell Hadidi (T 548), and al-Qitar. Within the Sweyhat Plain occupation resumed during the Iron Age and two small sites (Khirbet al-Hamrah 2 [SS 15] and SS 20B) produced distinctive and diagnostic pottery that could be placed within the first half of the first millennium B.C. An additional site (SS 23) discovered in 1992 exhibited a similar range of forms (not illustrated) and again can be regarded as Iron Age in date. The lack of a local Iron Age sequence initially necessitated the use of a detailed corpus published from Tell Abu Danne, located some 30 km to the east of Aleppo (Lebeau 1983). Distinctive types common to both sites are listed in table 6.4. As a result of the publication of major studies of Iron Age ceramics from Syria and Lebanon (Lehmann 1998, 1996) and also northern Syria, Iraq, and southern Turkey (Hausleiter and Reiche 1999), it is possible to place the pottery from sites in the Sweyhat area into a broader ceramic context.

Table 6.4. Counts of Main Forms Recorded at Khirbet al-Hamrah 2 (SS 15) and SS 20B

Type Description	SS 15 (fig. 6.17)	Total	SS 20B (fig. 6.16)	Total
Standard Iron Age bowl	Fig. 6.17:4, 5, 6, 7, 25, 26, 27, 30	8	Fig. 6.16:2, 3, 30	3
Internally-thickened bowl	—	0	Fig. 6.16:6, 7, 31, 32, 33, 34	6
Indented-rim bowl	—	0	Fig. 6.16:5, 28, 29	3
Hole-mouth jar	Fig. 6.17:31	1	Fig. 6.16:27	1
Handled jar	Fig. 6.17:17, 18	2	Fig. 6.16:17, 18, 19	3
Pithos or large bowl	Fig. 6.17:19, 20, 21, 22, 23	6	Fig. 6.16:22, 23, 24, 25	4
Simple Iron Age jar rim	(total only)	8	(total only)	10
Other Iron Age handles	—	2	—	—

Bowls with an open profile dominate the assemblages and are typified by three basic forms:

Standard Iron Age Bowls

Standard Iron Age bowls with internally- and externally-thickened rims have good parallels in Late Assyrian or slightly later assemblages of northern Iraq (Curtis 1989, figs. 28–29; Curtis and Green 1997, figs. 29–31, 33, 35) and from Sultantepe in the Turkish Balikh Valley (Lloyd and Gokçe 1953, fig. 7:14–20). Equivalent forms at Tell Abu Danne (Abu Danne classes RL 27–28, 30) mainly fall within the date range 800–550 B.C. The form is also characteristic of Lehmann's assemblages 3 and 4 which continue until around 580 B.C. (Lehmann 1998, fig. 7).

Bowls with internally thickened rims were absent from Khirbet al-Hamrah 2 (SS 15) but were more common at SS 20B. Because the equivalent forms at Tell Abu Danne (BL 8) has a long time range, this disparity between the two sites, although it may represent a functional difference, may simply arise from the small size of the assemblages collected. Similar bowls from Jurn Kabir group B are thought to fall in the range tenth to mid-ninth centuries B.C. (Eidem and Ackermann 1999, fig. 6:10). Indented rim bowls (see table 6.4) only occur at SS 20B.

Hole-mouth Jar

Each site yielded a single example of a hole-mouth jar, a type that is equivalent to classes MM 3, MM 4, and MM 5 at Tell Abu Danne or group C at Jurn Kabir dated to the ninth to seventh centuries B.C. (Eidem and Ackermann 1999, fig. 9a:19–20). This form also occurred at Tell Rif'at and more recent studies of this material would place it into Lehmann's assemblages 1–4 (720–580 B.C.; Lehmann 1996, pl. 83:438a). Such hole-mouth vessels are also common at Tell Ahmar, where they are classed as cooking pots and are dated in the range 650–600 B.C. (Jamieson 1999, fig. 9).

Strap handles, usually affixed to simple jar forms, were a common type at both sites; this provides a marked contrast with the Early and Middle Bronze Ages where such handles were rare. In the Iron Age, handled vessels appear to have been much more common in western Syria (e.g., Lehmann 1996, pls. 83–86a), as well as to the north in the Turkish Euphrates Valley (Wilkinson 1990, fig. B.21), than in eastern Syria.

Pithos Rims

Also distinctive, and notably absent from Early and Middle Bronze Age sites, were heavy, coarse, usually chaff-tempered pithos rims (e.g., figs. 6.16:23, 6.17:21–23). They appear as a range of jar, and less commonly bowl forms, but owing to the problem of determining rim angle on some of these, the division between jar and bowl is not always clear. Nevertheless, the general rim type is well represented at Tell Abu Danne by a suite of forms: JP 3, JP 4, JG 1, and JG 2. Such types are also very common on sites in the Karababa area of southeast Turkey, where they were attributed to the Iron Age (Wilkinson 1990, figs. B.11:52, 55, B.12:9–10, 29, 31).

In addition to the above general classes, a number of individual profiles provided ceramic parallels outside the area. From Khirbet al-Hamrah 2 (SS 15), a simple bowl (fig. 6.17:1) is analogous to BL 13 at Tell Abu Danne, dated roughly to the eighth century B.C., or Jurn Kabir group A dated to the range eleventh to tenth century (Eidem and

Ackermann 1999, fig. 5: no. 13). From Khirbet al-Hamrah 2, a bowl or jar with a multiple grooved upper rim (fig. 6.17: no. 24), although resembling a Middle Bronze Age form, has parallels in ninth to eighth century contexts at Tell Abu Danne (Lebeau 1983, class CT 7). However, the possibility that the form continued from Middle Bronze to Iron Age times remains a possibility. Similar continuity could be argued for a jar (fig. 6.16:21) that would fit into Jurn Kabir group B, which is thought to fall in the range tenth to mid-ninth century B.C. (Eidem and Ackermann 1999). Finally, coarse finger-impressed strips on sherds of large pithos jars (fig. 6.16:26) can be paralleled at sites upstream, especially at Tell Ahmar, where they were of seventh century B.C. date (Jamieson 1999), as well as in the Karababa area, Turkey (Wilkinson 1990, figs. B.11:54, B.12:35, B.13:7), where they fell within the range Late Bronze Age to Hellenistic. These types have also been recorded farther west at Zincirli, Turkey (Lehmann 1996, pl. 67, forms 368, 369; ca. 720–580 B.C.).

Undistinguished simple jar rims were very common at both sites and the presence of handles on a number of them together with their corky, slightly porous fabric immediately distinguished them from Early to Middle Bronze Age equivalents.

To conclude, although there were slight differences between the counts of each form at the two sites (as well as SS 23), the assemblages are remarkably similar. In general, they resemble Late Assyrian assemblages of northern Iraq, but the geographically closer Tell Abu Danne assemblage provides better parallels. From the chronological ranges determined for equivalent Tell Abu Danne forms it appears that Khirbet al-Hamrah 2 (SS 15) and SS 20B were both occupied between the ninth and seventh century B.C., but the presence of a number of long-lived forms, especially those paralleled at Jurn Kabir, means that occupation as early as 1000 B.C. or as late as the sixth century B.C. cannot be discounted. Nevertheless, although some of the forms continued through much of the first millennium B.C., the generally coarse appearance of these vessels distinguishes them from the finer and smoother fabrics that were characteristic of the later, and particularly the Hellenistic, variants.

SS 26 (SWEYHAT SURVEY PERIODS X–XIII)

This disturbed and eroded site situated immediately above the level of the floodplain provides a problematic assemblage, which, although possibly plugging a gap in the occupational sequence, is sufficiently ambiguous to be treated with due caution. The site morphology suggests that its western side may have been eroded in antiquity by the Euphrates River and thus may have been considerably larger.

Unique within the survey area is the single coarse lug handle (fig. 6.19:6) that is virtually identical to early ceramic Neolithic lugs from Kumartepe within the Karababa area of southeast Turkey (Roodenberg, Wilkinson, and Bayrı-Baykan 1984). However, whether this is just a chance occurrence or the sherd once formed part of a larger site assemblage that has now been eroded away is difficult to determine.

The first millennium B.C. pottery, although quite abundant, is also problematic. The bowls are of Iron Age form; for example, figure 6.18:12 and figure 6.19:13 are equivalent to Pella Iron Age forms (McNicoll et al. 1992, pls. 64:7, 52:3) and figure 6.18:5, 7, to Tell Abu Danne BL 5 and CP 22 (Lebeau 1983). However, the assemblage is dominantly sand tempered and is of significantly finer and higher quality than the local Iron Age assemblages at Khirbet al-Hamrah 2 (SS 15) and SS 20B. Also, the presence of similar bowl forms from Hellenistic levels at Tell es-Sweyhat (Holland 1976, fig. 6:12, 22) and Tell Hammam et-Turkman level X (ibid., fig. 6:23–24; cf. Lázaro 1988, pl. 159:12–13) implies a long duration for many of the forms. Nevertheless, despite their sand temper, two forms (fig. 6.18:5, 8) include chaff temper and several (fig. 6.18:1–5, 7) have close parallels with Iron Age forms from northern Iraq (e.g., Curtis and Green 1997, figs. 29–31, 33, 35).

Most distinctive are the sharply carinated bowls and jars (fig. 6.19:15–17). These not only closely resemble Achaemenid bronze bowls from Deve Höyük (Moorey 1980, fig. 6), but also have slightly earlier parallels as well.[62] Although ceramic parallels are scarce, a good example from Late Assyrian Fort Shalmaneser, Nimrud, is very similar to figure 19:16–17 (Oates 1959, pl. 39:59). The chronological range is extended still further by the existence of Late Bronze and Early Iron Age parallels from Pella (McNicoll et al. 1992, pls. 49, 54) and Middle Bronze Age forms from Hammam et-Turkman period VII phase C (Curvers 1988, pl. 128:64–65). A further Iron Age parallel within the as-

---

62. Lehmann places these within his assemblages 3 and 4, that is, within the range 700–580 B.C. (Lehmann 1998, fig. 7:9–10), or perhaps slightly earlier, whereas at Jurn Kabir they fall much earlier, that is, within groups A and B of the eleventh to mid-ninth century B.C. (Eidem and Ackermann 1999, figs. 4:3, 6:1). Carinated fine ware jars also occur in seventh century B.C. levels at Tell Ahmar (Jamieson 1999), as well as Iron Age levels at Tell Sheikh Hassan (T 523) (E. Schneider 1999).

semblage is the hole-mouth jar (fig. 6.19:14), equivalent to MM 4 from Tell Abu Danne that falls within Lehmann's assemblages 1 to 4 (720–580 B.C.; Lehmann 1996, pl. 83).

Although some of the above exhibit Hellenistic parallels, no fully Hellenistic assemblage was evident, and it seems that there was a gap in occupation during the Hellenistic and Roman periods until the site was reoccupied in the Late Roman/Early Byzantine period as is indicated by the flanged dishes (fig. 6.19:1–2) and large bowls (fig. 6.19:4–5).

This assemblage is important because it provides evidence of settlement at floodplain level (cf. Tell Jouweif [SS 8] and Shams ed-Din Central Tell). A Late Iron Age date seems most likely, and although not definitely Achaemenid, the fine, well-made appearance of these evolved Iron Age forms, together with the absence of a Hellenistic assemblage, suggests a date between the Iron Age types of Khirbet al-Hamrah 2 (SS 15) and SS 20B and the fully Hellenistic (i.e., post-third century B.C.) assemblage of Khirbet Aboud al-Hazu (SS 6).

Khirbet Aboud al-Hazu (SS 6) (Sweyhat Survey Periods X–XI)

Although on first impression this appeared to be simply a Hellenistic/Roman site, detailed collection indicated an extended range of occupation from probably the Iron Age until at least the third century A.D. There is no indication, however, whether this approximately millennium-long occupation was continuous or not.

The small, possibly Iron Age assemblage included at least one example of the standard Iron Age open bowl (fig. 6.20:19), as well as a common Late Assyrian form with occasional chaff temper (fig. 6.20:18). The latter can be compared with class CP 14 from Tell Abu Danne and seventh century examples from Samaria-Sebaste (Crowfoot, Crowfoot, and Kenyon 1957, period VII). Figure 6.20:17 may also be an Iron Age form (Abu Danne BL 25). Other bowls (fig. 6.20:20, 22) have Hellenistic/Roman parallels at Tell Hammam et-Turkmen in period X (first century B.C. to third century A.D.), but they also may have Iron Age antecedents (Lázaro 1988, pls. 159:12, 160:22–26, respectively).

The Hellenistic pottery, which appeared to be much more common, primarily consisted of "common wares," that is, pottery that was not glazed, was coated with a red/black gloss, or brittle ware. Only a few vessels could be described as fine ware; these had fine bodies and pale red, pale brown, or mat black surface washes. Although not good examples of black or red gloss wares, they could be local imitations.

The most common bowl is the bowl with incurving rim, six of which were collected and two drawn (fig. 6.20:13–14). The bowls were tempered with moderately fine sand and were generally coated with a pale red or reddish brown wash on one or both surfaces. The form was common in the Hellenistic levels at Sweyhat Period C (Phase G in Holland 1976, fig. 6:5, 8–9, 13, 15) and in general is a very common Hellenistic diagnostic in the Levant and in greater Mesopotamia. The chronological range is from the fourth century until approximately the mid-second century B.C. (Hannestad 1983b: 15–17).[63]

Another characteristic Hellenistic form is the bowl with a modeled or molded rim interior. Figure 6.20:16 is in a moderately fine gray ware, whereas figure 6.20:12 is a slipped buff ware. Both have parallels in the Hellenistic corpus at Antioch and Samaria-Sebaste. At the former site these fall in the range fourth to second century B.C., whereas at the latter they are simply classed as pre-30 B.C. Such parallels, as well as later equivalents from Dura Europos (third century A.D.), are all in red or black gloss fine wares. Similar forms, but with simple rims and like the Sweyhat area examples not in red or black gloss ware, are common in northern Iraq. There they have a long history from perhaps the Achaemenid period until the mid-first century B.C. (L. McKenzie, pers. comm., 1989).

Another very common Hellenistic form in upper Mesopotamia is the indented jar rim with a characteristic fold-over rim. Of the six examples recorded, three (fig. 6.20:1–3) were drawn. Unfortunately, owing to their similarity to Bronze and Iron Age forms (e.g., table 6.2, Types J and K), they cannot be used on their own as diagnostics of Hellenistic occupation. But when they are present with independently dated Hellenistic types (and when Bronze Age forms are absent) they can each supply supporting evidence of Hellenistic occupation. In the north Jazirah of Iraq, although this form has earlier antecedents, the form illustrated here is a valuable diagnostic for the period fourth century to the first century B.C., after which developed forms continue into the Parthian period (Wilkinson and Tucker 1995: 118). Two examples have been published from Tell es-Sweyhat (Holland 1976, fig. 6:32–33), and the form is especially common at Tell Hammam et-Turkman level X (Lázaro 1988, pl. 165:80–92), as well as at numerous other sites in the Balikh Valley (Gerritsen 1996).

---

63. Note that earlier related forms were in use in western Syria during the Late Iron Age (ca. 720–650 B.C.; Lehmann 1996 types 127–29, pl. 22).

Owing to their scarcity, Hellenistic fine wares were not subdivided into groups but were classed together. None of the seven fine wares noted were sufficiently complete for illustration. Of these, none was a good example of black or red gloss ware, and instead the most common surface treatment was of red, reddish brown, pale red, or black wash (or paint) on a moderately fine body.

Strap handles were frequent, eight examples being of common plain ware, another being of brittle ware. Although the latter may suggest a Late Roman occupation for Khirbet Aboud al-Hazu (SS 6) (cf. those from the Karababa area; Wilkinson 1990, figs. B.15:33, B.16:5), the long time span of use for this ware from the first to the seventh century A.D. (Harper 1980: 335) could be consistent with a pre-third century A.D. date.

Taken together, the ceramic parallels suggest an occupation commencing perhaps as early as the seventh century B.C., and which followed on from the abandonment of Khirbet al-Hamrah 2 (SS 15) and SS 20B. However, the long life of some of the first millennium B.C. bowl forms suggests that initial occupation may not have occurred until later in the millennium. To judge by the abundance of Hellenistic pottery, the site attained its peak occupation at that time, after which occupation may have continued as late as the third century A.D., but probably not much later.

The small but distinctive group of pottery from Ramalah (SS 16B) was initially thought to be Hellenistic in date, but on reconsideration the internally-thickened rim bowls (fig. 6.20:26–31) resemble bowls of group B at Jurn Kabir dated to the tenth to mid-ninth centuries B.C. (Eidem and Ackermann 1999, fig. 6:10). Also, figure 6.20:32 resembles the carinated bowls illustrated for SS 26 and variously dated within the Iron Age (see above).

KHIRBET HAJ HASSAN (SS 10) AND SS 4 (MAINLY SWEYHAT SURVEY PERIOD XIII)

Khirbet Haj Hassan (SS 10) appears to be earlier than SS 4 and yielded a small but consistent collection of sherds (fig. 6.21). Brittle ware cooking pots are represented by figure 6.21:5, 7, 12–15, of which four (fig. 6.21:12–15) are handles characteristic of the Late Roman/Early Byzantine periods. The single keel rim bowl (fig. 6.21:18), although from its form appearing to fall in the same time range, is not in the more typical and diagnostic Late Roman C fabric. The painted body sherd of a scroll-painted amphora is again a common type for the period, being frequent in Early Byzantine levels at Dibsi Faraj (T 541) farther down the Euphrates Valley (Harper 1980, nos. 70–71) and as far east as the Balikh Valley (Bartl 1994, fig. 2:2–5). The large grooved-rim bowls in pale brown sandy ware are common on Late Antique sites in the region and appear to be the antecedents of the Abbasid forms present at Khirbet al-Hamrah (SS 7), Khirbet Dhiman (SS 11), and SS 12 (e.g., fig. 6.23:8).

SS 4, on the other hand, provides a smaller, less diagnostic assemblage that shows some signs of continuing into the Early Islamic period. The amphora (fig. 6.22:1) is probably Late Roman/Early Byzantine in date, as are the brittle wares: fig. 6.22:7–10 and 13–14. The distinctive brittle ware rim form (fig. 6.22:11) appears to be slightly later in date and compares with Early Islamic forms from Samarra, Iraq (Northedge 1981, fig. 245:5). It has been recorded at site 6 of the Late Antique and Early Islamic period near Kurban Höyük (Wilkinson 1990, fig. B.17:27–28) and appears to be antecedent to the hole-mouth Abbasid brittle ware illustrated by Whitcomb from Khirbet Dhiman (SS 11; fig. 6.27:6, 11–15).

The material from Khirbet Haj Hassan (SS 10) appears to be roughly contemporaneous to, or slightly later than, Late Roman levels at Tell es-Sweyhat from locus 3.3 in Trenches 1A1 and 1A2 that are dated to the period A.D. 350–400 (Holland, *Sweyhat* 2, Period B). SS 4, on the other hand, may have continued to be occupied into the Early Islamic period but apparently not as late as Khirbet al-Hamrah (SS 7), Khirbet Dhiman (SS 11), and SS 12.

KHIRBET DHIMAN (SS 11) AND KHIRBET AL-HAMRAH (SS 7) (SWEYHAT SURVEY PERIOD XIV)

Donald Whitcomb

The Lake Tabqa (renamed Assad) Reservoir Salvage Project encouraged a concentrated archaeological effort in the upper Euphrates Valley in the 1970s and 1980s. Major sites such as Balis (modern Meskene) and Qal'at Ja'bar (T 540) were investigated. Moreover, the intensive survey of this region revealed numerous smaller archaeological sites. This is a brief report on two small sites found in the vicinity of Tell es-Sweyhat in 1972. The inherent interest of these remains was noted at that time, but the relative lack of interest in the Islamic archaeology of this region did not encourage further study some twenty-five years ago. Happily, this situation has dramatically changed, especially with the publication of the Berlin conference by Bartl and Hauser (1996).

Two Farmsteads

The two sites, Khirbet Dhiman (SS 11) and Khirbet al-Hamrah (SS 7), lie on the alluvial terrace above the flood-plain of the Euphrates River (pl. 16). Both settlements are the inversion of the tells or mounds of the region; the ruins are low areas of grayish soil. Within each area are stone foundations and slightly raised features of bricky wash. These features were observed on the ground in 1972 and again in 1974 (by Tony J. Wilkinson); between these two surveys, their plans were easily traced on a series of aerial photographs in Chicago. This aerial perspective provides a structural clarity for these sites without excavation.

Khirbet Dhiman (SS 11) has three distinct blocks of structures grouped around a central building; on the western periphery stood a walled enclosure, about 70 × 70 m. An axial depression oriented east–west appears to have been a street. These structures appear to be blocks of two to four rectangular buildings (each 20–25 m on a side). This would seem to be a common size for courtyard houses (e.g., Déhès; Sodini et al. 1980, fig. 6).

Khirbet al-Hamrah (SS 7) follows the same plan with at least two housing blocks and a slightly smaller enclosure (this time on the southern edge). Again, the blocks are arranged in linear units of three and four houses and separated by street-like depressions.

The Ceramics

The clear structure of these sites suggests a relatively short period of occupation. The ceramics recovered from the sites indicate a congruity in their dating. Both sites were characterized by a high percentage of glazed ware, a splashed polychrome style of yellow or white base with green and brown accents. This ware is well known from excavations at Abu Gosh (de Vaux and Steve 1950) and Khirbet al-Mafjar in Palestine, where they indicate an important Abbasid occupation. More recently, the materials from Tell Yoqne'am (Qaymun; 23 km southeast of Haifa; Avissar 1996) have clearly demonstrated the transitional nature of this ware between Coptic glazed ware (a late Umayyad Levantine tradition; Whitcomb 1990/91) and the introduction of Samarran wares (an eastern tradition of the early ninth century).

This sequencing of Palestinian glazed wares is necessary to counteract the pervasive influence of the Samarran tradition in the archaeology of northern Syria. The work of Oliver Watson on ceramics from Tell Aswad at Raqqa leads him to segregate a yellow ware family as the earliest glazed tradition in north Syria, antecedent and distinct from the eastern developments focused on Samarra (1999: 81–87). Once this yellow ware (or common glazed ware) is defined, one begins to recognize this heuristic type in numerous excavations and surveys. Sherds are published from the Balikh survey (Bartl 1994, pl. 37) and from the work at Rusafa, particularly the mosque assemblage (Logar 1996, pls. 63–64). Among these publications, one must include that important Abbasid site of Qasr al-Hayr al-Sharqi, where type H-1 falls into this category. This may also be Ware F, a glazed fine red ware, found in the excavations at Balis (Leisten 1999–2000: 52), and similar sherds from Nisibis (Guérin 1996, group II, 33, 37–40).

The glazed sherds should also be seen as a crucial part of larger assemblages, which include so-called brittle wares, hard-fired red cooking wares. The types at these sites conform to early Abbasid forms (the slight overlap with the assemblage from Déhès confirms the earlier date for most of that material). Likewise one has specific types of basins, juglets, and moulded decoration that find parallels on many Syrian sites of the early Islamic period (e.g., the Rusafa mosque). The virtue of these two settlements is that, if they may be accepted as short occupations, these total assemblages should be contemporaneous and typical for the period A.D. 750–800.

Cities and Villages

The Islamic city of Balis (modern Meskene) is the nearest urban center and its morphology and the products of its kilns would be of prime importance for understanding the urban referent for these smaller settlements. The French excavations at Balis (1970–1973) provide some evidence of the *îlot*, a block of construction, ca. 20 m on a side (Raymond and Paillet 1995). The kilns discovered there were apparently of later date (Bartl 1994: 150–51).

These two archaeological sites appear to have been planned settlements of short duration in the late eighth century. Ruins of morphologically similar settlements were identified from the air by Poidebard (1934), blocks of houses arranged around rectangular central mounds (which he called "castra," though none are necessarily pre-Islamic). These ruins are very generally in the region of Balis and probably served as agricultural satellites for this commercial center during the Umayyad and Abbasid periods. As such, they may more properly be considered urban implantations, rather than farmsteads or villages.

SS 12 (SWEYHAT SURVEY PERIOD XIV)

The ceramic assemblage from SS 12 is primarily Early Islamic in date. It includes two jar rims of cream or very pale brown ware, a fabric type that tends to replace the pale brown wares of the Late Roman/Early Byzantine period. The range of brittle wares (fig. 6.30:1, 7–8, 13), although including possible Early Byzantine forms such as the strap handle (no. 13), appears to be somewhat later in date than those from SS 4 and Khirbet Haj Hassan (SS 10). For example, the two hole-mouth forms (fig. 6.30:7–8) resemble examples from Abbasid Khirbet Dhiman (SS 11; fig. 6.27:11–15). The glazed bowls (6.30:9–10, 14) are also Abbasid types comparable to those from Khirbet Dhiman as well as from the Early Islamic khan at Kurban Höyük (Algaze 1990, area D). A small flanged bowl (fig. 6.30:11) although resembling Early Byzantine forms, could also be Early Islamic, as could the large bowls (fig. 6.30:16–17).

SS 28 (SWEYHAT SURVEY PERIOD XV)

This small assemblage lacks the brittle wares that are characteristic of the Late Roman through Abbasid period, the only equivalent being a softer and less brittle cooking pot ware (fig. 6.31:2). The most diagnostic sherd from this group is the turquoise glazed bowl rim with black hanging swags (fig. 6.31:8), which probably falls within the range of frit wares of the eleventh to thirteenth century A.D. (Tonghini 1996). The relief-molded ware would fit within this time range also. Although large plain ware bowls are present, unlike at the Late Antique and Early Islamic sites of the area, these have a pronounced flange and feature wavy line incisions.

Together, this assemblage can be assessed as falling roughly within the range of the middle Islamic period, that is, they are post-Abbasid and were probably in use in the Zangid or Ayyubid periods.

6.B. SWEYHAT LANDSCAPE STUDIES POTTERY CATALOGS

CONVENTIONS

In fabric descriptions, colors were observed on the freshly broken edge of sherds. Temper is described according to its relative abundance: abundant, common, occasional, and rare. If no temper is mentioned it is absent or indeterminate. Rim diameters are only stated where a complete profile was not drawn; in such cases if no diameter is given, the rim diameter was indeterminate. For the Islamic ceramics, glaze conventions are adapted and modified from the original drawings by Whitcomb as follows:

Stipple: for yellow, or in one or two cases pale green, where that obviously forms the background color

Oblique hatching: green, closer where darker

Solid: black, grayish brown, brown, or dark gray

Vertical lines: blue

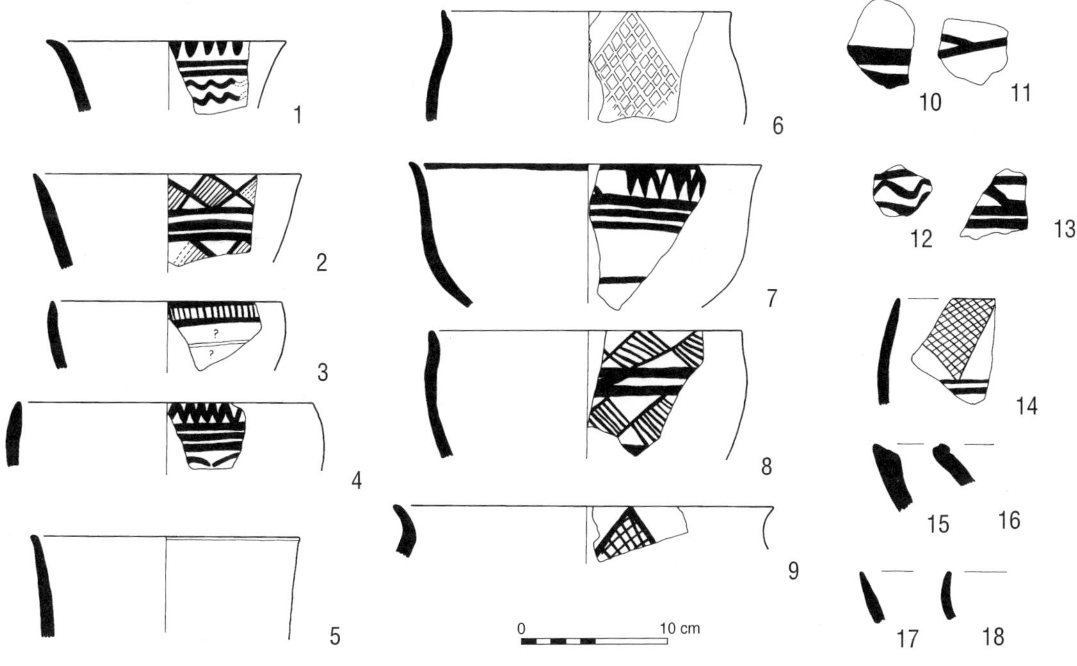

Figure 6.1. Pottery from SS 30. Sweyhat Survey Period II (Earlier Ubaid)

1. *Survey No. 2*. Rim of jar or bowl. Very hard black body partly vitrified green towards exterior; pale brown interior, pale green-slipped exterior. Common fine sand, some vesicles. Mat black painted broad bands and waves on exterior.

2. *Survey No. 1*. Bowl rim. Pale brown throughout with very pale green-slipped exterior. Fine fabric, rare medium-coarse sand; occasional fine voids. Mat dark gray-brown painted hatched diamond pattern on exterior.

3. *Survey No. 10*. Bowl rim. Pale red brown with pale brown surfaces. Occasional sand and rare large white inclusions. Very dull red painted lattice on exterior, partly faded; invisible where indicated by "??"

4. *Survey No. 7*. Bowl rim. Dull orange throughout. Moderately fine fabric, rare medium sand, occasional planar voids from chaff. Mat red paint in broad bands and running zigzag on exterior. Handmade.

5. *Survey No. 14*. Plain jar rim. Pale red brown, pale brown exterior. Moderately fine fabric, rare sand, occasional voids from fine chaff. Neat exterior beading.

6. *Survey No. 11*. Jar rim. Pale brown, pale yellow surfaces. Common fine/medium sand. Lattice painted in dull orange on exterior (now fugitive, shown in outline only). Handmade.

7. *Survey No. 5*. Bowl. Pale brown with yellowish surfaces. Occasional fine/medium sand and small voids. Horizontal bands and triangles in mat very dark reddish brown paint on exterior. Handmade.

8. *Survey No. 6*. Bowl. Pale red with pale brown core. Rare-medium sand temper, occasional voids and planar voids. Moderately fine fabric. Hatched diamond patterns in dark red mat paint on exterior.

9. *Survey No. 9*. Jar rim. Pale red brown body, pale yellow-slipped exterior. Occasional medium-coarse sand, some large irregular voids. Diamond on exterior infilled with crosshatching in dull red mat paint.

10. *Survey No. 17*. Body sherd. Pale brown, pale greenish-slipped exterior. Occasional medium sand. Broad bands in dark brown paint on exterior.

11. *Survey No. 18*. Body sherd. Hard grayish green body, pale brown surfaces. Abundant sand temper, partly vitrified. Dull black painted curvilinear bands on exterior.

12. *Survey No. 3*. Body sherd. Dark grayish brown, pale brown surfaces. Fine black sand temper. Curvilinear bands in mat black paint on exterior.

13. *Survey No. 4*. Body sherd. Pale grayish brown with pale brown interior and pale yellow-slipped exterior. Common black medium sand temper. Curvilinear bands in mat black paint on exterior.

14. *Survey No. 8*. Jar rim. Brown throughout. Moderately fine fabric, fine sand temper, occasional fine voids. Crosshatched lattice within diamond, painted in mat dark red on exterior. Handmade.

15. *Survey No. 15*. Bowl rim. Pale red brown throughout. Occasional fine sand, some fine voids.

16. *Survey No. 16*. Bowl rim. Pale grayish brown, locally reddened. Occasional fine/medium sand, rare voids.

17. *Survey No. 13*. Rim of small bowl. Pale brown with very pale brown surfaces. Moderately fine. Occasional sand and small voids.

18. *Survey No. 12*. Rim of small bowl. Pale brown, smooth pale yellow surfaces. Fine fabric, rare sand occasional small voids.

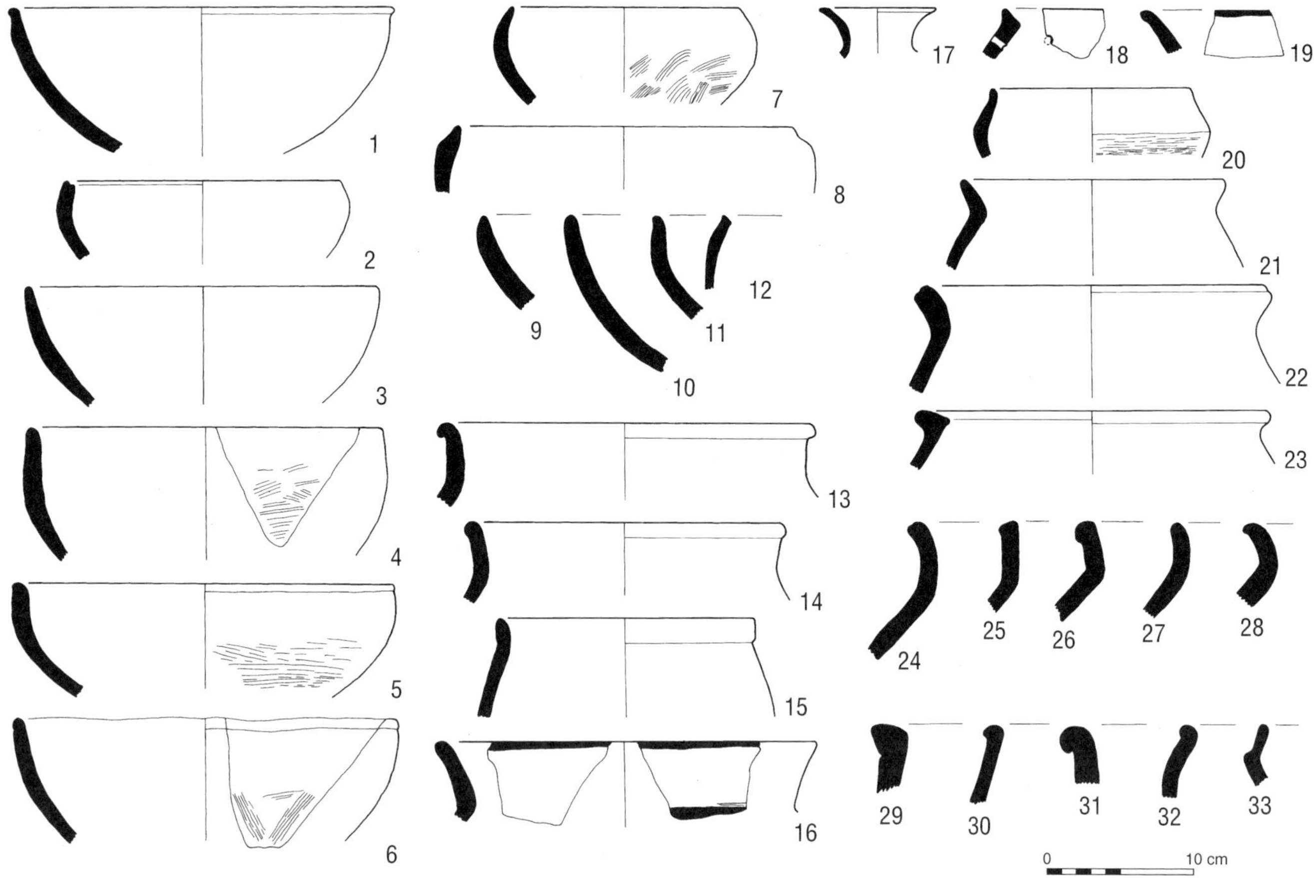

Figure 6.2. Pottery from SS 25. Sweyhat Survey Period III (Later Ubaid and Late Chalcolithic)

1. *Survey No. 10*. Open bowl. Pale brown, very pale brown surfaces. Common sand, rare fine chaff.

2. *Survey No. 11*. Bowl with grooved rim. Black, dark gray brown surfaces. Occasional fine sand and chaff.

3. *Survey No. 1*. Open bowl. Pale red brown throughout. Common chaff and medium sand. Flint-scraped lower body.

4. *Survey No. 2*. Bowl. Reddish brown throughout. Occasional chaff and fine sand. Flint-scraped lower body.

5. *Survey No. 5*. Open bowl. Pale red brown throughout. Dense, fine fabric, rare chaff, occasional fine, micaceous sand. Flint-scraped lower body. Slightly beaded-rim exterior.

6. *Survey No. 7*. Open bowl. Red brown and pale red brown surfaces. Dense fabric, fine/medium voids. Occasional micaceous fine sand. Common chaff impressions on surfaces. Flint-scraped lower exterior body. Beaded-rim exterior.

7. *Survey No. 8*. Rim of incurved bowl. Pale red brown, dark gray core. Rare chaff and occasional micaceous sand temper. Flint-scraped lower body.

8. *Survey No. 12*. Bowl rim. Black with dark gray surfaces, burnished exterior. Occasional chaff and fine sand. Handmade.

9. *Survey No. 3*. Bowl rim. Pale red brown throughout. Occasional chaff and rare large irregular voids, some white sand. Flint-scraped lower body. Diameter 30 cm.

10. *Survey No. 4*. Bowl rim. Pale red brown body and interior, pale brown exterior. Common chaff and medium Euphrates sand. Diameter 34 cm.

11. *Survey No. 6*. Bowl rim. Pale brown throughout. Fine sand with rare fine chaff temper. Flint-scraped lower body. Diameter 26 cm.

12. *Survey No. 9*. Grooved bowl rim. Pale red with very pale brown surfaces. Rare fine chaff and occasional fine/medium sand temper.

13. *Survey No. 18*. Rim of necked jar. Pale grayish brown with pale brown surfaces. Common fine chaff, occasional sand.

14. *Survey No. 25*. Jar rim. Pale red brown with very pale brown-slipped exterior. Occasional chaff temper.

15. *Survey No. 28*. Jar rim. Pale brown, very pale brown surfaces. Occasional medium sand and chaff temper. Hand finished.

16. *Survey No. 29*. Jar rim. Pale gray brown with very pale brown surfaces. Rare sand and indeterminate temper. Dark gray brown mat paint.

17. *Survey No. 21*. Jar rim. Very pale brown throughout. Occasional medium sand.

18. *Survey No. 16a*. Pierced ledge rim. Pale red brown body, very pale brown surfaces. Occasional medium sand and chaff temper. Pierced by 4 mm diameter perforation.

19. *Survey No. 23*. Flared jar rim. Very pale gray brown with very pale brown surfaces. Smooth, fine fabric, occasional fine sand. Very dark brown mat paint on exterior. Wheel thrown.

20. *Survey No. 14*. Rim of biconical bowl. Red brown with pale brown upper surfaces. Occasional chaff and fine sand. Horizontal scraping below carination.

21. *Survey No. 19*. Cooking pot rim. Black, bright red margins, pale brown exterior. Common chaff, occasional fine sand.

22. *Survey No. 20*. Jar rim. Brown body, pale brown surfaces. Common fine chaff voids, occasional sand.

23. *Survey No. 16b*. Rim of cooking pot. Reddish brown with dark reddish brown surfaces, some dark gray patches. Common medium-coarse sand. Occasional chaff and chaff voids.

24. *Survey No. 24*. Jar rim. Gray throughout. Common chaff. Oblique wiping on exterior. Diameter 30 cm.

25. *Survey No. 26*. Jar rim. Brown, pale brown surfaces. Abundant chaff, sparse mica. Diameter 26 cm.

26. *Survey No. 27*. Jar rim. Black core, pale red brown margins and exterior; pale brown interior. Abundant chaff temper. Roughly wheel finished. Diameter 26 cm.

27. *Survey No. 30*. Jar rim. Pale red brown with red brown margins and surfaces. Chaff temper, rare medium sand. Diameter 26 cm.

28. *Survey No. 31*. Jar rim. Red brown with pale brown core and surfaces. Common chaff. Diameter 26 cm.

29. *Survey No. 32*. Jar rim. Pale brown with reddened margins and pale brown surfaces. Occasional medium sand and voids from medium chaff. Diameter 32 cm.

30. *Survey No. 17*. Rim of bowl or casserole. Pale reddish brown with very pale brown surfaces. Occasional common chaff and sand. Diameter ca. 40 cm.

31. *Survey No. 22*. Rim of jar or casserole. Pale reddish brown with pale brown surfaces. Occasional sand and chaff temper.

32. *Survey No. 13*. Bowl rim. Black, gray margins and surfaces. Occasional chaff, common on interior. Occasional fine sand.

33. *Survey No. 15*. Rim of carinated bowl. Dark gray core, pale brown margins and surfaces. Lightly burnished exterior. Occasional fine sand and rare chaff.

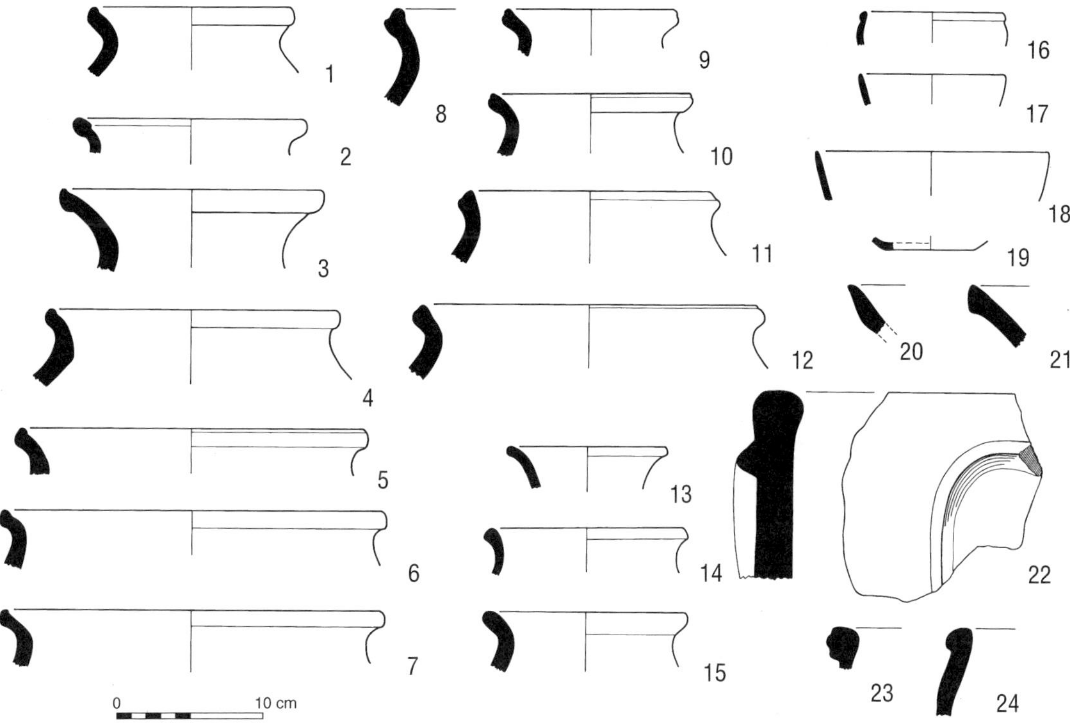

Figure 6.3. Pottery from SS 2. Sweyhat Survey Period V (Early Early Bronze Age)

1. *Survey No. 1/92*. Jar rim. Pink, pale yellow-slipped exterior. Common fine/medium sand; one calcite grit.

2. *Survey No. 10/91*. Jar rim. Pale brown throughout. Common sand temper.

3. *Survey No. 8/91*. Jar rim. Grayish brown body, pale brown surfaces. Occasional indeterminate sand temper.

4. *Survey No. 2/91*. Jar rim. Pale red brown and brown body; pale greenish brown slip on exterior, pale brown interior. Occasional Euphrates sand temper.

5. *Survey No. 11/91*. Jar rim. Gray core, pale red brown surfaces. Common Euphrates sand.

6. *Survey No. 8/92*. Jar rim. Pale brown with very pale brown surfaces. Fine sand temper.

7. *Survey No. 5/92*. Jar rim. Dark gray with pale greenish brown-slipped surfaces. Common fine/medium sand.

8. *Survey No. 2/92*. Rim of large jar. Pink with pale brown core; pale yellow-slipped surfaces. Common medium Euphrates sand. Roughly formed, wheel thrown with some surface blistering. Diameter ca. 32 cm.

9. *Survey No. 7/92*. Jar rim. Pale reddish brown, pale yellowish brown surfaces. Common medium sand, some pale yellow grog temper.

10. *Survey No. 5/91*. Jar rim. Pale greenish gray core, pale green exterior and interior. Common fine Euphrates sand.

11. *Survey No. 4/91*. Jar rim. Pale brown core becoming brown towards surfaces; pale greenish brown-slipped surfaces. Occasional Euphrates sand.

12. *Survey No. 6/92*. Jar rim. Gray, pale greenish brown surfaces. Common fine/medium sand.

13. *Survey No. 7/92*. Jar rim. Pale greenish brown, pale brown surfaces. Common fine sand.

14. *Survey No. 9/92*. Jar rim. Pale brown throughout. Occasional sand temper.

15. *Survey No. 6/91*. Jar rim. Pale red brown core with brown margins and pale greenish brown surfaces. Common Euphrates sand temper.

16. *Survey No. 13/91*. Rim of small bowl. Pale red brown throughout. Fine sand temper.

17. *Survey No. 12/91*. Fine bowl rim. Very pale brown throughout. Fine sand temper.

18. *Survey No. 11/92*. Rim of fine bowl. Very pale brown throughout. Hard; fine sand temper.

19. *Survey No. 15/91*. Flat base. Hard, pale brown body, pale gray brown exterior and interior surfaces. Fineware with some indeterminate fine sand temper.

20. *Survey No. n.a.* Band-rim bowl. Gray brown body, very pale brown surfaces. Common fine sand. Diameter ca. 26 cm.

21. *Survey No. 3/93*. Rim of flared jar or pedestal base. Gray brown with pale gray brown surfaces. Fine/medium sand with fine planar voids. Diameter 28 cm.

22. *Survey No. 17/91*. Storage jar. Dark gray core, red brown margins and brown exterior, dark red brown interior. Coarse grit and some chaff temper. Handmade with applied horseshoe handle. Diameter >30 cm.

23. *Survey No. 14/91*. Grooved-rim jar. Gray body; pale reddish brown surfaces. Common sand, some mica. Very battered, possibly field scatter. Diameter 28 cm.

24. *Survey No. 16/91*. Bowl rim. Pale gray brown surfaces and body. Occasional sand temper. Diameter ca. 20 cm.

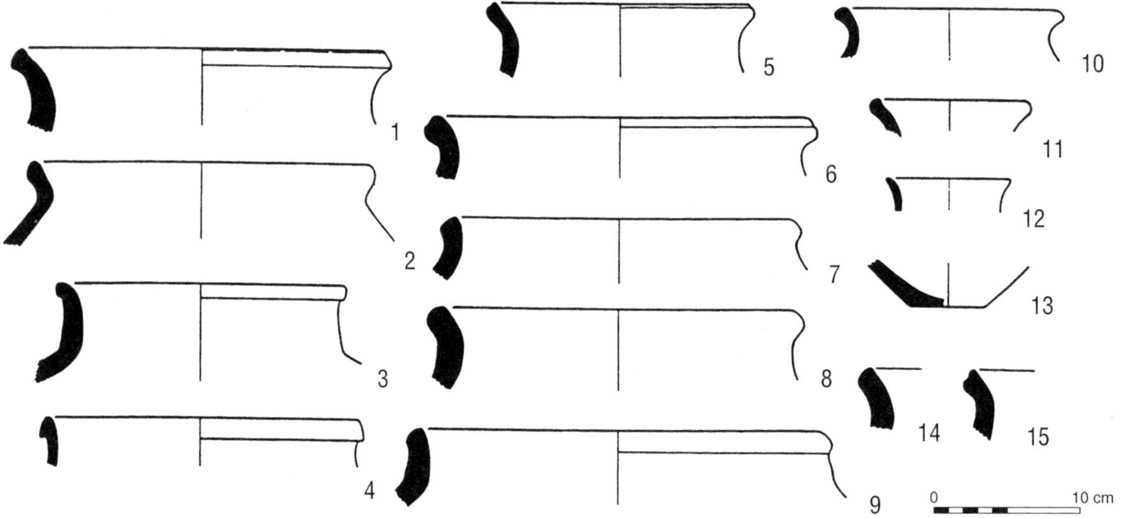

Figure 6.4. Pottery from Tell Hajji Ibrahim (SS 3). Sweyhat Survey Period V (Early Early Bronze Age)

1. *Survey No. 6/92*. Jar rim. Gray brown with pale brown surfaces. Common fine/medium sand.

2. *Survey No. 7/92*. Jar rim. Pale brown throughout. Common fine/medium sand.

3. *Survey No. 1/92*. Jar rim. Gray brown, pale brown surfaces. Common sand; occasional large irregular voids. Rather roughly made.

4. *Survey No. 5/92*. Jar rim. Pale greenish brown throughout. Abundant fine/medium sand, some dark minerals.

5. *Survey No. 4/92*. Jar rim. Red brown core, pale brown margins; pale green-slipped surfaces. Common sand.

6. *Survey No. 2/92*. Jar rim. Pale brown, very pale greenish brown-slipped surfaces. Abundant medium sand.

7. *Survey No. 3/91*. Jar rim. Pale red with brown core; pale greenish brown surfaces. Occasional fine sand.

8. *Survey No. 1/91*. Jar rim. Pale red body becoming brown towards exterior. Pale brown surfaces. Dense fabric with occasional medium sand. Very slight indentation in top of rim.

9. *Survey No. 2/91*. Jar rim. Dark greenish gray, pale greenish surfaces. Common black and translucent white grits; occasional planar voids.

10. *Survey No. 4/91*. Jar rim. Pale green throughout. Very pale greenish brown surfaces. Evenly fired; occasional fine/medium sand.

11. *Survey No. 6/91*. Jar rim. Very pale green, pale greenish brown surfaces. Dense fabric; occasional fine/medium sand.

12. *Survey No. 7/91*. Pale brown throughout, very pale brown surfaces. Occasional fine sand; rare planar voids.

13. *Survey No. 8/91*. Flat base. Pale reddish brown body; pale brown exterior; pale brown and pale red interior. Common medium sand with occasional mica.

14. *Survey No. 5/91*. Jar rim. Pale red brown body; very pale greenish brown surfaces. Common medium sand. Diameter >30 cm.

15. *Survey No. 3/92*. Jar rim. Gray-brown, pale brown margins, and very pale greenish-slipped exterior. Common fine/medium sand. Diameter indeterminate.

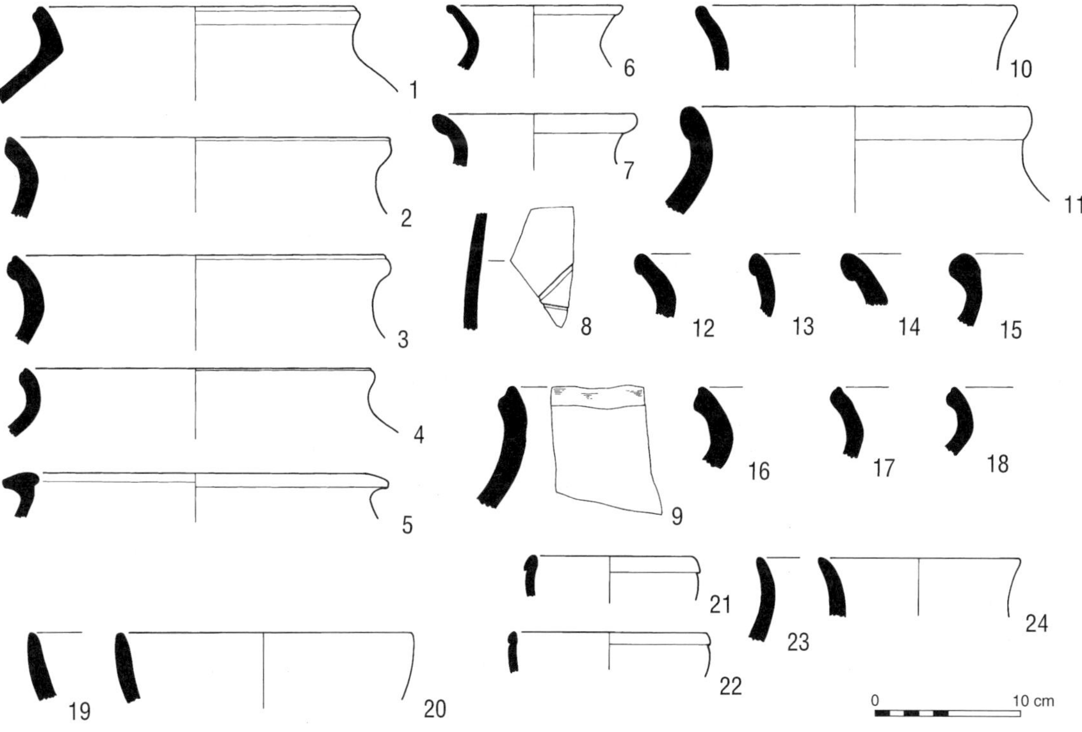

Figure 6.5. Pottery from SS 9. Sweyhat Survey Period V (Early Early Bronze Age)

1. *Survey No. 13/9B.* Beaded-jar rim. Gray-brown body, pale gray brown interior, very pale greenish exterior. Rare sand temper; occasional planar voids, possibly from chaff.

2. *Survey No. 14/9B.* Beaded-rim jar. Gray brown becoming pale brown at exterior margin; pale brown interior; pale green exterior surface. Hard, dense fabric with occasional irregular voids and Euphrates sand.

3. *Survey No. 17/9A.* Beaded-rim jar. Gray throughout, slightly reddened margins, very pale brown surfaces. Occasional medium sand, rare planar voids.

4. *Survey No. 18/9B.* Beaded-rim jar. Brown core, pale brown margins and surfaces. Moderately dense fabric with occasional medium Euphrates sand.

5. *Survey No. 22/9B.* Rim of jar/bowl. Pale red brown body, pale brown surfaces. Occasional coarse Euphrates sand.

6. *Survey No. 3/9A.* Jar rim. Dull greenish gray exterior half, very pale green interior half; very pale green surfaces. Dense fabric with occasional medium sand.

7. *Survey No. 4/9A.* Jar rim. Pale greenish brown throughout; very pale green surfaces. Abundant medium Euphrates sand.

8. *Survey No. 25/9A.* Body sherd. Brown core with reddish brown margins. Moderately fine, dense fabric with rare medium/coarse sand temper. Incised grooves ca. 1 mm wide, 0.5 mm deep.

9. *Survey No. 15/9A.* Beaded-rim jar. Dark gray body, pale brown surfaces. Occasional sand temper. One or two chaff impressions. Hand-formed rim. Diameter 35 cm.

10. *Survey No. 10/9B.* Jar rim. Pale greenish brown body, pale green surfaces. Moderately dense fabric; occasional medium Euphrates sand.

11. *Survey No. 7/9B.* Jar rim. Pale gray body, very pale brown surfaces. Rare sand and one or two chaff impressions.

12. *Survey No. 5/9B.* Jar rim. Brown with pale brown surfaces. Dense fabric, occasional medium sand. Diameter 26 cm.

13. *Survey No. 8/9B.* Jar rim. Pale green body, very pale green interior surface, pale brown exterior. Occasional medium Euphrates sand. Diameter 26 cm.

14. *Survey No. 6/9A.* Jar rim. Gray brown body, brown margins, pale brown surfaces. Rare sand, occasional fine planar voids.

15. *Survey No. 21/9B.* Jar rim. Pale greenish brown throughout, very pale brown surfaces. Occasional fine, rare medium sand.

16. *Survey No. 16/9B.* Beaded-rim jar. Pale brown body and interior surface, pale greenish exterior surface. Occasional medium Euphrates sand.

17. *Survey No. 11/9A.* Beaded-rim jar. Pale brown throughout. Common fine/medium sand. Diameter ca. 20 cm.

18. *Survey No. 19/9B.* Beaded-rim jar. Pale brown body, very pale green surfaces. Moderately dense with occasional sand. Diameter ca. 14 cm.

19. *Survey No. 1/9B.* Bowl rim. Pale gray, pale brown surfaces. Occasional medium sand with dark inclusions. Diameter 34 cm.

20. *Survey No. 2/9A.* Bowl rim. Very pale greenish brown throughout. Occasional medium Euphrates sand. Hand-finished with uneven rim.

21. *Survey No. 23/9A.* Jar rim. Pale brown with very pale brown surfaces. Occasional medium Euphrates sand.

22. *Survey No. 20/9B.* Beaded-rim bowl. Brown body, very pale brown surfaces. Moderately fine with fine sand temper.

23. *Survey No. 12/9B.* Jar rim. Brown with pale brown surfaces. Rare indeterminate sand. Irregular hand-formed rim.

24. *Survey No. 9/9B.* Jar rim. Very pale brown core, pale red brown margins, pale brown surfaces. Dense, moderately fine fabric, rare sand.

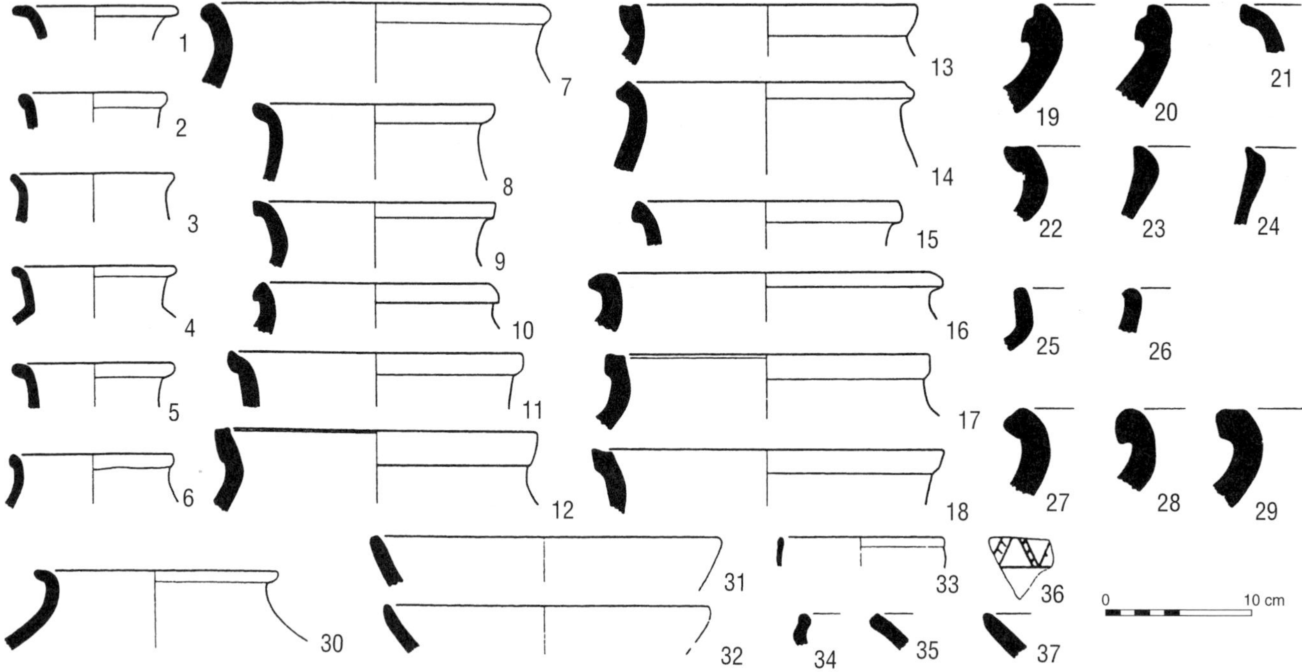

Figure 6.6. Pottery from SS 21. Sweyhat Survey Period V (Early Early Bronze Age)

1. *Survey No. 21.* Jar rim. Pale brown body, very pale brown surfaces. Occasional sand.

2. *Survey No. 22.* Jar rim. Brown body, pale brown surfaces. Common sand.

3. *Survey No. 7.* Jar rim. Pale red brown body, very pale brown surfaces. Occasional medium sand.

4. *Survey No. 17.* Folded-over jar rim. Pale green throughout. Hard, dense fabric, almost vitrified. Common medium sand, occasional lined vesicles.

5. *Survey No. 18.* Folded-over jar rim. Brown body, very pale brown surfaces. Moderately fine. Rare medium/coarse sand.

6. *Survey No. 6.* Folded-over jar. Pale brown body, very pale brown surfaces. Moderately fine fabric, occasional fine sand.

7. *Survey No. 19.* Jar rim. Pale reddish brown throughout, pale brown surfaces. Common Euphrates sand.

8. *Survey No. 15.* Folded-over jar rim. Brown body, pale brown interior surface, pale greenish exterior. Common Euphrates sand.

9. *Survey No. 35.* Jar rim. Pale brown body, very pale brown surfaces. Occasional medium sand.

10. *Survey No. 36.* Jar rim. Pale red brown body, very pale brown surfaces. Occasional fine/medium sand.

11. *Survey No. 16.* Jar rim. Gray becoming brown towards vessel interior; pale green-slipped surfaces. Dense, rare medium sand.

12. *Survey No. 23.* Jar rim. Pale reddish brown body. Very pale brown surfaces. Occasional medium sand and voids.

13. *Survey No. 24.* Jar rim. Gray core, pale greenish margins, pale green surfaces. Hard, abundant medium Euphrates sand.

14. *Survey No. 9.* Jar rim. Pale green throughout. Common medium Euphrates sand.

15. *Survey No. 10.* Jar rim. Pale brown body, locally reddish. Very pale brown surfaces. Occasional fine sand temper.

16. *Survey No. 37.* Jar rim. Brown body, very pale brown surfaces. Occasional sand and chaff temper.

17. *Survey No. 33.* Jar rim. Dark gray body, pale green surfaces. Occasional fine/medium sand.

18. *Survey No. 34.* Jar rim. Pale greenish brown body, pale green-slipped surfaces. Occasional medium sand.

19. *Survey No. 1.* Rim of large jar. Pale greenish gray body, pale brown interior, reddish and pale brown exterior. Occasional sand. Diameter 32 cm.

20. *Survey No. 2.* Rim of large jar. Gray core, pale brown margins and surfaces. Occasional medium sand. Diameter 46 cm.

21. *Survey No. 25.* Jar rim. Green body, pale green surfaces. Common fine/medium Euphrates sand. Diameter 30 cm.

22. *Survey No. 27.* Jar rim. Pale brown body, very pale brown surfaces. Common sand. Diameter 28 cm.

23. *Survey No. 28.* Rim of hole-mouth jar. Gray body, pale gray surfaces. Occasional medium sand. Diameter 26 cm.

24. *Survey No. 40.* Rim of hole-mouth jar. Handmade. Gray brown body with brown margins. Brown exterior and gray brown interior. Dense, fine fabric; common large black grits.

25. *Survey No. 38.* Jar rim. Dark gray body, pale green surfaces. Very hard, very dense, almost vitrified body. Common sand, some fine vesicles. Diameter 28 cm.

26. *Survey No. 42.* Jar rim. Pale greenish gray, pale brown surfaces. Moderately soft; occasional sand.

27. *Survey No. 11.* Jar rim. Pale gray core with pale brown margins; pale brown surfaces. Common Euphrates sand. Diameter 30 cm.

28. *Survey No. 13.* Jar rim. Gray brown core with reddish margins and pale brown towards surfaces; pale greenish brown surfaces. Dense fabric; common medium/coarse sand. Diameter 40 cm.

29. *Survey No. 39.* Jar rim. Dark gray core, brown margins, pale greenish brown surfaces. Common sand temper.

30. *Survey No. 20.* Jar rim. Pale brown core with reddened margins and pale brown surfaces. Occasional medium/coarse sand.

31. *Survey No. 43.* Bowl rim. Pale brown body and surface. Abundant fine/medium sand.

32. *Survey No. 44.* Bowl rim. Gray body, very pale grayish brown surfaces. Occasional fine sand and one or two large vesicles.

33. *Survey No. 47.* Rim of small bowl. Pale greenish body, pale brown surfaces. Occasional fine sand.

34. *Survey No. 45.* Bowl rim. Very pale greenish brown with very pale brown surfaces. Common very fine sand.

35. *Survey No. 46.* Bowl rim. Very pale greenish brown with very pale brown surfaces. Common very fine sand.

36. *Survey No. 48.* Body sherd. Pale brown with reddish interior margins; pale green exterior slip and pink interior. Occasional sand. Deeply incised ladder motif on exterior.

37. *Survey No. 29.* Bowl rim. Pale brown, very pale brown surfaces. Occasional medium sand. Diameter ca. 30 cm.

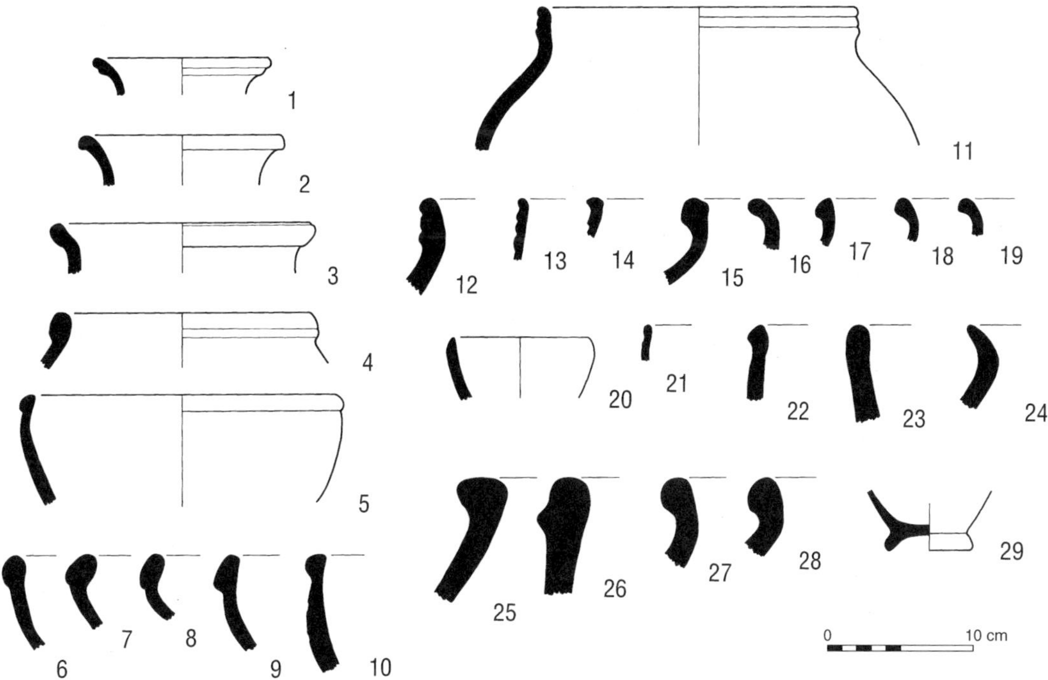

Figure 6.7. Pottery from Nafileh Village (SS 5). Sweyhat Survey Periods VI and VII (Mid-/Late Early Bronze Age) and VII (Late Early Bronze Age)

1. *Survey No. 11.* Flared-rim jar. Very pale green throughout. Occasional fine sand temper. Smooth surfaces.

2. *Survey No. 22.* Jar rim. Pale gray brown, pale brown surfaces. Moderately dense fabric; occasional fine sand; some dark, diffuse inclusions.

3. *Survey No. 23.* Jar rim. Reddish brown throughout; pale brown surfaces. Common fine Euphrates sand.

4. *Survey No. 24.* Jar rim. Brown, very pale brown exterior margins. Very pale green-slipped exterior. Very pale brown interior. Common fine sand, some mica.

5. *Survey No. 2.* Externally-thickened bowl rim. Pale brown, pale red interior margin; cream-slipped surfaces. Common fine sand temper.

6. *Survey No. 4.* Externally-thickened bowl rim. Pale reddish brown throughout; cream-slipped exterior. Occasional medium indeterminate sand. Diameter 26 cm.

7. *Survey No. 5.* Externally-thickened bowl rim. Brown body, pale red margins. Very pale brown-slipped surfaces. Common medium Euphrates sand. Diameter 28 cm.

8. *Survey No. 1.* Externally-thickened rim bowl. Pale brown core, dull red margins, pale brown-slipped surfaces. Common Euphrates sand temper. Diameter 30 cm.

9. *Survey No. 3.* Externally-thickened bowl rim. Pale greenish brown throughout. Common fine sand temper. Diameter 26 cm.

10. *Survey No. 6.* Externally-thickened bowl rim. Very pale brown throughout. Occasional fine/medium sand. Two broad impressed grooves around circumference. Diameter 28 cm.

11. *Survey No. 10.* Collared-rim jar. Pale green throughout, pale greenish brown surfaces. Abundant medium Euphrates sand.

12. *Survey No. 14.* Collared-rim jar. Pale greenish gray body, pale greenish surfaces. Common fine/medium sand. Diameter 26 cm.

13. *Survey No. 12.* Ribbed jar rim. Pale grayish brown throughout. Common medium sand temper.

14. *Survey No. 13.* Jar rim. Very pale greenish brown throughout. Occasional medium Euphrates sand. Diameter 14 cm.

15. *Survey No. 17.* Jar rim. Pale reddish brown throughout and interior surface. Very pale green exterior surface slip. Common fine/medium sand temper. Diameter 22 cm.

16. *Survey No. 18.* Jar rim. Green body with pale greenish brown surfaces. Dense fabric with white $CaCO_3$ inclusions, some lining voids. Slightly overfired. Diameter 22 cm.

17. *Survey No. 19.* Jar rim. Pale brown throughout, very pale brown surfaces. Occasional fine sand temper, rare chaff. Diameter 16 cm.

18. *Survey No. 20.* Jar rim. Very pale greenish brown throughout. Common fine/medium Euphrates sand. Diameter 18 cm.

19. *Survey No. 21.* Rim of cooking pot. Reddish brown body; brown/gray-brown/red brown surfaces. Moderately soft and friable; common coarse sand temper includes calcite. Diameter 20 cm.

20. *Survey No. 8.* Small bowl. Pale brown, very pale brown exterior, pale brown interior. Common medium sand, some mica.

21. *Survey No. 9.* Bowl rim. Pale green interior half, pale brown exterior half. Fine sand, moderately fine fabric, smooth surfaces.

22. *Survey No. 25.* Rim of straight-sided bowl. Dull reddish brown throughout, very pale brown interior, very pale green-slipped exterior. Common medium Euphrates sand, some white inclusions. Diameter 26 cm.

23. *Survey No. 7.* Simple bowl. Pale greenish brown throughout. Abundant medium Euphrates sand temper. Diameter 26 cm.

24. *Survey No. 26.* Jar rim. Pale reddish brown, pale brown surfaces. Moderately dense fabric; occasional fine/medium Euphrates sand. Diameter 20 cm.

25. *Survey No. 27.* Rim of coarse storage jar. Pale greenish brown throughout. Common chaff, occasional fine sand temper. Diameter 30 cm.

26. *Survey No. 28.* Rim of coarse bowl. Very pale green throughout. Occasional fine/medium sand temper. Diameter >30 cm.

27. *Survey No. 15.* Jar rim. Pale brown body, very pale greenish surfaces. Dense fabric, occasional fine/medium sand. Diameter 16 cm.

28. *Survey No. 16.* Jar rim. Pale brown, very pale green-slipped exterior. Laminar fabric; abundant medium Euphrates sand.

29. *Survey No. 29.* High ring base. Very pale brown throughout. Dense, moderately fine fabric with smooth surfaces; occasional fine/medium sand, rare voids.

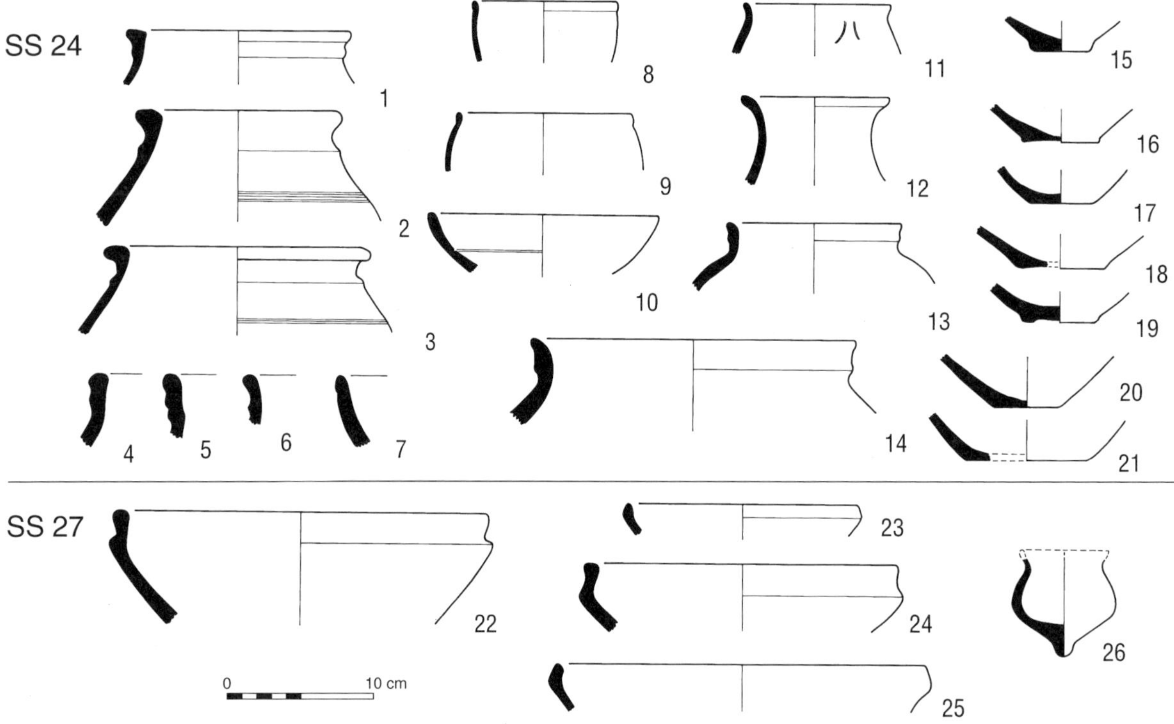

Figure 6.8. Pottery from SS 24 (nos. 1–21) and SS 27 (nos. 22–26). Sweyhat Survey Periods VII (Late Early Bronze Age) and VIII (Middle Bronze Age)

1. *Survey No. 7.* Rim of barrel jar. Pale red, very pale brown surfaces. Slightly crumbly with common medium sand.

2. *Survey No. 8.* Rim of barrel jar. Pale red brown, very pale brown surfaces. Fine/medium sand temper. Comb-incised exterior.

3. *Survey No. 11.* Rim of barrel jar. Pale brown, very pale greenish brown surfaces. Common medium Euphrates sand temper. Comb-incised exterior.

4. *Survey No. 12.* Jar rim. Gray brown, very pale greenish brown surfaces. Common fine/medium Euphrates sand. Slightly rolled. Diameter 22 cm.

5. *Survey No. 9.* Jar rim. Grayish brown, very pale brown surfaces. Dense; common medium Euphrates sand. Diameter 22 cm.

6. *Survey No. 10.* Jar rim. Pale reddish brown throughout. Common medium sand. Diameter 20 cm.

7. *Survey No. 4.* Bowl rim. Very pale greenish brown throughout. Occasional fine/medium sand. Angle approximate only.

8. *Survey No. 1.* Small bowl. Brown, pale brown surfaces. Occasional medium sand and voids.

9. *Survey No. 2.* Small bowl. Pale reddish brown, pale yellowish brown-slipped surfaces. Occasional medium sand.

10. *Survey No. 3.* Open bowl. Pale brown with pale yellowish brown-slipped interior. Common fine/medium sand.

11. *Survey No. 5.* Small jar. Pale brown, very pale brown surfaces. Occasional medium sand. Two curved incised lines on exterior.

12. *Survey No. 6.* Jar rim. Pale gray brown throughout. Common fine sand.

13. *Survey No. 13.* Jar rim. Dark gray brown, pale greenish surfaces. Abundant medium sand temper; common dark minerals. Hard, slightly vitrified surfaces.

14. *Survey No. 15.* Jar rim. Dark gray, pale greenish surfaces. Very hard with dense fabric; occasional sand; common small vesicles with pale brown lining.

15. *Survey No. 14.* Flat base. Pale brown, pale greenish brown surfaces. Occasional medium sand.

16. *Survey No. 18.* Slightly raised base. Dark greenish brown. Hard; abundant medium sand; occasional lined vesicles.

17. *Survey No. 17.* Flat base. Pale red brown throughout. Moderately dense; occasional medium sand.

18. *Survey No. 19.* Slightly raised base. Pink becoming cream towards exterior. Fine, smooth fabric; occasional white sand. Throwing rings on exterior.

19. *Survey No. 20.* Low ring base. Pale greenish brown throughout. Common medium sand.

20. *Survey No. 16.* Flat base. Pale brown, very pale brown surfaces. Common medium sand.

21. *Survey No. 21.* Slightly raised base. Very dark gray, pale greenish surfaces. Very hard, dense fabric. Overfired with common fired vesicles lined with pale brown.

22. *Survey No. 4.* Carinated bowl. Reddish brown with pale brown-slipped surfaces. Occasional sand.

23. *Survey No. 6.* Open bowl. Reddish brown with pale brown surfaces. Occasional sand.

24. *Survey No. 9.* Open bowl. Brown, yellowish brown-slipped surfaces. Abundant medium Euphrates sand.

25. *Survey No. 5.* Open bowl. Pale greenish brown, pale brown margins. Occasional sand temper.

26. *Survey No. 8.* Small nipple-based beaker (elliptical in plan). Brown, very pale yellowish brown-slipped surfaces. Smooth, occasional micaceous sand temper. Rim conjectural; rim dimensions 4 × 7 cm.

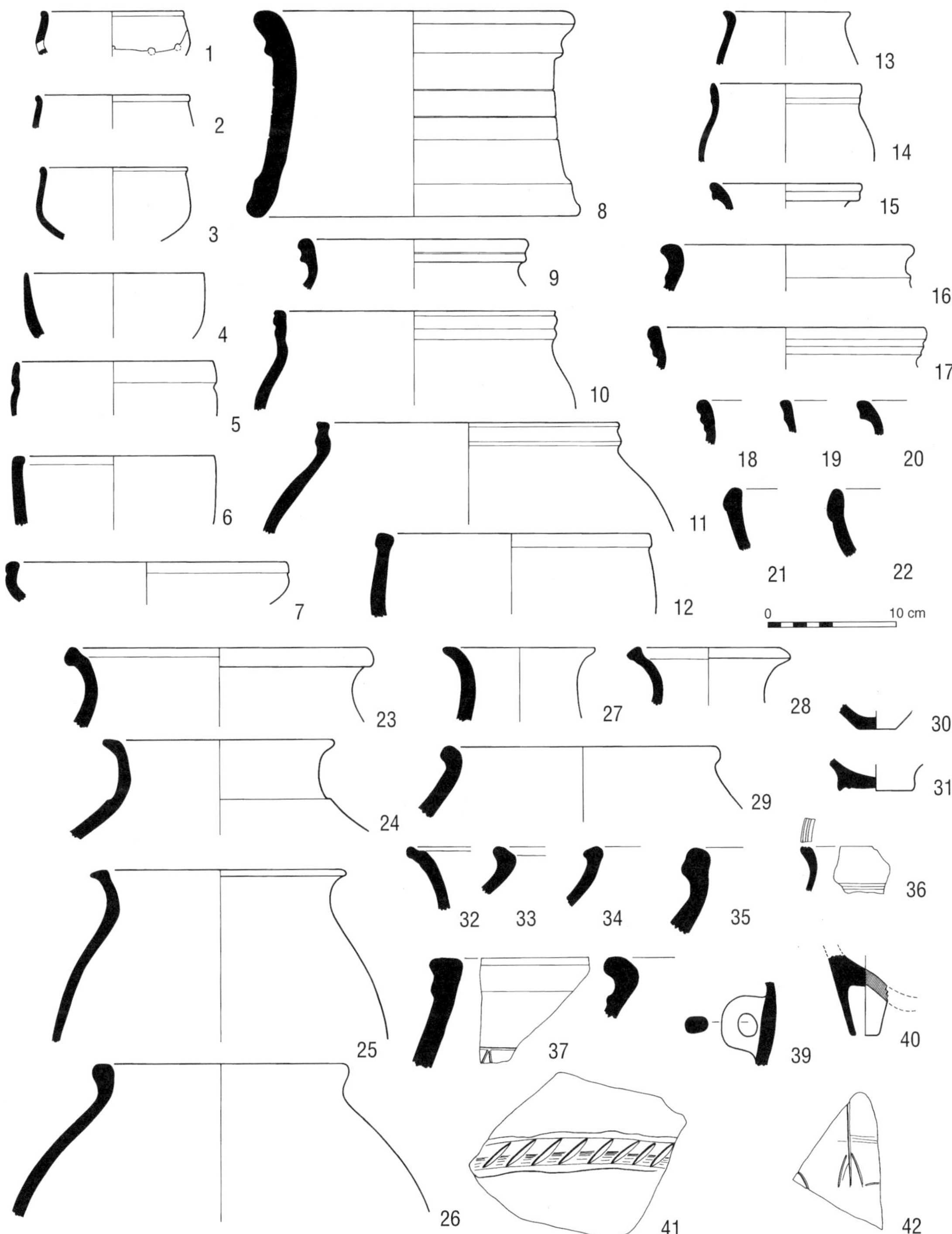

Figure 6.9. Pottery from SS 27 (*cont.*). Sweyhat Survey Periods VII (Late Early Bronze Age)
and VIII (Middle Bronze Age)

1. *Survey No. 11.* Colander bowl. Dark gray, gray surfaces. Common black sand. Holes pierced from interior.

2. *Survey No. 13.* Rim of small bowl. Brown, slightly reddened interior, very pale brown exterior. Abundant fine/medium sand; occasional planar voids.

3. *Survey No. 10.* Rim of small bowl (thickness approximate). Pale reddish brown, very pale brown surfaces. Sand temper.

4. *Survey No. 12.* Bowl rim. Dark grayish brown. Very dense and hard (slightly overfired); abundant sand, some vesicles.

5. *Survey No. 7.* Bowl rim. Pale greenish brown throughout. Common fine/medium sand, rare grog.

6. *Survey No. 17.* Bowl rim. Very pale brown throughout. Common fine sand. Slight beading on rim interior.

7. *Survey No. 2.* Bowl rim. Pale green throughout. Common medium Euphrates sand.

8. *Survey No. 32.* Potstand. Dark greenish brown, very pale greenish brown surfaces. Abundant Euphrates sand.

9. *Survey No. 22.* Jar rim. Reddish brown, red, and gray interior, very pale brown-slipped surfaces. Common medium sand.

10. *Survey No. 24.* Jar rim. Pale reddish brown, pale yellowish brown-slipped surfaces. Common Euphrates sand.

11. *Survey No. 25*. Jar rim. Pale brown throughout. Common indeterminate sand.

12. *Survey No. 15*. Bowl rim. Pale grayish brown with very pale brown surfaces. Common/abundant fine sand.

13. *Survey No. 14*. Rim of small jar. Very pale brown throughout. Fine sand, some coarse brown inclusions.

14. *Survey No. 28*. Jar rim. Pale red brown, very pale brown-slipped surfaces. Common sand.

15. *Survey No. 27*. Jar rim. Pale brown, very pale greenish brown surfaces. Common Euphrates sand.

16. *Survey No. 26*. Jar rim. Reddish brown throughout (surfaces obscured by lime concretion). Common fine/medium sand.

17. *Survey No. 20*. Jar rim. Reddish brown, pink interior, very pale brown-slipped exterior. Common medium sand includes occasional white sand.

18. *Survey No. 19*. Jar rim. Pale red brown body. Very pale brown surfaces. Common medium sand; occasional planar voids probably from chaff.

19. *Survey No. 21*. Jar rim. Pale brown, very pale brown surfaces. Common medium sand.

20. *Survey No. 23*. Jar rim. Brown, very pale brown surfaces. Common medium sand. Diameter 16 cm.

21. *Survey No. 3*. Bowl rim. Pale red brown, very pale yellowish brown-slipped surfaces. Common medium sand. Diameter 32 cm.

22. *Survey No. 1*. Bowl rim. Pale brown core, pale red margins and surfaces. Moderately fine fabric; sand temper includes white inclusions. Diameter 28 cm.

23. *Survey No. 37*. Jar rim. Pale brown, pale greenish brown exterior. Occasional medium Euphrates sand.

24. *Survey No. 38*. Jar rim. Pale red brown with pale yellowish brown surfaces. Common medium sand.

25. *Survey No. 33*. Jar rim. Hard, red brown, pale brown surfaces. Moderately smooth; occasional sand. Some irregular voids.

26. *Survey No. 42*. Jar rim. Gray with pale brown margins and surfaces. Indeterminate medium sand temper.

27. *Survey No. 34*. Jar rim. Pale red brown with very pale brown-slipped exterior. Medium sand temper.

28. *Survey No. 31*. Jar rim. Pale brown, very pale brown surfaces. Moderately fine fabric; occasional fine sand.

29. *Survey No. 39*. Jar rim. Pale brown, very pale greenish brown-slipped exterior. Occasional fine/medium sand.

30. *Survey No. 48*. Small flat base. Pale brown throughout. Occasional fine/medium sand. Moderately rolled.

31. *Survey No. 49*. Low ring base. Pale red, pale greenish brown-slipped surfaces. Moderately fine; occasional fine/medium sand.

32. *Survey No. 36*. Jar rim. Brown, slightly reddened interior, pale brown exterior. Medium sand temper. Diameter 16 cm.

33. *Survey No. 41*. Rim of cooking pot. Reddish brown with pale brown surfaces. Moderately soft; abundant coarse white calcite grits.

34. *Survey No. 40*. Rim of cooking pot. Dark gray core, brown and grayish brown variegated surfaces. Moderately soft abundant angular white grits. Diameter 26 cm.

35. *Survey No. 43*. Jar rim. Pale greenish brown throughout. Abundant medium Euphrates sand. Diameter 36 cm.

36. *Survey No. 18*. Jar rim. Grayish brown, pale brown surfaces. Common fine/medium sand. Comb-incised exterior and grooves in top of rim. Diameter 14 cm.

37. *Survey No. 30*. Rim of barrel jar. Brown with slightly reddened interior, very pale greenish brown-slipped exterior. Abundant Euphrates sand. Deeply scored lines on exterior. Diameter 44 cm.

38. *Survey No. 29*. Rim of barrel jar. Reddish brown with brown margins, very pale brown surfaces. Common medium sand; sparse chaff. Diameter 28 cm.

39. *Survey No. 44*. Ring handle. Pale brown throughout. Occasional fine/medium sand.

40. *Survey No. 45*. Conical foot or stand. Gray with reddish margins and surfaces. Smoothed with wooden tool. Occasional sand temper; chaff impressions on surfaces.

41. *Survey No. 47*. Body sherd. Pale brown, pale greenish brown-slipped surfaces. Occasional fine medium sand. Deep oblique slashes on raised cordon. Cordon edges smoothed with wooden baton.

42. *Survey No. 46*. Body sherd. Pale red with very pale brown surfaces; occasional sand and fine pores. Incised lines on exterior.

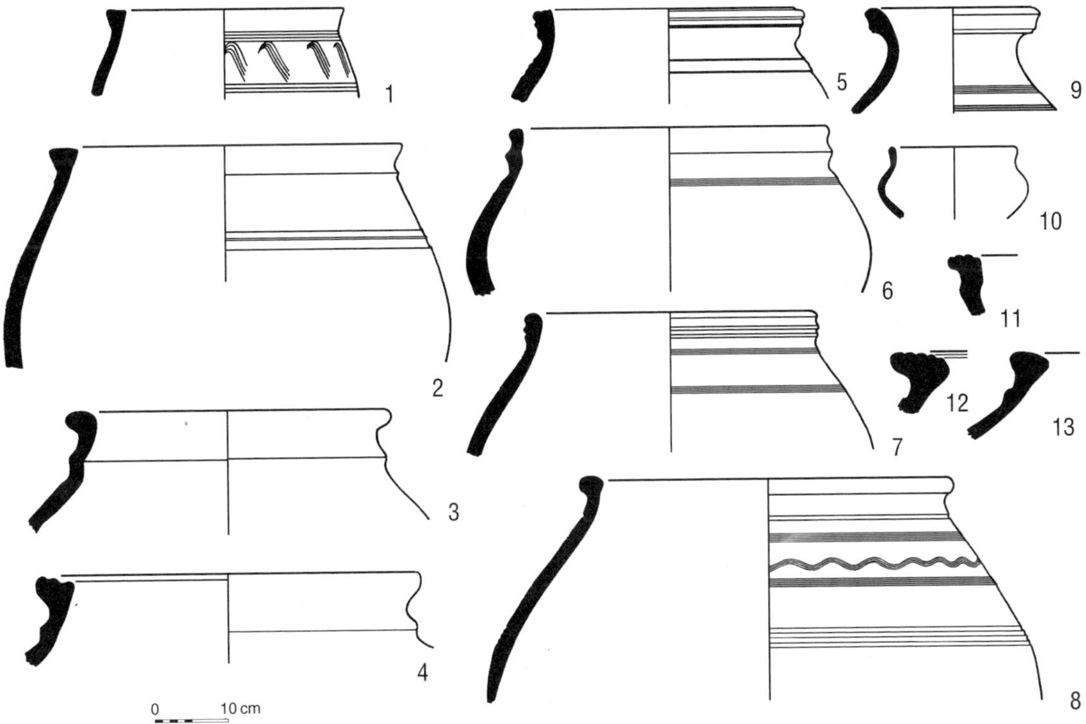

Figure 6.10. Pottery from Tell Jouweif (SS 8) Area A and Area B. Sweyhat Survey Period VIII (Middle Bronze Age)

1. *Survey No. A2*. Jar rim. Reddish brown body, pale greenish brown-slipped surfaces. Abundant medium Euphrates sand. Shallow comb-incised lines and waves on exterior.

2. *Survey No. A1*. Barrel jar rim. Pale brown body and interior surface, very pale greenish brown-slipped exterior. Common medium Euphrates sand. Broad, shallow grooves on exterior.

3. *Survey No. A13*. Jar rim. Dark reddish brown body, pale red brown and pale brown surfaces. Dense fabric; occasional medium sand. Hard, moderately smooth and very highly fired.

4. *Survey No. 6*. Jar rim. Grayish brown body, dull greenish-slipped surfaces. Common medium sand temper, rare chaff impressions.

5. *Survey No. B9*. Jar rim. Pale reddish brown body, pale brown interior surface, very pale green-slipped interior. Common fine/medium Euphrates sand includes mica. Broad complex impressed grooves on exterior.

6. *Survey No. B4*. Jar rim. Reddish brown core, pale brown exterior margins, very pale green-slipped surfaces. Deep parallel combed incisions. Common medium Euphrates sand.

7. *Survey No. B2*. Jar rim. Pale brown body and interior surface, very pale brown exterior surface. Moderately dense, occasional sand. Deep parallel combed incisions on exterior.

8. *Survey No. B1*. Jar rim. Pale reddish brown body, pale brown interior surface, very pale brown exterior. Occasional fine medium sand. Regular, neat combed incisions on exterior.

9. *Survey No. B7*. Jar rim. Pale brown body, very pale green-slipped surfaces. Abundant fine/medium Euphrates sand. Parallel shallow combed incisions on exterior.

10. *Survey No. B8*. Rim of small bowl. Pale reddish brown exterior margin merging into pale brown interior margin. Pale reddish brown and pale brown patchy exterior. Very pale greenish-slipped interior. Common fine/medium Euphrates sand, some mica.

11. *Survey No. A5*. Bowl rim. Grayish brown body, pale greenish gray interior, very pale brown-slipped exterior. Common Euphrates sand.

12. *Survey No. A7*. Jar rim. Dull red body, very pale brown-slipped surfaces. Common Euphrates sand, rare chaff impressions. Diameter ca. 46 cm.

13. *Survey No. A8*. Jar rim. Pale grayish brown body, dull green-slipped surfaces. Abundant medium Euphrates sand. Diameter ca. 38 cm.

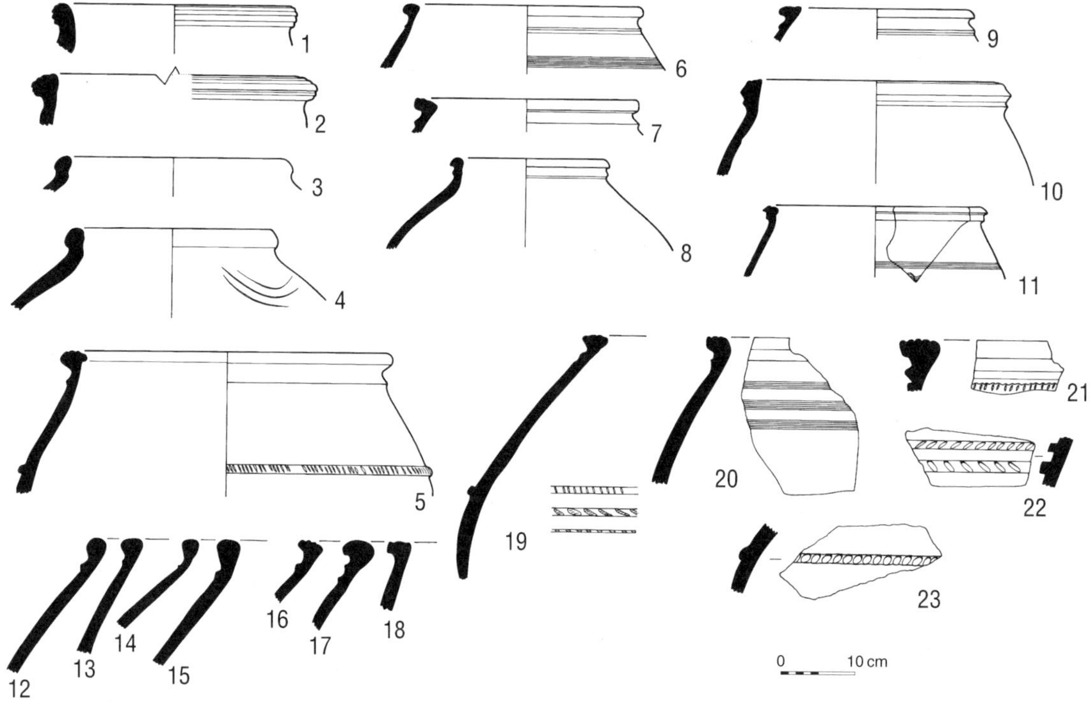

Figure 6.11. Pottery from Tell Jouweif (SS 8) Area B. Sweyhat Survey Periods VI (Mid-/Late Early Bronze Age), VII (Late Early Bronze Age), and VIII (Middle Bronze Age)

1. *Survey No. B17.* Grooved jar rim. Pale gray brown core with slightly reddened margins. Common medium Euphrates sand.

2. *Survey No. B15.* Grooved jar rim. Pale brown body, pale greenish brown-slipped surfaces. Common medium Euphrates sand. Grooves incised and slightly folded over. Diameter 48 cm.

3. *Survey No. B19.* Jar rim. Gray brown body, pale greenish-slipped exterior, brown interior. Common Euphrates sand, rare voids.

4. *Survey No. B11.* Jar rim. Pale red brown body, pale greenish brown-slipped interior and exterior. Common sand; one or two large voids. Deep, hanging swag-like incisions on exterior.

5. *Survey No. B16.* Rim of large storage jar. Dark gray becoming pale grayish brown and light brown on exterior margin, brown on interior margin. Poorly fired. Occasional indeterminate sand, occasional chaff. Applied strip cut by deep oblique incisions. Below this, abrupt angle in pot wall produced with wooden tool.

6. *Survey No. B3.* Rim of barrel jar. Pale red brown body, very pale red brown interior, pale yellowish brown exterior surface. Common medium Euphrates sand. Broad incised grooves on exterior.

7. *Survey No. B18.* Jar rim. Dark grayish brown body, dull green exterior slip, brownish black interior surface, partly smoke-blackened. Occasional sand and chaff temper.

8. *Survey No. B14.* Jar rim. Pale brown body becoming redder towards interior margin. Occasional sand; occasional chaff temper; some medium/large voids.

9. *Survey No. B12.* Jar rim. Pale brown throughout, very pale brown interior, pale greenish brown-slipped exterior. Common medium Euphrates sand and occasional chaff.

10. *Survey No. B5.* Jar rim. Pale brown body, very pale brown interior, pale green exterior. Occasional medium Euphrates sand; occasional chaff impressions on surfaces.

11. *Survey No. B10.* Jar rim. Pale brown body, very pale brown interior, pale greenish brown-slipped exterior. Common medium sand. Combed linear and wavy comb-incised decoration on exterior.

12. *Survey No. 92.1.* Storage jar rim. Pale brown, very pale greenish-slipped surface. Fine/medium sand, rare chaff. Diameter 36 cm.

13. *Survey No. 92.2.* Storage jar rim. Pale red, pale brown-slipped surfaces. Common sand, rare chaff. Diameter 46 cm.

14. *Survey No. 92.3.* Storage jar rim. Pale brown throughout. Common sand, occasional chaff. Diameter 30 cm.

15. *Survey No. 92.4.* Storage jar rim. Pale red, pale brown-slipped surfaces. Common medium sand. Diameter 42 cm.

16. *Survey No. 92.5.* Storage jar rim. Brown, pale brown exterior, pale reddish brown interior. Common sand, occasional chaff. Diameter 50 cm.

17. *Survey No. 92.6.* Storage jar rim. Pale reddish brown, very pale brown-slipped surfaces. Common sand. Diameter 46 cm.

18. *Survey No. 92.7.* Storage jar rim. Grayish brown, pale brown surfaces. Sand temper, occasional chaff. Diameter 50 cm.

19. *Survey No. n.a.* Storage jar rim. Pale red, pale brown surfaces. Sand temper, rare chaff. Diameter 28 cm.

20. *Survey No. 92.9.* Storage jar rim. Pale brown, slightly reddened interior. Mainly sand temper. Linear comb-incisions on exterior. Diameter 40 cm.

21. *Survey No. 92.8.* Storage jar rim. Gray brown throughout. Common sand, occasional chaff. Diameter ca. 62 cm.

22. *Survey No. 92.10.* Body sherd of large storage jar. Brown throughout. Sand temper. Cordons cut by shallow oblique impressions.

23. *Survey No. B8.* Body sherd. Pale brown body, dull brown interior, pale greenish-slipped exterior. Common Euphrates sand temper. Rare chaff. Deep finger-impressions on applied strip. Incidental finger impressions on body (below, but not illustrated).

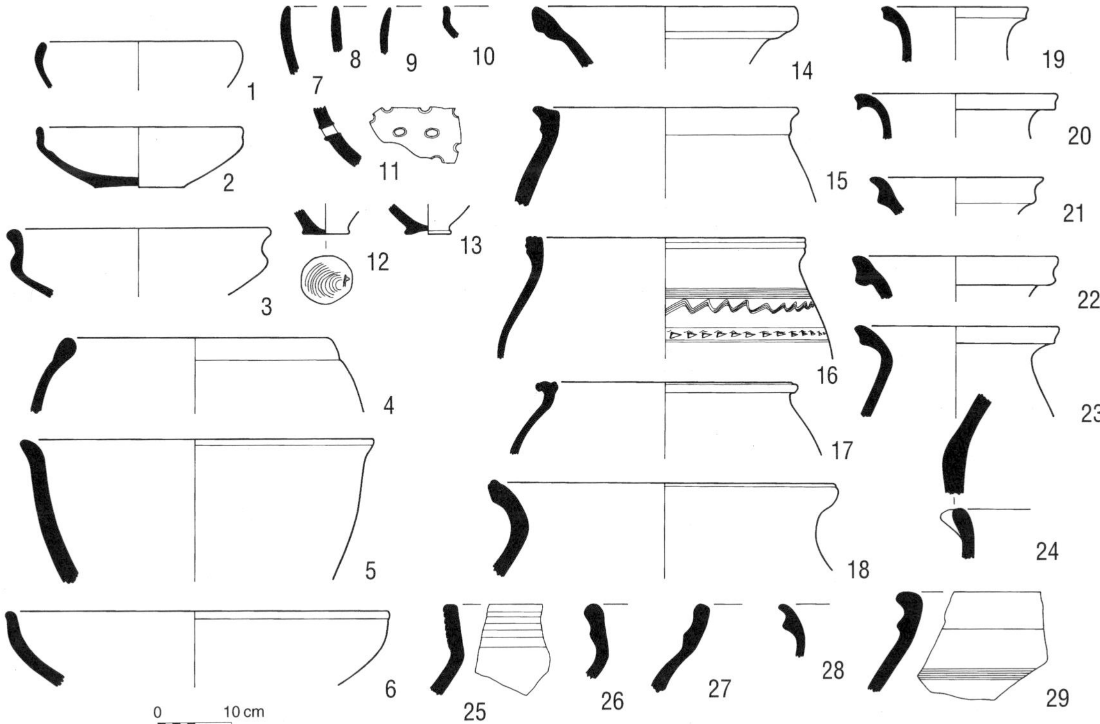

Figure 6.12. Pottery from Tell Jouweif (SS 8) Area A and Area C. Sweyhat Survey Periods V (Early Early Bronze Age), VI (Mid-/Late Early Bronze Age), VII (Late Early Bronze Age), and VIII (Middle Bronze Age)

1. *Survey No. C10.* Bowl with incurved rim. Brown, pale yellow surfaces. Sand temper includes occasional white $CaCO_3$ inclusions.

2. *Survey No. C2.* Open bowl. Brown, slightly reddened margins. Pale reddish brown surfaces; exterior surface pale brown in places. Occasional often coarse white $CaCO_3$ sand. Some surface spalling.

3. *Survey No. C1.* Rim of carinated bowl. Pale brown with very pale brown surfaces. Common medium Euphrates sand; rare large voids.

4. *Survey No. C9.* Rim of globular bowl. Pale reddish brown body, pale brown surfaces. Common Euphrates sand.

5. *Survey No. C8.* Bowl rim. Very pale brown throughout. Common fine sand. Exterior surface finished with wooden tool.

6. *Survey No. C7.* Bowl rim. Gray core, brown margins, pale brown interior surface, pale green-slipped exterior. Indeterminate sand temper. Pottery badly split maybe due to defects in clay body.

7. *Survey No. C3.* Bowl rim. Pale greenish body, very pale green surfaces. Common fine sand. Diameter 12 cm.

8. *Survey No. C4.* Bowl rim. Pink body, very pale brown exterior, pale reddish brown interior. Common Euphrates sand some mica. Diameter 12 cm.

9. *Survey No. C5.* Bowl rim. Brown with pale brown surfaces. Common sand temper; occasional white inclusions. Diameter ca. 10 cm.

10. *Survey No. C6.* Bowl rim. Brown body and interior surface. Very pale greenish brown-slipped exterior. Occasional medium white $CaCO_3$ sand. Diameter 12 cm.

11. *Survey No. C11.* Body sherd of colander bowl. Reddish brown body, pink interior. Very pale brown-slipped exterior. Occasional Euphrates sand. Perforations have surrounding rim on both interior and exterior.

12. *Survey No. C21.* Flat string-cut base. Pale grayish brown body, pale brown surfaces. Moderately fine fabric, fine sand temper.

13. *Survey No. C22.* Low ring base. Gray brown with reddish margins. Common medium Euphrates sand temper.

14. *Survey No. C27.* Jar rim. Reddish brown body, pale brown-slipped surfaces, tendency to pink on interior. Common Euphrates sand.

15. *Survey No. C17.* Jar rim. Very pale red brown body and interior, pale brown exterior surface. Common fine sand temper.

16. *Survey No. C12.* Jar rim. Pale red brown body, pale brown surfaces. Common Euphrates sand temper. Comb-incised exterior with deep triangular notches taken out from lower band.

17. *Survey No. C13.* Jar rim. Very pale greenish brown throughout. Occasional medium sand temper. Impressed grooves on top of rim.

18. *Survey No. C23.* Jar rim. Cooking pot ware. Very dark gray body, gray and pale brown patchy surfaces. Moderately soft, common sand inclusions include calcite crystals.

19. *Survey No. C15.* Jar rim. Pale red brown body, very pale red brown interior surface, pale brown exterior. Moderately fine fabric, occasional fine sand.

20. *Survey No. C19.* Jar rim. Pale red brown body, very pale brown surfaces. Common fine/medium Euphrates sand.

21. *Survey No. A9.* Jar rim. Dark grayish brown body, pale green-slipped surfaces. Overfired, slightly vitrified body. Very hard abundant sand temper.

22. *Survey No. A12.* Jar rim. Very pale brown throughout. Common medium Euphrates sand.

23. *Survey No. A10.* Jar rim. Pale gray brown body, dull greenish-slipped surfaces. Abundant medium Euphrates sand.

24. *Survey No. C26.* Rim of "triangular-lugged cooking pot." Gray-brown body, dark gray exterior, gray brown interior. Common sand temper includes white sand. Lightly polished exterior. Weak triangular lug.

25. *Survey No. C16.* Jar rim. Dark gray brown core, brown margins, pale reddish brown interior, very pale brown exterior. Common Euphrates sand temper.

26. *Survey No. A3.* Jar rim. Pale yellowish brown body and surfaces. Common medium Euphrates sand.

27. *Survey No. C18.* Jar rim. Pale reddish brown body, very pale brown-slipped surfaces. Common Euphrates sand temper.

28. *Survey No. A11.* Jar rim. Pale reddish brown body, very pale yellowish brown-slipped surfaces. Moderately fine fabric; common medium Euphrates sand. Diameter 12 cm.

29. *Survey No. A4.* Jar rim. Dark reddish brown body, brown surfaces. Common Euphrates sand. Shallow linear comb incision on exterior. Diameter 26 cm.

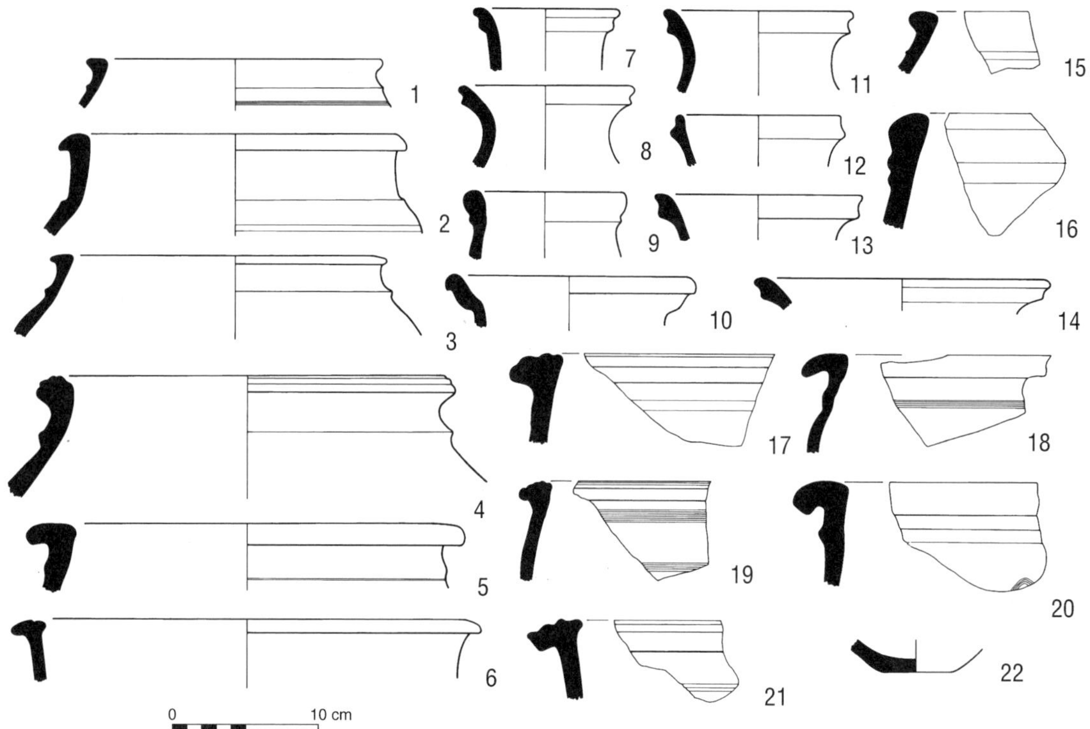

Figure 6.13. Pottery from Tell Ali al-Haj (SS 17). Sweyhat Survey Periods VI (Mid-/Late Early Bronze Age),
VII (Late Early Bronze Age), and VIII (Middle Bronze Age)

1. *Survey No. 38.* Jar rim. Pale red brown, pale yellow-slipped exterior. Occasional sand. Comb-incised exterior.

2. *Survey No. 4.* Jar rim. Pale brown with very pale brown surfaces. Moderately dense; common sand temper. Two parallel incised lines on shoulder.

3. *Survey No. 15.* Jar rim. Pale greenish brown throughout. Smooth; fine sand temper, occasional planar voids. Shallow incised groove at base of extant body.

4. *Survey No. 21.* Jar rim. Pale grayish brown, very pale brown surfaces. Common fine/medium Euphrates sand; very rare chaff impressions.

5. *Survey No. 37.* Jar rim. Pale green throughout. Common sand and occasional planar voids.

6. *Survey No. 26.* Large bowl rim. Reddish brown, very pale brown surfaces. Occasional sand temper.

7. *Survey No. 32.* Jar rim. Pale reddish brown interior and body, very pale red brown exterior. Occasional fine/medium sand.

8. *Survey No. 28.* Jar rim. Pale greenish brown throughout. Common medium sand, rare chaff.

9. *Survey No. 30.* Jar rim. Pale reddish brown, very pale brown surfaces. Occasional sand temper and small voids.

10. *Survey No. 34.* Jar rim. Pale brown, reddened margins; pale yellowish brown-slipped surfaces. Common medium Euphrates sand.

11. *Survey No. 27.* Jar rim. Pale greenish brown throughout. Occasional sand and chaff temper.

12. *Survey No. 29.* Jar rim. Brown very pale brown surfaces. Occasional medium sand.

13. *Survey No. 33.* Jar rim. Pale brown, very pale yellowish brown surfaces. Occasional medium sand, rare large voids.

14. *Survey No. 31.* Jar rim. Pale brown, very pale brown surfaces. Occasional medium sand temper.

15. *Survey No. 24.* Jar rim. Pale reddish brown, very pale brown surfaces. Occasional fine/medium sand; rare voids and grog. Diameter 24 cm.

16. *Survey No. 44.* Rim of large barrel jar. Pale reddish brown, pale brown surfaces. Occasional sand and chaff temper.

17. *Survey No. 6.* Storage jar rim. Pale brown core, slightly reddened margins. Common medium sand temper. Diameter ca. 46 cm.

18. *Survey No. 20.* Rim of large jar or bowl. Pale red, cream-slipped exterior, pink interior. Common Euphrates sand. Parallel grooving on exterior. Diameter ca. 36 cm.

19. *Survey No. 18.* Rim of large jar. Pale reddish brown, reddish margins, pink surfaces. Occasional fine/medium sand. Diameter 36 cm.

20. *Survey No. 48.* Rim of large jar. Grayish brown, reddened interior margins, very pale green-slipped surfaces. Occasional sand, rare chaff. Curved comb incision on exterior. Diameter ca. 50 cm.

21. *Survey No. 49.* Rim of large jar. Pale greenish brown throughout. Occasional medium sand. Comb-incised exterior. Diameter ca. 50 cm.

22. *Survey No. 16.* Flat base. Brown, very pale brown surfaces, common Euphrates sand. Fine throwing rings on base.

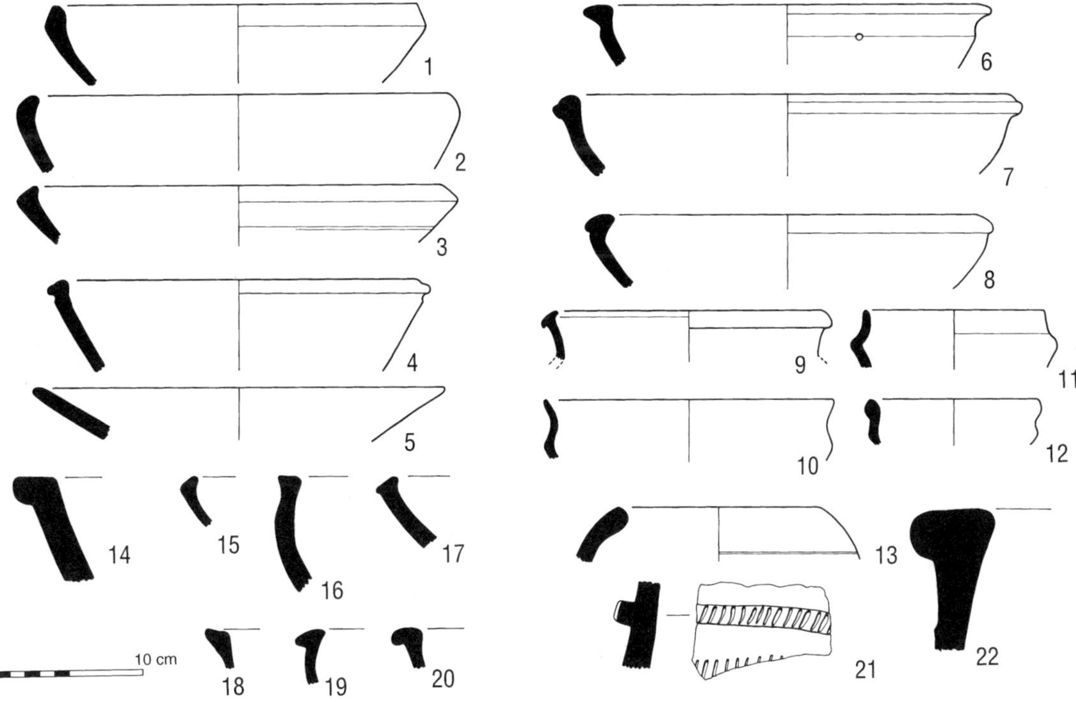

Figure 6.14. Pottery from Tell Ali al-Haj (SS 17) (*cont.*). Sweyhat Survey Periods IX (Late Bronze Age) and X (Iron Age)

1. *Survey No. 50.* Bowl rim. Pale reddish brown, pale brown surfaces. Moderately fine fabric. Occasional fine/medium sand temper; occasional irregular voids.

2. *Survey No. 51.* Bowl rim. Reddish brown with pale red surfaces. Occasional sand and planar voids.

3. *Survey No. 52.* Bowl rim. Pale reddish brown, pale brown surfaces. Moderately fine fabric, fine sand temper. Throwing rings on exterior.

4. *Survey No. 22.* Bowl rim. Very pale brown throughout. Fine sand temper; rare irregular voids.

5. *Survey No. 8.* Plate. Pale reddish brown, pale brown surfaces. Occasional medium sand.

6. *Survey No. 35.* Bowl. Gray, pale grayish brown surfaces. Occasional fine/medium sand temper. Pierced hole of unknown function in body.

7. *Survey No. 19.* Bowl rim. Pale red, very pale brown surfaces. Fine/medium micaceous sand temper.

8. *Survey No. 36.* Bowl. Pale brown core, reddened margins. Common fine sand.

9. *Survey No. 46.* Bowl or jar rim. Brown, very pale brown surfaces. Moderately fine, occasional sand, fine chaff voids.

10. *Survey No. 41.* Rim of carinated bowl. Brown, very pale yellowish brown-slipped surfaces. Abundant Euphrates sand temper.

11. *Survey No. 42.* Rim of carinated bowl. Brown, pale brown surfaces. Common medium sand.

12. *Survey No. 40.* Rim of small bowl. Pale reddish brown with yellowish brown core. Common Euphrates sand.

13. *Survey No. 12.* Hole-mouth bowl. Reddish brown, very pale brown surfaces. Moderately smooth fabric, rare small voids. Deep impressed groove on exterior.

14. *Survey No. 10.* Rim of large bowl. Pale greenish brown throughout. Common chaff temper. Diameter ca. 50 cm.

15. *Survey No. 23.* Bowl rim. Pale brown throughout. Common fine Euphrates sand, rare fine chaff.

16. *Survey No. 17.* Bowl rim. Brown, pale brown surfaces. Fine sand temper. Diameter ca. 36 cm.

17. *Survey No. 47.* Bowl rim. Brown, very pale brown surfaces. Moderately fine, rare sand, occasional voids.

18. *Survey No. 39.* Bowl rim. Pale reddish brown, pale yellowish brown-slipped surfaces. Common sand. Diameter 32 cm.

19. *Survey No. 43.* Bowl rim. Brown core, yellowish brown margins, very pale brown surfaces. Occasional sand and voids.

20. *Survey No. 5.* Bowl rim. Pale red, very pale brown surfaces. Sand temper; occasional white inclusions and rare fine chaff. Diameter ca. 30 cm.

21. *Survey No. 13.* Body sherd. Brown with reddened margins, pale brown interior. Occasional sand and chaff temper. On applied cordon deep curvilinear slashes ca. 1 mm. Lower range of slashes impressed from left.

22. *Survey No. 9.* Rim of large storage jar. Pale brown throughout. Common sand and chaff temper. Diameter 44 cm.

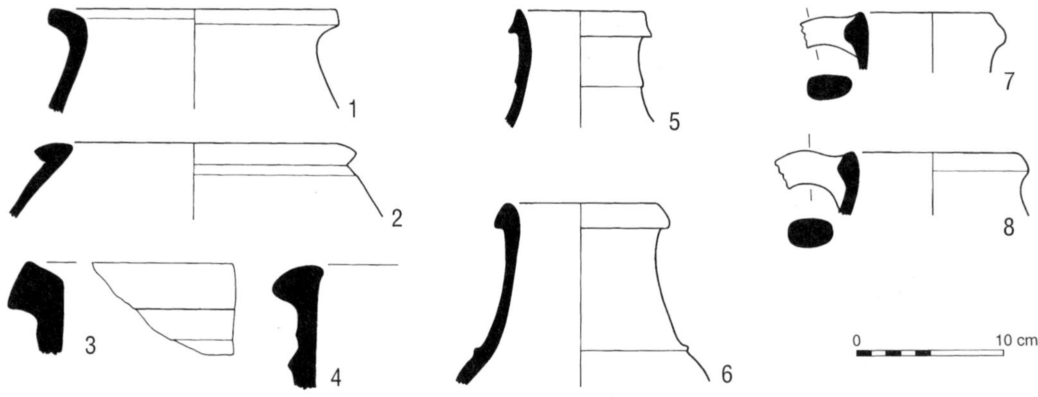

Figure 6.15. Pottery from Tell Ali al-Haj (SS 17) (*cont.*). Sweyhat Survey Periods IX (Late Bronze Age), X (Iron Age), and XI/XII (Hellenistic/Roman)

1. *Survey No. 3.* Jar rim. Gray core, slightly reddened margins, pale brown-slipped surfaces. Common chaff temper, occasional sand.

2. *Survey No. 25.* Rim of jar or bowl. Greenish brown, locally reddened. Pale greenish brown surfaces. Occasional medium sand.

3. *Survey No. 7.* Rim of storage jar. Gray core, slightly reddened margins, pale brown surfaces. Mixed chaff and coarse sand temper. Diameter 50 cm.

4. *Survey No. 11.* Rim of large jar or bowl. Pale brown, very pale greenish brown surfaces. Dense and hard; occasional sand; occasional chaff impressions and voids. Diameter >52 cm.

5. *Survey No. 1.* Jar rim. Pale brown, very pale brown-slipped surfaces. Common medium sand.

6. *Survey No. 2.* Jar rim. Dark gray, reddened margins, pale reddish brown surfaces. Moderately soft. Mainly coarse white inclusions; some fine micaceous sand and fine vegetable inclusions.

7. *Survey No. 14.* Rim of Hellenistic/Roman jug. Pale red brown, very pale brown surfaces. Occasional fine sand. Oval-sectioned handle.

8. *Survey No. 45.* Rim of Roman/Hellenistic jug. Red brown, cream-slipped surfaces. Occasional sand, rare large irregular voids. Oval-sectioned handle.

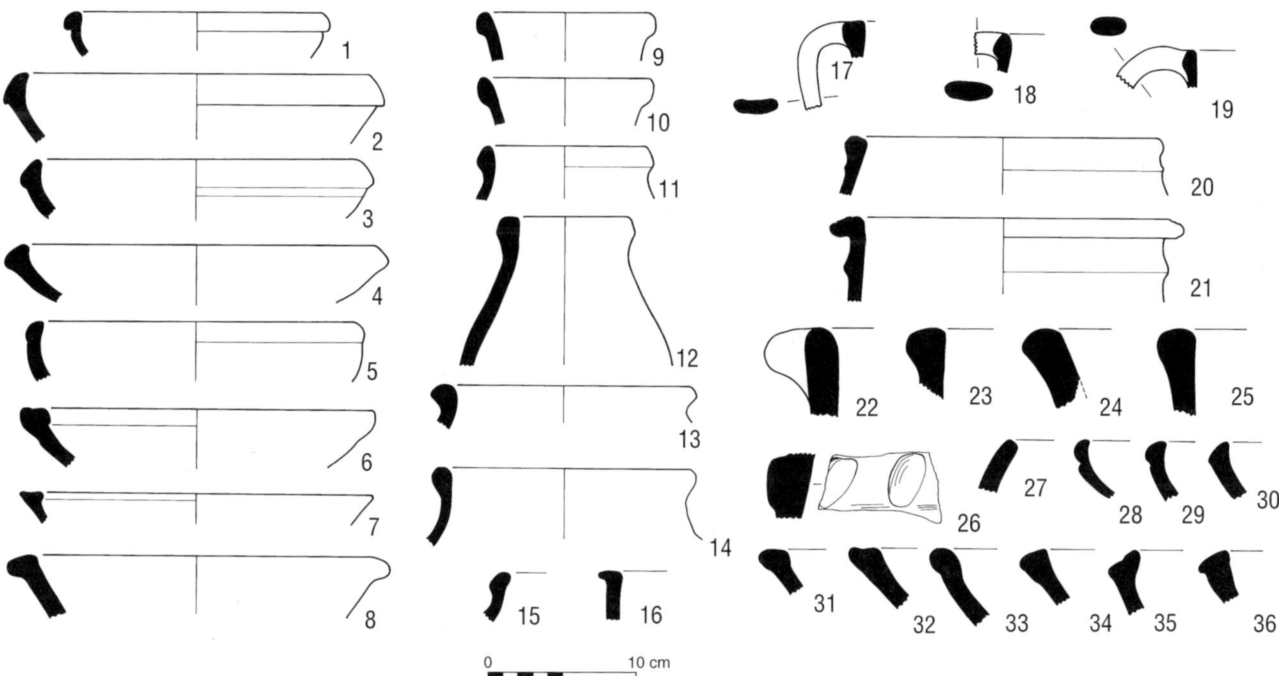

Figure 6.16. Pottery from SS 20B. Sweyhat Survey Period X (Iron Age)

1. *Survey No. 4.* Bowl rim. Dark gray body, pale gray surfaces. Moderately hard, occasional indeterminate sand.

2. *Survey No. 1.* Bowl rim. Pale reddish brown, pale brown surfaces. Occasional fine sand with mica.

3. *Survey No. 2.* Bowl rim. Pale brown core, reddish margins, pale brown surfaces. Occasional medium/coarse Euphrates sand.

4. *Survey No. 18.* Bowl rim. Pale brown core, pale reddish brown margins. Very pale brown surfaces. Occasional fine sand (some white inclusions); occasional irregular voids.

5. *Survey No. 3.* Bowl rim. Very pale greenish brown, very pale brown surfaces. Common fine sand.

6. *Survey No. 11.* Rim of bowl with internally thickened rim. Brown body, very pale brown surfaces. Occasional fine sand temper; irregular voids.

7. *Survey No. 12.* Rim of bowl with internally thickened rim. Pale reddish brown body, very pale brown surfaces. Moderately fine fabric; occasional medium sand.

8. *Survey No. 13.* Rim of bowl with internally thickened rim. Brown body, very pale brown surfaces. Common fine/medium sand.

9. *Survey No. 22.* Jar rim. Brown body, pale brown surfaces. Common fine, rare medium sand.

10. *Survey No. 23.* Jar rim. Pale reddish brown body, pale brown surfaces. Occasional medium sand temper.

11. *Survey No. 25.* Jar rim. Brown body, pale brown surfaces. Common fine sand and fine irregular voids.

12. *Survey No. 21.* Jar rim. Very pale reddish brown body and interior, pale brown exterior. Abundant medium/coarse sand (some reddish).

13. *Survey No. 24.* Jar rim. Pale brown, very pale brown surfaces. Occasional sand and rare voids.

14. *Survey No. 35.* Jar rim. Pale reddish brown body, pale brown surfaces. Moderately fine fabric; occasional white sand and irregular voids.

15. *Survey No. 32.* Jar rim. Pale gray brown body, very pale brown surfaces. Common fine/medium sand. Diameter ca. 18 cm.

16. *Survey No. 27.* Jar rim. Pale reddish brown body, very pale brown surfaces. Occasional fine/medium sand.

17. *Survey No. 37.* Jar rim and handle. Pale brown body, very pale brown surfaces. Fine sand temper.

18. *Survey No. 38.* Jar rim and handle. Pale greenish gray body, very pale brown surfaces. Occasional fine/medium sand. Diameter 10 cm.

19. *Survey No. 36.* Jar rim and handle. Dark greenish gray body, pale green surfaces. Hard, dense fabric. Common Euphrates sand. Diameter ca. 36 cm.

20. *Survey No. 33.* Jar rim. Dull reddish brown body, pale brown towards interior, pale gray brown surfaces. Common fine white sand temper; occasional fine voids.

21. *Survey No. 34.* Jar rim. Pale reddish brown body, very pale brown-slipped exterior. Pale reddish brown body. Common medium Euphrates sand.

22. *Survey No. 40.* Rim of large jar or bowl. Reddish brown body, pale brown surfaces. Common chaff. Large lug affixed to rim. Diameter ca. 36 cm.

23. *Survey No. 41.* Rim of large jar. Reddish brown body, very pale brown surfaces. Common chaff, occasional mica. Diameter ca. 40 cm.

24. *Survey No. 43.* Rim of large jar or bowl. Brown core, pale reddish brown margins, very pale brown surfaces. Rare chaff, occasional sand. Diameter ca. 48 cm.

25. *Survey No. 42.* Rim of large jar. Brown body, pale brown surfaces. Abundant chaff temper.

26. *Survey No. 39.* Body sherd of pithos. Pale brown throughout. Occasional chaff and sand. Added cordon decorated with impressed ovals.

27. *Survey No. 20.* Rim of hole-mouth jar. Gray body, pale brown surfaces. Occasional fine/medium dark sand.

28. *Survey No. 9.* Bowl rim. Gray brown body, pale gray brown surfaces. Occasional fine sand temper.

29. *Survey No. 5.* Bowl rim. Pale brown core, pale reddish brown margins, pink surfaces. Occasional fine, rare medium sand.

30. *Survey No. 6.* Bowl rim. Reddish brown body, pale brown surfaces. Occasional medium sand.

31. *Survey No. 10.* Rim of bowl with internally-thickened rim. Pale reddish brown body, pale brown surfaces. Common fine sand (some white); also large voids containing secondary white concretions. Diameter ca. 34 cm.

32. *Survey No. 8.* Rim of bowl with internally-thickened rim. Pale reddish brown body with pale brown surfaces. Moderately fine fabric. Occasional fine, rare medium sand. Diameter ca. 34 cm.

33. *Survey No. 16.* Bowl rim. Brown core, reddish brown margins, very pale brown surfaces. Occasional medium sand. Diameter ca. 32 cm.

34. *Survey No. 17.* Bowl rim. Pale brown core, reddish margins, pale brown surfaces. Common medium sand, some white. Diameter ca. 34 cm.

35. *Survey No. 7.* Bowl rim. Brown body, pale brown surfaces. Occasional sand, some mica. Occasional large, irregular voids. Diameter 34 cm.

36. *Survey No. 15.* Bowl rim. Brown body, very pale red brown surfaces. Common fine/medium sand temper; occasional small voids. Diameter 30 cm.

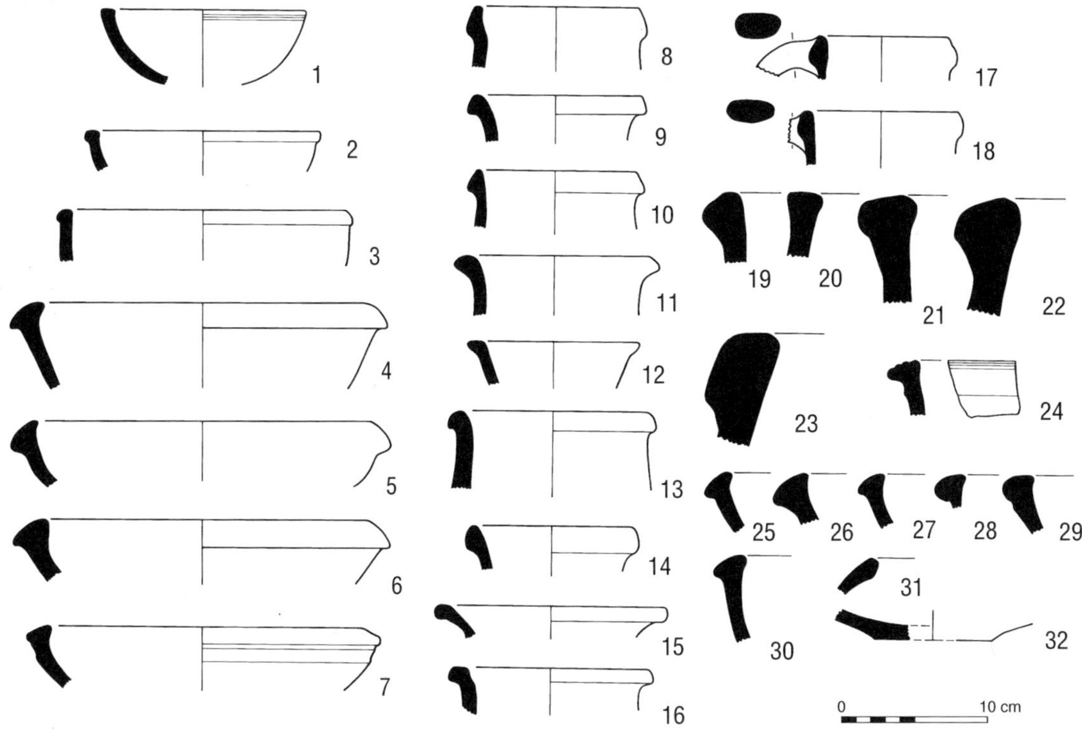

Figure 6.17. Pottery from Khirbet al-Hamrah 2 (SS 15). Sweyhat Survey Period X (Iron Age)

1. *Survey No. 10.* Bowl rim. Pale reddish brown, pale brown surfaces. Fine sand temper.

2. *Survey No. 14.* Bowl rim. Pale reddish brown, pale brown surfaces. Moderately fine, occasional voids.

3. *Survey No. 13.* Bowl rim. Grayish brown body, pale brown surfaces. Occasional sand temper.

4. *Survey No. 1.* Bowl rim. Pale brown core, reddened margins. Moderately fine; fine sand temper.

5. *Survey No. 2.* Bowl rim. Dark gray core, reddened margins, pale reddish brown surfaces. Poorly fired, occasional chaff.

6. *Survey No. 3.* Bowl rim. Pale brown, reddened margins, pale brown surfaces. Sparse temper but occasional voids.

7. *Survey No. 9.* Bowl rim. Pale grayish brown, pale brown surfaces. Moderately fine fabric, rare fine sand.

8. *Survey No. 28.* Jar rim. Pale brown throughout, common chaff temper. Hollow on rim interior.

9. *Survey No. 22.* Jar rim. Brown, pale brown surfaces. Fine sand temper.

10. *Survey No. 21.* Jar rim. Pale brown throughout. Moderately fine fabric; occasional fine sand and voids.

11. *Survey No. 20.* Jar rim. Pale reddish brown, pale brown surfaces. Occasional fine/medium sand.

12. *Survey No. 16.* Rim of jar or bowl. Very pale brown throughout. Occasional fine sand temper.

13. *Survey No. 23.* Jar rim. Pale reddish brown, pale brown surfaces. Moderately fine fabric; occasional fine sand.

14. *Survey No. 25.* Jar rim. Pale reddish brown body, pale brown surfaces. Occasional fine sand.

15. *Survey No. 26.* Jar rim. Very pale grayish brown body, pale brown surfaces. Fine sand temper.

16. *Survey No. 27.* Jar rim. Pale grayish brown body. Gray brown and pale brown surfaces. Common fine sand.

17. *Survey No. 34.* Jar rim with handle. Very pale greenish brown body, very pale brown surfaces. Common fine sand temper. Oval-sectioned handle.

18. *Survey No. 35.* Jar rim with handle. Pink body, pale brown surfaces. Common fine/medium sand temper, some white inclusions. Oval-sectioned handle.

19. *Survey No. 36.* Rim of large jar. Pale reddish brown body, pale brown surfaces. Common chaff, some micaceous sand. Diameter ca. 40 cm.

20. *Survey No. 37.* Rim of large jar. Pale reddish brown body, pale brown surfaces. Common chaff temper, occasional fine sand. Diameter ca. 38 cm.

21. *Survey No. 38.* Rim of large jar or bowl. Pale reddish brown body, pale brown surfaces. Occasional chaff and fine/medium sand temper. Diameter ca. 46 cm.

22. *Survey No. 40.* Rim of large jar. Reddish brown body, pale brown margins and surfaces. Common chaff temper.

23. *Survey No. 41.* Rim of large jar. Very pale brown throughout, common chaff temper. Diameter ca. 50 cm.

24. *Survey No. 15.* Bowl rim. Very pale grayish brown body and exterior, pale brown interior surface. Occasional indeterminate sand and fine voids. Rim top scored by shallow grooves. Diameter ca. 34 cm.

25. *Survey No. 4.* Bowl rim. Reddish brown, pale red brown interior, pale brown exterior. Moderately fine fabric, occasional voids. Diameter 28 cm.

26. *Survey No. 5.* Bowl rim. Dark grayish brown with brown margins. Pale gray brown surfaces. Fine sand temper; common mica. Diameter 30 cm.

27. *Survey No. 6.* Bowl rim. Pale brown, very pale brown surfaces. Moderately fine fabric, fine sand temper. Diameter 24 cm.

28. *Survey No. 7.* Bowl rim. Pale red brown and pale brown body, pale brown surfaces. Occasional sand.

29. *Survey No. 8.* Bowl rim. Reddish brown body, pale brown surfaces. Occasional medium sand and irregular voids. Diameter ca. 30 cm.

30. *Survey No. 11.* Bowl rim. Reddish brown body, pale brown surfaces. Occasional fine sand includes white sand.

31. *Survey No. 17.* Rim of hole-mouth jar or bowl. Grayish brown body, pale brown surfaces. Coarse sand temper, occasional mica.

32. *Survey No. 31.* Flat base of shallow bowl. Grayish brown body, reddish brown/pale brown exterior, pale brown interior. Occasional fine sand with mica.

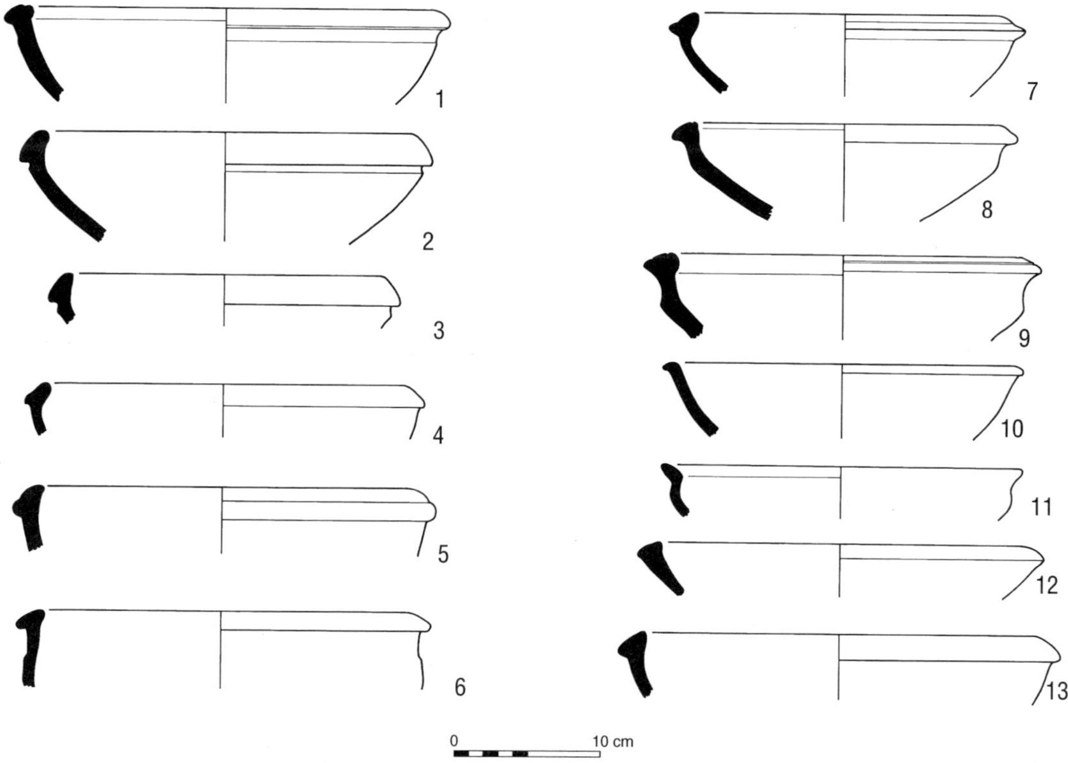

Figure 6.18. Pottery from SS 26. Sweyhat Survey Period X (Iron Age)

1. *Survey No. 29.* Bowl rim. Pale green throughout. Occasional fine/medium sand. Smooth surfaces.

2. *Survey No. 30.* Bowl rim. Pale reddish brown, pale brown surfaces. Occasional medium sand.

3. *Survey No. 14.* Bowl rim. Reddish brown, pale red surfaces. Occasional fine sand; smooth surfaces.

4. *Survey No. 9.* Bowl rim. Red brown body, pale brown surfaces. Occasional sand; smooth surfaces.

5. *Survey No. 22.* Bowl rim. Brown throughout. Occasional chaff temper.

6. *Survey No. 4.* Bowl rim. Pale reddish brown with very pale reddish brown surfaces. Common sand, 50% white.

7. *Survey No. 23.* Bowl rim. Brown, pale gray brown surfaces. Fine sand temper, fine voids, some mica. Smooth surfaces, throwing lines on exterior.

8. *Survey No. 24.* Bowl rim. Pale reddish brown body, pale brown surfaces. Occasional chaff and sand temper. Throwing lines on exterior.

9. *Survey No. 25.* Bowl rim. Pale reddish brown, pale brown surfaces. Common fine/medium sand. Shallow grooves in top of rim.

10. *Survey No. 21.* Bowl rim. Reddish brown body, pale brown surfaces. Smooth, occasional fine sand.

11. *Survey No. 16.* Bowl rim. Reddish brown, pale brown surfaces. Occasional medium sand.

12. *Survey No. 6.* Bowl rim. Reddish brown, pale reddish brown interior, very pale brown surfaces. Sparse fine/medium sand.

13. *Survey No. 7.* Bowl rim. Pale greenish gray throughout. Fine sand temper.

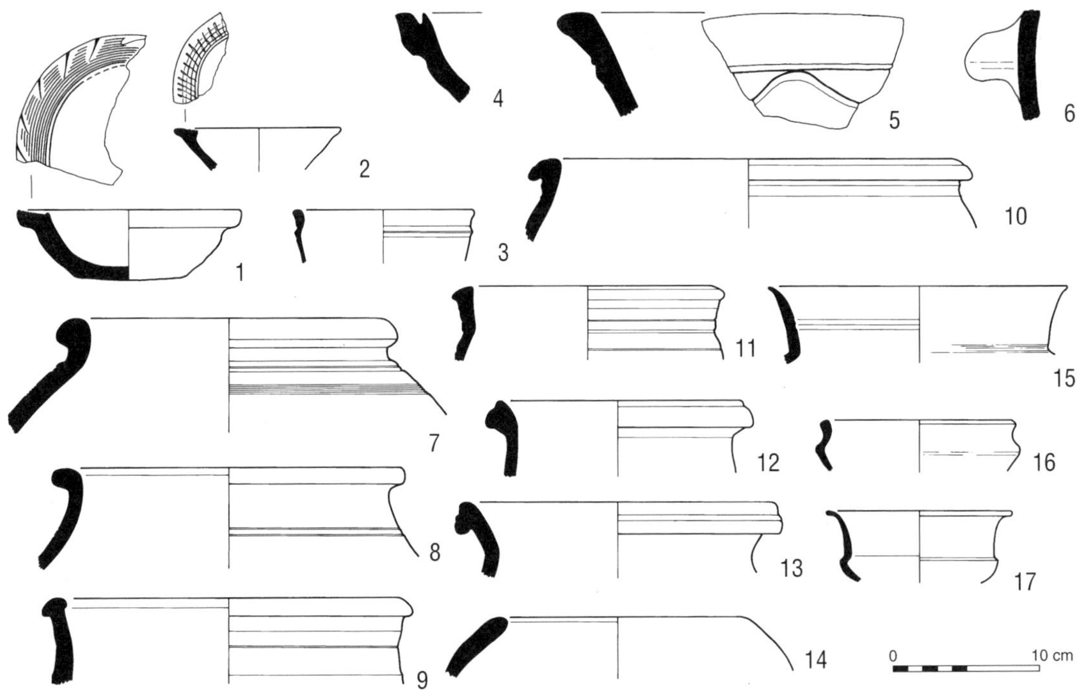

Figure 6.19. Pottery from SS 26 (*cont.*). Sweyhat Survey Periods X (Iron Age) and XIII (Late Roman/Early Byzantine)

1. *Survey No. 10.* Flanged dish. Reddish brown body, pale brown surfaces, fine sand temper. Flange decorated with circumference grooves cut by broad, oblique slashes.

2. *Survey No. 28.* Flanged dish. Pale greenish gray throughout. Very hard and dense. Common medium sand. Flange decorated with occasional circumference grooves cut by numerous radial incisions.

3. *Survey No. 19.* Rim of brittle ware jar. Reddish brown throughout. Very hard, rare fine sand.

4. *Survey No. 26.* Rim of large bowl. Pale reddish brown, very pale yellowish brown-slipped surfaces. Common medium sand. Diameter 54 cm.

5. *Survey No. 27.* Rim of large bowl. Dark brown with brown surfaces. Dense fabric; fine micaceous sand. Shallow incised wavy lines on exterior. Diameter 46 cm.

6. *Survey No. 3.* Lug handle from Neolithic(?) jar. Moderately hard, brown, pale grayish brown surfaces. Occasional coarse black inclusions. Roughly made. Estimated jar diameter 26 cm.

7. *Survey No. 1.* Jar rim. Pale greenish brown, pale brown surfaces. Occasional chaff and sand temper. Comb-incised exterior.

8. *Survey No. 2.* Jar rim. Pale greenish brown, olive brown surfaces. Occasional medium sand. Two shallow incised lines on exterior.

9. *Survey No. 15.* Jar rim. Pale brown, reddish brown exterior margin, brown exterior surface, pale brown interior surface. Fine sand temper.

10. *Survey No. 5.* Jar rim. Pale greenish gray throughout. Common medium sand.

11. *Survey No. 11.* Jar rim. Red brown body, pink interior. Smooth, fine sand temper.

12. *Survey No. 8.* Jar rim. Reddish brown, very pale brown surfaces. Occasional fine/medium sand.

13. *Survey No. 13.* Jar rim. Pale brown, pale greenish brown surfaces. Occasional fine sand.

14. *Survey No. 12.* Hole-mouth jar. Pale reddish brown body, brown surfaces. Occasional medium/coarse sand. Rings on interior and exterior surfaces suggest vessel was wheel thrown.

15. *Survey No. 20.* Jar rim. Gray core, pale greenish surfaces. Rare medium black inclusions.

16. *Survey No. 17.* Carinated bowl rim. Red brown body, pale brown surfaces. Fine sand. Rim either heavily abraded or broken.

17. *Survey No. 18.* Carinated bowl rim. Brown body, very pale brown surfaces. Smooth, fine sand temper.

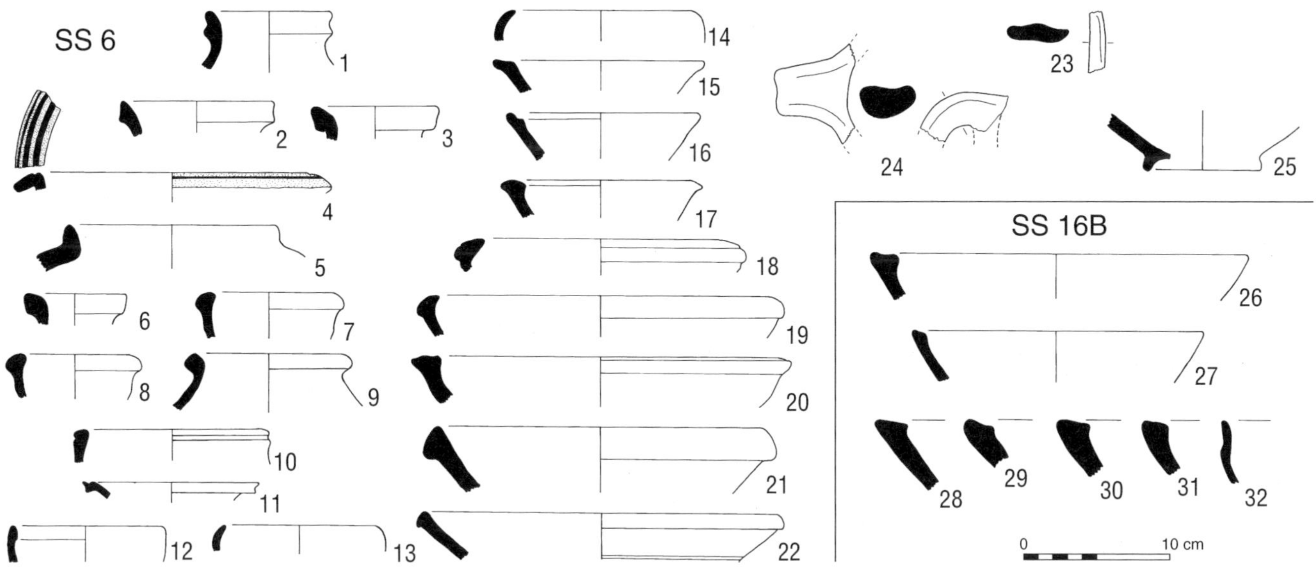

Figure 6.20. Pottery from Khirbet Aboud al-Hazu (SS 6) (nos. 1–25) and Ramalah (SS 16B) (nos. 26–32). Sweyhat Survey Periods XI (Hellenistic) and XII (Roman)

1. *Survey No. 1.* Jar rim. Brown with very pale brown-slipped surfaces. Moderately fine fabric, occasional sand temper and irregular voids.

2. *Survey No. 3.* Jar rim. Pale brown core with dull red margins and pink surfaces. Abundant medium Euphrates sand temper.

3. *Survey No. 4.* Jar rim. Brown core with reddish margins, pale brown surfaces, locally slightly pink. Dense moderately fine fabric, occasional medium sand. Rim formed by folding over.

4. *Survey No. 2.* Jar rim. Pale reddish brown with pale brown exterior, dark red (stipple) and dark reddish brown (solid) paint on top of rim and exterior. Fine fabric, occasional sand temper, and fine voids.

5. *Survey No. 22.* Rim of cooking pot. Dark grayish brown tending to dull red brown exterior margins; dark gray interior, brown exterior. Occasional sand and indeterminate inclusions.

6. *Survey No. 20.* Jar rim. Pale brown, very pale brown surfaces. Common medium/coarse sand temper.

7. *Survey No. 19.* Jar rim. Pale red brown body, pale brown surfaces. Common fine/medium sand, occasional irregular voids, some large.

8. *Survey No. 17.* Jar rim. Black body, pale green surfaces. Very hard almost vitrified body; occasional white sand. Overfired but not a waster.

9. *Survey No. 21.* Jar rim. Pale red brown body, mat pale brown surfaces. Common fine/medium sand.

10. *Survey No. 16.* Jar rim. Very pale reddish brown, pale brown-slipped surfaces. Occasional sand temper, one or two pieces of grog.

11. *Survey No. 18.* Bowl rim. Black body, pale greenish on parts of rim exterior, elsewhere black surfaces. Very hard fine fabric, sub-vitrified. Rare indeterminate inclusions. Fabric similar to no. 17, below.

12. *Survey No. 11.* Bowl rim. Pale brown throughout, very pale brown-slipped surfaces. Common indeterminate pale brown inclusions; occasional irregular voids of all sizes.

13. *Survey No. 6.* Incurved rim bowl. Pale red tending to pale brown outer margin; mat pale brown exterior, dull red interior wash or paint extends up to rim. Fine fabric, no discernible temper, rare small voids.

14. *Survey No. 5.* Incurved rim bowl. Dull red core, pale brown margins. Evenly fired fine fabric, no discernible temper. Dull red wash or paint on exterior and interior.

15. *Survey No. 14.* Bowl rim. Pale red brown body, mat pale brown surfaces. Common sand. From Area E.

16. *Survey No. 10.* Bowl rim. Dark gray throughout, pale gray surfaces. Moderately fine fabric, occasional voids, very sparse temper.

17. *Survey No. 12.* Bowl rim. Pale grayish brown, evenly fired body, pale brown mat surfaces. Occasional medium sand and voids.

18. *Survey No. 8.* Bowl rim. Pale red brown with pale brown surfaces. Occasional sand and irregular voids; occasional chaff impressions on exterior.

19. *Survey No. 7.* Bowl rim. Pale reddish brown evenly-fired body; mat very pale brown surfaces. Moderately fine fabric, rare sand temper. Top of rim very slightly beveled.

20. *Survey No. 13.* Bowl rim. Pale red brown body, pale brown surfaces with red wash or paint on interior to within 8 mm of rim. Occasional fine/medium white sand temper.

21. *Survey No. 9.* Bowl rim. Pale brown core, pale red margins, mat pale brown surfaces. Moderately fine fabric, occasional indeterminate sand temper.

22. *Survey No. 15.* Bowl rim. Pale brown body, very pale brown-slipped surfaces. Occasional medium sand. Impressed groove on exterior. (From Area E)

23. *Survey No. 25.* Brittle ware handle. Very dark reddish brown body with very dark red brown-slipped surfaces. Occasional fine sand temper.

24. *Survey No. 24.* Jug rim and handle. Pale gray brown body, very pale brown-slipped surfaces. Common fine/medium Euphrates sand.

25. *Survey No. 23.* Ring base. Dull orange exterior half, pale brown interior half, dull red surfaces; exterior surface smoothed. Rare sand and white inclusions; occasional planar voids.

26. *Survey No. 4.* Bowl rim. Brown reddish brown exterior, occasional medium sand.

27. *Survey No. 6.* Bowl rim. Brown reddish brown interior, pale brown surfaces. Moderately fine fabric, occasional sand and irregular voids. Diameter 16 cm.

28. *Survey No. 1.* Bowl rim. Pale red throughout. Occasional medium sand and irregular voids. Diameter 40 cm.

29. *Survey No. 2.* Bowl rim. Pale brown, very pale brown surfaces, occasional medium sand. Diameter 30 cm.

30. *Survey No. 3.* Bowl rim. Brown throughout, common medium sand. Diameter 30 cm.

31. *Survey No. 5.* Bowl rim. Pale reddish brown, very pale brown interior, pale red brown exterior. Occasional medium sand and irregular voids. Diameter 30 cm.

32. *Survey No. 7.* Rim of carinated bowl. Pale brown throughout. Common medium sand.

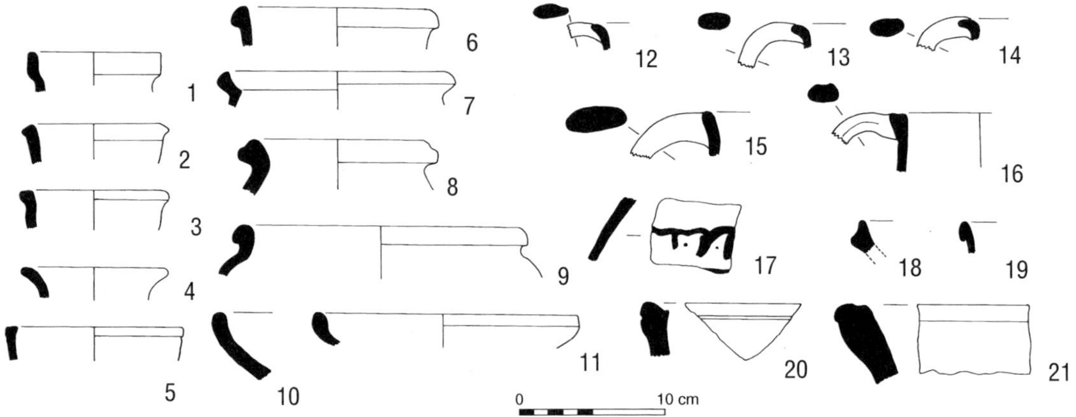

Figure 6.21. Pottery from Khirbet Haj Hassan (SS 10). Sweyhat Survey Period XIII (Early Byzantine)

1. *Survey No. 9.* Jar rim. Pale reddish brown throughout. Moderately fine, dense fabric; occasional sand.

2. *Survey No. 8.* Jar rim. Dull red body and interior, pale brown surfaces. Moderately fine fabric with occasional fine sand.

3. *Survey No. 6.* Brown body, very pale brown-slipped surfaces. Occasional sand temper.

4. *Survey No. 11.* Jar rim. Brown body, very pale brown surfaces. Common very fine sand, rare medium sand.

5. *Survey No. 17.* Brittle ware jar rim. Red body, dull black-slipped exterior and top, dull red interior. Very hard fine fabric. Occasional large black-coated voids.

6. *Survey No. 10.* Jar rim. Brown body, very pale brown surfaces. Occasional Euphrates sand temper.

7. *Survey No. 18.* Rim of brittle ware jar. Dull red body becoming black towards exterior; mat black exterior, dull red interior. Fine micaceous sand temper includes some white sand.

8. *Survey No. 13.* Jar rim. Pink body, pale reddish brown interior, very pale brown exterior. Moderately dense, common Euphrates sand.

9. *Survey No. 12.* Jar rim. Dull reddish brown body, pale brown interior, very pale greenish brown-slipped exterior. Common medium Euphrates sand, some large voids.

10. *Survey No. 1.* Bowl rim. Pale reddish brown body, pale brown exterior, very pale brown interior. Common medium Euphrates sand.

11. *Survey No. 2.* Bowl rim. Very pale grayish brown with very pale brown surfaces. Moderately fine fabric, fine sand temper.

12. *Survey No. 19.* Brittle ware rim and handle. Red brown body, dull black exterior and top, dull red interior. Occasional fine sand.

13. *Survey No. 20.* Brittle ware rim and handle. Very dark gray brown body, dull gray surfaces, becoming dull red towards interior. Fine sand temper includes some white inclusions.

14. *Survey No. 21.* Brittle ware rim and handle. Dull reddish brown body. Mat black surfaces. Moderately hard, occasional voids, rare medium sand.

15. *Survey No. 15.* Brittle ware handle and rim. Bright red body and interior surface, dull red exterior surface. Occasional medium sand and voids.

16. *Survey No. 16.* Buff ware handle and jar rim. Pale brown throughout. Occasional medium Euphrates sand. Very pale brown-slipped surfaces. Diameter 12 cm.

17. *Survey No. 14.* Body sherd of scroll-painted amphora. Pink core, pale brown margins and interior surface, very pale brown-slipped exterior. Occasional sand temper, some weak yellowish inclusions. Rough scrolls executed on exterior with dark brown paint.

18. *Survey No. 5.* Fragment of keel-rim bowl. Pale red brown body, pink interior, very pale brown exterior. Common fine Euphrates sand. Note: this is not Late Roman C ware.

19. *Survey No. 7.* Rim of small jar. Dull red body and interior, pale brown exterior. Occasional sand temper includes some fine white inclusions.

20. *Survey No. 3.* Rim of large bowl. Pale reddish brown body, pale brown surfaces. Occasional medium sand temper. Deep incised groove on perimeter of rim. Diameter 38 cm.

21. *Survey No. 4.* Rim of large bowl. Pale brown body and interior; very pale brown-slipped exterior. Common medium Euphrates sand. Diameter ca. 50 cm.

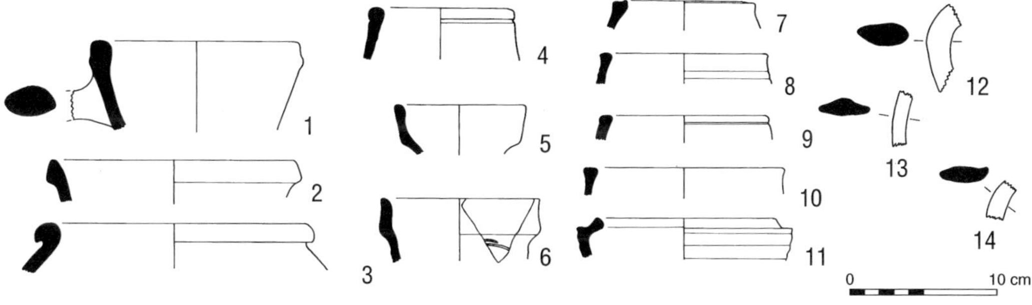

Figure 6.22. Pottery from SS 4. Sweyhat Survey Periods XIII (Late Roman/Early Byzantine) and XIV (Early Islamic)

1. *Survey No. 8*. Rim of jar or amphora. Very pale brown throughout. Common medium Euphrates sand temper. Common planar voids.

2. *Survey No. 4*. Jar rim. Very pale brown throughout. Rare/occasional fine/medium Euphrates sand.

3. *Survey No. 1*. Jar rim. Brown, pale brown surfaces. Occasional grit, rare voids.

4. *Survey No. 3*. Jar rim. Brown, very pale brown surfaces. Fine sand temper, occasional voids. Rim scored by very deep groove on exterior.

5. *Survey No. 5*. Jar rim. Very pale brown throughout. Occasional medium sand, some very fine mica.

6. *Survey No. 2*. Jar rim. Pale reddish brown throughout, very pale brown surfaces. Fine sand temper. Impressed wavy line on exterior.

7. *Survey No. 12*. Brittle ware jar rim. Pale red brown body, dull red brown surfaces. Fine/medium sand temper.

8. *Survey No. 14*. Brittle ware jar rim. Dark red brown body, dull red brown exterior, dull red interior. Common fine sand, some mica.

9. *Survey No. 13*. Brittle ware jar rim. Dark red brown body, dull red brown exterior, red brown interior. Fine sand temper.

10. *Survey No. 11*. Brittle ware jar rim. Red body, mat black exterior, dull red interior. Fine sand temper, some large irregular voids.

11. *Survey No. 9*. Rim of brittle ware cooking pot. Red body, pale red surfaces. Evenly fired, sand temper.

12. *Survey No. 7*. Buff ware handle. Reddish brown body, pale brown surfaces. Common medium sand.

13. *Survey No. 6*. Brittle ware handle. Red interior, evenly fired, dull red exterior. Occasional medium sand.

14. *Survey No. 10*. Brittle ware handle. Red body, dull red surfaces. Occasional fine/medium sand temper, some mica.

ISLAMIC POTTERY CATALOGS

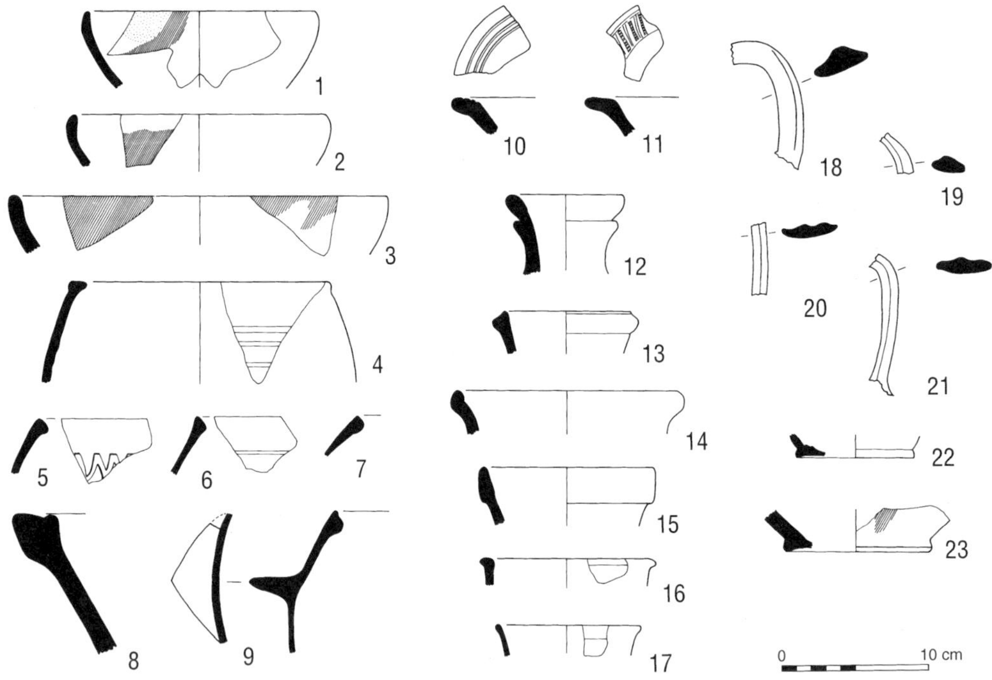

Figure 6.23. Pottery from Khirbet al-Hamrah (SS 7). Sweyhat Survey Period XIV (Early Islamic)

1. *Survey No. G13.* Rim of glazed bowl (two sherds). Pale reddish brown body, pale brown exterior. Moderately fine sand temper, rare voids. Interior has very dark thick green glaze (hatched) dribbled over cream slip or degraded white glaze. Lighter, (greenish) glaze stippled.

2. *Survey No. G14.* Rim of glazed bowl. Pale brown body, very pale brown exterior. Moderately fine ware with fine sand temper. Green glaze (hatched) on interior becoming paler above where apparently slightly obscured by CaCO$_3$.

3. *Survey No. F15.* Rim of glazed bowl. Pale reddish brown body. Moderately fine with fine sand temper. Interior has green glaze which dribbled over rim to exterior where it occurred in scattered patches over pale brown body.

4. *Survey No. F9.* Brittle ware hole-mouth jar. Reddish brown and dark brown body, mainly dark reddish brown interior. Dull black exterior. Hard; common micaceous very fine sand. Very weakly corrugated interior.

5. *Survey No. F10.* Brittle ware hole-mouth jar. Bright reddish brown body, dark reddish brown interior, dull black exterior. Very hard; sparse fine sand temper. Impressed rocker pattern on exterior. Diameter 18 cm.

6. *Survey No. G11.* Brittle ware hole-mouth jar. Dark reddish brown exterior half, reddish brown inner half; dull red interior surface, dull reddish brown exterior surface. Moderately hard, occasional medium sand temper. Diameter 16 cm.

7. *Survey No. F12.* Brittle ware hole-mouth jar. Bright reddish brown body, dull red surfaces. Hard; common medium sand. One shallow impressed line on exterior. Diameter 18 cm.

8. *Survey No. F1.* Rim of large bowl. Pale reddish brown body, very pale brown surfaces. Occasional fine/medium sand temper. Diameter ca. 40 cm.

9. *Survey No. G19.* Brittle ware hole-mouth jar. Bright red body, dull red surfaces. Very hard, fine fabric; occasional fine sand temper. Triangular ledge handle appears to be integral part of body.

10. *Survey No. G6.* Rim of flanged dish. Pale grayish brown body, pale brown surfaces. Occasional sand temper and voids. Lightly incised grooves on upper face of flange. Diameter 14 cm.

11. *Survey No. G7.* Rim of flanged dish. Pale brown body, very pale brown surfaces. Occasional fine sand, one inclusion of pink grog. Flange decorated with lightly-incised radial lines and short impressed grooves. Diameter 14 cm.

12. *Survey No. G4.* Jar rim. Pale reddish brown body, very pale brown surfaces. Occasional fine/medium sand.

13. *Survey No. F5.* Jar rim. Pale reddish brown body, very pale brown surfaces. Moderately fine fabric, fine sand temper.

14. *Survey No. G2.* Jar rim. Pale grayish green with pale brownish green surfaces. Occasional sand temper. Slight hollow on rim interior.

15. *Survey No. F3.* Jar rim (angle approximate). Very pale brown throughout. Moderately fine fabric, occasional large voids.

16. *Survey No. G18.* Brittle ware jar rim. Bright reddish brown body, dull black exterior, dull red interior. Moderately hard; common medium sand temper.

17. *Survey No. F17.* Brittle ware jar rim. Bright red body, dull red surfaces. Hard; occasional sand and off-white inclusions.

18. *Survey No. F8.* Buff ware handle. Pale brown body, very pale brown surfaces. Occasional sand temper.

19. *Survey No. F22.* Brittle ware handle. Bright reddish brown body, dull black surfaces. Rare medium sand; occasional micaceous fine sand. Conspicuous finger-smoothing on handle exterior.

20. *Survey No. F21.* Brittle ware handle. Bright reddish brown body, dull black surfaces. Common fine micaceous sand, rare medium sand; some planar voids. Note central groove.

21. *Survey No. G20.* Brittle ware handle. Dull reddish brown body. Dull black and brownish black surfaces. Rare medium, occasional fine sand temper.

22. *Survey No. G23.* Low cream ware base. Very pale brown with cream surfaces. Moderately fine with occasional fine sand temper. Deep incisions on vessel interior.

23. *Survey No. G16.* Ring base. Pale brown body, very pale brown surfaces. Occasional fine/medium sand temper; occasional irregular voids. Dribble of green glaze on exterior.

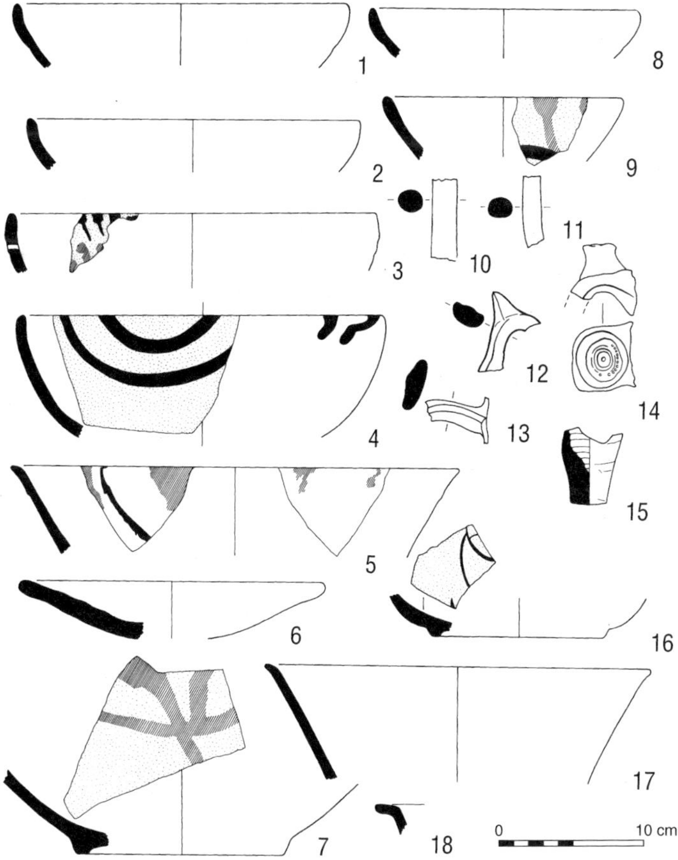

Figure 6.24. Pottery from Khirbet Dhiman (SS 11). Sweyhat Survey Period XIV (Early Islamic)

1. *Survey No. D12.* Rim of glazed bowl. Pale brown body. Moderately fine fabric, some fine sand. Exterior: green glaze splashed over cream slip. Interior: pale brown variegated glaze over cream slip (glazes abraded and only partially present therefore not shown).

2. *Survey No. C5.* Rim of glazed bowl. Very pale reddish brown body. Moderately fine ware, little discernible temper. Moderately shiny green glaze on exterior and interior surfaces (glaze not shown on drawing).

3. *Survey No. A4.* Rim of glazed bowl. Pale brown body. Moderately fine, fine sand temper and rare medium sand. Interior glazed with green and dark brown splashes on cream slip (under) glaze. Sherd pierced by mending hole (not shown).

4. *Survey No. C4.* Glazed bowl. Pale reddish brown body, brown mat exterior with a few dribbles of brown/black glaze from interior. Occasional sand temper; some voids, occasionally large. Interior covered with thin moderately shiny light green glaze (stipple) decorated with hanging swags (curved bands) of very dark grayish brown glaze.

5. *Survey No. C2.* Rim of glazed bowl. Very pale brown body. Moderately fine ware with occasional fine sand temper. Interior has thick white glaze with dark green and dark grayish brown glazed plumes. Exterior has similar white glaze below rim thinning to off-white below. Splashes of green glaze spill over to exterior just below rim. The low radial ridge on interior of bowl is characteristic of equivalent bowls of Mesopotamian manufacture.

6. *Survey No. D1.* Plain bowl. Brown body, very pale brown surfaces. Occasional fine sand. Vestiges of rounded base.

7. *Survey No. C12.* Ring base of glazed bowl. Dull reddish brown body, pale brown exterior. Moderately fine fabric, fine sand temper. Interior glazed with yellow decorated with broad green glazed bands.

8. *Survey No. D13.* Rim of glazed bowl. Brown body. Moderately fine fabric. Interior decorated with yellow and green glaze over cream slip (eroded therefore not illustrated). Exterior plain with single scrap of green glaze remaining.

9. *Survey No. D10.* Rim of green glazed bowl. Pale brown body, very pale brown exterior. Fine fabric, no discernible temper. Interior glazed white; exterior with green and black bands over pale green white glaze.

10. *Survey No. D18.* Fine rod handle. Pale brown with cream surfaces. Moderately fine with occasional fine voids.

11. *Survey No. D16.* Fine rod handle. Very pale brown with cream surfaces. Moderately fine with occasional fine voids.

12. *Survey No. B19.* Handle. Very pale green throughout. Fine fabric, some fine sand. Knob applied as separate item, then smoothed.

13. *Survey No. D17.* Brittle ware handle. Bright red body, dull red surfaces. Occasional fine sand and very fine mica.

14. *Survey No. A14.* Turban handle. Brown body, very pale brown surfaces. Fine medium Euphrates sand temper. Turban, applied as separate item, decorated with incised circles and small impressed circles.

15. *Survey No. C13.* Base of amphora(?). Pale yellowish brown body with cream exterior surface. Occasional fine sand.

16. *Survey No. C11.* Base of glazed bowl. Reddish brown body, pale brown exterior. Common fine/medium sand, some white $CaCO_3$ sand. Mat (through weathering) yellow and green glaze on interior decorated with thin brown curving lines.

17. *Survey No. C10.* White glazed bowl. Pale yellowish brown body. Occasional indeterminate sand temper. Thick white glaze on interior and upper part of exterior. Glaze thins and becomes transparent over lower part of exterior. Glaze moderately shiny.

18. *Survey No. D11.* Rim of glazed plate or dish. Pale reddish brown body. Moderately fine fabric. Green and very pale green splashed interior; yellow and green splashed exterior, not illustrated because partly eroded. Diameter 30 cm.

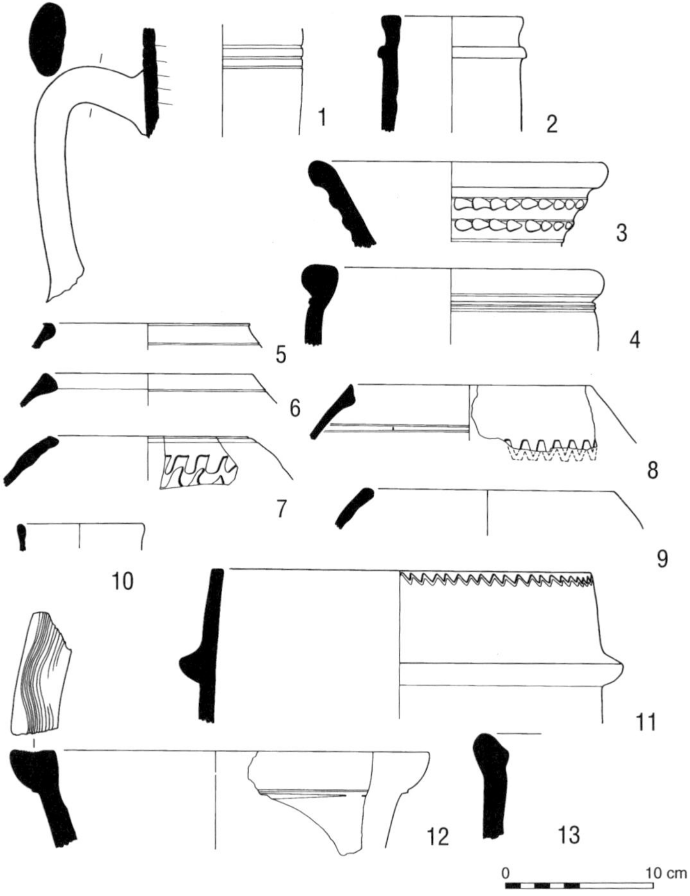

Figure 6.25. Pottery from Khirbet Dhiman (SS 11) (*cont.*). Sweyhat Survey Period XIV (Early Islamic)

1. *Survey No. C1*. Handle of large jar. Pale reddish brown body, brown interior, very pale brown-slipped exterior. Rare grog and chaff temper; some fine sand. Voids filled with CaCO₃ concretions. Neck diameter ca. 11 cm.

2. *Survey No. C8*. Jar rim. Pale reddish brown body, very pale brown surfaces. Moderately fine fabric, fine sand, occasional irregular voids.

3. *Survey No. C3*. Jar rim. Very pale brown with pale greenish brown-slipped surfaces. Moderately fine, some fine/medium sand. Decorated with deep tear-shaped depressions on rim exterior.

4. *Survey No. C9*. Jar rim. Very pale yellowish green body, very pale brown surfaces. Occasional medium sand temper. Deep incised grooves on exterior.

5. *Survey No. D6*. Brittle ware hole-mouth jar rim. Reddish brown body, dull red surfaces. Fine sand temper. Single deep groove on exterior.

6. *Survey No. D8*. Brittle ware hole-mouth jar rim. Bright red body, dull red surfaces. Occasional fine, rare medium sand. Groove incised on exterior.

7. *Survey No. D9*. Brittle ware hole-mouth jar rim. Reddish brown body, dull dark red exterior, red interior. Hard, fine fabric. Rocker pattern impressed on exterior.

8. *Survey No. C7*. Hole-mouth cooking pot (i.e., brittle ware variant). Dark brown core with dull red margins and dull red interior surface, mat black-slipped exterior. Occasional fine/medium micaceous sand. Deeply impressed rocker pattern on exterior.

9. *Survey No. D5*. Brittle ware hole-mouth bowl. Reddish brown body, dull red interior, mat black exterior. Occasional sand temper.

10. *Survey No. D7*. Brittle ware jar rim. Dull red body, dull dark red exterior, dull red interior. Hard, fine fabric, rare grog or sand temper.

11. *Survey No. C6*. Lugged cooking pot. Dark brown core, black margins and surfaces. Occasional grit temper includes CaCO₃ grits to 3 mm. Deep, wavy line incised immediately below rim. Large crescentic lug.

12. *Survey No. D2*. Rim of large bowl. Greenish cream body, cream surfaces. Fine sand temper, some irregular voids. Combed wavy line on top of rim, shallow incisions on exterior.

13. *Survey No. D3*. Rim of large bowl. Brown body, pale brown wiped surfaces. Fine sand temper, some fine voids. Diameter 40 cm.

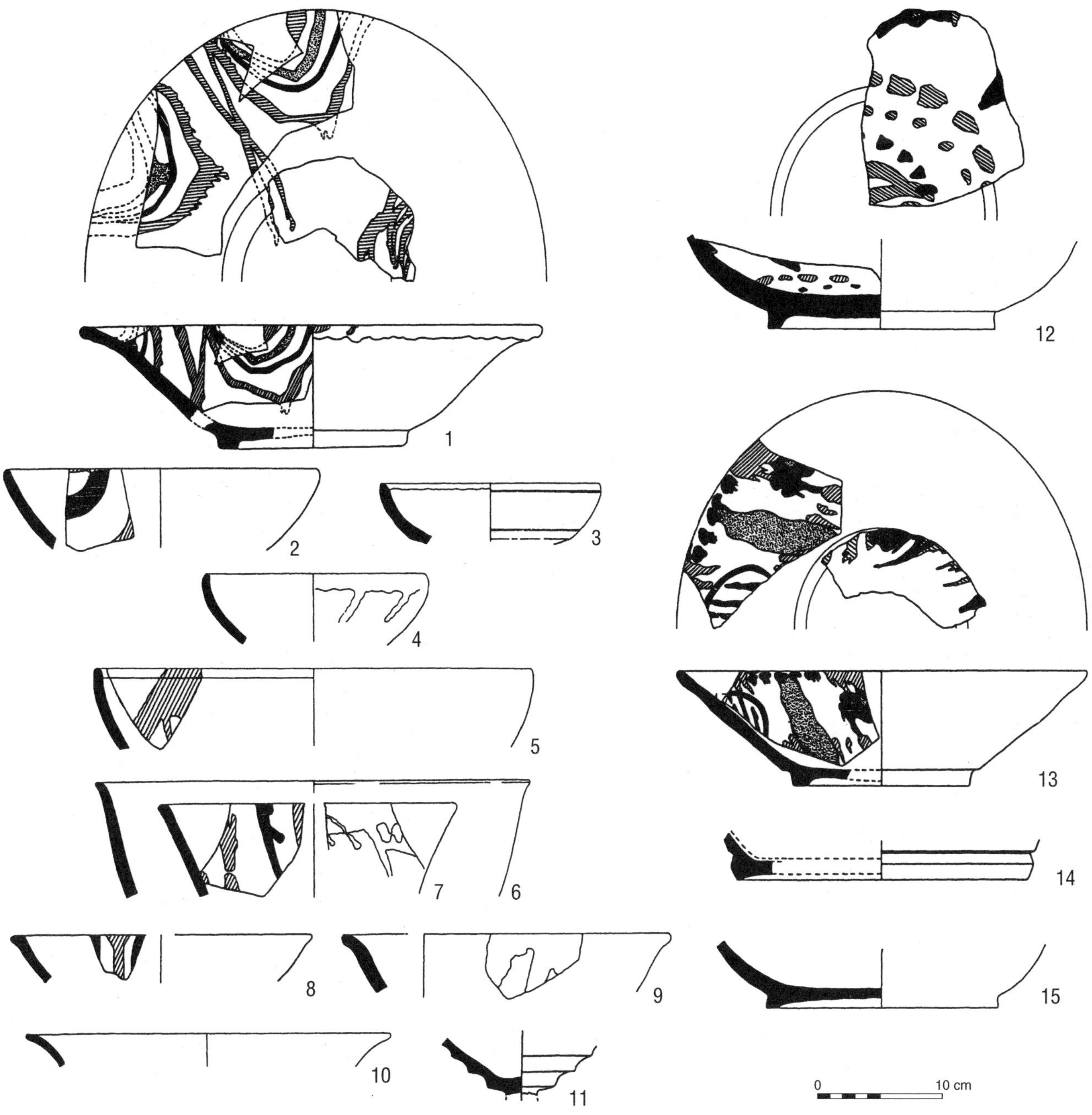

Figure 6.26. Pottery from Khirbet Dhiman (SS 11) (*cont.*). Sweyhat Survey Period XIV (Early Islamic)

1. *Survey No. 1*. Orange buff ware. Green, yellow, purple glaze on interior and rim. Moderate medium sand.

2. *Survey No. 22*. Orange tan ware. Yellow, with green, purple glaze on interior.

3. *Survey No. 37*. Orange tan ware. Opaque white glaze on interior. Moderate medium sand.

4. *Survey No. 51*. Orange tan ware. Opaque white with traces of green glaze on interior and rim. Moderate medium sand.

5. *Survey No. 12*. Orange tan ware. Yellow, with green glaze on interior. Moderate medium sand.

6. *Survey No. 43*. Orange tan ware. Green glaze on interior and exterior. Moderate medium sand.

7. *Survey No. 11*. Orange tan ware. Yellow, with green glaze on interior and rim. Moderate medium sand.

8. *Survey No. 9*. Orange tan ware. Dark yellow, with green and purple glaze on interior. Moderate medium sand

9. *Survey No. 42*. Orange tan ware. Green with olive green glaze on interior. Moderate medium sand.

10. *Survey No. 53*. Orange tan ware. Opaque white glaze on interior and exterior. Moderate medium sand.

11. *Survey No. 63*. Orange tan ware. Dark yellow glaze on interior; green glaze on exterior. Moderate medium sand.

12. *Survey No. 6*. Orange tan ware. Dark yellow, with green, purple glaze on interior. Moderate medium sand.

13. *Survey No. 2*. Orange tan ware. Opaque white, with green, yellow, purple glaze on interior. Moderate medium sand.

14. *Survey No. 80*. Orange tan ware. Opaque white glaze (traces on interior). Moderate medium sand.

15. *Survey No. 5*. Orange tan ware. Green glaze on interior and exterior. Moderate medium sand.

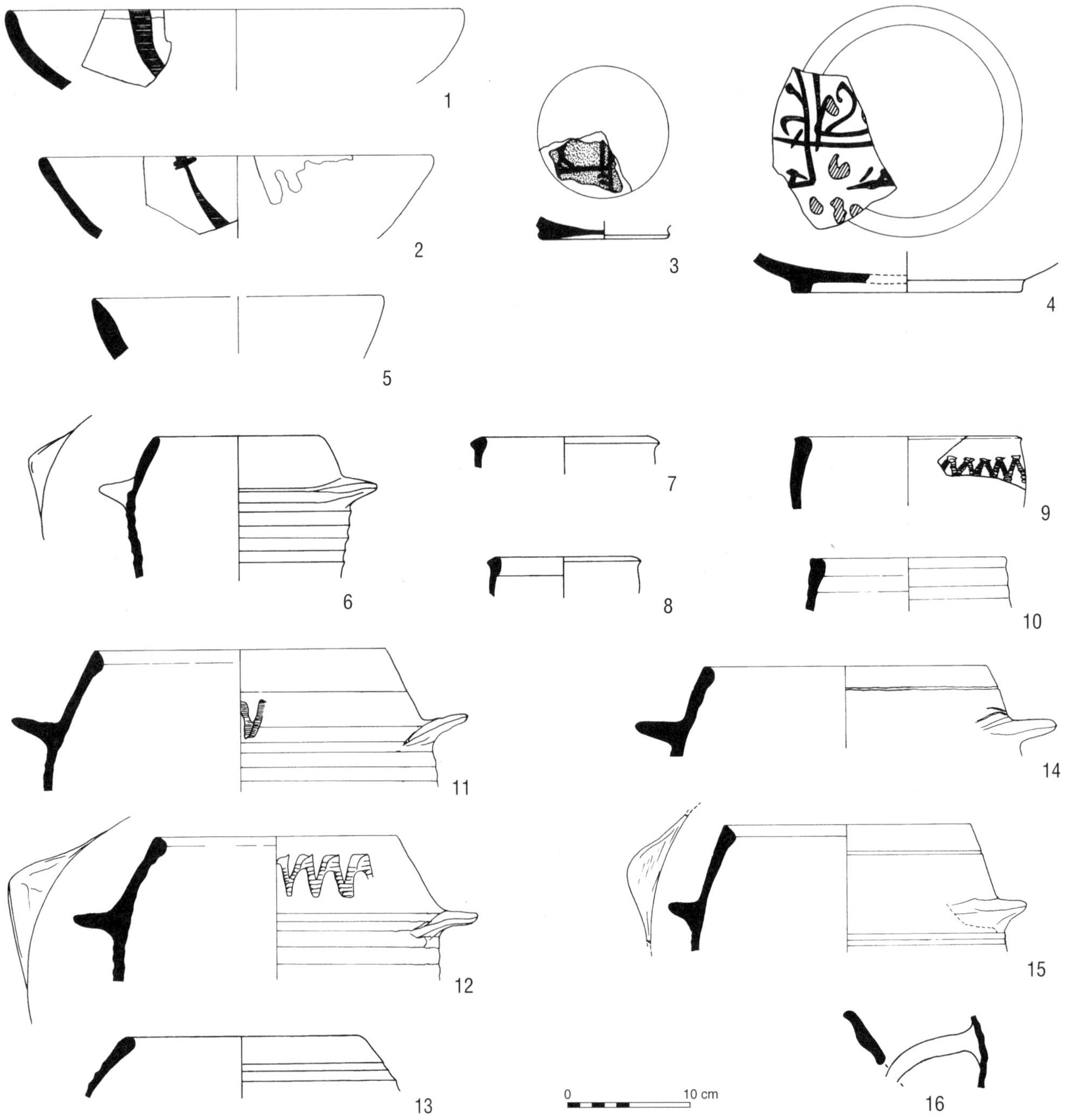

Figure 6.27. Pottery from Khirbet Dhiman (SS 11) (*cont.*). Sweyhat Survey Period XIV (Early Islamic)

1. *Survey No. 57.* Orange tan ware. Yellow, with brown glaze on interior. Moderate medium sand.

2. *Survey No. 52.* Buff ware. Green, with brown glaze on interior and rim. Moderate medium sand.

3. *Survey No. 65.* Orange tan ware. Greenish yellow, with brown glaze on interior. Moderate medium sand.

4. *Survey No. 66.* Orange ware. Yellow, with green, brown glaze on interior. Moderate medium sand.

5. *Survey No. 30.* Dark red ware. Common medium sand.

6. *Survey No. 93.* Dark red ware. Blackened exterior. Common medium sand.

7. *Survey No. 101.* Dark red ware. Common medium sand.

8. *Survey No. 96.* Dark red ware. Common medium sand.

9. *Survey No. 26.* Dark red ware. Common medium sand.

10. *Survey No. 39.* Dark red ware. Common medium sand.

11. *Survey No. 8.* Dark red ware. Blackened exterior. Common medium sand.

12. *Survey No. 7.* Dark red ware. Blackened exterior. Common medium sand.

13. *Survey No. 92.* Dark red ware. Common medium sand.

14. *Survey No. 56.* Dark red ware. Common medium sand.

15. *Survey No. 48.* Dark red ware. Common medium sand.

16. *Survey No. 91.* Dark red ware. Common medium sand.

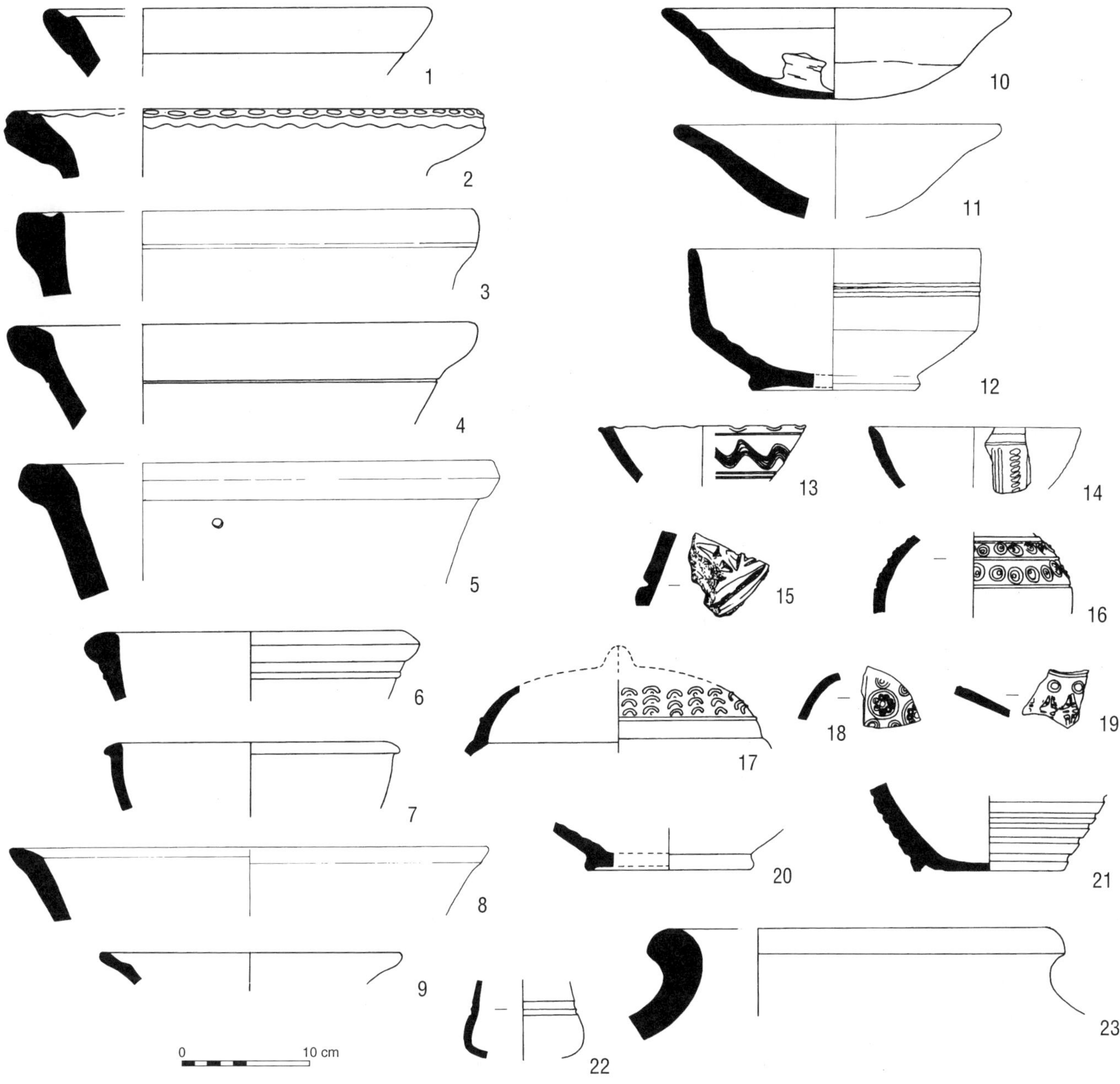

Figure 6.28. Pottery from Khirbet Dhiman (SS 11) (*cont.*). Sweyhat Survey Period XIV (Early Islamic)

1. *Survey No. 73.* Buff ware. Moderate medium sand.

2. *Survey No. 74.* Buff ware. Moderate medium sand.

3. *Survey No. 32.* Buff cream. Moderate medium sand.

4. *Survey No. 72.* Buff ware. Moderate medium sand.

5. *Survey No. 20.* Cream ware. Repair hole. Moderate medium sand.

6. *Survey No. 98.* Buff ware. Moderate medium sand.

7. *Survey No. 99.* Buff ware. Moderate medium sand.

8. *Survey No. 21.* Buff ware. Moderate medium sand.

9. *Survey No. 94.* Buff ware. Moderate medium sand.

10. *Survey No. 61.* Buff ware. Burnt on rim. Moderate medium sand.

11. *Survey No. 33.* Buff ware. Moderate medium sand.

12. *Survey No. 60.* Orange ware. Incised bands. Moderate medium sand.

13. *Survey No. 83.* Buff ware. Comb-incised. Moderate medium sand.

14. *Survey No. 58.* Buff ware. Molded exterior. Moderate medium sand.

15. *Survey No. 102.* Buff ware. Excised decoration. Moderate medium sand.

16. *Survey No. 70.* Orange tan ware. Traces of green glaze on interior and exterior. Moderate medium sand.

17. *Survey No. 84.* Buff ware. Cream slip on exterior. Molded decoration. Moderate medium sand.

18. *Survey No 75.* Buff ware. Molded decoration. Moderate medium sand.

19. *Survey No. 69.* Buff ware. Moderate medium sand.

20. *Survey No. 86.* Buff ware. Moderate medium sand.

21. *Survey No. 62.* Buff orange ware. Moderate medium sand.

22. *Survey No. 78.* Buff ware. Moderate medium sand.

23. *Survey No. 81.* Buff ware. Moderate medium sand.

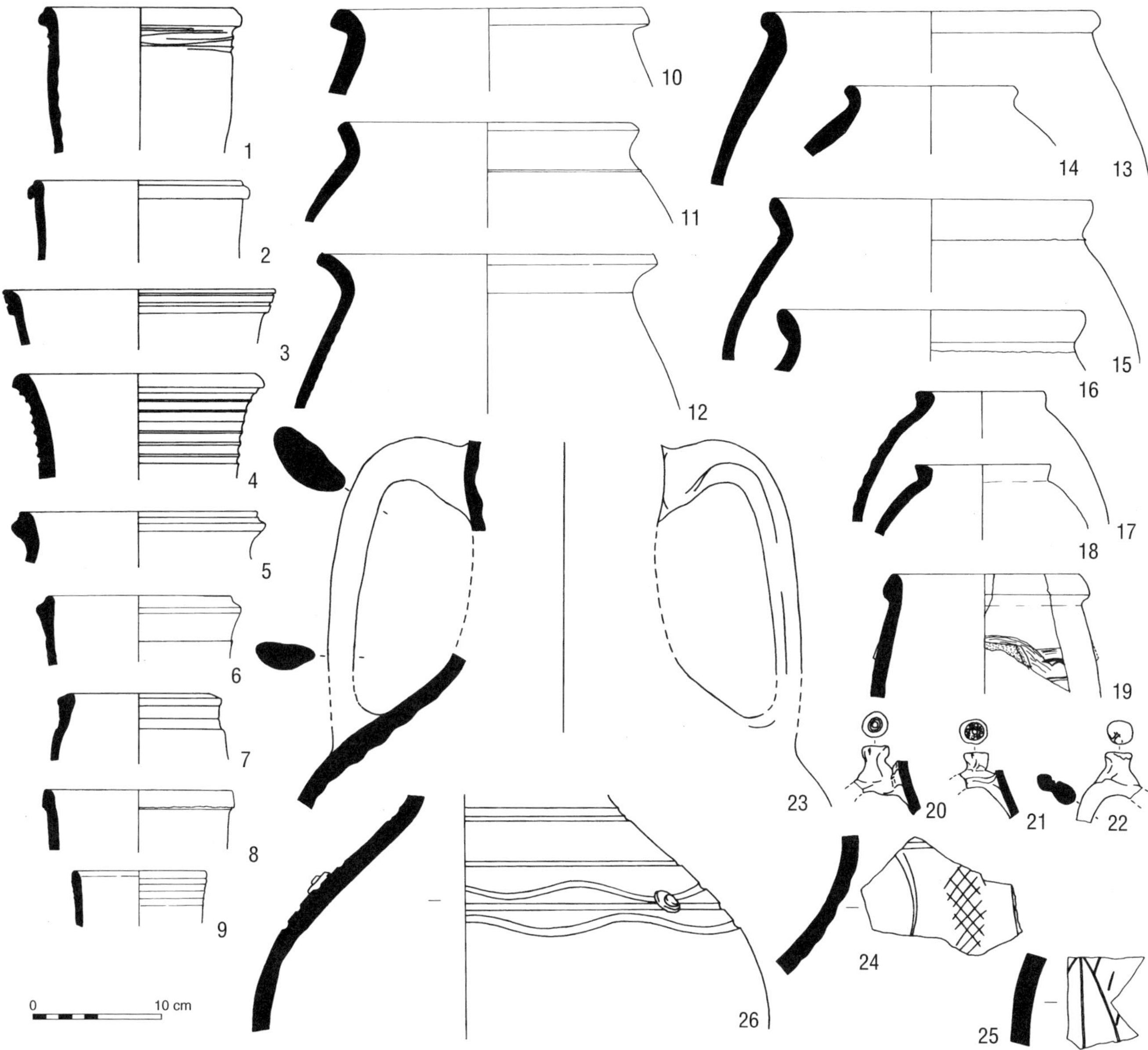

Figure 6.29. Pottery from Khirbet Dhiman (SS 11) (*cont.*). Sweyhat Survey Period XIV (Early Islamic)

1. *Survey No. 88*. Buff ware. Moderate medium sand.
2. *Survey No. 89*. Buff ware. Moderate medium sand.
3. *Survey No. 100*. Buff ware. Moderate medium sand.
4. *Survey No. 87*. Buff ware. Moderate medium sand.
5. *Survey No. 95*. Buff ware. Moderate medium sand.
6. *Survey No. 13*. Orange tan ware. Moderate medium sand.
7. *Survey No. 97*. Buff ware. Moderate medium sand.
8. *Survey No. 36*. Buff ware. Moderate medium sand.
9. *Survey No. 44*. Buff ware. Moderate medium sand.
10. *Survey No. 41*. Buff ware. Moderate medium sand.
11. *Survey No. 45*. Buff ware. Moderate medium sand.
12. *Survey No. 46*. Buff ware. Moderate medium sand.
13. *Survey No. 64*. Buff ware. Moderate medium sand.
14. *Survey No. 38*. Cream ware. Moderate medium sand.
15. *Survey No. 34*. Orange tan ware. Moderate medium sand.
16. *Survey No. 54*. Orange tan ware. Moderate medium sand.
17. *Survey No. 4*. Buff ware. Moderate medium sand.
18. *Survey No. 16*. Buff ware. Moderate medium sand.
19. *Survey No. 35*. Buff ware. Moderate medium sand.
20. *Survey No. 77*. Buff ware. Molded impression on top of handle. Moderate medium sand.
21. *Survey No. 67*. Buff ware. Molded impression on top of handle. Moderate medium sand.
22. *Survey No. 76*. Buff ware. Molded impression on top of handle. Moderate medium sand.
23. *Survey No. 82*. Orange tan ware. Moderate medium sand.
24. *Survey No. 85*. Buff ware. Incised decoration. Moderate medium sand.
25. *Survey No. 79*. Buff ware. Incised decoration. Moderate medium sand.
26. *Survey No. 71*. Buff ware. Incised and appliqué decoration. Moderate medium sand.

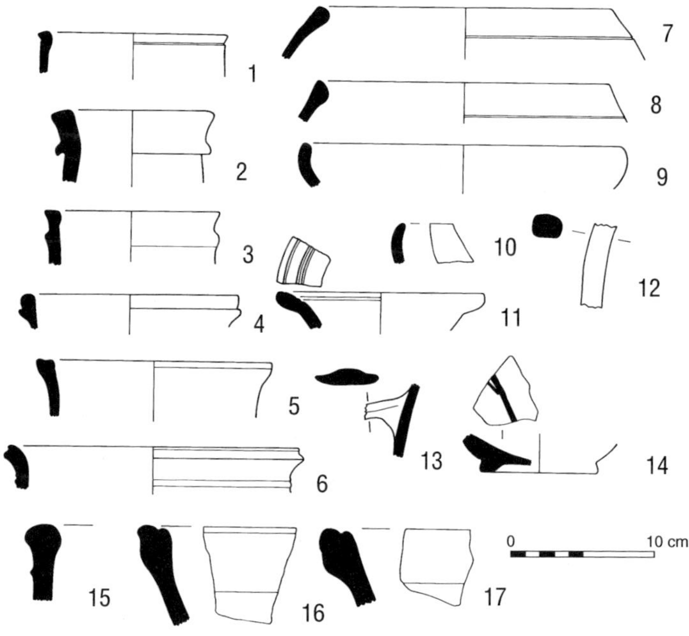

Figure 6.30. Pottery from SS 12. Sweyhat Survey Period XIV (Early Islamic)

1. *Survey No. 14*. Brittle ware jar rim. Reddish body, mat black exterior, dull red interior. Very hard, fine, dense fabric.

2. *Survey No. 3*. Jar rim. Pale greenish cream body and surfaces. Occasional fine sand and fine voids.

3. *Survey No. 2*. Jar rim. Greenish cream body and surfaces. Moderately fine fabric, occasional fine sand.

4. *Survey No. 5*. Jar rim. Grayish green, pale greenish brown surfaces. Occasional fine sand temper.

5. *Survey No. 1*. Jar rim. Pale brown core, pink margins. Pale brown interior surface, very pale brown-slipped exterior. Moderately fine fabric. Occasional fine sand, rare voids.

6. *Survey No. 4*. Jar rim. Pale brown body, very pale brown surfaces. Occasional sand temper.

7. *Survey No. 12*. Brittle ware hole-mouth jar rim. Red body, dull red surfaces. Moderately hard, occasional sand temper. Shallow groove on exterior.

8. *Survey No. 13*. Brittle ware hole-mouth jar rim. Dull red body, dark dull red surfaces. Fine, hard, dense fabric. Narrow groove on exterior.

9. *Survey No. 10*. Bowl rim. Reddish brown body. Smooth, moderately fine. Rare micaceous fine sand (note: this may have lost its glaze as a result of weathering).

10. *Survey No. 11*. Bowl rim. Pale reddish brown body, pink surfaces. Rare fine sand temper. Vestigial greenish yellow glaze on exterior. Diameter indeterminate.

11. *Survey No. 9*. Small flanged bowl. Pale reddish brown body, slightly brown towards core; pale yellowish brown-slipped exterior, dull red interior. Common medium/coarse sand. Shallow incised grooves on top of flanged rim.

12. *Survey No. 16*. Glazed rod handle. Dark grayish brown body. Occasional fine sand and voids. Shiny leaf green glaze all over.

13. *Survey No. 15*. Brittle ware handle. Brick red body and interior surface, dull red exterior surface. Occasional medium sand and voids.

14. *Survey No. 17*. Ring base of glazed bowl. Pale yellow body, moderately soft. Occasional medium sand temper. Thick grayish white glazed interior with gray glazed plume (shown black). Thin off-white glaze on exterior and beneath base.

15. *Survey No. 6*. Jar rim. Pale brown body, very pale brown-slipped surfaces. Moderately fine fabric, occasional fine sand. Diameter 18 cm.

16. *Survey No. 7*. Rim of large grooved-rim bowl. Brown body, pale greenish brown-slipped surfaces. Common Euphrates sand temper. Diameter ca. 46 cm.

17. *Survey No. 8*. Rim of large grooved-rim bowl. Pale reddish brown body, very pale brown surfaces. Occasional sand temper.

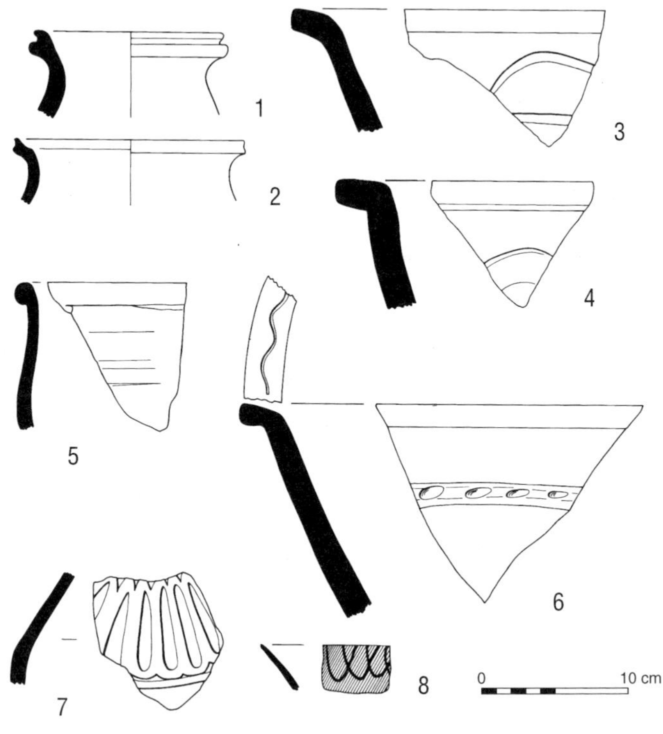

Figure 6.31. Pottery from SS 28. Sweyhat Survey Period XV (Middle Islamic)

1. *Survey No. 2*. Jar rim. Brown with pale greenish brown exterior. Fine sand and occasional grog temper.

2. *Survey No. 6*. Jar rim of cooking pot ware. Dark gray with reddened margins and surfaces. Slightly granular fabric; temper indeterminate.

3. *Survey No. 3*. Rim of large bowl. Brown, pale brown surfaces. Fine sand temper; occasional large irregular voids. Impressed curvilinear decoration on exterior. Diameter 44 cm.

4. *Survey No. 1*. Rim of large bowl. Pale greenish brown throughout. Common fine sand. Very shallow curved impression on exterior. Diameter ca. 44 cm.

5. *Survey No. 8*. Jar rim. Pale greenish brown throughout. Moderately fine fabric, no visible temper. Roughly formed on wheel; rim is uneven and features an applied pellet below the lip. Diameter 16 cm.

6. *Survey No. 4*. Rim of large bowl. Very pale yellowish brown throughout. Fine sand temper. Small fingertip impressions on very low exterior band; shallow impressed meander on upper face of rim. Diameter 46 cm.

7. *Survey No. 7*. Body sherd of "relief molded ware." Very pale brown with almost cream surfaces. Moderately fine fabric; very sparse chaff impressions (note: on close examination the lobate ridges appear to be applied, not molded).

8. *Survey No. 5*. Rim of small bowl. Very pale yellow or cream "fritware," slightly granular in appearance. On exterior black hanging swag decoration on turquoise background both glazed over with clear glaze. Obscure horizontal bands in black, fugitive on interior (only exterior drawn). Diameter 26 cm.

7. THE EVOLUTION OF THE SETTLEMENT PATTERN AROUND TELL ES-SWEYHAT

7.A. INTRODUCTION

This section describes the ebb and flow of settlement over the last seven thousand years or so. Emphasis is placed upon the development of settlement on the semi-arid plain around Sweyhat, and conversely its retreat off the plain towards the moister floodplain zone. The field data provide clear evidence for complex, alternating patterns of colonization, urbanization, dispersal, and collapse. These developments are then examined in *Section 9: Tell es-Sweyhat in Its Regional Context* in terms of changing environment, socio-cultural, and demographic factors, all of which may have influenced the spread or decline of settlement.

Before describing the settlement phases it is necessary to point out that the settlement pattern has been established by varying intensities of survey. The area of approximately 4 km radius around Tell es-Sweyhat was surveyed intensively by means of numerous transects on foot. Elsewhere, the area was surveyed either by car or by extensive pedestrian surveys, thereby supplementing the surveys of van Loon, Rihaoui, and others. Limited survey was completed on the west bank to the north of Tell Hadidi (T 548), but the scouring action of the river, and the rise of Lake Assad behind the Tabqa Dam, have probably resulted in large-scale loss of settlement from the floodplain. Only the area of ancient floodplain between Shams ed-Din Southern Site and Cemeteries (SS 22) and Tell Jouweif (SS 8) (fig. 7.5) ap-

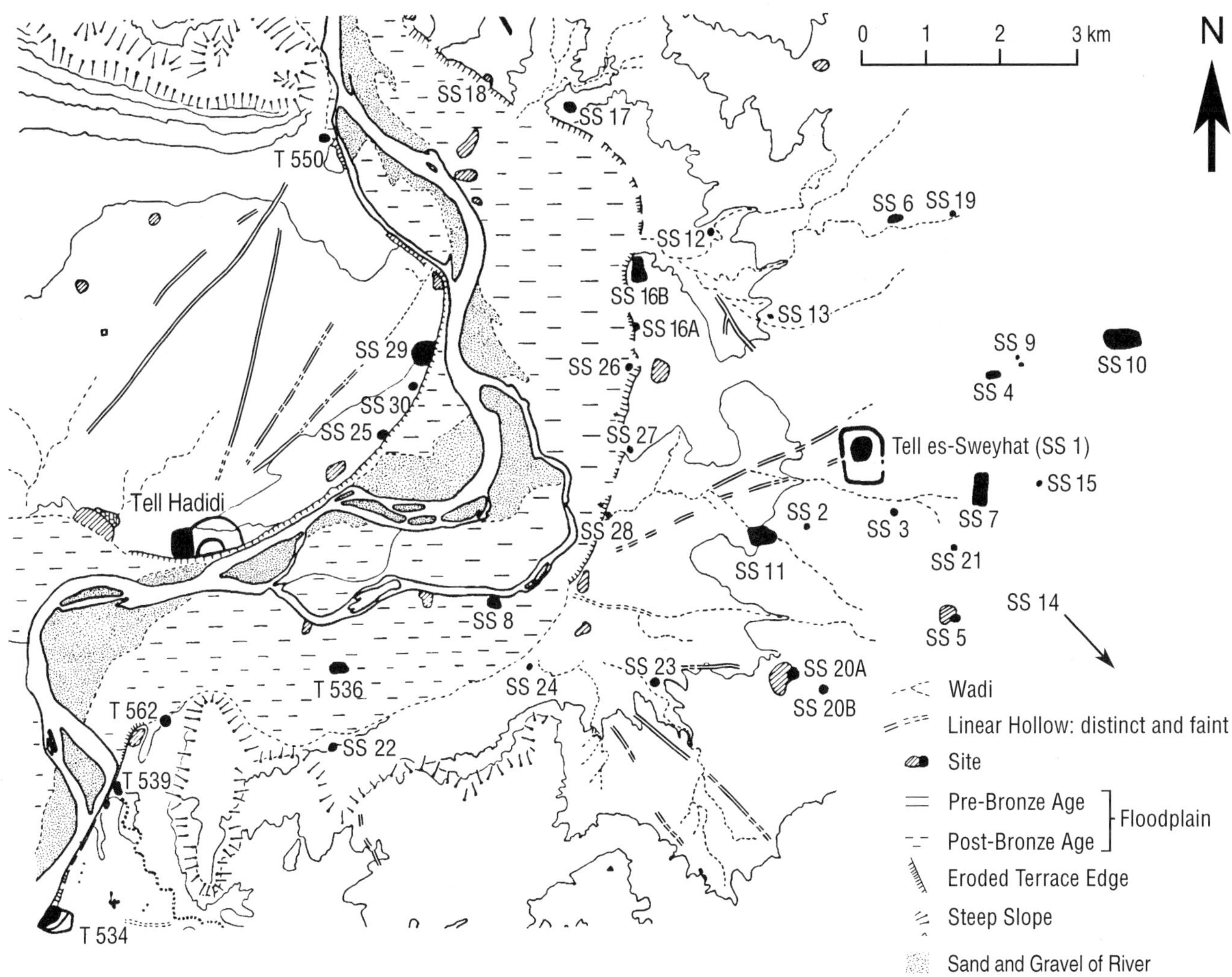

Figure 7.1. Archaeological Sites Recorded during the 1974 and 1991 Surveys

133

pears to be sufficiently intact for sites to remain in place, but even here owing to the steady aggradation of fine sediments washed from the slopes to the southeast, smaller sites similar to SS 25 and SS 30 could have been buried. Nevertheless, geomorphological surveys demonstrate that the primary area of interest, namely the Sweyhat Plain (and also that around Tell Hadidi), has only experienced minor aggradation, thus leaving a potentially more complete record of settlement. For summary data on the Sweyhat Survey sites, see tables 7.2–3.

7.B. LATER PREHISTORIC AND CHALCOLITHIC (SWEYHAT SURVEY PERIODS I–III)

Traces of pre-Bronze Age settlement are slight, being limited to small, virtually flat sites along the edges of the main river terrace. Their absence from the floodplain can probably be ascribed to the constant fluvial reworking of the alluvium (*Section 2.B.2: The Alluvial Plain*), an assertion that is supported by the presence of a single ceramic Neolithic lug handle at SS 26 (*Section 6.A: Pottery of the Chalcolithic to Late Roman Periods*, SS 26). This implies that SS 26 may have originally included a Neolithic component, which has since been eroded away. To date, no occupation earlier than approximately early third millennium has been found at Tell es-Sweyhat, despite the excavation of a 6.4 m deep sounding at the center of the tell (Trench IIA, Holland 1976) and a sounding to virgin soil in Trench IC.[64] However, the termination of excavations in IIA some 5.0 to 7.0 m above the level of virgin soil suggests that there is still room for a modest sized pre-Bronze Age tell to exist. This uninterpretable evidence aside, the only hints of pre-Bronze Age occupation on the plain are occasional, ambiguous chaff-tempered sherds among the small assemblages from SS 13 and Khirbet Aboud al-Hazu 2 (SS 19: fig. 7.1) and a very sparse scatter of chaff-tempered sherds along the northern bank of the Wadi Nafileh some 300–400 m to the southwest of the present village.

Present evidence suggests that before the Bronze Age the Sweyhat Plain was either unoccupied or was very sparsely and episodically settled, perhaps by pastoral nomadic groups. Those early sites that do remain are limited to the edge of the Euphrates terrace.

7.B.1. HALAF (SWEYHAT SURVEY PERIOD I)

The only site of the Halaf period remaining is Shams ed-Din Tannira (T 562; fig. 7.1), which although not included in the survey, does occur within the overall area under consideration (see *Appendix B: Site Gazetteer* for details and references). The estimated area of 2–4 ha makes this is a large site for its period, with occupation being confined to three phases of the later Halaf. Excavations exposed a full inventory of buildings, occupation levels, storage features, and domestic structures suggestive of sedentary occupation. On the other hand, the presence of an unusually large proportion of wild animal remains within the faunal assemblage (Uerpmann 1982) suggests either that it occupied a marginal location or that it had a specialized function. Its position on an ecological boundary gave the inhabitants easy access to grasses and scrubland on the steppe to the east and riverine woodland and marshes to the west (ibid., p. 42). This pattern of site location and resource accessibility was also characteristic of other Chalcolithic sites in the area.

7.B.2. UBAID (SWEYHAT SURVEY PERIOD II)

Painted Chalcolithic pottery of Ubaid period type came from a single small flat site located on the west bank of the river (fig. 7.2: SS 30). Its terrace edge position, undistinguished appearance, poor surface definition, and meager pottery assemblage resembled equivalent Ubaid occupations discovered in the Kurban Höyük area along the banks of the Turkish Euphrates River (Sites 11 and 25 in Wilkinson 1990: 90–91). Like any site located near the terrace edge, SS 30 may simply have been the upper component of a larger floodplain site, now eroded away. Excavations at the main sites of Tell Hadidi (T 548), Tell es-Sweyhat, and Tell Ali al-Haj (SS 17) give no hint of occupation earlier than the Uruk, thus there is no evidence that an Ubaid center existed within the area. However, because the floodplain has undergone a considerable amount of erosion, it is possible that a significant number of early settlements may have been lost.

---

64. Supported by excavations directed by Richard Zettler (Armstrong and Zettler 1997: 12–13).

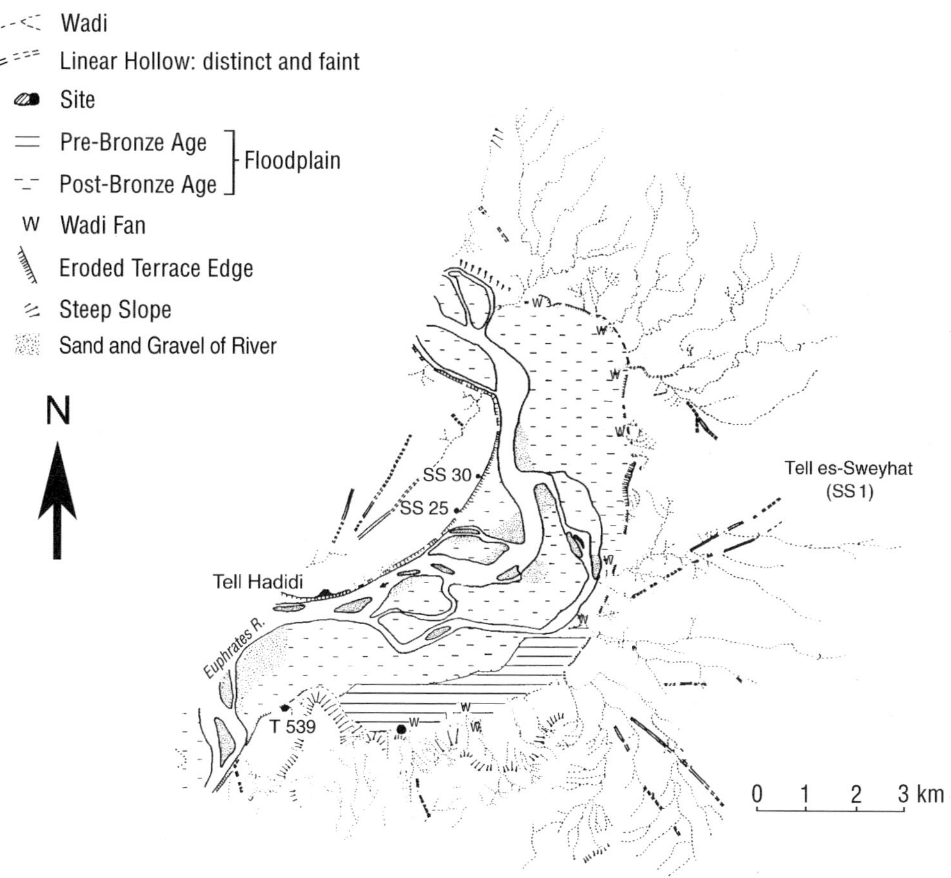

Figure 7.2. Distribution of Sites with Ubaid and Late Chalcolithic Pottery (Sweyhat Survey Periods II and III)

7.B.3. LATE CHALCOLITHIC (SWEYHAT SURVEY PERIOD III)

The Late Chalcolithic period is also weakly represented within the surface assemblages, but in 1992 a large collection of simple open bowls was recognized at SS 25 along the embankment of a modern irrigation channel on the west bank of the Euphrates River (fig. 7.2). Its position within a kilometer of SS 30 suggests that an extensive Chalcolithic settlement may exist in this area, although from its flat nebulous form it is unlikely that it includes the remains of many substantial buildings. The absence of Amuq F chaff-tempered[65] forms suggests that the SS 25 assemblage occupied an earlier phase of the Late Chalcolithic that predates the major developments at Habuba Kabira (T 509/513), Jebel Aruda (T 527), and Tell Sheikh Hassan (T 523) a short distance downstream.

Within the area shown in figure 7.2, beveled-rim bowls have come from the base of Tell Hadidi (T 548) (trench R) and a small site at Shams ed-Din Tannira (T 562). Tell Hadidi also yielded an Uruk ceramic cone (area B) and part of a drooping spout (fig. 7.3, area M: Dornemann 1988: 16). Dornemann does not consider this to be a full Uruk occupation comparable to those of Habuba Kabira (T 509/513) and Jebel Aruda (T 527) but regards it as continuing and extending that tradition into Early Bronze I, that is, to around the turn of the third millennium. In terms of the ceramic indicators used by the Sweyhat Survey, this occupation would be classified within the Late Chalcolithic (of southern tradition, that is, Period IV), therefore placing it shortly before the early Early Bronze Age occupation to be described below. In general, traces of settlement are fragmentary at best, and given the absence of Uruk type pottery from Tell es-Sweyhat or sites on the surrounding plain,[66] it originally seemed that the plain remained largely unoccupied by sedentary settlement during the entire Chalcolithic period. However, radiocarbon assay of carbonized material from Tell Hajji Ibrahim (SS 3) suggests that the plain was probably first settled in the final third of the fourth millennium B.C. (M. Danti, pers. comm., August 1999; see *Section 6.A: Pottery of the Chalcolithic to Late Roman Periods,* fn. 57).

---

65. As in the well-known casseroles, platters, and coarse jars of the Amuq sequence (Braidwood and Braidwood 1960), or more recently from Tell Haji Nebi Tepi (Pollock and Coursey 1995).

66. But two beveled-rim bowl fragments have been recorded from the lower levels at Tell Hajji Ibrahim (SS 3) (M. Danti, pers. comm.).

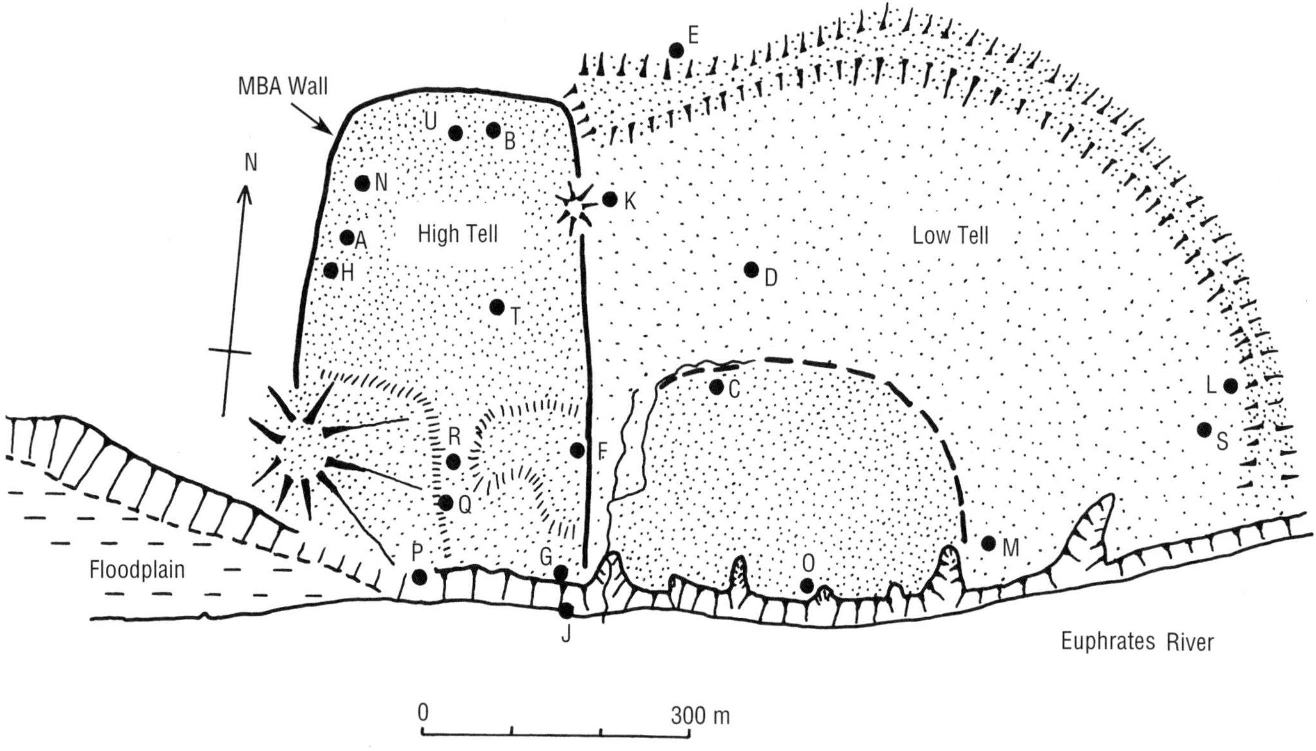

Figure 7.3. Sketch Map of Tell Hadidi (T 548) from Aerial Photograph; Details of Excavated Trenches (Lettered) and
Other Features from Dornemann 1985: 54

In summary, Chalcolithic settlement formed a sparse scatter along the edge of the river terraces and there is no evidence for a settlement hierarchy. The relevance of this pattern to the larger regional context is elaborated below in *Section 9: Tell es-Sweyhat in Its Regional Context*.

7.C. THE EARLY EARLY BRONZE AGE (SWEYHAT SURVEY PERIOD V)

Ceramic parallels for this period are discussed in *Section 6.A.2: The Early Bronze Age*. The early Early Bronze Age occupies roughly the first half of the third millennium B.C., but owing to the apparently localized pottery style zones at this time, few external parallels can be cited. Nevertheless, the sites indicated in figure 7.4, although not necessarily contemporaneous, are sufficiently consistent in their pottery assemblages to be placed within a 400 to 500 year span contemporary with the Ninevite V of northern Iraq, period V at Kurban Höyük, period G of the Amuq, and Porter (1999) phases one and two.

This period includes the first definite occupation at Tell es-Sweyhat. Although the occupied area cannot be ascertained, the presence of this pottery in Trench IIA, compared with its limited occurrence in Trench IC, suggests a site area of ca. 2 ha or perhaps as much as the area of the tell.[67] At the same time Tell Hadidi (T 548) was large, with occupation covering perhaps the entire site area; buildings were particularly well defined in area RII. On the east bank river terrace around Tell es-Sweyhat, smaller settlements were located at SS 2, Tell Hajji Ibrahim (SS 3), SS 9, Khirbet Aboud al-Hazu 2 (SS 19), SS 21, and Shams ed-Din Southern Site and Cemeteries (SS 22). Although the settlement pattern around Tell es-Sweyhat is limited, the areas of the site territories can be estimated by the construction of Thiessen polygons and by the estimation of settlement sustaining areas. Thiessen polygons define territorial boundaries on the assumption that they lie halfway between sites, irrespective of their size.[68] In figure 7.4 circles show approxi-

---

67. Thus Zettler (1997: 169) estimates the phase 1 occupation as no larger than the area of the high mound, which would put it in the range of up to 11–13 ha.

68. This technique entails taking the halfway point along the straight-line distance between two sites, and then drawing an orthogonal line to produce a boundary between the two sites. By

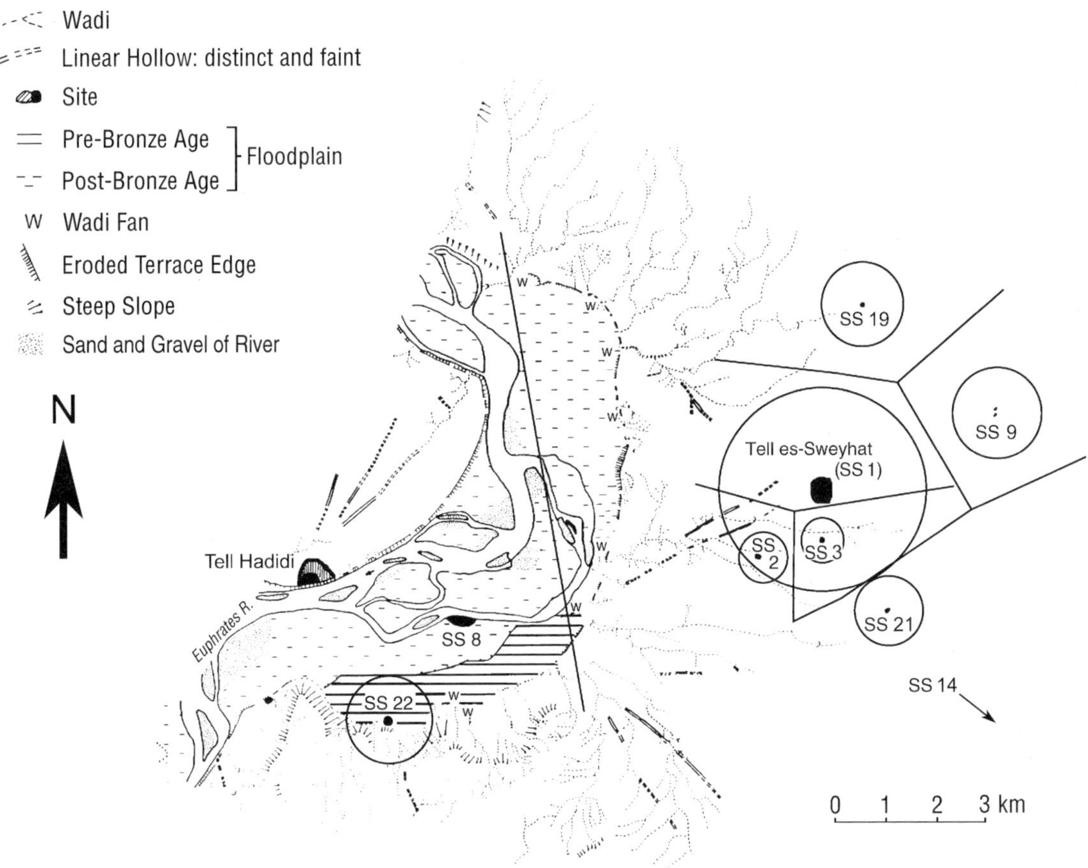

Figure 7.4. Distribution of Sites with Early Early Bronze Age Pottery (Early Third Millennium B.C.; Sweyhat Survey Period V). Territorial Boundaries Generated by Thiessen Polygons. For Sustaining Areas (Circles), See Text

mately the area of land required to support the inhabitants of each contained site assuming that each hectare of site would have been occupied by 100 people, and each person required roughly 250 kg of cereals per year.

These techniques suggest that each site was surrounded by a small territory of ca. 1 ha radius and sustaining areas, calculated from the site area (see below), ranged from 0.4 to 1.4 km radius. The small, prominent mounds at SS 2 and Tell Hajji Ibrahim (SS 3) were either contained within the modest-sized territory of Tell es-Sweyhat, as suggested by sustaining areas, or the site's own cultivated area must have been very limited, as implied by the Thiessen polygons. SS 2, Tell Hajji Ibrahim, and SS 9 are all very prominent with a distinctive steep-sided morphology which suggests that substantial walls may partly have determined their form. This was confirmed by excavation of Tell Hajji Ibrahim in 1993 by Danti (1997), who showed that the site's earlier phases comprised large buildings, perhaps interpreted as granaries. If these sites were in fact fortified granaries, they may have performed a specialized function similar to Tell Raqa'i (0.5 ha, 7.0 m high) in the middle Khabur Valley (Schwartz and Curvers 1992).

Although Tell Hadidi (T 548) ultimately grew to exceed Tell es-Sweyhat in size, the location of their mutual territorial boundary[69] along the center of the floodplain suggests that each commanded its own respective territory on the west and east banks, respectively. Site 22, covering some 150 × 90 m, was of intermediate size and enclosed within a fortification wall (Meyer 1991 and this volume, *Appendix A: Sweyhat Survey Site Catalog*).

In contrast to the Chalcolithic period, settlement blossomed during the early third millennium. The spread of settlement onto the Sweyhat Plain suggests that agricultural production was increased at this time by taking in new lands. There is no evidence from field scatters to show whether intensive manuring was practiced or not, but from the lack of early Early Bronze Age types within the field scatters it seems either that cultivation was of low intensity and did not include manuring or, that if manuring was practised, it simply employed animal manures without the inclusion

---

progressively constructing such boundaries between all sites of a period, one produces geometric boundaries between all sites,

unweighted according to site area. In other words large sites do not have territories any larger than small sites.

69.   That is, according to Thiessen polygons.

of household refuse. Such a practice may have occurred prior to the use of dung as fuel, when more dung was available to be applied to fields.

7.D. THE MID-/LATE AND LATE EARLY BRONZE AGE (SWEYHAT SURVEY PERIODS VI–VII)

Although the production of a full ceramic sequence from Tell es-Sweyhat must await the final analysis of excavated pottery from all excavations, it is possible to relate surface collections to assemblages excavated from Tell es-Sweyhat[70] and Tell Hadidi (T 548) to make a preliminary periodization (see *Section 6: The Ceramic Sequence from Surveyed Sites*). The following impression is gained from the collected pottery and a preliminary interpretation of the excavations.

A little after the middle of the third millennium, that is, during Sweyhat Survey Period VI, settlement at Tell es-Sweyhat was mainly confined to the main tell and covered an estimated area of 6–15 ha.[71] Then, by the third quarter of the third millennium, settlement had spread on to much of the northern and eastern lower town (pl. 16; Zettler 1997: 169). The pre-existing Sweyhat Survey Period V sites (SS 2 and SS 9) were abandoned by the time metallic ware came into common use,[72] whereas Tell Hajji Ibrahim (SS 3) continued in use into the mid-/late Early Bronze Age as is shown by the presence of metallic ware vessels (Danti 1997). In the place of these sites, satellites grew up at some 3–4 km distance in the mid-/late Early Bronze Age, at Nafileh Village (SS 5), Tell Othman (SS 20A),[73] and probably at Tell Jouweif (SS 8), as well as at Tell Ali al-Haj (SS 17) by the Middle Bronze Age. On the west bank of the Euphrates River, Tell Hadidi (T 548) became a substantial settlement (*Azu* of the Ebla texts) during Early Bronze III and IV and although its maximum area during the mid-/late third millennium is uncertain, according to Dornemann (1992; fig. 7.3) the site attained roughly 58 ha, or about half the size of Mari.

Tell es-Sweyhat attained its maximum size during the last third, probably the last quarter of the third millennium (see *Section 1.E: Archaeological and Historical Context*). Whether this means that both Tell Hadidi (T 548) and Tell es-Sweyhat attained their maximum size simultaneously is unclear (see further discussion in *Section 9.B: Long-term Trends in Settlement*). At Tell es-Sweyhat the construction of defenses around the lower town in the form of a casemate wall (to the north) or earthen ramparts (on the east) extended the occupied area to at least 31 ha, a significant part of which (but not all) was inhabited (Zettler 1997: 2–4). An additional extension to the south may have extended the site's area still farther by perhaps as much as 10 ha. The pre-existing Sweyhat Survey Period VI satellite communities remained occupied and additional small settlements grew up at SS 24 and SS 27 on the boundary between the floodplain and steppe. Thus the dispersed straggle of small Sweyhat Survey Period V settlements had by Sweyhat Survey Periods VI or VII been transformed into a hierarchy comprising a center at Tell es-Sweyhat and satellites at Nafileh Village (SS 5), Tell Othman (SS 20A), and SS 27. Other sites such as Tell Ali al-Haj (SS 17) and Tell Jouweif (SS 8) appear to have developed on major routes indicated on the ground by hollow ways. Although nothing is known of the morphology of the satellites, both Tell Jouweif and, more clearly Tell al-ʿAbd (T 535, fig. 9.1), appear to have been fortified. The wall at the latter site, originally exposed by erosion by Lake Assad and refined by excavation, was constructed of large foundation stones with a mudbrick superstructure, eventually reaching a width of 10 m (Finkbeiner 1995). A similar but less obvious feature at Tell Jouweif could be traced by rough alignments of large limestone blocks enclosing an area of very approximately 100 m in length (fig. 8.1c).

The large Bronze Age center of Tell Hadidi (T 548) can be seen in aerial photographs to comprise a massive semi-circular enclosed space to the east (Low Tell in fig. 7.3), with a central higher mound (including areas C and O), and a walled high tell to the west. It is not certain that habitation was continuous across the entire enclosed area, and part of the interior also included tombs. In addition, the western end appears to have been modified by the construction of the

---

70. The main reference sequence from Tell es-Sweyhat employed here is that of Holland, *Sweyhat* 2, which supersedes the earlier preliminary reports in Levant (Holland 1976, 1977).

71. According to Zettler 1997: 169, it covered 10–15 ha during the third quarter of the third millennium B.C.

72. For the use of the term "metallic ware," see *Section 6.A: Pottery of the Chalcolithic to Late Roman Periods*, fn. 58.

73. Unfortunately, the sparse surface pottery meant that only a small collection is available for dating from Tell Othman (SS 20A; see Holland, *Sweyhat* 2, fig. 6:8–13). These appear to represent a fairly generic range of early and mid-/late Early Bronze Age sherds. No clearly Middle Bronze Age II sherds were noted. It therefore seems likely that Tell Othman may have been established during the early Early Bronze Age, and like Tell es-Sweyhat, continued in use into the mid-/late Early Bronze Age.

fortified Middle Bronze Age town (fig. 7.3). Three hollow ways radiating to the northeast may have operated as both local routes or more long-distance links, an example of the latter being the easternmost feature which trends towards Tell Ali al-Haj (SS 17). The existence of such a link, presumably via a ford or boat crossing, implies that not only was there active communication between the two banks of the river, but also that Tell Hadidi and Tell Ali al-Haj (SS 17) may have existed along a long-distance route running from southwest to northwest.

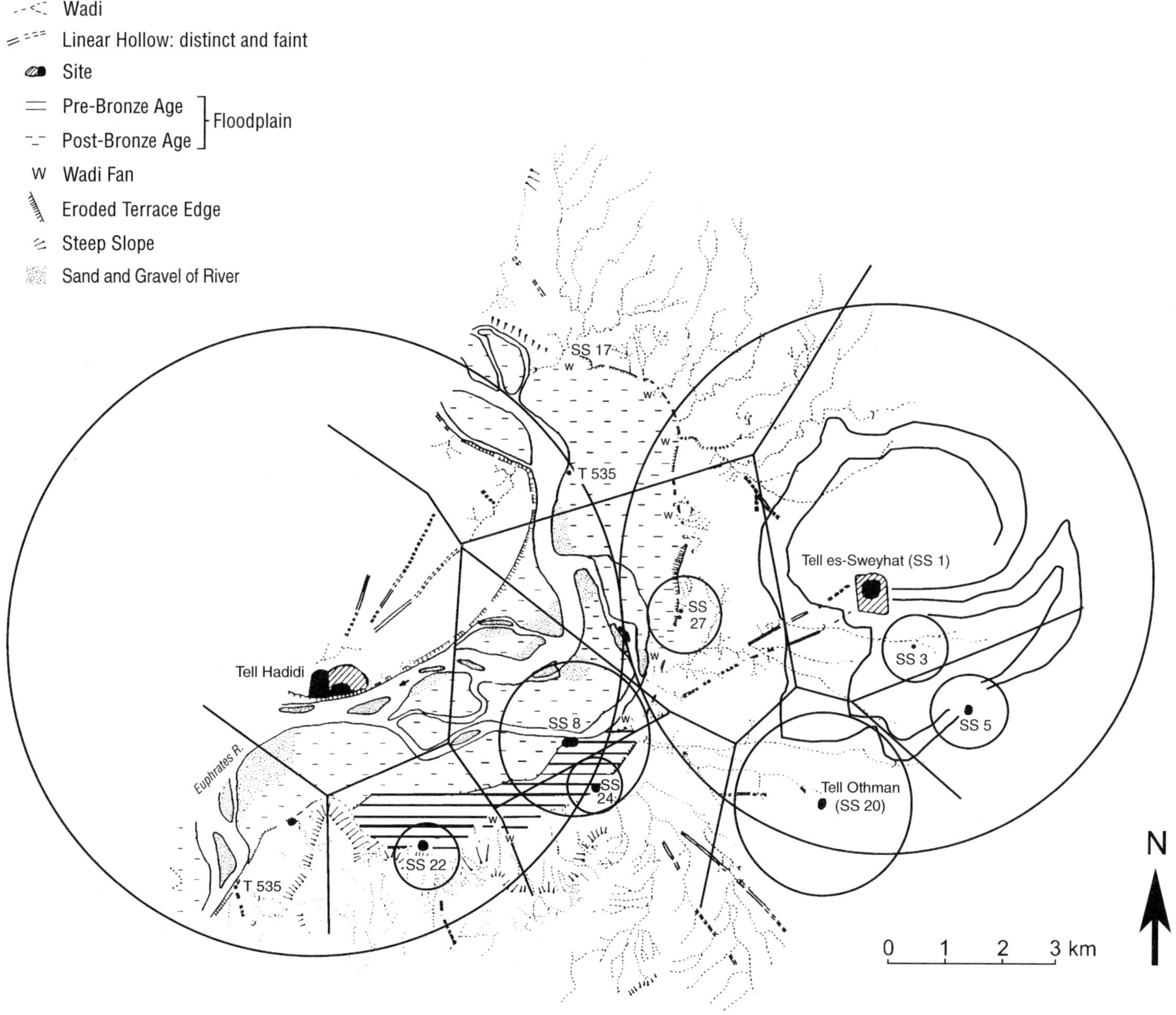

Figure 7.5. Distribution of Sites with Mid-/Late Early Bronze Age Pottery (Later Third Millennium B.C.; Sweyhat Survey Periods VI and VII) Showing Hypothetical Territorial Boundaries, Potential Sustaining Areas, and the Zone of Intensive Cultivation around Tell es-Sweyhat

Table 7.1. Calculated Sustaining Areas for Mid-/Late Early Bronze Age Sites in the Area of Tell es-Sweyhat*

Site	Area (ha)	Calculated Population**	Cultivated Area Required (ha)	Radius of Cultivation (km)
Tell es-Sweyhat (SS 1)	31.0	3,100	6,200	4.4
Tell es-Sweyhat (SS 1)	31.0	6,200	12,400	6.3
Nafileh Village (SS 5)	0.4	40	80	0.5
Nafileh Village (SS 5)	0.4	80	160	0.7
Tell Jouweif (SS 8)	1.7	170	340	1.0
Tell Jouweif (SS 8)	1.7	340	680	1.5
Tell Ali al-Haj (SS 17)	3.0	300	600	1.4
Tell Ali al-Haj (SS 17)	3.0	600	1,200	2.0
Tell Othman (SS 20A)	1.8	180	360	1.1
Tell Othman (SS 20A)	1.8	360	720	1.5
Shams ed-Din (SS 22)	0.5	50	100	0.6
Shams ed-Din (SS 22)	0.5	100	200	0.8
SS 24	0.2	20	40	0.4
SS 24	0.2	40	80	0.5
SS 27	0.4	40	80	0.5
SS 27	0.4	80	160	0.7
Tell Hadidi	40.0	4,000	8,000	5.0
Tell Hadidi	40.0	8,000	16,000	7.1
Tell Hadidi***	50.0	5,000	10,000	5.6
Tell Hadidi***	50.0	10,000	20,000	8.0

*Assumptions: minimum viable crop yield: 300 kg/ha. Seed grain for following year: 50 kg. Minimum annual production: 250 kg. Annual cereal requirement per person is also taken as 250 kg. If biennial fallow is assumed, 2 ha supports 1 person during a year of poor yields.

**Site population densities are assumed to be 100 and 200 person per ha of site.

***Note that two area estimates have been included for Tell Hadidi.

Three estimates for the later third millennium B.C. site territories are shown in figure 7.5. First are Thiessen polygons which define territorial boundaries on the assumption that they lie halfway between sites, irrespective of their size. Although useful heuristically, the polygons are somewhat arbitrary in their allocation of space, thus large sites such as Tell es-Sweyhat are shown with insufficient land to support them, whereas tiny settlements such as SS 24 (0.2 ha) are well surrounded by arable land. This discrepancy is emphasized by calculated sustaining areas as tabulated in table 7.1. In figure 7.5 circles show approximately the area of land required to support the inhabitants of each contained site with a staple cereal-based diet, assuming that each hectare of site would have been occupied by 100 people, and each person required roughly 250 kg of cereals per year (see table 7.1 for details). The area can now be seen to fall into two major contributory areas, that surrounding Tell es-Sweyhat and that around Tell Hadidi (T 548). Each large sustaining area then includes satellite communities as follows:

Tell es-Sweyhat: Tell Hajji Ibrahim (SS 3), Nafileh Village (SS 5), Tell Othman (SS 20A), and SS 27

Tell Hadidi: Tell Jouwief (SS 8), Shams ed-Din South Site and Cemeteries (SS 22; pl. 13), SS 24, and Tell al-'Abd (T 535)

In addition, Tell Ali al-Haj (SS 17) lay outside the potential sustaining area of both sites, roughly an equal distance from them. Given the location of the satellite sites within the potential sustaining area of each of the two centers, it could be concluded that each would be supplying the nearest central settlement with crops. Whether the satellite sites supplied the central settlements is a matter for debate, but it raises the interesting issue that east bank sites such as Tell Jouweif (SS 8) may have been economically tied to Tell Hadidi (T 548) on the opposite bank rather than supplying Tell es-Sweyhat. Such a potential linkage suggests a greater integration of the two communities than had formerly been suspected. Although it might be argued that such a cross river linkage seems unlikely, it must be noted that the pairing of the large settlements of Tell es-Sweyhat and Tell Hadidi on opposite banks of the river implies a considerable amount of cross river activity (see *Section 9.B.2: Early Bronze Age Twin Towns and Late Bronze Age Strongholds*). Furthermore, admittedly for a more recent seagoing empire, it can be noted that the rank-size hierarchy of settlements in colonial period North America was convex because the primate city which administered them was London, on the other side of the Atlantic (Johnson 1981: 171). This underscores that when considering settlement systems, one should consider the entire administrative or economic system that is involved. Presumably, of course, the movement of food crops from satellite to center would have varied with time, as would the level of "control" exerted by the centers. Nevertheless, these calculations suggest that a distinct hierarchy of settlements probably existed, and that smaller sites (with the exception of Tell Ali al-Haj [SS 17]) were probably economically tied to the main centers of Tell es-Sweyhat and Tell Hadidi as suppliers of food crops. An additional complication derives from the presence of pasture and grazing herds that would further blur the boundary between settlement territories (see *Section 9.B: Long-term Trends in Settlement*).

Finally, part of the area of inferred Early Bronze Age cultivation is represented by off-site field scatters which in *Section 4.F: Discussion and Conclusion* are argued as being the result of past manuring activities. This scatter, although only mapped within the area of Tell es-Sweyhat, emphasizes how the inferred intensive cultivation extends beyond the notional territorial boundaries imposed by Thiessen polygons but remains within the calculated sustaining areas. The field scatters imply that during the period of maximum occupation the Sweyhat Plain was continuously cultivated over a broad area rather than as belts of cultivation along selected wadis and zones of soil moisture enhancement. The absence of traces of canals as well as convenient water sources for irrigation, and the presence of field scatters at elevations above what could be irrigated by runoff, indicate that most likely this area was used for rain-fed cultivation. Between the zone of significant field scatter, defined here as the second, third, and fourth quartile ranges, and the limit of the sustaining area spread a zone of land characterized by relatively sparse (or absent) off-site sherds. This zone could have been the outer zone of low intensity, perhaps long fallowed cultivation, probably with intermittent pasture (see *Section 9: Tell es-Sweyhat in Its Regional Context*).

Table 7.1 indicates that if site population densities of much greater than 100 persons/ha had existed, the sustaining areas of Tell es-Sweyhat and Tell Hadidi (T 548) would overlap, thereby implying that there would have been competition for food and shortages in bad years. Although such an eventuality is possible, I consider it more likely that settlement populations were closer to the lower limit (100 persons/ha). This is because geophysical survey has shown that by no means all of the lower town at Tell es-Sweyhat was occupied by a dense scatter of habitations (Zettler 1997: 170). Furthermore, within the mound center, some of the built environment was probably given over to public buildings characterized by a lower population density. The potential response of such land use systems to climatic fluctuations is elaborated in *Section 9.G: Long-term Settlement and Environmental Change*.

The inclusion of part of the floodplain within the sustaining areas of Tell es-Sweyhat and Tell Hadidi (T 548) implies that in order to supply the centers with sufficient food from within a reasonable distance it would have been necessary to grow some of the food on the floodplain. Unfortunately, as discussed in *Section 2.B.2: The Alluvial Plain*, although such cultivated land almost certainly existed it is likely that the evidence has been erased by riverine erosion.

In addition Tell es-Sweyhat, being in such a marginal location close to the open steppe, must have received a significant amount of food from pastoral activities or hunting. Beyond the Sweyhat Plain, Danti (2000, 1997) argues that the area between the Balikh and the Euphrates Rivers was probably utilized as a long-term pastoral resource. Danti's surveys demonstrate that some of the southeast draining valleys contained occasional tells, totaling fifteen in number and up to a maximum area of 15+ ha, which included occupation from as early as the earlier phases of the Early Bronze Age, but not earlier. In addition there is evidence for possible water harvesting structures as well as some undated animal corrals (Danti 2000, pp. 270–72). Overall, settlements in this zone of upland steppe settlement were able to benefit from the availability of seasonal water supplies and presumably groundwater in the wadis. Such settlements probably relied upon pockets of cultivable land in the wadi floors as well as extensive pastoral resources on the steppe, and it seems that in the third millennium B.C. this area represents a more attenuated zone of agro-pastoral activity than occurred along the Euphrates River and its terraces. Further discussion of pastoralism and agricultural production is reserved for *Section 9.A: The Landscape and Economy of Tell es-Sweyhat in the Late Third Millennium B.C.*

In summary, the region of Tell es-Sweyhat during the later third millennium comprised dual centers located on opposite banks of the river. Each probably had just sufficient land within 4–5 km to supply basic cereal and legume supplies, and within this zone were a number of satellite communities that probably were tributary to the main centers. Cultivation on the floodplain would have contributed to the food budget of both Tell es-Sweyhat and Tell Hadidi (T 548), and this would have been supplemented by a significant amount of food from pastoral activities and hunting, although the amount of this contribution remains uncertain (see *Section 9.A: The Landscape and Economy of Tell es-Sweyhat in the Late Third Millennium B.C.*) The location of Tell Hadidi, Tell es-Sweyhat, Tell Jouweif (SS 8), and perhaps Tell Ali al-Haj (SS 17) along the alignment of hollow way routes suggests that their growth may be related to the presence of route systems. Whether these were long-distance routes is not clear, but if they were, it would appear that both sites may have been associated with increased trade and/or long-distance movements of goods.

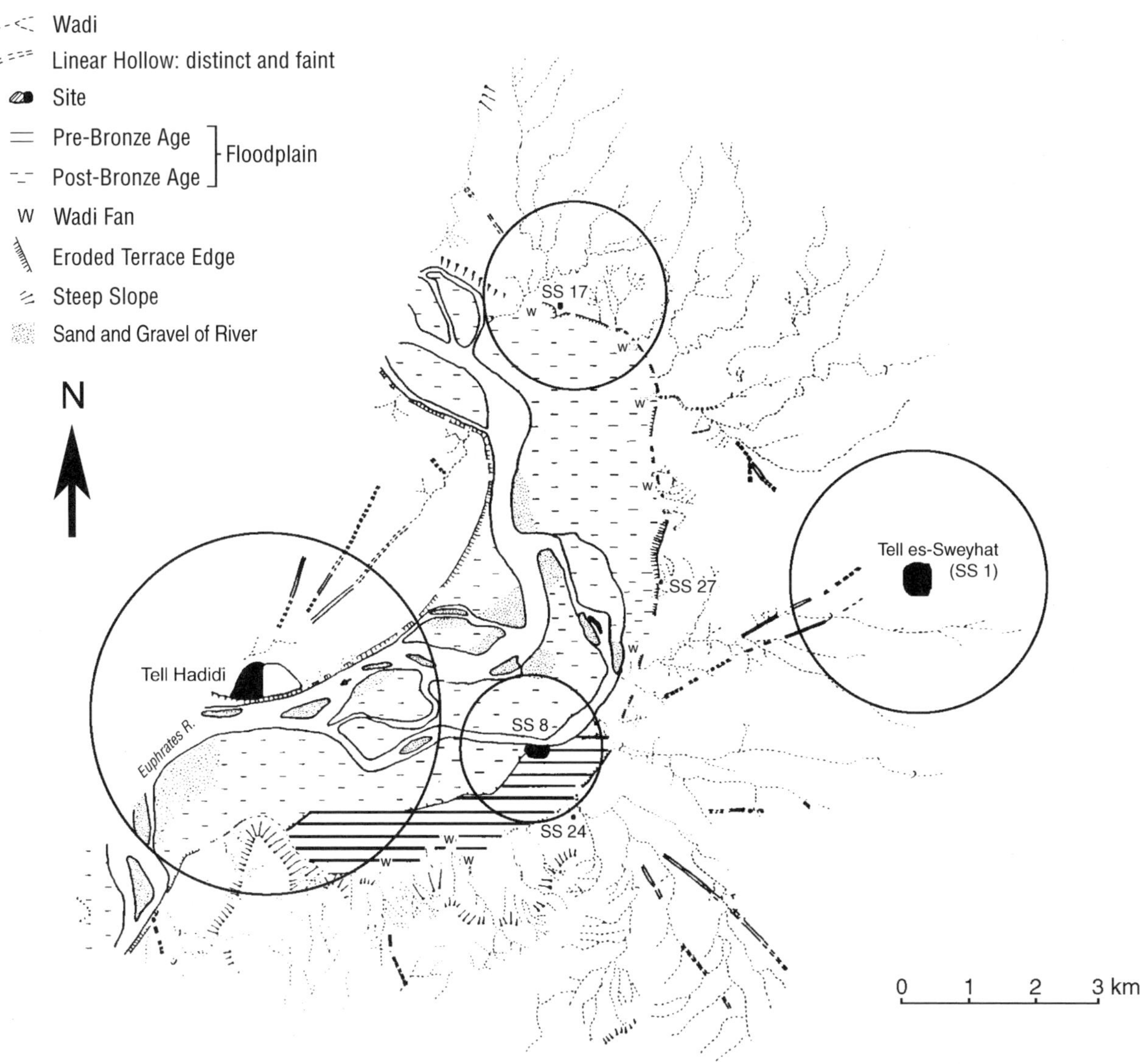

Figure 7.6. Distribution of Sites with Middle Bronze Age and Late Bronze Age Pottery
(Sweyhat Survey Periods VIII and IX) Showing Site Sustaining Areas

7.E. THE MIDDLE AND LATE BRONZE AGE
(SWEYHAT SURVEY PERIODS VIII–IX)

The peak in settlement that characterized the final third of the third millennium ushered in a period during which the main centers apparently shrunk and a number of smaller sites were abandoned. Given the coarse-grained nature of the survey data, negative records are difficult to assess. Nevertheless, this period did not see a wholesale collapse but rather a decline in urbanization from large, probably unsustainable centers down to smaller settlements that were easier to provision in such marginal terrain.

The outer town at Tell es-Sweyhat had probably ceased to be occupied after the turn of the second millennium. Evidence for continued occupation into the Middle Bronze Age is equivocal but may take the form of a series of building levels in Operations 1, 12, and 20 on the high tell which date from the early years of the second millennium B.C. (Armstrong and Zettler 1997: 27–30). However, their spatial extent cannot be determined, neither can the spatial extent of settlement, if any, after the end of the Early Bronze Age. At Tell Hadidi (T 548), on the other hand, the extensive Early Bronze Age occupation was followed during the Middle Bronze Age by a phase of fortified occupation on the diminished main western tell covering some 12–15 ha. The Middle Bronze Age[74] fortification wall enclosed the raised west end of the site, making a distinct cut through the pre-existing Early Bronze Age occupation (fig. 7.3).

Not only was Tell es-Sweyhat reduced to a small occupation during the Middle Bronze Age and abandoned entirely by the "early years of the second millennium B.C." (Armstrong and Zettler 1997: 30), but its satellite settlements, Nafileh Village (SS 5) and Tell Othman (SS 20A), were also abandoned. This almost total desertion of the plain is evident from the absence of barrel jars from these three sites. The only sites occupied during the Middle Bronze Age are the well-attested occupations at Tell Jouweif (SS 8) and Tell Ali al-Haj (SS 17) and minor occupations at SS 24 and SS 27 within the Euphrates floodplain or immediately adjacent on the terrace edge. This more attenuated settlement system was presumably still served by the route systems represented by the hollow ways.

The lack of Middle Bronze Age diagnostic sherds from the field scatters implies that manuring with settlement-derived refuse was minimal, probably because settlement on the plain was limited or completely absent. A speculative scenario for the agriculture of the final phase of settlement is that the reduced sustaining area required for cultivation was more likely to have been concentrated along wadis and in areas that would receive occasional floods. Hence, although there is no evidence for runoff farming, crop production probably benefited from soil moisture enhancement that would lessen the risk of crop failure in dry years.

The reduced sustaining areas of Tell Hadidi (T 548) fell well short of any satellite sites of the previous Early Bronze Age occupation and coincided roughly with the Thiessen territorial boundaries of the previous phase.

The minimal pattern of Middle Bronze Age settlement on the east bank was further reduced during the Late Bronze Age down to a settlement of unknown size at Tell Ali al-Haj (SS 17). Tell es-Sweyhat was totally abandoned during the early part of the Middle Bronze Age, and although settlement at Tell Jouweif (SS 8) apparently continued throughout the Middle Bronze Age, Late Bronze Age pottery is absent.

On the west bank, on the other hand, Tell Hadidi (T 548) expanded again around 1500 B.C. to occupy both high and low tells, although the precise limits remain uncertain.

The trend in settlement within the area of Tell es-Sweyhat and Tell Hadidi (T 548) area parallels that sketched for inland Syria which suggests a "major decline in sedentary population [...] at the end of the Middle Bronze Age and the beginning of the Late Bronze Age" (McClellan 1992: 168). However, that this is not a total decline is suggested as follows. Although Tell es-Sweyhat and its surrounding plain appear to have been abandoned by or before the early-second millennium B.C., major occupation continued during the Late Bronze Age at Tell Hadidi, Tell Mumbaqa (T 534), some 10 km downstream from Tell es-Sweyhat, and at al-Qitar, an equivalent distance upstream. The second millennium decline can be seen as a two component process: first, an abandonment of settled areas away from the river; second, a concomitant expansion of fortified settlements at intervals overlooking the Euphrates River. The implications of this settlement shift are considered in *Section 9.D: Settlement Decline in the Second Millennium B.C.*

74.　Middle Bronze Age I and IIA according to Dornemann 1985:
　　54; ca. 2000–1775 B.C.

7.F. THE IRON AGE (SWEYHAT SURVEY PERIOD X)

The abandonment of the Sweyhat Plain, which probably occurred during the early part of the Middle Bronze Age (i.e., early second millennium B.C.), was followed, during the Iron Age, some 700 to 900 years later, by a phase of recolonization. The three or four small sites recorded during the survey compare with a meager record of two possible occupations recorded during the van Loon survey for the entire area of Lake Assad. The attributions of van Loon (1967: 4) are rendered more tenuous being simply based upon two ceramic figurines of "Assyrian, Babylonian or Persian" date. The first figurine, a horseman (from Tell Dhahir [T 536] near Tell Jouweif [SS 8]), and the second a plaque of a naked woman of the Assyrian-Parthian period (from Rimalah, site T 554), are both poorly dated. This together with the general ignorance of local Iron Age pottery at the time of van Loon's survey clearly inhibited the identification of sites, therefore the gap in occupation within the area of Lake Assad is probably more apparent than real. However, a later publication benefiting from a considerable amount of subsequent rescue excavation still only gives five Iron Age sites for the upper Lake Assad area (Dornemann 1985: 52–53). Of these sites, one occupation is mis-attributed to Tell es-Sweyhat, for which there is no evidence for Iron Age occupation.

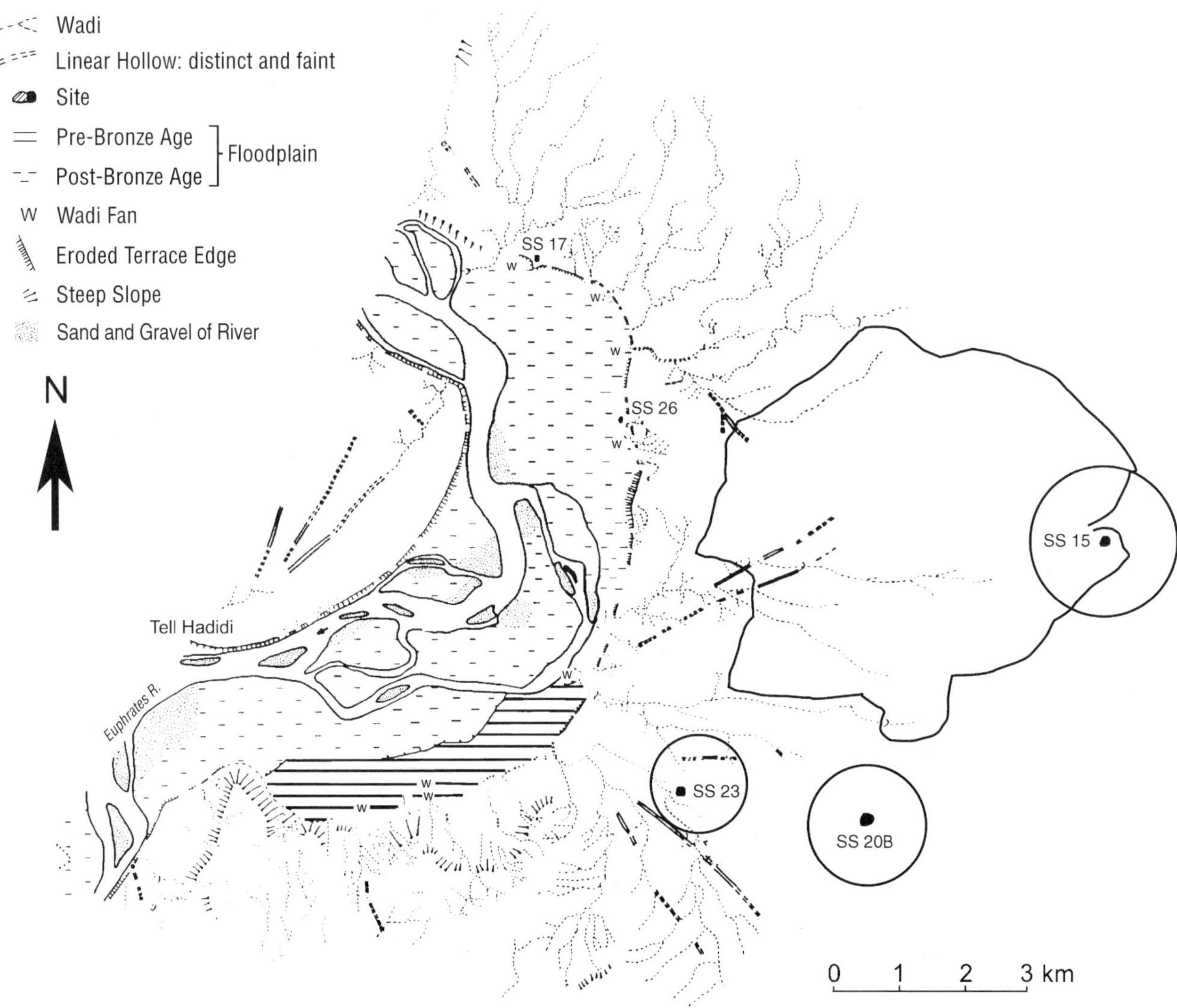

Figure 7.7. Distribution of Sites with Iron Age Pottery (Sweyhat Survey Period X) with Associated Sustaining Areas.
Note the Irregular Solid Line Indicates the Approximate Limit of Dense Field Scatters and therefore
Intensive Cultivation around Bronze Age Tell es-Sweyhat

The Iron Age sites in the Sweyhat area were either un-mounded or low rounded tells and must represent little more than farmsteads or hamlet-sized communities. Calculated sustaining areas indicate that crop production could have been limited to the slightly moister valley bottom lands within a short distance of the settlement. Beyond half or one kilometer of the sites the landscape must have been open for occasional opportunistic long fallow cultivation, or more likely, permanent steppe pasture.

The former Late Bronze Age sites of al-Qitar, Mumbaqa (T 534), and Tell Hadidi (T 548) show no signs of Iron Age habitation,[75] but a small number of probable Iron Age sherds from Tell Ali al-Haj (SS 17) and SS 26 (*Section 6.A: Pottery of the Chalcolithic to Late Roman Periods*) suggest that dispersed settlement was also present along the floodplain margins.

The evidence from the Sweyhat Survey, although not yet subdividable into phases of the Iron Age, clearly suggests that after the substantial fortified sites of the Late Bronze Age collapsed, a straggle of small hamlet or village-size communities developed. Although these sites indicate a recolonization of the plain, nothing suggests that this was an imperial resettlement scheme as probably occurred in northern Iraq during the Neo-Assyrian period (Wilkinson 1995: 144–49). Rather, these settlements which developed in locations that were favorable for consistent crop yields may simply represent the small self-sufficient communities that were established following the collapse of the fortified Late Bronze Age centers or alternatively may be a result of the resettlement of nomads. This picture is thus similar to that recorded for the uplands west of the Jordan in the southern Levant, where colonization of marginal land occurred in the late second and early first millennium B.C. (Finkelstein 1995a). In the context of Late Bronze Age collapse, the picture around Tell es-Sweyhat agrees with that suggested by McClellan (1992: 168) that "rather than viewing the twelfth century as the period of catastrophic collapse, we should consider it as the end of a decline which commenced much earlier."

Interestingly, as is shown in figure 7.7, Khirbet al-Hamrah 2 (SS 15), Tell Othman (SS 20A), and SS 23 all grew up some distance from Tell es-Sweyhat. If this is not simply due to chance factors, it suggests the possibility that marginal lands were selected for occupation perhaps because the formerly occupied lands in and around Tell es-Sweyhat were unavailable. Such a situation may have resulted because the area of Tell es-Sweyhat may have continued under the de facto ownership of the previous occupants, but now as pasture lands, which were used seasonally. The new settlements, established by communities unrelated to the Tell es-Sweyhat lineage, would therefore have been forced into the lands that were beyond those used by the former occupants. Although it is uncertain whether such rights can have persisted over virtually a millennium, a similar pattern of occupation has been recognized in the Balikh Valley to the east for the same period (Wilkinson 1995).

In the case of the upper Lake Assad area, progressive decline during the Middle and Late Bronze Ages, which culminated in the development of Late Bronze Age strongholds such as Mumbaqa (T 534), al-Qitar, and Tell Hadidi (T 548), was apparently followed by the collapse of those centers and the dispersal of the population into small self-sufficient rural communities.

7.G. THE HELLENISTIC, ROMAN, AND EARLY BYZANTINE PERIODS (SWEYHAT SURVEY PERIODS XI–XIII)

In contrast to the meager pattern of Iron Age occupation, that of the late first millennium B.C. and the early first millennium A.D. comprises a well-developed spread of settlements of various size and form. The presence of Late Iron Age pottery at SS 26 implies some degree of continuity of occupation during the first millennium B.C., although there is little evidence for continuity in the form of continuous stratigraphic sequences on any other sites.

The settlement pattern in figure 7.8 comprises a range of dated occupations from Hellenistic (third to second centuries B.C.) through Roman to Late Roman/Byzantine (fourth to sixth centuries A.D.). The pattern is not necessarily complete, however, and it is likely that multi-period tells such as Tell Ali al-Haj (SS 17) and Tell Othman (SS 20A) include a wider range of occupations than indicated. Individual phases for each site and period are given in tables 7.2 and 7.3.

---

75. But a *bīt ḫilāni* of the Iron Age was recorded from level 3 at Tell Sheikh Hassan (T 523; see *Appendix B: Site Gazetteer*). In addition, several other Iron Age phases have been recorded by excavations of various sites such as Tell al-ʿAbd (T 535) in the upper Lake Assad area (see *Appendix B: Site Gazetteer* and *Section 9: Tell es-Sweyhat in Its Regional Context*).

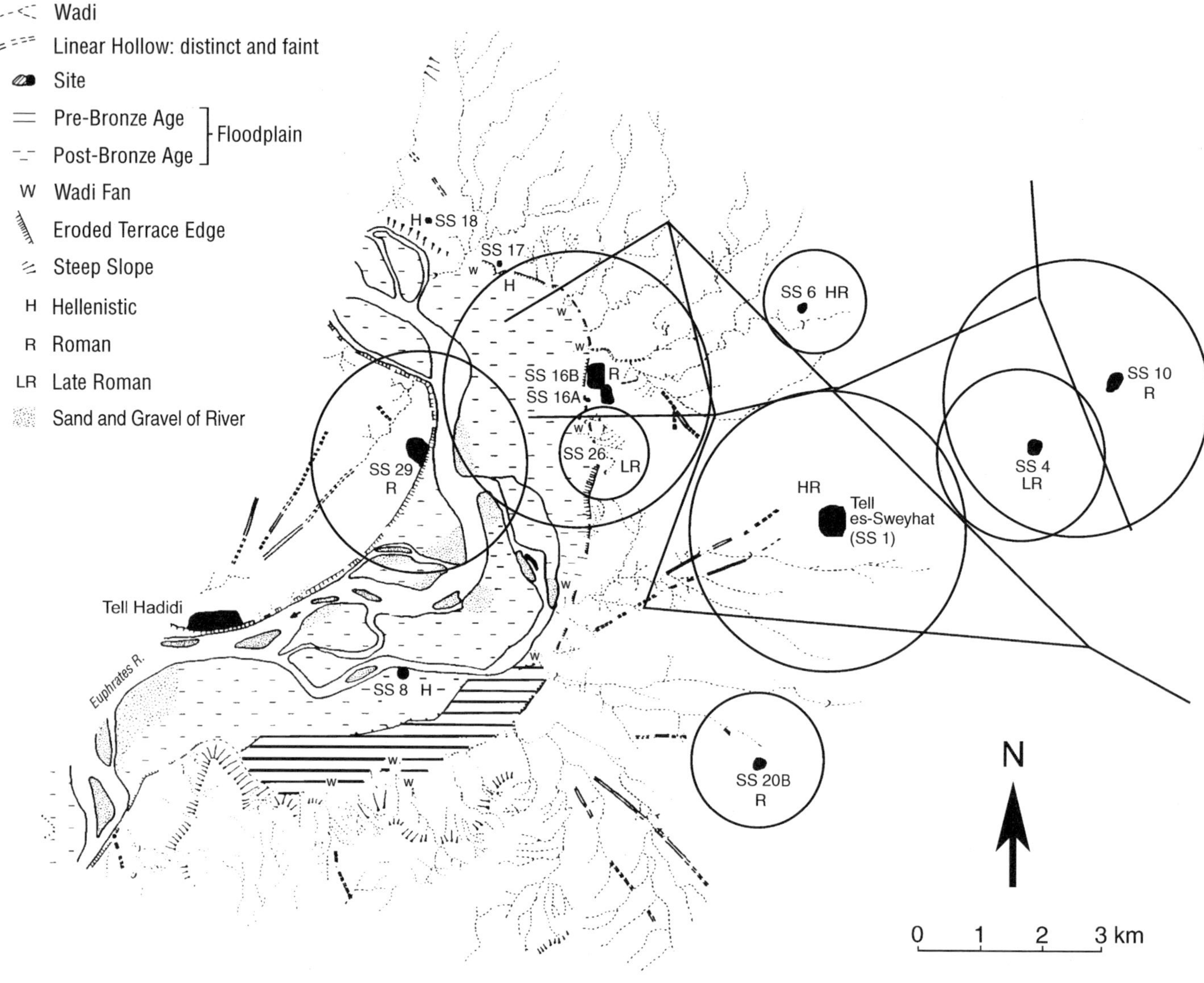

Figure 7.8. Distribution of Sites with Hellenistic and Roman Pottery (Sweyhat Survey Periods XI, XII, and XIII) with Hypothetical Territorial Boundaries and Potential Sustaining Areas

Hellenistic occupation is well attested on the summit of the main mound at Tell es-Sweyhat, where the cultural remains were interpreted as being the remnants of a watch post or watchtower (Holland, *Sweyhat* 2, Chapter 8, Period C, Early Hellensitic Period). This occupation included a large assemblage of Early Hellenistic wares as well as a hollow horse or camel rider figurine (Holland 1976: Area II Phase G; Holland, *Sweyhat* 2, Chapter 5, pl. 132:9). In addition, on the southern slopes of the tell thin cultural deposits of Roman (first to second centuries A.D.) and Late Roman (fourth century) date were excavated (Holland, *Sweyhat* 2, figs. 258–65).

For the first time since the Early Bronze Age it is possible to make some assessment of the form and function of the settlements because, on the largely single period occupations at least, individual buildings and walls are frequently evident. Disregarding the multi-period occupations at Tell es-Sweyhat, Tell Othman (SS 20A), Tell Ali al-Haj (SS 17), and Tell Hadidi (T 548), it is possible to classify the sites into the following morphological types (fig. 7.8):

Type *a*   Fortified sites with substantial enclosure walls: Khirbet Aboud al-Hazu (SS 6), Mishrifat (SS 16A), and Shajara Saghira (SS 29). In addition Ramalah (SS 16B), with a roughly rectilinear plan and a rampart wall or bank along its northern side, may have been fortified.

Type *b*   Small unenclosed village-like settlements with a dispersed layout of individual buildings: SS 4 and Khirbet Haj Hassan (SS 10). This type continues into the Early Islamic period (see Khirbet al-Hamrah [SS 7] and Khirbet Dhiman [SS 11], below).

Site morphology in combination with the settlement pattern suggests that Hellenistic/Roman settlement falls into two groups:

Group *a*   This consists of an alignment of fortified sites from Shajara Saghira (SS 29; pl. 14) in the southwest through Mishrifat (SS 16A) on the eastern bank of the river to Khirbet Aboud al-Hazu (SS 6) in the northeast. The SS 16A–C site complex comprises two elements: an earlier Hellenistic phase (Ramalah [16B]), which although on a grid plan with a rampart to the north lacks true fortifications, and a later pentagonal fortified stronghold (Mishrifat [16A]), 60 m across, overlooking the river. This dressed limestone construction on an eroded limestone bluff was built in the first or second century A.D. and clearly had a military function. Presumably it was constructed to guard the river crossing when the Jazirah was incorporated into the Roman Empire by Marcus Aurelius during the second century A.D. (Egami, Masuda, and Iwasaki 1979: 14). Bearing in mind the problems inherent in drawing straight lines between three points, the presence of three walled or fortified sites in a line suggests that these sites may have been aligned along a Roman route. Although no major route is known on this alignment, part of the route between Carrhae (modern Harran, Turkey) and the small town of Eragiza (TAVO map B VI 1) falls on this line. Therefore, it remains a possibility that these sites (Shajara Saghira, Mishrifat, Khirbet Aboud al-Hazu) may have developed along a minor Roman route. Interestingly, the pattern of modern field boundaries[76] as well as the orientation of the Early Islamic sites of Khirbet Dhiman (SS 11) and Khirbet al-Hamrah (SS 7) were also parallel to this alignment, which provides a hint that perhaps some of the field boundaries that exist today may be a relict feature determined as early as the Roman/Hellenistic period.

Group *b*   An alignment along an extrapolated hollow way exists at Tell es-Sweyhat, SS 4, and Khirbet Haj Hassan (SS 10). In this case none of the occupations are enclosed or fortified (although the Hellenistic site of Tell es-Sweyhat has been interpreted as a watchtower and an undated rectangular structure was noted near the summit) and instead they all exhibit an irregular layout reminiscent of a non-military function.

The landscape of the Hellenistic/Roman period can therefore be classified into a possible military route with associated fortified structures to the north and a southern group of sites along a roughly parallel route represented in part by a hollow way leading to the northeast. Additional sites of indeterminate function existed at Tell Ali al-Haj (SS 17), Dahrat er-Ramile (SS 18), SS 20B, SS 26, and Tell Hadidi (T 548). The use of the road and its fortification may correspond to the second century A.D. incorporation of the province of Mesopotamia into the Roman Empire. According to surface ceramics at SS 4 and Khirbet Haj Hassan (SS 10) (*Section 6.A.3: Middle Bronze Age and Later Assemblages*), occupation at these sites and at Tell es-Sweyhat represents a later development that took place gradually in the century or two after the inception of the province of Mesopotamia. Thus we may be able to distinguish the formation of a civil zone of settlement behind (i.e., southeast) and parallel to that of the Roman military occupation.

The Hellenistic and Roman landscape may also have included the wine presses described in *Section 5.A: Wine Presses*. Although only those at SS 26 can be approximately dated (by their association with the adjacent Iron Age to Late Roman/Byzantine site), the others are probably of Hellenistic/Roman type. As noted in *Section 3.C: Irrigation Agriculture*, the presence of wine presses implies that the growing and processing of grapes took place along the edge of the floodplain. The presses, together with numerous Hellenistic, Roman, and Byzantine tombs along the bluffs, provide further confirmation for a flourishing and moderately wealthy society. The presence of settlements on most parts of the Sweyhat Plain indicates that climatic conditions remained suitable for settlement and presumably agriculture. Like their Iron Age counterparts, the inhabitants could have placed most of their fields in the zones of soil moisture enhancement along wadis, but calculated sustaining areas suggest that it would also have been necessary to cultivate some of the slightly more elevated and drought prone soils away from the wadis (fig. 7.8). It should be emphasized, however, that sustaining areas, being calculated from standardized site population densities, may be exaggerated for the dispersed and extensive Hellenistic/Roman sites compared with the more compact and presumably more densely populated sites of the Bronze Age. Nevertheless, the combination of Thiessen polygons and sustaining areas demonstrates that a significant area of the plain would have been cultivated. Unlike the pattern of Late Roman rural settlement recognizable in southeastern Turkey (Wilkinson 1990, chapter 5), however, these settlements do not appear to have been surrounded by significant field scatters. This absence of field scatter implies that systems of cultivation during the Hellenistic/Roman period were of moderate to low intensity and that there were probably sufficient domestic animals to provide manure for the land without the need for farmers to resort to the application of other forms of domestic waste to fields.

---

76.   As recognized on recent satellite images such as the SPOT image (see Zettler 1997, fig. 1.2) or the declassified CORONA images.

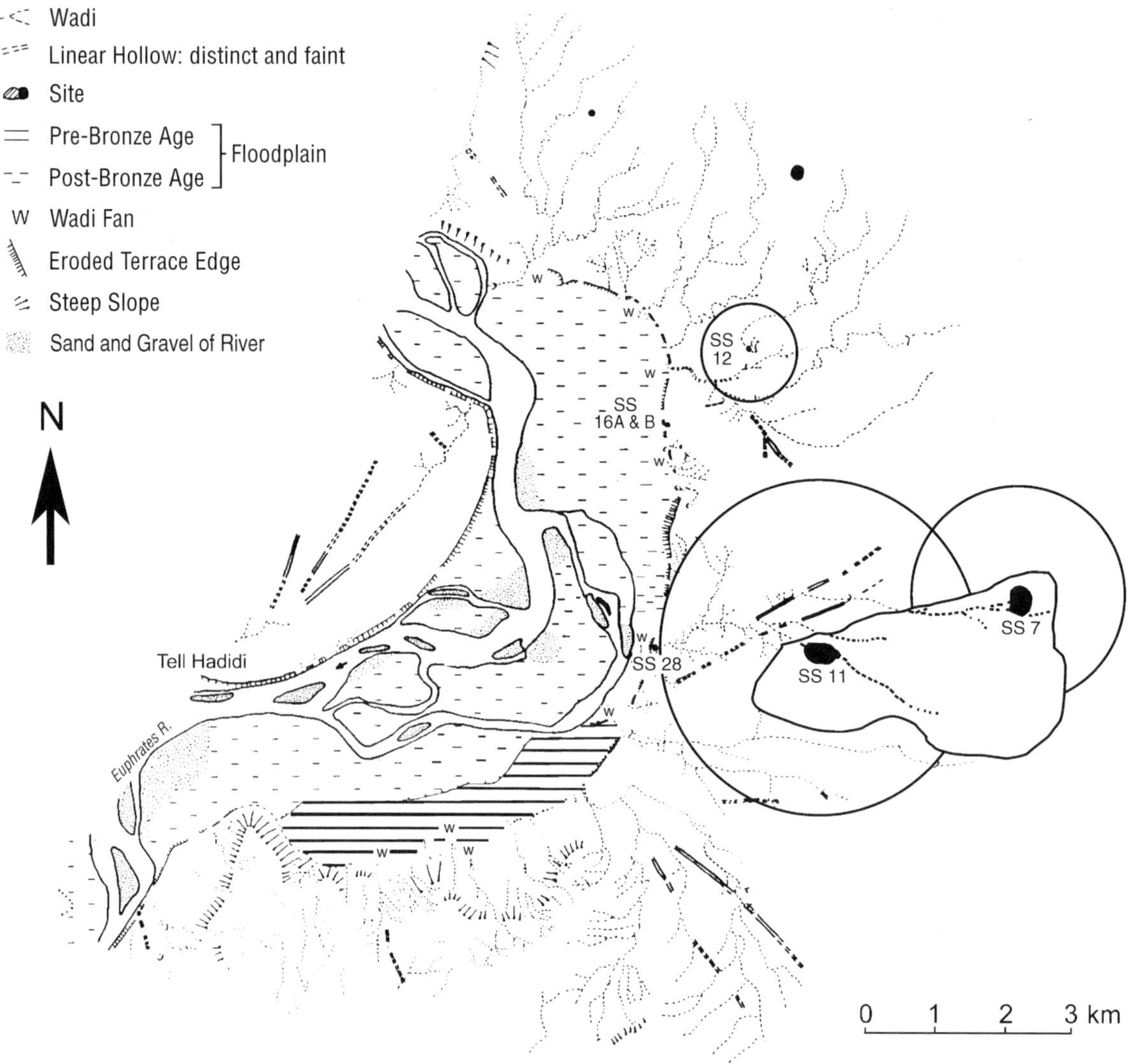

Figure 7.9. Distribution of Sites with Early Islamic (Sweyhat Survey Period XIV) and Middle Islamic (Sweyhat Survey Period XV) Pottery, with Sustaining Areas and Area where Islamic Diagnostics Occur within the Field Scatters (Irregular Solid Line Surrounding Khirbet Dhiman [SS 11] and Khirbet al-Hamrah [SS 7])

7.H. THE ISLAMIC PERIOD (SWEYHAT SURVEY PERIODS XIV–XV)

Ceramically, the Late Roman/Byzantine material culture merges almost imperceptibly with that of the Early Islamic period, but with new forms of brittle and various buff wares continuing through with relatively little change. The major indicator of a changeover from the preceding period to that of the Islamic period is the appearance of significant numbers of Islamic glazed wares. Using these wares and other selected factors, it is possible to recognize a significant change in the settlement pattern.

The two large Early Islamic sites, Khirbet al-Hamrah (SS 7) and Khirbet Dhiman (SS 11), exhibit no pre-Islamic occupations and are both located towards the presumed territorial margins of the Late Roman settlements. Because the territorial boundaries are hypothetical, being based upon Thiessen polygons and calculated sustaining areas, it is not possible to say just how close they were to such limits. This is unfortunate because settlement on territorial boundaries can result from colonization in which adventitious groups settle on neutral or unoccupied terrain. Conversely, the establishment of "daughter settlements" within the parent catchment but towards the boundary is a well-attested process when communities grow and it is necessary to cultivate new land (Grossman 1971). However, the observation that the Late Roman sites apparently died (or at least have no Islamic pottery) shortly after Khirbet al-Hamrah (SS 7) and Khirbet Dhiman (SS 11) developed suggests that they are not parent settlements. Instead the more plausible interpretation is that the Early Islamic sites represent new foundations on land that was marginal during the Roman period. On the other hand, although SS 12 also exhibits a marginal position (with respect to Mishrifat [SS 16A]), in this case Mishrifat continued to be occupied into the Early Islamic period.

On the west bank, Tell Hadidi (T 548) was occupied during both the Roman and Islamic periods. Although a large area has been assigned to this occupation (Dornemann 1985: 54), the continuity and intensity of this occupation is not known. Two other presumed Islamic settlements have not been surveyed but were identified on the basis of their distinctive ground plan on aerial photographs (un-numbered sites to north in fig. 7.9). These settlements now appear to be inaccessible below the modern villages of al-Mengal and Khirbeh.

All three of the larger Early Islamic sites (Khirbet al-Hamrah [SS 7], Khirbet Dhiman [SS 11], and SS 12) lack enclosure walls and form dispersed scatters of buildings, roughly on the same alignment but not necessarily on a planned grid. House mounds with internal depressions range from 20 to 25 sq. m, and each presumably comprised a courtyard dwelling occupied by a family of five to six people. Khirbet al-Hamrah sits astride two wadis and the presence of excavated depressions along both suggests that groundwater or runoff was extracted from them. Similarly, Khirbet Dhiman (SS 11), when first visited in 1974, showed evidence of a hollow way on the wadi just upstream of the site. The aerial photographs also suggest the presence of two "streets" parallel to the long axis of the settlement. The northern "street" leads towards a large building enclosure or courtyard building situated at the west end of the village (fig. 7.10). The presence of relief carved stones suggests that this was a building of some status, possibly a sheikh's dwelling or some form of khan. SS 12, which was also unenclosed, simply comprised a scatter of small buildings around one large building (18 sq. m) of dressed limestone block construction. Extensively robbed for building stone, the disturbed remains include numerous grooved and rebated building blocks[77] that were either original fixtures in the building or had been brought from sites in the vicinity for its construction. The small size of this site and the dominance of a single large, evidently high status building (an Islamic palace according to Egami, Masuda, and Iwasaki 1979) argues against this being a village site. Instead it could be the residence of an affluent sheikh.

Sustaining areas for the Early Islamic settlements can be calculated using the size and estimated number of building units and then cross-checked against the site area as before. In order to estimate site population, individual 20–25 sq. m house plans can be identified on aerial photographs and in the field. On the assumption that each module corresponds to a courtyard dwelling capable of accommodating a family of six, the total population of each site can be calculated by dividing the site area by the area of a standard house module (400–625 sq. m) multiplied by six. Because this unrealistically allows for zero public open space, an arbitrary 25% of the total site area has been allocated as open space. This allowance entails reducing the gross estimate by multiplying by 0.75. The resultant population estimates of 360–563 for Khirbet al-Hamrah (SS 7) and 864–1,350 for Khirbet Dhiman (SS 11) are close to the 500 and 900 that would be arrived at using an assumed population density of 100 persons per site hectare. The slight overlap of the sustaining areas suggests that either these population estimates are excessive, or territories were not circular. The presence of small numbers of Islamic ceramics within the field scatters suggests that cultivation extended more to the south than to the north (fig. 7.9). Such a distribution might result because of the existence, when Khirbet al-Hamrah and Khirbet Dhiman were established, of the Late Roman communities and their fields to the north and west. Thus it became necessary for the Islamic communities to open up new cultivated fields on vacant land to the south.

The ceramics from Khirbet al-Hamrah (SS 7), Khirbet Dhiman (SS 11), and SS 12 suggest a short-lived occupation within the eighth to tenth centuries A.D. Following their collapse only one site on the eastern bank, SS 28, a small settlement of Middle Islamic date, was occupied. This was probably contemporary with or slightly earlier than the Ayyubid occupation at Tell Hadidi. The location of SS 28 within a valley leading down to the floodplain left the remainder of the plain unoccupied. Thus with the abandonment of the three Early Islamic sites (Khirbet al-Hamrah, Khirbet Dhiman, and SS 12), the plain was deserted for the first time since around 1000 B.C. This situation, with sparse occupation occurring at the boundary between the floodplain and the steppe, most closely resembles that of the Chalcolithic period. By the time the area was visited by Gertrude Bell in the early twentieth century, the area was entirely deserted except for occasional nomads of the Walda and ʿAnayzah tribes (Bell 1911: 41).

---

77. Possibly belonging to a wine or olive press and similar to examples illustrated in Frankel 1999.

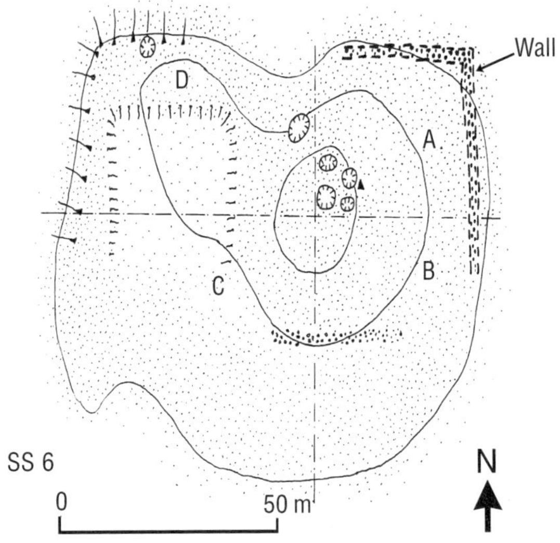

Khirbet Aboud al-Hazu (SS 6): Hellenistic, Roman

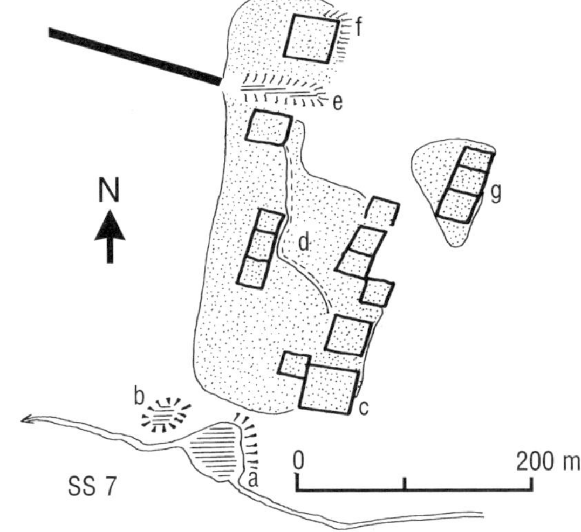

Khirbet al-Hamrah (SS 7): Early Islamic

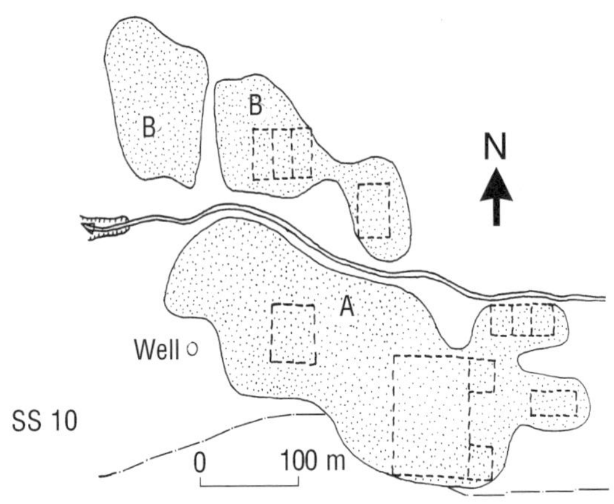

Khirbet Haj Hassan (SS 10): Late Roman

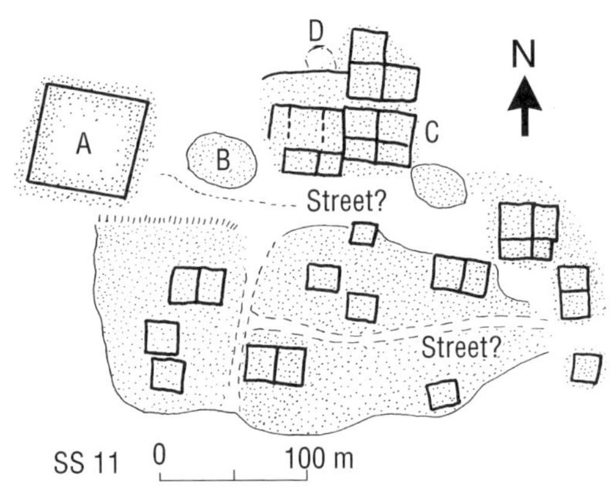

Khirbet Dhiman (SS 11): Early Islamic

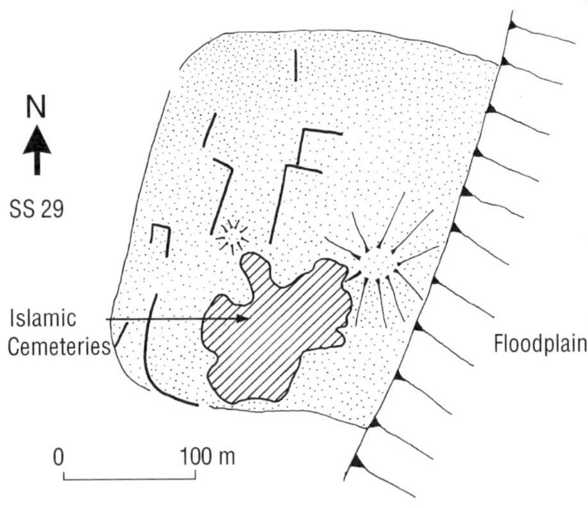

Shajara Saghira (SS 29): Roman

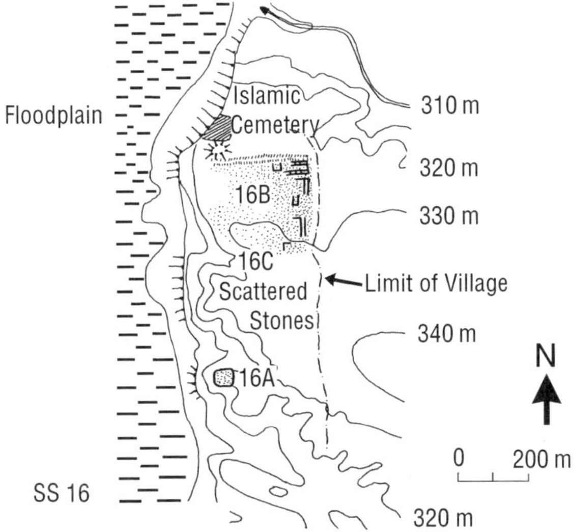

Mishrifat (SS 16A): Roman, Late Roman, Early Islamic; Ramalah
(SS 16B): Hellenistic; SS 16C: Hellenistic with Some Late Iron Age

Figure 7.10. Sketch Plans of Selected Hellenistic, Roman, Byzantine, and Early Islamic Sites. Stippling Indicates Verified Occupation, Straight Lines Indicate Wall Alignments, and Letters Indicate Ceramic Collection Areas Allocated in the Field. For Detailed Discussion of the Sites, See *Appendix A: Sweyhat Survey Site Catalog*. Not to Same Scale

7.I. DISCUSSION

The Sweyhat Survey has demonstrated that phases of colonization of the plain apparently alternated with episodes of desertion. In terms of sedentary settlement, the plain was deserted throughout the Early Holocene and Chalcolithic, during much of the second millennium B.C., and between the tenth and twentieth centuries A.D.

The first phase of colonization of the Sweyhat Plain during the early third millennium B.C. appears to have followed very shortly after the collapse of the phase of southern Uruk settlement at Habuba Kabira South (T 513) and Jebel Aruda (T 527), but whether the establishment of settlements on the Sweyhat Plain was a direct result of the withdrawal of southern Uruk administration is a matter for debate.

The second millennium decline, as noted above, forms part of a sporadic decline of the former centers that eventually resulted in the collapse of the Late Bronze Age strongholds in the area around the twelfth century B.C. This decline is part of a regional trend that, although much debated, is unresolved. In the Sweyhat area the decline was a two phase process: first the desertion of the plain occurred during the second millennium B.C.; second, Late Bronze Age strongholds along the river collapsed around or somewhat before the twelfth century B.C. The collapse of such strongholds coincides with a period of unrest, drought, and famine that has been cataloged by Neumann and Parpola (1987: 162) and ascribed by them to a period of warm dry winters and drought between 1200 and 900 B.C. (For a discussion of possible relationships between settlement and climate in the region, see *Section 9.G: Long-term Settlement and Environmental Change.*) Furthermore, campaigns in pursuit of the Aramaeans, together with increased incidence of crop failures and possibly even famines, could have made marginal settlements untenable. Therefore, whether or not climatic change was the cause of the desertion, it may well have perpetuated it.

The settlement pattern that developed within the Jazirah in the Iron Age appears to form part of a major structural transformation that occurred in many parts of the Jazirah of northern Iraq and Syria following a significant period of decline in the second millennium B.C. This decline resulted in the appearance of a distinctive pattern of small, dispersed rural settlements and some sprawling small towns across the landscape. On the Sweyhat Plain, the pattern of small Iron Age settlements of Sweyhat Survey Period X was then continued, probably with no discernible gap, by a similar pattern of small dispersed rural settlement in the Hellenistic, Roman, Byzantine, and Early Islamic periods.

The next stage of desertion started during approximately the tenth century A.D., so that by the eleventh/twelfth centuries the Sweyhat Plain was deserted, a situation that prevailed throughout most of the second millennium A.D. until the period of modern settlement began earlier in the twentieth century.

Table 7.2. Sweyhat Survey Site Dimensions and Main Periods of Occupation (Minor Occupations in Parentheses)

Sweyhat Survey Site (SS)	*Length in Meters*	*Width in Meters*	*Area in Hectares*	*Sweyhat Survey Period(s) of Occupation*
Tell es-Sweyhat (SS 1)	630	550	31.00	V, VI, VII, VIII, XI, XII, XIII[†]
(Tell es-Sweyhat, Main Tell [SS 1]	—	—	6.00	—)
SS 2	60	55	0.30	V
Tell Hajji Ibrahim (SS 3)	50	50	0.20	V, VI
SS 4	180	100	1.00	XIII, (XIV)
Nafileh Village (SS 5)	70	70	0.40	VI, VII
Khirbet Aboud al-Hazu, Areas A–D (SS 6)	100	70	0.70	X, XI
Khirbet Aboud al-Hazu, Area E (SS 6)	70	50	0.35	XIII
Khirbet al-Hamrah (SS 7)	450	180	5.00	XIV
Tell Jouweif (SS 8)	180	120	1.70	V, VI, VII, VIII, (XI)
Tell Jouweif (SS 8)*	180	150	2.00	V, VI, VII, VIII, (XI)
SS 9, Mound A	50	50	0.20	V
SS 9, Mound B	50	50	0.20	V
Khirbet Haj Hassan (SS 10)	500	280	10.00	XII–XIII
Khirbet Dhiman (SS 11)	420	280	9.00	XIV
SS 12	100	80	0.80	XIV
SS 13	40	40	0.20	(III[?]–IV[?]), V
SS 14	20	20	0.05	V–VI(?)
Khirbet al-Hamrah 2 (SS 15)	70	60	0.40	X
Mishrifat (SS 16A)	70	70	0.50	XIII, XIV
Ramalah (SS 16B)	300	250	7.50	X
SS 16C	N/A	N/A	3.75	XI
Tell Ali al-Haj (SS 17)	200	200	3.00	VIII, IX, X, (XI)
Dahrat er-Ramile (SS 18)	—	—	0.50**	XI
Khirbet Aboud al-Hazu 2 (SS 19)	80	70	0.40	(III?–IV?), V
Tell Othman (SS 20A)	150	150	1.80	V–VI
SS 20B	100	80	0.60	X
SS 21	100	80	0.60	V
Shams ed-Din Southern Site and Cemeteries (SS 22), Area A	150	90	1.00	V
Shams ed-Din Southern Site and Cemeteries (SS 22), Areas B–D	—	—	0.50**	VI
SS 23	80	80	0.50	X
SS 24	40	40	0.20	VII, VIII
SS 25	80	80	0.50	III
SS 26	70	70	0.70	X–XIII
SS 27	100	50	0.40	VII, VIII
SS 28	80	60	0.40	XV
Shajara Saghira (SS 29)	300	200	5.00	XII, XIII
SS 30	80	80	0.50	II

[†]That is, main tell and outer town.

*Estimate before erosion by river.

**Poorly defined sites in field, therefore area arbitrarily assigned.

Table 7.3. Site Periodization for Sweyhat Survey Area

Sweyhat Survey Period	Cultural Period	Occupied Sites (SS)*	Number
I	Halaf	—	0
II	Ubaid	SS 30	1
III	Late Chalcolithic	SS 25	1
IV	Uruk	—	0
V	Early Early Bronze Age	SS 1, 2, 3, 8, 9, 13, 14, 19, 20A, 21, 22A	11
VI	Mid-/Late Early Bronze Age	SS 1, 3, 5, 8, 20A, 22B–D	6
VII	Late Early Bronze Age	SS 1, 5, 8, 24, 27	5
VIII	Middle Bronze Age	SS 1, 8, 17, 24, 27	5
IX	Late Bronze Age	SS 17	1
X	Iron Age	SS 6A–D, 15, 16B, 17, 20B, 23, 26	7
XI	Hellenistic	SS 1, 6A–D, 16C, 18, 26	5
XII	Roman	SS 1, 10, 26, 29	4
XIII	Late Roman and Early Byzantine	SS 1, 4, 6E, 10, 16A, 26, 29	7
XIV	Early Islamic	SS 7, 11, 12, 16A	4
XV	Middle Islamic	SS 28	1

*For areas of individual sites, see table 7.2.

8. THE ANCIENT AGRICULTURAL ECONOMY: BIOLOGICAL REMAINS

8.A. INTRODUCTION

In contrast to the sparse data available from pollen analysis, other biological remains, namely, carbonized plant remains and animal bones, provide a wealth of information that supply clues to the ancient environment and economy of the region. Fortunately, the peak of activity in the upper Lake Assad area coincided or followed shortly after an upsurge of interest in environmental archaeology. Although sampling procedures were not standardized, we do at least have a reasonable body of data to work with, and not only has Tell es-Sweyhat provided a range of data from a number of studies, but other sites along the river have also been investigated (van Zeist and Bakker-Heeres 1985). Here the ancient economy is analyzed within its environmental context, with special reference being made to Tell es-Sweyhat and Tell Jouweif (SS 8). The latter site, which is located on the floodplain, provides data on the Middle Bronze Age riverine economy. We summarize the faunal and carbonized plant remains from Tell es-Sweyhat, this subject having been discussed in more detail by Naomi Miller (herein, below; 1997a–b; 1993) and Jill Weber (1997). Although the database is small, Tell Jouweif must have existed within an environment that differed somewhat from that at Tell es-Sweyhat on the dry steppe. In order to place the two sites within a broader temporal and spatial context, the data described are then compared with a number of sites from the Euphrates and Balikh Valleys.

Reports employed for this analysis are as follows: Tell Jouweif (SS 8), conducted by Naomi Miller (1993), the updated version of which is published in its entirety here; Tell es-Sweyhat reports are Miller 1997a–b, Weber 1997, Hide 1990, Buitenhuis 1988 and 1983, and van Zeist and Bakker-Heeres 1982.

Tell Jouweif (SS 8) provided an ideal contrast to Tell es-Sweyhat because being on the floodplain, it could be expected to have existed within a slightly more verdant environment than that which prevailed in the region of Tell es-Sweyhat on the high terrace to the west. Sampling was made possible by the presence of a high cut eroded by the river on the southwest side of the mound (pl. 15). This massive section, although obscured in places by collapsed material as well as chutes of debris eroded from the bluffs above, provided sufficient exposures to give an overall snapshot view of the stratigraphy (fig. 8.1c). We are grateful to Dr. Adnan Bounni, then Director of Excavations in the Department of Antiquities, Damascus, for supplying permission for this sampling operation with short notice in October 1992. The six sample positions indicated in figure 8.1c were primarily from Middle Bronze Age levels and therefore unfortunately do not coincide precisely in date to the main occupation at Tell es-Sweyhat, dated to the latest phases of the Early Bronze Age in the final quarter of the third millennium B.C. Prior to sampling, the area around each sample point was cleaned and a basket (*zanbil,* ca. 8.4 to 8.8 kg) of soil was taken from the cleaned area and floated using the local lake water as the flotation medium, due care being taken to ascertain that no carbonized plant material was in the water as contaminant. We are therefore confident that the samples well reflect the strata from which they were sampled. The following samples were taken:

Sample *1*   2.0–2.5 m below soil surface of top of mound. Pale gray ash overlying black charcoal-rich deposit. The black deposit that was sampled was below a series of compressed mud surfaces and above similar surfaces which included charcoal lenses. The black deposit was cut by a pit to the north, but this pit was not sampled. Visible inclusions included small pieces of what appeared to be brushwood and small oval pellets resembling carbonized goat droppings.

Sample *2*   2.4–2.5 m below soil surface at top of section. Dark gray ashy layer with common flecks of charred material within banded accumulation 1+ m thick, of stratified, horizontally-bedded ash and charcoal layers. One or two sherds of plain simple ware and one Early Bronze/Middle Bronze Age jar rim were noted.

Sample *3*   2.5–2.6 m below top of section. Black layer, rich in charred material. From same sequence as Sample 2 and immediately below it.

Sample *4*   4.3–4.5 m below top of section. Variegated layers variously gray, olive brown, and dark gray ashy deposits, flecked with common charred material. Charred material common to abundant and includes cereal grains and some wood charcoal.

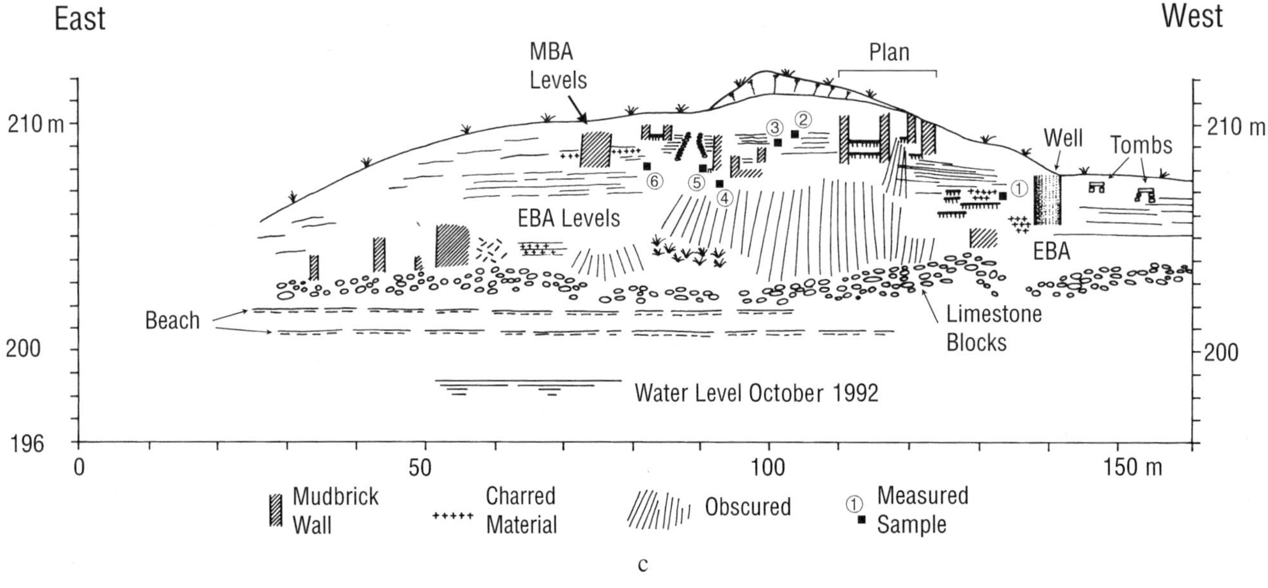

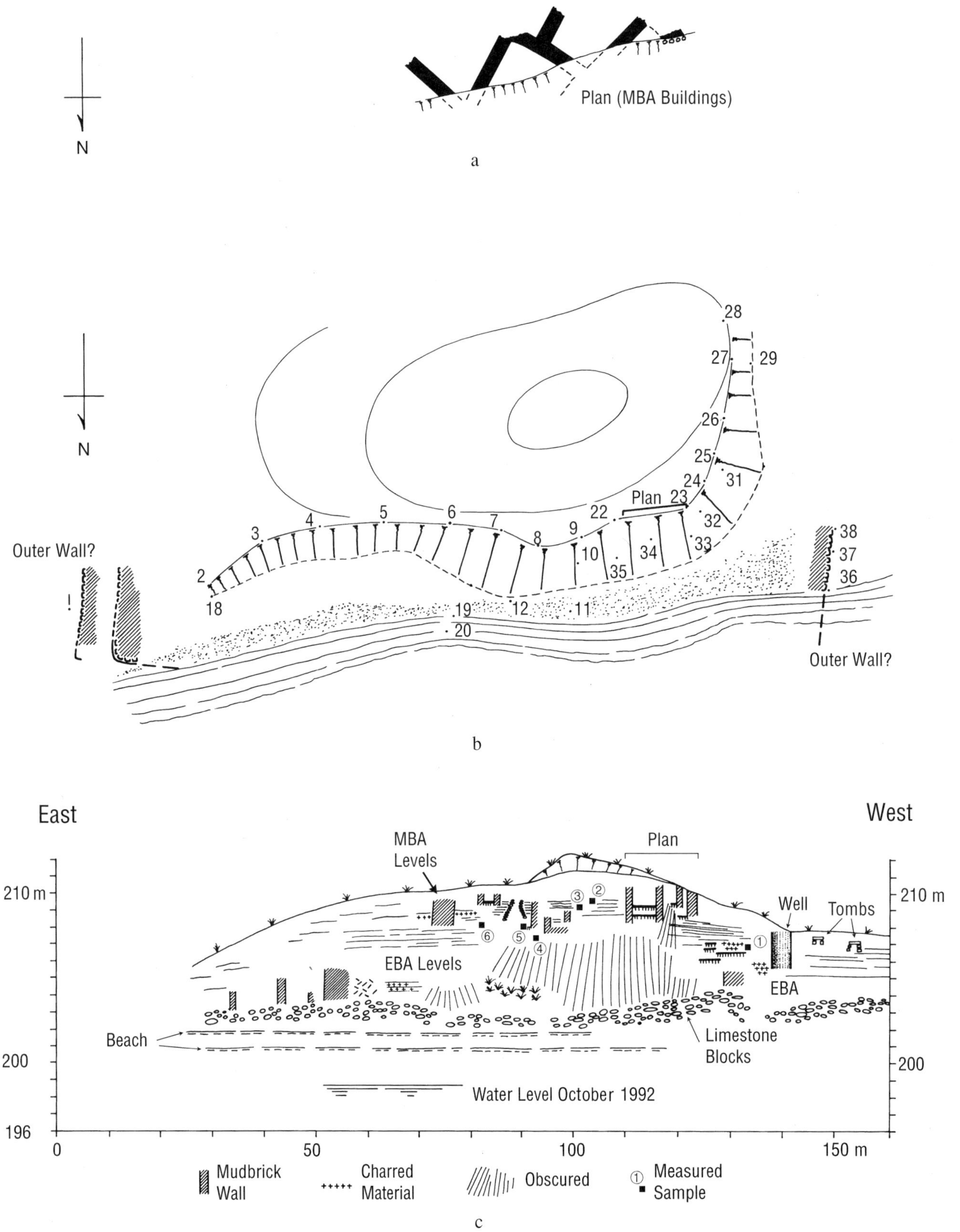

Figure 8.1. Tell Jouweif (SS 8) October 1992: (*a*) Detail of Wall Plan of Middle Bronze Age Buildings, (*b*) Plan of Site and Surveyed Features, (*c*) Sketch Section of Riverward Face

Sample 5   3.9–4.0 below top of section. Gray ashy deposit adjacent to and against mudbrick wall and overlying possible floor. Situated above a series of horizontal layers, mainly of mineral material, apparently forming a series of built-up surfaces. Charred material, although common in section, seems less abundant than in Samples *1–4*.

Sample 6   2.2–2.4 m below top of section. Gray ashy stratum, ca. 50 cm thick, accumulated against a mudbrick wall that runs behind the section. Charred material, including brushwood, is common in section below an upper phase of mudbrick walls and ovens.

Of these, Sample *1* was an isolated sample from later Early Bronze Age or early Middle Bronze Age deposits near the west end of the section, whereas Samples *2–6* were closely associated with Early Bronze/Middle Bronze and earlier Middle Bronze Age levels within the site center. Of these, Samples *2–5* were from sub-horizontal ashy deposits, apparently associated with or immediately predating the Middle Bronze Age mudbrick walls indicated in figure 8.1. Sample *6* was taken from directly against a mudbrick wall, not illustrated in figure 8.1c.

8.B. FLOTATION SAMPLES FROM THE 1992 EXCAVATION AT TELL JOUWEIF

Naomi F. Miller

Six flotation samples from the cut face of the tell were extracted and examined for this report (table 8.1).[78] The goal of this exploratory analysis is to determine whether there are any observable differences between the Tell Jouweif (SS 8) assemblage and those of nearby Early Bronze Age Tell es-Sweyhat or the other roughly contemporary sites farther downstream (Selenkahiye [T 507, EBA] and Tell Hadidi [T 548, MBA]). A fair amount of previous archaeobotanical research provides the basis for comparisons (Miller 1997b; Hide 1990; van Zeist and Bakker-Heeres 1985).

8.B.1. LABORATORY PROCEDURES

Each flotation sample consists of the material that was extracted from one *zanbil* of earth averaging 8.6 kg in weight. Most of the samples were too large to sort completely and so were split in a cardboard rifflebox. The non-sorted portions of the samples have been kept.

8.B.2. THE PLANT REMAINS

With few exceptions, the taxa recovered are known from the other sites along the middle Euphrates Valley. The bulk of the remains, in terms of absolute quantity and frequency of occurrence, both wild and cultivated, come from two families: grasses and legumes; this is also true of Middle Bronze Age samples from Tell Hadidi (T 548). For details about morphology, habitat, and possible economic uses, see van Zeist and Bakker-Heeres 1985, 1984, 1982; Hide 1990; identifications are based on illustrations in these works, other reports and seed atlases, and seeds in the comparative collection housed at MASCA.

---

78.   Revised version of MASCA Ethnobotanical Laboratory Report 12 (Miller 1993). Naomi F. Miller is a Senior Research Scientist at the Museum Applied Science Center for Archaeology (MASCA), The University of Pennsylvania Museum, Philadelphia, Pennsylvania.

Table 8.1. Overview of Flotation Samples from Tell Jouweif (SS 8)

Sample Number	*1*	*2*	*3*	*4*	*5*	*6*
Soil volume (fraction of *zanbil*)	0.23	1.00	0.22	0.40	1.00	0.13
Volume analyzed (cc)	125	75	100	50	100	100
Charcoal (g, >2 mm)	1.35	7.54	5.40	7.79	4.91	7.69
Seed (g, >2 mm)	0.69	0.16	2.13	0.37	0.57	0.27
Other (g, >2 mm)	0.21	0.03	0.63	0.06	0.23	0.06
Dung (g, >2 mm)	3.82	0.00	3.58	0.00	1.57	3.21
Wild/weedy seed (no.)	296	7	166	70	93	34
Charred plant material (>2 mm, g/*zanbil*)	9.78	7.73	37.09	20.55	5.71	61.69
Seed/charcoal (g/g)	0.51	0.02	0.39	0.05	0.12	0.04
Seed/other (g/g)	3.29	5.33	3.38	6.17	2.48	4.50
Other/charcoal (g/g)	0.16	0.00	0.12	0.01	0.05	0.01
Weed seed/charcoal (no./g)	219	1	31	9	19	4

Table 8.2. Charred Remains

Sample Number	1	2	3	4	5	6	Ubiquity
CULTIGENS							
Hordeum (g)[1]	0.12	0.10	1.45	0.14	0.16	0.20	1.00
Triticum (g)	—	—	+	—	—	—	0.17
Cereal, indeterminate (g)[2]	0.07	0.04	0.80	0.03	0.06	—	0.83
Lens	—	—	1	—	1	1	0.50
Lathyrus	—	—	2	—	—	—	0.17
Fabaceae, large seeds (estimate)	—	1	2	1	—	—	0.50
WILD AND WEEDY							
Cf. *Anthriscus*	1	—	—	—	—	—	0.17
Bupleurum	—	—	—	—	1	—	0.17
Centaurea	—	—	—	—	—	1	0.17
Asteraceae indet.	—	—	1	—	—	—	0.17
Heliotropium	1	—	—	—	—	—	0.17
Arnebia	2	—	—	—	—	—	0.17
Aellenia (perianth)	14	—	—	—	—	—	0.17
Atriplex[3]	19	—	—	—	1	—	0.33
Chenopodiaceae	—	—	—	—	—	1	0.17
Cyperaceae	12	—	—	—	—	—	0.17
Alhagi	17	—	—	2	60	4	0.67
Astragalus	1	—	—	2	1	—	0.50
Cf. *Onobrychis*	3	—	—	—	1	1	0.50
Prosopis (estimate)[4]	20	—	5	4	1	1	0.83
Trifolium/Melilotus-type	—	1	4	8	2	2	0.83
Trigonella	11	—	4	—	—	2	0.50
Fabaceae, miscellaneous	32	—	3	18	—	1	0.50
Cf. *Teucrium*	1	—	—	—	—	—	0.17
Cf. *Glaucium*	—	1	2	—	—	—	0.33
Plantago	—	—	—	1	—	—	0.17
Aegilops	3	1	31	2	—	—	0.67
Bromus	—	—	—	1	—	—	0.17
Cf. *Eremopyrum*	18	2	69	4	1	—	0.83
Hordeum	1	—	—	—	—	—	0.17
Phalaris	1	—	—	8	2	—	0.50
Secale	1	—	—	—	—	—	0.17
Cf. *Setaria*	—	—	—	1	—	—	0.17
Poaceae, miscellaneous	46	1	15	15	12	5	1.00
Polygonaceae/Cyperaceae	19	—	—	—	—	—	0.17
Androsace	2	—	1	—	1	—	0.50
Adonis	—	1	3	—	—	—	0.33
Ceratocephalus	—	—	18	—	—	—	0.17

Table 8.2. Charred Remains (*cont.*)

Sample Number	1	2	3	4	5	6	Ubiquity
WILD AND WEEDY (*cont.*)							
Ceratocephalus	—	—	18	—	—	—	0.17
Cf. *Ranunculus*	1	—	—	—	—	—	0.17
Rubus	4	—	—	—	—	—	0.17
Sanguisorba minor-type[5]	1	—	2	3	—	—	0.50
Galium	1	—	—	—	—	—	0.17
Cf. *Thymelaea*	3	—	—	—	—	—	0.17
Valerianella coronata-type	2	—	—	—	—	2	0.33
Unknown, miscellaneous	59	—	8	1	10	14	n/a

MISCELLANEOUS CHARRED PLANT PARTS

Sample Number	1	2	3	4	5	6	Ubiquity
Aegilops, glume base	14	4	22	3	3	—	0.83
Hordeum, internode	187	2	49	6	7	23	1.00
Hordeum, dense-eared internode	45	2	21	—	—	—	0.50
Triticum monococcum/ dicoccum, spikelet fork	1	—	—	—	—	1	0.33
Straw nodes	93	—	113	9	8	21	0.83
Cf. *Alhagi*, pod segment	1	—	—	—	—	—	0.17
Fabaceae, pod fragments (g)	—	—	—	—	0.15	—	0.17
Arnebia decumbens-type, uncharred	—	1	1	4	—	—	0.50
Thorns, miscellaneous	(several)	—	—	—	4	—	0.33
Leaves (cf. *Alhagi*)	—	—	—	—	78	—	0.17

Notes

[1] *Hordeum* count may be estimated using the average weight at Tell Jouweif (SS 8) of 0.007 g/caryopsis.

[2] Cereal count may be estimated using an average weight of 0.007 g/caryopsis, assuming indeterminate cereal to be mostly *Hordeum*.

[3] Sample *5* had a single *Atriplex* only; Sample *1* had closed perianths of both *Atriplex* and *Aellenia* that would contain one seed each.

[4] *Prosopis* count estimates based on 0.019 g/seed (average from Tell Jouweif samples).

[5] *Sanguisorba minor*-type (= *Poterium lasiocarpum*) is equivalent to SLK 67–S157 illustrated in van Zeist and Bakker-Heeres 1985, fig. 4.8.

CULTIGENS

Cereals, primarily barley (*Hordeum vulgare*), predominate in the samples (table 8.2). Unfortunately, most of the material is fragmented or greatly distorted by puffing; some of the seeds look (literally) chewed. Although a few grains look twisted, the barley at Tell Jouweif (SS 8) appears to be the two-row type (*H. vulgare* var. *distichum*), as at the other Bronze Age sites in the upper Lake Assad area.

In addition to the barley grains, two types of barley internodes were observed. The "dense-eared" type has very little space between glume bases. A single internode could be from the six-row type (*H. vulgare* var. *hexastichum*).

One grain that resembles bread/hard wheat (*Triticum aestivum/durum*) was also observed. As is the case at the other sites, wheat would seem to have been a minor crop at best.

A small number of pulses was encountered — three lentils (*Lens*) and two grass peas (*Lathyrus*). Both of these types are known from other sites in the area, where they occur in similar low proportions.

WILD AND WEEDY PLANTS

Plants of fields, other disturbed ground, steppe, and moist areas are represented in the wild and weedy plant assemblage (table 8.3). Few types are restricted to one or another habitat. For example, *Alhagi* and *Prosopis* are native steppe plants, but they are also persistent weeds in cultivated fields because it is difficult to destroy their deep taproots.

Most of the wild plants are grasses or forbs (herbaceous broad-leaved plants), though a few shrubs are represented. Table 8.3 provides summary information about the plant types. Some of the plants warrant separate discussion here; for more detailed information on individual taxa, read the reports of van Zeist cited above.

Aellenia

A plant part enclosing a seed or achene has been identified as *Aellenia* (Chenopodiaceae) based on its "hard bony perianth, 5-pitted at base" (Zohary 1966: 167). The specimens are consistent with *A. autrani*. Many members of the genus are steppe and desert plants; *A. autrani* also grows in cultivated ground.

Atriplex

Atriplex has many representatives in the Middle East. Members of this Chenopodiaceae genus occur in steppe and cultivated ground, and many are salt tolerant as well (Davis 1967: 305 ff.). *Atriplex* seeds are reported from the much earlier sites of Mureybit (T 502–504) and Tell Aswad (van Zeist and Bakker-Heeres 1984, 1982). At Tell Jouweif (SS 8), in addition to a single seed in Sample 5, nineteen fruiting perianth segments were seen that most closely resemble *A. turcomanica* collected near Malyan, Iran. McCorriston (1995) reports a related type, *A. leucoclada* from sites in the Khabur Valley. As there is one seed per flower, I have added the *Atriplex* fruits to the seed counts.

Alhagi

Alhagi (camelthorn) is a spiny perennial. It has not yet been reported from the middle Euphrates sites, but there is no reason to doubt its presence. In addition to the seed, a pod fragment and leaves that probably belong to the genus were observed.

Secale

One fairly large grass caryopsis that resembles rye was encountered. Although not reported from the Bronze Age sites, Hillman did find some wild rye at Abu Hureyra (T 545; Hillman, Colledge, and Harris 1989).

Ceratocephalus

Seeds of this small member of the Ranunculaceae are identified. I have also seen it at Umm al-Marra (Miller 1996 as Umm-10) and at Tell es-Sweyhat (Miller 1997b).

Sanguisorba minor

Three samples yielded seeds that look like those seeds depicted in van Zeist's articles: from Selenkahiye (T 507; SLK 67-S157, illustrated in fig. 4.8) or Mureybit (T 502–504; Mb'73, G9, illustrated in fig. 5.14). Joy McCorriston (pers. comm.) suggests the type to be *Sanguisorba minor/Poterium lasiocarpum*, which seems likely. The type is a good grazing plant (Townsend and Guest 1966: 141).

Table 8.3. Summary Descriptions of Wild and Weedy Taxa from Tell Jouweif (SS 8)

Taxon	Life Form*	Common Name; Habitat (if restricted)
Apiaceae	—	Carrot family
Cf. *Anthriscus*	h	—
Bupleurum	h	—
Asteraceae	—	Daisy family; typically plants of open ground
Centaurea	h	—
Asteraceae indet.	—	—
Boraginaceae	—	Borage family
Arnebia	h	(Only charred specimens included in totals)
Heliotropium	h	—
Chenopodiaceae	—	Goosefoot family
Aellenia	h, w	—
Atriplex	h, w	—
Cyperaceae	h	Sedges; usually associated with moist areas (stream sides, irrigation ditches, high water table)
Fabaceae	—	Legume, pea family
Alhagi	w	Camelthorn; deep taproot, common in degraded steppe and fields
Astragalus	h, w	—
Cf. *Onobrychis*	h	—
Prosopis	w	Deep taproot, common in degraded steppe and fields
Trifolium/Melilotus	h	Clover; fields and fairly moist areas
Trigonella	h	—
Fabaceae miscellaneous	—	—
Lamiaceae	—	Mint family
Cf. *Teucrium*	h	Sub-shrub
Papaveraceae		Poppy family
Cf. *Glaucium*	h	—
Plantaginaceae	—	—
Plantago	h	Plantain; typically associated with agricultural disturbance or moist area
Poaceae	h	Grass family; typically plants of open ground
Aegilops	h	Goat-face grass
Bromus	h	Brome grass
Cf. *Eremopyrum*	h	—
Hordeum	h	Wild barley
Phalaris	h	—
Secale	h	Wild rye
Cf. *Setaria*	h	—
Poaceae miscellaneous	h	—
Polygonaceae/Cyperaceae	—	Buckwheat family/Sedge family
Primulaceae	—	Primrose family
Androsace	h	—
Ranunculaceae	—	Buttercup family
Adonis	h	—
Cf. *Ceratocephalus*	h	Open places
Cf. *Ranunculus*	—	Buttercup
Rosaceae	—	Rose family
Rubus	w	Bramble; would grow along the river
Rubiaceae	—	—
Galium	h	Cleavers
Thymeleaceae	—	—
Cf. *Thymelaea*	h	—
Valerianaceae	—	—
Valerianella	h	—

* Life form: h = herbaceous, w = woody

WOOD CHARCOAL

For this preliminary study, five pieces of charcoal from each of the flotation samples were examined (table 8.4). In identifying wood charcoal, it is generally a good idea to consider only those pieces that have at least one growth ring, so as not to underestimate the types that are difficult to identify from tiny fragments. There are a few shrubs (e.g., sagebrush [*Artemisia*]) that do not have distinct growth rings, which renders the rigid application of this rule problematic, and many of the pieces selected for identification did not have complete growth rings. Identification also requires adequate reference and comparative material, which was not readily available. Thus, despite the fact that many of the pieces are relatively large (caught in 4.75 mm mesh), I could not identify most of the pieces I picked out.

Among the identified pieces were taxa that are known from the other sites in the area: poplar or willow (*Populus* or *Salix*), tamarisk(?) (cf. *Tamarix*), elm family (Ulmaceae), oak (*Quercus*), and at least one shrub taxon, the goosefoot family (Chenopodiaceae). The first three would have grown in riparian forest. Oak might have drifted downstream (van Zeist and Bakker-Heeres 1985), or scattered oaks may have grown nearby. The member of the Chenopodiaceae would have grown out on the steppe.

Table 8.4. Charcoal from Tell Jouweif (SS 8)

Sample Number	*1*	*2*	*3*	*4*	*5*	*6*
COUNT						
Populus/Salix	—	2	—	(1)	1	2
Cf. *Tamarix*	—	—	—	3	—	2
Ulmaceae	—	2	1	—	—	—
Quercus	—	—	—	—	2	—
Chenopodiaceae	2	—	—	—	—	—
Unknown	3	1	4	2	2	1
WEIGHT EXAMINED (G)						
Populus/Salix	—	0.19	—	(noted)	0.05	0.13
Cf. *Tamarix*	—	—	—	0.68	—	0.36
Ulmaceae	—	0.24	0.20	—	—	—
Quercus	—	—	—	—	0.43	—
Chenopodiaceae	0.35	—	—	—	—	—
Unknown	0.20	0.08	0.32	0.62	0.39	0.10
Amount analyzed	0.55	0.51	0.52	1.30	0.87	0.59
Total weight of sample	1.35	7.54	5.40	7.79	4.91	7.69

8.B.3. THE SIGNIFICANCE OF INDIVIDUAL TAXA FOR ENVIRONMENTAL OR ECONOMIC RECONSTRUCTION

Quantifying archaeobotanical data in a meaningful way is not easy, especially when few samples are available. Even if a seed type is numerous, it may occur in only one or two samples. At Tell Jouweif (SS 8) more than half of the genera appear in only one sample. For example, a single *Bupleurum* seed occurs in Sample *5* and none other. Only one type, domesticated barley, occurs in all six samples. Absolute quantities of seeds are therefore best interpreted in conjunction with a ubiquity analysis of the assemblage as a whole. For example, the nineteen *Atriplex* fruits in Sample *1* could come from a single branch tossed into a fire, whereas the *Eremopyrum* is found in five out of six samples, occurring in some quantity in two of them. At least for the deposits analyzed to date, one might conclude that *Eremopyrum* was the more significant or useful plant.

At this preliminary stage in the research, it is advisable to interpret the data with some caution. A quick glance at the results from other sites shows that Tell Jouweif (SS 8) fits well within the normal range of taxa.

8.B.4. THE SAMPLES

Because the flotation samples were taken from deposits cut by the river, it is more difficult to fit them into a functional cultural space than if they had been excavated from a horizontal exposure. Nevertheless, based on the descriptions furnished in *Section 8.A: Introduction*, Wilkinson suggests that the samples were associated with surfaces (probably external) that were accumulating debris as sub-horizontal layers adjacent to mudbrick buildings. The deposits were charcoal-rich but not necessarily burned in situ. The deposits may therefore represent a wide range of debris — fuel, crop-processing remains, other trash (cf. Miller 1984; Hillman 1984, 1981).

An analysis of the composition of the samples compared to that of other sites in the region can, however, narrow the range of possibilities. In contrast to Tell Jouweif (SS 8), the deposits from the northwest terrace and the lower town of Tell es-Sweyhat excavated in 1989 yielded very few cultigens, generally under 10% of the total, whether or not the problematic uncharred borages are included (Hide 1990). Neither are the Tell Jouweif samples comparable to those identified by van Zeist and Bakker-Heeres at Tell es-Sweyhat because the latter are virtually pure crop samples from a burnt building; even the samples with the highest proportions of cultigens at Tell Jouweif do not exhibit the crop purity of those samples. Though the Tell Hadidi (T 548) samples are somewhat more mixed than the Tell es-Sweyhat crop samples, they too seem to have primarily crop plant remains. On the other hand, sample composition of Tell es-Sweyhat trashy deposits excavated in 1991 and 1993 (Miller 1997b), from the Selenkahiye (T 507) "refuse deposits near the town wall" (van Zeist and Bakker-Heeres 1985: 272), and the "cultural fill" deposits (ibid., p. 276) bear a striking resemblance to those from Tell Jouweif: barley predominates, but substantial numbers of wild seeds and rachis fragments are present.

The question remains, of course, what is the nature of that settlement debris. As I have discussed elsewhere, barring convincing contextual evidence to the contrary, one's first assumption in characterizing charred debris is that it comes from fuel — charcoal, dung, or brush (Miller 1991, 1984). Charcoal from settlement debris is almost certainly fuel remains. Four of the Tell Jouweif (SS 8) samples also contain significant quantities of dung — a few are intact, readily recognizable carbonized sheep/goat pellets — and relatively high quantities of a substance that has the fibrous texture of dung (see table 8.5). Furthermore, a dung-like residue coats many of the charred remains. The ratio by weight of dung to charcoal is also rather high.

Seeds are most likely to come from intentional burning of dung or brush fuel, or from burnt crop-processing debris. It is not obvious in mixed samples how one might distinguish these sources. For now, I only deal with dung and brush. Much of the charcoal in Samples *1* and *5* consists of twiglet fragments, which might be from brush fuel. Brush fires would presumably be fueled by otherwise non-useful plants. In the Tell Jouweif (SS 8) samples, *Alhagi*, with its sharp-tipped branches, is the most obvious candidate. The other genera in the assemblage are for the most part suitable fodder plants. Aside from dung itself, the use of dung fuel may be inferred from the seeds of fodder plants.

If seeds originated in dung fuel, one might expect seeds and dung to co-occur. As Bottema (1984) demonstrates, however, sheep dung does not always contain many seeds. At Tell Jouweif (SS 8), even though a large amount of dung is in the samples, dung fragments and wild/weedy seeds are totally unassociated. Nevertheless, and without going into all the arguments here, I maintain that many seeds are likely to have originated in dung fuel (Miller 1996, 1984); variation between individual samples can mask regularities that characterize entire assemblages. If this reasoning is valid, seed to charcoal ratios could indicate relative proportions of dung and wood fuel in comparisons between sites.

In Miller 1997b, I provide some quantitative information that allows comparison between the Tell es-Sweyhat and the Tell Jouweif (SS 8) samples with respect to seeds and charcoal. The seed/charcoal ratio (by weight) of seventeen samples from Tell es-Sweyhat Operation 1 averages 0.70 (Miller 1997b). Seventeen other Tell es-Sweyhat debris samples analyzed by Christine Hide (1990) yield an average of 0.67 (1.52 if one includes an outlier). At Tell Jouweif, with only six samples, the comparable figure is 0.19, which is quite a bit lower. This lower sampling could support the hypothesis that wood fuel (presumably from riverine sources) was more available at Tell Jouweif than at Tell es-Sweyhat. The difference between the sites is probably real because a major determinant of fuel use is availability, and even 3 or 4 km would make a difference to the person carrying the fuel. (See also Miller 1990a: 82 for a discussion of firewood use in the city and the countryside.) Similarly, the weed seed count to charcoal weight is higher on average at Tell es-Sweyhat than at Tell Jouweif.

Note further that at Tell Jouweif (SS 8) the average ratio of wild seeds (count) to cereal (weight) is 447, at Tell es-Sweyhat it is more than twice that (Miller 1997b). If the seeds reflect animal fodder, a speculative but plausible explanation may be proposed: Tell es-Sweyhat, heavily dependent on pastoral production, sent animals out to graze in steppe pasture. Tell Jouweif is located more favorably for agriculture (Wilkinson, pers. comm.) and is geographically constrained by the Euphrates River on the west and the territory of Tell es-Sweyhat on the east. Its animals were therefore more likely to be fed straw and graze on field stubble, and the proportion of wild seeds relative to cereal is relatively low. This line of argument is more fully developed in Miller 1997a.

Unfortunately, it is next to impossible to eliminate all other factors, and crop-processing debris could be mixed in with fuel debris samples. That we are not dealing with pure crop-processing debris tossed onto a wood-fueled fire is, however, suggested by the fact that the samples contain a range of seed sizes (cf. Hillman 1984).

Table 8.5. Charred Dung from Tell Jouweif (SS 8)*

Sample Number	*1*	*2*	*3*	*4*	*5*	*6*
Sheep/goat pellets (no.)	10	—	—	—	1	—
Sheep/goat pellets (g)	0.87	—	—	—	0.06	—
Sheep/goat pellet fragments (g)	1.31	—	—	—	—	—
Other dung(?) fragments (g)	1.64	—	3.58	—	1.51	3.21
Dung/charcoal (g/g)	2.83	—	0.47	—	0.32	0.42

*Weight in grams of pieces larger than 2 mm.

8.B.5. SUMMARY OF MAIN RESULTS

The Tell Jouweif (SS 8) assemblage fits comfortably within the range of materials and deposits found at other Bronze Age sites in the region. The six samples can probably best be characterized as burnt settlement debris, primarily fuel remains. Located directly on the river, Tell Jouweif may have had broader access to wood fuel than Tell es-Sweyhat, though the taxa collected were the same. Arguing against this conclusion is the relatively large amount of dung relative to charcoal.

8.C. LONG-TERM TRENDS IN THE PLANT AND ANIMAL ECONOMY

Tony J. Wilkinson

It is now possible to place the results from Tell Jouweif (SS 8) within a broader framework. In order to obtain a long-term perspective on the changing agricultural environment, particular emphasis is placed upon Tell es-Sweyhat and nearby sites, or on those with a similar mean annual rainfall (table 8.6).

The closest evidence for the Early Holocene plant economy comes from Jerf al-Ahmar (T 559) and Halula, two small aceramic Neolithic sites dated to the Pre-pottery Neolithic A, and early Pre-pottery Neolithic B, respectively. Jerf al-Ahmar is ca. 12 km northwest of Tell es-Sweyhat and Halula is some 18 km northwest; both were within the area to be flooded behind the new Tishrin Dam. Carbonized plant remains from levels dated between 9,800 and 9,200 B.P. (uncalibrated radiocarbon years) indicate that wild cereals (einkorn wheat, rye, and barley) and pulses (lentils, pea, and bitter vetch) were exploited (Willcox 1996). In addition, grains of morphologically domestic emmer (*Triticum dicoccum*), naked wheat (*Triticum durum*), and two-row barley (*Hordeum distichum*) were found at Pre-pottery Neolithic B Halula. The two-row barley was also recorded from earlier Pre-pottery Neolithic B and Pre-pottery Neolithic A Djaʿde, located farther upstream. Interestingly, pulses such as lentil, pea, and bitter vetch were common at all three sites, and although it is not clear whether they were cultivated or gathered, they appear to have formed a significant part of the plant economy (Miller 2002). Similarly, wild vine and even parts of olive stones were noted at Halula and Djaʿde. These data supplement the information from Mureybit (T 502–504) and Abu Hureyra (T 545), both of which are located within the more arid areas to the south of Tell es-Sweyhat.

The presence of wild einkorn and wild rye suggests cooler, moister conditions (Willcox 1996: 150). This observation is supported by the analysis of charcoals that indicate ash, vine, elm, plane, and perhaps olive, all of which today are found significantly farther north. Furthermore, almond, *Pistacia* type *atlantica*, and deciduous oak at present only occur at higher, moister altitudes within the region. Although it is evident that the degradation of vegetation probably accounts for some of these differences between the aceramic Neolithic and that of the Bronze Age (or the present day), the ecological requirements of most of these plants are incompatible with the present day climatic range; therefore, a shift in climate seems to have occurred.

Similarly, aceramic Neolithic levels at Abu Hureyra (T 545), located in a slightly drier location[79] southeast of the bend of the Euphrates River, yielded a wide range of carbonized plant remains (table 8.6). These included domestic rye, breadwheat, emmer wheat, some einkorn, domestic barley, lentils (with wild more frequent than domestic types), domestic chick pea, field bean, and perhaps wild vine (Hillman 2000: 418–20). The last named would probably have grown among the valley bottom woodland or scrub.

Farther to the east, but at an equivalent latitude and rainfall, the carbonized plant remains from early ceramic Neolithic Damishliyya (ca. 6000 B.C.) showed a significant percentage of lentils (17.5%). In addition, wheat (*Triticum dicoccum* and *aestivum*) predominated over barley. Early Halaf and Halaf levels at Sabi Abyad show a significant decline in pulses, but emmer wheat continued to predominate over barley to a significant degree. During the Chalcolithic period a decline in wheat followed and by the Early Bronze Age and Middle Bronze Age, as at Tell es-Sweyhat, barley overwhelmingly dominated the assemblage of carbonized plant remains and presumably the local plant economy (see van Zeist and Waterbolk-van Rooijen 1996, 1989; van Zeist and Bakker-Heeres 1985; also Wilkinson 1998, fig. 10).

Table 8.6. Major Crops in the Area of Tell es-Sweyhat for Sites Receiving Mean Annual Rainfall Close to 250 mm

	PPNA	PPNB	PPNB	Early Ceramic Neolithic	Early Halaf	Ubaid	Late Chalcolithic	EBA	MBA
	Jerf al-Ahmar (T 559)	*Dja'de*	*Abu Hureyra* (T 545)	*Damishliyya*	*Sabi Abyad*	*Tell Hammam et-Turkman*	*Tell Hammam et-Turkman*	*Tell es-Sweyhat* (SS 1)	*Tell Jouweif* (SS 8)
Wild wheat/rye[1]	*	*	*	—	—	—	—	—	—
Wild barley[2]	*	*	*	—	—	—	—	—	—
Domestic or wild lentil[3]	*	*	*	*	+	—	—	+	*
Domestic or wild pea[4]	*	*	*	*	—	—	—	*	—
Almond[5]	*	*	—	—	—	—	—	—	—
Pistachio[6]	*	*	*	—	—	—	—	—	—
Wild grape[7]	*	*	?	—	—	—	—	—	—
Domestic emmer[8]	—	—	*	**	**	*	**	—	—
Domestic einkorn[9]	—	—	*	—	*	—	*	—	—
Bread/hard wheat[10]	—	—	*	*	*	*	—	*	+
Two-row barley[11]	—	—	*	*	*	***	***	***	***
Grass pea[12]	—	—	*	—	—	—	—	*	*

+	Trace	1.	*Triticum* or *Secale*
*	Present in small quantities	2.	*Hordeum spontaneum*
**	Present in large quantities	3.	*Lens orientalis/culinaris*
***	Dominant (>50%)	4.	*Pisum sativum/humile*
		5.	*Amygdalus*
		6.	*Pistachia terebinthus/atlantica*

7.	*Vitis sylvestris*
8.	*Triticum dicoccum*
9.	*Triticum monococcum*
10.	*Triticum aestivum/durum*
11.	*Hordeum vulgare*
12.	*Lathyrus sativus*

---

79.   Mean annual rainfall ca. 200 mm.

8.C.1. CARBONIZED PLANT REMAINS FROM TELL ES-SWEYHAT

The plant remains from Tell es-Sweyhat provide a varied range of evidence for third and perhaps early second millennium crop utilization that contrasts markedly with that from the aceramic Neolithic, ceramic Neolithic, and Halaf periods in the region. The following results are summarized from Miller 1997a–b, Hide 1990, and van Zeist and Bakker-Heeres 1985.

Using samples from the original excavations directed by Thomas Holland, van Zeist and Bakker-Heeres found concentrations of two-row barley and *Lathyrus sativus* (grass pea); although six-row hulled barley may have been present, this is not certain. Both were found in what appears to have been storage contexts, and the barley (two-row) was in association with a storage jar and possible scoop (Holland 1976: 59). I presume that if grain was stored in jars, it was for human consumption rather than for animal feed.

Similarly, Miller's (1997a–b) analyses of samples from the later seasons show that in all contexts investigated, be they from storage or refuse contexts, barley predominated. Wheat represented only a small proportion of the identified cereals. If the seed remains are from burnt dung, the predominance of barley is to be expected because this would have been the main animal feed crop used. On the other hand, if sheep were grazed on the harvested fields, then the dung would contain a more representative suite of the cereal crops grown. If this were the case, then the overwhelming presence of barley in all samples suggests that barley was likely to have been the main crop plant grown. In summary, because barley appears to predominate in all contexts — crop storage, animal feed, and on the fields themselves — it seems that barley was the dominant cereal crop, whereas wheat was at best only a minor crop.

Legumes — lentil, field pea, or bitter vetch — were present in only very small amounts. However, the presence of a pure sample of *Lathyrus* (grass pea from storage vessels in Room 6, Area IV) suggests that this legume was used for human food (see below). As would be expected from the prevailing environment, fruit seeds were vary sparse and only single examples of fig and grape seeds were found. This contrasts with the large numbers of grape seeds found at Kurban Höyük, located to the north within a significantly moister environment (Miller 1986).

Of the weedy plants in later third millennium contexts at Tell es-Sweyhat, leguminous weeds were common, and although some may have been weeds of fields, others such as *Trigonella* were probably derived from the steppe (Miller 1997a). Although the variety of grasses is high, they do not appear to have been as important as the leguminous weeds. However, in the earlier third millennium contexts at neighboring Tell Hajji Ibrahim (SS 3), grass seeds form an important part of the carbonized assemblage, more so in fact than from other sites along the Syrian Euphrates River. It is tempting to see this higher occurrence of grass seeds as indicating that during the early third millennium B.C., the steppe was grassier and then became more degraded during the later part of the millennium, though Miller leans toward the interpretation that the Tell Hajji Ibrahim grasses came from agricultural fields and may even be crop-processing debris (Miller 1997b: 103–04).

The carbonized plant remains reveal no evidence for irrigation, and in fact it has been pointed out that the barley grains from Tell es-Sweyhat and Selenkahiye (T 507) were notably smaller than those from moister areas upstream at Tepecik and Korucetepe (van Zeist and Bakker-Heeres 1985).

On the basis of a long program of analyses of carbonized plant remains from along the Turkish and Syrian Euphrates River, Miller argues that a significant proportion of the plant seeds and crop grains arrive on site as a result of the burning of dung as fuel (Miller 1997a; Miller and Smart 1984). This dung burning is particularly significant in the area of Tell es-Sweyhat, where she argues that fuel woods had probably been used up at an early date, and it resulted in a high amount of carbonized seeds of weeds in proportion to those of domestic grains in the samples. In contrast, for the Chalcolithic and earlier Early Bronze Age periods at, for example, Kurban Höyük, fragments of wood charcoal were much more common because at such times there was sufficient wood and scrub available for use as fuel, and dung could be applied to the fields. For later third millennium levels at Tell es-Sweyhat, the high proportion of seeds to both charcoal and domestic grain suggests that a significant amount of animal grazing took place on the open steppe, that is, beyond the cultivated zone around the site (Miller 1997b).

However, if a significant proportion of the grains recorded by flotation had been recycled by animals, what were the main plant foods? At Tell es-Sweyhat the presence of barley and *Lathyrus* in domestic storage contexts with storage jars (Hide 1990; Holland 1976: 57–59) suggests that both were used as food. Barley, although quite tasty, is rather difficult to process. Nevertheless, when mixed with wheat it makes an excellent loaf,[80] and Hide points out its use in

---

80. I have eaten barley bread myself in Baghdad and can vouch for
     its wholesomeness.

porridge (see Renfrew 1973: 81). Also in southern Iraq during the mid-twentieth century, much more barley was consumed as human food than wheat (Poyck 1962: 66), mainly in the form of unleavened bread. Clearly, however, it was regarded as the lower status food, and whereas farm owners consumed 32 kg of barley to 13.2 kg of wheat per annum, tenants consumed barley at a ratio of 46.5 kg barley to 10.7 kg wheat (Poyck 1962, table 4.21; cf. Harlan 1995, who quotes barley as the food of the poor and soldiers). If malted, barley could also have been used in the manufacture of beer.

Lathyrus, being present in a cleaned form in storage contexts, also appears to have been eaten by the residents of Tell es-Sweyhat. Today the seeds are ground for use in breads, for example, in Ethiopia; therefore, they may be regarded as being, in part, a food crop. Although toxic in large quantities, with a tendency to cause paralysis (lathyrism: Renfrew 1973: 118), these seeds have been cultivated over a wide area from southwest Europe to central Asia. Because of this tendency for *Lathyrus* seeds to result in paralysis, they are unlikely to have formed a primary plant food, and therefore they could be taken as another indication of the marginal and potentially impoverished (at least at times) nature of the settlement. Given the marginal environment, it is not surprising that lentils are uncommon at Tell es-Sweyhat (nor are they common in equivalent levels at Tell Hammam et-Turkman in the Balikh Valley: van Zeist, Waterbolk-van Rooijen, and Bottema 1988). However, large samples were recorded from Middle Bronze Age levels at Tell Hadidi (T 548). Whether, however, these Tell Hadidi lentils were locally grown under rain-fed conditions, were irrigated,[81] or were imported from moister areas upstream is unclear.

There is little evidence from the region for post-Bronze Age crop cultivation. At Tell Hadidi (T 548) the Roman period carbonized plant assemblage "did not differ essentially from that of the Bronze Age," namely being hulled barley, free-threshing wheat, lentil, field pea, grass pea, and probably bitter vetch (van Zeist and Bakker-Heeres 1985: 308). In addition, one seed of mulberry (*Morus*) may represent a Roman addition to the domesticated plant community. As for earlier periods, distinct indicators of irrigation were absent, despite the view that canals were in use in the Euphrates Valley from the Roman period (van Zeist and Bakker-Heeres 1985), and that the presence of wine presses (discussed in *Section 5.A: Wine Presses*) also implies that there was valley floor irrigation. Although two internodes of six-row barley were recorded in Roman levels at Tell Hadidi, they are not regarded as sufficient evidence for irrigation.

8.C.2. FAUNAL REMAINS

Two studies have been made of the faunal remains from Tell es-Sweyhat. Each has used different bone assemblages, and each has provided markedly different results. The earlier study on the bone remains from the excavations directed by Thomas Holland, show, as would be expected, a heavy reliance upon animal husbandry, particularly the rearing of sheep and goats (sheep/goat ranged from 66 to 93% of identified bones; Buitenhuis 1983).[82] These ovicaprids are thought to have been reared for both meat and secondary products such as wool and milk. *Bos taurus,* domestic cattle (at 9–12% of the identified bone assemblage), and pig (usually <1%), were of lesser importance. On the other hand, hunted mammals and birds formed only 2.5% of the animal remains. Equids were common, however, attaining some 8.4% of the assemblage during the early Early Bronze Age. Because none of the equid bones showed traces of butchering, and few were burned, Buitenhuis concludes that equids were not eaten but rather were employed for transport. This proposition leads to the attractive conclusion that the equids, particularly the domestic ass (*Equus asinus,* but also perhaps mules), were used as transport animals, and that Tell es-Sweyhat might have been a way-station along some major transport route. The status of some of the *Equus,* such as the wild *Equus hemionus,* remains unclear.

In contrast, Jill Weber's analyses of the more recent excavations directed by Richard Zettler, shows distinct differences. According to the Pennsylvania excavations some 11% of food remains were from wild animals.[83] Furthermore, equids, which appear to have formed a significant amount of the food remains, were primarily wild onager (*E. hermionus*). Significantly, these wild equids attain their maximum percentage when Tell es-Sweyhat was at its largest

---

81. However, I know of no traditional examples of lentil irrigation in the region at present, and Poyck (1962) in his studies of modern agriculture in southern Iraq provides no examples of lentil cultivation in the irrigated zone.

82. This compares with 65% sheep/goat from mid-third millennium B.C. Gritille (Stein 1987), 71% from mid-third millennium B.C. Kurban Höyük (period IV), and 51% from later third/early second millennium B.C. Kurban Höyük (period III: Wattenmaker 1987). Both of these sites are located in significantly moister areas along the Turkish Euphrates River.

83. That is, the number of individual specimens (NISP), but when bone weight is employed this percentage rises to 34% (Weber 1997: 141).

extent, and presumably its population was at its highest (Weber 1997: 141). Tell Hajji Ibrahim (SS 3), by contrast, had a much more typical faunal assemblage, exhibiting an almost 100% reliance on domestic animals. Most of the food would have in fact come from cattle, sheep/goats, and domestic pig (Weber 1997), with a surprisingly large reliance being on the latter, given the rather arid and desolate setting for the site today.

The considerable difference between the two Tell es-Sweyhat assemblages are unlikely to result solely from differences between the two faunal analysts (although some differences, e.g., in the interpretation of the equid remains and butchering marks, might be accounted for in this way). Furthermore, the data that do bear comparison, those from Tell Hajji Ibrahim (SS 3), are from the earlier third millennium B.C., rather than the late. It therefore appears that there were probably marked variations within Tell es-Sweyhat, between different rubbish deposits or activity areas of the site. Such variations have also been noted (albeit not quite as distinct) at Tell Leilan, where "high status" areas on the high mound yielded a fauna rich in sheep/goat bones, with some 22% domestic pig, whereas "low status" areas of the lower town showed much more pig (Zeder 1995).

Such differentiation is not surprising, as is shown by the following example of traditional animal husbandry at the village of Tell Toqaan, south of Aleppo. Sweet (1974: 89–90) demonstrates that in this village, two basic classes of animal husbandry existed. A "peasant group" depended upon working animals for power, that is, for plowing, operating irrigation wheels, threshing, and carrying grain to market. These working animals consisted of cattle and oxen, the non-descript village horse, donkeys, mules, and camels. In addition, there were dogs and cats, as well as small household flocks of sheep and goats. The pastoralist sector, on the other hand, comprised mobile pastoralists who depended mainly upon sheep (and a few goats) for subsistence and surplus, and traditionally upon camels for transport. Peasant work animals needed grass of higher quality and more green fodder than sheep, goats, and camels, and they did not graze on the stubble of fallow fields (ibid., p. 96). Having been attached to the village for much of the year, most pastoralists then started to move east towards the pastoral reserves at the beginning of autumn rains. In recent years, however, expansion of cultivation has reduced open pasturage and fewer pastoralists move east, and then not until the spring.

Therefore, in the context of Tell es-Sweyhat, the Tell Toqaan model suggests that first we might expect to see a local sedentary householder economy based upon the peasant group of animals. These animals would also include pig (not of course present in traditional Islamic villages) and comprise a core of animals for traction, probably oxen, but perhaps equids. In addition to having their own small flocks of sheep, families with significant links with nomadic pastoralists would then perhaps have more sheep, and some families may only have resided within the town for part of the year, being out on the steppe for the remainder of the year. Such families would therefore bring their large flocks with them or would have pastured them in the area. Even today, one or two families in Nafileh are temporary residents, moving in to village houses for part of the year, in this case from villages farther away on the steppe to the northeast. To this dual economy it appears that we should also add in this marginal location a significant hunting element that would result in wild animals being brought to the settlement. Whether the bones of wild animals resulted from local families going out and hunting on the steppe or the riverine plains or were a result of trade with nomadic pastoralists cannot be determined.

8.C.3. CONCLUSIONS

Putting the data from the aceramic Neolithic Euphrates sites with those from ceramic Neolithic, Halaf, and later sites around Sabi Abyad, we get a distinct impression of a more verdant Early Holocene environment, with a more diversified plant economy, more trees (in the earliest period at Jerf al-Ahmar [T 559]), and probably a moister climate. The tree cover as inferred by Willcox (1996) can be compared with the models of Hillman (2000) that show the possible forest distribution at around 9000 B.C. (uncalibrated). These place Tell es-Sweyhat and Jerf al-Ahmar close to the boundary between forest and woodland and oak-pistachio park woodland, with pistachio-almond woodland steppe extending across the entire Balikh Valley and much of the Jazirah (Hillman 1996, fig. 10.10b).[84] In the Syrian Balikh Valley, by the Halaf period, the plant economy appears to have been dominated by wheat, which itself then retreats

---

84. Hillman reconstructs a dense woodland (including montane forest, eu-Mediterranean sclerophyllous woodland, and xeric deciduous oak Rosaceae woodland) over the area of the Turkish Euphrates Valley north of Carchemish to include the area of the Karababa Dam. The area of Tell es-Sweyhat, Jerf al-Ahmar (T 559), and the bend of the Euphrates River would be oak-tere-binth-Rosaceae park woodland, that is, a mosaic of woodland and open areas dominated by annual grasses. It is also likely to have been an area endowed with extensive stands of wild cereals. For detailed estimates of the vegetation of the region, see Hillman's (2000) reconstructions.

from the record, becoming less than 10% during the Early and Middle Bronze Age. This decrease in wheat, with a commensurate increase in barley, may not simply be the result of a climatic shift; rather it appears that during the Middle Holocene there was some drying of the regional climate, as well as a significant degradation of the vegetation and a reduction of woody plants. In terms of the local subsistence economies it appears that there has been a progressive narrowing of the range of cropping opportunities, so that by the late third millennium B.C. the economy was focused more on the production of cereals, specifically barley. This focus on grain production might, in part, be accounted for by the extension of cultivation to the drier terraces and steppelands farther away from the river that would have required a shift towards the use of the more drought-tolerant barley.

Clearly by the Early and Middle Bronze Age, both in the Balikh Valley at Tell Hammam et-Turkman and at Tell es-Sweyhat/Tell Hadidi (T 548), there had been a significant shift towards not only cereal cultivation, but cereal cultivation dominated by barley. This shift is in line with the contemporary land use that again is dominated by barley cultivation. The high proportion of seeds of steppe plants suggests that dung was being used as fuel (which is confirmed by the recognition during excavation of carbonized dung pellets at Tell Jouweif [SS 8]) and that there was little wood remaining in the areas for use as fuel (*Section 8.B: Flotation Samples from the 1992 Excavations at Tell Jouweif;* Miller 1997a–b). Furthermore, the higher quantities of grass seeds from Tell Hajji Ibrahim (SS 3) suggests that the steppe was relatively less degraded during the first half of the third millennium B.C. Then, by the time Tell es-Sweyhat attained its maximum size during the final quarter of the millennium, the grass steppe had become somewhat degraded.[85] All the plant remains underscore a marginal environment, in which the pastoral component was significant. Irrigation was not practiced and the traditional dry-farmed barley was probably used both as human food and fodder for animals. In addition, Miller's work (herein and 1997a–b) demonstrates that the flocks probably grazed to a significant degree on the outlying steppe. From the presence of a significant amount of wild animals, we can also conclude that some households at least were acquiring wild animals, either by hunting or by trade with communities that did hunt. Whether the site had a significantly large equid population engaged in transport (and perhaps trade) remains an attractive, albeit unproven, proposition. The significance of these various features to the local economy is elaborated in *Section 9: Tell es-Sweyhat in Its Regional Context.*

---

85. In general, heavy grazing can eliminate both annual and perennial grasses, although there are contradictions to this in the literature (Hillman 1996, n. 7). Note that McCorriston (1992) has also observed significant degradation of the environment of the Khabur Valley by the Halaf period.

9. TELL ES-SWEYHAT IN ITS REGIONAL CONTEXT

There are few synthetic studies of the archaeology of Syria, and in order to perceive general patterns of development, it is usually necessary to wade through detailed and often preliminary reports on excavations. The upper Lake Assad area is no exception, and therefore in order to place Tell es-Sweyhat within its regional setting, basic data on sites from the area between Selenkahiye (T 507) and al-Qitar (fig. 9.1) have been compiled by Clemens Reichel (*Appendix B: Site Gazetteer*). These data are synthesized here in order to provide an overview of settlement changes through the Holocene. A general discussion of interactions between environmental conditions, historical developments, and the political economy of the region follows.

But first it is necessary to draw together the strands of the field evidence that enable a tentative reconstruction of the local agricultural landscape in the area of third millennium B.C. Tell es-Sweyhat.

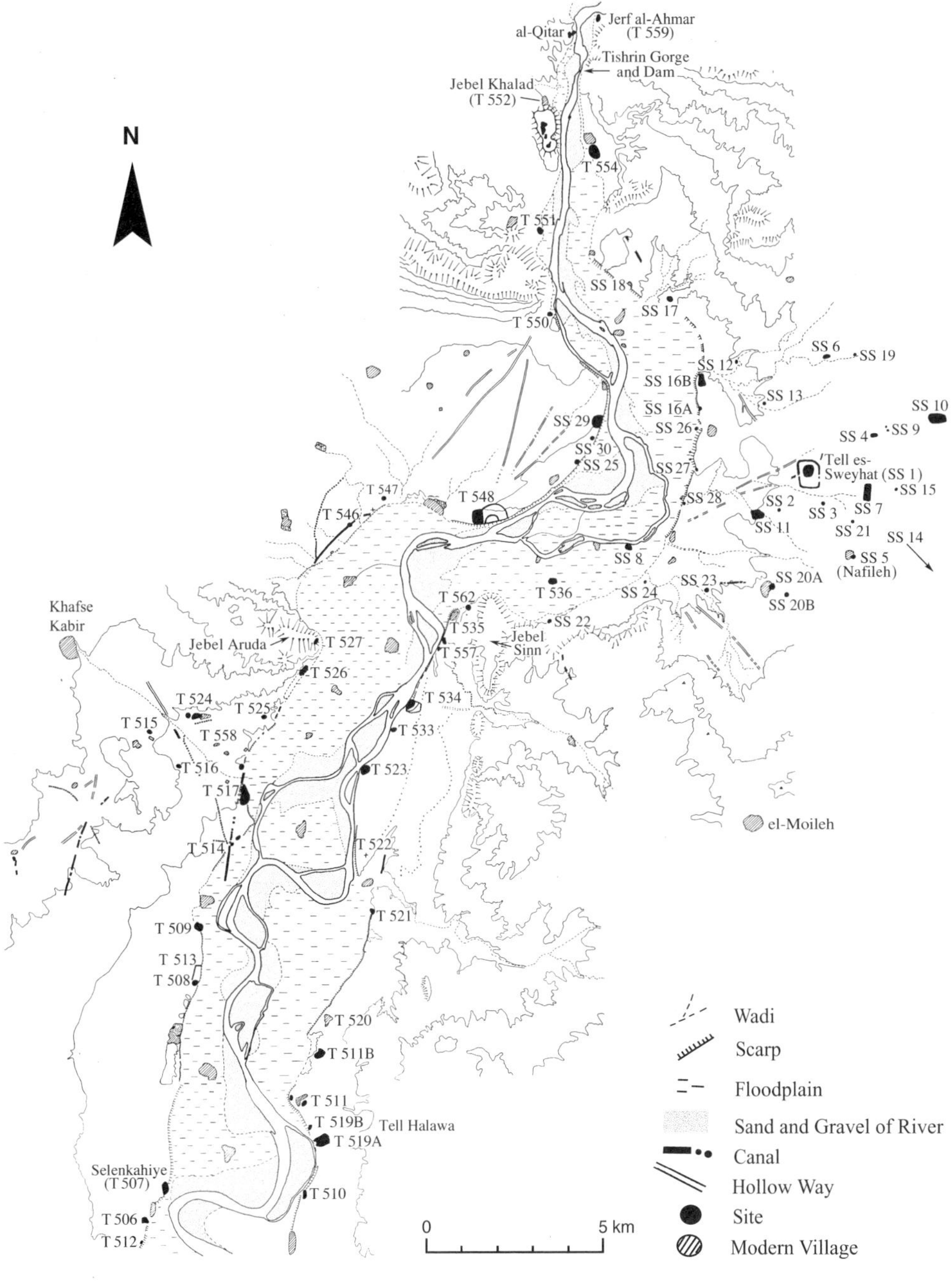

Figure 9.1. Archaeological Sites in the Upper Lake Assad Area

171

9.A. THE LANDSCAPE AND ECONOMY OF TELL ES-SWEYHAT
IN THE LATE THIRD MILLENNIUM B.C.

Using evidence drawn from *Sections 4* and *8,* as well as information published from campaigns at Tell es-Sweyhat by Zettler (1997), it is now possible to attempt a general reconstruction of the landscape for the period when Tell es-Sweyhat attained its maximum size during the last quarter of the third millennium B.C. These land use zones (Zones *1–6*) are indicated in figure 9.2 (see also accompanying caption).

Zone 1

Off-site sherd scatters[86] suggest that Zone *1* was intensively cultivated land that received significant inputs of manure probably in the form of organic waste from the site (*Section 2: The Physical Environment*). As is traditional practice in much of the Middle East today, the compost applied probably included ash from the household middens. According to Miller (1997b), the main crops were probably barley, small amounts of wheat, and perhaps some legumes. Zone *1*, extending some 2–3 km from the site, might have been cultivated every second year, thereby allowing a year for the land to recuperate and to accumulate a small reserve of moisture. Alternatively, increased applications of manure would have allowed for annual crop cultivation to take place. This would have been at the expense of crop stability, however, because effective soil moisture would have been slightly less as a result of violation of fallow which would have lessened the carry-over of soil moisture from the fallow year.

Zone 2

Zone *2* is situated between Zone *1* and the limit of the sustaining area of Tell es-Sweyhat, which is estimated to be in the range of 4.4 to 6.3 km radius from the site.[87] Zone *2* was probably mainly devoted to low intensity cultivation with perhaps some open land for pasture. In this area fields may have stood fallow for extended periods, as in the outer areas of the Aşvan village territory (cf. Hillman 1973a: 227).

Zones 3 and 4

There is little to distinguish Zone *2* from Zone *3*, except that the latter extended to rolling ground to the southwest of Tell es-Sweyhat and also on to the lower colluvial and gravel fan slopes at the foot of the escarpment. Zone *3* probably represented an inner zone of long-term steppe pasture that would have been available for grazing year round. It then merged into the outer pasture zone via a transition zone today represented by rocky slopes of the fringing escarpment. Zones *3* and *4* were probably the steppelands that were used as pasture for the flocks that grazed on steppe plants such as the legumes *Trigonella* and *Astragalus* recorded in the carbonized plant remains from Tell es-Sweyhat (Miller 1997b: 102).

Zone 5

Zone *5* is the riverine zone described in *Section 2.B: The Euphrates Terraces*. This would have consisted of a varied ecosystem of pasture, riparian brushwood or woodland, with perhaps the addition of rain-fed and flood-irrigated cultivation. Flood irrigation, if practiced, however, may simply have been used for certain types of legumes as noted by d'Hont (1994) for the Middle Euphrates Valley. There is no reason to assume that all of Zone *5* would have been under the control of the inhabitants of Tell es-Sweyhat; rather it was probably shared with Tell Hadidi and also used by inhabitants of small sites located either on the floodplain itself or on the adjacent terrace bluffs (e.g., SS 24 and SS 27). The fallow deer recorded from Tell es-Sweyhat may have lived within the riparian woodland of this zone, which, according to the small samples of charcoal from Tell Jouweif (SS 8) and Tell es-Sweyhat may have been willow/poplar and tamarisk (*Section 8: The Ancient Agricultural Economy*).

---

86.   Defined as the second, third, and fourth quartiles of field scatters mapped in figure 4.1.

87.   Calculated as the amount of land that could support the estimated population of the 31 ha site assuming a population of 100 persons per site ha. Alternatively this area could extend to 6.3 km distance if the site had been occupied by 200 persons per occupied ha. I have not included estimates for the area of the southern extension of the site, but inclusion of population estimates for this area might compensate for some of the spaces in the lower town occupation. The larger sustaining area estimate, being based on an assumed dense occupation of the lower town, however, seems unlikely because recent geophysical prospections coupled with control excavations suggest that the lower town was not densely occupied but instead may have included areas of open space (see Peregrine et al. 1997: 80–81)

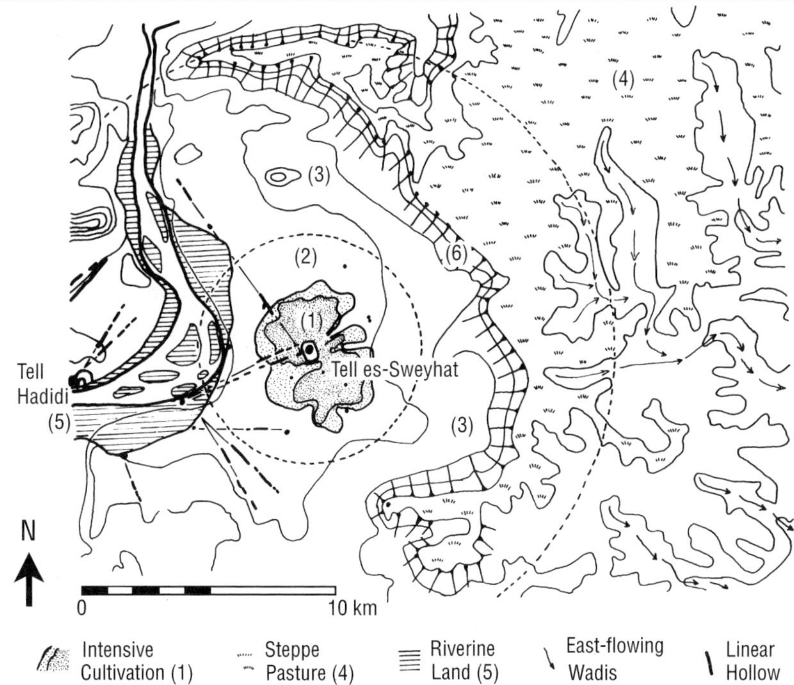

Zone 1	Intensive cultivation that had received frequent application of fertilizers as indicated by field scatters; perhaps under annual cultivation during some periods. Between 0 and 3 km from Tell es-Sweyhat. Mainly on deep reddish calcareous loams.
Zone 2	Low intensity cultivation and fallow. Negligible field scatters. Between the limit of Zone 1 and approximately 4.4 km from the site. Combination of deep calcareous loams and gentle stony colluvial slopes.
Zone 3	Probably under fallow or low intensity cultivation. Also includes inner pastoral zone. Roughly 4.4 to 8.0 km from site depending upon topography; mainly confined to the north, east, and south of the site. Zone 3 occupies rolling terrain with thin soils, stony colluvial slopes, and gravel fans issuing from plateau. Steppe legumes in the carbonized plant remains at Tell es-Sweyhat probably came from Zones 3 and 4.
Zone 4	Upland steppe pasture. Outer pastoral zone. On limestone plateau and usually >8 km from the site. Steppe legumes in the carbonized plant remains at Tell es-Sweyhat probably came from Zones 3 and 4. Zone 4 may have been the zone where onager and gazelle were hunted.
Zone 5	Riparian zone of Euphrates floodplain. Floodplain cultivation, pasture, and brushwood. In recent past some of this cultivation was devoted to flood irrigated legumes such as lubiya (beans), and it is likely that this land would have been ideal for legumes in the past. Mainly deep silt/clay soils of floodplain, including all levels of floodplain described in *Section 2.B.2: The Alluvial Floodplain*. Note that this land must have been within the territories of several sites, located both on the Pleistocene terrace and on the higher floodplain. Probably some fallow deer lived in gallery woodland of willow/poplar and tamarisk.
Zone 6	Steep scarp slopes and other pasture land, including dry wadis draining the plateau. Zone 6 is probably where onager and gazelle were hunted. Zones 4 and 6 form a single landscape complex, with Zone 6 being more eroded than Zone 4.

Basis for Estimated Sustaining Areas

Tell es-Sweyhat and the lower town are assumed to have been occupied over a total area of 31 ha only. Assuming a staple food requirement of 250 kg per person, allowing for seed etc. and normal surplus, 1 ha would supply requirements for one person, but to allow for fallow, this area would be cultivated only every second year. Assuming an on-site population of 100 persons per ha, the radius of the sustaining area would be 4.4 km; if 200 persons per ha, 6.2 km.

Figure 9.2. Reconstruction of Land Use Zones around Late Early Bronze Age Tell es-Sweyhat

Zone 6

Finally, merging into Zones *3* and *4*, is a miscellaneous steppe/pasture zone that includes east-draining dry wadis. This area would probably have been used as supplementary grazing and also might have been inhabited by flocks of onager (*Equus hemiones*) and gazelle (*Gazella*) that were apparently hunted in large amounts by the inhabitants of Tell es-Sweyhat (Weber 1997: 136–38).

It is now evident from carbonized plant remains, animal bones, and the land use map (fig. 9.2) that Tell es-Sweyhat was presumably supported by a mixed farming economy which comprised both intensive cultivation on the deeper more fertile soils around the site and extensive outer zones of low intensity cultivation and/or pasture beyond. The site was virtually surrounded to the northwest, north, east, and south by high steppelands that would have constrained the extension of cultivated land but would have been available for grazing and hunting. In terms of area alone such pastures would have been significantly more extensive than the inner cultivated zone. Although the outer zones as reconstructed are quite speculative, the model demonstrates that the important bioarchaeological analyses of Miller (1997a) and Weber (1997) can be readily incorporated into a general mixed farming model which also supports the interpretations of Danti and Zettler (1998) that the site had a significant reliance on wild and pastoral resources.

However, Danti's model for Early Bronze Age land use emphasizes that despite the extensive area of surrounding steppe, a basic constraint on pastoral production would have been the availability of fodder for supplementary feeding in late winter and early spring in the form of crop residues and barley (Danti 2000: 39–40). This practice would therefore have made considerable inroads into available cereal supplies that would not only have been required for human food but also would have been needed to make straw temper for mudbrick. A necessary result of any increase in population and an expansion of the agro-pastoral system would be the expansion of barley production (in the form of annual cropping of barley) and an increase in rates of stocking on the surrounding steppe rangeland (i.e., Zones *3, 4,* and *6*; see Danti 2000: 310). Such an expansion would have had a twofold effect. First, the demand for cereals would have been significantly higher than that posited in the original land use model (Wilkinson 1994, fig. 9.3). An increase in animals would, in turn, increase the demand for animal feed and would have increased the need for the intensification

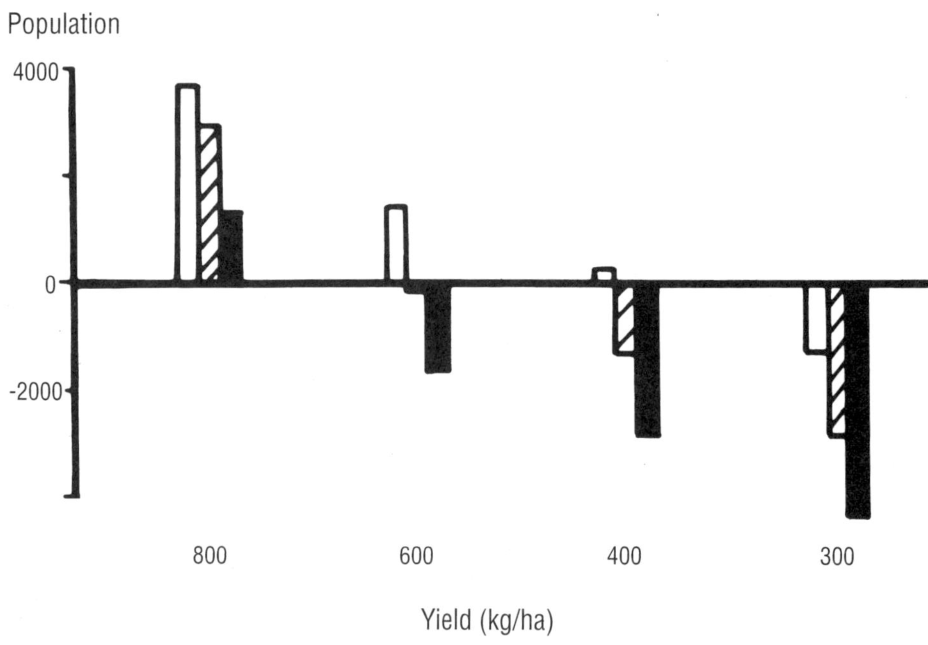

Figure 9.3. Surplus and Deficit Production for a 4 km Cultivated Catchment around Tell es-Sweyhat Assuming Different Levels of On-site Population and Variations in Crop Yield from 300 to 800 kg per ha. Population Densities Are: White Bars = 100 Persons per ha; Hatched Bars = 150 Persons per ha; and Black Bars = 200 Persons per ha. High Yields (e.g., 800 kg per Cultivated ha) Are Assumed to Take Place Mainly during Moister Years and Lower Yields (e.g., 300 kg per Cultivated ha) during Dry Years (from Wilkinson 1994, fig. 15)

Table 9.1. Sweyhat Settlement Area Data

Sweyhat Survey Period = Cultural Period	*Occupied Sites (SS Sites)*	*Area Per Site (ha)*	*Total Area (ha)*	*Mean Area (ha)*
I = Halaf	—	—	—	—
II = Ubaid	SS 30	0.5	0.50	0.50
III = Late Chalcolithic	SS 25	0.5	0.50	0.50
IV = Uruk	—	—	—	—
V = Early Early Bronze Age	SS 1, 2, 3, 8, 9, 13, 14, 19, 20A, 21, 22A	6.0*, 0.3, 0.2, 0.85*, 0.2, 0.2, 0.05, 0.2, 0.4, 0.6, 0.5	9.5	0.86
VI = Mid-/Late Early Bronze Age	SS 1, 3, 5, 8, 20A, 22B–D	15.0*, 0.2, 0.4, 1.7, 1.8, 0.5	17.90	2.98
VII = Late Early Bronze Age	SS 1, 5, 8, 24, 27	31.0, 0.4, 1.7, 0.2, 0.4	33.70	6.74
VIII = Middle Bronze Age	SS 1, 8, 17, 24, 27	6.0, 1.7, 3.0, 0.2, 0.4	11.30	2.26
IX = Late Bronze Age	SS 17	3.0	3.00	3.00
X = Iron Age	SS 6A–D, 15, 16B, 17, 20B, 23, 26	0.7, 0.4, 7.5, 1.5*, 0.6, 0.5, 0.7	11.90	1.70
XI = Hellenistic	SS 1, 6A–D, 16C, 18, 26	3.0*, 0.7, 3.75*, 0.5, 0.7	8.65	1.73
XII = Roman	SS 1, 10, 26, 29	3.0*, 10.0, 0.7, 5.0	18.70	4.68
XIII = Late Roman/Early Byzantine	SS 1, 4, 6E, 10, 16A, 26, 29	3.0*, 1.0, 0.35, 10.0, 0.5, 0.7, 5.0	20.55	2.94
XIV = Early Islamic	SS 7, 11, 12, 16A	5.0, 9.0, 0.8, 0.5	15.30	3.83
XV = Middle Islamic	SS 28	0.4	0.40	0.40

* Partial site area used for period. For example, area of Tell es-Sweyhat in Sweyhat Survey Periods V, VI, and VII taken as 6 ha, 15 ha, and 31 ha, respectively.

of cereal production that could potentially constrain the amount of food available for human consumption. Second, there would have been a tendency to overgraze the surrounding steppelands, which would have resulted in severe degradation of the plant cover, which in turn may have contributed to soil erosion (Danti 2000: 65). Although the mid-third millennium B.C. settlement at Tell es-Sweyhat (Sweyhat Survey Period VI: estimated to occupy some 15 ha) would have been comfortably supported by the available cultivable land and pasture, the expansion that occurred in the late third millennium B.C. (Sweyhat Survey Period VII) would have severely constrained the availability of surplus cereal. This strain on the food supply would have encouraged the adoption of annual cropping and therefore could have moved the system toward a state of greater instability so that there would have been a greater likelihood of crop failure during drier years, even more so than in the original model (Wilkinson 1994). As a result, only if on-site population densities were low (ca. 100 persons per hectare; white bars in fig. 9.3) would there have been sufficient production to supply the inhabitants of the town, but even then only in wet or normal years.

The above summary analysis underscores the marginal nature of the Tell es-Sweyhat economy. Even though the wider steppe to the east between the Euphrates and the Balikh Valleys beyond would have been potentially available as pasture land, this land could only have been utilized if there were some degree of mobility of the population. Such mobility would have entailed part of the community being absent for long periods of time with a commensurate decrease in population at Tell es-Sweyhat itself as well as perhaps social cohesion. Nevertheless, the availability of such open land provides a marked contrast with areas of northern Iraq and northeast Syria (e.g., around Tells al-Hawa and Hamoukar) where in the third millennium B.C. grazing land was in much shorter supply (Wilkinson 2000b, fig. 3).

9.B. LONG-TERM TRENDS IN SETTLEMENT

A major problem for the interpretation of the settlement record along much of the Syrian Euphrates River is that an unknown part of the archaeological record is either missing or is archaeologically invisible. To allow for this problem the archaeological record of the area is subdivided into three broad zones:

Zone *a*   Sedentary settlement on the main Euphrates terraces. Virtually all of the Sweyhat Survey sites (*Appendix A: Sweyhat Survey Site Catalog*) fall within this zone that also includes the boundary between the floodplain and the fringing bluffs as well as the Pleistocene terrace itself. Zone *a* contains the archaeologically visible and potentially quantifiable part of the archaeological record.

Zone *b*   Areas of the floodplain that probably formerly housed sedentary settlements which have since been eroded by the active channel of the Euphrates River (see *Section 2: The Physical Environment*). This zone includes rare residuals of ancient floodplain that have remained un-eroded over the millennia. Such a relict floodplain can be postulated to have existed, first from the residuals of ancient floodplain such as that upon which Tell Jouweif (SS 8) rests (see *Section 8: The Ancient Agricultural Economy*), and secondly from the distribution of traditional villages (fig. 2.4). The latter distribution demonstrates that the part of the floodplain zone above flood level represents a logical and desirable locus for settlement. However, because the ancient floodplain has been almost entirely lost as a result of riverine erosion (particularly the mega-floods demonstrated by Tipping [in Peltenburg et al. 1997] at Jerablus Tahtani; see *Section 2: The Physical Environment*), the former existence of settlements within it can only be hypothesized.[88]

Zone *c*   The area of terrace and neighboring steppe "behind" Zone *a*. This zone was probably occupied or used by nomads to varying degrees in the past. Such nomadic groups would presumably camp on the terraces or floodplain and bring their flocks to water along the river (d'Hont 1994; Matthews 1978) or to watering holes inland (Danti 1997: 92). These steppe areas would then presumably have become the long-term seasonal territory of many tribes. At times of dense sedentary settlement on the terraces, there would have been restricted space for the nomads and their herds. However, because long-term links between the nomadic and sedentary groups were often strong and connected by family or tribal lineages, one can imagine that there was considerable interaction between the sedentary and nomadic groups. The traces of nomadic groups are more subtle and difficult to date than those of sedentary communities, especially because all traces of their sites have frequently been removed by modern plowing (Hole 1991; see Cribb 1991 for archaeological evidence for nomadic groups). Nevertheless, Danti's recognition of a zone of agro-pastoral activity in the steppe to the east of Tell es-Sweyhat, as well as the presence of a slight Early Bronze Age settlement at SS 14 on the bluff southeast of Tell es-Sweyhat suggest that nomadic groups may therefore have formed a potentially large but only hazily visible presence in the population record (Danti 2000; Danti and Zettler 1998). In addition, occasional sparse scatters of coarse chaff-tempered pottery both along the Wadi Nafileh and at smaller sites such as SS 13 and Khirbet Aboud al-Hazu 2 (SS 19) could be the remains of Late Chalcolithic camps. Unfortunately, at present such fragmentary and ephemeral traces are difficult to diagnose, either chronologically or functionally.

Because the settlement record along the Euphrates Valley may be underrepresented as a result of the problems noted above, any attempt to produce long-term population estimates based on aggregate site area per period should be treated with caution. Bearing this caution in mind, figure 9.4 provides a general estimate of long-term settlement for

---

88.   Such loss of the floodplain and associated settlements may explain why large Bronze Age cemeteries such as those at Tawi (between T 521 and T 522 in figure 9.1) remain without any nearby contemporaneous settlement remains. If these were not the cemeteries of mobile pastoralists (itself, of course, a possibility), they may well have been the burial grounds of communities that resided on parts of the floodplain that have since been eroded away.

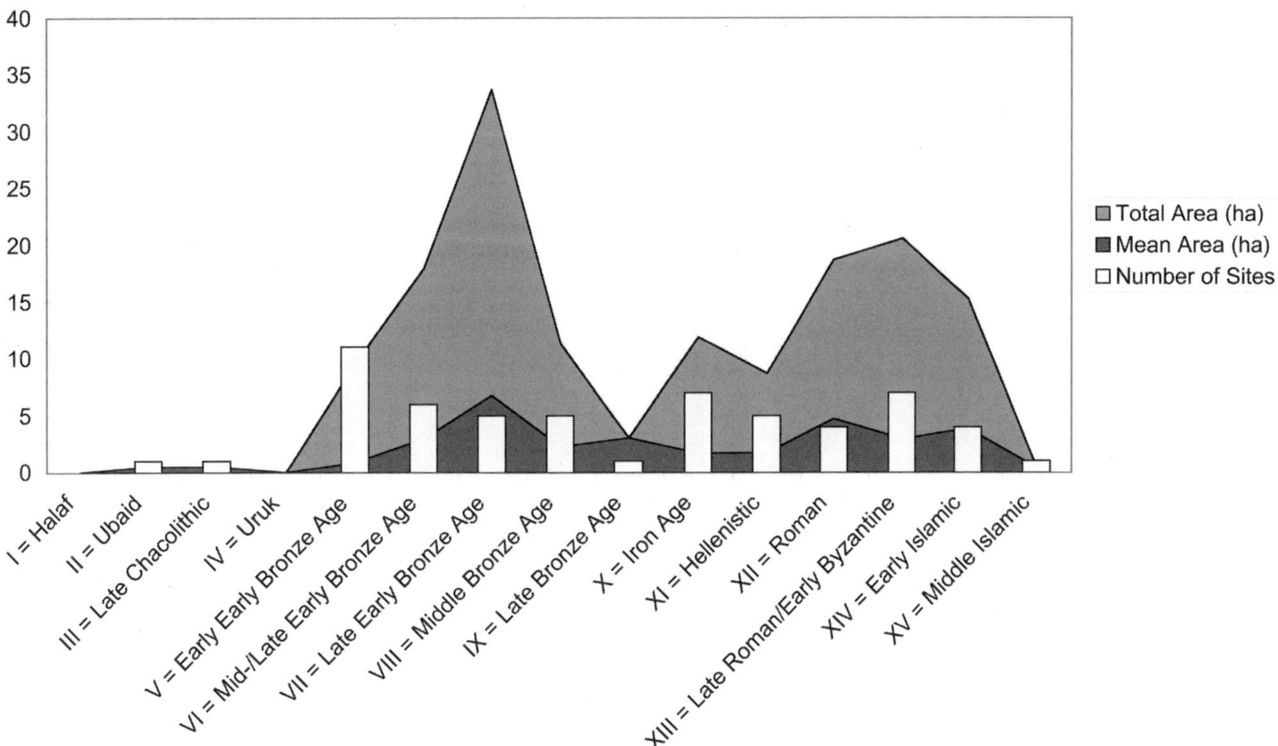

Figure 9.4. Aggregate Settlement Area, Mean Area, and Number of Sites for the Area of the Sweyhat Survey
(Data from Table 9.1; see *Appendix A: Sweyhat Survey Site Catalog*)

the area of the Sweyhat Survey (i.e., for SS 1–30; see fig. 7.1) in terms of: (a) The number of sites and (b) aggregate settlement area (in ha) for all sites according to the ceramic period. Because Tell es-Sweyhat is by far the largest site, it dominates the record for certain periods. As a result, although the quantity of sites attains a peak in the early third millennium B.C., both aggregate settlement area and mean site area peak in Sweyhat Survey Period VII (table 9.1; i.e., during the later EBA or EB/MB transition). There is evidence for a settlement decline in the Middle Bronze Age (Sweyhat Survey Period VIII), although this decline is not necessarily the case for the Lake Assad region in general (see below), so that settlement apparently reached its minimum during the Late Bronze Age (Sweyhat Survey Period IX). Thereafter a significant rise in the number of sites occurred during the Iron Age (Sweyhat Survey Period X), although mean site size at this time was only in the region of 1–2 ha. In general, during the first millennia B.C. and A.D., the population of the Sweyhat survey area was relatively large but fluctuating, and not as high as during the second half of the third millennium B.C. The fluctuations indicated in figure 9.4 for the period after 1000 B.C. may in part result from uncertainties in the ceramic types diagnostic of the specific periods (e.g., Hellenistic and Roman) that may result in greater weight being given to one period rather than another. Therefore, this long period may best be regarded as a broad phase during which the Tell es-Sweyhat area was settled by a significant population that lived in some four to six small, dispersed, and rather straggling villages. Settlement then plummeted at the end of the Early Islamic period (Sweyhat Survey Period XIV), that is, during the Middle Islamic period, after which the plain was abandoned.

To provide a broader picture of settlement for the upper Lake Assad area, the number of sites is simply plotted according to ceramic phase.[89] Because a small number of large sites can accommodate a much larger population than a large number of small sites (see, e.g., fig. 9.4; Wilkinson and Tucker 1995, fig. 50), these data cannot be used as a proxy for the number of inhabitants in the area. The data provide an impression of the amount of sedentary settlement, in this case that which occurs on terraces fringing the floodplain. Settlement trends based on the number of sites provide a mixed signal; for example, the presence of few sites means that either sedentary settlement was limited or was confined to a few large nucleated communities (in which case it is noted). Conversely, a large number of sites implies either that there was much sedentary settlement or that settlement was in the form of numerous small dispersed sites.

---

89. Here the quantity of sites occupied per period is broken down into those sites where the evidence is in the form of excavated levels, and those where the evidence is in the form of surface remains or artifacts that are out of context.

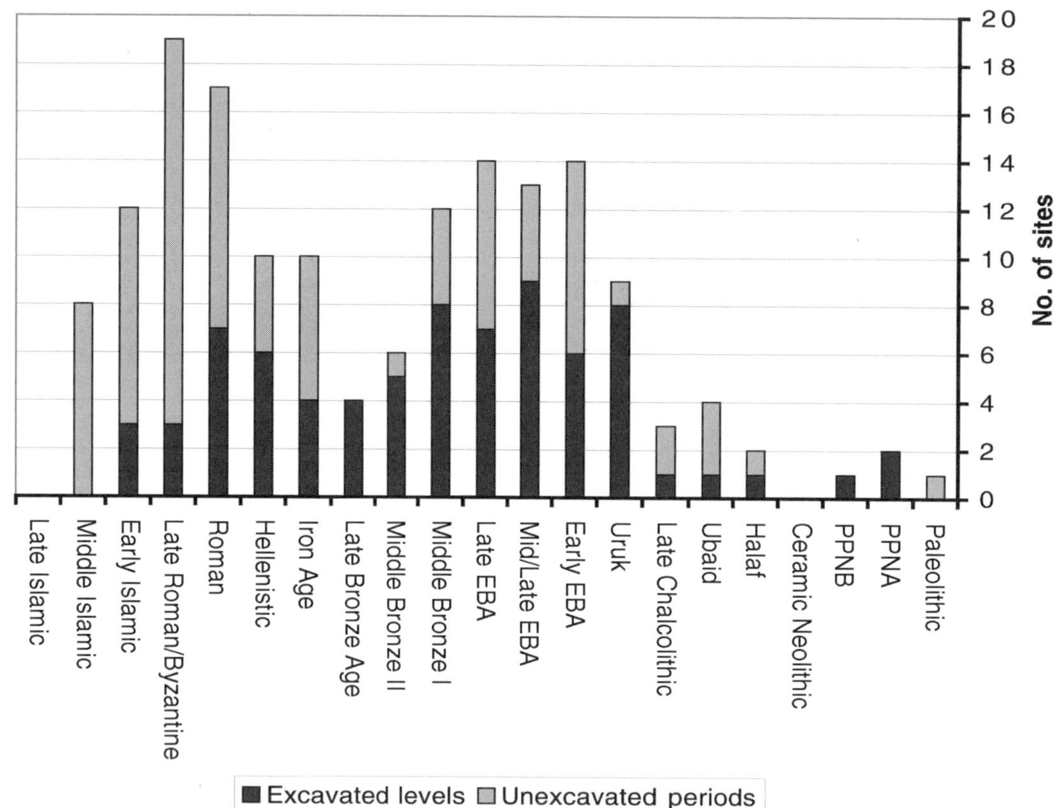

Figure 9.5. Number of Sites according to Ceramic Period for the Sweyhat Survey and Upper Lake Assad Areas Combined. Compiled from *Appendix A: Sweyhat Survey Site Catalog* and *Appendix B: Site Gazetteer*, Respectively

Finally, during those periods when the fringing Pleistocene terraces were almost devoid of archaeological sites, one may infer that sedentary settlement was virtually absent, was confined to the floodplain, or that nomadic populations were substantial. The following eight settlement phases are recognizable for the area of the upper Lake Assad (fig. 9.5).[90]

PHASE 1

During the Upper Paleolithic to Late Chalcolithic periods few settlements were on the Pleistocene terraces. Of these, most Upper Paleolithic and Neolithic sites were situated around the major bend in the Euphrates River at Mureybit (T 502–504), Abu Hureyra (T 545), and Dibsi Faraj East 1 (T 542) and are therefore not dealt with herein. Some settlements may also have existed on the floodplain but are now lost.[91] This latter zone would have provided a verdant environment, albeit one in which the annual flood (in the spring) would have come at a difficult time for irrigation. Nevertheless, prehistoric settlements on the floodplain could have engaged in opportunistic flood recession agriculture.

---

90. Plotted according to those sites recorded in the upper Lake Assad area (i.e., the sites recorded in *Appendix B: Site Gazetteer*), combined with sites recorded in the Sweyhat Survey (i.e., the sites in *Appendix A: Sweyhat Survey Site Catalog*).

91. It is possible that during the aceramic Neolithic, the early Holocene Euphrates River flowed along a dynamic and mobile braided channel, which would have deterred humans from settling the floodplain. As a result, sedentary settlement may have been forced to take place on the adjacent Pleistocene terraces. Then, with the development of a more stable floodplain during the later phases of the Neolithic and the Chalcolithic, sedentary settlement might have occurred on the floodplain with the result that settlements could have abandoned the terraces and moved on to the floodplain only to have been removed by subsequent erosion. Of relevance here is the presence of a single Neolithic lug handle from SS 26 on the edge of the floodplain (*Section 6: The Ceramic Sequence from Surveyed Sites*). In a similar vein, Akkermans (1999) convincingly argues that either riverine deposition or erosion has resulted in the loss of many prehistoric sites along the Euphrates Valley compared with the less dynamic Balikh River.

PHASE 2

During the Uruk period a major phase of settlement occurred in the area of Habuba Kabira South (T 513), Jebel Aruda (T 527), and Sheikh Hassan (T 523) (the so-called "Uruk triangle"; fig. 9.6). This development, which is similar to that of another enclave near Carchemish (Algaze, Breuninger, and Knutstad 1994: 10–12), occurred on the main river terrace in an area that would have been both on the margins of the floodplain and on the geographical margin of dry farming. To date, one of the few Late Chalcolithic sites recorded is SS 25, situated on the west bank of the main Euphrates terrace (figs. 7.2, 9.1). SS 25, however, is fairly early in the Late Chalcolithic sequence and probably predates the main phase of local Late Chalcolithic occupation at Haci Nebi Tepe (Stein 1999). If there had been a local Late Chalcolithic population on the floodplain at this time, the southern Uruk occupation would therefore represent a "break-out phase" during which a second tier of settlement was established away from and above the floodplain on the Pleistocene terrace. During what may have been slightly wetter conditions during the fourth millennium B.C., rain-fed cultivation was feasible, although risky, on the surrounding Pleistocene terraces so that the Uruk/Late Chalcolithic settlement system may have been agriculturally self-sufficient. The presence of Amuq F chaff-faced storage jars within Habuba Kabira South, together with an absence of agricultural tools, has led Sürenhagen to conclude that this site of some 6,000–8,000 people was dependent upon supply from local Late Chalcolithic communities (Sürenhagen 1986: 21–23). Although Sürenhagen infers that such supplier communities were on the extensive plains stretching to the west towards the Jabbul Plain, surveys around Umm al-Marra suggest that Late Chalcolithic settlements were limited in number. That is, thirteen Late Chalcolithic sites were identified, and none of southern Uruk type, compared with forty-seven of the mid-/late Early Bronze Age (Schwartz et al. 2000: 449–50). Overall it seems unlikely that the Jabbul Plain can have been the food supply zone for the Uruk sites in the Lake Assad area (G. Schwartz, pers. comm., December 1997). Alternatively, therefore, the above model suggests that communities on the floodplain could also have existed at this time and could have provided agricultural staples for Uruk settlements located on the terraces and limestone high points.[92] This model is dismissed by Schwartz (2001b: 259–60) who argues that the Uruk colonies of Habuba Kabira and Jebel Aruda developed because the region around the bend of the Euphrates River was relatively vacant for settlement at the time in contrast with the more densely populated areas in eastern Syria. Given, however, the significant amount of settlement loss that has probably occurred due to riverine deposit and erosion, this argument is founded on an imperfect database.

The location of Habuba Kabira South (T 513) at the southern edge of the rain-fed farming zone forms a classic position for a "gateway community" (Algaze 1993: 61–63; Lupton 1996: 56; after Burghardt 1971). Habuba Kabira South and its adjacent settlements would therefore have been ideally positioned to benefit from exchange between any nomadic groups that might have existed at this time, and sedentary "local Late Chalcolithic" communities that existed to the north (perhaps again on the floodplain). Furthermore, Habuba Kabira South occupies a position where traffic from the eastern Jazirah crossing the Euphrates River would then have struck across the Jabbul/Aleppo Plain. This traffic may have provided an additional reason for its growth. Thus the spectacular growth of this concentration of southern Uruk communities may be ascribed to the combined location advantages of a gateway community and a Euphrates River crossing point on a major east–west route.

PHASE 3

Collapse of the Uruk colonies around Habuba Kabira (T 509/513) was followed by a phase in which small early Early Bronze Age settlements became dispersed across the main Euphrates terrace around Tell es-Sweyhat. Radiocarbon dates from Tell Hajji Ibrahim (SS 3) suggest that settlement commenced roughly at the time of the later phases of Uruk settlement (albeit associated with a rather different ceramic assemblage); therefore, this early Early Bronze Age phase of dispersal can be seen to be contemporary with, or to have followed on immediately after, the collapse of southern Uruk type settlements without a discernible gap (Danti 2000, table 5.1).

The early Early Bronze Age settlements (i.e., Sweyhat Survey Period V), which were particularly conspicuous on the plain around Tell es-Sweyhat, were not simply villages or farmsteads but may have functioned as specialized places apparently used for storage and processing of grain, perhaps for local pastoral communities (Danti 1997; Danti and Zettler 1998: 224). The frequent but small sites of this period may not therefore have housed a particularly large number of people, and overall this phase may represent a slight trough in sedentary population between the more popu-

---

92. It should be emphasized, however, that such an argument from silence should be treated with caution. I am not saying that floodplain settlements necessarily existed at any time of the archaeological record. Rather, they may or even probably did exist and to ignore their potential existence could be misleading.

lated phases of the Uruk period and the mid-/late third millennium B.C. However, the presence of a substantial occupation at Tell Hadidi testifies to the existence of some form of settlement hierarchy during the early third millennium B.C.

PHASE 4

Following collapse, decline, or withdrawal of the Uruk period sites and the establishment and dispersal of early Early Bronze Age communities away from them, a large number of nucleated settlements grew up throughout the upper Lake Assad area, mainly on the Pleistocene terraces, but also on parts of the floodplain. The steep slopes of their prominent tells suggest that they were surrounded and constrained by defensive walls such as those already recorded at Tell al-ʿAbd (Finkbeiner 1995) and Jerablus Tahtani (within the Tishrin Dam area; Peltenburg et al. 1996). Among these numerous tells were the nucleated and paired settlements that grew up at Tell Hadidi/Tell es-Sweyhat and Halawa (T 519A)/Selenkahiye (T 507) during the middle of the third millennium B.C., the locations of which are some distance beyond the sites of the Uruk triangle (fig. 9.6).

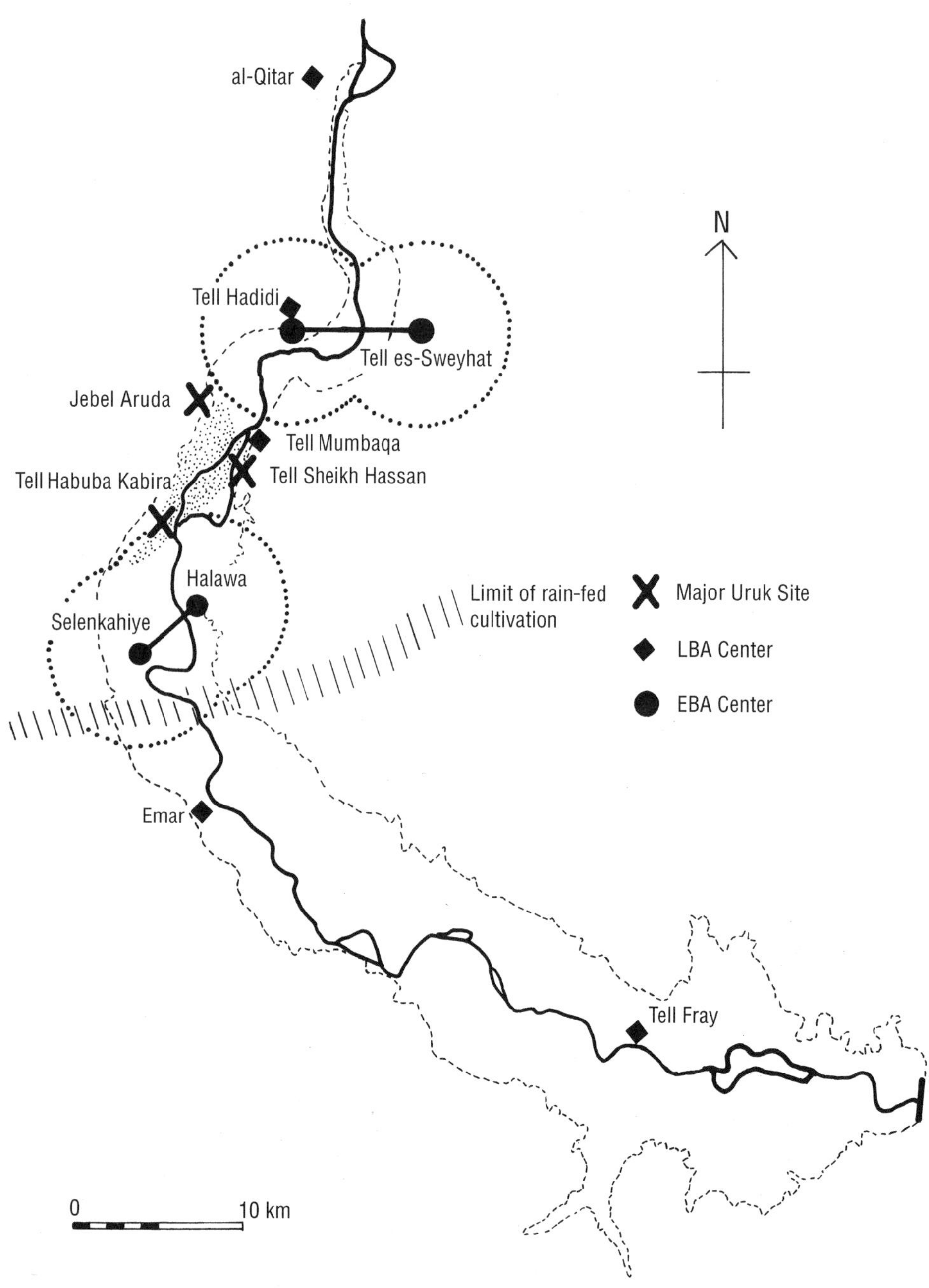

Figure 9.6. Upper Lake Assad Area Showing Major Sites of the Uruk Triangle, Paired Early Bronze Age Sites, and Late Bronze Age Strongholds

Unequivocal evidence for occupation of the floodplain during the mid-/late third millennium B.C. comes from the presence of Tell Jouweif (SS 8) and Tell Dhahir (T 536) on a relict sector of ancient floodplain to the southeast of Tell Hadidi. Such settlements along with Tell Kabir in the Tishrin Dam area (Porter 1995) demonstrate that the floodplain zone was clearly capable of being occupied, at least episodically, during the Bronze Age.

During this phase of settlement expansion, occasional Early Bronze Age tells developed in the steppe between the Balikh and the Euphrates Rivers (Danti 2000: 266–79), which, as noted above, suggests that this area was settled by a sparse scatter of agro-pastoral communities and an unquantifiable number of pastoral nomadic groups.

PHASE 5

Settlement on the Sweyhat Plain, and in the upper Lake Assad area in general, apparently attained a peak during the final third or quarter of the third millennium B.C. This was a time when settlement was also considerable in the Carchemish/Birecik area (Algaze, Breuninger, and Knutstad 1994: 14–17) and reached a peak (in terms of the number of sites) in the Jabbul Plain (Schwartz et al. 2000: 450). On the other hand, farther to the northeast around Kurban Höyük, by the final quarter of the third millennium population was dispersed mainly in rural settlements (Wilkinson 1990; Algaze, Misir, and Wilkinson 1992). In the Lake Assad area by the end of the third millennium B.C. or the initial stages of the second, both total aggregate settlement area and the number of occupied sites had then apparently dwindled, but the precise number of sites that were occupied at this time is unclear. Possible mechanisms for settlement change in the final third of the third millennium are elaborated below.

PHASE 6

During the second millennium, certainly around Tell es-Sweyhat and apparently also along the remainder of the Euphrates Valley in the upper Lake Assad area, settlement retreated towards the edge of the Pleistocene terraces overlooking the floodplain. Settlement continued to be in the form of both large and small tells such as Tell Hadidi and Tell Mumbaqa (T 534), but by the second half of the millennium a distinctive pattern of fortified settlements was present at Tell Fray (T 532), Emar (with its fort at Qal'at Ferq'ous), Tell Mumbaqa, Tell Hadidi, al-Qitar, and Tell Bazi (for Tell Bazi, see Einwag and Otto 1999). If the additional small site of Tell Ali al-Haj (SS 17) is added it becomes evident that by the Late Bronze Age the paired Early Bronze Age towns had been replaced by an alternating series of Late Bronze Age strongholds up- and downstream on opposite banks of the river (fig. 9.6). With the exception of Tell Hadidi and Tell Mumbaqa, both of which were occupied during the Middle Bronze Age, these settlements again respected the territories of the preceding Early Bronze Age communities.

PHASE 7

In the first millennium B.C. the five small, dispersed settlements that developed on the Sweyhat terrace, although puny in aggregate area (fig. 9.4), are important because they significantly increase the total number of Iron Age sites recorded in the Lake Assad area (fig. 9.5). This pattern of dispersed Iron Age settlement then developed without obvious discontinuity into the similarly dispersed pattern of Hellenistic and Roman settlement. Because of the different levels of survey intensity between the Sweyhat Plain and the Lake Assad area in general, it is difficult to compare the two areas, but around Tell es-Sweyhat the increase in settlement of the Late Roman to Early Byzantine and Early Islamic periods compares in broad outline with a similar trend in the Balikh Valley (Bartl 1994, 1996) and the Kurban Höyük area (Wilkinson 1990; Gerber 1996). On the other hand, its settlement contrasts in detail with these areas because in the Birecik and Carchemish areas a marked Early Byzantine peak was followed by a virtual collapse of settlement in the Early Islamic period (Algaze, Breuninger, and Knutstad 1994: 21–23; Algaze, Misir, and Wilkinson 1992; Wilkinson 1990). In the Tell es-Sweyhat area there was no such collapse; neither was there a massive surge in settlement during the Early Islamic period as occurred in the Balikh Valley (Bartl 1996, 1994). Rather, in the upper Lake Assad area, and particularly the area of the Sweyhat Survey, there was a broad peak in settlement that corresponded to the Roman, Early Byzantine, and Early Islamic periods.

Such contrasting demographic trajectories may be a result of different socio-political conditions and varying levels of investment that took place within the Islamic/Byzantine frontier region (the Thugir) during the seventh to ninth centuries A.D., as well as attacks by the Sasanian kings Chosroes I and II in the sixth and seventh centuries A.D. After the Early Islamic period, settlement then declined overall, until both the Sweyhat Plain and the upper Lake Assad area became thinly inhabited by the mid-/late Islamic period, especially so after about the thirteenth century A.D.

PHASE 8

Finally, during the mid-/late Islamic period sedentary population had decreased to such an extent that settlement was either restricted to the floodplain alone or was primarily nomadic, a situation that persisted until the early travelers reported similar conditions in the nineteenth and early twentieth centuries A.D.

9.B.1. SETTLEMENT SUCCESSION AND LAND HOLDINGS

During much of the time span between the Uruk period and the Iron Age, settlement showed a sequential development with the successor settlement of each phase being located towards the fringe of the territory of the preceding communities (fig. 9.6). Thus the settlements of the Uruk triangle — Habuba Kabira (T 509/513), Jebel Aruda (T 527), and Tell Sheikh Hassan (T 523) (including Tell Kannas [T 508] Tell al-Hajj [T 517] and Shams ed-Din Tannira [T 562]) — were replaced by twin centers of the Early Bronze Age at Tell Hadidi/Tell es-Sweyhat and Halawa (T 519)/Selenkahiye (T 507), both pairs being situated beyond the inferred territorial limits of the Uruk triangle sites and to the north and south of them, respectively. Following the decline of many Middle Bronze Age settlements, Tell Mumbaqa (T 534) grew to its maximum size during the Late Bronze Age, Tell Hadidi continued through the early second millennium and was re-fortified and expanded in the Late Bronze Age, whereas al-Qitar and Emar (modern Meskene) grew up well beyond the earlier centers. Although not all sites shifted to the territorial boundaries of pre-existing communities, there was again a tendency for the successor settlements to shift to a point well beyond the previous locus of settlement.

This pattern may be the result of the operation of some form of social memory, as follows: following the abandonment of settlements, their former inhabitants would be absorbed by the nomadic communities. These populations could then have retained ties, affiliations, or rights to the territories of the former centers, thereby rendering them inaccessible for new phases of sedentary settlement. Subsequently, when conditions favorable to sedentary settlement returned, other social groups would either establish new settlements, not on the original tell, but on territorial boundaries where cultivable land and/or grazing rights were still available. Alternatively, as discussed for the Uruk period above, following the collapse of the centers on the terraces, the main locus of population might have retreated once more to the floodplain, where they were no longer visible. Such settlements might then have retained rights to the lands of the former centers, either for supplementary cultivation or grazing.

9.B.2. EARLY BRONZE AGE TWIN TOWNS AND LATE BRONZE AGE STRONGHOLDS

The mid-/late third millennium B.C. settlement hierarchy of the Lake Assad area was dominated by Tell Hadidi (T 548), followed by Tell es-Sweyhat, Selenkahiye (T 507), and Halawa (T 519); the remaining sites at 5 ha or less were therefore significantly smaller (fig. 9.7). These four major sites formed conspicuous pairs, Tell Hadidi and Tell es-Sweyhat being occupied contemporaneously during the early Early Bronze Age, mid-/late Early Bronze Age, and late Early Bronze Age, whereas Selenkahiye and Halawa were contemporaneous during the late Early Bronze Age, and perhaps mid-/late Early Bronze Age and Middle Bronze Age I. The common periods when both pairs of twin towns were functioning were therefore mid-/late Early Bronze Age and late Early Bronze Age (table 9.2).

Pairing is also apparent for the Uruk period when Habuba Kabira South (T 513) and Tell Sheikh Hassan (T 523) developed on opposite banks of the Euphrates River, but it is unclear whether the same mechanisms that operated in the Early Bronze Age can be applied to these settlements.

The pattern of twin Early Bronze Age towns can be compared with similar pairings noted near Kurban Höyük as follows: Lidar/Gritille, Samsat/Şaşkan Büyüktepe, and Kurban Höyük/Birecik (Wilkinson 1990: 101).[93] Although cross river spacing at 1.5–2.7 km in the Karababa area was much less than the 4–8 km recorded in the Lake Assad area, the pairing of settlements is still evident in the latter area (fig. 9.6).

In the interior of the United States, river towns also developed in pairs that superficially resemble those in the Lake Assad area (Burghardt 1959). Although any analogies between recent capitalist economies and ancient pre-capitalist polities must be treated with caution, some conclusions inferred for the U.S. situation may be pertinent to the Syrian Euphrates settlements. Rivers act either as conduits for goods transported along them or as barriers for land traffic

---

93. See also the twin Roman towns of Zeugma/Apamea to the north
    near Birecik, Turkey, which were associated with a former
    bridging point (D. Kennedy 1998).

that has to cross them. In the latter case, if the river is not bridged, any goods transported must be unloaded and re-loaded into boats, rafts, or keleks and then reloaded at the other side. At such break-of-bulk points communities then develop and grow as a result of the proceeds derived from servicing the traders and their caravans. Although at first glance the distance of 8 km between Tell Hadidi and Tell es-Sweyhat might argue against these settlements being really twinned, the actual mechanics of the river crossing can be narrowed down by the interpretation of linear hollows in the landscape. As shown in the Sweyhat landscape and land use maps (figs. 5.1, 9.2), Tell es-Sweyhat was approached by two linear hollows that trend from northeast to southwest. One proceeded to a gap in the outer wall (arguably a west gate), and the second bypassed the walls on the north side. Therefore, if these linear hollows were Bronze

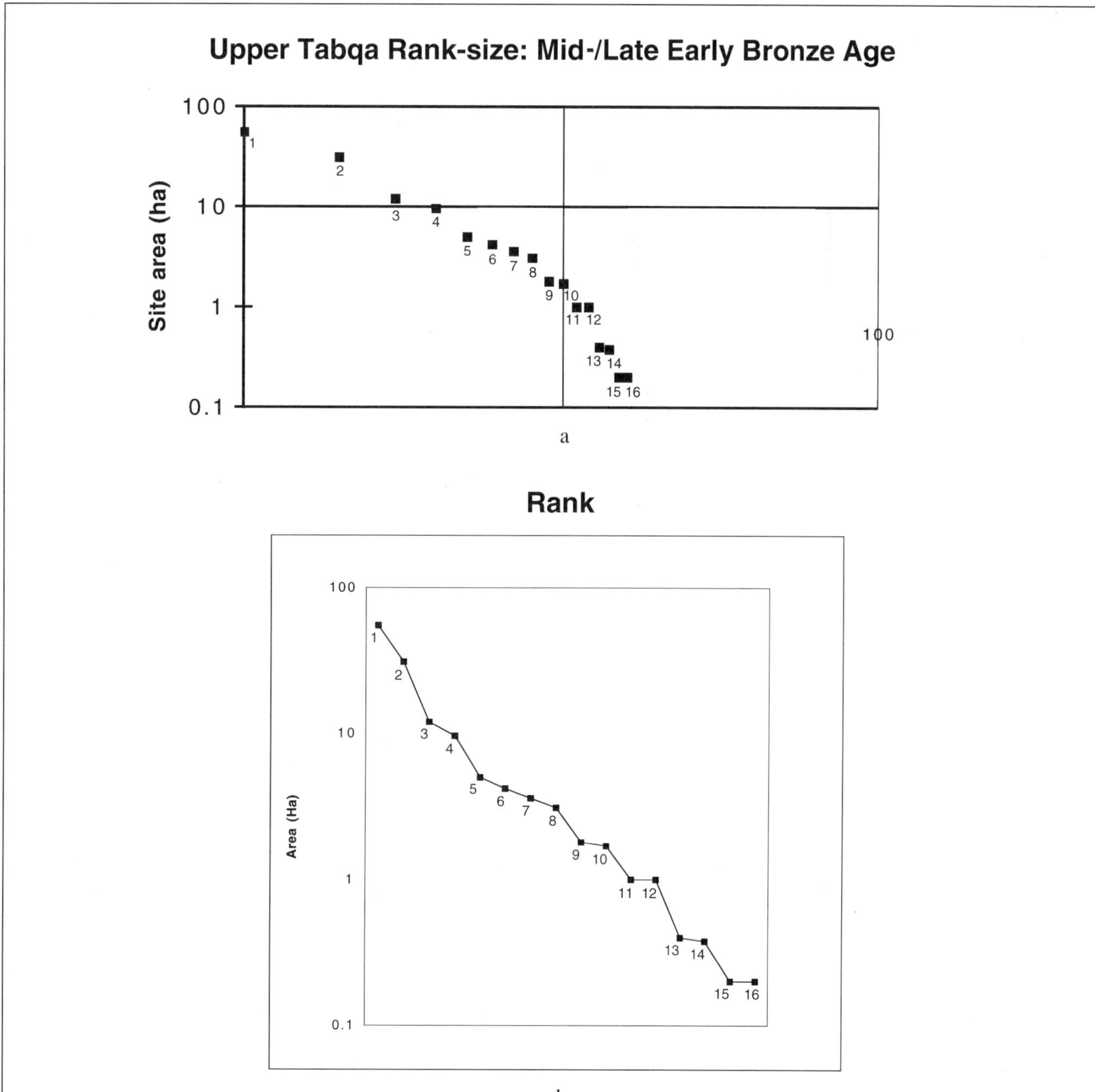

Figure 9.7. (*a*) Rank-size Curve for Sites of the Mid-/Late Early Bronze Age according to a Log-log Scale and (*b*) the Same Distribution Plotted with a Logarithmic Axis for Site Area and a Normal Scale for Sites

1 = Tell Hadidi (T 548)	5 = Tell Mumbaqa (T 534)	9 = Tell Othman (SS 20A)	13 = SS 27
2 = Tell es-Sweyhat (SS 1)	6 = Tell Habuba Kabira (T 509)	10 = Tell Jouweif (SS 8)	14 = Nafileh Village (SS 5)
3 = Selenkahiye (T 507)	7 = Tell al-ʿAbd (T 535)	11 = Shams ed-Din (SS 22)	15 = Tell Hajji Ibrahim (SS 3)
4 = Halawa Tell A (T 519A)	8 = Tell Ali al-Haj (SS 17)	12 = Halawa Tell B (T 519B)	16 = SS 24

Table 9.2. Approximate Dates of Occupation for Major Bronze Age Sites in the Upper Lake Assad Area

Date B.C.	Habuba Kabira T 509	Sheikh Hassan T 523	Jebel Aruda T 527	Tell Hadidi T 548	Tell es-Sweyhat SS 1/T 585	Halawa T 519	Selenkahiye T 507	Tell Mumbaqa T 534	al-Qitar	Emar T 518
4000										
3900										
3800										
3700										
3600										
3500										
3400										
3300										
3200										
3100										
3000										
2900										
2800										
2700										
2600										
2500										
2400										
2300										
2200										
2100										
2000										
1900										
1800										Texts
1700										
1600										
1500										
1400										
1300										Texts
1200										
1100										
1000										

Legend:
- Major (50%), well-attested occupation
- Moderate (25%), significant occupation; area uncertain
- Minor (12.5%) or uncertain occupation*

*In many cases represented by extreme spread of radiocarbon determinations.

Sources: See *Appendix B: Site Gazetteer* for all sites (with references) except al-Qitar and Emar. For Habuba Kabira (T 509/513), Tell Hadidi, al-Qitar, Mumbaqa (T 534), and Emar, see also Dornemann 1997; Margueron and Sigrist 1997; McClellan 1997); for Sheikh Hassan (T 523), see Boese 1995.

Age tracks as has been argued elsewhere (*Section 5: The Archaeological Landscape II;* Wilkinson 1993), it is evident that traffic would have passed along this route towards the terrace edge and the floodplain beyond. The actual crossing and break-of-bulk point would therefore have been at Tell Jouweif (SS 8) rather than at Tell es-Sweyhat itself. From this reasoning, it therefore seems possible that Tell es-Sweyhat could have functioned as a place of commerce, administration, customs point, or lodgings, the point where goods were actually loaded on to the boats being at or near Tell Jouweif.

In the United States, when twin cities grew up, the crossing point usually became bridged, and the town on the commercially or agriculturally more productive bank then outgrew the town situated on the less productive bank. In the context of mid-/late Early Bronze Age upper Lake Assad area, Tell Hadidi exhibited a maximum size of 55 ha compared to Tell es-Sweyhat's 31 ha, whereas Selenkahiye (T 507) with a walled area of some 12 ha, compared with some 9.5 ha for Halawa Tell A (T 519A). Therefore, bearing in mind the uncertainties of site contemporaneity, it appears that in aggregate, the west bank (Shamiyah) towns were both larger than their east bank (Jazirah) counterparts. This westward location of the larger sites may imply that the more productive hinterlands at this time were in the Shamiyah and more specifically the Jabbul plains to the west where rainfall was higher and more reliable and the political economies within the orbit of Ebla were more conducive to long-term settlement. Similarly, the Tell Hadidi/Tell es-Sweyhat pairing in the better-watered northern area was larger perhaps because of the higher agricultural productivity of these lands.

If the settlement pair of Tell Hadidi/Tell es-Sweyhat represents a crossing point of the Euphrates River, the details of such a situation require elaboration. First, the most convenient location for the actual crossing would have been at Tell Jouweif (SS 8), from which Tell Hadidi could be reached after a short overland trip across the floodplain and a boat trip or fording across the river. Tell es-Sweyhat, rather than representing the actual eastern crossing point, could therefore have functioned as an overnight stopping point where there was sufficient food for provisioning any caravan, as well as space for pasture, and protection in the form of a walled enclosure. Therefore, a degree of flexibility is assumed in this crossing scenario, travelers from the east could come from the steppe below SS 14 direct to Tell es-Sweyhat. Travelers could then have continued on to Tell Jouweif in order to cross to Tell Hadidi. Alternatively, they could go straight along the linear hollow routes to Tell Jouweif where they could make a direct crossing. Transit from west to east could be effected by crossing from Tell Hadidi to Shams ed-Din Southern Site and Cemeteries (SS 22), from whence another route led to the east, or travelers could continue upstream to Tell Jouweif or Tell es-Sweyhat, but only if a night's sleep or extra provisioning was required.

If Tell es-Sweyhat did function in any way as a route station, its location in the center of a broad cultivable plain surrounded by potential pasture land (i.e., the inner pasture zone) may have been because a greater agricultural productivity was required for provisioning additional travelers. In other words, for a way station to be capable of provisioning travelers, a location within an agriculturally and pastorally productive area is probably more important than a position immediately on the riverbank. In addition, because the Euphrates region may have been undergoing a phase of expansion during the late third millennium (Algaze, Breuninger, and Knutstad 1994), the growth of Tell es-Sweyhat (perhaps to include the provisioning of caravans) may also partly have been tied into north–south trade from the Carchemish/Birecik area. Although the specific functional details of Tell es-Sweyhat as a paired river crossing town remain elusive, the general scheme provides a plausible overall interpretation for its growth.

During the Late Bronze Age, when strongholds were distributed on alternating banks of the river, locational factors were apparently different. Again employing the United States analogy of Burghardt (1959), such a distribution would imply that the Late Bronze Age settlements were port towns for handling goods being transported along the river. This would support Dornemann's suggestion (1980: 231) that during the Mitannian period Tell Hadidi was oriented towards trade and contacts along the Euphrates River (see below). Although accepting that river traffic may have been a factor in the development of these towns, more generally these sites could be viewed as being fortified towns that developed to control the Euphrates River at certain key points. On the other hand, the absence of twin settlements on the opposite bank suggests that there may have been insufficient cross-channel traffic to generate break-of-bulk points and settlements that grew therefrom.

However, if the paired settlement did grow in response to a major crossing of the river, it is logical to examine how Tell es-Sweyhat and its neighbors fit into the pattern of inter-regional trade.

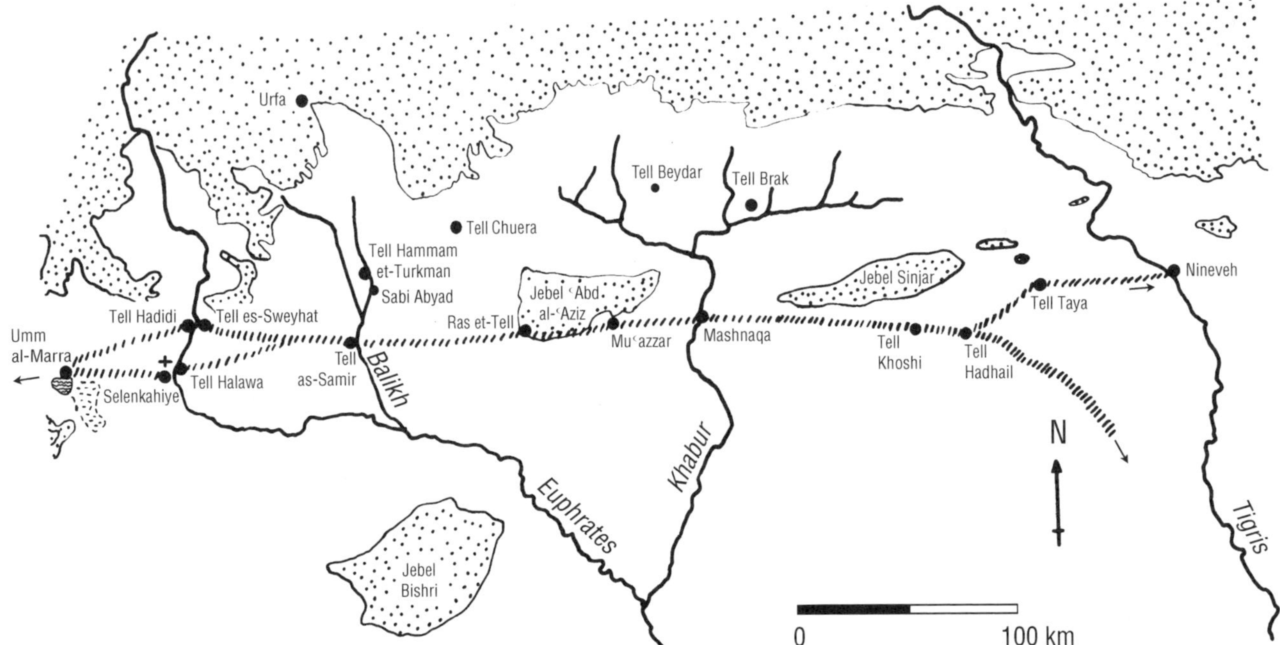

Figure 9.8. Suggested East–West Route across the Jazirah from Nineveh on the Tigris River to Major Crossing Points of the Euphrates River around Upper Lake Assad

9.C. TRANSPORT AND ROUTE SYSTEMS IN CONTEXT

The Tell es-Sweyhat survey area has provided a small number of linear hollow features that suggest the existence of relict route systems (*Section 4: The Archaeological Landscape I*). These are shown in figure 9.2 with thin lines indicating the overall trajectory of the inferred routes. Three main groups of southeast–northwest oriented linear hollows imply that traffic came from the southeast towards Shams ed-Din Southern Site and Cemeteries (SS 22), or converged on Tell Jouweif (SS 8). In both cases these routes could have led to a crossing point on the east bank of the Euphrates River linking to Tell Hadidi on the west bank. Tell es-Sweyhat itself appears to have been linked with Tell Jouweif and the same crossing point by two parallel linear hollows. There is no sign that these hollows continued to the northeast, although it is feasible that such a route would have led to a pass over the plateau and then in an easterly direction across the Jazirah (but see below). However, from the linear hollows it appears that the main route from Tell es-Sweyhat led to the northwest via Tell Ali al-Haj (SS 17) towards the Tishrin Gorge and onwards up the Euphrates Valley towards Tell Banat.

The apparent pairing of Tell Hadidi and Tell es-Sweyhat, as well as Halawa (T 519) and Selenkahiye (T 507), suggests that both pairs could have developed because a major route system crossed the Euphrates River at these points. Landscape studies in Syro-Mesopotamia suggest that long-distant route systems often formed multiple features so that there was never any single route (Wilkinson 1993), but instead travelers had a choice of routes. One such east–west route can be inferred to have reached the Euphrates River in the upper Lake Assad area (figs. 9.1 and 9.8). This route is not reconstructed from physical features on the ground but rather is inferred from the alignment of a series of large sites that are situated along the major hill ranges of the Jebel ʿAbd al-ʿAziz and Jebel Sinjar. Moving east from the Lake Assad area, a northern route would lead southeast from Tell Jouweif (SS 8) to skirt the plateau below SS 14, to turn to the east via traditional wells at Bir Mjeibna and Abu Chaaf (Danti 1997, fig. 5.1) and thence east to the Balikh Valley. Similarly, the route from Halawa and Selenkahiye may have trended east-northeast towards the same wells where the two routes may have converged. This combined east–west route would then have crossed the Balikh River at or near Tell as-Samir (BS 83; Curvers 1991). This site, the largest Early Bronze Age site in the Syrian part of the Balikh Valley,[94] has a 10 ha lower town to the east (BS 84) that was occupied through most of the third millennium B.C. (Balikh periods VIA–D; Curvers 1991). A direct route to the east from Tell as-Samir would then have crossed the steppe to the footslopes of the Jebel ʿAbd al-ʿAziz below the ceremonial/religious Early Bronze Age sites of Jebelet al-Beidha (Moortgat-Correns 1972) towards the *Kranzhügel* of Muʿazzar[95] and on to the Khabur Valley in the vicin-

---

94.   With the exception of Tell Biʾa that strictly speaking belongs to   95.   See Kouchoukos 1998: 368.
      the Euphrates Valley sites.

ity of Mashnaqa. Finally, the route would have followed an eastward course towards the foothills of the Jebel Sinjar, past the two major walled settlements of Tell Khoshi and Tell Hadhail (Lloyd 1938, sites 64 and 41, respectively), below the extensive site of Tell Taya (Reade 1973, 1968) until the Tigris River was reached at Nineveh. The final stretch of this route has only been confirmed by independent evidence (in the form of hollow ways) in the area to the west of Nineveh (Altaweel, 2003). Nevertheless, such a route would logically tie together an otherwise curious alignment of unusually large sites, the growth of which is difficult to explain.[96] Because the sites along this alignment cannot all be demonstrated to have been in use during the late third millennium when Tell es-Sweyhat was at its maximum extent, it is probably better to regard this route as being in use over much of the Early Bronze Age. Traffic could have stimulated the initial development of paired settlements, and then the route could have continued in use, perhaps episodically, through the remainder of the third millennium B.C. Such a route through the semi-arid steppe should hardly be considered unusual because it parallels a later Neo-Assyrian route through Tell Malhat al-Deru, already noted by Kühne (1995).

To the west of the Lake Assad area the postulated east–west route would then have crossed the northern Jabbul Plain through Umm al-Marra (Curvers and Schwartz 1997) and on to Aleppo and thence to the Mediterranean via the southern Amuq Plain.

9.D. SETTLEMENT DECLINE IN THE SECOND MILLENNIUM B.C.

Historical evidence implies that the upper Lake Assad area experienced a significant shift in its administration between the mid- to late third millennium B.C. and the rise of the Assyrian Empire. During the second half of the third millennium B.C., Tell es-Sweyhat (perhaps *Burman* of the Ebla texts) fell within the orbit of Ebla; during the second millennium there was then a significant re-orientation towards Mari, and then by the mid-second millennium B.C. it came under Hittite rule, which was administered from Carchemish to the north. Finally, around 1200 B.C. the area was close to the administrative reach of the Middle Assyrian Empire, although it did not necessarily fall within it. Such shifts and re-alignments must have had a significant influence on the settlement pattern, as described below.

For many parts of the Jaziran region there appears to have been a significant decline in sedentary settlement during approximately the middle of the second millennium, B.C. This pattern has been characterized by Buccellati:

> "After the fall of Mari and then of Terqa as the capital of the Middle Euphrates (by the middle of the 2nd Millennium B.C.E.), the entire region underwent a devolution process of de-urbanization. The tribes moved their geographical focus to the west, where they eventually established (by about 1300 B.C.E.) the first true steppe-based state, the kingdom of Amurrum" (Buccellati 1997: 110; see also Buccellati 1990a).

This devolution was also examined by Thomas McClellan (1992) who shows that in Syria there was a major decline in sedentary population at the end of the Middle and the beginning the Late Bronze Age. Similar trends can be seen in Jordan (Ibach 1987: 199) and Palestine (Finkelstein 1995b). The well-known twelfth century collapse (Drews 1993) appears to have been at the end of a decline that started much earlier (McClellan 1992).

A number of detailed surveys have been conducted, some published, since McClellan's study (1992). The surveys show that after a peak in settlement in the Old Assyrian and Old Babylonian periods, a number of areas experienced a significant decline between the end of the Old Babylonian and the beginning of the Middle Assyrian periods, a phase that corresponds to that of the Mitannian state.

In northern Iraq, after a substantial peak in settlement during the early second millennium B.C. (characterized by the presence of Khabur Valley wares on sites), settlements dwindled so that by the Middle Assyrian period occupation was at a long-term minimum (Wilkinson and Tucker 1995, chapter 7). Similarly, Meijer's survey of the Khabur Valley suggests that its eastern part was heavily populated during the Old Babylonian/Old Assyrian periods with numerous sites being occupied (Meijer 1986; Eidem and Warburton 1996). The area then experienced a substantial decline during the Late Bronze Age (Meijer 1986, period 10, fig. 10). In contrast, according to Lyonnet's (1996) large-scale reconnaissance and a more detailed survey around Tell Beydar (Wilkinson 2000a), much of the western Khabur Valley was sparsely occupied during the Middle and Late Bronze Age until there was a marked population increase in the Iron Age. Closer to Tell es-Sweyhat to the west, the survey of the Jabbul Plain shows that settlement reached its minimum,

---

96.   Alternative explanations might include, for example, an external stimulus such as overland trade, or perhaps, exchange of commodities between sedentary groups to the north and nomads to the south.

in terms of the number of sites, during the Late Bronze Age, when only eleven sites were occupied (Schwartz et al. 2000: 451). In the Balikh Valley, the survey of Akkermans (analyzed in Curvers 1991) shows that following an Old Babylonian (MBA) peak in settlement in which there appears to have been substantial competition for water, settlement progressively dwindled through the mid-/late second millennium until by the time of the Middle Assyrian settlement around the thirteenth century B.C., the valley supported a significantly smaller population, and the southern irrigated part of the valley had declined more than the northern rain-fed zone (Lyon 2000). Thus it seems that a decrease in sedentary settlement may also have corresponded to the decline of the infrastructure of irrigation. Finally, only a short distance to the north of Lake Assad within the Carchemish/Birecik area, Algaze and colleagues have shown that the Late Bronze Age exhibited the lowest aggregate settlement area of all periods since and including the aceramic Neolithic (Algaze, Breuninger, and Knutstad 1994, fig. 18).

In the upper Lake Assad area, there was a decline in the number of sites through the Bronze Age until the Late Bronze Age witnessed the smallest number of sites (fig. 9.5). However, this decline may not be as massive as appears from the number of sites because many sites (such as Tell Mumbaqa [T 534]) were substantial, exhibiting a fairly dense urban fabric of buildings as well as strong defensive walls. Furthermore, Emar (modern Meskene) and Tell Fray (T 532) grew up downstream of the major bend of the Euphrates River, in what must have been the irrigated zone.[97] Therefore, although there appears to have been a decline in settlement during the Late Bronze Age, this decline should not be overemphasized. Rather, what is clear is that compared to the Early Bronze Age, the Late Bronze Age represents a settlement transition during which a significant change in the structure and possible function of settlements occurred.[98] First, what had been a clear pairing of sites during the Early Bronze Age became a pattern in which Late Bronze Age sites were arranged at intervals often on alternate banks of the river. Second, many of these sites appear to have been large strongholds or fortresses. Therefore, during the Late Bronze Age when the Mitannian kingdom was being taken over by the Hittites, cross river trade was probably insufficient to result in the growth of twin towns on opposite banks. This provides a marked contrast with the inferred flourishing long-distance commerce and strong interregional linkages that prevailed in the Early and Middle Bronze Age. Such a pattern of alternating strongholds may therefore have been a product of increased movement up and downstream along the Euphrates River (Burghardt 1959), which could, in turn, reflect a greater degree of linkage with the Hittite administrative center at Carchemish. Alternatively, the presence of fortifications or fortified high points at al-Qitar, Tell Hadidi, and Mumbaqa could be taken to suggest that a considerable degree of insecurity prevailed either in the Mitannian period or when Hittite armies were making their presence known in the area, such as at the time of Mursili I's campaign during the sixteenth century B.C. or later during the Hittite Empire in the fourteenth century B.C.

Although Emar had been ruled by the Hittites via the king of Carchemish since Mursili II[99] (1339–1306 B.C.; Margueron 1995: 127), none of the Lake Assad sites, Emar included, can be regarded as fully Hittite. Unfortunately, with the exception of Emar, few tablets of this era have been recovered from sites in the area; we know of only a single Middle Assyrian tablet from al-Qitar,[100] while the "tablet building" at Tell Hadidi is regarded by the excavator as Mitannian. Mumbaqa (T 534) also expanded in the second half of sixteenth and first half of fifteenth centuries when it was known either as Uru or Ekalte,[101] according to the campaign of Thutmose III in 1458 B.C. Mumbaqa's material culture, being of Middle Bronze II and Late Bronze Age material, places it roughly contemporaneous with occupations at al-Qitar and Tell Hadidi (de Feyter 1989; *Appendix A: Sweyhat Survey Site Catalog*). De Feyter suggests that the location of Mumbaqa between the emerging nations of the Hurrians in northeast Syria and kingdoms of Yamhad (modern Aleppo) and western Syria encouraged the growth of the town, and furthermore he suggests that the site became a crossing point and harbor on the Euphrates River. It should be cautioned, however, that although cross river traffic must have existed, it does not appear to have been sufficient to stimulate the growth of twin towns that existed in the Early Bronze Age.

---

97. It now appears from the recent excavations that there was also Early Bronze Age occupation in parts of the site of Emar.

98. I have deliberately not calculated aggregate site areas for sites in the Lake Assad area because, as in earlier periods, many sites may have been eroded away by the Euphrates River. In this case, the calculation of aggregate settlement area through time as a proxy for settlement population may provide a spurious impression of accuracy.

99. Or perhaps from the reign of Šuppiluliuma I (1380–1340 B.C.; Margueron and Sigrist 1997: 236–37). Occupation at the site continued until ca. 1187 B.C.

100. Snell 1983/84: 159–60. Tell Shiukh Fawqani is the only other site in this part of the Euphrates Valley to exhibit an unambiguous Middle Assyrian occupation (Morandi Bonacossi 2000a: 223).

101. See de Feyter 1989: 252; alternatively Yakultum ca. 1815–1761 B.C. (E. N. Cooper 2001: 82).

At Tell Fray (T 532) to the southeast of Emar (modern Meskene), the discovery of cuneiform texts of the twelfth/thirteenth century B.C. provided a name for that site (Yakharisha), the names of its satellite settlements, and suggestions that a canal was in operation adjacent to the site (Bounni 1979a). Therefore, at this stage of the Late Bronze Age the Euphrates floodplain between Tell Fray and Emar was under irrigation. Emar, on the floodplain beyond the limit of rain-fed cultivation, also relied upon irrigation for at least part of its food supply (*Section 3.C: Irrigation Agriculture*). Therefore, at the threshold of the Middle Assyrian conquest when the Balikh Valley was depopulated and was probably experiencing a decline in irrigation, the Lake Assad area must have had a significant population who were in part housed within a series of fortified sites. The distribution of these sites at alternating points along the river suggests that they were more oriented towards the oversight of transport up and down than across the river. That this structural reorganization had occurred as early as the Mari texts is indicated by references to a vigorous riverine trade in grain between Carchemish and Mari at the time of Zimri-Lim (Molina 1999). By the Late Bronze Age the area of Emar then came under some degree of Hittite control from Carchemish; again this Hittite control would have maintained a north–south orientation of administration and information flow.

More generally, during the Late Bronze Age, the settlement pattern of the Jazirah to the east suggests a period of generally thinning population as well as greater insecurity. Despite this apparent demographic decline in the Jazirah, the second half of the second millennium B.C. should not be viewed as a total societal or economic collapse because many centers such as Tell Brak, Tell Fakhariyyah, and Emar (modern Meskene) continued to be occupied, at least up until 1200 B.C. Furthermore, at Tell Brak, trade continued and technological developments were often of considerable sophistication (Oates, Oates, and McDonald 1997). It is perhaps significant that the Lake Assad area was situated near the boundary between an eastern Jaziran zone that experienced mid-second millennium B.C. decline, and a western area (from the Jabbul Plain to the Mediterranean Sea), where such a decline was less evident. Hence, sites like Umm al-Marra, although in a climatically marginal situation, showed if not complete continuity, then at least occupation in every ceramic phase of the second millennium B.C. (Curvers and Schwartz 1997). The Amuq Plain appears to have had a significant occupation through most of the second millennium B.C. (Braidwood 1937) and sites such as Alalakh became major centers until they suffered major decline around 1200 B.C. (Woolley 1953). On the other hand, at Tell Afis, to the west of Aleppo, although a period of short-lived destruction is recorded at the end of the Late Bronze Age (around 1200 B.C.), the settlement then experienced a long phase of uninterrupted settlement that corresponded to the formative phases of the Syro-Hittite state (Venturi 1998: 134–37).

9.E. THE UPPER LAKE ASSAD AREA IN THE POST-HITTITE PERIOD

The period following the collapse of the Hittite Empire is regarded as a dark age. Nevertheless, a line of local kings can be traced at Carchemish, and these kings probably held the Euphrates Valley from Malatya to Meskene (Hawkins 1995: 88). It has also been argued that a phase of urbanization occurred in northern Syria during the Early Iron Age,[102] which resulted in new urban foundations or the re-planning of old centers. In terms of the settlement pattern of the upper Lake Assad area, however, the post-Hittite period is indeed a dark age with relatively little evidence of occupation. Although an Iron Age *bīt ḫilāni* is reported from Tell Sheikh Hassan (T 523) (Boese 1995), this is thought to date to the eighth or seventh century B.C., when the area was under Assyrian rule. Tell Ali al-Haj (SS 17), being of Late Bronze Age and Iron Age date, may have been occupied for part or all of the span between the Hittite and the Neo-Assyrian empires, but this is unclear from the surface materials. Therefore, through what is without doubt a very murky archaeological prism, it seems that the dark age between the thirteenth and tenth centuries B.C. may have been filled in by the occupation at Tell Ali al-Haj and the re-settlement of the Sweyhat Plain.

Of similarly vague date are the Iron Age sites around Tell es-Sweyhat (*Section 7.F: The Iron Age*). The broad chronological range of the surface ceramics makes it difficult to place these sites in either the Neo-Assyrian period or that preceding it, but a number of types dated to the first centuries of the first millennium B.C. suggests that this phase of settlement *might* predate the inclusion of the area into the Neo-Assyrian Empire during the reign of Shalmaneser III (858–824 B.C.). Consequently, the re-appearance of small settled communities could be either the result of a spontaneous settlement by Aramaeans on the climatically marginal plain of Sweyhat or part of a more systematic settlement that occurred more generally during the Neo-Assyrian period during the ninth to seventh century B.C. A similar upsurge of Iron Age settlement has been recorded in many parts of Syria both to the east (Wilkinson and Barbanes 2000; Morandi Bonacossi 2000b), as well as to the west of Tell es-Sweyhat (Schwartz et al. 2000: 452).

---

102. Iron Age I according to Mazzoni 1995.

9.F. LATER SETTLEMENT AND ECONOMY

Surveys and excavations in the Near East have frequently neglected the pattern of later occupations, which is regrettable, because in addition to the obvious merits of the cultures themselves, the settlement record from these periods provides a valuable yardstick with which earlier settlement can be measured. Susan Alcock (1994: 188) summarizes scanty and frustrating data from survey literature to suggest that over wide areas of the eastern Mediterranean and Near East, despite a wide range of regional trajectories, the dominant trend during the Hellenistic period was towards higher levels of urbanization, increasing population, and more intensive land use. This trend was also the case in Syria, in part because of the implantation of new cities by the Seleucid rulers (ibid., p. 181; Grainger 1990: 110–19). Clearly the data from the Sweyhat area can throw light on this question.

Following the re-occupation of the Sweyhat Plain during the first half of the first millennium B.C., settlement gained momentum in the Hellenistic/Roman period, so that during the Hellenistic to Early Islamic period the Sweyhat Plain, and indeed the steppe well to the east (Danti 2000: 271), was occupied by a dispersed pattern of settlements. Not only did this include villages and farmsteads, but several possible pastoral camps have also been recognized (ibid., p. 271). This re-expansion appears to have been part of a widespread pattern of dispersed rural settlement common for Hellenistic/Roman/Byzantine times throughout much of the Near East,[103] and the pattern around Tell es-Sweyhat provides a marked contrast with the nucleated tell-based occupations of the Bronze Age. A similar rapid growth in Hellenistic/Roman times has also been observed in the Carchemish/Birecik area (Algaze, Breuninger, and Knutstad 1994), the Jabbul Plain (Gerritsen, MacCormack, and Schwartz 2000), the Balikh Valley (Wilkinson 1998), the Amuq Plain (Casana 2003), and in the Kurban Höyük area (Wilkinson 1990), which underscores the widespread nature of this phenomenon. Whether this dispersion was simply a bi-product of the freedom of location that was made possible under Hellenistic/Roman administration is not clear. However, because large territories were under the control of a single overall administration, it is likely that the increased security offered by the Roman Empire encouraged the growth of rural settlements in this formerly marginal area. In addition, if the economy was increasingly monetized during these later periods (Greene 1986: 45–65), then settlements in locations such as the Sweyhat Plain would have benefited from the increased fiscal flexibility of the economy. This could enable deficits in grain production to be met by purchases of grain from markets along the Euphrates or Balikh Rivers (where irrigation certainly was practiced at this time), or from more verdant parts of the rain-fed zone. To what degree this settlement entailed the deliberate settlement of pastoral nomadic groups under the relative stability of the Roman administration is difficult to say, but it seems likely that at least part of this phenomenon results from such sedentarization. Although there was a slight increase in Hellenistic/Roman settlement, it is not as great as what came later in the Late Roman/Early Byzantine period (figs. 9.4–5). The upper Lake Assad area provides some support for the suggestion of Alcock's (1994) that Hellenism did bring a growth in rural settlement, but it is important to note that this growth was, in turn, built upon an earlier growth that took place in the Iron Age. Furthermore, it was during the Iron Age that the fundamental change in settlement structure from that of the Bronze Age occurred. This dominantly dispersed or non-tell pattern of settlement then continued through the post-Iron Age periods of occupation throughout many parts of the Jazirah.

Interestingly, the distribution of later settlements appears to fall on a series of east-northeast alignments, namely, through Mishrifat/Ramalah (SS 16A–B) and Khirbet Aboud al-Hazu (SS 6) (Hellenistic/Roman), SS 4 and Khirbet Haj Hassan (SS 10) (Roman/Late Roman), and Khirbet Dhiman (SS 11) and Khirbet al-Hamrah (SS 7) (Early Islamic). This pattern of settlement distribution roughly parallels the modern day field boundaries, which follow similar alignments. The southward shift of sites from the Hellenistic/Roman period to the Early Islamic period suggests that as in the Bronze Age, each successive phase of settlement may have resulted in a lateral shift to just beyond the potential territorial limits of the previous phase. Because of the problems inherent in assuming continuity between the modern field boundaries and those a thousand years earlier, there is no evidence to demonstrate that the modern field pattern has been directly inherited from the earlier one. Alternatively, such shifts in settlement alignment may be related to shifts in the location of roads, but if this was the case, the traces of such roads appear to have been lost. Nevertheless, such potential landscape continuities deserve investigation in the future. There is no reason to assume a completely sedentary population during the Hellenistic through Islamic period and, as in the Bronze Age, during periods of rapidly changing settlement there may have been continued circulation of populations into the nomadic communities of the re-

---

103. Greene 1986: 170. Of course, fluctuations were apparent; for example, in Greece there was a decline between expansion in the Hellenistic period and another expansion in the Late Roman (Alcock 1993). For a considerable increase in Hellenistic/Roman settlement, see Gerritsen, MacCormack, and Schwartz 2000: 452–55.

gion. Finally, with the total abandonment of the plain by the Middle Islamic period, we see the area becoming available again for use as a pastoral resource.

9.G. LONG-TERM SETTLEMENT AND ENVIRONMENTAL CHANGE

9.G.1. UPPER LAKE ASSAD AREA

Being situated close to the limit of viable rain-fed agriculture, Tell es-Sweyhat makes a valuable test case for various theories concerning the relationship between increases and decreases of human settlement and changes in climate. At face value it is reasonable to suggest that if rainfall fluctuates significantly through time (see *Section 2.A.1: Climate and Climatic Change* for discussion), during periods of significantly low rainfall communities in the rain-fed farming zone would have been stressed to a point that crop failure was likely. This would have resulted in significant shortfalls in the production of staple crops that in turn could have resulted in widespread famines and even population collapses. In the Syrian-Iraqi Jazirah it is possible to recognize a southern limit beyond which settlement is either attenuated on the steppe or is concentrated along river valleys. In the latter situation, raised soil moisture favored better pastures and higher crop yields and there was also a potential supply of water for watering flocks and for irrigation. Therefore, if a limit to rain-fed cultivation can be recognized, it follows that any change in climate would result in a change in the productivity of the agricultural systems and a shift in such a boundary. However, because settlement in such marginal zones can only take place when political, social, and economic conditions allow occupation to take place, these factors should also be taken into account (see Lewis 1988).

To test the relationship between climate and settlement, the number of settlements through the Holocene is compared with the closest well-dated climate proxy record, that from Lake Van (Lemcke and Sturm 1997, fig. 5; *Section 2.A.1: Climate and Climatic Change*). Although probably the most reliable proxy record to be established in the region to date, the core may be too distant from the Sweyhat area to provide a reliable record. Nevertheless, at least the broad features of post mid-third millennium B.C. decline are supported by another proxy record, that of Soreq Cave near Jerusalem (Bar-Matthews, Ayalon, and Kaufman 1998).[104]

The number of sites (as indicated in figs. 9.4–5) plotted according to the approximate length of their respective periods is shown in figure 9.9. Also superimposed (along the top) are major phases of occupation at Abu Hureyra, located just round the main bend of the Euphrates River (T 545 in fig. 1.2). In figure 9.9 both atmospheric humidity and the number of archaeological sites increase towards the top. Although the Natufian or late Upper Paleolithic settlement of Abu Hureyra 1 was occupied around ca. 11,000 B.P.,[105] the only other similarly dated settlements recorded in the Lake Assad area were the early Natufian Dibsi Faraj East 1 (T 542) and Late Natufian Mureybit 1A (T 502–504) (ca. ninth millennium B.C.). The extreme dry episode registered is interpreted as the Younger Dryas event, during which climate in northwest Europe was cooler and drier than both earlier and later. According to Moore and Hillman (1992), this climatic reversal, which occurred around the time that the Upper Paleolithic settlement of Abu Hureyra 1 was occupied, caused the forest steppe west of that site to retreat farther to the west. The Younger Dryas must have had a severe impact on the Upper Paleolithic 2 hunter-gatherers of the region, but the site of Abu Hureyra itself was not deserted (Moore and Hillman 1992: 490).

Significantly, therefore, occupation in the upper Lake Assad area started before and continued through the Younger Dryas, but remained at a fairly low level (one to two sites only) during the Pre-pottery Neolithic A and Pre-pottery Neolithic B. Settlement was even less in the early ceramic Neolithic, and it may be significant (although this can hardly be argued from fig. 9.9) that this decrease in settlement corresponded to a decline in humidity around 8,800 B.P. This climatic event may, in turn, correspond to a similar event noted in a number of parts of the globe (Alley et al. 1997).[106] Although atmospheric humidity fluctuated around fairly low levels during the Pre-pottery Neolithic, it is significant that carbonized plant remains from sites of this period in the Tishrin Dam area show a slightly more wooded landscape than modern rainfall could support (Willcox 1996). This was a period when woodland was only slowly increasing on the Anatolian Plateau around Lake Van (Landmann et al. 1996, fig. 2).

---

104. Although impressive, these quantitative records depend on a number of assumptions that could eventually be superceded.

105. Date uncalibrated; see Moore 1992, fig. 1. Otherwise, dates on the Lemke and Sturm graph are in varve years before present and archaeological periods have been converted to calendar years by calibration to match with these. Early Holocene dates for archaeological sites are approximate and according to table 1 in Schwartz and Weiss 1992.

106. According to the less well-dated sequence of Courty 1994, this drying event was around 8,000–7,000 B.P.

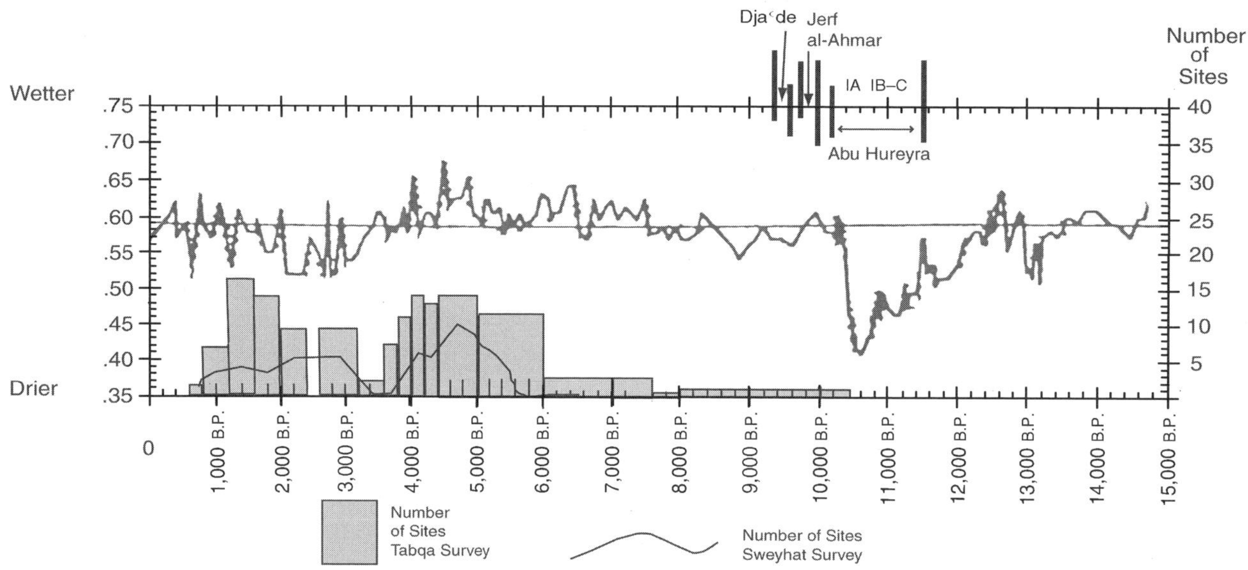

Figure 9.9. Number of Sites in the Upper Lake Assad and Sweyhat Survey Areas Compared to Possible Climatic Phases as Recorded in Lake Van, Turkey (Climatic Curve from Lemcke and Sturm 1997, fig. 5) (Note that Uncertainties in the Dating of the Early Part of the Van Core Render the Correlations between the Dates of the Aceramic Neolithic Sites and the Climate Curve Problematic)

If the Lake Assad area experienced the Younger Dryas to the same extent as Lake Van, communities must have been stressed to a considerable degree, therefore the limited settlement at this time is hardly surprising. Climate during this period may be seen as an inhibitor to some degree. Similarly, throughout the Pre-pottery Neolithic A, Pre-pottery Neolithic B, and ceramic Neolithic, the somewhat dry conditions may also have discouraged settlement. Altogether, although there was a dearth of settlement in the region around the time of the Younger Dryas, even this extreme event did not cause total social disruption; rather, it might have acted as a spur towards cereal cultivation as well as the development of the Neolithic economies (Hillman 1996: 195; Blumler 1996: 41).

On the Anatolian Plateau, the period from around 7,500 B.P. witnessed both increased humidity and a high cover of woodland. Nevertheless, it is clear that in the Lake Assad area this period of optimal climate and presumably verdant vegetation cover did not encourage a substantial spread of settlement, which remained modest in scale during the Halaf and Ubaid periods (fig. 9.9). Whether the sparse scatter of sites of the ceramic Neolithic and Halaf is representative of the original settlement pattern in the Lake Assad area is difficult to judge. Nevertheless, because Halaf settlement tends to thin significantly to the south of the 300 mm rainfall isohyet (Nieuwenhuyse 2000), this absence may also be real. More generally, the distinct spread of settlement that occurred in the Euphrates Valley in Turkey and in the Balikh Valley of Syria[107] during the Halaf and Ubaid appears to have occurred when environmental conditions may have allowed settlement of the terraces. In the upper Lake Assad area, this spread of settlement only took place to a minor degree, because either population levels were low or settlements were mainly restricted to the floodplain and have since been lost by increased erosion and deposition as described above.

The substantial rise in visible sedentary settlement that occurred during the fourth millennium B.C. was manifest in terms of both the number of sites, and to judge from the size of the sites, in the aggregate area also. This period of settlement increase does not appear to be the result of an especially favorable climate but more likely is specific to the nature of the Uruk colonial process, whether it was for economic, political, or military reasons (Algaze 1993). This massive apparent increase in settlement may not have been quite as great as it seems because settlement may have existed on the floodplain through much of the Holocene but has probably been lost by erosion. It is possible that the

---

107. For example, the upper tier of Halaf settlement near Kurban Höyük (Wilkinson 1990), and the significant extension of Halaf settlement in the Balikh Valley (Akkermans 1993).

floodplain was moderately populated by the indigenous Halaf, Ubaid, and Late Chalcolithic communities throughout but is underrepresented in the archaeological record. If this were the case, then the sudden appearance of southern Uruk communities on the terrace around Habuba Kabira (T 509/513)/Sheikh Hassan (T 523) may represent an additional population that built their settlements on the dry terraces which fringed the already populated floodplain. Although speculative, this phenomenon has been recorded elsewhere in the Jazirah with the Uruk settlements appearing towards the settlement boundaries of pre-existing communities.[108]

The number of settlements increased in the early Early Bronze Age and fluctuated only slightly for the remainder of the third millennium. The early Early Bronze Age increase does not necessarily represent an increase in population because many of these settlements were small and dispersed, often being little more than granaries (Danti 1997). With the decline or collapse of the Uruk entity in the region, rather than undergoing a massive depopulation the inhabitants shifted to a more dispersed rural settlement pattern. Because many settlements of this phase, for example, those at Tell Hadidi and Tell es-Sweyhat, remain entombed beneath later Bronze Age occupations, we cannot estimate the full scale of such centers in the early third millennium B.C. It can be concluded that whereas the apparent collapse of the Uruk colonies may have occurred when there was a slight drying of atmospheric conditions, the early Early Bronze Age phase of dispersed settlement took place when moister environmental conditions allowed settlement to take place on the plain.

The episodes of settlement growth and nucleation that were characteristic of the second half of the third millennium occurred during declining albeit fluctuating humidity. For example, an environmental fluctuation occurring around 2400–2200 B.C. (fig. 9.9) may correspond to a major dustfall event recorded by Courty (1998) in the Jazirah to the east. More specifically, Weiss et al. (1993) suggest that a sustained spell of aridity during the final quarter of the third millennium led to collapse of urban-scale settlements over virtually the entire rain-fed Near East. Whatever produced such events, dated stratigraphically between the late Early Dynastic and Akkadian periods,[109] it appears that there was little prolonged effect on settlement around Tell es-Sweyhat.

From about the middle Early Bronze Age to the onset of the Iron Age (4,400 until 3,000 B.P. in fig. 9.9), atmospheric conditions were both liable to wide fluctuations and appear to have been somewhat drier than formerly. Despite the onset of these more inclement conditions,[110] the Sweyhat Plain was indeed settled and a large town grew up in an area that, according to all available evidence, was devoted to dry farming and pastoralism rather than large-scale irrigation (see *Sections 4.E: The Dates of the Off-site Sherd Scatters* and *8.C: Long-term Trends in the Plant and Animal Economy;* Miller 1997a–b). It must be emphasized, however, that the survey record is not sufficiently fine-grained to demonstrate the existence of any short-term negative trend in settlement. In fact, probably the most marked decline of settlement in western Syria appears not to have been around 2400–2350, nor 2200, but rather around 2000 B.C., when large urban-scale settlements appear to have been replaced by smaller rural settlements (Cooper 1998). Although the 2000 B.C. decline does correspond to a marked drop in humidity in the Lake Van climate proxy record, judging from the single visible spike, this again was only a short-lived event.

Interestingly, in the steppelands to the southeast of Aleppo, Bernard Geyer and colleagues have documented an extension of settlement during the end of the Early Bronze Age (late EB IV) at roughly the same time as the maximum extent of occupation at Tell es-Sweyhat (Geyer and Calvert 2001). In this case, despite the limitations of the dry climate of the area, agro-pastoral groups had established settlements across a wider area of the steppe than had been occupied during earlier and possibly somewhat moister phases.

In summary, during the final quarter of the third millennium B.C., inclement environmental conditions appear to have been over-ridden by human factors. For example, agricultural technology in the form of applications of compost, manure, or household refuse fertilizer probably increased agricultural production, albeit at the expense of the stability of long-term yields. In other words, by shifting production towards a more intensive farming regime, although annual production may have been higher, crop failures may have been more likely as a result of reductions in nutrient status and soil moisture, as discussed in *Section 3.D: Climate and Climatic Change.*

The growth of population in the Lake Assad area that occurred during the final third of the third millennium approximately coincided with increases in settlement in the Carchemish/Birecik area (Algaze, Breuninger, and Knutstad

---

108. Such an association has been noted in the field near Kurban Höyük (Wilkinson 1990), in the Balikh Valley, in the north Jazirah, Iraq, and in the Tell Beydar area (Wilkinson 2000a).

109. As opposed to at the end of the Akkadian period as originally suggested by Weiss et al. 1993.

110. More recent support for a drier episode around the late third millennium B.C. has come from the southern Levant; see Bar-Matthews, Ayalon, and Kaufman 1998.

1994), which may be related to the abrupt decline of settlement that occurred in the Khabur Valley at around this time. A similar EB IV increase that occurred in the Jabbul Plain to the west may also represent part of this movement but alternatively may have occurred as early as 2500 B.C. (G. Schwartz, pers. comm.). Although the duration, scale, timing, and degree of late third millennium B.C. devolution of settlement continues to be debated (Weiss et al. 1993; Butzer 1997), population decline in the Khabur Valley could have been matched by increases in populations elsewhere, resulting from perhaps a shift in trade routes, movements of populations, or differential population growth.

The period of declining atmospheric moisture that occurred after 4,000 B.P. (fig. 9.9) is roughly paralleled by a progressive decline of settlement through the Middle Bronze Age, so that by the final quarter of the second millennium B.C. the number of sites was at its lowest for any point since the Ubaid. Claiming that the mid-second millennium decline in settlement could relate to the more arid conditions that prevailed in the Jazirah may be justified. On the other hand, in the Lake Assad area, the third quarter of the second millennium B.C. may be regarded as a phase of settlement nucleation rather than simply diminution. Furthermore, the record for the final part of the second millennium is blurred by uncertainties in chronology because the Iron Age settlements can be dated to only within the range of 1200 to 700 B.C. Nevertheless, according to figure 9.9, with the exception of two moist spikes, it appears that conditions were fairly dry throughout this period.[111] Despite such apparently drier conditions, settlement did continue, and although sites in climatically marginal locations such as Tell es-Sweyhat were abandoned in the early second millennium, other sites such as Tell Brak in similar marginal locations were occupied through most of the second millennium B.C. up until Middle Assyrian times (Oates, Oates, and McDonald 1997). During the second millennium B.C., low rainfall could therefore have inhibited settlement, especially during the final stages of the millennium when sedentary settlement appears to have declined significantly.

After the Iron Age, population increase partly accords with increasing atmospheric humidity. The Lake Van proxy record shows a drier but strongly fluctuating period after about 1400 B.C., and by the Hellenistic period climatic conditions were especially dry. It was during the earlier first millennium B.C., during an apparently drying phase, that the Sweyhat Plain was reoccupied. However, much of this settlement was in the form of dispersed small and medium-sized settlements, especially during the Iron Age when settlements were particularly small. For the upper Lake Assad area in general, the Iron Age pattern of dispersed settlement was maintained during the Hellenistic period,[112] after which settlement increased further during the Roman, Late Roman, and Byzantine periods. This expansion of Roman settlement corresponds to a period during which there was no obvious trend in atmospheric humidity in the Lake Van record, although other records have picked up a slight increase in humidity, albeit one marked by noticeable fluctuations.[113] There followed a decline in settlement numbers from Late Roman/Byzantine to Early Islamic times in the upper Lake Assad area in general (fig. 9.5), but the Sweyhat Plain continued to be well settled throughout the Early Islamic period (fig. 9.4; *Sections 7.G: The Hellenistic, Roman, and Early Byzantine Periods* and *7.H: The Islamic Period*). A sharp drop in atmospheric humidity registered at Lake Van around A.D. 800 may correspond to an overall decline in the number of settlements in the Sweyhat area, which was matched albeit in a more subdued manner in the Lake Assad area in general.[114] Settlement decline then became manifest during Middle and Late Islamic times, by which time the region was very thinly inhabited, but this desertion corresponds to no obvious climatic trend.

Despite the dry and capricious environmental conditions, from the first millennium B.C. onwards communities on the Sweyhat Plain appeared to have been capable of producing sufficient staple foods to provide basic support. In addition, increasingly monetized exchange systems would have allowed communities to buy food from areas that were producing surpluses. During this long phase, population increase may have resulted in more settlement on the plain. By the Islamic period, farmsteads may even have been developed as noted by Whitcomb (*Section 6.A.3: Middle Bronze Age and Later Assemblages*). During the twelfth/thirteenth century A.D., population on the plain retreated so that either

---

111. But see Neumann and Parpola (1987) for evidence of moist conditions during the Neo-Assyrian period.

112. Depending upon whether the data are plotted for the Sweyhat Survey area, for the upper Lake Assad sites alone, or for both sets combined.

113. At this time the Lake of Antioch appears to have developed or risen, conditions in the Jazirah were perhaps slightly moister (Rösner and Schäbitz 1991), the Dead Sea was high (Frumkin et al. 1994), and conditions in the southern Levant were slightly cooler and more humid (Yakir et al. 1994). In addition, evidence

for a slight humic phase in the Palmyra basin during the Roman period took the form of an organic silt dated to 1860 ± 70 or 1930 ± 30 B.P. (Besançon et al. 1997: 19).

114. Unfortunately, the Middle Islamic record for the upper Lake Assad area in figure 9.5 may overrepresent the actual situation because the original van Loon survey frequently describes sites simply as "Islamic." In such cases I have chosen to plot these as both Middle and Early Islamic. This is not the case for the Sweyhat Survey, where the site periodization is subdivided.

nomadism or town life in parts of Syria to the west may have become a more viable option for the displaced population.

Although there are some tantalizing correspondences between settlement numbers and climate — specifically in the mid-/late second millennium B.C. as well as presumably during the Younger Dryas — there is no linear correspondence between humidity (at Lake Van at least) and settlement. The period of later second millennium B.C. atmospheric drying accords quite well with the depressing succession of drought and famines noted in the texts for the end of the second millennium B.C. (Neumann and Parpola 1987), but there is no sign in the climatic record of the verdant times that apparently followed during the first millennium B.C. Overall it seems that during some periods the sedentary population may have succumbed to climatically driven production failures, at other times they were able to over-ride any detrimental features of the climate. In the latter case, if the area were undergoing re-population, soil organic matter and vegetation would have recovered sufficiently for agriculture and pastoralism to be conducted more successfully than during the end of a long period of intensive occupation that resulted in degraded soils (see below). Furthermore, initial smaller populations would concentrate their cultivation and pasture in localized niches along wadis where soil moisture concentration was favorable to crop growth, rather than on the slightly more elevated but somewhat drought-prone soils beyond (*Section 3.D: Climate and Rain-fed Agriculture*). Certainly during pioneer phases of settlement on the Sweyhat Plain (as occurred during the early Early Bronze Age and again in the Iron Age), soil organic matter and nutrient levels would have been raised sufficiently to provide bumper crops, at least for a few years.[115] Finally, the wide range of adaptive strategies available — soil bunds to conserve and direct water, increased storage of staples, different levels of reliance upon pastoral strategies, trade, and potentially more monetized economies from the Iron Age — may have enabled communities to survive in an otherwise inhospitable climate.

Recent geomorphological observations raise the possibility that major floods occurred along the Euphrates Valley during the Middle Holocene and may have had a detrimental effect on settlement (Oguchi and Oguchi 1998; Peltenburg et al. 1996). Flood horizons, which appear to have occurred as high as some 15 m above present river level,[116] were clearly the result of major events that occurred at very long return intervals. In addition to threatening or destroying sedentary settlement on the floodplain and potentially initiating an outward movement of migrants from the riverine zone, such events could have exacerbated the scouring of floodplains and the removal of any associated settlements. It remains a possibility that growth of settlement on terraces such as the Sweyhat Plain may have been partly a response to devastating floods along the floodplain. However, given the limited evidence for floodplain settlement, which partly may be because of such floods and the poor dating of the mega floods, any such relationship must remain hypothetical.

9.G.2. THE SWEYHAT SURVEY AREA

To refine the relationship between settlement and climate, aggregate settlement area for the Sweyhat Plain has been plotted through time and can be compared with climatic phases (fig. 9.9). Even allowing for variations in population density on sites of different periods, the broad pattern is quite clear. There was little or no sedentary settlement on the plain during the moderately verdant Halaf, Ubaid, and Late Chalcolithic periods. Settlement increased abruptly in the early Early Bronze Age, that is, either during the later stages of the Uruk colonies or after their collapse. An increase in aggregate settlement area followed, as well as a concentration of population at Tell es-Sweyhat during the erratically drying final stages of the third millennium B.C. This increase can be compared with the extension of settlement at the end of the Early Bronze Age in the dry steppe southeast of Aleppo (Geyer and Calvet 2001). As the environment became increasingly dry during the second millennium B.C., settlement then disappeared from the plain entirely. It was during the later part of this period in the Late Bronze Age that occupation became concentrated in the nucleated strongholds at Tell Hadidi and Tell Mumbaqa (T 534), as well as at Emar downstream. The desertion of the Sweyhat Plain during the early second millennium B.C. corresponds quite well to a phase of climatic drying. The spread of small sites during the early first millennium took place in a dry but fluctuating environment. Hellenistic settlement, which extended to the plain for some 3 km from the bluffs, again appears to have occurred during a some-

---

115. A similar situation has been recorded in arid parts of central Syria in the mid-twentieth century A.D. during recent phases of agricultural colonization (Métral 2000: 130).

116. According to Oguchi and Oguchi 1998: 309 and 313 for the Tishrin Dam area upstream, but more realistically to some 4 m above floodplain level according to Carter and Tipping 1997. The high figures supplied by Oguchi and Oguchi are, as yet, not confirmed by other studies and need to be supported by other evidence such as the use of slack water deposits to indicate high palaeo-flood stages.

what dry phase, but by the Roman and especially the Late Roman period slightly more humid conditions may have allowed or encouraged the spread of settlement into the drier steppe margins, as has been reported for the steppe of north central Syria (Geyer and Rousset 2001). The Early Islamic settlement, which clearly contained a substantial population (although perhaps not as large as settlement areas would suggest), occurred during a phase of fluctuating albeit possibly drier climate.

9.G.3. SETTLEMENT AND ENVIRONMENTAL CHANGE: SOME GENERAL CONCLUSIONS

In order to interpret the record of settlement more comprehensively, it is necessary to look at a wider range of influences that include social factors, the political economy, as well as environmental fluctuations. No single factor can satisfactorily account for the changes in long-term settlement, either on the Sweyhat Plain or in the upper Lake Assad area in general. Potentially, however, it may be possible to understand this pattern as the result of a number of broad influences as follows: For sedentary settlement to occur, it is necessary that environmental conditions allow it. The local soil conditions and climate must be suitable for crops to be grown for sufficient time to support the communities in question. The environmental factor can be seen as either allowing settlement or inhibiting it. However, an area is not occupied unless social, economic, or political factors are conducive. The need to settle an area is influenced by the existence of key resources (mineral, agricultural, water) or an overspill of population from elsewhere. Overpopulation can be a significant driving agency because if population increases above a certain level, then areas that were formerly not settled are then occupied. Hence, the increase in settlement shown in figures 9.4–5 could be seen as being the result of natural population increase or the arrival of populations from other areas. If major floods had inundated settlements on the floodplain, then the displaced communities may have chosen to settle on adjacent alluvial terraces. Alternatively, economic conditions (themselves perhaps partly related to climate) may have encouraged nomadic communities to settle or for people to immigrate from elsewhere. In addition, technologies such as irrigation or manuring could have been used to enhance inclement environments so that occupation could take place, at least as long as the need remained or the technology was in place. The first obvious sign that technology was specifically introduced to offset the environmental limitations occurred in the second millennium B.C. with the appearance of a canal near Tell Fray (T 532) and textual evidence for irrigated fields around Emar (see *Section 3.C: Irrigation Agriculture*). The only investigated example of a canal within the upper Lake Assad region is the Nahr al-Maslama, dug probably from Habuba Kabira (T 509/513) down to Dibsi Faraj (T 541) and Abu Hureyra (T 545) during Byzantine or Early Islamic times (Harper 1975). This canal appears to be an attempt to increase agricultural production specifically to irrigate land beyond the limits of rain-fed cultivation. The paucity of evidence for irrigation along the Euphrates River contrasts with the Balikh Valley to the east, where large canal systems dug in the Parthian/Hellenistic and Late Antique/Early Islamic periods allowed settlement to extend away from the Balikh River (Wilkinson 1998). The lack of evidence may again be the result of erosion of the floodplain and its associated landscape features by the Euphrates channel.

If economic conditions changed and a monetized exchange system was introduced, the import of food over longer distance would become more financially viable. Hence, in pre-Iron Age economies, when the economy was driven by the local production, exchange, or redistribution of staple goods, the import of food from distant sources may have been more difficult. On the other hand, if a settlement formed part of a commercialized economy supplying goods such as olives (in the Roman period) that could be exported to distant markets, the procurement of supplies would have been more flexible.

Clearly, numerous factors can enable communities to subsist and sometimes even thrive in seemingly marginal areas. A key factor is, of course, the diversified economic strategies that the communities can choose to adopt. So-called agro-pastoral strategies that employ both sedentary cultivation and pastoral activities can be used to increase the flexibility of human groups in such areas (Wachholtz 1996). It is likely that by opportunistically cultivating the land, but also by owning large numbers of animals that can graze wide areas of the steppe and seek out better grazing lands, communities survive even when settlements primarily reliant on rain-fed cultivation may fail. Although environmental conditions must have played a significant role in the long-term survival of settlements in the semi-arid parts of Syria, social, economic, and cultural practices must have been capable of over-riding climatic limitations. Such complicating factors must therefore have contributed to what appears to be a fairly blurred correspondence between environmental conditions and settlement.

9.H. SUMMARY AND CONCLUSIONS

Analysis of the settlement landscape within some 15 km radius around Tell es-Sweyhat suggests that the site was supported by a mixed economy which comprised sedentary intensive cultivation and agro-pastoral activities around the site itself, pastoral activities on the river terrace up to the plateau steppe, and hunting in the hinterlands beyond. Long-distance trade and exchange may have been conducted, in part, along the alignments of settlements across the Jazirah (fig. 9.8). Sedentary merchant communities, travelers, and their animals would, on the one hand, have facilitated trade and exchange but equally would have placed a demand on the settlement for animal fodder and pasturage as well as food for humans. In the summer, additional pasture would have been provided by grazing on the harvested cereals. Even a failed cereal crop could have been turned for a profit if it were used for grazing. As argued by Danti (1997), the pastoral component was probably significant, and as the sedentary population ebbed and flowed over long time periods, it is possible that the nomadic communities would have grown and declined in a complementary fashion, perhaps increasing in numbers during phases of sedentary decline and declining during periods of urban growth when sedentarization became an attractive option.

Pastoral groups could have played a significant role in the local economies by exchanging animals and their products with the sedentary communities and by placing a substantial demand on local grain supplies, thereby perhaps encouraging intensification of cultivation. Mobile pastoral groups would also have supplied supplementary manure for fields as well as provided protection for trade caravans passing through the region (cf. Curtin 1984). Furthermore, during periods of climatic stress when the local inhabitants may have had to sell or exchange animals for scarce (therefore expensive) reserves of grain, some segments of the community, perhaps the elites, traders, or pastoral nomadic groups, may have gained large numbers of animals, and therefore wealth. This could therefore have swollen the reserves of animals for certain individuals while impoverishing others, and at the same time would have propelled parts of the society towards pastoralism (Mortimore 1989; Gallant 1991).

In addition, pastoral groups would probably have played a "protective" role throughout the Jazirah and specifically along the putative long-distance route between Nineveh and the Lake Assad area mapped out above (fig. 9.8). From their southern location it is likely that most of the sites along this route would have been close to extensive areas of pastoral steppe that would have placed them in a position to benefit (or suffer) from interactions with mobile groups. In addition to benefiting from pastoral resources, proximity to cultivable land would have been advantageous, but their climatically marginal locations would have rendered these communities vulnerable to runs of dry years or prolonged drought that would have placed a stress on agricultural production and may have precipitated localized collapse. One such regional collapse, that of the Khabur Valley around the end of the Akkadian period (Weiss et al. 1993), may have encouraged growth in the region between the Lake Assad and Carchemish areas by contributing population who could either have swelled the ranks of the pastoral groups or settled along the Euphrates River.

As noted above, there were probably many routes in operation throughout the Jazirah during any single phase of the Early Bronze Age, and vagaries in political conditions, shifting tribal alliances, and changing patterns of belligerence from nomadic groups would favor certain routes over others. It can be argued that long-distance trade and exchange may originally have contributed to the development of the sites in the Uruk triangle (Algaze 1993), as well as the growth of the Tell Hadidi/Tell es-Sweyhat and Halawa (T 519)/Selenkahiye (T 507) paired settlements. Despite the apparent atmospheric drying that occurred during the later third millennium B.C., settlement on the Sweyhat Plain appears to have continued throughout the Early Bronze Age, perhaps because long-distance trade as well as exchange with pastoralists contributed sufficient wealth to buy food during times of stress. Ironically, climatically "marginal" settlements like Tell es-Sweyhat may have been in a more advantageous position during such periods than settlements in moister areas simply because the latter communities may have been more reliant upon production of staple crops. On the other hand, sites such as Tell es-Sweyhat that could tap into long-distance "network economies" and their associated wealth may have been less vulnerable to the vagaries of local climatic fluctuations (Butzer 1997). Ultimately, however, large settlements in such agriculturally marginal locations were vulnerable to fluctuations in both climate and economic conditions and were therefore ideal candidates for desertion (Danti 2000; Wilkinson 1994).

Overall, during the entire 11,000 years of the Holocene period, the Sweyhat Plain was colonized by two distinct waves of settlement: one during the Early Bronze Age and initial Middle Bronze Age (ca. 3000 to 1900 B.C.), and a second from the Iron Age to the Early Islamic period (ca. 1000 B.C. to A.D. 900/1000). Interestingly, these two cycles closely resemble those recorded by the number of settlements in the upper Lake Assad area as a whole (fig. 9.5), as well as elsewhere in the region.

The second wave of settlement to the river terrace plain around Tell es-Sweyhat during the first millennium B.C., and its continuation thereafter, demonstrates quite clearly that the area was capable of being settled even during those periods when, according to proxy climate records from Lake Van and Soreq Cave, the Near East was rather dry. This appears to have been the period when environmental conditions in the Sweyhat region were least propitious for sedentary settlement.

In summary, the Sweyhat Survey has had to deal with a settlement universe transformed by complex taphonomic processes and which therefore is not fully visible today. Furthermore, these settlements belonged to a set of complex interacting economies based upon a mix of sedentary cultivation, pastoral production (both nomadic and sedentary), and more network-based wealth economies that provided links with a much wider economic sphere. The archaeological record comprises a complex pattern of settlement and retreat that responded to both socio-economic and environmental factors in complex and often unanticipated ways. The situation was further complicated by events in other areas, themselves relating to complex local economies that must have influenced the upper Lake Assad area by contributing immigrants during times of stress and by withdrawing populations when conditions in those places were propitious for growth.

APPENDIX A: SWEYHAT SURVEY SITE CATALOG

SS 1–30

SS 1: TELL ES-SWEYHAT

Wilkinson Tabqa Number: T 585 *Illustration:* Figures and plates, passim

Holland/Whitcomb Survey Number: 2[1]

Period: Third–Early Second Millennium B.C., Hellenistic, Roman (Sweyhat Survey Periods V–VIII, XI–XIII)

Miscellaneous: Possibly ancient Burman. In van Loon's (1967: 12) survey, the site appears to have been identified as T 539 "Msheyrfe Seghire" (cf. Holland 1976: 36–37), which is identified as Mishrifat (SS 16A) herein. Also called Tall as-Sweat, Tall as-Swehat, Tell es-Soueihat, Tall Suwehat

DESCRIPTION

The site consists of a central high mound, 15 m high, covering some 5–6 ha, and a lower outer town area extending over some 700×600 m (ca. 31 ha; Holland 1976). In addition, a rather indistinct area to the south (referred to as the lower town south in Zettler 1997: 4) covered an additional 10 ha. The outer town is surrounded by a very low enclosure wall, which is at its most subdued to the east where sediments washed from the east may have obscured it to some degree. The site is the largest on the plain and sits roughly centrally within it. Parts of the main mound and outer wall have been excavated under the direction of Thomas Holland (1976; 1977; *Sweyhat* 2). In addition, parts of the high mound and outer town have been excavated and explored by geomagnetic prospection under the direction of Richard Zettler (1997).

SS 2

Wilkinson Tabqa Number: T 563 *Illustration:* Figures 2.7, 4.1, 4.12–13, 7.1, 7.4, 9.1

Holland/Whitcomb Survey Number: 9

Period: Early Early Bronze Age (Sweyhat Survey Period V)

Miscellaneous: Recorded as 7 p 45 in the 1974 survey[2]

DESCRIPTION

Small mound, ca. 1.3 km southwest of Tell es-Sweyhat, 55 m north–south, 60 m east–west, 1.5 m high. The mound has a rounded symmetrical profile. Common large stones on the surface are up to 80 cm in size. Occasional to common sherds and occasional flints were seen. The surface is disturbed by six or seven robber pits. In 1974 one of these pits exposed stratified ash layers and some mudbrick. The site is situated immediately south of shallow swale. Holland/Whitcomb survey in 1972 provided similar early Early Bronze Age pottery.

---

1. Unpublished report and field notes from 1972 by Thomas Holland and Donald Whitcomb, on file at the Oriental Institute, University of Chicago; see Holland, *Sweyhat* 2, Chapter 1.

2. The 1974 survey is reported on in Holland 1976: 68–70.

SS 3: TELL HAJJI IBRAHIM

Wilkinson Tabqa Number: T 564   *Illustration:*   Figures 2.7, 4.1, 4.12–13, 7.1,
Holland/Whitcomb Survey Number: 18   7.4–5, 9.1, 9.7
Period: Early Early Bronze Age; minor mid-/late Early
                   Bronze Age; Roman/Byzantine cemetery
                   (Sweyhat Survey Periods V and VI)

DESCRIPTION

Small mound, ca. 0.9 km southeast of Tell es-Sweyhat, ca. 50 m diameter and 1.5 m high (Danti 1997: 89–94;
Danti 2000: 105–95). The mound appears prominent owing to its position overlooking a shallow wadi that runs
along the south edge of Tell es-Sweyhat. Five or six large stones (maximum 100 cm long axis) on the surface
were strewn on the south and west slopes. A robber pit on the southwest slopes exposed 50 cm of occupation deposits and ash, overlaid by 50 cm of developed soil. Pottery was quite sparse but sufficient to distinguish the site
from a field scatter. Occasional flints but no tools were seen. The visit by Holland and Whitcomb in 1972 provided
confirmation of early Early Bronze Age date, together with one later Early Bronze Age comb-incised ware. Excavation by Michael Danti in 1993 demonstrated two phases of early Early Bronze Age occupation and a later phase
dating to around the mid-Early Bronze Age (Danti 1997). The early phase structures were interpreted as silos or
storerooms, whereas the later buildings were described as multiple-room residences.

SS 4

Wilkinson Tabqa Number: T 565   *Illustration:*   Figures 2.7, 4.1, 4.12–13, 7.1,
Holland/Whitcomb Survey Number: 13   7.8, 9.1
Period: Late Roman, Early Byzantine, Early Islamic
                   (Sweyhat Survey Periods XIII and XIV)
Miscellaneous: Recorded as 17 P 77 in 1974 survey

DESCRIPTION

Area of low mounding, 2 km east-northeast of Tell es-Sweyhat on the north bank of a wadi that now flows along
the north side of Tell es-Sweyhat. The site extends over ca. 180 m east–west and 100 m north–south, maximum
height 70 cm. Abundant large stones litter the surface, and the topography is roughly formed into building
mounds. Occasional wall footings were evident. Two or three outliers of minor buildings were evident to the east
of the site. The visit by Holland and Whitcomb in 1972 produced a brittle ware sherd of probable Early Islamic
date (Holland, *Sweyhat* 2, fig. 8:18).

SS 5: NAFILEH VILLAGE

Wilkinson Tabqa Number: T 566   *Illustration:*   Figures 2.7, 4.1, 4.5, 4.12–13,
Holland/Whitcomb Survey Number: 22   7.1, 7.5, 9.1, 9.7
Period: Late Early Bronze Age (Sweyhat Survey Periods VI and VII)

DESCRIPTION

Low mound ca. 70 m in diameter in prominent location on south side of Wadi Nafileh, 2.5 km south-southeast of
Tell es-Sweyhat. The depth of occupation is estimated at ca. 1 m. The site is located in the village of Nafileh and
because it is within an area of housing, pottery is scarce but more common on the eroding slopes, especially those
overlooking the wadi. The underlying natural mounding may be a relict bluff of the Pleistocene Euphrates Valley.
A tomb cut in the limestone rock is probably Roman/Hellenistic in date.

SS 6: KHIRBET ABOUD AL-HAZU

Wilkinson Tabqa Number:	T 567	*Illustration:*	Figures 2.7, 4.1, 4.5, 4.12–13,
Holland/Whitcomb Survey Number:	—	7.1, 7.8, 7.10, 9.1, A.2
Period:	Hellenistic; sparse Iron Age and Roman
(collection areas A–D: Sweyhat Survey
Periods X, XI; collection area E: Sweyhat
Survey Period XIII)
Miscellaneous:	Recorded as 3 p 63 in 1974 survey

DESCRIPTION

3.2 km north of Tell es-Sweyhat, roughly rectangular mound of overall dimensions 100 m east–west and 65–70 m north–south, 2 m high, but appears more prominent from the wadi which runs to the south. A low depression halfway along the north edge of the site may be a gateway. Mound morphology, together with elongate scatter of limestone along the north and east sides, suggests an outer enclosure wall ca. 2 m thick. A possible enclosure or building in the west half of the site is indicated by hachures (fig. A.2). Pits dug in mound summit intercept occupation deposits. Collection areas were A (northeast), B (southeast), C (southwest), and D (northwest). An additional low mound located to the west of the main site (E) is overlaid by a twentieth century house (now abandoned). A modern well is located between the house and the wadi. For the valley section to the south, see figure 2.9.

SS 7: KHIRBET AL-HAMRAH

Wilkinson Tabqa Number:	T 568	*Illustration:*	Figures 2.7, 4.1, 4.12–13,
Holland/Whitcomb Survey Number:	12	7.1, 7.9–10, 9.1, A.1, A.3;
Period:	Late Byzantine/Early Islamic (mainly	plate 16
Sweyhat Survey Period XIV)
Miscellaneous:	Recorded as 10 p 35 in 1974 survey

DESCRIPTION

1.7 km east-southeast of Tell es-Sweyhat, extensive site of low building mounds, 450 m north–south, 180 m east–west, maximum height of mounding 2 m. Frequent building mounds are evident and these enable the site to be subdivided into the following features:

a. Depression alongside south wadi, now heavily plowed; no obvious upcast; possibly intended to trap water flowing along wadi.

b. Minor earthen depression.

c. Square earthen enclosure, 30 m square, ca. 60 cm high.

d. Extensive area of low building mounds with intervening depressions.

e. Elongate depression along wadi. Surface of depression some 0.75 m below plain level, 2.5 m below highest adjacent mounding. Upcast on northwest side includes limestone chips and fine-medium gravel located along south edge of Feature *f*. This upcast appears to have been dug from the wadi bed. The hollow is either a water catchment basin or a large well.

f. Large enclosure of earth and stone, ca. 60 m square, 1.5 m maximum height.

g. Building mound ca. 60 cm square, 80 cm high.

A modern well is located to the west of Feature *g*. Note three additional sherds drawn from 1972 Holland/Whitcomb survey confirm a Byzantine–Early Islamic date (Holland, *Sweyhat* 2, fig. 8:15–17).

SS 8: TELL JOUWEIF

Van Loon Tabqa Number: T 537   *Illustration:*   Figures 1.2, 2.6–7, 5.1,
Holland/Whitcomb Survey Number: 5   6.10–12, 7.1, 7.4–6, 7.8,
Period: Sparse(?) early Early Bronze Age, mainly late Early Bronze Age   8.1, 9.1, 9.7; plates 1, 4, 15
               and Middle Bronze Age, very sparse Hellenistic (Sweyhat Survey
               Periods V, VI, VII, VIII, XI)
Miscellaneous: Also spelled Juaf, Joueif, Jweif, Jweyf; called Shams ed-Din East Tell by van Loon (but see *Appendix B: Shams ed-Din Site Complex, Description*)

STATE OF RESEARCH

Visited by Rihaoui in 1963, van Loon in 1964, and Strommenger in 1968. Surveyed by Holland and Whitcomb in 1972 (Holland, *Sweyhat* 2). Collected as part of the Sweyhat Survey in 1991; sampled for paleobotanical and related material in 1992.

LOCATION

The site is located 6 km southwest of Tell es-Sweyhat upon the residual of a relict Euphrates floodplain on the east bank overlooking the Euphrates River. The altitude of the site was recorded at ca. 298 m a.s.l.

DESCRIPTION

High tell, 180 × 120 m (before formation of Lake Assad) with a 240 m east–west extension; it is partly covered with a modern cemetery. The northern part of the tell was cut by the Euphrates River on the northwest side, revealing a 7 m high section (in 1991) with a continuous sequence of ash layers, a building of burnt mudbrick (or baked brick), a stone-lined well, numerous indeterminate walls and other features, and limestone foundations. An entire suite of rooms was exposed by robbing on top of the section (fig. 8.1c). On the beach of Lake Assad abundant large boulders appear to have been eroded from walls by the lake. Two or three large walls remain intact, and part of this scatter may belong to a large enclosure wall (cf. Tell al-ʿAbd). The mound summit is covered by Islamic(?) graves. Pottery collection areas were A (summit), B (base of occupation along cut), and C (beach with pottery eroded from site). During the 1992 season, the site was sampled for carbonized plant remains as described in *Section 8*. For ceramics from the 1972 Holland and Whitcomb survey, see Holland, *Sweyhat* 2, figure 6:14–18, which supply supporting information for an early Early Bronze Age date. Strommenger mentions Roman sherds on the surface of the tell. Collections in 1991 and 1992 produced mainly mid-/late Early Bronze Age and Middle Bronze Age pottery; Hellenistic sherds were very sparse. Sherds belonging to the "classical" and "Arab" period were found during the construction of a pumping station for irrigation to the east of the tell. Rihaoui mentions rock caves close by that he dates to the Roman or Byzantine period.

LITERATURE

Heinrich et al. 1969: 32–33, figs. 5–6; Holland, *Sweyhat* 2; Rihaoui 1965: 108 (no. 17); van Loon 1967: 13 (no. 537).

SS 9

Wilkinson Tabqa Number: T 569   *Illustration:*   Figures 2.7, 4.1, 4.12–13, 6.5,
Holland/Whitcomb Survey Number: 14   7.1, 7.4, 9.1
Period: Early Early Bronze Age (Sweyhat Survey Period V)
Miscellaneous: Mound A recorded as 1 p 93 and Mound B as 2 p 93 in 1974 Survey

DESCRIPTION

Two small mounds, 2.7 km northeast of Tell es-Sweyhat, situated on opposite sides of a wadi; a second wadi runs to the south of Mound A. Mound A (to south) and Mound B (to north) are both ca. 50 m diameter and 1.5 m high. The surfaces are littered with subrounded limestone fragments, occasionally up to 80 cm long axis. Mound A has more robber pits than Mound B. In 1974 one pit in Mound A revealed stratified ash and occupation deposits. One large fragment of a fossiliferous limestone grindstone was seen on Mound A. A possible circular enclosure of large limestone fragments to the southwest of Mound B may be a late animal pen. According to a local informant, a 10 m square building with four doors was exposed within living memory in the wadi between Mounds A and B. The building was subsequently plowed out. A 10 m long wall, northwest–southeast (103° magnetic), of limestone cobbles, 10–30 cm, was evident immediately south of the southern wadi. This possible water diversion structure or check dam is undated.

SS 10: KHIRBET HAJ HASSAN

Wilkinson Tabqa Number: T 570   *Illustration:* Figures 2.7, 4.1, 4.5, 4.12–13,
Holland/Whitcomb Survey Number: 15   6.21, 7.1, 7.8, 7.10, 9.1, A.4
Period: Late Roman–Early Byzantine (Sweyhat
    Survey Periods XII and XIII)
Miscellaneous: Recorded as 3 p 93 in 1974 survey

DESCRIPTION

Extensive area of low building mounds, ca. 4 km east-northeast of Tell es-Sweyhat, overall dimensions 500 m east–west, 280 m north–south, maximum mound height 60 cm. The site is situated 1.5 km southwest of village of Haj Hassan on main wadi leading southwest towards Tell es-Sweyhat. The site consists of numerous low mounds with occasional wall traces and footings; some building plans are discernible (see sketch plan, fig. A.4). A modern well in the southwest part of the site is now dry but may be a re-excavated Roman feature. A 15 m deep well was cut through angular limestone gravels above, and below through white limestone. The site appears to have developed on a fan of limestone gravels. The site is considerably damaged by plowing since a last visit in 1991 (M. Danti, pers. comm.). One Roman pot stand is illustrated in Holland, *Sweyhat* 2, fig. 8:19.

SS 11: KHIRBET DHIMAN

Wilkinson Tabqa Number: T 571   *Illustration:* Figures 2.7, 4.1, 4.12–13, 6.24–29,
Holland/Whitcomb Survey Number: 10   7.1, 7.9–10, 9.1, A.1, A.5; plate 16
Period: Early Abbasid (Sweyhat Survey Period XIV)
Miscellaneous: Also called Khirbet Dhima; recorded as 5 p 43 in 1974 survey

DESCRIPTION

Extensive area of low building mounds, 1.5 km southwest of Tell es-Sweyhat, overall dimensions 500 m northeast–southwest, 320 m northwest–southeast, maximum mound height 1.5 m. The site is situated on a faint wadi trace that now appears to flow through the site. In 1974 a circular hollow was noted at the northeast end of site with a possible diversion channel to the south. This hollow is similar to the hollow noted at Khirbet al-Hamrah (SS 7) (Feature *a*) and may be either a water collection basin or a pit dug in clay for mudbricks. At the west end of the site a 70 m square enclosure (B) remains with each linear mound being 1.2–1.5 m high. Indeterminate scatters of stone occur within the interior courtyard. The width of the enclosure mound, including the soil washed from the walls, is 14 m. This mounding may include a range of rooms (cf. Area D building at Kurban Höyük [Marfoe 1990, fig. 124]). A single dressed and decorated stone was noted along the east wall mound of structure A. The remainder of the site comprises a scatter of modest-sized building mounds; for example, B is a rectangular building mound, and C is a grid plan of buildings of modular size 20–25 m across, which probably were courtyard houses. Pottery from Mound C came from modern plunder pits dug along walls, the upcast of which comprised brown loams and ashes, which include common charcoal lumps. Mound D is an area of gray soil with abundant pottery; very sandy with common Euphrates gravel; this deposit may be cleanout from a now infilled well. The remainder of the site was not collected. The northeast end of the site is clipped by the modern metalled road.

SS 12

Wilkinson Tabqa Number: T 572   *Illustration:*   Figures 2.7, 6.30, 7.1, 7.9, 9.1
Holland/Whitcomb Survey Number: —
Period: Early Islamic (Sweyhat Survey Period XIV)
Miscellaneous: Recorded as 9 p 33 in 1974 survey

DESCRIPTION

Low mound of white soils and dressed stone, ca. 4 km northeast of Tell es-Sweyhat, overall extent 100 m east–west, 65 m north–south (probably the "Islamic palace" of Egami, Masuda, and Iwasaki 1979, pl. 2). The site over-looks and is on the north side of a deeply incised wadi cut in limestone. The main mound of the site has been ex-tensively robbed to reveal a well-constructed central building 18 × 18 m. Dressed limestone blocks vary over a range of sizes: 90 × 45 × 35 cm, 115 × 50 × 40 cm, and 130 × 50 × 35 cm. The upper wall courses were of very pale brown mudbrick with cream lime mortar. Several interior stones were channeled and grooved for an unknown function, but they may have been robbed out of an olive press, wine press, or similar installation. Interior walls were inferred from robber pits and linear mounds within the main mounded area.

Other mounds adjacent to this central building include a possible enclosure to the north. The linear mound is of pale brown and white soil and probably accommodated a range of rooms of mudbrick. A second low mound to the northwest may be a courtyard building, again of mudbrick.

SS 13

Wilkinson Tabqa Number: T 573   *Illustration:*   Figures 7.1, 9.1
Holland/Whitcomb Survey Number: —
Period: Late Chalcolithic(?) through early Early Bronze Age (Sweyhat Survey Periods III[?], IV[?], V)

DESCRIPTION

Possible site evident as area of low mounds and occasional large stones, ca. 2.3 km north-northwest of Tell es-Sweyhat (SS 1), located on north bank of shallow un-incised wadi, overall diameter 30–50 m, ca. 20–30 cm high. Two groups of large limestone stones may have been plowed or robbed from building foundations. One such stone, with a deep central hollow, is either a door socket or a large mortar stone. The surface scatter includes com-mon flints and common pottery, but the latter is not significantly greater than the local field scatter. A small num-ber of pieces of chaff-tempered and softer pottery suggests, but does not prove, a prehistoric presence, perhaps Late Chalcolithic. Eleven sherds were found, of which two were rims. It is difficult to distinguish between a puta-tive prehistoric scatter and the probably Early Bronze Age field scatter. This site may have been a small prehis-toric (Late Chalcolithic?) settlement overwhelmed and partly destroyed by Early Bronze Age cultivation and plowing.

SS 14

Wilkinson Tabqa Number: T 574   *Illustration:*   Figures 7.1, 7.4, 9.1
Holland/Whitcomb Survey Number: —
Period: Early Early Bronze Age (Sweyhat Survey Periods V[?] and VI[?])

DESCRIPTION

Located on spur of limestone escarpment with a large cairn of stones. Small site on hilltop overlooking Nafileh from the southeast. The adjacent land surfaces are uncultivable lithosols and water sources are absent and must also have been absent in the past. The site forms a roughly rectilinear pattern of stone walls of haphazard stones one course deep. The earth-fast stones are extremely weathered. At the north end of the site a roughly circular cairn of loose stones appears to be a later construction. One or two Euphrates cobbles among the site scatter must be manuports of unknown function. The sherd scatter is sparse, and sherds are small, battered, and highly weath-ered. The sherds are not simply from a single vessel because their thickness varies from 3 to 8 mm (modal thickness 5–6 mm). The overall extent of the built structure is 20×20 m. Although the structure may have formed a dwelling or watchpost, the remains are difficult to interpret. The sherds are all plain simple ware, and the single rim sherd suggests an early Early Bronze Age date, but this suggestion is very tentative.

SS 15: KHIRBET AL-HAMRAH 2

Wilkinson Tabqa Number: T 575   *Illustration:*   Figures 2.7, 4.1, 6.17, 7.1, 7.7, 9.1
Holland/Whitcomb Survey Number: —
Period: Iron Age (Sweyhat Survey Period X)

DESCRIPTION

Small low mound, ca. 2.5 km east of Tell es-Sweyhat, roughly 70 m east–west, 60 m north–south, 1 m high. Stones are common on the surface; two or three are very large, up to 80 cm across. The site is located in an area of very gently sloping terrain with cultivable loam soils; it appears to be on the lowest fringes of the cobble fans debouching from the plateau to the east.

SS 16A–C

The site is located on the Euphrates bluffs ca. 3.5–4.0 km northwest of Tell es-Sweyhat. At present the site is partly obscured by the expanded modern village of Roumeilah. The site is subdivided into an excavated citadel (Mishrifat [SS 16A]), an extensive site within the village (Ramalah [SS 16B]), and a disturbed area (SS 16C) to the west of SS 16B.

SS 16A: MISHRIFAT

Van Loon Tabqa Number: T 539   *Illustration:*   Figures 2.7, 5.1, 7.1–2, 7.8–10,
Holland/Whitcomb Survey Number: 16   9.1, A.6
Period: Late Roman/Byzantine/Early Islamic (XIII and XIV)
Miscellaneous: Also spelled Mechrefat; also called Msheyrfe Seghir, Mushrafe Saghir, Mishrifah Saghir, and Mechrefat Chams el-Dine; new village where site is located is called Roumeilah

STATE OF RESEARCH

Visited by Rihaoui in 1963 and van Loon in 1964; surveyed and excavated by the Japanese Archaeological Mission since 1975; collected by the Sweyhat Survey in 1991. Note that Holland, *Sweyhat* 2, fig. 8:6–7, includes two sherds dating to the final quarter of the third millennium B.C.

LOCATION

Located on the east bank of the Euphrates River on an isolated limestone residual along bluffs of the river terrace ca. 1.1 km north of modern village of Msheyrfe Saghir, 2.5–3.0 km southeast of site of Tell Ali al-Haj (SS 17), with deep eroded valleys to the north and south. The site area described by a Japanese team (Mishrifat; Egami, Masuda, and Iwasaki 1979) includes Mishrifat (SS 16A) and Ramalah (SS 16B), which extends to the north across the river terrace; it exposed a ca. 70×70 m area of limestone ashlar fortification wall reminiscent of Dibsi Faraj. The altitude of the site was recorded at 320.0–330.0 m a.s.l.; compare the floodplain at ca. 300.0 m and northwest of tell at 297.7 m a.s.l.

DESCRIPTION

Mishrifat (SS 16A). Three levels were excavated; the lowest level is described first:

Level III: A massive wall built of square limestone blocks exposed on the north and east sides of the tell appears to form a pentagonal enclosure wall surrounding the top of the tell. The wall follows a "zigzag line" that may be explained by the presence of towers or bastions. A gate was exposed at the east side; the interior has two building phases (buildings A–D).

Finds from the earlier phase include a stone amulet with Aramaic inscription and fragments of first to second century A.D. amphorae including one with a pointed base. Finds from the later phase between Building A and the limestone wall include glass vessel fragments, pointed bone implements, and 298 Roman copper coins dating to the third century A.D. (Antonius Gordianus III [238–244], Julius Philippus [244–249], Trajanus Decius [249–251]); in Building D, a limestone sculpture with a Syriac inscription was found.

Level II: No associated building was unearthed; finds include pottery and coins that date to the Byzantine period.

Level I: Stone foundations of houses overlay a limestone wall; finds include fragments of glazed and buff pottery, glass bracelets, a glass jar with handle, a gold earring, and coins.

Suggested dates: Level III early First to second century A.D., Trajan (89–117?)
  Level III late Third century (evidence of coins)
  Level II Byzantine
  Level I Early Islamic

The site has been interpreted as a military outpost.

LITERATURE

Egami, Masuda, and Iwasaki 1979; Rihaoui 1965: 108 (no. 18); van Loon 1967: 12 (no. 539).

SS 16B: RAMALAH

Tabqa Number: —   *Illustration:*   Figures 2.7, 5.1, 6.20, 7.1,
Holland/Whitcomb Survey Number: 3   7.8–10, 9.1, A.6
Period: Late Iron Age and/or Hellenistic (mainly Sweyhat Survey Period X)
Miscellaneous: Also spelled Ramaleh

STATE OF RESEARCH

Visited by Holland and Whitcomb (1972); collected by the Sweyhat Survey in 1991.

LOCATION

Located on high gravel terrace between old metalled road and bluffs. At present the site extends beneath the village where it is visible in spaces between houses.

DESCRIPTION

In aerial photographs, wall alignments of individual buildings are evident as rectilinear traces (fig. A.6), to the northwest of which appears to be a larger built structure with rather diffuse walls. Traces of numerous walls constructed of large subrounded boulders (0.5–1.0 m) originally collected from the deposits of the nearby Pleistocene terrace. Buildings are eroded down to foundation level; sherds are moderate to common but trampled into small fragments. Slight low occupational mounding occurs towards the northwest end of the site. In 1972 Holland and Whitcomb reported "handaxes and Hellenistic figurines."

LITERATURE

Holland, *Sweyhat* 2, Ramaleh, fig. 9:9–10, pl. 132c–f

SS 16C

Tabqa Number: —   *Illustration:*   Figures 5.1, 7.10, A.6
Holland/Whitcomb Survey Number: —
Period: Hellenistic (XI), with perhaps Late Iron Age

DESCRIPTION

The site, a subdivision of SS 16B, is a disturbed area to the southwest comprising buildings and perhaps graves.

SS 17: TELL ALI AL-HAJ

Wilkinson Tabqa Number:	T 560	*Illustration:*	Figures 1.2. 5.1. 6.13–15, 7.1,
Holland/Whitcomb:	—		7.5–8, 9.1, 9.7
Period:	Sparse Early Bronze Age(?) and Middle Bronze Age at base; much Late Bronze Age into		
	Early Iron Age; sparse Hellenistic (Sweyhat Survey Periods VIII, IX, X, and XI)		
Miscellaneous:	Called Tell el-Naj on topographic maps		

STATE OF RESEARCH

Visited by Rihaoui in 1963 and van Loon in 1964; surveyed and excavated by the Japanese Archaeological Mission since 1975.

LOCATION

Tell Ali al-Haj is located to the east of the village of Roumeilah at the edge of the "second" river terrace. The site is situated on a moderately dissected terrace surface ca. 22 m above the floodplain. The terrace edge is fringed by steep but not vertical bluffs; a moderately mature floodplain extends to the south. Tell Ali al-Haj is separated from Dahrat er-Ramile (SS 18) by a northeast–southwest wadi (Wadi ʿAlawi es-Sulum).

DESCRIPTION

Medium-sized tell, ca. 200 m diameter and 7–8 m high, immediately east of one of the Rumeilah villages on the terrace overlooking the Euphrates River. The Japanese team (Egami, Masuda, and Iwasaki 1979; Masuda 1983), which excavated the site, dug a large excavation trench. The lower settlement spreads as a virtually flat site to the north; a slight rise on the terrace to the north may be part of an outer enclosure wall. A bulldozed area to the south on the edge of the bluffs is of indeterminate date. One or two ceramic wasters of unknown date were recorded on the surface of the tell. The altitude of Tell Ali al-Haj was recorded at 334 m a.s.l. at the top of the mound.

DESCRIPTION

The site is comprised of a settlement and several burials (rock tombs also referred to as "circular stone features").

Settlement (Tell Ali al-Haj). A complex morphology of the terrace by site may comprise additional occupation areas. These include, to the north, a short length of elongate mound (roughly east–west), which may form outer ramparts. The tell has eight building levels (I–VIII), uncovered without reaching virgin soil. Level VI has a substantial mudbrick wall surrounding(?) houses (cf. Masuda 1983, pl. 1); three houses with a total of eleven rooms were excavated. Levels VII and VIII below appear to have a similar layout.

Finds and Dates. In levels VII–VI, terra-cotta house models (marked on Masuda 1983, pls. 1–2), similar to those found at Assur (Ishtar Temple) and Emar, indicate a date of the settlement within the middle of the third millennium B.C. (ED III–Early Akkadian). Little is published on later levels, but a Hellenistic settlement seems to have been at Dahrat er-Ramile. See *Section 6: The Ceramic Sequence from Surveyed Sites* for additional details on Middle Bronze Age, Late Bronze Age, and Iron Age occupations.

Burials:

a) Circular Stone Features: Total of twenty-three of these features were discovered in this area. Situated along the edges of second river terrace, three were excavated (labeled B–D in Egami, Masuda, and Iwasaki 1979, pl. 8a). the diameter of the circles is between 9 and 10 m. One or more burial chambers made of boulders were exposed from beneath the circles. Up to thirty-nine human bodies were found within one chamber (burial C-I). Cist graves (B-III–V) and a jar burial (B-VI, outside stone circle) were also observed.

  The finds include terra-cotta lamps, glass (fragments and beads), a figurine of a goddess holding spear and wearing helmet, and a coin with Greek "M" on it.

b) Rock Tombs E-1 and E-2: Both tombs were cut into the limestone cliff of the terrace (ca. 1.5 km south of Tell Ali al-Haj; cf. Egami, Masuda, and Iwasaki 1979, pl. 2). Both tombs were entered by passageway. Tomb E-1 has sixteen funerary niches, E-2 has three. The finds include pottery, glass-wares (goblet with stem, bottles), terra-cotta lamps, fragments of human bones; one relief fragment showed a funerary figure (surface find). The finds indicate a Late Roman or Byzantine date for both burial types. However, aspects of internal chronology between these two types have not yet been adequately solved.

LITERATURE

Egami, Masuda, and Iwasaki 1979; Masuda 1983, pls. 1–7; Rihaoui 1965: 108 (no. 20).

SS 18: DAHRAT ER-RAMILE

Wilkinson Tabqa Number: T 587   *Illustration:*   Figures 1.2, 7.1, 7.8, 9.1
Holland/Whitcomb Survey Number: —
Period: Hellenistic (Sweyhat Survey Periods XI and perhaps XII/XIII)
Miscellaneous: Also spelled Roumālah, Roumeilah, Rumeilah

LOCATION

Dahrat er-Ramile is located to the east of the village of Roumeilah at the edge of the "second" river terrace. The site is situated on a moderately dissected terrace surface ca. 22 m above the floodplain. The terrace edge is fringed by steep but not vertical bluffs; a moderately mature floodplain extends to the south. Dahrat er-Ramile is separated from Tell Ali al-Haj (SS 17) by a northeast–southwest wadi (Wadi ʿAlawi es-Sulum).

DESCRIPTION

Site merely consists of a scatter of large building stones along the edge of the terrace and adjacent slopes. No mounding is discernible, and other evidence of occupation is slight because the site is, in part, beneath houses of a modern village. Pottery includes Hellenistic bowls, brittle ware, and one fragment of a Hellenistic terra-cotta plaque. The altitude of Dahrat er-Ramile was recorded at 325 m a.s.l.

SS 19: KHIRBET ABOUD AL-HAZU 2

Wilkinson Tabqa Number: T 576   *Illustration:*   Figures 2.7, 4.1, 4.5, 4.12–13, 7.1,
Holland/Whitcomb Survey Number: —   7.4, 9.1
Period: Late Chalcolithic(?) through early Early Bronze Age (Sweyhat Survey Periods III–IV[?] and V)

LOCATION

The site is located ca. 1 km east of Khirbet Aboud al-Hazu (SS 6) and 3.5 km north-northeast of Tell es-Sweyhat.

DESCRIPTION

A very low site, it consists of a group of very small mounds, all but one (18 m diameter) of which are little more than cairns. A number of small cairns occur around the periphery of the site and although these may have formed part of a perimeter wall, this is very tenuous. The intervening space, 70 m east–west × 80 m north–south, is covered by a sparse scatter of pottery and flints. The pottery has an ill-defined chaff-tempered component (Chalcolithic?) and some probably early Early Bronze Age sherds.

SS 20A–B

SS 20A: TELL OTHMAN

Van Loon Tabqa Number: T 538   *Illustration:*   Figures 2.7, 4.5, 4.12–13, 5.1,
Holland/Whitcomb Survey Number: 11   7.1, 7.5, 9.1, 9.7
Period: Early to late Early Bronze Age (Sweyhat Survey Periods V–VII)

STATE OF RESEARCH

Visited by van Loon in 1964, and various members of Sweyhat team in 1970s, 1980s, and 1990s, including the original Holland and Whitcomb survey in 1972.

LOCATION

East bank of the Euphrates River on an inland edge of the terrace ca. 3.5 km away from the riverward edge, approximately 3.3 km south of Tell es-Sweyhat, and 4.2 km east-southeast of Tell Jouweif within the modern village of Tell Othman. Limestone slopes rise gradually towards the south. The altitude of the site was recorded at ca. 324 m a.s.l.

DESCRIPTION

The height of the prominent tell was 9 to 12 m (heavily cut and damaged on its summit), 150 m diameter and ca. 9 m high. No obvious lower, outer mounding was evident, but it could lie beneath the houses of the village. Traces of rubble and mudbrick were on the surface. The site is heavily cut by pits on the north side, which expose some mudbrick and ash layers. The houses of the village have encroached virtually up to the summit of the mound on the south side. Pottery is nowhere abundant. In 1972 Holland and Whitcomb recorded additional pottery of early Early Bronze Age (one cooking pot), mid-/late Early Bronze Age, and indeterminate date. Holland (*Sweyhat 2*, fig. 6:8–13) dates the pottery within the range of Early Bronze Age II to Early Bronze Age IVB. Van Loon suggests an Islamic date.

The low Iron Age site (SS 20B) to the southeast was not recorded by van Loon.

Note: An area of low stony mounding within an area of limestone crust ca. 1 km south of the village exhibiting occasional robber pits appears to be an area of ancient tombs.

LITERATURE

Holland, *Sweyhat* 2; van Loon 1967: 15 (no. 538).

SS 20B

Wilkinson Tabqa Number: T 586   *Illustration:* Figures 2.7, 4.12–13, 6.16, 7.1,
Holland/Whitcomb Survey Number: —   7.7–8, 9.1
Period: Iron Age (Sweyhat Survey Period X)

DESCRIPTION

1.5 m high mound, 100 m east–west and 80 m north–south. The area is located 800 m southeast of Tell Othman (SS 20A), between village and new metalled road. A surface scatter includes a few large, irregular stones up to 60 cm. Pottery is moderately common.

SS 21

Wilkinson Tabqa Number: T 577   *Illustration:* Figures 2.7, 4.1, 4.12–13, 6.6,
Holland/Whitcomb Survey Number: —   7.1, 7.4, 9.1
Period: Early Early Bronze Age (Sweyhat Survey Period V)

DESCRIPTION

Low mound, ca. 100 m diameter and 80 cm high. The site is located ca. 1 km north of Nafileh, a few hundred meters south of a swale that leads towards Tell Hajji Ibrahim. From the east the site appears as a low grayish mound. Common pottery and flint were seen, no obvious concentrations of stones. One or two quernstones of limestone and a few rubbing stones of Euphrates cobbles were recorded. Vesicular basalt was rare. Occasional pottery wasters were observed.

SS 22: SHAMS ED-DIN SOUTHERN SITE AND CEMETERIES

Wilkinson Tabqa Number: 561   *Illustration:*   Figures 5.1, 7.1, 7.4–5, 9.1,
Holland/Whitcomb Survey Number: 4   9.7, A.7; plates 8, 10, 13
Period: Area A: Early Early Bronze Age (Sweyhat Survey Period V);
            remainder of site: Early and Mid-/Late Early Bronze Age (Sweyhat Survey Periods V[?] and VI)

STATE OF RESEARCH

Excavated by J. W. Meyer in 1975 (see *Appendix A: SS 22*), visited by Holland and Whitcomb in 1972 (Site 4).

LOCATION

On low limestone slopes and spur on the east bank of the Euphrates River, the tell is ca. 1.3 km south of Shams ed-Din Central Tell (T 536) and 3.5 km south-southeast of Tell Hadidi (T 548; but on the opposite side of the river). These slopes merge into the floodplain via pale-colored silt and sand fans washed from adjacent limestone slopes. The site is situated in a stable location unaffected by the erosion caused by the Euphrates River. The adjacent limestone terrain has low agricultural potential and cultivation must have occurred on the floodplain to the north (fig. A.7). The altitude of the site was recorded at 312 m a.s.l.

DESCRIPTION

Area A. Elongate low mound 190 m northeast–southwest (1992 estimate: 150 m), ca. 90 m east–west, locally robbed. The area is located on a spur of bedrock between two valleys and overlooks gently aggrading slopes leading down to the ancient floodplain. The tell has two summits and a steep slope in the south; the slope in the north is gradual, allowing no exact delimitation of settlement size. The entire mound appears to consist of cultural deposits, little disturbed by the robber trenches. In 1988 the water of the lake washed away its northwestern edge, exposing parts of the city wall. The wall was 1.0 m wide, followed the contours of the hill, and was preserved for a length of 150.0 m. The wall, reported by a German excavation team, was not evident by the Sweyhat Survey in 1992. The area is clearly an occupation mound in contrast to the heavily robbed tomb groups excavated by Meyer to the east (fig. A.7). Among the sherds collected on the surface by Meyer was one incised sherd (bird?) with a seal impression (spiral and rosette). The tell dates to the early Early Bronze Age, equivalent to the early phases at Tell es-Sweyhat; the remainder of the site and at least some of the cemeteries are later (EB III/IV). For additional pottery, see Holland, *Sweyhat* 2, fig. 7.

Area B. Small area of occupation on a hilltop to the south of Area A. Common sherds of Early Bronze Age pottery were recorded, but some may have been robbed from tombs.

Area C. Lower and mid-slopes to south of Area A. A scatter of sherds and one or two grindstone fragments may also indicate an Early Bronze Age occupation area.

Area D. Area of low mounding (at least partly natural) to the west of Area A with a moderate scatter of Early Bronze Age pottery.

Cemetery A: Cemetery A is located southeast of the tell in a depression between the saddle on which the tell is located and the lowest step of the terrace.[3] The burials were in a chamber burial with entrance shaft, cist graves, and pit graves covered with stone slabs; most graves were robbed. The cemetery extends ca. 20 m north–south and 140 m east–west (i.e., extent of robbed graves). During the 1972 survey of Holland and Whitcomb, vessels labeled "S. Din Cem." can be ascribed to a cemetery adjacent to the tell (Holland, *Sweyhat* 2, site 4). Thirty sherds provide a good range of early, middle, and late Early Bronze Age pottery, but not necessarily a complete sequence (Holland, *Sweyhat* 2, fig. 7:1–29). These sherds complement and extend the range of forms reported in Meyer 1991. The cemetery was excavated by the German team as Shams ed-Din South; see the map in Meyer 1991, fig. 3.

Cemetery B: Cemetery B is located ca. 100 m south of Cemetery A on the northeast extension of the western hills (Jebel Sinn of Shams ed-Din). Robbed graves were between some ruins of a modern village; three graves at the very southern end were documented (nos. 60–62); the burials were in chambers and not cist graves.

---

3.   Compare Meyer 1991: 18, fig. 5, nos. 1–56.

Cemetery C:　Cemetery C is located on the northern extension of the western hills on a small spur projecting northwards and flanked by two wadis to the east and west.[4] Limestone outcrops appear on the surface. A former road to Mumbaqa (T 534) cuts the site into two halves. The area is disturbed by robber trenches. The site extends ca. 150 m north–south and 70 m east–west. Burials were oriented along the slope of the spur; the burials were in chambers (nos. 70–93) with an entrance shaft pointing outwards, cist graves (nos. 94–120), and pit graves (un-numbered).

See also *Appendix B: Shams ed-Din Central Tell, Commentary.*

LITERATURE

Holland, *Sweyhat* 2; Meyer 1991.

SS 23

Wilkinson Tabqa Number:　　578　　　　　　　*Illustration:*　　Figures 2.7, 7.1, 7.7, 9.1
Holland/Whitcomb Survey Number:　　—
Period:　Iron Age or perhaps some Late Bronze Age(?) (Sweyhat Survey Period X)

DESCRIPTION

Virtually flat site, 2 km west of Tell Othman (SS 20A), ca. 80 m diameter, on the north bank of a wadi draining a large catchment to the south of Tell Othman. Common limestone fragments (maximum size 30 cm) were seen, many of which eroded from bedrock. The poorly defined site lacks distinctive soil coloration. The site lies close to the boundary between the Euphrates terrace deposits and limestone slopes; the latter have sparse field scatter suggestive of cultivation in antiquity. Pottery is only occasionally present but sufficient to indicate probable sedentary occupation; some sherds exhibit occasional fresh breaks. Three fist-sized quern fragments were recorded. No obvious water source was present and water probably came from wells in antiquity.

SS 24

Wilkinson Tabqa Number:　　579　　　　　　　*Illustration:*　　Figures 2.7, 6.8, 7.1, 7.5–6,
Holland/Whitcomb Survey Number:　　—　　　　　　　　　　　　　　　　　9.1, 9.7
Period:　Late Early Bronze Age or Early Bronze/Middle Bronze Age (Sweyhat Survey Periods VII and VIII)

DESCRIPTION

On west side of a large wadi where it debouches onto the floodplain near Tell Jouweif (SS 8). The small, virtually flat site on the northeast facing slopes overlooks the wadi. A low mound with outcropping blocks of limestone lies immediately to the west, but the only consistent scatter of sherds is from the flat area on the slopes. Sherds were mainly from a disturbed and robbed area; no occupation deposits were visible. Although the range of sherds suggests occupation rather than graves, this is not entirely clear. The complex of circular stone structures and tumuli in this area also suggests the presence of cemeteries, but this suggestion is not certain. The occupation of the site is contemporary with the main occupation at Tell es-Sweyhat.

4.　Meyer 1991, fig. 29.

SS 25

Wilkinson Tabqa Number: 580   *Illustration:*   Figures 6.2, 7.1–2, 9.1
Holland/Whitcomb Survey Number: —
Period: Late Chalcolithic and pre-Uruk (Sweyhat Survey Period III)

DESCRIPTION

On west bank of the Euphrates River on the main terrace, 3 km northeast of Tell Hadidi. The site is virtually flat, which from a distance is evident as an area of extensive scatter of large limestone blocks that in fact have eroded from terrace deposits. The site is visible along an east–west modern irrigation canal, which has exposed and disturbed dark brown cultural deposits containing numerous large sherds and one or two quern fragments. The site is very ill-defined on the ground, a rough estimate of size being 1 ha in area.

SS 26

Wilkinson Tabqa Number: 581   *Illustration:*   Figures 2.7, 5.1, 5.2, 6.18–19,
Holland/Whitcomb Survey Number: —   7.1, 7.7–8, 9.1; plate 7
Period: Late Iron Age through to Late Roman/Early Byzantine (Sweyhat Survey Periods X, XII, and XIII)

DESCRIPTION

Small site, ca. 0.5 km south of Mishrifat (SS 16A) and 3.5 km west-northwest of Tell es-Sweyhat. The site is located on a fan of a small wadi where it debouches onto the floodplain. A pipe section indicates that limestone fan gravels extend to 2+ m below the level of the floodplain. The site is partly trimmed by the Euphrates River to the west, more recently disturbed by a modern pipe trench, and heavily disturbed and eroded by the lake. Although pottery is abundant, much has been abraded by lakeside erosional processes. In the field emphasis was placed upon collection of freshly disturbed material. Gray ashy deposits with limestone are exposed to the south; the west area is strewn with angular limestone and large pottery fragments. Common Late Roman/Byzantine roof tiles and occasional quern fragments were observed, as was one basalt rotary quern ca. 40 cm in diameter. To the southwest human tombs are disturbed with skeletal fragments strewn around. On the upslope part of the site two rock-cut wine presses were exposed (see *Section 5.A: Wine Presses*).

SS 27

Wilkinson Tabqa Number: 582   *Illustration:*   Figures 2.7, 5.1, 6.8–9, 7.1, 7.5–6,
Holland/Whitcomb Survey Number: —   9.1, 9.7; plates 11–12
Period: Predominantly Late Early Bronze Age and Early Bronze/Middle Bronze Age
         (Sweyhat Survey Periods VII and VIII)

DESCRIPTION

On the bluffs, 3 km west of Tell es-Sweyhat on the edge of the modern village of Mishrifah Kabir. The main site (Area A) is on a hilltop overlooking the floodplain, ca. 100 × 50 m in area. At present the site is partly disturbed by bulldozing for new houses, but the very disturbed soil appears to come from the site, which has a moderate scatter of pottery on adjacent limestone slopes. Common querns and ashy occupation deposits were observed. Occasional pottery is also present on the lower rock-cut slopes (Area B) where a large wadi debouches onto the floodplain in the vicinity of abundant rock-cut tombs (*Section 5.C: Tombs*). Additional material was present on a small disturbed conical mound (Area C), partly disturbed, to the south. The occupation of the site was contemporary with the main occupation at Tell es-Sweyhat.

SS 28

Wilkinson Tabqa Number:	583	*Illustration:*	Figures 2.7, 5.1, 6.31, 7.1, 7.9,
Holland/Whitcomb Survey Number:	—		9.1; plate 9

Period: Mainly Middle Islamic (Sweyhat Survey Period XV)

DESCRIPTION

On the north bank of a large wadi tributary to the Euphrates River, a little north of Shams ed-Din village and 3.5 km west-southwest of Tell es-Sweyhat. On the Euphrates terrace, the site extends over 60 × 80 m. Occupation deposits, mainly fine ash layers, form an apron over the south facing slopes overlooking the wadi. In 1991/92 the site was cut by the shoreline of the lake. One or two quern fragments were observed. Robber pits on the upper site expose probable wall foundations of roughly-hewn stones. The site postdates Khirbet al-Hamrah (SS 7) and Khirbet Dhiman (SS 11) (ninth–eleventh century A.D.?).

SS 29: SHAJARA SAGHIRA

Van Loon Tabqa Number:	549	*Illustration:*	Figures 7.1, 7.8, 7.10, 9.1, A.8;
Holland/Whitcomb Survey Number:	—		plate 14

Period: Roman and Late Roman (Sweyhat Survey Periods XII and XIII)
Miscellaneous: Also spelled Schajara Saghira; also called Khirbet al-Hajj al-Saled

LOCATION

The village of Shajara Saghira is situated on the west bank of the Euphrates River on a spur of the river terrace 24 m above the floodplain, 5 km northeast of Tell Hadidi (T 548), virtually opposite Mishrifat (SS 16A). The site is located by van Loon ca. 250–300 m to the south of and separated from the village by an east–west wadi. The terrace, which is little dissected, is littered with boulders (see *Section 2*) and has been trimmed vertically by the recent passage of the Euphrates River. Before the rise of Lake Assad, the site partly overlooked the river and floodplain. The terrace edge to the south has a number of low mounds along it that partly correspond to Chalcolithic sites SS 25 and SS 30. The altitude of the site was recorded at 320 m a.s.l. on the terrace and 296 m a.s.l. on the floodplain ca. 700–800 m to the south.

DESCRIPTION

A low tell (ca. 2 m high) forms the center of the site on the edge of the terrace. The site was partly disturbed by robbing. The surrounding outer town extending over roughly 200 × 200 m (or slightly more) is comprised of occasional walls of large limestone blocks removed from the underlying terrace. One or two low building mounds and low platform-like areas were observed. Occasional querns were found on the surface; large pieces of worked stone and dressed masonry were sparse. Pottery and Late Roman roof tiles were abundant. Numerous subrecent graves were found in the southern part of the site.

Rihaoui and van Loon may refer to different areas. Rihaoui's description refers to the actual village and its agricultural hinterland, while van Loon refers to an area ca. 250–300 m to the south of the village. Both mention traces of buildings made of rough stone; van Loon notes "many large rectangular buildings," a heavy concentration of flat and semi-cylindrical roof tiles, a few sherds, and "some vesicular basalt hand mill fragments." Rihaoui mentions a great number of potsherds and flints and indicates a Roman date.

LITERATURE
Rihaoui 1965: 109 (no. 27); van Loon 1967: 13 (no. 549).

SS 30

Wilkinson Tabqa Number:	584	*Illustration:*	Figures 6.1, 7.1–2, 9.1
Holland/Whitcomb Survey Number:	—		
Period:	Mainly Ubaid (Sweyhat Survey Period II)		

DESCRIPTION

The site is located on the terrace on the west bank of the Euphrates River between SS 25 and Shajara Saghira (SS 29), possibly merging with the southern limits of the latter. The site is virtually flat with an indeterminate perimeter and estimated area of 100 m, some 50–100 m back from the bluffs. Prehistoric painted pottery and common pottery were on the surface, but only occasional large sherds. Evidence of obvious occupation is little.

MISCELLANEOUS SITES

The following sites, which have been reported by other surveys (mainly Holland and Whitcomb 1972), cannot be fixed precisely. They are noted here for the sake of completeness and for future reference.

TELL WALID ASAF

Wilkinson Tabqa Number: 588   *Holland/Whitcomb Survey Number:*   1

DESCRIPTION

The site is located on the east side of the Euphrates River behind the village of Shams ed-Din; its precise location is not known. On a high rock ridge cut by a wadi are rock-cut tombs and an area of sherd concentration. Five sherds appear to be Hellenistic in date (Holland, *Sweyhat* 2, fig. 9:4–8).

RASM AL-ʿABD MUSTAHA

Wilkinson Tabqa Number: 589   *Holland/Whitcomb Survey Number:*   6

DESCRIPTION

The site appears as a slight rise in the fields, 2 km north of Tell Hadidi (T 548), near the modern village of Rasm al-Mustaha; the site is approached by several modern viaducts. Of the two sherds drawn, both appear to be post-Iron Age, and Holland places them in the Hellenistic period (Holland, *Sweyhat* 2, fig. 8:22–23). Note that this may be the same site as Resm al-ʿAbd Mustaha (T 546), but because their locations do not tally they have been assigned separate numbers.

ZAROB

Wilkinson Tabqa Number: 590   *Holland/Whitcomb Survey Number:*   17

DESCRIPTION

Located on the road roughly northeast of Tell es-Sweyhat (SS 1), near to the village of Shallal and directly west of the road by a deep wadi. Its precise location is unknown, but from the description the site appears to be outside the area of the Sweyhat Survey. The site consists of a mound, 70 × 100 × 3 m, flanked by lower ruins to the north and west. The finds include stone foundations but little pottery. The total extent of the site is ca. 300 × 400 m. Of the two illustrated sherds, J/1 is a white glazed Islamic bowl and the other is a coarse necked jar of Iron Age or Hellenistic/Roman date (Holland, *Sweyhat* 2, fig. 8:20–21).

UMM JEHASH

Wilkinson Tabqa Number: 591   *Holland/Whitcomb Survey Number:*   20

Description

Located near the modern village of the same name, ca. 1 km east of Tell Jouweif (SS 8), probably on or near the edge of the Pleistocene terrace. The site was not recorded by the Sweyhat Survey. Pottery dates range from Hellenistic to mid-Islamic (Holland, *Sweyhat* 2, fig. 8:27–28).

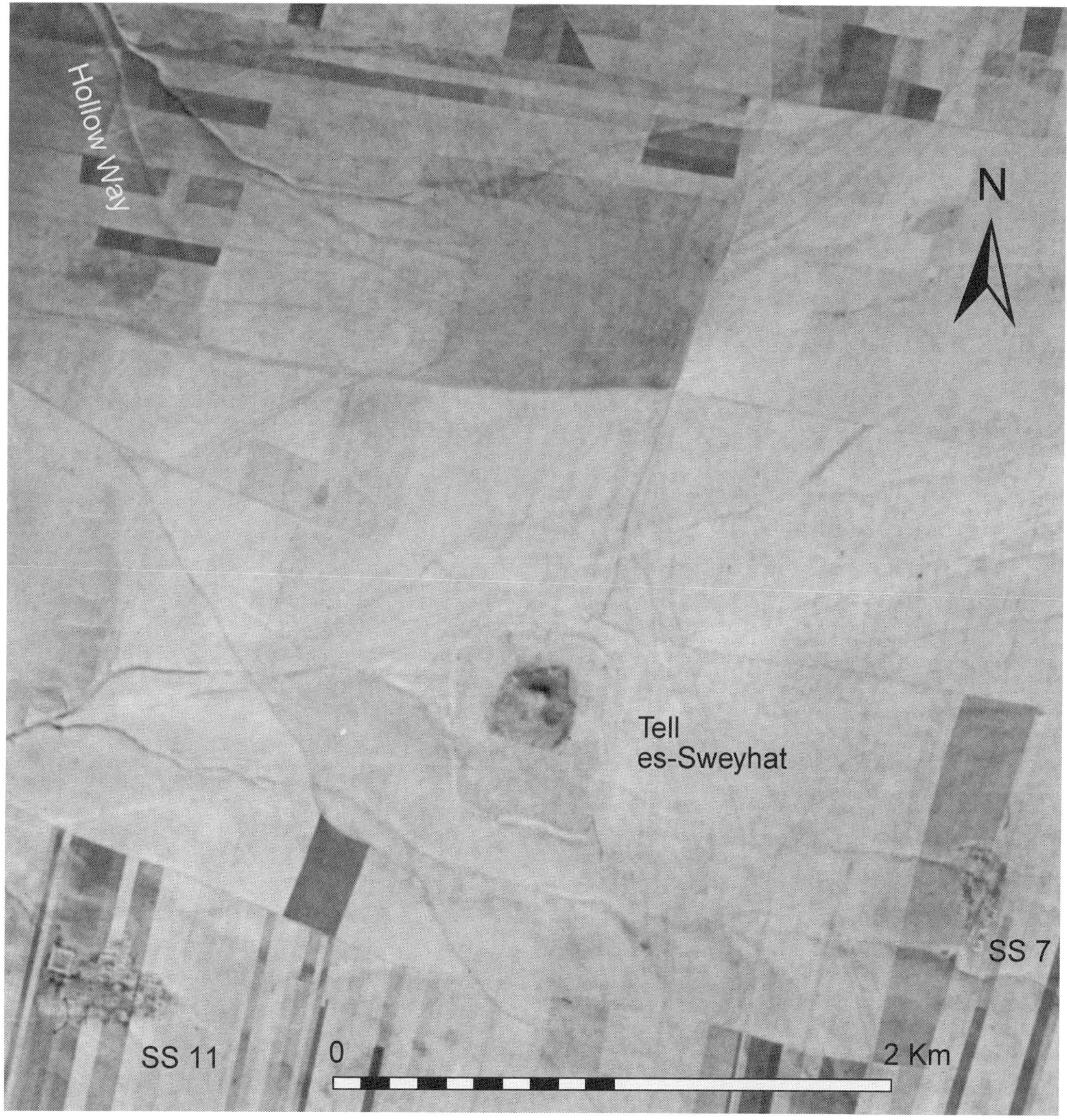

Figure A.1. Tell es-Sweyhat Showing the Faint Trace of the Outer Enclosure Wall around the Central Tell (Dark Area). Note the Trace of a Hollow Way to the Northwest as Well as Two Early Islamic Sites (Khirbet al-Hamrah [SS 7] and Khirbet Dhiman [SS 11]) to the Southeast and Southwest, respectively. Produced by Jason Ur, Oriental Institute CAMEL Laboratory; Courtesy of U.S. Geological Survey

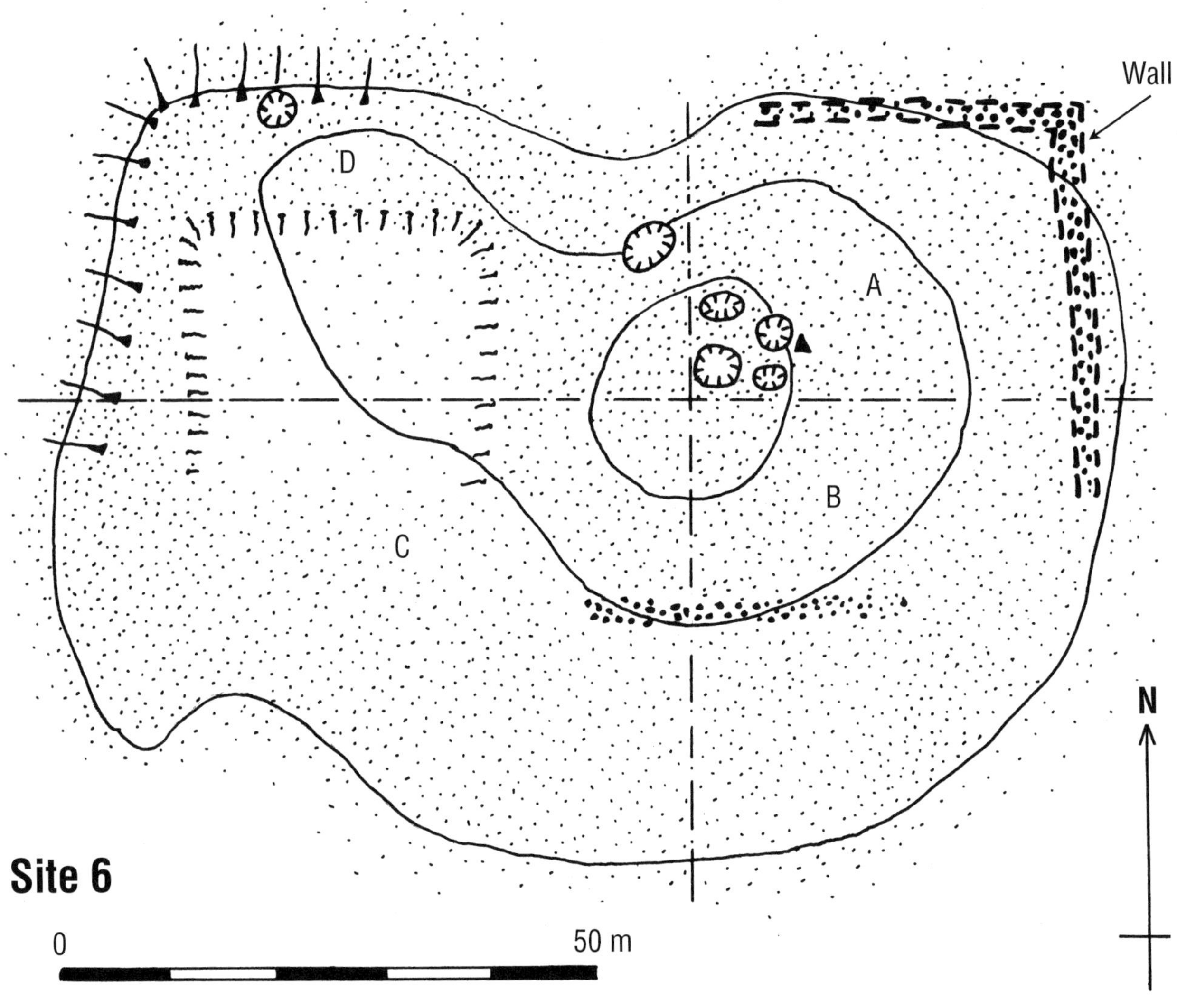

Figure A.2. Sketch Plan of Khirbet Aboud al-Hazu (SS 6) from Aerial Photgraphs and Field Observation.
Letters Indicate Collection Areas

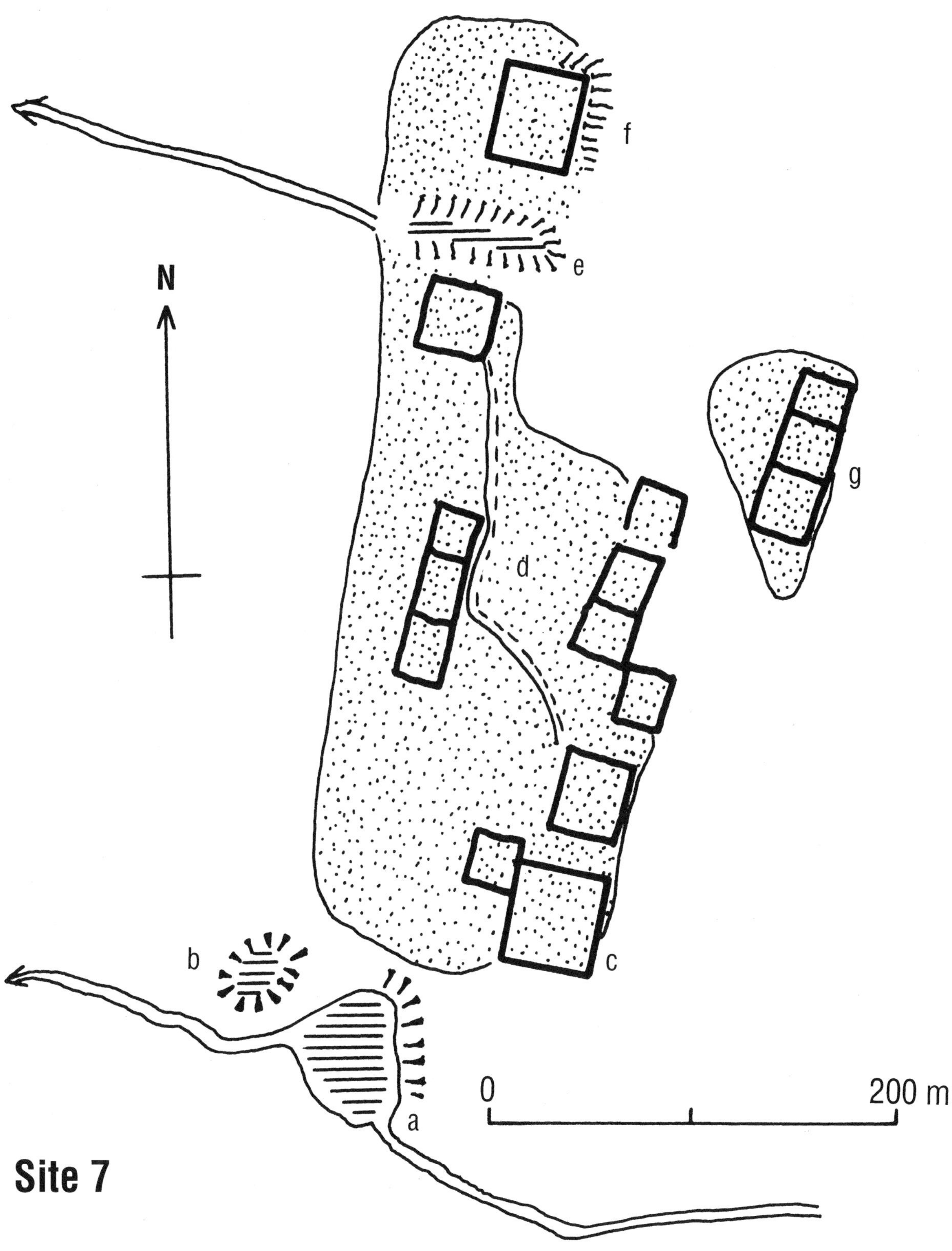

Figure A.3. Sketch Plan of Khirbet al-Hamrah (SS 7) from Aerial Photgraphs and Field Observation.
Letters Indicate Site Features

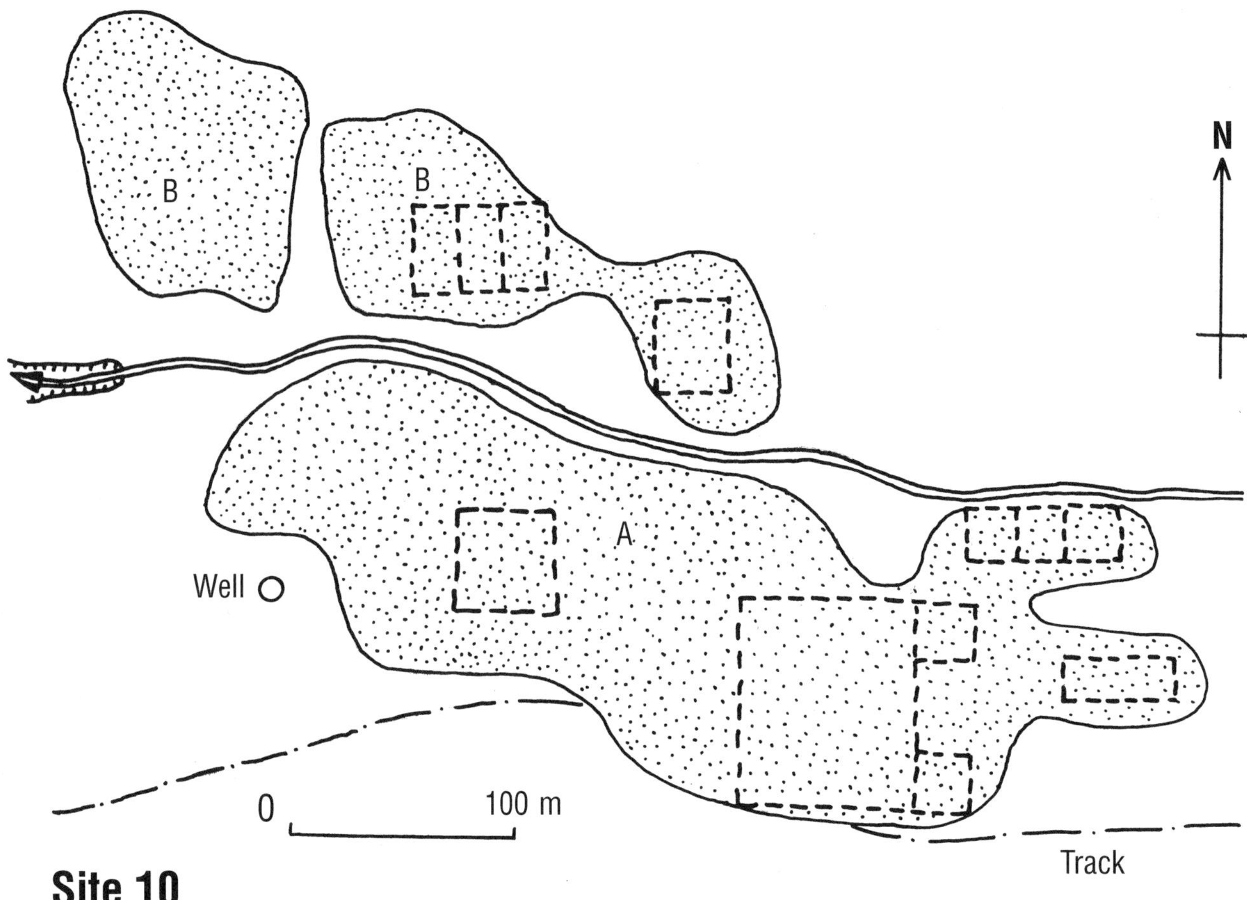

Figure A.4. Sketch Plan of Main Building Mounds of Khirbet Haj Hassan (SS 10). Letters Indicate Collection Areas

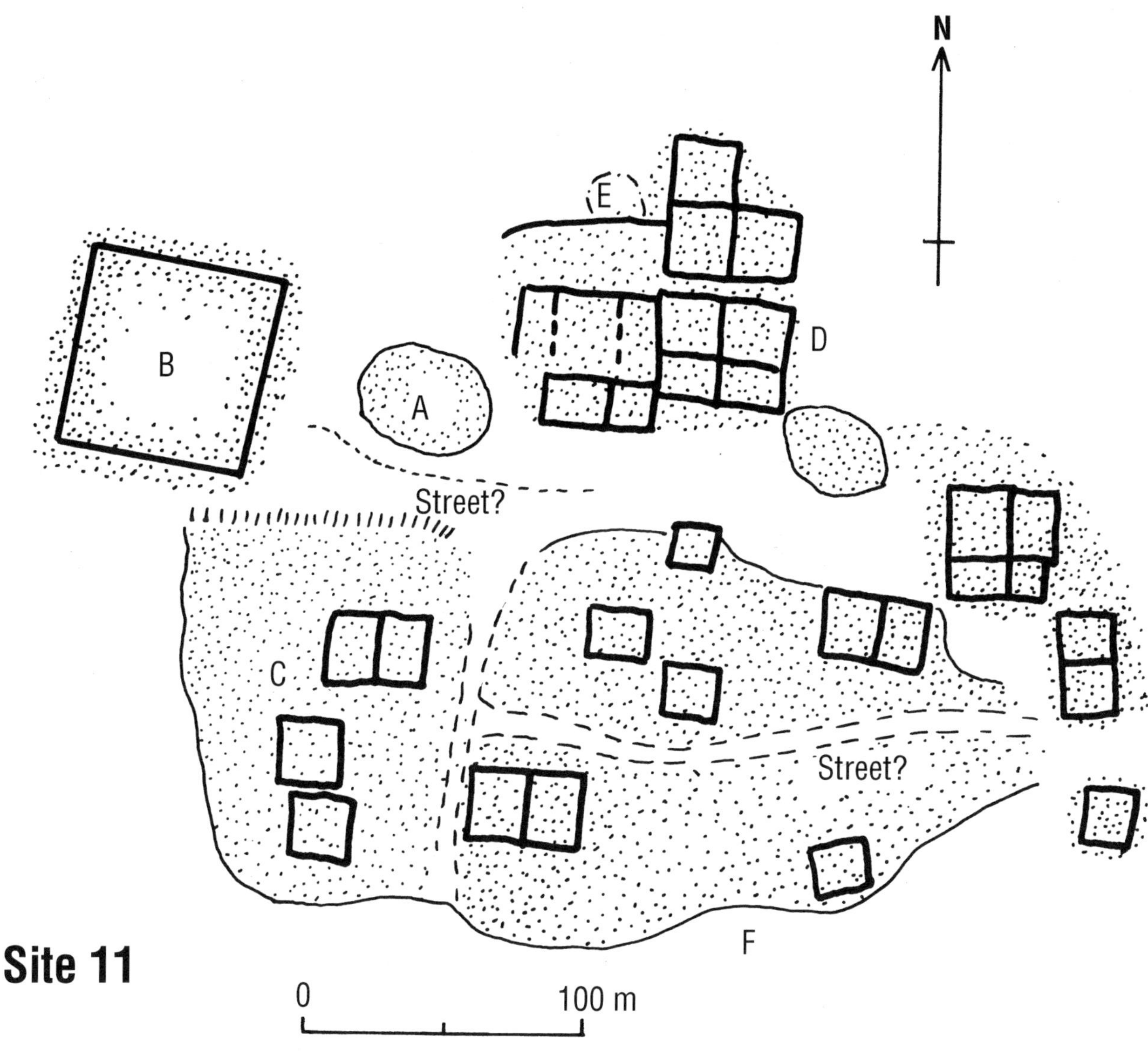

Figure A.5. Sketch Plan of Khirbet Dhiman (SS 11) from Aerial Photographs and Field Observation. Letters Indicate Features

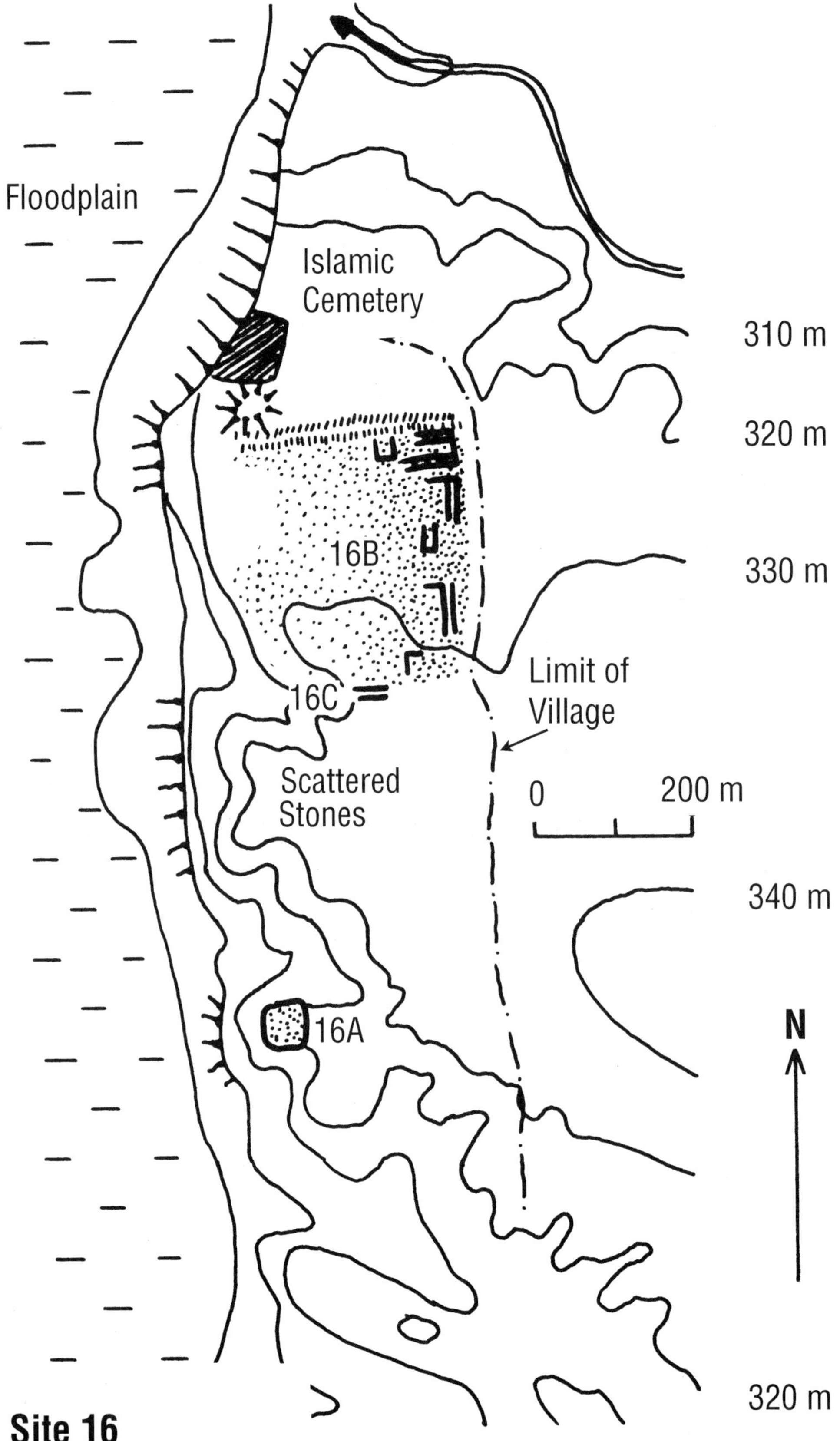

Figure A.6. General Plan of Mishrifat (SS 16A), Ramalah (SS 16B), and SS 16C, Based upon Original Map from Egami, Masuda, and Iwasaki 1979, Aerial Photographs, and Field Observations

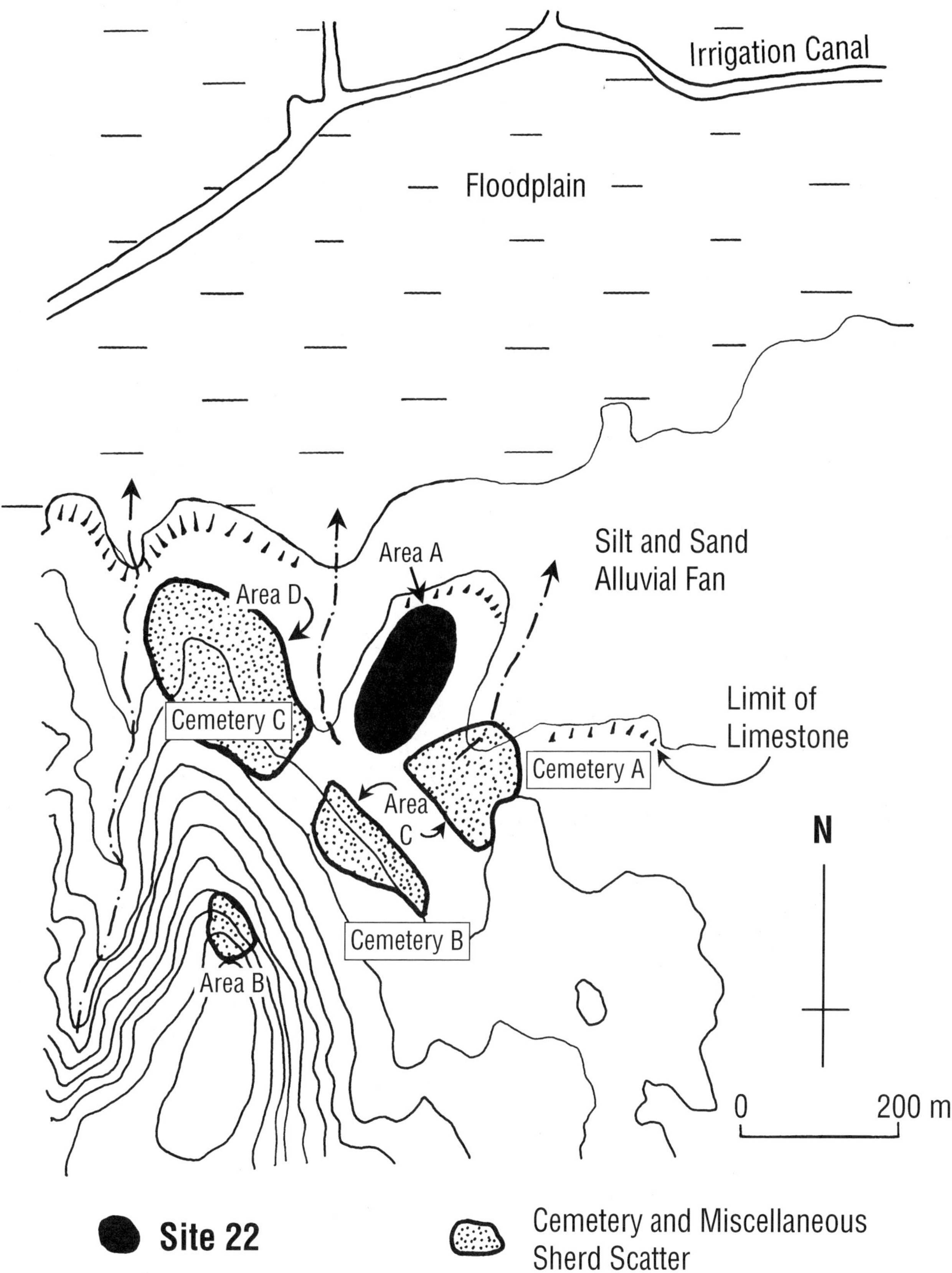

Figure A.7. General Plan of Shams ed-Din Southern Site and Cemeteries (SS 22), Based upon Original Map from Meyer 1991, Aerial Photographs, and Field Observations

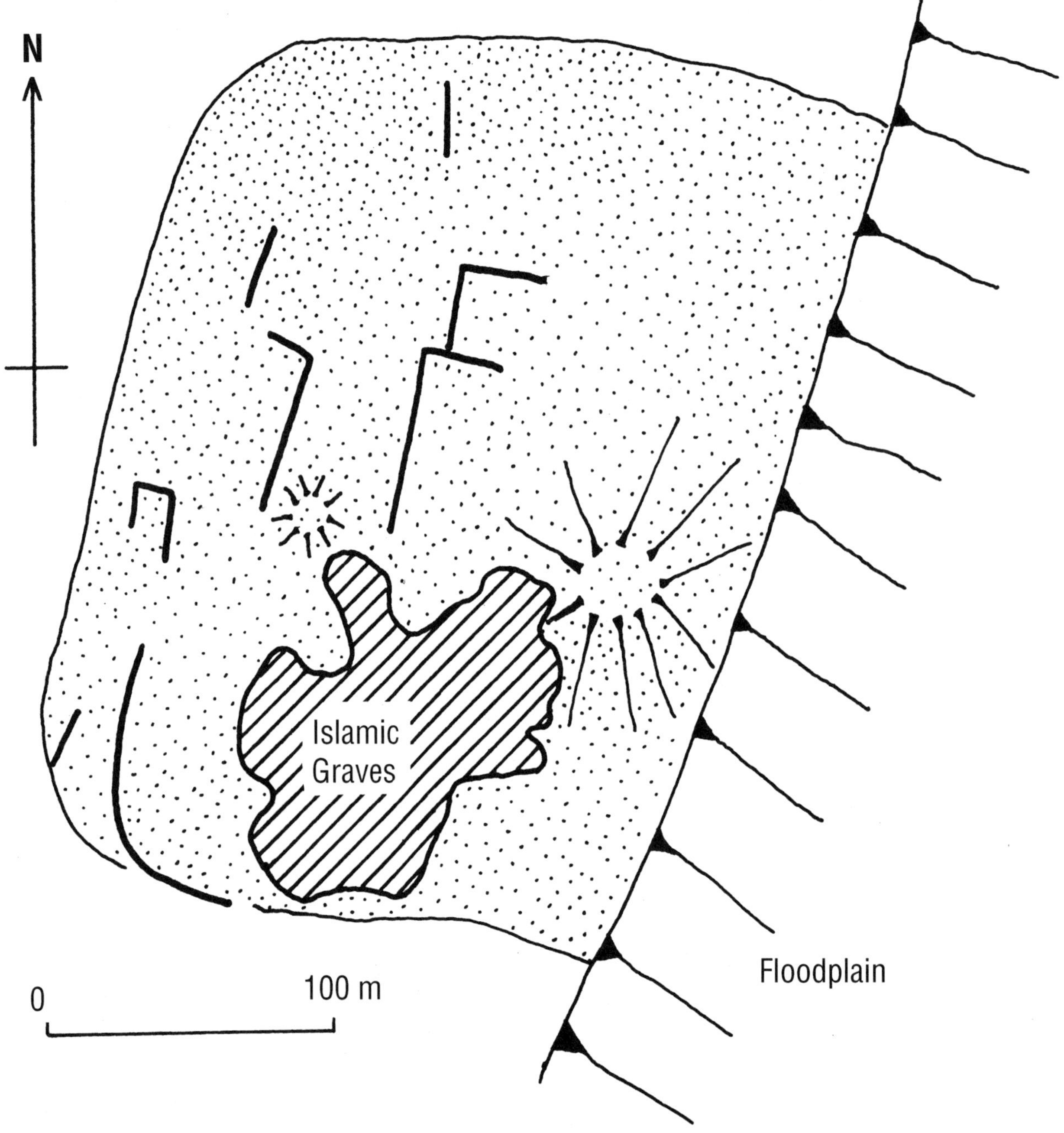

Figure A.8. Sketch Plan of Shajara Saghira (SS 29) from Aerial Photographs and Field Observations

APPENDIX B: SITE GAZETTEER

Clemens D. Reichel

The site gazetteer lists sites primarily in the upper Lake Assad area, with some exceptions. Data for the Sweyhat Survey and miscellaneous sites are given in *Appendix A: Sweyhat Survey Site Catalog*. Tabqa numbers were assigned by van Loon from T 501 to T 556 to sites in the area to be affected by flooding after the building of the Tabqa Dam; Wilkinson continues the numbers up to T 591 (i.e., T 557–T 591). Tabqa sites T 501–T 591 are listed in table B.2. See the *Index of Geographical Names* for page and figure references.

The gazetteer was compiled from data available during the 1990s, when the main text was written, until 1999, when the manuscript was finally revised. Dates for cultural periods are those of the investigators of the sites in question. Although this inevitably results in some inconsistencies in terminology (e.g., Palestinian versus Mesopotamian), the original intent of the authors is preserved without imposing new and possibly inaccurate perceptions.

Table B.1. Summary of Sites Listed in the Site Gazetteer

Site Name	Tabqa Number (SS No.)	Period Occupied
ʿAbd, Tell al-	T 535	EBA, MB I, Iron Age, Hellenistic, Roman, Byzantine
Aboud al-Hazu, Khirbet	T 567 (SS 6)	Hellenistic, Roman
Aboud al-Hazu 2, Khirbet	T 576 (SS 19)	Late Chalcolithic, early EBA
ʿAnab as-Safinah	T 557	Ubaid, Roman, Byzantine, Islamic
Abu Dara West	T 525	Byzantine, Islamic
Ali al-Haj, Tell	T 560 (SS 17)	EBA, MBA, LBA, Iron Age, Hellenistic
Aruda Kabira	T 558	Roman, Islamic
Aruda, Jebel	T 527	Uruk
Dahrat er-Ramile	T 587 (SS 18)	Hellenistic
Dhiman, Khirbet	T 571 (SS 11)	Early Abbasid
Habuba Kabira South	T 513	Late Chalcolithic, Uruk
Habuba Kabira, Tell	T 509	Uruk, EBA, MBA
Habuba Saghira/Aruda Saghira	T 514	—
Hadidi, Mazraʿat	T 547	Paleolithic, Neolithic, Late Chalcolithic, early EBA
Hadidi, Tell	T 548	Uruk, EBA, MBA, LBA, Hellenistic, Byzantine, Early Islamic
Hajj, Tell al-	T 517	Ubaid, Uruk, MBA, LBA, Iron Age, Persian, Hellenistic, Roman, Late Roman
Hajj Hassan, Khirbet	T 570 (SS 10)	Late Roman–Early Byzantine
Hajji Ibrahim, Tell	T 564 (SS 3)	EBA, Roman/Byzantine
Halawa South Site	T 519	Unknown
Halawa Tell A	T 519A	Mid-EBA, late EBA, MBA I, Roman
Halawa Tell B	T 519B	End of Uruk, early EBA, Roman
Halawa Village Sites	T 511	Roman, Byzantine
Halawa, Hweyjet	T 511B	Roman, Byzantine
Halawa, Hweyjet, Northern Village	T 520	Islamic
Halula	—	PPNB, Ceramic Neolithic, Halaf, Ubaid
Hamrah, Khirbet al-	T 568 (SS 7)	Late Byzantine, Early Islamic
Hamrah 2, Khirbet al-	T 575 (SS 15)	Iron Age
Hweysh, Khirbet	T 510	Roman, Byzantine, Islamic
Jafla, Tell	T 521	Pre-Hellenistic
Jerf al-Ahmar	T 559	PPNA, PPNB
Jouweif, Tell	T 537 (SS 8)	EBA, MBA, Hellenistic, Byzantine, Islamic
Kannas, Tell	T 508	Uruk, Agade (Mid–Late EBA), Old Babylonian (MBA), Roman, Islamic, Byzantine
Khafse Saghire	T 515	Roman
Khaled, Jebel	T 552	Hellenistic, Roman

Table B.1. Summary of Sites Listed in the Site Gazetteer (*cont.*)

Site Name	Tabqa Number (SS No.)	Period Occupied
Mishrifat	T 539 (SS 16A)	Roman, Byzantine, Early Islamic
Mumbaqa, Tell	T 534	EBA, MBA, LBA, Byzantine, Hellenistic, Roman, Islamic
Nafileh Village	T 566 (SS 5)	Late EBA
Othman, Tell	T 538 (SS 20A)	EBA, Late Roman, Byzantine
Rimalah	T 554	Roman, Islamic
Rasm al-ʿAbd Mustaha	T 589	Hellenistic
Resm al-ʿAbd Mustaha	T 546	—
Ramalah	SS 16B	Late Iron Age, Hellenistic
Salama, Khirbet	T 516	Byzantine
Selenkahiye	T 507	EBA
Shajara Saghira	T 549 (SS 29)	Roman
Shams ed-Din Central Tell	T 536	Late EBA, early MBA
Shams ed-Din Southern Site and Cemeteries	T 561 (SS 22)	Early EBA, mid-EBA
Shams ed-Din Tannira	T 562	Uruk, Halaf
Shash Hamdan	T 550	Roman, Byzantine, Islamic
Sheikh Hassan, Tell	T 523	PPNA, Halaf, Ubaid, Uruk, Iron Age, Persian, Hellenistic, Roman, Islamic
SS 2 (see *Appendix A*)	T 563 (SS 2)	Early EBA
SS 4 (see *Appendix A*)	T 565 (SS 4)	Late Roman, Early Byzantine, Early Islamic
SS 9 (see *Appendix A*)	T 569 (SS 9)	Early EBA
SS 12 (see *Appendix A*)	T 572 (SS 12)	Early Islamic
SS 13 (see *Appendix A*)	T 573 (SS 13)	Late Chalcolithic, EBA
SS 14 (see *Appendix A*)	T 574 (SS 14)	Early EBA
SS 16C (see *Appendix A*)	—	Late Iron Age, Hellenistic
SS 20B (see *Appendix A*)	T 586 (SS 20B)	Iron Age
SS 21 (see *Appendix A*)	T 577 (SS 21)	Early EBA
SS 23 (see *Appendix A*)	T 578 (SS 23)	Iron Age
SS 24 (see *Appendix A*)	T 579 (SS 24)	Late EBA, EBA/MBA
SS 25 (see *Appendix A*)	T 580 (SS 25)	Late Chalcolithic, pre-Uruk
SS 26 (see *Appendix A*)	T 581 (SS 26)	Late Iron Age, Late Roman, Early Byzantine
SS 27 (see *Appendix A*)	T 582 (SS 27)	Late EBA, EBA/MBA
SS 28 (see *Appendix A*)	T 583 (SS 28)	Middle Islamic
SS 30 (see *Appendix A*)	T 584 (SS 30)	Ubaid
Sukhni	T 524	Byzantine
Sweyhat, Tell es- (see *Appendix A*)	T 585 (SS 1)	Early EBA–MBA, Hellenistic, Late Roman
Taʿas	T 526	Roman, Byzantine, Early Islamic, Ayyubid
Tawi (al-Itre)	T 522	Byzantine
Tawi Burial Complexes	—	EBA
Umm Jehash	T 591	Hellenistic–mid-Islamic
Walid Asaf, Tell	T 588	Hellenistic
Wreyda	T 506	Islamic
Wreyda South Site	T 512	Unknown
Yusef Pasha	T 553	—
Zarob	T 590	Iron Age, Hellenistic, Roman, Islamic
Zmaleh, Khirbet	T 551	Unknown
Zreyjiye	T 533	"Proto-literate," Roman, Byzantine

ʿABD, TELL AL-

Van Loon Tabqa Number:	535	*Illustration:*	1.2, 5.1, 7.5, 9.1, 9.7
Miscellaneous:	Also called Shams ed-Din South Tell		

STATE OF RESEARCH

Visited by Maurits van Loon in 1964; first excavated in 1971/72 by the Syrian Archaeological Excavation Service under Adnan Bounni; subsequent extensive excavations between 1992 and 1994 by the University of Tübingen under Uwe Finkbeiner.

LOCATION

On the east bank of the Euphrates on the river terrace ca. 10 m above the floodplain. Before the rise of Lake Assad, the site overlooked the river at the crossing point between Jebel Sinn (to the east) and Jebel Aruda. The terrace is trimmed by the Euphrates River on the north side. An incised wadi is immediately to the south. The rising lake level has eroded it substantially and turned it into an island (as seen in 1994). The altitude was recorded at 310.4 m a.s.l. at the top and 295.0 m a.s.l. at the base.

DESCRIPTION

Rounded form; dimensions north–south: 210 m, east–west: 220 m. A spur of the site extends to the east. The site has a gentle slope to the east and north, a steep slope to the west and south.

   a. Excavations by Bounni:

In the south, where cut by a wadi, seven 10 × 10 m squares were excavated. Soundings were made on the tell and in the surrounding area. The average depth of cultural deposit was 4–5 m, in three levels:

Level 3: Pebble pavements, circular enclosures, mudbrick walls, stone foundations. The pottery shows little variety and simple execution.[1] Radiocarbon dates range between 2450 B.C. ±60 years and 2195 B.C. ±60 years (uncalibrated). Bounni suggests a date between Early Dynastic III and Akkadian (or EB III); calibration of the radiocarbon dates would place this date considerably earlier.[2]

Level 2: Mudbrick walls (occasionally plastered); ovens, storage pits, pottery, terra-cotta figurines of humans and animals. The pottery includes plain goblets with ring base datable to ca. nineteenth century B.C.; the level has three sub-phases, though generally thin layers of cultural deposit. The suggested date is twenty-first to nineteenth century B.C.

(hiatus)

Level 1: Hellenistic(?); very disturbed due to erosion. Brick walls, pavements, rough stone foundations, channels, ovens (tannurs), and mud deposits with Hellenistic sherds. The evidence suggests a rural economy and pottery production.

  b. Excavations by Finkbeiner:

EBA II–III: Monumental fortification walls could be traced from the north edge (Area I) along the entire eastern edge of the site to the south. Two construction phases were observed. In the younger phase, a glacis was added. Next to a gateway through the fortification in the north several phases of a large "palatial" building were observed. In the eastern center part of the site (Area III), five building phases of a domestic quarter were excavated.

MBA: Little architecture was preserved (Area II), but Middle Bronze Age pottery (e.g., combed-incised ware) was abundantly attested in the secondary fill from Iron Age terracing.

(hiatus)

Iron Age: The site was resettled around 700 B.C. (based on presence of Cypriot-geometric pottery), and occupation continued through the Persian period.

---

1. Compare Bounni 1979b: 53.

2. Curvers (1989: 177) considers a date as early as the beginning of the third millennium B.C.

Hellenistic–Roman: Remains of largely domestic architecture and local Hellenistic pottery (fish plates) were observed. In the Roman period, the Early Bronze Age fortifications were reused and reconstructed.

     c. Observations by van Loon:

Byzantine: Van Loon mentions "sherds Byzantine (red/black corrugated) and later)."

Foot of eastern slope: A necropolis, with ten tombs oriented east–west, was constructed of roughly worked and vertically placed limestone slabs, covered with the same kind of slabs; one or two skeletons were observed. The burial gifts include pots, stone and bronze beads, shell discs, and bronze pins.

LITERATURE

Anonymous 1978/79b: 177; Bounni 1974c; Bounni 1979b; Curvers 1989: 177; Finkbeiner 1994; Finkbeiner 1995; Finkbeiner 1997; van Loon 1967: 13–14 (no. 535).

ABOUD AL-HAZU (SS 6), KHIRBET

See *Appendix A: SS 6.*

ABOUD AL-HAZU 2 (SS 19), KHIRBET

See *Appendix A: SS 19.*

ʿANAB AS-SAFINAH

Wilkinson Tabqa Number:	557	*Illustration:*	Figure 9.1
Miscellaneous:	—		

STATE OF RESEARCH

Excavations by the Syrian Archaeological Excavation Service under Adnan Bounni in 1971/72.

LOCATION

Located on the east bank of the Euphrates River on the edge of a moderately incised river terrace. The site is located on a spur of a terrace next to a wadi, ca. 250–300 m south of Tell al-ʿAbd (T 535).

DESCRIPTION

The site forms a small mound with an elongated mound or earthworks of unknown function extending to the southeast summit of the mound. Late Islamic burials and a stela with an Arabic inscription were observed.

Sherds decorated with black and brown paint and of Ubaid type were common (Bounni 1979b: 55), but no structures were noted.

A Byzantine charnel house included hundreds of skeletons, some in coffins, buried in sandy soil, associated with lamps of Byzantine/Islamic type (fifth to seventh century A.D.), glass bracelets, metal jewelry, and amulets; the burials were disturbed.

Below the charnel house was a tomb made of limestone blocks with an entrance, dromos, and two funerary rooms (sculptures now restored in the citadel of Qalʿat Jaʿbar [T 540]). The finds include glass vessels (vases, goblets). A coin of Emperor Gallus (A.D. 251–253) gives a *terminus post quem* for the date of the tomb, but the tomb is clearly pre-Christian. A second tomb was found in 1972.

In the area of ʿAnab as-Safinah were several tumuli surrounded by stone circles, paralleled by tumuli found at Tell Jouweif (SS 8), Tell Mumbaqa (T 534), Selenkahiye (T 507), and Tell Ali al-Haj (T 560): the diameter of the circles is 9 m maximum, encircling a conical tumulus, covering two or three individual tombs made of stone or mudbrick, robbed in antiquity. The suggested date is Late Roman/Byzantine(?).

LITERATURE

Bounni 1974a; Bounni 1979b.

ABU DARA WEST

Van Loon Tabqa Number:	525	*Illustration:*	Figure 9.1
Miscellaneous:	—		

STATE OF RESEARCH
Visited by van Loon in 1964.

LOCATION
The site is on the west bank of the Euphrates River, ca. 400 m from the edge of a moderately dissected area of terrace, ca. 18 m above the floodplain. The terrace bluffs were steep and moderately eroded. The site is located 1.5 km north-northwest of the village of Abu Dara, ca. 1.7 km east of Sukhni (T 524). The altitude was recorded at ca. 308 m a.s.l.

DESCRIPTION
Small tell ca. 90 m in diameter, 4 m high. The eastern portion is low. Sherds were of red and black ware. Roof tiles and stone counterweights with two grooves were observed. The suggested date is Byzantine/Islamic.

LITERATURE
Van Loon 1967: 7 (no. 525).

ALI AL-HAJ (SS 17), TELL

See *Appendix A: SS 17.*

ARUDA KABIRA

Wilkinson Tabqa Number:	558	*Illustration:*	Figures 1.2, 9.1
Miscellaneous:	Also spelled Aroudda Kabira, ʿAruda Kabira		

STATE OF RESEARCH
Visited by Rihaoui in 1963.

LOCATION
Located on the west bank of the Euphrates River, 5 km southeast of the modern town of Khafseh, ca. 400–500 m north of Nahr al-Homr, ca. 800 m southeast of Sukhni (T 524). The altitude of the site was recorded at 314.3 m a.s.l.

DESCRIPTION
Described as an "agglomeration of *khirbets*" with several mounds, some in the plain. Fragments of columns and tiles were dated to the Roman period; some pottery was also of Islamic date.

LITERATURE
Rihaoui 1965: 109 (no. 31).

ARUDA, JEBEL

Van Loon Tabqa Number:	527	*Illustration:*	Figures 9.1, 9.6
Miscellaneous:	Also called Sheikh ʾArud, Jebel (Jabal) ʿAruda		

STATE OF RESEARCH
Visited by van Loon in 1964, excavated by van Driel (University of Leiden) between 1972 and 1982.

LOCATION
Located on the west bank of the Euphrates River, overlooking the floodplain, and 60 m above it, on the easternmost limestone spur of the Jebel Aruda. The east-facing slopes are very steep.

DESCRIPTION

Three main areas were excavated: temple area, northern houses, and southern houses.

Temple Area[3]

The temple area was at an excellent state of preservation, though the western half at the slope had been eroded. The area was surrounded by a religious precinct wall decorated with niches, preserved to the full height of 2.30 m (rounded wall tops) with gates in the south and west. Secondary rooms were in the south. The eastern extent of the wall was unknown. To the south of the southern entrance was a stairway leading up 2.50 m onto a mudbrick wall that retained the stone fill of a platform; the purpose of the stairway or platform was unknown. Two building phases were noted:

First Phase. Platform (ca. 0.25 m high) with temple (Red Temple) on it. The Red Temple (13.00 × 12.20 m) was tripartite and its outer front niche-decorated. The temple had three doors on its west side and a central room with a rectangular platform. West of the temple was a kitchen building (Lower Building I) consisting of a wide room with a separate courtyard in front.

Second Phase. Large parts of the temple area were filled in with stones, especially Lower Building I and its courtyard and the building of Lower Building II. The "Gray Temple" north of the Red Temple was a tripartite structure, with two entrances on its west side, an "altar" against the southern wall of its central room, and a long narrow room(?) to the south along the southern side of the room. A long mudbrick wall was added to the western gate of the temenos, which extended as far as the natural outcrop of rock.

Destruction of the site appears to have been non-violent: the whole complex was emptied, leveled, and filled in with large mudbricks forming part of a large terrace; the extent of and superstructures on this terrace are unknown. The non-violent destruction accounts for paucity of finds (flower pots, seal impressions).

Northern Houses[4]

Residential quarter with streets (no. 65 in the south, no. 21 in the center of the excavated area), at least eight houses adjoining each other were uncovered (NA–NH). Houses are of the same Uruk type as in Habuba Kabira South, mainly comprising a central courtyard surrounded by a reception room, smaller domestic rooms, and a tripartite house structure. Rectangular and pan-shaped fireplaces are located in the central rooms of the tripartite units and the reception rooms (cf. Habuba Kabira South); this area was destroyed by fire.

Southern Houses (= Area DD)[5]

The terrain has been leveled extensively by cutting a step into the rock and building a stone terrace down the slope of the hill; buildings are therefore largely on one level with narrow and irregular alleys (nos. 82, 102, 128). Seven houses were excavated (S I–VII), each with the same basic features as in the northern houses. The most complete plan was recovered in the northern part of this area (squares E–G / 2–6, building has formerly been called T I); T-shaped middle room in the tripartite unit is also to be found in the adjoining building (T II) to the west.

In the southeast (squares F–G / 95–96) was a shrine surrounded by adjacent rooms with ovens (marked S VIII on plan).

Radiocarbon dates for area DD (houses T I, T II) are 3210–3260 and 3200–3350 B.C. (calibrated),[6] for the Red Temple 3030–3220 B.C. (calibrated),[7] putting the houses in area DD at a slightly earlier date than the Red Temple; seals show Uruk-style processions and Jemdet Nasr-style animal files and women; note the presence of numerical tablets (some with seal impressions) but the absence of clay bullae.

LITERATURE

Anonymous 1978/79a; Hanbury-Tenison 1983, figs. 1–27, tables 1–4; Kalsbeek 1980 (3 figs.); van der Leeuw 1974: 79–80; van Driel 1977; van Driel 1980; van Driel 1981/82; van Driel 1982; van Driel 1983; van Driel 1984; van Driel 1993; van Driel and van Driel-Murray 1979; van Driel and van Driel-Murray 1983, maps 1–3.

---

3. Compare plan in van Driel and van Driel-Murray 1979.

4. Compare van Driel and van Driel-Murray 1983, map 2.

5. Compare plans following van Driel and van Driel-Murray 1979; see also van Driel and van Driel-Murray 1983, map 3.

6. 4495 ±35 B.P. (GrN-7989) and 4490 ±35 B.P. (GrN-8463) (van Driel and van Driel-Murray 1979: 24).

7. 4410 ±80 B.P. (GrN-8464); this sample, however, has been classified as "bad sample" (van Driel and van Driel-Murray 1983, map 3).

DAHRAT ER-RAMILE (SS 18)

See *Appendix A: SS 18.*

DHIMAN (SS 11), KHIRBET

See *Appendix A: SS 11.*

HABUBA KABIRA SOUTH

Van Loon Tabqa Number: 513   *Illustration:*   Figure 9.1
Miscellaneous: —

STATE OF RESEARCH

Visited by van Loon in 1964; excavated by E. Heinrich and E. Strommenger (Deutsche Orient-Gesellschaft) between 1969 and 1974.

LOCATION

Located on the west bank of the Euphrates River on the lower extension of the river terrace (the Mureybit Formation of the main terrace) some 600 m south of Tell Habuba Kabira (T 509). The site is close to the river but is protected from floodwaters and level with the river terrace. Tell Kannas (T 508) in the southern part of the site is discussed separately (see below).

DESCRIPTION

The total area of settlement is ca. 18 ha, of which some 20,000 sq. m (ca. 15%) have been excavated.

City Wall

The inner wall was 3 m wide with bastions or towers and niche decorated; the outer wall was ca. 0.7 m wide with two gates in the west (Habuba Gate and Kannas Gate). Access to the city was also provided on the eastern side from the river through two wadis, one north of Tell Kannas (corresponding to the Kannas Gate) and presumably leading up from a harbor and the second to the south of Tell Kannas.

City Quarters

The city quarters were dominated by a 5 m wide north–south street with gravel pavement that leads, in the north, through a wadi to the terrace, turns southwest, later south, and continues as far as the east–west street between the Kannas Gate and the "harbor." House fronts appeared to be regular. The oldest (apparently unfortified) settlement was concentrated in the north at the eastern edge of the river terrace; three to five sublevels ("*Benutzungsebenen*") were distinguished (Heinrich et al. 1971: 38). Houses showed a typical Uruk-style layout with a square court surrounded by two broad rooms and a tripartite house structure as in Jebel Aruda (see above). Pan-shaped fireplaces were in the court and rooms (Strommenger 1976: 17–19). Some houses (in areas Z, AA, CC) were burnt with their contents preserved within them. Workshops west of Tell Kannas produced game boards (Strommenger 1976: 20–21).

City Area South of Tell Kannas

No sherds were observed on the surface. Parts of this area were thought to have been used for plantations. A sounding in this area cut an east–west ancient irrigation canal that was suggested to have been fed by the Euphrates River (Strommenger 1980: 35); though it is difficult to conceive how the water would have been raised across a 10 m difference in elevation between river terrace and floodplain. Mechanical devices to raise water the 10 m difference are not yet attested for the Uruk period.

Finds

Uruk pottery includes beveled-rim bowls, flower pots, conical cups, water bottles with bent spouts, and re-served slip pottery; red-slipped pottery only occurred in the lower level of the city area (Strommenger 1970: 61–66; Seidl 1971; Sürenhagen 1978). Considerable amounts of Late Chalcolithic chaff-faced ("Amuq F") ware indicate interaction with local Late Chalcolithic culture (Sürenhagen 1986: 24). Other artifacts include cylinder seals, jar sealings ("international style" with human and animal figures), clay bullae, inlays, baked clay tokens with string holes, and numerical tablets. Functional differences between Habuba Kabira South and Jebel Aruda have been suggested based on differences in seal motifs, the presence or absence of clay tokens, and different percentages of local Late Chalcolithic pottery in the pottery assemblages (Sürenhagen 1986: 23–24; Schwartz and Weiss 1992: 232).

Date and Chronology of the Site

An uncalibrated radiocarbon date of 5,085 ±65 B.P. from the site seems fairly early (see Frangipane and Palmieri 1989). The earliest pottery assemblage compares to the Uruk VII–VI assemblage; the presence of nu-merical tablets, however, points towards an occupation of the site until Uruk IV (see Schwartz and Weiss 1992: 232–33). Three phases of occupation can be distinguished, but the layout of houses remains largely identical with no major break in between. The total length of occupation was suggested to have been more than 150 years (Sürenhagen 1978: 48–49; Strommenger 1980: 65).

LITERATURE

Curvers 1989: 178; Frangipane and Palmieri 1989; Frank 1975, pls. 1–4; Heinrich 1970a: 27–37; Heinrich et al. 1971: 37–43; Heinrich et al. 1973: 11–38, 68; Ludwig 1980; Ludwig and Strommenger 1970: 132–33; Riederer 1976; Rihaoui 1965: 110 (no. 32); Schwartz 1992; Seidl 1971; Strommenger 1970: 61–66; Strommenger 1973; Strommenger 1974; Strommenger 1974/77; Strommenger 1975, figs. 1–14; Strommenger 1976, figs. 1–12; Strommenger 1979; Strommenger 1980; Strommenger and Sürenhagen 1970; Sürenhagen 1975; Sürenhagen 1978; Sürenhagen 1986; van Loon 1967: 9 (no. 509 = Tell; no. 513 = South Site).

HABUBA KABIRA, TELL

Van Loon Tabqa Number: 509   *Illustration:*   Figures 1.2, 9.1, 9.6–7

Miscellaneous: —

STATE OF RESEARCH

Visited by Rihaoui in 1963 and van Loon in 1964; excavated by the Deutsche Orient-Gesellschaft between 1968 and 1974.

LOCATION

Located on the west bank of the Euphrates River on the lower extension of the river terrace (the Mureybit Formation of the main terrace), which grades down to the floodplain. No evidence of significant lateral erosion of the tell or adjacent terrace was observed. The site is located some 500 m to the south of the modern village and 1.5 km north of Tell Kannas (T 508). The altitude at the foot of the tell was recorded at 291 m a.s.l., at the floodplain 288 m a.s.l.

DESCRIPTION

The diameter of the site was ca. 230 m, and it covered ca. 3 ha, rising a maximum of 14 m above the floodplain. The top and west slopes were covered by a modern cemetery; excavations therefore had to be largely confined to the east and southeast sides. Twenty building levels were distinguished (from earliest to latest):[8]

Level 1:   Few remains, presumably contemporary with Habuba Kabira South and Tell Kannas, were uncovered, including *Riemchen*-bricks, clay cones (out of context), and pottery (including a sherd incised with a pictogram). A gap was noted[9] between this level and succeeding levels.

Levels 2 and 3:   Two buildings (Northern and Southern) adjoined each other. The eastern wall was the outer wall of the settlement. The Northern building was an industrial complex (pottery?) with fireplaces and working areas. The Southern building showed a defensive character with interior walls reinforced with pillars inside; destruction by fire preserved parts of the inventory (pottery, benches, and fireplaces). The Southern building seems to have had functional and both living and working areas. Dates suggested for this level range between Early Sumerian (Heusch 1980) and Early Dynastic (Curvers 1989).

Level 4:   Rebuilding of buildings from previous level.

Level 5:   The outer wall was reinforced in the east (pillar in southeast corner of outer wall); change from pottery production to production of jewelry.

Level 6:   The outer wall in the east was reinforced by adding 1.0–1.2 m to its width. A gate was constructed towards the Euphrates River in the area of the Northern building. Grave contents (beads, bronze needles, terra-cottas, and brown and black pottery) at that level compare to the assemblages from contemporary burials at Habuba Kabira South.

Level 7:   Further reinforcement of the outer wall. The Southern building remained in existence, with its rooms and activity areas increased in size. A textile dying industry (basins in floor, traces of color) was introduced.

Level 10:   Following a distinctive stratigraphic break, buildings were restructured, some of them with stone foundations. A gateway at the eastern entrance was constructed with an entrance room; to its south a terrace with a well in it was constructed and surrounded by a strong wall that was reinforced by pillars. Substantial changes in the area of the Southern Building were made, including a new building in the area of the Northern building. At this level this settlement reached its greatest extension. Houses are also attested outside of the walled town. A clay cone with incised inscription suggests a date of or before Ur III.[10]

---

8.   The following description (from bottom to top) follows the level designation used by Heusch 1980, which differs totally from the one used in the field.

9.   Heinrich et al. 1971: 9, levels called 7/8 and 6.

10.   Heinrich et al. 1973: 10; Sürenhagen 1973: 36–37.

Level 11:   Buildings were destroyed by flooding.[11] The gate was walled up. A massive building to the north (only exposed at one corner of excavation) was constructed. The Northern and Southern buildings joined together for first time.

Level 14:   Complete reconstruction of the fortification wall in the east. The Northern and Southern buildings disappeared. The settlement density within the city appears to decrease. Date of level: Isin/Larsa–Old Babylonian period.

LITERATURE

Curvers 1989; Heinrich 1970a: 27–37; Heinrich et al. 1970: 30–57; Heinrich et al. 1971: 8–36; Heinrich et al. 1973: 36–67; Heusch 1980; Ludwig and Strommenger 1970: 131–32; Strommenger 1973: 168–70; Strommenger 1979; Sürenhagen 1973; van Loon 1967: 14 (no. 521); von Schuler et al. 1969.

HADIDI, MAZRAʿAT

Van Loon Tabqa Number: 547   *Illustration:*   Figure 9.1
Miscellaneous: Holland/Whitcomb Survey Number 8

STATE OF RESEARCH

Visited by Rihaoui in 1963, by van Loon in 1964, by a team from the Deutsche Orient-Gesellschaft in 1968, and by Holland and Whitcomb in 1972.

LOCATION

On west bank of the Euphrates River about 1 km west-southwest of the village of Hadidi, at a point where the Wadi ʿAyn al-Jamus joins the Euphrates floodplain. The site is located on a spur of an alluvial fan terrace sloping towards the river valley, which forms an intermediate step between the higher terrain and the river valley. Van Loon's (1967: 18) survey map shows an ancient canal between Mazraʿat Hadidi and Resm al-ʿAbd Mustaha (T 546).

DESCRIPTION

Van Loon describes the site as measuring 200 m northeast–southwest and 50 m northwest–southeast. The map drawn up by the Deutsche Orient-Gesellschaft team, however, suggests a much larger area that also includes the area of the modern village. A wide scatter of artifacts includes flints (Paleolithic to Neolithic), chipped stones, and pottery sherds (including handmade and straw-tempered vessels). The artifacts appear to lie on natural soil with no signs of architecture visible (though Rihoui mentions a "petit tell," which may be the same site).

According to van Loon, the site was occupied during the Paleolithic, Neolithic, Chalcolithic, and Early Bronze Age. Holland describes pottery dating to the Late Chalcolithic and Early Bronze Age I (five illustrated sherds: MH/1–5; Holland, *Sweyhat* 2, fig. 8:1–5). One vessel described there as Early Bronze Age IVA (ibid., fig. 8:4) could also be in the Late Chalcolithic/early Early Bronze Age range.

LITERATURE

Heinrich et al. 1969: 31–32, fig. 3; Holland, *Sweyhat* 2; Rihaoui 1965: 109 (no. 29); van Loon 1967: 11 (no. 547).

---

11.   Or level 14(?); compare Heinrich et al. 1971: 10.

HADIDI, TELL

Van Loon Tabqa Number: 548   *Illustration:*   Figures 1.2, 2.6, 3.1–2, 5.1,
Miscellaneous: Holland/Whitcomb Survey Number 7;   7.1–9, 9.1–2, 9.6–8
          also spelled Ḥadīdī; ancient name Azu

STATE OF RESEARCH

Visited by Rihaoui in 1963 and van Loon in 1964; excavated by Henk Frankel for the University of Leiden from 1972 to 1974 and by Rudolph Dornemann (Milwaukee Public Museum) between 1972 and 1978.

LOCATION

Located on the west bank of the Euphrates River on the edge of the terrace ca. 27.0 m above the floodplain. The terrace is little dissected, but the river has trimmed the bluffs vertically. The site overlooks the Euphrates River, with a higher tell to the west, and a lower tell to the east. Hollow ways radiate to the northeast and north (*Section 5.D. Linear Hollows*). The soundings and area excavations are designated areas A–U (see fig. 7.3). The altitude of the higher tell was recorded at 317.5 m a.s.l.

DESCRIPTION

Early Bronze Age

The size of the site is ca. 135 acres (50–60 ha) (cf. map in Dornemann 1985); the earliest evidence comes from area R II (south central area of the high tell):

Stratum 1:   Early Bronze Age I; Nine architectural levels; pottery compares to Sweyhat Area IIA preliminary phases A–C (Holland 1976, fig. 4:1–30), Halawa Tell B, Amuq G, and includes beveled-rim bowls.

Stratum 2:   Early Bronze Age II–III; Pottery assemblage compares to Sweyhat Area IIA preliminary phases D–F (ibid., figs. 4:31–41, 5: 1–42), Halawa Tell B, Mumbaqa *Steinbau* level 4, end of Amuq H (includes comb-incised bands on pottery).

Stratum 3:   Early Bronze Age IV; Few remains were found.

Other Areas: Area B: Robbed Early Bronze Age III/IV tombs were discovered.

Area L: In tomb I, Early Bronze Age III pottery ("metallic ware") and imported vessels with tall narrow spouts were recovered.

Area E: Tomb E I was slightly later than tomb L I.

Numerous handmade figurines were found (EB III/IV).

Around 2000 B.C., the Early Bronze Age city was destroyed.[12]

Middle Bronze Age

During Middle Bronze Age I (stratum 4), the size of the city was drastically reduced (ca. 55 acres, or even less to 12–15 ha). Restricted to the higher tell, in Middle Bronze Age II (stratum 5) an elaborate fortification was constructed (cut in areas B and F). Middle Bronze Age IIB pottery shows close parallels to Tell Halawa and Tell Mumbaqa. A clay mold-impressed plaque from this period has stylistic similarities to the investiture scene painting at Mari palace.[13] Occasional Middle Bronze Age II painted pottery has close parallels at Ugarit, and Middle Bronze IIIB pottery compares to pottery of the Zimri-Lim period at Mari.

Late Bronze Age

The city regained its approximate former size (cf. fig. 7.3 and map in Dornemann 1985: 54).

Stratum 6:   (= LBA IA and B). In area H, the "tablet building" had fourteen tablets[14] dating to the fifteenth century B.C., the time of Hittite domination. The architecture and artifacts tie in with al-Qitar, Tell Mumbaqa (T 534), Meskene/Emar, Qalʿat Ferqʾous, and Tell Fray (T 532).

Sparse remains date to Late Bronze Age II, Iron Age, Persian, and Hellenistic periods.

---

12. Dornemann 1985: 51.   14. Whiting 1979: 144–49.

13. Dornemann 1983, fig. 29.

Stratum 7:   Roman remains found to the south of the high and low tells; sparse remains from the Byzantine and Early Islamic period were observed.

Stratum 8:   Ayyubid (A.D. 1174–1263) occupation.[15]

LITERATURE

Dornemann 1978; Dornemann 1979; Dornemann 1980, pls. 1–10; Dornemann 1981, figs. 1–16; Dornemann 1981/82, figs. 25–30; Dornemann 1983; Dornemann 1985; Dornemann 1988; Dornemann 1989; Dornemann 1990; Dornemann 1992; Dornemann 1993; Dornemann 1997; Franken 1978; Heinrich 1969: 30–32, fig. 3; Rihaoui 1965: 109 (no. 24); van der Leeuw 1974; van Loon 1967: 11 (no. 551); Whiting 1979.

HAJJ, TELL AL-

Van Loon Tabqa Number: 517   *Illustration:*   Figures 1.2, 9.1
Miscellaneous: Also spelled al-Ḥağ, al-Hadsch; Roman name possibly Eragiza

STATE OF RESEARCH

Visited by van Loon in 1964, excavated by a Swiss team in 1971/72 (terminated prematurely due to the construction in 1972 of a water-pumping station on, and a canal right through, the tell).

LOCATION

Situated on the west bank of the Euphrates River on the terrace ca. 12 m above the floodplain. The steep riverward slopes of the tell and its peculiar oval form suggests that the tell was truncated in antiquity and was formerly larger. The tell is approximately 350 m west of the western branch of the river, ca. 1.7 km away from the higher terrace, and 3.8 km north of Tell Habuba Kabira (T 509); immediately west of the site an underground *qanat*-like canal flowed southward.

DESCRIPTION

The tell is large and of ovoid shape, measuring 400 m from north to south, and 200 m from east to west, with a steep slope against the river. The upper and lower town is distinguishable in the aerial photograph. The surrounding terrain includes traces of two square built structures of unknown date. The following periods are represented:

Ubaid Period: Ubaid sherds.[16]

Uruk Period: Beveled-rim bowls were found on the eastern part of the mound (Z–A+ / 20), as well as reddish, smooth incised fragments comparable to those found at Tell Habuba Kabira (T 509), an eye idol,[17] and spouted vessels. The extension of the Uruk settlement was at least over 300 m (evidence from sounding in C / 20a).[18]

Early Bronze Age (third millennium B.C.): Very little occupational material was found; the excavators assume a serious decline — if not a break — in settlement continuity.[19]

Middle–Late Bronze Age (second millennium B.C.): Continued occupation from the early second millennium onwards to the Roman period; the sounding in W / 26–27 and X–A+ / 15–16 showed second millennium fortifications. Among the finds were a relief of Astarte,[20] a liver model,[21] figurines, reliefs, and clay models.[22]

Early Iron Age (early first millennium B.C.): Cypriot pottery (bichrome III–IV) was found on the surface on the east side of the mound.

Persian Period: Finds include a late Astarte relief and rider figurines.[23]

---

15.   Late Bronze Age II onwards taken from table in Dornemann 1985.

16.   Spycher in Bridel et al. 1974: 9, 44, pl. 8a–b.

17.   Stucky 1975: 179, pl. 9a.

18.   Spycher in Bridel et al. 1974: 45–46, figs. 7–14.

19.   Stucky in Bridel et al. 1974: 49.

20.   Stucky 1975: 179, pl. 9b.

21.   Bridel et al. 1974: pl. 12c.

22.   Stucky in Bridel et al. 1974: 49–51.

23.   Stucky in Bridel et al. 1974: 51–52, fig. 17.

Hellenistic Period: Mudbrick walls were found in the upper and lower town, but no coherent structure was recovered. Among the finds were coins, terra-cotta lamps, and pottery.[24]

Late Hellenistic: An outer city wall was found with a shell of two mudbrick walls with a rubble core.

Roman: An inner wall was constructed around the upper town with gates in the west and north and a bastion on the northwest corner (N 26/27). Three building periods were observed; a paved street framed by large square stones leads to the northern gate (cut in P–R 30), to the west of which is a house. The finds date from the first to the second century A.D. To the east of the northern gate, large stone slabs that underlie later buildings are possibly part of a Hellenistic(?) public square. *Upper Town:* Heaps of stone balls of various sizes (for slings and catapults) were found inside the wall. The official headquarters possibly reached in S / 19 includes a mass of stamped bricks of a *cohors secunda pia fidelis*, the presence of which predates A.D. 88.[25] West of the upper town a house and street were exposed in I–K / 21–22. A slope (glacis) towards the wall of the upper town was observed. In the moat of the inner wall a column prism with Greek inscriptions was found, suggesting the presence of a Greek-speaking population in the upper town.

Late Roman (fourth–fifth century A.D.): Only the upper town was inhabited. Coins were found, and subterranean burial chambers south of the city were possibly of the same date.

LITERATURE

Bridel et al. 1974; Bridel and Stucky 1980; Heinrich et al. 1969: 30, fig. 2; Krause, Schuler, and Stucky 1972; Krause, Schuler, and Stucky 1973, pls. 1–18; Spycher in Bridel et al. 1974; Stucky 1972; Stucky 1974: 11 (no. 12); Stucky in Bridel et al. 1974; Stucky 1975, pls. 1–11; van Loon 1967: 16 (no. 53).

HAJJI IBRAHIM (SS 3), TELL

See *Appendix A: SS 3.*

HAJ HASSAN (SS 10), KHIRBET

See *Appendix A: SS 10.*

HALAWA SOUTH SITE

Van Loon Tabqa Number: 519   *Illustration:* —

Miscellaneous: —

STATE OF RESEARCH

Visited by van Loon in 1964; but see Halawa Tell A and Halawa Tell B.

LOCATION

Located on the east bank of the Euphrates River, 1 km south of Halawa village on a natural rise, 10.5 m high.

DESCRIPTION

The length of the site from east to west is ca. 300 m, from north to south is ca. 100 m. A wall, 18 m long and made of roughly dressed stones, was interpreted as the corner tower of a fortress (Halawa Tell B). About 50 m to the south on the other rise (Halawa Tell A) is another foundation made of large conglomerate blocks. A robbed cemetery (of unknown date) is located on the heights to the east of the road.

LITERATURE

Van Loon 1967: 9 (no. 519).

---

24. Stucky 1975: 167.

25. Compare arguments in Stucky 1975: 168.

HALAWA TELL A

Van Loon Tabqa Number: 519A   *Illustration:*   Figures 9.1, 9.7
Miscellaneous: —

STATE OF RESEARCH

Visited by Rihaoui in 1963 and by van Loon in 1964; excavated by W. Orthmann (University of Saarland) from 1977 to 1982.

LOCATION

Located on the east bank of the Euphrates River on a natural mound that is part of the natural river terrace, 1 km south-southeast of Halawa village, and 400 m south-southeast of Halawa Tell B. To the south is a large and deep wadi. The nearby upper river terrace consists of limestone covered with an uneven layer of conglomerate; this layer in turn is overlaid by sedimentary layers (reddish clay with bands of fine gravel).

DESCRIPTION

The site measures between 300 and 400 m in diameter. The city wall consists of a glacis, lower wall, circuit, main wall, and inner reinforcements; the main wall is 1.75–2.60 m wide, made of mudbrick on gravel foundation (Orthmann 1989: 12, fig. 3l; 17, fig. 5). A tower is located in square J.0g (trench F) and a gate in square Q.7e.

Excavations (Levels from Top to Bottom):

> *Square Q:* Excavations in a larger area (Orthmann 1981: 9–37; Orthmann 1982: 144f.; Orthmann 1989: 19–56):

>> *Top Level*: Roman graves (cist graves, pit graves with covering limestone slab).

>> *Level 1* (Orthmann 1982: 127, pl. 2, plan): The walls are close to the surface. Two court houses were uncovered of which only the foundations survive. The pottery corresponds to Hama H–F. The level is dated to the end of Middle Bronze Age I (1800 B.C.) (Orthmann 1981: 27; 1989: 20).

>> *Level 2* (Orthmann 1989: 21, fig. 6, plan): 5,000 sq. m were excavated, and two sub-phases (b and c) were identified. About eighty small house units were excavated, with narrow streets and alleys. No evidence of destruction between the sub-phases was unearthed, rather organic rebuilding occurred. The level is dated to early Middle Bronze Age I (Orthmann 1989: 28).

>> *Level 3* (Orthmann 1989: 34, fig. 15, plan): About 2,000 sq. m were excavated, and three phases (a–c) were identified with phase 3c being built on virgin soil. The city wall had a gate (phases 3c and b). About twenty houses were excavated, with streets and alleys. The finds include pottery, grindstones, and terra-cottas and generally indicate a higher social class than level 2. The pottery corresponds to graves found around the tell. The level is dated to Early Bronze Age IV (phase 3c corresponds to Mardikh IIB1, phases 3b–a to Mardikh IIB2).

> *Square R:* Located adjacent to square Q, a comparison of the stratigraphy with square Q indicates that levels 1 and 3 are present while level 2 is absent (Orthmann 1989: 57–61).

> *Square T:* Excavated over a three year period, three areas (T.3e–5e) were uncovered and the remains of buildings were found on five levels (Orthmann 1982: 146):

>> *Level 1:* Terra-cottas and pottery suggest a late Early Bronze Age IV–Middle Bronze Age I date.

>> *Level 2:* Substantial layer of debris with pits dug into it.

>> *Levels 3–4:* Very fragmentary.

>> *Level 5:* Architectural remains include a large room (cultic function?); the pottery dates to the middle Early Bronze Age (EB II or EB III?).

> *Squares L and M:* Located west of the town area, three levels were uncovered. The top level corresponds to square Q, level 3. Architectural remains suggest the presence of a domestic quarter street with a temple (north Syrian *Antentempel*). A stela fragment was found dating to the Akkadian period (Orthmann 1985: 470–71).

Literature

Curvers 1989: 177–78; Lüth 1989; Meyer 1982; Meyer 1987/88; Meyer and Orthmann 1983; Orthmann 1978/79; Orthmann 1981; Orthmann 1981/82; Orthmann 1982, plans 1–9, figs. 1–24; Orthmann 1984; Orthmann 1985; Orthmann 1989; Rihaoui 1965: 107 (no. 11).

HALAWA TELL B

Van Loon Tabqa Number: 519B   *Illustration:*   Figures 9.1, 9.7
Miscellaneous: —

State of Research

Excavated by W. Orthmann (University of Saarland).

Location

Located on the east bank of the Euphrates River, on a rising land at the edge of the river terrace, ca. 600 m south-southeast of Halawa village, ca. 400 m north-northwest of Halawa Tell A; defined in the north and south by gullies. The altitude at the top of mound was recorded at 310.1 m a.s.l.

Description

Size: Ca. 100 × 100 m.

Fortification Wall. Washed free by the rising lake level in the west of the site, great limestone blocks of the wall were filled in with rubble and clay, and the wall was reinforced with bastions; a mudbrick wall was built on top of the stone wall (stone wall = foundation?), and an artificial rampart was noted on the east side of the site.

Periodization from Bottom to Top (following Orthmann 1989: 85):

Period I: Levels 4 and 3a–b

Level 4: Level 4 was reached in square BM 6b; it was built on virgin soil with no plan. The level is dated to the end of the Uruk period or shortly thereafter.

Level 3a–b (Orthmann 1989, pl. 12): A fortification wall was unearthed in square BM 2b/3b and traced along the northern side of the site. The excavated features consist of small rooms with no coherent building plans except that in the north buildings were oriented on a rectilinear grid. The southern area features occasional semi-circular walls; room 312 contained a wall painting. The finds include a copper ax from level 3b, a zoomorphic vessel, and a mold for metal casting. This occupation level was destroyed by fire.

Period II: Levels 2a–b and 1a–c

Level 2a–b: The city wall was rebuilt. Terracing occurred in large areas, and a 1 m high mudbrick platform was constructed in the middle of the site with a temple (*Bau II*) measuring 10 × 12 m (inside) on it. The temple's outside was decorated with niches, inside a podium at its northern side. To the east of *Bau II* another "temple" was built on a platform (*Kleiner Tempel*). South of the temples were a street and houses.

Level 1c: Due to the considerable rise of the terrain around the sanctuary a new terrace was built for *Bau II* and ramps were added on its east and west sides.

Level 1b: The terrace was widened; an ash layer (indicator of a destruction?) in the *Kleiner Tempel* was leveled probably in response to a permanent rise of the terrain.

Level 1a: Changes were made in the eastern part of the sacred area, the terrace was widened, and a building with two rooms was added. The southern front of the *Kleiner Tempel* was decorated with pillars.

Level 1 is dated to early Early Dynastic (ED I/II).

Roman period: Graves were observed.

LITERATURE

Curvers 1989: 177–78; Lüth 1989; Meyer 1982; Meyer 1987/88; Meyer and Orthmann 1983; Orthmann 1978/79; Orthmann 1981; Orthmann 1981/82; Orthmann 1982, plans 1–9, figs. 1–24; Orthmann 1984; Orthmann 1985; Orthmann 1989; Rihaoui 1965: 107 (no. 11).

HALAWA VILLAGE SITES

Van Loon Tabqa Number:	511	*Illustration:*	Figures 1.2, 9.1, 9.6, 9.8
Miscellaneous:	—		

STATE OF RESEARCH

Visited by van Loon in 1964.

LOCATION

Two sites within the southern part of the village of Halawa, ca. 100 m apart from each other, a southern and western site.

DESCRIPTION

Much pottery visible, other finds include flat and semi-cylindrical roof tiles, a limestone column, two basalt querns, a cross in a circle (in stone), a pottery flask, and a base of a glass vessel. The sherds (described for both Halawa Village Sites and Hweyjet Halawa [T 511B]) were wheel made, grit tempered buff, bright red slipped, red/black corrugated, with large painted loops. Some 500 m to the north, at the northern edge of the village, two limestone columns and fossiliferous limestone bases in situ suggest the presence of a building. Finds suggest a Roman/Byzantine date of the site.

LITERATURE

Van Loon 1967: 8 (no. 511).

HALAWA, HWEYJET

Van Loon Tabqa Number:	511B	*Illustration:*	Figures 1.2, 9.1
Miscellaneous:	Also spelled Hawije, Hweije, and Hweijet		

STATE OF RESEARCH

Visited by van Loon in 1964.

LOCATION

Located on the east bank of the Euphrates River, near the center of the modern village of Hweyjet Halawa, ca. 1.1 km north of Halawa Tell B, 4.9 km southeast of Tell Habuba Kabira (T 509), 4.0 km southeast of Tell Kannas (T 508), and ca. 1.3 km north of Halawa village.

DESCRIPTION

Mudbrick wall exposed in cut (corner rests on a stone block), with bricks measuring 50×8 cm. Nearby flat and semi-cylindrical roof tiles, ornate marble columns, and a mosaic floor (5×7 m) were observed. A conglomerate millstone, 2 m diameter, 50 cm thick, square hole in its middle, was found at the near north side of the village. The sherds (described for both Halawa Village Sites and Hweyjet Halawa [T 511B]) were wheel made, grit tempered buff, bright red slipped, red/black corrugated, with large painted loops. Finds suggest a Roman/Byzantine date of the site.

LITERATURE

Van Loon 1967: 8 (no. 511).

HALAWA, HWEYJET, NORTHERN VILLAGE

Van Loon Tabqa Number: 520   *Illustration:*   Figure 9.1
Miscellaneous: Also called Hawiǧet

STATE OF RESEARCH
Visited by van Loon in 1964.

LOCATION
Located on the east bank of the Euphrates River at the edge of the lower terrace, ca. 2.3 km north-northeast of Halawa village (measured from village site), at the northern (main) village of Hweyjet Halawa.

DESCRIPTION
Site located in the area of the cemetery of the modern village (northern part) on natural isolated bluff ca. 10 m above the village, ca. 50 m in diameter, on a thin occupation deposit. The sherds were wheel made, grit tempered buff, painted (one sherd), gritty red slipped, and glazed and blue glazed. The finds suggest an Islamic date for this site.

LITERATURE
Van Loon 1967: 10 (no. 520).

HALULA

Tabqa Number: —   *Illustration:*   —
Miscellaneous: —

STATE OF RESEARCH
First investigated in 1986 by the archaeological mission of Melbourne University at al-Qitar; in 1989 by M. C. Cauvin (Centre National de la Recherche Scientifique), Ahmet Taha (Palmyra Museum), and M. Molist (Universitat Autònoma de Barcelona); and excavated in 1991 and 1992 by the Universitat Autònoma de Barcelona.

LOCATION
Located on the west bank of the Euphrates River, north of al-Qitar (not indicated in fig. 9.1).

DESCRIPTION
The dimensions of the site are 360 × 300 m, 8 m high. Pre-pottery Neolithic B occupation was reached in two areas:

Sectors I–III (southern area of tell): 169 sq. m were excavated, and continuous occupation was noted. A rectangular mudbrick building of multi-room type on stone foundations with plastered walls and floors was excavated; the domestic units contain ovens, fire pits, silos, and burials (mainly infants). Finds include lithics (Byblos and oval-shaped arrowheads, sickle blades, cores, debris) made of flint and obsidian, stone implements, clay animal figurines, and grinding stones. Uncalibrated radiocarbon dates (upper sequence) were 8,500–7,900 B.P., suggesting a date to the "upper to the middle phases" of Pre-pottery Neolithic B for this sector.

Sector VII: 108 sq. m were excavated and revealed complex stone architecture, with walls preserved up to 1.3 m. The architecture was non-domestic in character, possibly of a fortification. The finds consisted mostly of lithic products (Amuq arrowheads, sickle blades, retouched blades), bone implements, and handmade pots. Wild animals were the main food source (cattle, equids, fallow deer, gazelle); domestication of sheep, goats, and possibly cattle occurred between the lower and upper Pre-pottery Neolithic B phases. The presence of free-threshing bread wheat/hard wheat, emmer wheat, and possibly einkorn (Willcox 1996) was noted. The date of this sector is "final PPNB" (late eighth millennium).

Neolithic occupation levels (Halaf–Ubaid) was reached in several soundings on the upper part of the tell where a stone wall was found associated with three phases:

Phase a   Initial construction possibly dating to Pre-pottery Neolithic B
Phase b   Intermediate phase with dark-faced burnished ware
Phase c   Late Halaf to Ubaid

LITERATURE
Molist Montaña 1994; Molist Montaña 1996; Willcox 1996.

HAMRAH (SS 7), KHIRBET AL-

See *Appendix A: SS 7.*

HAMRAH 2 (SS 15), KHIRBET AL-

See *Appendix A: SS 15.*

HWEYSH, KHIRBET

Van Loon Tabqa Number: 510   *Illustration:*   Figure 9.1
Miscellaneous: —

STATE OF RESEARCH
Visited by van Loon in 1964.

LOCATION
Located on the east bank of the Euphrates River, ca. 2.5 km south-southwest of Halawa Tell A (T 519A), 1.5 km north of the modern village of Hweysh on a steep bluff of the edge of the lower river terrace.

DESCRIPTION
The site measures 500 m north–south, 100 m east–west, height ca. 5 m. The northern half of the site forms an 80 m long separate hillock, isolated by a wadi to the east.
Traces of 40 cm wide walls built of rubble were visible on the surface. The pottery was described as including wheel-made, grit-tempered buff, bright red-slipped, red/black-corrugated, large loop-painted, glazed, and relief-decorated ware. Several roof tiles were observed.
Finds suggest occupation during the Roman, Byzantine, and Islamic periods.

LITERATURE
Van Loon 1967: 10–11 (no. 510).

JAFLA, TELL

Van Loon Tabqa Number: 521   *Illustration:*   Figures 1.2, 9.1
Miscellaneous: Also spelled Jafle, Jefle, and Djafla

STATE OF RESEARCH
Visited by Rihaoui in 1963.

LOCATION
Located on the east bank on the edge of the terrace overlooking the river and ca. 11 m above it, 4.9 km east of Tell Habuba Kabira (T 509), 4.0 km south of Tell Sheikh Hassan (T 523), ca. 600–700 m south of the village of Tawi

'Abdullah al-Ahmar. The bluffs were trimmed vertically as a result of recent erosion by the Euphrates River. The site overlooks a large area of the floodplain. The altitude of the site was recorded at 310 m a.s.l., on the floodplain 300 m, and to the west at 290 m a.s.l.

DESCRIPTION

Described as an extensive site dominated by a prominent conical tell with a cemetery on its summit. On the surface were roughly dressed stones, traces of a (fortification?) wall, and pottery, some of it dating to the pre-Hellenistic period.

LITERATURE

Rihaoui 1965: 107 (no. 12).

JERF AL-AHMAR

Wilkinson Tabqa Number: 559   *Illustration:*   Figures 9.1, 9.9
Miscellaneous: —

STATE OF RESEARCH

Discovered in 1989 and originally investigated by Thomas McClellan and Anne Porter, and since 1994 by the Franco-Syrian expedition, directed by D. Stordeur.

LOCATION

Located on the east bank of the Euphrates River immediately to the north of the site of the Tishrin Dam, ca. 1 km northeast of al-Qitar in the north of the upper Lake Assad area.

DESCRIPTION

The site consists of two rises separated by a wadi. Two trenches were excavated revealing five occupation levels. Building plans indicate the presence of round houses ("Natufian" and PPNA) and rectangular houses (late PPNA and PPNB). Three skulls were discovered in a pit hearth filled with pebbles, which was situated on the exterior of the house. The finds were similar to those from the Pre-pottery Neolithic A levels at Mureybit (T 502–504). A grooved stone showed figurative decoration with a quadruped framed by chevrons and a bird of prey.

The faunal remains indicate that dogs were the only domesticated animal species, while wild aurochs, equids, and gazelles were hunted. Floatation samples suggest that wild barley (*Hordeum spontaneum*) was the most common plant food, but wild wheats, grasses, and pulses were also gathered.

LITERATURE

Stordeur 1996; Willcox 1996.

JOUWEIF (SS 8), TELL

See *Appendix A: SS 8.*

KANNAS, TELL

Van Loon Tabqa Number: 508   *Illustration:*   Figures 1.2, 9.1
Miscellaneous: Also spelled Qannas

STATE OF RESEARCH

Visited by Rihaoui in 1963 and van Loon in 1964; excavated by the Comité belge de recherches historiques, épigraphiques, et archéologiques en Mésopotamie from 1967 to 1974.

LOCATION

Located within the Uruk settlement of Habuba Kabira South (T 513), ca. 1.5 km south of Tell Habuba Kabira (T 509), therefore, technically not a separate site. The altitude at the top of the mound was recorded at 308 m a.s.l.

DESCRIPTION

The site covers about 1 ha and rises some 16 m above the city area of Habuba Kabira South. Four main occupation phases were recorded:

Uruk Period: The site was occupied by a cultic complex. Walls were preserved up to a height of 2 m and three building phases could be distinguished:

1. *East Temple:* A tripartite building (15.70 × 14.40 m) with a magazine room built against its western side were excavated. This room was later destroyed by fire and abandoned; finds from it include storage jars and sealings. Two more magazine rooms were located to the south.
2. *North Temple* (18.30 × 16.40 m): Adjoining north of the East Temple and the magazine room, with a single entranceway from the west. The central room, decorated with niches, includes two fireplaces.
3. *South Temple:* Possibly part of a larger unit to the west that had been destroyed by fire and leveled completely. A large rectangular room or court (14.10 × 10.20 m) featured an elaborate niche decoration inside. A small corridor in the northeast corner led to a small chamber. Finds correspond in date to those from Habuba Kabira South.

Agade–Old Babylonian Period: Immediately above the Uruk levels, a building was constructed on top of the mound that includes several occupation levels. The building consisted of an enclosure wall (mudbricks on stone foundations) that had rooms built against its inside that opened towards a courtyard. This building was interpreted by the excavators as a fortified magazine; signs of a gradual impoverishment over time were noted by the excavators (Finet 1980: 111). Finds include human- and animal-shaped foundation figurines; burials were found both inside and outside of the enclosure wall.

Roman Period: Burials were oriented east–west; finds include coins dating to Nero, but no traces of architecture were uncovered.

Islamic Period: The remains include numerous tombs of various types and qualities and a mudbrick house with stone foundations.

LITERATURE

Finet 1972, figs. 1–17, plan; Finet 1973; Finet 1974; Finet 1975; Finet 1977; Finet 1980; Finet 1993; Rihaoui 1965: 110 (no. 33); Trokay 1981, figs. 1–12; van Loon 1967: 15 (no. 508).

KHAFSE SAGHIRE

Van Loon Tabqa Number: 515   *Illustration:*   Figure 9.1
Miscellaneous: Also spelled Khafse Seghire; also called Hafsa (Khafje)

STATE OF RESEARCH

Visited by van Loon in 1964.

LOCATION

Situated towards the south edge of a broad, open valley. The site is 500 m northeast of the village of Khafse Saghire and is located within an irrigated area (site visibility poor) that shows evidence of recent *qanat* and well excavations. The altitude of the site was recorded at ca. 322 m a.s.l.

DESCRIPTION

Small, low mound (2 m high), dimensions 40 × 50 m; about 100 m to its south an ancient reservoir is indicated by broad mounds of upcast soil, with outflow going east towards the Euphrates River. Two parallel earthworks next to the site may relate to the same feature. In a nearby cemetery a large limestone block with two grooves has been re-used as a headstone. The site assemblage includes flat and semi-cylindrical roof tiles; sherds include wheel-made, grit-tempered buff, bright red-slipped, and red/black-corrugated and buff-corrugated wares. Suggested date: Roman/Byzantine.

LITERATURE

Van Loon 1967: 10 (no. 515).

KHALED, JEBEL

Van Loon Tabqa Number:	552	*Illustration:*	Figure 9.1
Miscellaneous:	Also called Jerf Khalad; Graeco-Roman Betanati (Bemmaris)(?)		

STATE OF RESEARCH

Surveyed, described, and excavated by G. W. Clarke (Australian National University).

LOCATION

Situated on the limestone hills on the west bank of the Euphrates River, opposite Ramalah (SS 16B), south of the modern village of Khirbet Khaled. The altitude of the site was recorded at ca. 410–420 m a.s.l.

DESCRIPTION

Site extends over a total area of rock outcrop of ca. 50 ha, some three-fifths of which show signs of occupation. The total length of the outcrop and enclosed hilltop is ca. 1,500 m north–south. It rises 125 m above the riverbank and attains a maximum altitude of 417 m a.s.l. Aerial photographs show at least one major building and a virtually continuous grid pattern of buildings extending over several hectares. Access is provided on the eastern side by two flights of stairs (presumably indicated by broken lines on Clarke's map); this side of the mound is protected by the proximity of the river and the steep slope. The site is defended by ca. 4 km of walls ca. 3 m wide with remains of twenty-eight interval towers. Each measures ca. 3 × 3 m and is made of carefully dressed limestone blocks (1.10 × 0.40 m), but which are now severely robbed. A massive gate complex provided access through the west wall. The southern part of the mound (Jebel al-Meghr) is dominated by a walled acropolis covering some 2.2 ha. Within the acropolis, a large building with a Doric-order colonnaded courtyard appears to have formed a palatial house or administrative building. About 100 m north of it are the ruins of another, smaller building which may be identified as a rural temple on the basis of column drums and lengths scattered around. On the northeast side of the acropolis a grid of streets is visible on the surface. Several cisterns were found in this area, including one on the acropolis.

Also excavated were the remains of three private buildings of a domestic quarter, a building that initially served some commercial function, and a commercial building (stoa). The private houses, which were situated on sloping ground facing south across to the acropolis, were shown to be on a Hippodamian grid plan.

Burial areas include a necropolis in a valley to the west. In the entrance area in the east, several tumulus graves were mostly robbed, whereas at the western side of the mound, cist graves were laid out in rows cut into the rock. Everywhere on the site is evidence of extensive quarrying of the limestone outcrop and several quarry galleries have been turned into rooms with windows and steps inside. A six-roomed feature in the southeast of the site was decorated with pillars, with one room equipped with a barrel vault. This vault appears to have been used, at least initially, for burials. North of the ravine at the eastern side, three rooms, which were cut into the rock and were interconnected by doorways, may have served a religious function. This assumption is supported by the presence, below these rooms, of a tomb, part of the walls and ceiling of which were painted. In addition to a bas-relief cross and Christian graffiti (Clarke 1984/85, figs. 2–3), two Syriac inscriptions were found (Muraoka 1984/85).

The sherd collection was described by van Loon as wheel-made, grit-tempered buff wares (including ring bases and pointed bases) and bright red-slipped wares. From much larger excavated assemblages, Clarke suggests a Middle to Late Hellenistic date. The site could be identified with Graeco-Roman Betanati (Bemmaris). The planned layout of this town, with its acropolis enclosed within the main town area, differs from other early Seleucid foundations. The site is considered to be a purely Greek foundation and was not expanded from an earlier local community. Clarke (1994) regards it as being a Macedonian military colony of similar function to Dura Europos.

LITERATURE

Clarke 1984/85; Clarke 1994; Clarke 1999a; Clarke and Conner 1995; Mairs 1995; Muraoka 1984/85; Rihaoui 1965: 108 (no. 23); van Loon 1967: 10 (no. 552).

MISHRIFAT (SS 16A)

See *Appendix A: SS 16A.*

MUMBAQA, TELL

Van Loon Tabqa Number: 534   *Illustration:*   Figures 1.2, 7.1, 9.1, 9.6–7

Miscellaneous: Also spelled Mumbaqat, Moumbaqat, Munbaqa, and Munbayah; ancient name Ekalte or Uru

STATE OF RESEARCH

Visited by van Loon in 1964; excavated by the Deutsche Orient-Gesellschaft between 1969 and 1994.

LOCATION

The site lies on the river terrace, 3 km southeast of the village of Mumbaqa. The site was approximately 24 m above the floodplain, 322 m a.s.l. at the summit of the mound (*Kuppe*), compared to 312–314 m a.s.l. at the river terrace and 287 m a.s.l. on a river island ca. 500 m to the west. Before the formation of Lake Assad, the site had already been trimmed by the Euphrates River. To the east, between the site and Jebels Sinn and Ghirre, a 1 km wide valley parallel to the river at 305–310 m may be a relict (Pleistocene) channel of the Euphrates (fig. 2.2). South of Tell Mumbaqa this feature is flanked by steep slopes on its west side; its gradient, like the Euphrates Valley, is towards the south. A dark soil mark trending towards the site from the east may be either a hollow way or a non-sinuous infilled wadi.

DESCRIPTION

The emphasis of the excavators was on the study of architecture. The site chronology was studied in terms of stratigraphy ("horizons") rather than cultural periods and a comprehensive study of the phases at Mumbaqa is still missing. Dates in the following descriptions are based on occasional references and should be treated with caution.

The following structures or areas have been excavated:

Kuppe Nord (northern part of summit):

Steinbau 1–3: Buildings of rectangular shape, consisting of a main room and an anteroom at the entrance, interpreted as temples (cf. *Antentempel* at Tell Chuera), and dated to Middle Bronze Age–Late Bronze Age.

Steinbau 1:[26]   Size: 26.00×12.50 m; a sounding inside the main room revealed nine "horizons" (H_0–H_8, with subdivisions) and earlier buildings; the *Steinbau* itself belongs to H_4/$H_{4.1}$; later[27] this division was modified and replaced with phases; phase 1 = H_1–H_2; phase 2 = H_2–H_4; phase 3 = $H_{4.1}$–H_7; phase 4 pottery corresponds to Habuba Kabira level 6 (= Early Dynastic?); north of *Steinbau 1* (square 27/37) is a tumulus, presumably dating to phase 3 or 4.[28]

Steinbau 2:[29]   (Square 20–23/31–33). Size: 33.40×14.80 m; similar construction as *Steinbau 1* but larger (main room 17.0×8.5 m, anteroom: 5.00×8.50 m), main room contained

---

26. Machule, Wäfler, and Rhode 1974: 11–29; Orthmann 1976: 26–29; Orthmann and Kühne 1974: 58–77.

27. Orthmann 1976.

28. Orthmann and Kühne 1974: 65–70.

29. Orthmann 1976: 29–32; Orthmann and Kühne 1974: 77–79.

an altar, three levels were exposed there (Level 2 dated to "Middle Syrian period" [ca. 1400–1200 B.C.]).

Steinbau 3:[30]   (Squares 26–29/37–40). Size: 29 × 15 m, northern part destroyed, internal layout differs from other two buildings due to the presence of three small rooms instead of a cella; Level 3 dated to Late Bronze II.

West of *Steinbau 3:* Cultic building made of mudbrick dating to the Middle Bronze Age (phase H_6–H_5); south of it Late Bronze Age domestic architecture (House V) with five phases (H_5–H_1); fire destruction in H_4, subsequent reconstruction in H_3 coincides with construction of *Steinbau 3*.[31]

Below and adjacent to *Steinbau 3:* Older building complex made of mudbrick, with several rooms; two phases were observed, both dating to the Early Bronze Age.

Kuppe (summit):[32] Apart from the northeast gate, this is the highest point of the tell. Excavations revealed domestic architecture with houses of irregular shape, an east–west street (2 m wide), and a double fortification wall with gates. Top of summit has nine levels (top level and building levels 1–8), with top level consisting of five phases, the oldest of which probably does not predate the first century B.C. Evidence from pottery and seals suggests that Levels 1–8 all belong to Early Bronze Age IVA and B, roughly contemporary with the Akkadian period.

Kuppe Süd (southern part of summit):[33] Mostly Late Bronze Age domestic(?) architecture (House P with kitchen and "butchering room") with two main streets and several alleys; test trench in 26/20–24 showed four levels with Level I = Islamic, Level II = Late Bronze Age I, Level III = Early Bronze Age IV, Level IV = Early Bronze Age III;[34] Early Bronze Age architecture is directly overlaid by Late Bronze Age architecture. A Roman sarcophagus was unearthed in 16/28. A subsequent Islamic settlement covered most of *Kuppe Süd*.

Innenstadt (inner city, south and east of *Kuppe Süd*):[35] Several test trenches indicate domestic (House Q) and possibly an administrative building built on virgin soil and dated to the Late Bronze Age.

Northeast Gate:[36]   A gate with two door chambers was found at a place where the inner and outer fortification walls joined. Two levels: Level 5 (= Middle Bronze Age?) had a gate that was built at the same time as the eastern extension of the city. Level 4 (= Late Bronze Age) had a blocked gate of different use; pottery includes Cypriot white slip II ware (LBA I).[37] The gate was rebuilt in the classical period.

Southeast Gate:[38]   Of unusual shape, this gate was presumably not the main gateway in the south. The gate was comprised of a simple passageway flanked in the south by a building consisting of a forecourt with ovens, a hall with central fireplace, and three subsidiary rooms. Three phases, tentatively dated to the Late Bronze Age, were identified.[39]

Ibrahim's Garden:[40]   A Late Bronze Age suburb in the southwest consisted of tripartite houses (A–E, E1, K, L, N, O, R, S, U) with a fireplace in the central rooms, several streets and plaza, and a mudbrick city wall with tower. Six phases were observed (IG 0–V),[41] all dating to the Late Bronze Age. Gravel fill between IG II and III suggested a discontinuity of settlement reported elsewhere as well.[42] Several cuneiform tablets (land/house purchases, loans, adoptions) were recovered from IG II.

---

30.   Machule et al. 1991: 73–76.

31.   Machule et al. 1992: 13–14.

32.   Eichler et al. 1984: 66–78; Machule et al. 1988: 13–21; Machule et al. 1990: 11–19; Machule, Czichon, and Werner 1989: 76–77; Machule et al. 1986: 68–98; Machule, Wäfler, and Rhode 1974: 45–47.

33.   Machule et al. 1991: 77–81.

34.   Machule et al. 1988: 15–17.

35.   Machule et al. 1991: 83–85.

36.   Kühne 1980; Orthmann 1976: 33–35; Orthmann and Kühne 1974: 79f.

37.   Machule and Wäfler 1983: 127.

38.   Orthmann 1976: 35–38.

39.   Compare Machule and Wäfler 1983: 127.

40.   Eichler et al. 1984: 78–93; Machule et al. 1987: 101–24; Machule et al. 1991: 85–90; Machule et al. 1992: 33–40; Machule et al. 1988: 28–37; Machule et al. 1990: 29–41; Machule, Czichon, and Werner 1994: 57–59; Machule et al. 1986: 99–122.

41.   Machule et al. 1990: 29.

42.   On *Kuppe*.

Houses on Inner Fortifica-   The structure of the houses was similar to those at Ibrahim's Garden; pottery was of
tion Wall (F–F$_1$, M$_1$):[43]   Late Bronze Age date.

Aussenstadt:[44] Two houses and a street were partly uncovered (G and J); two phases (AS I and II) were identified and a third phase (AS III) covered the AS II ruins. The *Aussenstadt* was dated to the Late Bronze
Age (slightly later than *Innenstadt* and Ibrahim's Garden). The presence of a natural gravel hill and an adjacent wadi within the area of the *Aussenstadt* is seen by the excavators as evidence for occasional flooding of this area predating the Late Bronze Age city expansion into this area.

History and Chronology of the Site: At present the earliest evidence appears to come from *Steinbau* Phase 4 (=
EB II/III?) and from *Kuppe Süd* (EB III). A preliminary assessment of the city's phases (now probably to
be revised) was given in 1976 after the end of the first series of excavations:[45]

Mumbaqat IV: "Early Syrian" (ca. 2500–2100 B.C.). This phase includes precursors of *Steinbau 1*
and burial tumuli around the city.

Mumbaqat III: "Old Syrian" (ca. 2000–1600 B.C.). This phase presumably includes the remainders of
Steinbau 1 and *2* and the inner (and outer?)[46] fortification walls.

Mumbaqat II: "Middle Syrian" (ca. 1600–1200 B.C.). This phase saw the greatest expansion of the
city with suburbs (Ibrahim's Garden, *Aussenstadt*) and *Steinbau 3*; note that a hiatus in
Late Bronze Age settlement was observed in Ibrahim's Garden and other parts of the
city.

(hiatus)

Mumbaqat I: Roman/Byzantine phase includes burial chambers and traces of buildings visible on
the surface.

LITERATURE

Anonymous 1978/79c; Becker, Fassbinder, and Chouker 1994, figs. 1–8b; Bell 1911; Boessneck and Peters 1988;
Boessneck and von den Driesch 1986; Curvers 1989: 178–79; Czichon and Werner 1998; Eichler et al. 1984, figs.
1–25; de Feyter 1989, figs. 1–50; Frank et al. 1982; Heinrich 1970a; Heinrich 1970b; Heinrich 1970c, pl. 10;
Karstens 1990; Karstens 1992, figs. 1–2; Koelling and Kunze 1986; Kühne 1980, pls. 1–8; Küster 1989; Ludwig
and Strommenger 1970: 134; Machule 1984, figs. 46–47; Machule 1993/94; Machule 1994, figs. 1–7; Machule et
al. 1986, figs. 1–41; Machule et al. 1987, figs. 1–32; Machule et al. 1988, figs. 1–31; Machule et al. 1990, figs. 1–
22; Machule et al. 1991, figs. 1–16; Machule et al. 1992, figs. 1–18; Machule et al. 1993, figs. 1–18; Machule et
al. 1996, figs. 1–10; Machule, Czichon, and Werner 1989, figs. 1–12; Machule, Czichon, and Werner 1994, figs.
1–7; Machule and Rentschler 1971, pls. 7–9; Machule and Wäfler 1978, figs. 1–3; Machule and Wäfler 1983;
Machule, Wäfler, and Rhode 1974, figs. 29–66; Mayer 1990; Mayer 1993; Mayer-Opificius 1989, figs. 1–4;
Orthmann 1974; Orthmann 1975, figs. 1–21, pls. 1–16; Orthmann 1976, figs. 1–12; Orthmann and Kühne 1974,
figs. 1–41; Riederer 1976; Seidl 1969, figs. 26–29; Strommenger 1970; Strommenger 1973: 169–70;
Strommenger 1976; von Soden 1982; Wäfler 1980, figs. 1–3; Wäfler 1982.

NAFILEH VILLAGE (SS 5)

See *Appendix A: SS 5.*

OTHMAN (SS 20A), TELL

See *Appendix A: SS 20A.*

---

43.   Machule et al. 1987: 80–85.

44.   Machule et al. 1987: 92f.; Machule et al. 1991: 91–92.

45.   Orthmann 1976: 43.

46.   Compare Kühne's reassessment in Margueron 1980: 217.

RASM AL-ʿABD MUSTAHA

See *Appendix A: Miscellaneous Sites.*

RIMALAH

Van Loon Tabqa Number: 554
Miscellaneous: Also called Ramale, Rmale

Illustration: Figures 1.2, 2.7, 9.1

STATE OF RESEARCH

Visited by Rihaoui (1963) and van Loon (1964).

LOCATION

On the east bank of the Euphrates River on a very low terrace south of the modern village of Ramāle, opposite Jebel Khalad (T 552). Situated on the riverward end of an alluvial fan merging into a very low Euphrates terrace slightly trimmed by the river. The site was approximately 7–8 m above river level.

DESCRIPTION

The site consists of a mound with an extensive low site to the southeast. The mound was described as rising to 10 m above the terrace; its diameter was ca. 150 m. The mound is partly covered by a modern cemetery, finds from which include a pottery figurine of a horseman. The southern area was covered with pottery; the presence of wasters and slag in its eastern part suggests an area of pottery production. Date: Roman/Islamic (van Loon)

Note that Rihaoui refers to a village on a small tell "situé à l'extérieur de la region du Basin."

LITERATURE

Rihaoui 1965: 108 (no. 21), van Loon 1967: 13 (no. 554).

SALAMA, KHIRBET

Van Loon Tabqa Number: 516
Miscellaneous: —

Illustration: Figure 9.1

STATE OF RESEARCH

Visited by van Loon in 1964.

LOCATION

Located on the southern slopes of a broad, open valley leading to the northwest away from the Euphrates River, 150–200 m southeast of the village of Khirbet Salama (itself 1.4 km east-southeast of Khafse Saghire [T 515]). The altitude of the site was recorded at 312–313 m a.s.l.

DESCRIPTION

Small one-period site on a natural mound. The mound is low and rounded and includes numerous minor depressions (possibly, but not necessarily, robber holes); its diameter was ca. 50 m, and its height ca. 4–5 m. A *qanat* was noted to the east of the mound. Surface scatter includes flat roof tiles. Sherds include wheel-made, grit-tempered, buff red/black-corrugated, and gritty red-slipped wares. Date: Byzantine.

LITERATURE

Van Loon 1967: 11 (no. 516).

SELENKAHIYE

Van Loon Tabqa Number: 507   *Illustration:*   Figures 1.2, 3.1, 9.1, 9.6–8
Miscellaneous: —

STATE OF RESEARCH

Visited by Rihaoui in 1963 and by van Loon in 1964; excavated by M. N. van Loon (Oriental Institute of the University of Chicago) in 1967 and by M. N. van Loon (University of Amsterdam) in 1972, 1974, and 1975.

LOCATION

Located on the right bank of the Euphrates River, ca. 8.5 km northeast of Meskene, ca. 4.0 km west-southwest of Halawa Tell A (T 519A), on the edge of the lower river terrace above the floodplain; at this point the great bend of the Euphrates River reaches its westernmost point which reduces the floodplain to a small strip.

DESCRIPTION

Low, long site, roughly rectangular in size, with a modern cemetery on the southern part. The size of the site is 600 m north–south, 250 m east–west, ca. 5 m high. The site perimeter was defined by surrounding "[…] pronounced ridges, which form a rectangle […]," presumably the line of the citadel wall surrounding the main mound, with an extensive outer town to its west.

Five phases were distinguished (bottom to top):[47]

Phase I: Immediately above virgin soil, a house with a stable built of baked brick was uncovered in O26–P26, finds from it include a limestone mold for casting pendants, a pebble-paved court with ovens, and two shaft tombs; on the southern edge of the site were houses in W42, X42, and V45, the latter one containing a tub that possibly was used for beer-making. The house in X42 was destroyed by fire.

Phase II: The first construction of a citadel wall was attested along the western side of the citadel (P26–Q26 and W42/43), along with pebble-paved courtyards, stone foundations, and a mudbrick wall in the western part of the site (U21). In the south a "tower" (W43) and a street with gateway through the wall (V–X42/43) were found. Outside the citadel were large ash deposits and substantial architecture in X45. Phase II was thoroughly destroyed (large amount of ashes in U21) and the citadel wall was razed below its foundation.

Phase III: Different architectural layout from previous occupation. In the northeast a mudbrick citadel wall was constructed along the northern and western edge (Y07–SS07, T06, P–Q26), built on pebbles, ca. 1.90–2.30 m wide, with several "towers" (in Y07–Z07, T06, P–Q23/24) and a guard house (in P–Q23/24 phase III or IV?; van Loon 1979: 97). Several houses were found along the inner side of the citadel wall (P–Q26 and T04–06). In the western part of the site (W12) several rooms and a courtyard were built on virgin soil; finds from here include a sherd with an impression of an Early Dynastic cylinder seal. Squares T21 and U21 contained houses, one with clay figurines (foundation deposits?) below a doorsill, and a street with pebble pavement. In the south a fortress ("portico building") was associated with a heavy fortification wall; one of its rooms contained numerous sealings with impressions of local stamp seals and of Akkadian cylinder seals.

Phase IV: Occupation continued from phase III. In the northeast the citadel wall was strengthened by filling in the rooms built along it, doubling its width (T04–T06), and the floor level along it was substantially raised by 2 m. Numerous shaft tombs were dug in Q26. In the west domestic architecture with bread ovens was found, one room filled with broken storage jars and charred grain. The courtyard of one of the houses contained a tomb shaft with two tombs. To the west a street and houses unearthed in V20, Q21–V21, and U22 continued to exist from phase III. In U22 a grave was found containing a Middle Bronze Age dagger and a chlorite cylinder seal. In the south, reconstruction and further strengthening of the southern fortress was done. Large amounts of ash and mudbrick tumble found all over the site indicate a violent destruction of this occupation phase.

Phase V: Clearly separated from phase IV by a destruction ash layer. Scanty remains of re-occupation unconnected to the previous architecture were found close to the surface. Among the finds were donut-

---

47.   Description follows van Loon 1979 unless otherwise indicated.

shaped objects made of basalt in T04 and several figurines. The citadel wall was haphazardly reconstructed without a stone foundation, enclosing a smaller area than in phase IV (Q21, P–Q23/24, P–Q26). A guard's house was uncovered in Q21. Shallow circular graves were found along the western edge (W12) and more burials were noted in P–Q23/24. Traces of re-occupation of a domestic nature were recovered in the area of the southern fortress.

Outer City: Remains of domestic(?) architecture were traced in a bulldozer trench up to 250 m west of the western edge of the citadel (square KK29), but their correlation with the main mound remains uncertain.

Dating: Radiocarbon dates (B.C., all MASCA corrected, but note that the inconsistencies may in some cases be the result of the use of old wood for dating):

Phase I:	2384, 2316
Phase IV:	2557, 2335, 2125
Phase V:	2413, 2340

Pottery: The pottery from the earlier phases was correlated by Schwartz (2001a) with Hama J 8–6, Amuq I, Mardikh IIB1, and the later phases with Hama J 4–1, Amuq J, Mardikh IIB2, Early Bronze Age Sweyhat, and Hadidi.

Sculpture: A fragment of a statue from W42 (van Loon 1979, fig. 17) shows a tasseled garment comparable to votive statues from pre-Sargonic Mari, and the lower part and base of another statue fragment from X43 (van Loon 1979, fig. 18) displayed elements characteristic of Akkadian or Ur III sculpture;[48] both fragments were found in phase III but considered heirlooms from phase II.

Seal Impressions: A seal impression on a jar shoulder showing a hero fighting with bulls or caprids (van Loon 1979, fig. 16) from V42 (phase II) seems Early Dynastic II in date and may be an heirloom from the earliest level. Another sealing, found in phase III in W44, can be dated to the early Akkadian period (van Loon 1979, fig. 21).

The occupation levels at Selenkahiye therefore span the later part of the third millennium, roughly equivalent to the late Early Dynastic to Ur III periods in southern Mesopotamia.

LITERATURE

Amiet 1976; Ducos 1968; Ducos 1973; Schwartz 2001a; van Loon 1968a; van Loon 1969a; van Loon 1969b; van Loon 1973; van Loon 1977/78; van Loon 1978/79; van Loon 1979; van Loon 2001; van Zeist 1968; van Zeist 1973.

SHAJARA SAGHIRA (SS 29)

See *Appendix A: SS 29.*

SHAMS ED-DIN CENTRAL TELL

Van Loon Tabqa Number:	536	*Illustration:*	Figures 1.1, 2.6, 7.1, 9.1
Miscellaneous:	Holland and Whitcomb Survey 21; also spelled Chams ed-Dine, Sams ed-Din, Shams Eddine; also called Tell Dhahir (according to Bell 1911: 43 and local inhabitants in 1992), Tell az-Zaher, Tell Zaher, Tell Zaidan, Tell Zeydan, and Zeidan		

STATE OF RESEARCH

Visited by van Loon in 1964, first noted by Gertrude Bell in 1911, also visited in 1972 by Holland and Whitcomb.

---

48. Compare Akkadian parallels (Amiet 1976, fig. 15a [Maništusu])
and the Statue of Puzureštar and Ištup-ilum of Mari dating to Ur
III or later (Strommenger and Hirmer 1962, figs. 153–55).

LOCATION

Located on the east bank of the Euphrates River on the floodplain terrace. At present the site forms an island within Lake Assad. The altitude of the site at the summit was recorded at 303 m a.s.l., at the base of the tell, 295 m a.s.l., and at river level ca. 290 m a.s.l.

DESCRIPTION

The diameter of the site was 140 m and its height 9 m, with the northern part steeper than the southern. Low mounding also extended to the south and southeast as a crescent-shaped low settlement. Before the rise of Lake Assad, the site was surrounded by irrigated gardens. The site was partly covered with a modern cemetery. The site consisted of loose, ashy soil with many small sherds; sherds were wheel-made, grit-tempered buff wares; one straw-tempered sherd was observed. Wasters indicate pottery production occurred on the site. Bell (1911: 43) notes a "heap of unsquared building stone." The visit by Whitcomb and Holland in 1972 produced a female plaque figurine. The pottery was described as late Early Bronze Age, transitional Early Bronze Age–Middle Bronze Age, and early Middle Bronze Age; the wares were gritty, pink buff, fine pinkish buff, and gritty pinkish brown ware, the latter of which was comb-incised. The wares fit the range of types excavated from late Early Bronze Age, Early Bronze Age–Middle Bronze Age, and early Middle Bronze Age levels at Tell es-Sweyhat (Holland, *Sweyhat 2*, fig. 9:1–3).

COMMENTARY

The name Shams ed-Din has been attributed to a great number of sites over a large area, thereby causing some confusion. Herein the following sites are included within the rubric Shams ed-Din:

> Shams ed-Din Central Tell (T 536)
> Shams ed-Din Tannira (T 562)
> Shams ed-Din Southern Site and Cemeteries (SS 22, T 561)

The following sites, occasionally referred to as Shams ed-Din, have been listed under their alternative names:

> Tell al-ʿAbd (T 535): called "Shams ed-Din South Tell" by van Loon (1967).
> Tell Jouweif (SS 8, T 537): called "Shams ed-Din East Tell" by van Loon (1967).
> Mishrifat (SS 16A, T 539): called "Mechrefat Chams el Dine" by Rihaoui (1965).
> Zreyjiye (T 533): called "Zreijiet Chams el Dine" by Rihaoui (1965).

Note also that Rihaoui (1965) mentions three Shams ed-Din sites that cannot be identified with certainty without his map: "Chams el Dine" (possibly Shams ed-Din Central Tell), "Chams el Dine (No. 2)" (possibly the Shams ed-Din Southern Site and Cemeteries [SS 22, T 561]), and "Chams el Dine (2)."

LITERATURE

Bell 1911; Holland, *Sweyhat 2*; Rihaoui 1965; van Loon 1967: 13 (no. 536).

SHAMS ED-DIN SOUTHERN SITE AND CEMETERIES (SS 22)

See *Appendix A: SS 22.*

SHAMS ED-DIN TANNIRA

Wilkinson Tabqa Number: 562   *Illustration:*   Figures 7.1, 9.1
Miscellaneous: —

STATE OF RESEARCH

Excavated by Helga Seeden and Selma al-Radi (American University at Beirut) in 1974.

LOCATION

On the east bank of the Euphrates River on the terrace ca. 10 m above the floodplain, approximately 200–250 m east of the village of Tannira (wadi between village and site), and ca. 1 km north of Tell al-ʿAbd (T 535). The site sits at the edge of the lowest step of moderately dissected terrace that has been trimmed vertically by the river.

About 600 m to the west of the outcrop of Jebel Sinn of Shams ed-Din (SS 22). The altitude of the site was recorded at 300–305 m a.s.l., the floodplain at 290 m a.s.l.

DESCRIPTION

Flat settlement with thin levels of cultural deposit; total area up to 25,000 sq. m, extending ca. 240 m north–south, and 220 m east–west. Two areas were excavated:

Area A: Seven 5 m squares were excavated in square A 5; the earliest occupation, resting on the conglomerate of the river terrace, was reached 1 m below the surface. Finds include pottery rings and worked obsidian pieces. Above this level three architectural levels were observed, containing round houses as well as rectangular dwellings with hearths, round storage pits, gravel and mud floors, and ashy lenses. Both architecture and finds identify this area as domestic.

Area B: Virgin soil was not reached. Two building levels were recovered with a hiatus between them. The levels consisted of a freestanding limestone wall, ovens, cooking places, storage areas, and mud and lime plaster floors. Area B has been identified as an "industrial" area (baking and cooking, possibly pottery kilns?).

Pottery: Halaf pottery was found in all levels (1,000–3,000 sherds per square). Neutron activation analysis indicates two variants, one presumably of local production, the other imported from outside the Euphrates Valley (possibly from the Khabur). Stylistic parallels in decoration with Ugarit may indicate contact with the west.[49]

Stone Artifacts: Chert and obsidian scrapers, drills, graving tools, sickle blades, and retouched blades were recovered; notched tools are ca. 30% of total number; stone vessels were also found.

Bone: Single tool.

Faunal Analysis: 1,730 bones were recovered. Among wild animals was a predominance of small equids (*Equus hemionus*), gazelle, and fallow deer. Domesticated animals include sheep, goat, cattle, pig, and dog.[50]

Post-Halafian Occupation: Two later graves were dug into the Halafian level in A 5;[51] Meyer mentions an Uruk settlement at Tannira noted during a survey,[52] an observation supported by the record of eight beveled-rim bowls from squares A 1 and A 2 (Gustavson-Gaube 1981: 78). During a site visit in 1994, members of the Tell al-ʿAbd excavation team noted numerous Uruk sherds along the lakeshore that bordered and partially flooded the site at that time.

LITERATURE

Akkermans 1989a: 81; Azouri and Bergman 1980; Gustavson-Guabe 1981; Meyer 1991; al-Radi and Seeden 1974; al-Radi and Seeden 1980; Seeden 1978/79; Seeden 1982; Uerpmann 1982.

SHASH HAMDAN

Van Loon Tabqa Number: 550   *Illustration:*   Figures 5.1, 7.1, 9.1
Miscellaneous: —

STATE OF RESEARCH

Visited by Rihaoui in 1963 and van Loon in 1964, mapped by the Deutsche Orient-Gesellschaft in 1968, and recorded by the Sweyhat Survey team in 1991.

LOCATION

On the west bank of the Euphrates River on a natural limestone hill at the foot of the pass between Jebel Tariq az-Zor (northwest) and Jebel al-Jirn (southeast), ca. 1.9 km west of the village of Roumeilah.

---

49. Compare Seeden 1978/79: 166; Gustavson-Gaube 1981 for a detailed discussion.

50. Uerpmann 1982: 10, table 2.

51. Al-Radi and Seeden 1980: 117.

52. Meyer 1991: 13.

DESCRIPTION

The site appears to follow the contours of the mountain down to the river in the east and a wadi to the south. The site area was partly disturbed by an Islamic cemetery. Remains of buildings of square stone blocks were noted. Finds included flat roof tiles and painted wheel-made sherds that are obviously late in date. A Roman/Byzantine rock-cut tomb cut into a bluff to the south of Shash Hamdan was recorded by the Sweyhat Survey team in 1991 (see *Section 5.C. Tombs and Cemeteries*). Strommenger and Heinrich assigned a Roman or later date, van Loon a Byzantine date.

Rihaoui mentions a "great khirbet" (location uncertain) south of Shash Hamdan on a rocky elevation (Jebel al-Jirn?). Flints and pottery sherds painted red and incised were of distinctively Halafian character; also found was the head of a horse figurine (suggested date: second millennium B.C.).

LITERATURE

Heinrich et al. 1969: 33, fig. 4; Rihaoui 1965: 109 (no. 25); van Loon 1967: 11 (no. 551).

SHEIKH HASSAN, TELL

Van Loon Tabqa Number: 523   *Illustration:*   Figures 1.2, 9.1, 9.6
Miscellaneous: Holland and Whitcomb Survey Number 19 (Holland, *Sweyhat* 2, fig. 8:24–26); also
                              spelled Cheikh Hassan, Sheykh Hasan, Šeḫ Hassan

STATE OF RESEARCH

Visited by Rihaoui in 1963 and van Loon in 1964, excavations by Bounni in 1971/72, J. Cauvin in 1976, and J. Boese (ten campaigns between 1984 and 1994).

LOCATION

Located on the east bank of the Euphrates River on the edge of the river terrace ca. 11 m above the floodplain, 3.5 km east-northeast of Tell al-Hajj (T 517), and 2 km southwest of Tell Mumbaqa (T 534). The altitude of the site was recorded at 312.5 m a.s.l. on the hilltop, compared with 300.0 m a.s.l. on the terrace ca. 200 m south of it, and 289.0 m a.s.l. on the floodplain ca. 500 m west of the site. The terrace is the same terrace as that at Tell Mumbaqa, and as at that site, to the east is located a broad valley probably representing a relict channel of the Euphrates River. Before Lake Assad was formed, the river ran by the west side of the tell and trimmed the terrace into vertical bluffs.

DESCRIPTION

Stratigraphic Sequence (note: the excavations by Cauvin and Boese have not yet been correlated stratigraphically, and the numbered levels given below refer to Boese's excavation sequence exclusively):

Aceramic Neolithic: 1976 soundings on the western slope of the mound; two soundings supply a lithic assemblage comparable to Mureybit IIIb:

Sondage nord: Building with a grid of small square rooms;[53] several building levels. The building material consists of flat stones and wooden beams packed into clay, very similar to Mureybit XIV–XVII.

Sondage sud: Two successive levels of architecture:

Lower Level: Building with rectilinear walls made of "cigar-shaped" cut stones on a foundation of large pebbles. The rooms are less rectangular than trapezoid; due to the insufficient size of the excavated area the overall shape has not been recognized but could be circular.

Upper Level: Two major walls of large stones; the walls are rectilinear and parallel, 3.50 m apart; clay floor.[54]

---

53. Cauvin 1980, fig. 3.

54. Cauvin 1978: 42.

Finds: Human bones (lower jaws; studied in Clère, Adeleine, and Ferembach 1985) and lithic tools (grindstones studied in Nierlé 1982: 177–216).

The finds from *sondage sud* date to Pre-pottery Neolithic A.

Halaf and Ubaid Periods: Sherds found in later context.

Middle–Late Uruk (Levels 4–22):

Levels 22–17:   No architecture found, date ascertained by pottery (square 1833).

Level 15:   Earliest architectural remains (square 1833) (Boese 1995: 94).

Levels 14–13:   First city wall with city gate; continues into level 6.

Levels 11–10:   Mud floor, ovens, fire places, pottery (beveled-rim bowls) in square 1932; in square 1933 (Level 11) a fireplace was associated with beveled-rim bowls; in Level 10, a building destroyed by fire contained complete storage vessels filled with grain and implement tools.

Level 12:   Large building.

Levels 9–8:   Tripartite buildings (Boese 1995: 136–37).

Level 7:   Substantial building (square 2032).

Level 6:   A "stone building" (square 2032) against the city wall contained beveled-rim bowls and two corroded copper weapons; city wall with niches (square 2032 IV, 2031 II and III; tower or gate in square 1832); mudbrick terrace in squares 2133 and 2033. One-room sanctuary with infant burials (squares 21–22/32–33; Boese 1995: 134–36, 158–60, 166–68, figs. 4–6).

Level 5:   Finds include a ram-headed figure.

Level 4:   Hearths, ovens; finds include a mace-head.

(hiatus)

Iron Age

Level 3:   "Building" (or "Palace") A: substantial tripartite building of *bīt ḫilāni*-type in square 2131 I–IV (overlying Uruk city wall), minimum dimensions: 21 × 31 m. Walls ca. 1.3 m thick (cf. Zinçirli, *Ḫilāni* II and III). The level is dated to the first millennium B.C.; note, however, the paucity of diagnostic finds — eighth/seventh century B.C.(?) (Boese 1995: 132–34; 143, fig. 2; 144, fig. 3).

Persian Period: "Persian" style reliefs found in secondary context (Boese 1995: 95).

Level 2:   Hellenistic.

Level 2e–c: "Older" Hellenistic settlement layers (Boese 1995: 130).

Level 2b–a: Substantial building ("Palace") extending over at least 40 m; Level 2a building has a courtyard paved with baked bricks, extending over more than 30 m; the level is dated to the Hellenistic period, third–second century B.C.

Level 1:   Islamic tombs; Roman child burial, Hellenistic and Roman pits cut into level 2; stone foundations were called Level 1c (squares 2131 I and IV, 2133 III and IV).

LITERATURE

Boese 1986/87, figs 1–42; Boese 1987/88, figs. 1–22; Boese 1995; Cauvin 1978; Cauvin 1978/79; Cauvin 1980; Clère, Adeleine, and Ferembach 1985; Nierlé 1982: 177–216; Rihaoui 1965: 107 (no. 13); van Loon 1967: 15–16 (no. 523).

SS 2, 4, 9, 12, 13, 14, 16C, 20B, 21, 23, 24, 25, 26, 27, 28, and 30

See *Appendix A: SS 2, 4, 9, 12, 13, 14, 16C, 20B, 21, 23, 24, 25, 26, 27, 28,* and *30.*

SUKHNI

Van Loon Tabqa Number:	524	*Illustration:*	Figure 9.1
Miscellaneous:	Also spelled Sakhni, Sukni		

STATE OF RESEARCH

Visited by van Loon in 1964.

LOCATION

On the west bank terrace of the Euphrates River ca. 10 m above the floodplain. Approximately 200–250 m east of the village of Tannira (a wadi is between the village and site), and ca. 1 km north of Khirbet Salama (T 516). At the edge of the lowest step of a moderately dissected terrace that has been trimmed vertically by the river. About 600 m west of an outcrop of the Jebel Sinn. The altitude of the site was recorded at 300–305 m a.s.l., of the floodplain 290 m a.s.l.

DESCRIPTION

Southern Tell. Small tell (120 × 140 m), 8 m high. Flat roof tiles were found on the site; a *qanat* runs east–west ca. 200 m south of village (on map). A low north–south ridge on which the village sits has Byzantine sherds over its whole length (ca. 500 m); a grinding stone was found in the village.

LITERATURE

Van Loon 1967: 14 (no. 524).

SWEYHAT, TELL ES-

See *Appendix A: SS 1.*

TAʿAS

Van Loon Tabqa Number:	526	*Illustration:*	Figures 1.2, 9.1
Miscellaneous:	Also spelled Taʿass, el-Tafs (village) on map		

STATE OF RESEARCH

Visited by van Loon in 1964; later excavations by the University of Leiden during the early 1970s.

LOCATION

The site extends along the footslopes of Jebel Aruda overlooking the Euphrates floodplain, ca. 1.0–1.4 km northwest of the modern village of el-Tafs. The site is located on a narrow terrace (ca. 9 m above the floodplain), backed to the west by heavily eroded limestone slopes. The terrace is moderately dissected and incised wadis have contributed numerous small wadi fans to the adjacent floodplain. Linear dark and pale soil markings on the floodplain may indicate the course of a relict canal, now presumably veiled by floodplain sediments. The altitude of the site was recorded at 300 m a.s.l.

DESCRIPTION

A medieval settlement extending over the length of 1 km and a width of several hundred meters; in the north it was partly covered by a recent cemetery; most of it appears to date to the Early Islamic (ninth century A.D.) and Ayyubid (twelfth–thirteenth century A.D.) periods. Three soundings were made revealing the following features:

1. Christian building dating to the early Islamic (Umayyad) period. Finds include fragments of a polychrome wall painting and fragments of a Greek-Byzantine cross.

2. Domestic building, burnt. Finds include complete set of glass vessels.

3. Pottery kiln, three furnaces with fire room below. Numerous fragments of wasters.

Rihaoui and van Loon mention sherds and tiles of high quality dating to the Roman, Byzantine, and Islamic periods; van Loon assumes that the center of the site was in the north and was covered by a cemetery. A visit by Wilkinson in September 1993 showed that the site extended northeast–southwest for several hundred meters along the terrace edge (fig. 9.1: broken line). Cultural deposits, although scarce, were noted. Finds and sherds were quite dense and include a number of querns. Together these observations suggest that the scatter represents in situ occupation and not simply "background noise." Ceramics include glazed Early Islamic sherds, as well as Early Byzantine/Late Roman C wares. One infilled well was observed.

LITERATURE

Franken 1983; Rihaoui 1965: 109 (no. 30); van der Leeuw 1974; van der Leeuw 1976; van Loon 1967: 14 (no. 526).

TAWI (AL-ITRE)

Van Loon Tabqa Number: 522   *Illustration:*   Figure 9.1
Miscellaneous: —

STATE OF RESEARCH

Visited by van Loon in 1964.

LOCATION

On the east bank at the edge of a moderately dissected terrace overlooking the river and ca. 12 m above it, 2.5 km south of Tell Sheikh Hassan (T 523), 3.6 km east-southeast of Tell al-Hajj (T 517). The altitude of the village was recorded at 314.4 m a.s.l., compare to 285.4 m a.s.l. at the Euphrates Valley 500 m northwest of the village and 294.7 m a.s.l. in the wadi east of the site.

DESCRIPTION

The site as described by van Loon is said to be east of the road ca. 1 km north of the village. The site consists of "3 groups of stones" — remains of houses and/or tombs, roughly dressed stones, flat roof tiles, and glass. The suggested date is Byzantine.

LITERATURE

Van Loon 1957: 14 (no. 521).

TAWI BURIAL COMPLEXES

Tabqa Number: —   *Illustration:*   —
Miscellaneous: —

STATE OF RESEARCH

Excavations by Orthmann and Kampschulte in the late 1970s in squares 2/W (Area A), 7/P and 7/O (Area B), 5/L (Area C), 12/H (Area E), and 13/L (Area F).

LOCATION

On the east bank of the Euphrates River extending over the river terrace and rolling hills around the modern village of Tawi 'Abdullah al-Ahmar and Tell Jafla (T 521). Six major burial complexes are distributed over a wide area around Tell Jafla south of Tawi:

Area A: Area of village of Tawi 'Abdullah al-Ahmar.

Area B: Area north and east of Tell Jafla; two centers.

Area C: Two hills south of Tell Jafla separated by a depression; the altitude was recorded at 313 m a.s.l. Relatively even distribution of graves suggests a coherent burial complex.

Area D: On both sides of a small subsidiary valley of a large wadi running east–west. Two separate sites, the larger complex was on a spur northwest of the valley.

Area E: Flat terrain with four obvious site areas.

Area F: Area with five conglomerations of burials.

In addition, a rectangular complex mound, ca. 400–500 m to the southeast of Tell Jafla (T 521), appears to be part of a fortified building.

DESCRIPTION

Grave Types:

Pit graves: Most were covered by a stone slab, usually containing one body with rare cases of secondary inhumations.

Cist graves: Rare.

Gallery graves: These graves appear to be concentrated in Areas A, B, and F. Their size exceeds 4 m; sometimes cut into rock, elsewhere walled up with stone walls. In contrast to the graves at Tell Hadidi (T 548) and Tell Mumbaqa (T 534), no entrance shafts were found.

Shaft graves: Shaft graves with an adjacent chamber — a type frequent at Halawa (T 511) — were only found in square 7/O.

Finds: Pottery, bronze pins, pearls.

Date: Early Bronze Age (authors avoid a detailed definition of periods); burials in 2/W are older, called "Early Syrian I," the others are called "Syrian II and III."

LITERATURE

Kampschulte and Orthmann 1984.

UMM JEHASH

See *Appendix A: Miscellaneous Sites (T 591).*

WALID ASAF, TELL

See *Appendix A: Miscellaneous Sites (T 588).*

WREYDA

Van Loon Tabqa Number: 506   *Illustration:*   Figures 1.2, 9.1
Miscellaneous: Also called Warde Saghire, Wreyda Saghire; also spelled Wreida, Wreyde

STATE OF RESEARCH

Visited by van Loon in 1964. A group of tombs in the vicinity of Wreyda and Wreyda South Site (T 512) were excavated in 1979 by W. Orthmann (University of Saarland).

LOCATION

On the west bank of the Euphrates River, ca. 1 km south-southwest of Selenkahiye (T 507) on the edge of the lower river terrace above the floodplain, separated from the modern village of Wreyda by a small valley just north of it. The highest point of the site was ca. 7 m above the floodplain.

DESCRIPTION

The site is 60 m in diameter, 4 m high, with a "flat extension" 40 m eastwards of the site. The finds include recent pottery, and some flints were on the surface. The site is dated to the Islamic period.

In the vicinity of Wreyda and Wreyda South Site, tombs within an Early Bronze Age cemetery were excavated in 1979. Five two or three chamber tombs were published with associated ceramic groups (Orthmann and Rova 1991). The graves contained large numbers of mid-/late Early Bronze Age ceramics, stone figurines, and metal grave goods. Ceramics found in them were mainly of "EB IV" types.

LITERATURE

Orthmann and Rova 1991; van Loon 1967: 16 (no. 506).

WREYDA SOUTH SITE

Van Loon Tabqa Number: 512   *Illustration:*   Figure 9.1
Miscellaneous: Also spelled Wreyde

STATE OF RESEARCH

Visited by van Loon in 1964.

LOCATION

On the west bank of the Euphrates River, ca. 1.5 km south-southwest of Selenkahiye, 700 m south-southwest of modern village of Wreyda on the edge of the lower river terrace above the floodplain.

DESCRIPTION

Described as three hillocks, 3.50 m high, ca. 75 m apart. No artifacts were collected, so the dates of these sites are unknown.

LITERATURE

Van Loon 1967: 16 (no. 512).

ZAROB

See *Appendix A: Miscellaneous Sites (T 590).*

ZMALEH, KHIRBET

Van Loon Tabqa Number: 551   *Illustration:*   Figure 9.1
Miscellaneous: Also spelled Zmale; also called Shash Kabir

STATE OF RESEARCH

Visited by Rihaoui in 1963 and van Loon in 1964.

LOCATION

About 700 m east of modern Khirbet Zmaleh on the plain between mountain ridges. The site is situated where a wadi debouches as an alluvial fan on the low undulating terrace ca. 5 m above the floodplain terrace. The site was trimmed to the east by the Euphrates River. The altitude of the site was recorded at 305 m a.s.l.

DESCRIPTION

The site is a low mound with rough stone wall foundations on the surface, including a door threshold and round building, extending 120 m northwest–southeast and 50 m northeast–southwest. The date of the site is unknown.

LITERATURE

Rihaoui 1965: 109 (no. 24); van Loon 1967: 11 (no. 551).

ZREYJIYE

Van Loon Tabqa Number:	533	*Illustration:*	Figure 9.1
Miscellaneous:	Also spelled Zreyiye, Zreijiet Chams el Dine; also called "north site" by van Loon (see *Appendix B: Shams ed-Din Central Tell, Commentary*)		

STATE OF RESEARCH

Visited by Rihaoui in 1963 and van Loon in 1964.

LOCATION

On the east bank of the Euphrates River on the same terrace as Tell Mumbaqa (T 534). Approximately 900 m southwest of Tell Mumbaqa and 1.1 km northeast of Tell Sheikh Hassan (T 523). The altitude of the site was recorded at ca. 298 m a.s.l., of the nearby floodplain 290 m a.s.l.

DESCRIPTION

Van Loon describes the site as being 60 m north of a village. The site is triangular in shape (150 m east–west, 100 m north–south, 1.50 m high), cut by an irrigation canal. Traces of "fortification-type walls" (large, roughly-shaped stones) remain at the southwest and southeast corners; lighter stone house wall foundations were near the southwest corner. Among the finds were a large stone door socket and vesicular basalt handmill fragments. Sherds were straw- and grit-tempered, wheel-made, buff (including ring and pointed bases), and painted (horizontal zones). Also present were bright red-slipped and red/black-corrugated wares. The artifact assemblage suggests occupations during the "Proto-Literate," Roman, and Byzantine periods.

Rihaoui describes several mounds belonging to an ancient city; the outlines of a rectangular building were visible on the surface. Stone blocks and sherds belonging to the Roman and Islamic periods were observed.

LITERATURE

Rihaoui 1965: 107 (no. 14); Stucky et al. 1972; van Loon 1967: 16 (no. 533).

Table B.2. List of Sites with Tabqa Numbers in the Lake Assad Area

Tabqa numbers from T 501 to T 556 were assigned by van Loon to sites in the area to be affected by flooding after the building of the Tabqa Dam; Wilkinson continues the numbers up to T 591 (i.e., T 557–T 591). Sites in the upper Lake Assad area are treated in this volume; sites in the lower Lake Assad area are located to the south of Wreyda South Site (T 512) and Khirbet Hweysh (T 510) and are not treated in this volume. See the *Index of Geographical Names* for page and figure references.

Tabqa Number	*Name*	*Sweyhat Survey Number*	*Holland/Whitcomb Survey Number*	*Location*
Van Loon				
501	Qubab	—	—	Lower Lake Assad area
502	Mureybit Ferry Site	—	—	Lower Lake Assad area
502a	Mureybit Gas Station Site	—	—	Lower Lake Assad area
503	Mureybit School Site	—	—	Lower Lake Assad area
504	Tell Mureybit	—	—	Lower Lake Assad area
505	Mureybit North Site	—	—	Lower Lake Assad area
506	Wreyda	—	—	Upper Lake Assad area
507	Selenkahiye	—	—	Upper Lake Assad area
508	Tell Kannas	—	—	Upper Lake Assad area
509	Tell Habuba Kabira	—	—	Upper Lake Assad area

Table B.2. List of Sites with Tabqa Numbers in the Lake Assad Area (*cont.*)

Tabqa Number	Name	Sweyhat Survey Number	Holland/Whitcomb Survey Number	Location
Van Loon (*cont.*)				
510	Khirbet Hweysh	—	—	Upper Lake Assad area
511	Halawa Village Sites	—	—	Upper Lake Assad area
511B	Hweyjet Halawa	—	—	Upper Lake Assad area
512	Wreyda South Site	—	—	Upper Lake Assad area
513	Habuba Kabira South	—	—	Upper Lake Assad area
514	Habuba Saghira/Aruda Saghira	—	—	Upper Lake Assad area
515	Khafse Saghire	—	—	Upper Lake Assad area
516	Khirbet Salama	—	—	Upper Lake Assad area
517	Tell al-Hajj	—	—	Upper Lake Assad area
518	Meskene Qadime	—	—	Lower Lake Assad area
519	Halawa South Site	—	—	Upper Lake Assad area
519A	Halawa Tell A	—	—	Upper Lake Assad area
519B	Halawa Tell B	—	—	Upper Lake Assad area
520	Hweyjet Halawa, Northern Village	—	—	Upper Lake Assad area
521	Tell Jafla	—	—	Upper Lake Assad area
522	Tawi (al-Itre)	—	—	Upper Lake Assad area
523	Tell Sheikh Hassan	—	H/W 19	Upper Lake Assad area
524	Sukhni	—	—	Upper Lake Assad area
525	Abu Dara West	—	—	Upper Lake Assad area
526	Taʿas	—	—	Upper Lake Assad area
527	Jebel Aruda	—	—	Upper Lake Assad area
528	Wadi al-Makrum	—	—	Lower Lake Assad area
529	Radde Kabira	—	—	Lower Lake Assad area
530	Mureybit East Site	—	—	Lower Lake Assad area
531	Kisret Mureybit	—	—	Lower Lake Assad area
532	Tell Fray	—	—	Lower Lake Assad area
533	Zreyjiye	—	—	Upper Lake Assad area
534	Tell Mumbaqa	—	—	Upper Lake Assad area
535	Tell al- ʿAbd	—	—	Upper Lake Assad area
536	Shams ed-Din Central Tell	—	H/W 21	Upper Lake Assad area
537	Tell Jouweif	SS 8	H/W 5	Upper Lake Assad area
538	Tell Othman	SS 20A	H/W 11	Upper Lake Assad area
539	Mishrifat	SS 16A	H/W 16	Upper Lake Assad area
540	Qalʿat Jaʿbar	—	—	Lower Lake Assad area
541	Dibsi Faraj	—	—	Lower Lake Assad area
542	Dibsi Faraj East 1	—	—	Lower Lake Assad area
543	Ghazale Sharqiye Southwest Site	—	—	Lower Lake Assad area
544	Ghazale Sharqiye Southeast Site	—	—	Lower Lake Assad area
545	Abu Hureyra	—	—	Lower Lake Assad area
546	Resm al-ʿAbd Mustaha	—	—	Upper Lake Assad area

Table B.2. List of Sites with Tabqa Numbers in the Lake Assad Area (*cont.*)

Tabqa Number	Name	Sweyhat Survey Number	Holland/Whitcomb Survey Number	Location
Van Loon (*cont.*)				
547	Mazra'at Hadidi	—	H/W 8	Upper Lake Assad area
548	Tell Hadidi	—	H/W 7	Upper Lake Assad area
549	Shajara Saghira	SS 29	—	Upper Lake Assad area
550	Shash Hamdan	—	—	Upper Lake Assad area
551	Khirbet Zmale	—	—	Upper Lake Assad area
552	Jebel Khaled	—	—	Upper Lake Assad area
553	Yusef Pasha	—	—	Upper Lake Assad area
554	Rimalah	—	—	Upper Lake Assad area
555	Kreyn	—	—	Lower Lake Assad area
556	Banat Abu Hureyra	—	—	Lower Lake Assad area
Wilkinson				
557	'Anab as-Safinah	—	—	Upper Lake Assad area
558	Aruda Kabira	—	—	Upper Lake Assad area
559	Jerf al-Ahmar	—	—	Tishrin Dam area
560	Tell Ali al-Haj	SS 17	—	Upper Lake Assad area
561	Shams ed-Din Southern Site and Cemeteries	SS 22	H/W 4	Upper Lake Assad area
562	Shams ed-Din Tannira	—	—	Upper Lake Assad area
563	—	SS 2	H/W 9	Upper Lake Assad area
564	Tell Hajji Ibrahim	SS 3	H/W 18	Upper Lake Assad area
565	—	SS 4	H/W 13	Upper Lake Assad area
566	Nafileh Village	SS 5	H/W 22	Upper Lake Assad area
567	Khirbet Aboud al-Hazu	SS 6	—	Upper Lake Assad area
568	Khirbet al-Hamrah	SS 7	H/W 12	Upper Lake Assad area
569	—	SS 9	H/W 14	Upper Lake Assad area
570	Khirbet Haj Hassan	SS 10	H/W 15	Upper Lake Assad area
571	Khirbet Dhiman	SS 11	H/W 10	Upper Lake Assad area
572	—	SS 12	—	Upper Lake Assad area
573	—	SS 13	—	Upper Lake Assad area
574	—	SS 14	—	Upper Lake Assad area
575	Khirbet al-Hamrah 2	SS 15	—	Upper Lake Assad area
576	Khirbet Aboud al-Hazu 2	SS 19	—	Upper Lake Assad area
577	—	SS 21	—	Upper Lake Assad area
578	—	SS 23	—	Upper Lake Assad area
579	—	SS 24	—	Upper Lake Assad area
580	—	SS 25	—	Upper Lake Assad area
581	—	SS 26	—	Upper Lake Assad area
582	—	SS 27	—	Upper Lake Assad area
583	—	SS 28	—	Upper Lake Assad area
584	—	SS 30	—	Upper Lake Assad area

Table B.2. List of Sites with Tabqa Numbers in the Lake Assad Area (*cont.*)

Tabqa Number	Name	Sweyhat Survey Number	Holland/Whitcomb Survey Number	Location
Wilkinson (*cont.*)				
585	Tell es-Sweyhat	SS 1	H/W 2	Upper Lake Assad area
586	—	SS 20B	—	Upper Lake Assad area
587	Dahrat er-Ramile	SS 18	—	Upper Lake Assad area
588	Tell Walid Asaf	—	H/W 1	—
589	Rasm al-ʿAbd Mustaha	—	H/W 6	—
590	Zarob	—	H/W 17	—
591	Umm Jehash	—	H/W 20	—

APPENDIX C: SELECTED SOIL
AND SEDIMENT DESCRIPTIONS

Section 1

LOCATION

Section 1 was exposed in the alluvial plain near Dibsi Faraj (T 541), west of the pumping station, 7 m from the Euphrates River, and close to the white limestone bluffs northwest of Dibsi Faraj (fig. 2.4) in October 1973. This section is therefore to the southeast of Emar (Meskene) and beyond the main upper Lake Assad area under discussion. It is included to illustrate the less pedogenically altered phases of the floodplain deposits.

DESCRIPTION

0–0.70 m	Mixture of white silt and sand, with occasional limestone gravel, mixed as result of cultivation over the last 100 or so years.
0.70–2.50 m	Alternating layers of light yellowish brown (10YR 6/4 [dry]) to dark yellowish brown (10YR 4/4 [moist]) Euphrates silts; light brownish gray (2.5Y 6/2 [dry]) to olive brown (2.5Y 4/4 [moist]) fine sand, and white (10YR 8/1 [dry]), pale brown (10YR 6/3 [moist]) silts. The last named appear to have been washed from the adjacent limestone bluffs.
2.50–5.20 m	Moderately poorly sorted fine-coarse limestone sand and gravels. Hard, white with abundant root holes, some infilled by overlying sediment. These locally-derived deposits overly bedded deposits of Euphrates sand and silt.

INTERPRETATION

Note that pedogenic features are minimal throughout, implying that the deposits are of relatively recent origin and have not been transformed by soil-forming processes except for by localized biological activity. Elsewhere the floodplain sediments are dominated by dark yellowish brown Euphrates silts, not altered by pedogenic activity, underlain by fine to medium Euphrates sands and well-rounded medium to coarse Euphrates cobbles.

Section 2

LOCATION

Section 2 was exposed in a pit at the base of occupation (see fig. 2.11) in Trench IC at Tell es-Sweyhat.

DESCRIPTION

1. Occupation deposits within Trench IC.

2. Brown undifferentiated loam.

3. Thin bed of water-laid silt.

4. Cross-bedded medium grained sand.

5. Thin layer of gray ash.

6. Brown undifferentiated loam.

7. Well-sorted sand and fine gravel.

8. Reddish yellow (7.5YR 6/6 [dry]) and strong brown (7.5YR 5/6 [moist]) fine-medium sand, capped by a thin layer of laminated silt.

9. Brownish yellow (10YR 6/6 [dry]) and yellowish brown (10YR 5/6 [moist]) fine sand loam, imbedded with rare charcoal flecks.

10. Light brown (7.5YR 6/4 [dry]), strong brown (7.5YR 5/6 [moist]), sandy loam with small (< 5 mm) lenses of fine silt, with related accumulations in insect burrows.

11. Brownish yellow (10YR 6/6 [dry]) and yellowish brown (10YR 5/6 [moist]) soft massive sandy loam with occasional charcoal flecks.

12. Same as Layer 10 but with less distinct silt lenses (possibly concentrations within insect holes), occasional very fine charcoal flecks.

13. Reddish yellow (7.5YR 6/6 [dry]) and strong brown (7.5YR 5/6 [moist]) poorly sorted sandy loam with weak silt coatings on sand grains. Common flecks of charcoal, but these are interpreted to probably have been washed in.

14. Reddish yellow (7.5YR 6/6 [dry]) and strong brown (7.5YR 5/6 [moist]) massive loam with occasional to rare charcoal fragments.

15. Reddish yellow (7.5YR 6/6 [dry]) and strong brown (7.5YR 5/6 [moist]) crumbly silt loam with fine granular structure and occasional to common clusters of crystals, probably gypsum.

INTERPRETATION

Layer 4 is either an aeolian sand or a low-energy fluvial sand (i.e., wadi sand) capped by an overlying silt (Layer 3) which indicates a decrease in flow energy. Layer 7 was deposited in an episodic flow channel of a wadi, in this case of moderate energy flow, which followed on from Layer 8, a low-energy sand with decreasing flow-energy towards the top. Layers 9–13 are of indeterminate origin but appear to be very low energy sandy loams containing some indications of human activity in the form of small charcoal flecks. Because pedogenic features (such as soil structure and secondary mineral accumulations) are minimal, these five layers cannot be regarded as true soils, although they may have been cultivated. Layers 14 and 15 are interpreted as a buried soil A horizon (14), above a relict subsoil B/C horizon (15). Unlike most pedogenic carbonate accumulations that are evident as aggregates of silt-sized calcite crystals or off-white soft concretions of calcium carbonate, these form clusters of small needle-shaped crystals of gypsum. Gypsum crystals as components of a gypsic horizon commonly occur in semi-arid soils with rainfall of < 300 mm rainfall, being at increasingly shallow depths as rainfall decreases (Retallack 1990: 166). The source of the gypsum is probably gypsum-rich aeolian dust, which is then translocated to various depths within the soil profile by percolating rainwater (Dixon 1994: 100).

Prior to the growth of the mound it appears that soils probably formed in a semi-arid environment similar to that of the present day. An accumulation of sand, silt, and fine gravel deposits resulting from episodic flow of water along a shallow swale accumulated above these soils, and with time increasing quantities of charcoal were incorporated into the sediment matrix. By the time Layer 5 accumulated, occupation in the vicinity was significant.

Section 3

LOCATION

Section 3 is a soil profile from the south edge of Nafileh Village (SS 5; fig. 9.1). This profile is described in order to show the nature of soil development in the area today, and to provide a comparison with the buried soil below Tell es-Sweyhat described above.

DESCRIPTION

0–28 cm   Yellowish brown (10YR 5/6 [moist], 10YR 7/6 [dry]) soft sandy loam; occasional medium gravel; common fine root hairs. Single-grain to very weak subangular blocky structure. Slightly irregular diffuse boundary. Ap horizon.

28–60 cm   Strong brown (7.5YR 5/6 [moist], 7.5YR 6/6 [dry]) loam. Moderate fine subangular blocky structure; common white $CaCO_3$ soft concretions, slightly elongate in vertical plane. Rare stones; occasional fine root hairs. Moderately firm. Distinct horizontal lower boundary. Bca horizon.

60–90+ cm   Reddish yellow (7.5YR 6/6 [moist], 7.5YR 7/6 [dry]) loamy sand with abundant sugar-like gypsum crystals in a very sparse brown matrix. Massive structure; very sparse fine roots. By horizon.

Note: A second profile 35 m to the southeast includes a fine gravel layer from the Wadi Nafileh below 70 cm.

Section 4

LOCATION

Section 4 is a soil profile from the eastern lower town of Tell es-Sweyhat.

DESCRIPTION

18–28 cm	Light brown (7.5YR 6/4 [dry]) and dark brown (7.5YR 4/4 [moist]), perceived redder than 0–18 cm), sandy loam, moderately gritty. Moderately firm with coarse subangular blocky structure and common biopores and other evidence of biological activity. Occasional potsherds and stones. Occasional fine root hairs.
28–33 cm	Elongate lenses of mainly Euphrates gravel, 3–20 mm long axis. Occasional fragments of charcoal. Some pale brown matrix as for 18–28 cm. The presence of charcoal implies these are not simply lenses of fluvial gravel.
33–38 cm	Light brown (7.5YR 6/4 [dry]) and dark brown (7.5YR 4/4 [moist]) sandy loam as for 18–28 cm. Elsewhere in the section at 36–43 cm are accumulations of dark gray ash. To the south a 6 cm thick lens of fine to 1 cm limestone gravel may represent a localized interval of fluvial activity.
38–46 cm	Pink (7.5YR 7/4 [dry]) to light brown (7.5YR 6/4 [dry]) and dark brown (7.5YR 4/4 [moist]) to strong brown (7.5YR 5/6 [moist]) loam and silt loam. Moderately firm, weak subangular blocky structure. Occasional weak $CaCO_3$ soft concretions. Approximately the level of the buried old ground surface.
46–70 cm	Reddish yellow (7.5YR 7/6 [dry]) and strong brown (7.5YR 5/6 [moist]) clay loam. Medium-coarse subangular blocky structure. Occasional moderately developed white soft concretions of $CaCO_3$, which also occurs as filaments and other minor concretions.
70–86 cm	As for 46–70 cm but without $CaCO_3$ soft concretions. Under hand lens, occasional fine root voids and fine-medium Euphrates sand inclusions were observed.
86–140 cm	Light brown (7.5YR 6/4 [dry]) and strong brown (7.5YR 5/6 [moist]) sandy clay loam. Massive, breaks reluctantly to very coarse subangular blocky structure. Common sugar-like and sheet-like crystals of gypsum throughout give sandy texture.
140–190 cm	Very hard, otherwise as for 86–140 cm, but with occasional fine-medium subrounded limestone pebbles. Well-developed fine-medium subangular blocky structure. Translucent crystals of gypsum both dispersed through matrix and as clusters. Some needle-shaped gypsum crystals also. Occasionally gypsum crystals dominate the soil matrix.

INTERPRETATION

The upper 33 cm represents an accumulation in the presence of sparse local occupation, with 0–18 cm being a modern Ap horizon weakly transformed by plowing. The buried old land surface (38–46 cm: IIA) is underlain (47–70 cm) by an old subsoil enriched in $CaCO_3$ (IIBca). This subsoil, in turn, is underlain by a deep subsoil horizon enriched in pedogenic gypsum (IICg). Although there are minor differences, this is the same basic sequence evident below the main Tell es-Sweyhat mound (Trench IC in *Section 2.C. The Soils*) and in the Nafileh Village (SS 5) soil pit (Section 3). The implication is that there has been no significant change in the processes of soil formation between the pre-Early Bronze Age (early phase) (in the case of Trench IC), the pre-Early Bronze Age (later phase) in the case of the outer town sequence, and the present day (Section 3, Nafileh Village).

Section 5

LOCATION

 Section 5, 1.0 m × 1.5 m (see fig. 2.10), was exposed in Trench S5.

DESCRIPTION

0–5 cm	Very pale brown (10YR 7/4 [dry]) and yellowish brown (10YR 5/6 [moist]) fine sandy loam, single grained structure with occasional large clods. Very soft and loose with gradual lower boundary.
5–30 cm	Very pale brown (10YR 7/4 [dry]) and yellowish brown (10YR 5/6 [moist]) fine sandy loam with well-developed coarse-medium subangular blocky structure. Peds slightly hard. Common insect burrows and holes, and occasional fine root holes. Straight, distinct lower boundary to the following horizon.
30–60 cm	Very pale brown (10YR 8/4 [dry]) and yellow (10YR 7/6 [moist]) fine sand, structureless to massive, breaking to large structural units above and single grained beneath. The lower portion of the profile is slightly moist. Rare insect and root holes. Deposit is sandy, apparently calcite sand; it is hard above and softer beneath.

Sherd counts in arbitrary 20 cm units: 0–20 cm: 16; 20–40 cm: 1; 40–60 cm: 0.

Section 6

LOCATION

 Trench S6. 1.0 × 1.5 m (see fig. 2.10).

DESCRIPTION

0–20 cm	Yellow (10YR 7/6 [dry]) and yellowish brown (10YR 5/6 [moist]) fine sandy loam with slightly loose surface soil tending to weak medium subangular blocky structure beneath. Occasional cherty fine gravels. Clear wavy boundary below.
20–44 cm	Reddish yellow (7.5YR 7/6 [dry]) to strong brown (7.5YR 5/6 [moist]) loam, moderately firm, breaking to weak to moderate medium subangular blocky structure. Contains occasional to common off-white soft calcium carbonate concretions. Occasional root holes and one 8 cm diameter animal burrow. Lower portion of this horizon is slightly moist. Distinct wavy boundary below.
44–70 cm	Reddish yellow (7.5YR 6/6 [dry but slightly moist in profile]) to strong brown (7.5YR 5/6 [moist]) sandy loam breaking to weak medium subangular blocky structure. In section, peds slightly hard to hard. Calcium carbonate/gypsum forms common to abundant crystals dispersed throughout the loam matrix above, and below these merge to form clusters. In the lower layers are some occasional concentrations of reddish yellow clay loam.

Sherd counts in arbitrary 20 cm units: 0–20 cm: 25; 20–40 cm: 5 (includes 2 rims); 40–60 cm: 1.

INDEX OF GEOGRAPHICAL NAMES

249, 260; figs. 7.1, 7.8, 7.10, 9.1, A.8; pl. 14

Shajara Formation — 20; fig. 2.8

Shallal — 214

Shamiyah — 4, 6, 185

Shams ed-Din (modern village) — 213–14; figs. 1.2, 3.1

Shams ed-Din Central Tell (T 536) — 5, 20–23, 97, 210, 224, **249–50**, 250, 259; figs. 1.1, 2.6, 7.1, 9.1

Shams ed-Din East Tell — *see* Jouweif, Tell

Shams ed-Din South Tell — *see* ʿAbd, Tell al-

Shams ed-Din Southern Site and Cemeteries (SS 22, T 561) — 8, 20, 55–56, 80 and fn. 52, 133, 136, 140, 152–53, 175, 185–86, **210–11**, 224, 250, 260; figs. 5.1, 7.1, 7.4–5, 9.1, 9.7, A.7; pls. 3, 10, 13; *see also* ʿAbd, Tell al-

Shams ed-Din Tannira (T 562) — 8, 20, 41, 85, 88, 134–35, 182, 224, **250–51**, 260; figs. 7.1, 9.1

Shams Eddine — *see* Shams ed-Din Central Tell

Shash Hamdan (T 550) — 80, 224, **251–52**, 260; figs. 5.1, 7.1, 9.1

Shash Kabir — *see* Zmaleh, Khirbet

Sheikh ʾArud — *see* Aruda, Jebel

Sheikh Hassan, Tell (T 523) — 5, 8, 86, 94, 96 fn. 62, 135, 145 fn. 75, 179, 182, 184, 189, 193, 224, 240, **252**, 255, 258, 259; figs. 1.2, 9.1, 9.6; pl. 2

Shenef, Khirbet-esh — 41

Sheykh Hasan — *see* Sheikh Hassan, Tell

Shioukh Tahtani — 79

Sinjar, Jebel — 46, 186–87; figs. 2.1, 9.8

Sinn, Jebel — 210, 225, 244, 251, 254; fig. 9.1

Sohar — 33

Soreq Cave — 15–16, 191, 198

Söğütlü, marsh of — 15

Soueihat, Tell es- — *see* Sweyhat, Tell es-

SS 1 (T 585) — *see* Sweyhat, Tell es-

SS 2 (T 563) — 55–56, 84, 87, 89, 90–91, 103, 136–38, 152–53, 175, **199**, 224, 253, 260; figs. 2.7, 4.1, 4.12–13, 7.1, 7.4, 9.1

SS 3 (T 564) — *see* Hajji Ibrahim, Tell

SS 4 (T 565) — 29, 55–56, 66, 84, 98, 100, 123, 146–47, 152–53, 175, 190, **200**, 224, 253, 260; figs. 2.7, 4.1, 4.12–13, 7.1, 7.8, 9.1

SS 5 (T 566) — *see* Nafileh Village

SS 6 (T 567) — *see* Aboud al-Hazu, Khirbet

SS 7 (T 568) — *see* Hamrah, Khirbet al-

SS 8 (T 537) — *see* Jouweif, Tell

SS 9 (T 569) — 31, 55–56, 66, 72, 84, 87, 89–91, 105, 136–38, 152–53, 175, **202–03**, 224, 253, 260; figs. 2.7, 4.1, 4.12–13, 6.30, 7.1, 7.4, 9.1

SS 10 (T 570) — *see* Haj Hassan, Khirbet

SS 11 (T 571) — *see* Dhiman, Khirbet

SS 12 (T 572) — 55–56, 84, 98–99, 149, 152–53, 175, **204**, 224, 253, 260; figs. 2.7, 6.30, 7.1, 7.9, 9.1

SS 13 (T 573) — 56, 67, 73, 87, 89, 90–91, 134, 152–53, 175–76, **204**, 224, 253, 260, 276; figs. 7.1, 9.1

SS 14 (T 574) — 56, 152–53, 175–76, 186, **204**, 224, 253, 260; figs. 7.1, 7.4, 9.1

SS 15 (T 575) — *see* Hamrah 2, Khirbet al-

SS 16A (T 539) — *see* Mishrifat

SS 16B — *see* Ramalah

SS 16C — 20, 56, 147, 152–53, 175, 205, **206**, 224, 253; figs. 5.1, 7.10, A.6

SS 17 (T 560) — *see* Ali al-Haj, Tell

SS 18 (T 587) — *see* Dahrat er-Ramile

SS 19 (T 576) — *see* Aboud al-Hazu 2, Khirbet

SS 20A (T 538) — *see* Othman, Tell

SS 20B (T 586) — 29, 55–56, 84, 94–98, 117, 147, 152–53, 175, **209**, 224, 253, 261; figs. 2.7, 4.12–13, 6.16, 7.1, 7.7–8, 9.1

SS 21 (T 577) — 55–56, 60, 84, 87, 89–91, 106, 136, 152–53, 175, **209**, 224, 253, 260; figs. 2.7, 4.1, 4.12–13, 6.6, 7.1, 7.4, 9.1

SS 22 (T 561) — *see* Shams ed-Din Southern Site and Cemeteries

Upper Lake Assad from Tell Jouweif (SS 8), Looking South, ca. 1991

Upper Lake Assad, Looking toward Jebel Aruda (T 527) from Tell Sheikh Hassan (T 523), ca. 1991

View West from Shams ed-Din (Near Site SS 22) toward the Main Terrace of the Euphrates on the West Bank.
Note: Taken at Time of Low Lake Level, Autumn 1992

Euphrates Valley South of Tell es-Sweyhat (SS 1), View Looking North across Relict Early Floodplain with Tell Jouweif
(SS 8: Asymmetric Light Mound) to Left of Center

View across the Southeastern Portion of the Lower Town of Tell es-Sweyhat (SS 1) and Cultivated Steppe beyond,
toward Limestone Escarpment to East, Autumn 1974

Valley Fill of Northern Wadi Showing Upper Loam (Deposit *c*) Overlying Gravel Fill (Deposit *b*). See Figure 2.8

Spout and Collecting Basin of Wine Press p 101b near SS 26

Treading Floor and Collecting Basin of Wine Press 22 p 103, Cut in Limestone along Floor of Euphrates Bluffs

Limestone Quarries along Limestone Bluffs of Euphrates Valley to North of SS 28

Pock-marked Area of Plundered Early Bronze Age Tombs to East of Shams ed-Din Southern Site and Cemeteries (SS 22)

Vaulted Tomb Cut in Limestone of Euphrates Bluffs near SS 27

Vaulted Tomb Cut in Limestone of Euphrates Bluffs near SS 27. Note that Tomb Is Heavily Truncated to the Left by the Erosive Action of the Euphrates River

Early Bronze Age Southern Site and Cemeteries at Shams ed-Din (SS 22) Visible
as Low Gray Rise to Right of Center, Looking North

Roman Site of SS 29 on West Bank of Euphrates River with Modern Tombs in Left Foreground and Rows of Weathered Stones of Building Walls in Mid-ground

Middle Bronze Age Floors and Associated Walls Exposed by Erosion at Tell Jouweif (SS 8)

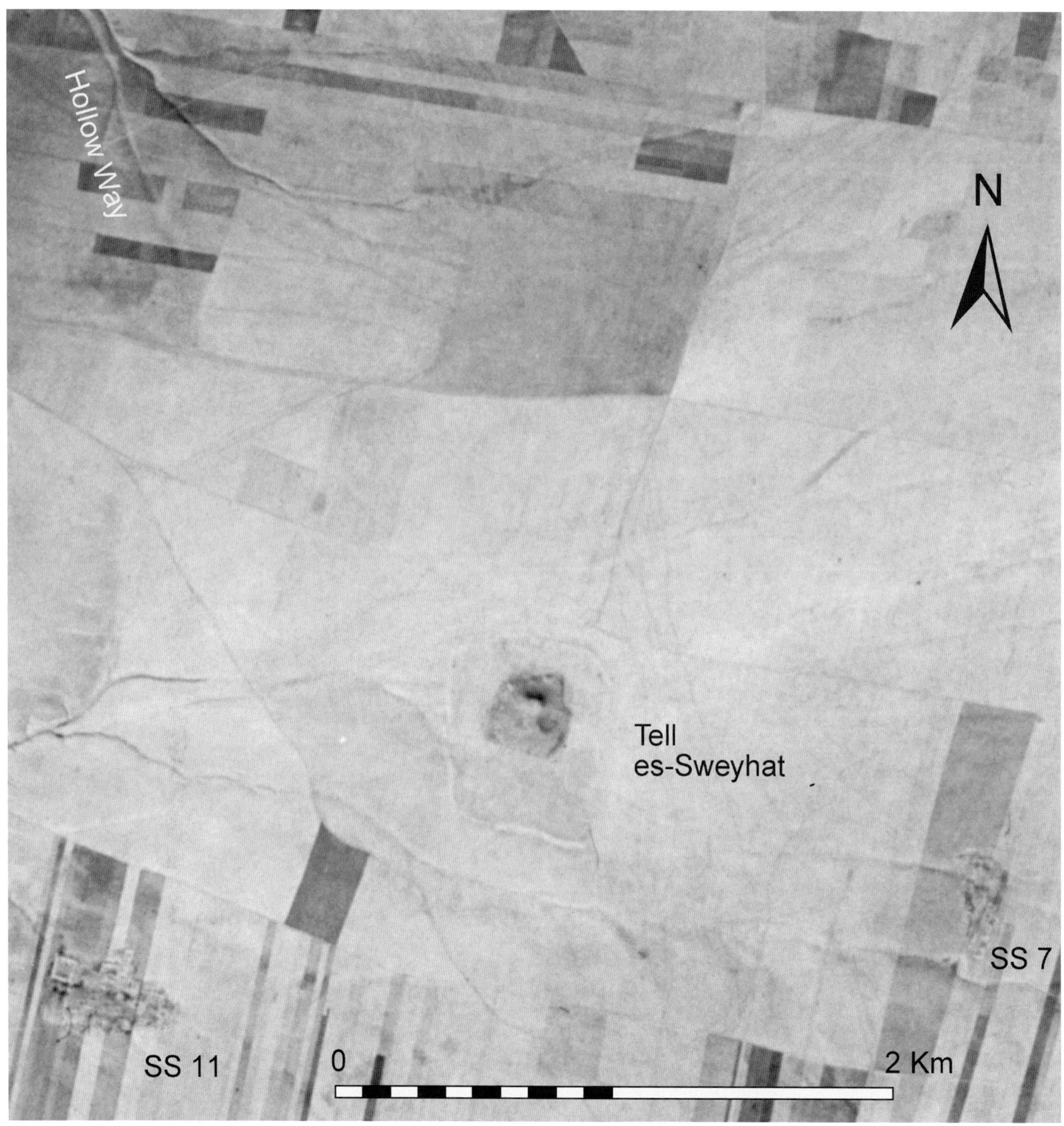

Satellite Photograph of Tell es-Sweyhat (SS 1) Showing the Faint Trace of the Outer Enclosure Wall around the Central
Tell (Dark Area). Note the Trace of a Hollow Way to the Northwest as Well as Two Early Islamic Sites (Khirbet
Dhiman [SS 11] and Khirbet al-Hamrah [SS 7]) to the Southwest and Southeast, Respectively. Produced by
Jason Ur, Oriental Institute CAMEL Laboratory; Courtesy of U.S. Geological Survey